Human Development in Multicultural Contexts: A Book of Readings

Human Development in Multicultural Contexts: A Book of Readings

Edited by

Michele A. Paludi

Union College

Upper Saddle River, New Jersey 07458

Library of Congress Cataloging-in-Publication Data

Human development in multicultural contexts : a book of readings /
edited by Michele A Paludi.
p. cm.
Includes bibliographical references and indexes.
ISBN 0-13-019523-5
1. Developmental psychology—Cross-cultural studies. I. Paludi, Michele Antoinette.

BF713.5 .H79 2001
155—dc21

2001021904

VP/Editorial Director: Laura Pearson
Senior Acquisitions Editor: Jennifer Gilliland
Assistant Editor: Nicole Girrbach
VP/Director of Production and Manufacturing: Barbara Kittle
Managing Editor: Mary Rottino
Senior Production Editor: Shelly Kupperman
Prepress and Manufacturing Manager: Nick Sklitsis
Prepress and Manufacturing Buyer: Tricia Kenny
Director of Marketing: Beth Gillett Mejia
Senior Marketing Manager: Sharon Cosgrove
Cover Design Director: Jayne Conte
Cover Designer: Bruce Kenselaar
Art Director: Jayne Conte

For permission to use copyrighted material, grateful acknowledgment is made to the copyright holders listed on pages 259–261, which is considered an extension of this copyright page.

This book was set in 10/12 Baskerville by Pine Tree Composition, Inc., and printed and bound by R. R. Donnelley & Sons Company, Harrisonburg, PA. The cover was printed by Phoenix Color Corp.

Upper Saddle River, New Jersey 07458

Printed in the United States of America
10 9 8 7 6 5 4 3 2 1

ISBN 0-13-019523-5

Prentice-Hall International (UK) Limited, *London*
Prentice-Hall of Australia Pty. Limited, *Sydney*
Prentice-Hall Canada Inc., *Toronto*
Prentice-Hall Hispanoamericana, S.A., *Mexico*
Prentice-Hall of India Private Limited, *New Delhi*
Prentice-Hall of Japan, Inc., *Tokyo*
Pearson Education Asia Pte. Ltd., *Singapore*
Editora Prentice-Hall do Brasil, Ltda., *Rio de Janeiro*

To Rosa and John, my maternal grandparents,
for Antoinette, my mother,
And to
Lucia and Antonio, my paternal grandparents,
for Michael, my father,
And to
Antoinette and Michael
for
Rosalie, Lucille, and Me

Contents

Preface xiii

CULTURAL INFLUENCES ON DEVELOPMENT ACROSS THE LIFE CYCLE 1

INTRODUCTION 2

What Is Life-Cycle Developmental Psychology? 3

Multiculturalism in Life-Cycle Developmental Psychology 4

Multiculturalism in Life-Cycle Developmental Psychology: From Marginality to Inclusion 6

Placing Multiculturalism Within Developmental Psychology Courses 9

Rationale for the Selection of Readings 11

1 INFANCY 15

OVERVIEW: CULTURAL INFLUENCES ON DEVELOPMENT IN INFANCY 16

Physical Development in Infancy 16

Cognitive Development 17

  Focus on Infant-Directed Speech 17

Emotional Development 19

  Focus on Infants' Sleeping Arrangements 19

  Focus on Infant Temperament 20

Social Development 21

  Focus on Mother-Infant Attachment 21

  Focus on Play 23

READINGS 25

Functional Analysis of the Contents of Maternal Speech to Infants of 5 and 13 Months in Four Cultures: Argentina, France, Japan, and the United States 25

Marc H. Bornstein / Joseph Tal / Charles Rahn / Celia Z. Galperín / Marie-Germaine Pêcheux / Martine Lamour / Sueko Toda / Hiroshi Azuma / Misako Ogino / Catherine S. Tamis-LeMonda

Cultural Variations in Infants' Sleeping Arrangements: Questions of Independence 31

Gilda A. Morelli / Barbara Rogoff / David Oppenheim / Denise Goldsmith

Reactivity in Infants: A Cross-National Comparison 37

Jerome Kagan / Doreen Arcus / Nancy Snidman / Wang Yu Feng / John Hendler / Sheila Greene

Sleeping Out of Home in a Kibbutz Communal Arrangement: It Makes a Difference for Infant-Mother Attachment 41

Abraham Sagi / Frank Donnell / Marinus H. van IJzendoorn / Ofra Mayseless / Ora Aviezer

Play in Two Societies: Pervasiveness of Process, Specificity of Structure 45

Marc H. Bornstein / O. Maurice Haynes / Liliana Pascual / Kathleen M. Painter / Celia Galperín

Review Questions and Activities 51

Suggestions for Further Reading 51

2 PRESCHOOL YEARS 53

OVERVIEW: CULTURAL INFLUENCES ON DEVELOPMENT IN THE PRESCHOOL YEARS 54

Physical Development in the Preschool Years 54

Cognitive Development 55

- Focus on Language Advances 55
- Focus on Child Care 57

Emotional Development 59

- Focus on the Role of the Mother 59
- Focus on the Role of the Father 60

Social Development 61

- Focus on Play 61
- Focus on Preschoolers' Exposure to Real Violence 63

READINGS 65

Parents' Report of Vocabulary and Grammatical Development of African American Preschoolers: Child and Environmental Associations 65

Joanne E. Roberts / Margaret Burchinal / Meghan Durham

Child Care for Children in Poverty: Opportunity or Inequity? 70
Deborah A. Phillips / Miriam Voran / Ellen Kisker / Carollee Howes / Marcy Whitebook

Emotion Regulation in Early Childhood: A Cross-Cultural Comparison Between German and Japanese Toddlers 74
Wolfgang Friedlmeier / Gisela Trommsdorff

African American Fathers in Low Income, Urban Families: Development, Behavior, and Home Environment of Their Three-Year-Old Children 80
Maureen M. Black / Howard Dubowitz / Raymond H. Starr Jr.

Cultural Differences in Korean- and Anglo-American Preschoolers' Social Interaction and Play Behaviors 84
Jo Ann M. Farver / Yonnie Kwak Kim / Yoolim Lee

Effects of Community Violence on Inner-City Preschoolers and Their Families 88
Jo Ann M. Farver / Lucia X. Natera / Dominick L. Frosch

Review Questions and Activities 92

Suggestions for Further Reading 92

3 MIDDLE CHILDHOOD 94

OVERVIEW: CULTURAL INFLUENCES ON DEVELOPMENT IN MIDDLE CHILDHOOD 95

Physical Development in Middle Childhood 95

Cognitive Development 97
- Focus on Academic Achievement and Adjustment 97
- Focus on Language Development 100

Emotional Development 101
- Focus on Children of Divorce 101
- Focus on Self-Care After School 103

Social Development 104
- Focus on the Influence of a Peer Group 104

READINGS 107

Gender Effects in Children's Beliefs About School Performance: A Cross-Cultural Study 107
Anna Stetsenko / Todd D. Little / Tamara Gordeeva / Matthias Grasshof / Gabriele Oettingen

Phonetic Awareness: Knowledge of Orthography–Phonology Relationships in the Character Acquisition of Chinese Children 112
Hua Shu / Richard C. Anderson / Ningning Wu

A Prospective Study of the Effects of Marital Status and Family Relations on Young Children's Adjustment Among African American and European American Families 117

Daniel S. Shaw / Emily B. Winslow / Clare Flanagan

Children of the National Longitudinal Survey of Youth: Choices in After-School Care and Child Development 123

Deborah Lowe Vandell / Janaki Ramanan

Costa Rican Children's Perceptions of Their Social Networks 126

Melissa E. DeRosier / Janis B. Kupersmidt

Review Questions and Activities 130

Suggestions for Further Reading 130

4 ADOLESCENCE 131

OVERVIEW: CULTURAL INFLUENCES ON DEVELOPMENT IN ADOLESCENCE 132

Physical Development During Adolescence 133

Cognitive Development 135

  Focus on Body Image 135

Emotional Development 137

  Focus on Identity Development 137

  Focus on Adolescent Depression 139

Social Development 141

  Focus on Friendships and Membership in a Peer Group 141

  Focus on Sexual Activity and Risk-Taking Behavior 143

READINGS 147

Effects of Body Fat on Weight Concerns, Dating, and Sexual Activity: A Longitudinal Analysis of Black and White Adolescent Girls 147

Carolyn Tucker Halpern / J. Richard Udry / Benjamin Campbell / Chirayath Suchindran

The Collectivistic Nature of Ethnic Identity Development Among Asian-American College Students 154

Christine J. Yeh / Karen Huang

Depression in Adolescence 158

Anne C. Petersen / Bruce E. Compas / Jeanne Brooks-Gunn / Mark Stemmler / Sydney Ey / Kathryn E. Grant

Adolescent Same-Sex and Opposite-Sex Best Friend Interactions 170

Cami K. McBride / Tiffany Field

Searching for the Magic Johnson Effect: AIDS, Adolescents, and Celebrity Disclosure 173

Bruce Brown Jr. / Marc D. Baranowski / John W. Kulig / John N. Stephenson / Barbara Perry

Review Questions and Activities 178
Suggestions for Further Reading 179

5 ADULTHOOD 180

OVERVIEW: CULTURAL INFLUENCES ON DEVELOPMENT IN ADULTHOOD 181

Physical Development in Adulthood 182
- Focus on Physical Functioning 182

Cognitive Development 184
- Focus on Awareness and Utilization of Long-Term Care Services 184
- Focus on Objectified Body Consciousness 185

Emotional Development 187
- Focus on Continuity in Personality Across the Life Cycle 187
- Focus on Depressive Psychopathology in Older Adults 188
- Focus on Fear of Death 190

Social Development 191
- Focus on Family Violence 191
- Focus on Grandparenting 193
- Focus on the Experience of Bicultural Identity 194

READINGS 196

Constant Hierarchic Patterns of Physical Functioning Across Seven Populations in Five Countries 196
Luigi Ferrucci / Jack M. Guralnik / Francesca Cecchi / Niccoló Marchionni / Bernardo Salani / Judith Kasper / Romano Celli / Sante Giardini / Eino Heikkinen / Marja Jylhä / Alberto Baroni

Awareness and Utilization of Community Long-Term Care Services by Elderly Korean and Non-Hispanic White Americans 200
Ailee Moon / James E. Lubben / Valentine Villa

Women and Objectified Body Consciousness: Mothers' and Daughters' Body Experience in Cultural, Developmental, and Familial Context 205
Nita Mary McKinley

Age Differences in Personality Across the Adult Life Span: Parallels in Five Cultures 212
Robert R. McRae / Paul T. Costa Jr. / Margarida Pedroso de Lima / António Simões / Fritz Ostendorf / Alois Angleitner / Iris Marŭsić / Denis Bratko / Gian Vittorio Caprara / Claudio Barbaranelli / Joon-Ho Chae / Ralph L. Piedmont

Ethnicity, Gender, and Depressive Symptoms in Older Workers 216
Maria E. Fernandez / Elizabeth J. Mutran / Donald C. Reitzes / S. Sudha

Personality and Demographic Factors in Older Adults' Fear of Death 220
Victor G. Cicirelli

Changing Community Responses to Wife Abuse: A Research and Demonstration Project in Iztacalco, Mexico 226

Gillian M. Fawcett / Lori L. Heise / Leticia Isita-Espejel / Susan Pick

Raising Grandchildren: The Experiences of Black and White Grandmothers 231

Rachel Pruchno

Bicultural Identification: Experiences of Internationally Adopted Children and Their Parents 237

Myrna L. Friedlander / Lucille C. Larney / Marianne Skau / Marcus Hotaling / Marsha L. Cutting / Michelle Schwam

Review Questions and Activities 242

Suggestions for Further Reading 242

References 243

Credits 259

Index 263

Preface

Human Development in Multicultural Contexts highlights cultural influences on each of four major dimensions of development—the physical, cognitive, emotional, and social—during several stages of the life cycle: infancy, preschool, middle childhood, adolescence, and adulthood. This book of readings introduces students to theories, empirical research, and applications from a multicultural perspective that have become central to the field of life-cycle developmental psychology.

Each chapter of the book is in two parts: an overview, which is the editor's discussion of how that particular life stage traditionally has been researched within the four dimensions of development—and of some important multicultural correctives to these portrayals—and readings, a selection of articles (in excerpted format) that present specific multicultural studies. Thus this book of readings can provide you with resources, insights, and techniques with which to balance the perspectives on gender, race, ethnicity, class, and sex in your other courses.

It is assumed that students using *Human Development in Multicultural Contexts* have been introduced to the fundamentals of life-cycle developmental psychology through other textbooks and classes. This book of readings, therefore, is not intended to replace any textbook in developmental psychology; its goal is to supplement existing course materials by offering a multicultural perspective that has typically been lacking in textbooks on developmental psychology.

Each chapter opens with "Questions for Reflection" that will guide your reading. I have also provided you with suggestions for further reading and some activities and questions to serve as a review of each chapter.

Due to space limitations in this text, we were unable to reprint the readings in their entirety. We have provided you with the complete citation of the articles on the first page of each essay selection. I encourage you to continue your studies on multicultural issues in life-cycle developmental psychology by reading the articles in their entirety as they appeared in journal form. The authors provide a wealth of information on innovative research methodologies and suggestions for further research.

I also encourage you to pursue your own research in life-cycle developmental psychology from a multicultural perspective.

Acknowledgments

My own specialty within psychology is in developmental psychology. While I was being trained in graduate school (1976–1980), the field did not have the knowledge base we now have and continue to develop. As an undergraduate and graduate student, I was fortunate to have mentors who guided my thinking about life cycle development from a multicultural perspective, including William Dember, Philip Newman, Barbara Newman, Kathleen Burlew, Edward Klein, Judith Frankel, Kathy Borman, Dee Graham, Edna Rawlings, and Nancy Walbek. I have carried on this approach with students in my own courses in the psychology curriculum. It has been an honor for me to see many of these students pursuing research and teaching in life cycle development, keeping multicultural issues central, not marginal, to their work. They, in turn, will influence many other students to rethink and continue to modify life-cycle developmental theories and research.

Other students I have taught and mentored are working in advocacy positions, with rape crisis centers, battered women's shelters, or day care centers, while others work in business and academic positions, in which they advise and counsel employees and students and facilitate training programs in multicultural awareness that help break down barriers among individuals from varied cultural backgrounds. These advocates rely on the research and theories academicians have shared with the lay audience as well as with other academicians. So I have seen in many ways the impact one course or one textbook can have on helping people find ways to treat all individuals with respect and dignity regardless of sex, ethnicity, class, gender, and race. I hope this book of readings will encourage you to pursue research, teaching, and advocacy work in life-cycle developmental psychology.

No textbook is ever accomplished without the special help of many individuals. First, I wish to thank Jennifer Gilliland at Prentice Hall for her guidance, support, and encouragement. I have enjoyed working with Jennifer and her colleagues at Prentice Hall.

I also want to acknowledge the many students who have taught me about the psychology of gender, race, class, and ethnicity. They have increased my interest in life-cycle developmental psychology.

The following reviewers were most helpful: Brian Stagner/Texas A & M University; Jacqueline Lerner/Boston College; Gypsy Denzine/Northern Arizona University.

I extend special thanks to Fr. John Provost for sharing with me reference materials and his sage advice.

I applaud the authors of the articles reported and excerpted in this book of readings. They have greatly increased our understanding of life-cycle developmental psychology through their commitment to multicultural research.

My primary mentors were my parents, Antoinette Peccichio Paludi and Michael Paludi. They taught me by example as well as through their words. I never knew the full extent of their commitment to multicultural issues until my father died in 1980. At his wake, Charlie, my father's co-worker (they were skilled laborers at General Electric in Schenectady, New York) spoke to my mother. He told her that my father never denied the fact that Charlie was African American, but he also never treated him differently from other workers because of his race: all were treated with respect and dignity. He told my mother that my father set an example for how others on the job should treat him. During the years since, I have often thought about what a compliment this was to my father. I never had an opportunity to meet Charlie before the wake and I never saw him after the services, but I thank him so much for sharing this piece of my father with us. I realized during the course of working on this book that I have always wanted to write a book on life-cycle developmental psychology from a multicultural perspective as a tribute to the friendship and working relationship between my father and Charlie.

Finally, and most importantly, I thank Carmen Paludi Jr. for encouraging me to pursue editing this book, for listening to my ideas on an almost daily basis, and for bringing me laughter, friendship, and nurturance. This book is his as well as mine.

Michele A. Paludi

Human Development in Multicultural Contexts: A Book of Readings

What would it be like to have not only color vision but culture vision, the ability to see the multiple worlds of others?

Mary Catherine Bateson

Cultural Influences on Development Across the Life Cycle

INTRODUCTION

Look at the picture below for the next few minutes. What do you see? For example, how many children are there in this picture? Are they girls or boys? How many adults are there in the picture? What do you believe are the relationships among the children and adults—Are they parents and children? Siblings? Grandparents and children? And finally, where is this scene set?

When I have shown pictures similar to this one to students in various courses, students have generated responses such as these:

> "The mother, father, and their three sons and teenage daughter are sitting in their living room."
>
> "Grandma is visiting her daughter and son-in-law and their three sons. They are inside the home of her daughter and son-in-law."
>
> "One of the couple's sons is observing his mother, father, and two younger brothers visit with a family friend (female) in their den."

Were your responses similar to these?

Responses to this picture clearly suggest the ways in which we view events through the lens of our particular cultural experiences. What if I told you that this

picture is set outdoors—in fact, that a waterfall is present in the background? What if I also told you that the individuals are not related to each other? Also, did you notice the dog in the foreground?

Just as I have asked you to consider alternative descriptions to this scene, I will also ask you to view developmental psychology through a cultural lens as you read this book. For example, consider the following information and the cultural viewpoints suggested:

- In Belgium and France, accessibility to preschool is a legal right; and in Finland and Sweden, preschoolers of two employed parents have their day care provided.
- Native speakers of Japanese process information related to vowel sounds in the left hemisphere of the brain, while individuals of Japanese ancestry who learn Japanese as a second language process vowel sounds in the right hemisphere (as do North and South Americans and Europeans).
- Children who are bilingual show greater cognitive flexibility; they solve problems with greater creativity and versatility.
- African American men have the lowest cancer survival rate, while white European American women have the highest.
- Kipsigi infants in Kenya, Africa, are taught to sit up, stand, and walk early in infancy. They are placed in shallow holes in the ground that are designed to keep them in upright positions. Parents hold their infants with their feet touching the ground and they are pushed forward.
- In adulthood, African Americans report lower overall life satisfaction than do white Americans because of lower income, fewer job opportunities, and prejudice encountered throughout their lives.
- Life expectancy in the United States is approximately six years longer for white individuals than for people of color, for both women and men.

In *Human Development in Multicultural Contexts: A Book of Readings,* we will focus on these kinds of issues as we discuss life cycle development from a multicultural perspective.

WHAT IS LIFE-CYCLE DEVELOPMENTAL PSYCHOLOGY?

What is *life-cycle developmental psychology?* It is the scientific study of the patterns of growth, stability, and change that occur from conception through older adulthood and death. Specifically, this text addresses the life cycle in five stages: infancy, preschool, middle childhood, adolescence, and adulthood. The *infancy* stage extends from childbirth through toddlerhood or approximately the second year of life. The *preschool* period of development characterizes children 2 to 5 years of age. *Middle childhood* encompasses the years 6 to 11 and is also referred to as the "school-age period," emphasizing the advances that are made in children's mathematical, writing, and reading skills. *Adolescence* is a transitional stage between childhood and adulthood, usually from 11 or 12 through 18 or 20 years of age. *Adulthood* is the period from about 21 years to death. Certainly in adolescence and adulthood there are substages; for example, early and later adolescence and young, middle, and older adulthood are readily discernible. The age ranges listed here are averages. Some children, adolescents, and adults reach their respective milestone earlier than average, some later than average, and many just around the time of the average age.

Within each of these stages of the life cycle, psychologists study dimensions of development, generally designated physical, cognitive, emotional, and social development. *Physical development* includes the genetic foundations for development, physical growth of the body, development of the senses, and development in fine and gross motor skills and in bodily systems, as well as in health care. *Cognitive development* encompasses changes in the intellectual processes of thinking, remembering, learning, problem solving, and communicating. *Emotional development* refers to the development of attachment, trust, affection, aggression, emotional disturbances, temperament, and independence. *Social development* covers the socialization process, including the development of friendships, relationships (including marriage, parenting, and grandparenting), and careers or vocations.

Thus, when developmental psychologists study the infancy period, they may study infants' physical development, that is, for example, how infants push upward, sit up, crawl, and eventually walk. Developmentalists who study infants' cognitive development may research infants' use of representation and symbols, the development of their language from babbling to holophrases to telegraphic speech, or how infants begin to understand object permanence. Developmental psychologists who are interested in infants' emotional development may investigate temperaments and activity levels, the development of empathy, or the nature of infant attachments. Topics of infants' social development include the understanding of facial expressions and adaptation to day care.

Each of these dimensions—the physical, cognitive, emotional, and social—emphasizes certain aspects of our development. However, you will note that there is considerable *interdependence* among these dimensions. Aspects of social development are influenced by biological maturation and cognitive maturity. Cognitive development depends on social experiences. For example, many girls and women in North American culture report feeling dissatisfaction with their bodies. In fact, many adolescent girls perceive the normative physical developmental changes accompanying pubescence (including the redistribution of weight) as weight gain and a need to diet. Here we have an emotional response to a physical change that is also related to social factors, such as how the girls perceive themselves in terms of their attractiveness to boys.

MULTICULTURALISM IN LIFE-CYCLE DEVELOPMENTAL PSYCHOLOGY

Within each of the life stages and dimensions of development, we will focus on the ways in which culture influences development. The term *culture* here includes the ways an individual's sex, gender, race, ethnicity, and socioeconomic class affect the course of life cycle development. Because these terms are often used interchangeably, when in fact they are qualitatively different, each of these terms needs to be defined.

Sex versus Gender. In this text, the Doyle and Paludi (1997) framework is utilized: the word *sex* is used only when referring to biology specifically, that is, to *female* and *male*, and the term *gender* is used only when discussing social, cultural, and psychological aspects of the traits, norms, stereotypes, and roles of women and men, identified by the terms *feminine* and *masculine*. Sex is thus a biological construct; gender is defined in terms of its social, cultural, and psychological components. When we discuss "sex differences," the reference is to differences between males and females based on biological differences such as reproductive differences. Discussion of "gender differences" refers to differences that result from socialization experiences such as differences in career choices observed in men and women.

Race versus Ethnicity. The term *race* is a biological concept. It refers to classifications based on physical and structural characteristics. *Ethnicity* encompasses individuals' cultural background, religion, language, and nationality. Thus ethnicity refers to social characteristics, while race designates a group of individuals with specific physical characteristics. Note, however, that though race is a biological concept, it is never independent of environmental and cultural contexts. We cannot, therefore, attribute individuals' behavior to race only (Betancourt & Lopez, 1993). We must consider the environment in which the individual develops, including values, birth order, employment status of parent(s), and family life in which the child (with or without siblings) is being raised (e.g., with a single mother or father, by grandparents as parents, or by foster parents). Hispanic Americans, Asian Americans, and African Americans are typically considered as both racial and ethnic categories; Italian Americans, Irish Americans, and Polish Americans, for example, are typically understood to refer only to ethnic groups.

Socioeconomic Class. Individuals' social class is measured in terms of three dimensions: education, income, and occupation. An individual with a higher socioeconomic class status is one with more education, a higher income, and a professional occupation.

Life-cycle developmental psychologists may study the four dimensions in each of the stages of the life cycle within a particular sex or racial group, ethnic group, or socioeconomic class. For example, in one of the reading selections in this volume (see p. 65), "Parents' Report of Vocabulary and Grammatical Development of African American Preschoolers: Child and Environmental Associations," Joanne E. Roberts and her colleagues report on their study on the ways child and family factors affect language development in African American children between 18 and 30 months of age. Other developmental psychologists look for similarities as well as differences among various racial groups and ethnic groups and between females and males. In another reading in this text (see p. 212), "Age Differences in Personality Across the Adult Life Span: Parallels in Five Cultures," Robert R. McCrae and his colleagues discuss age differences in various personality constructs among women and men in Germany, Italy, Portugal, Croatia, and South Korea. It is through these comparisons that McCrae and his co-researchers can identify principles of development that are universal and those that are culturally determined.

MULTICULTURALISM IN LIFE-CYCLE DEVELOPMENTAL PSYCHOLOGY: FROM MARGINALITY TO INCLUSION

The field of life-cycle developmental psychology has not always taken into consideration the impact of sex, gender, race, ethnicity, and class in understanding how children, adolescents, and adults develop in cognitive, social, emotional, and physical ways. In fact, many criticisms of the field of developmental psychology (and of psychology in general) have been made about researchers who have taken an androcentric, gendercentric, ethnocentric, and/or heterosexist perspective (Graham, 1992; Landrine, 1995; Landrine, Klonoff, & Brown-Collins, 1995; MacPhee, Kreutzer, & Fritz, 1994; Worell, 1990). *Androcentrism* refers to the tendency, in both theories and research designs, to use boys and men as the prototype for humankind and girls and women as variants on the dominant theme. *Gendercentrism* is evident when separate paths of life cycle development are suggested for women and men because of their biological differences. *Ethnocentrism* is the proclivity in theories and research designs to assume identical development for all individuals across all ethnic, racial, and class groups. *Heterosexism* is evident in personality theories that assume that a heterosexual orientation is normative, while a lesbian or gay sexual orientation is deviant. The need for a multicultural perspective in developmental research has been identified in the literature.

According to McGoldrick, Giordano, and Pearce (1996):

> Our very definitions of human development are ethnoculturally based. Eastern cultures, for example, tend to define the person as a social being and categorize development by growth in the human capacity for empathy and connection. By contrast, many Western cultures begin by positing the individual as a psychological being and defining development as growth in the capacity for differentiation. African Americans have a communal sense of identity: "We are, therefore I am," which contrasts deeply with the dominant culture's individualistic "I think, therefore I am." (p. viii)

Sandra Graham's (1992) analysis of journals published by the American Psychological Association (APA) suggested a declining representation of African American research in six journals, including the widely respected journal *Developmental Psychology*. Graham also noted that fewer than one third to one half of the articles dealing with African Americans appearing in these psychological journals specified the socioeconomic class status of the research participants. Furthermore, most of the studies published were race-comparative studies—African Americans were always compared to other races, especially to whites broadly—rather than race-homogeneous studies. Such a methodology of always comparing races ignores within-group variation (Azibo, 1988; Campbell, 1967). For example, African American individuals are as varied, and as different among themselves, as are European American individuals. Individuals' experiences are extremely diverse; there are significant differences in the socialization experiences of individuals from all races and ethnicities.

MacPhee, Kreutzer, and Fritz (1994) analyzed volumes of the journals *Child Development* and *Developmental Psychology* published from 1982 to 1991. Their analysis found that information on family background was not present in the majority of studies. In addition, they found that less than one third of the research studies included low-income or ethnically diverse participants and that only those studies that did include ethnically diverse participants analyzed the data with respect to this dimension. MacPhee et al. noted:

> It is likely that 80% of research on child development is not generalizable to diverse groups. This would be especially true of research on cognitive development (notably infant perception), childhood, peer status, and normative adolescent development. . . . Most research with diverse groups focused on cross-cultural differences in language or social development, children at risk for or exhibiting developmental dysfunctions, or adolescent social problems. (p. 701)

These researchers also found that studies confounded socioeconomic class and ethnicity or socioeconomic class and race. Group differences were thus exaggerated because minority individuals are overrepresented in the lower social strata. The groups were also more likely to be clinical samples, that is, drawn from clinical trials and therefore not representative of more common environments such as schools and families (MacPhee et al., 1994).

Furthermore, DeFour and Paludi (1988) reported that it is important to avoid the use of value-laden language so as not to legitimize negative stereotyping of ethnic minorities. For example, the labels used to describe various lifestyle choices depend on the socioeconomic class and/or ethnicity or race of the individual being discussed. Young, unmarried African American mothers have been described in the context of a "broken home," while older, single European American mothers have been frequently discussed in the context of an "alternative" or "contemporary" lifestyle.

These findings suggest that a researcher is just as likely to be influenced by her or his cultural beliefs, values, and expectations as is anyone else in society. Such bias is referred to as *experimenter bias* (Doyle & Paludi, 1997). Experimenter bias may cause a researcher to look at a problem in only one way, while avoiding other possibilities. For example, the exclusion of lesbian couples, fathers, nonmarried heterosexual couples, single women, or gay couples in parent-infant studies suggests a bias in the researcher's plan or perspective. Experimenter bias may also show itself in the way a researcher words his or her questions. For example, requesting information about a participant's "marital status" denies gay and lesbian relationships as well as nonmarital heterosexual cohabitating relationships. If our questions are embedded with our personal bias, we are more likely to find answers that support our bias (Doyle & Paludi, 1997).

Saarni (1998) noted a North American bias in conducting research with other cultures. She reported that in the 61 studies about Chinese individuals published in the *Journal of Cross-Cultural Psychology,* 30% of the first authors lived in a Chinese society, while 56% of the first authors were residents of the United States. According to Saarni:

> The fact remains that conclusions about the inhabitants of a complex set of societies . . . are being drawn that may not reflect the informed observations of the people who live in these societies. (p. 648)

Cole and Tamang (1998) looked at children in Nepal interculturally: Their study investigated emotional-expressive behavior in Western, Tamang (the Buddhist majority of Nepal), and Chhetri-Brahmin (the Hindu minority of Nepal) children (1998). A review by Saarni (1998) of the Cole and Tamang study included the following comment:

> The outcome yielded a discussion that was sensitive to cultural nuance, to differences in socioreligious values, and to the interactive nature of what one is exposed to in rural village life and what one is socialized toward. At the conclusion of the article, I came away with a clearer sense of how this study encouraged cultural collaboration, in that considerable use of both naïve and expert local informants was evident in both the design and the interpretation of the collected data. (p. 649)

Accordingly, a number of developmental psychologists (as well as psychologists who specialize in other fields) have reexamined the existing body of theory and research methodologies and questioned to what degree it is relevant to their own concerns and life experiences. This questioning has provided the basis for new areas of scholarly work, focusing on populations who previously had been omitted from research participation and from the theoretical perspectives of "mainstream" psychology (Doyle & Paludi, 1997). Journals such as *Journal of Black Psychology, Psychology of Women Quarterly,* and *Journal of Cross-Cultural Psychology* attest to the fact that there is psychological research and theory focusing on ethnic minority women and men. Their work has provided answers to a set of research problems that did not come to light in traditional psychology and could not be solved by androcentric, ethnocentric, gendercentric, and heterosexist paradigms.

Integrating the scholarship on race, sex, ethnicity, and class into research on life-cycle developmental psychology adds an important dimension: It provides more understanding of the development of all people.

PLACING MULTICULTURALISM WITHIN DEVELOPMENTAL PSYCHOLOGY COURSES

In addition to integrating cultural research in the field of developmental psychology, there are distinct advantages in placing cultural material in the developmental psychology curriculum (Albert, 1988). For example, students can obtain information not available in their own culture or comparative information about the incidence of a particular psychological issue in a different culture. We can also discuss values, practices, or ideas common to a certain cultural group. Moreover, the generalizability of psychological research can be assessed by looking at research from several cultures.

MacPhee et al. (1994) described a project to integrate a multicultural perspective into human development courses at Colorado State University. They reported significant changes in students' attitudes toward poverty and racial minorities among students enrolled in these courses relative to students enrolled in human development courses that did not view development from a multicultural perspective. This project also helped to decrease students' ethnocentrism. Their critical thinking skills and awareness of poverty as a developmental risk factor were increased.

I too have had students increase their appreciation for cultural influences on life cycle development when the curriculum integrates the scholarship on race, ethnicity, sex, and socioeconomic class. I have been fortunate to teach a seminar on the psychology of race, gender, sex, ethnicity, and class at the undergraduate level. I specifically designed the course to offer students a more inclusive psychology, helping them, whether as future researchers or in other endeavors, expand their worldviews by introducing the life experiences of culturally diverse individuals. The course encouraged students to consider race, sex, gender, ethnicity, and class as important psychological variables and to note the traditional bias in older psychological theories and research paradigms. Such a more inclusive developmental psychology course challenges students to begin formulating researchable hypotheses of their own. Of course, for future psychologists, a more inclusive course has the added benefit of providing role models and mentors who can facilitate career development.

Cushner (1987) has described another approach to teaching about multicultural influences in psychology. He developed *culture assimilators,* which are critical incidents that describe a situation, followed by a list of interpretations or responses. The incident builds to a conclusion that involves misunderstanding or miscommunication among people from different cultures; the list of responses requires an analysis from the reader. The assimilators have proven to be useful in altering individuals' cognitive, affective, and behavioral processes. The following excerpt is an example of an assimilator; read it for the next few minutes.

> *Jane Jefferson from Australia had recently arrived in a Central American country on a job assignment for a multinational organization. Wanting to see something of the local culture, she went to the public market. She stopped at one stall, looked at some dresses, and*

chatted with the owner of the stall in her high-school level Spanish. As Jane left the stall without buying anything, the owner seemed to shout at her in an unpleasant tone. Jane began to develop negative feelings about her entire job assignment and about the country.

What is a good analysis of Jane's negative feelings?

1. Jane's company should never have sent to Central America a person whose Spanish was only high-school level.
2. Jane was the target of prejudice, possibly of jealousy, on the part of the stall owner.
3. Jane damaged a dress, and this was the target of the owner's anger.
4. The owner of the stall was having a bad day, and this was the cause of the anger.
5. Jane was overreacting to a very vivid, personal, but probably atypical event. (p. 222)

Which alternative did you select? Now, continue with the assimilator, as described by Cushner. Find the alternative you selected and then read the description that accompanies this number.

If you chose Number 1:

You chose Number 1. Although it may be true that no multinational organization should send out representatives who have a poor command of the local language, the fact remains that they often do. Language fluency probably contributed to the problem, but there is a better explanation. Please choose again.

If you chose Number 2:

You chose Number 2. This is possible. Visitors from highly industrialized countries, where the average standard of living is high, sometimes report that they are the target of jealousy when they go abroad. But this targeting is rarely true of all or even most people in any given culture, and there is no evidence in this story that the stall owner feels this way. Please choose again.

If you chose Number 3:

You chose Number 3. The story says Jane only looked at the dresses, and so this answer is unlikely. Please choose again.

If you chose Number 4:

You chose Number 4. This is a possibility, and it is the sort of thought Jane should explore before coming up with a more general conclusion about the country and the people as a whole. There is another explanation that involves Jane's thinking. Please choose again.

If you chose Number 5:

You chose Number 5. This is the best explanation. There is a strong tendency to react to vivid events that involve a person in a very direct way. The fact that Jane herself was the target of (what seemed to be) anger is a much stronger influence than less vivid, perhaps dull, information. For in-

> stance, Jane might have read in a survey report that most representatives of multinational organizations find this country a pleasure to live in and its citizens cooperative. This written report will be much less important in her mind than this one negative event in which she was directly involved. Given that Jane is a recent arrival and is still getting settled, the negative event will probably be even more influential in her thinking. The advice for sojourners is to ask themselves: "Am I overinterpreting a vivid, colorful event in which I was directly involved. Is there other information I should seek out before coming to a conclusion?" (p. 222)

How did you do with this assimilator? Do you find this is an effective way to learn about cultures?

RATIONALE FOR THE SELECTION OF READINGS

This book of readings introduces you to several theories, research studies, and applications that are part of the discipline of life-cycle development psychology, examining both traditional research findings and modifications to the existing body of knowledge that result from cultural approaches. Thus, throughout, a non-Eurocentric approach is the norm. This book also looks at several issues in life cycle development—for example, play, friendship formation, aggression, and violence—during more than one of the life stages, to highlight any continuity and/or discontinuity in development. We will see, for example, that violence among preschoolers may continue throughout childhood, adolescence, and into adulthood, expressing itself differently in each of these stages, either toward peers or, later, toward those with whom they are involved in romantic relationships. We will also see that excessive dieting and self-esteem issues in adolescence (primarily in girls) generally carry through to adulthood. In fact, research suggests girls' mothers are also dealing with weight concerns and feelings of unattractiveness and being less feminine; that is, similar issues are being dealt with at different life stages, coinciding with menarche (the first menstrual period, which signals reproductive maturity) and menopause (the cessation of the menses, the end of a woman's reproductive capacity).

Some of the readings are race-, class-, ethnicity-, and sex-homogenous; other articles are comparative. This is by intention, to give you the opportunity to read both kinds of research in developmental psychology. In addition, some articles describe cross-sectional research (i.e., research in which people of different ages are compared at the same point in time, thus providing information about age differences in development), while others describe longitudinal research (i.e., research in which the behavior of individuals is measured as they age, thus measuring age changes). It is important to note that cultural differences are not primarily differences in behavior; rather, they are differences in the meanings attributed and attached to identical behaviors.

Furthermore, some of the readings question the application of methodologies initially tested for individuals of one sex, race, or ethnicity in research on all individuals. For example, you will be reading about the Strange Situation, developed by Mary Ainsworth and her colleagues (e.g., Ainsworth & Bell, 1970) for use in determining types of attachments infants have with their mothers. This methodology was designed for research with infants in the United States. Thus a critical multicultural psychology leads to this question: Are infants from other countries being labeled incorrectly with this assessment tool because of limited cross-cultural utility and low validity (Kagan, 1984)? That is, are infants' attachment classifications a measurement fact or artifact?

With respect to methodology, the reading selections use several types of data collection techniques, including naturalistic observation, interviews, questionnaires and checklists, and standardized testing. *Naturalistic observation* involves research conducted in a natural setting by watching and recording behavior—for example, of mothers and children at home, adolescents with peers at school, or children interacting with peers and with adults in a neighborhood. In one of the readings in chapter 2, "African American Fathers in Low Income, Urban Families: Development, Behavior, and Home Environment of Their Three-Year-Old Children" by Maureen M. Black, Howard Dubowitz, and Raymond Starr Jr., mothers and their children were asked to play with blocks and a book while their interactions were videotaped.

The use of *interviews* involves face-to-face meetings between researchers and participants during which information given in answers to questions is recorded. For example, in their article (also in chapter 2), "Effects of Community Violence on Inner-City Preschoolers and Their Families," Jo Ann M. Farver, Lucia X. Natera, and Dominick L. Frosch interviewed mothers about the frequency of their exposure to violence, as victims of it, as primary witnesses to it, or as secondary witnesses who hear about violence in their neighborhood. *Questionnaires* and *checklists* are research methods that use written forms and responses to obtain relevant information from children, adolescents, and adults. In questionnaires, research participants provide written answers of various lengths to predetermined questions. Checklists provide a shortened version of questionnaires, by which researchers obtain participants' responses quickly. One example of the use of questionnaires is the reading in chapter 1 by Abraham Sagi, Frank Donnell, Marinus H. van IJzendoorn, Ofra Mayseless, and Ora Aviezer, "Sleeping Out of Home in a Kibbutz Communal Arrangement: It Makes a Difference for Infant-Mother Attachment." In this study, Sagi et al. used the Maternal Separation Anxiety Scale, Nursing Child Assessment Teaching Scales, and Infant Characteristics Questionnaire as part of their data collection techniques.

Standardized testing involves the use of tests to measure specific characteristics, such as intelligence or personality traits. For example, Joanne E. Roberts, Margaret Burchinal, and Meghan Durham, in their article, "Parents' Report of Vocabulary and Grammatical Development of African American Preschoolers: Child and Environmental Associations," describe testing participants with the Peabody Picture Vocabulary Test–Revised, the Sequenced Inventory of Communication Development–Revised, and the MacArthur Communication Development Inventory.

Some of the excerpted articles you will read describe research with individuals within the United States; many of the articles are international. Many of the authors are scholars at universities in countries other than the United States, including Argentina, France, Japan, Israel, the Netherlands, Italy, South Korea, Croatia, Germany, Portugal, and Mexico. The readings were chosen with special attention to Rubin's (1998) sentiment about researching development from a cultural perspective: namely, that researchers must ". . . examine the meaningfulness of the constructs that they study across the international divide. The efforts made in this regard will produce truly significant developmental outcomes" (p. 613).

Another goal of this selection of readings is to assist you in questioning the omission of cultural variables in other courses and textbooks in the psychology curriculum. The articles presented or recommended in this reader can be introduced into other courses in the psychology curriculum, including social psychology, clinical psychology, history of psychology, health psychology, psychology of gender, vocational psychology, personality, and statistics and experimental design. I encourage you to share what you are learning from this text in your other classes and when reading empirical research. Questions to ask include:

> What are the ethnic and racial backgrounds of the research participants in the experiments being discussed?
>
> Does the research focus on similarities between the sexes and among the racial or ethnic groups represented or are only differences noted?
>
> Are any differences due to sex, gender, race, class, or ethnicity inaccurately magnified to promote separation among individuals?

Halpern (1995, pp. 88–89) has provided researchers (and students) with a set of recommendations when planning, reading, and interpreting research. These recommendations include:

> Are main effects being moderated by unidentified interactions? For example, is the main effect of gender or ethnicity really the effect of socioeconomic status on gender or ethnicity? Would the effects of gender, for example, change if different age groups had been included as subjects? What other variables are confounded with gender and ethnicity? For example, African Americans in the United States take fewer college preparatory courses in high school than white students. Given the confounding of these variables, would at least part of the differences that are found be attributable to differential course-taking patterns? Are you careful to distinguish between research results and interpretations of research results? For example, the finding that women and men show different patterns of scores on the SATs does not necessarily mean that there are gender ability differences. All it does mean is at this time and with this test, there are "on the average" between-gender differences. Results of this sort indicate nothing about the cause of these differences.

On this last point, McHugh, Koeske, & Frieze (1986) have offered nonsexist guidelines for psychological research, including:

> Carefully examine the underlying values and assumptions in all research and state them explicitly.

Consider all possible explanations for sex-related phenomena, including social-cultural, biological, and situational factors.

Become aware of, consider, and devise studies of alternative and more complex models of causation.

Denmark, Russo, Frieze, & Sechzer (1988) have also provided researchers with guidelines to avoid sexism in psychological research. For example:

Research Methods:

Problem: The selection of research participants is based on stereotypic assumptions and does not allow for generalizations to other groups.

Example: On the basis of stereotypes about who should be responsible for contraception, only females are looked at in studies of contraception.

Correction: Both sexes should be studied before conclusions are drawn about the factors that determine use of contraception.

Guidelines offered by McHugh et al. (1986), Denmark et al. (1988), and Halpern (1995) provide the beginnings for an alternative approach to the study of human development. First and foremost, research is viewed as taking place within a well-defined cultural and social context, never totally free from the concerns and values of the larger society, including those of the researcher(s).

I urge you to keep a journal as you read this text and participate in your class. It is a reflective practice I recommend to all students. You may want to start by jotting down your answers to the following questions after each class discussion and reading.

What was the value of this issue to you as a whole?

How would you describe this discussion/reading to a friend?

Were any of the issues raised in class and/or in this text emotionally painful for you? Why?

Did the readings challenge your assumptions and attitudes about people who are of a different sex, race, ethnicity and/or socioeconomic class from you?

What did you learn and relearn about yourself today in terms of how your own cultural experiences have shaped your personality and interactions with peers?

Due to space limitations in this text, we were unable to reprint the readings in their entirety. We have provided you with the complete citation of the articles on the first page of each essay selection. I encourage you to continue your studies on multicultural issues in life-cycle developmental psychology by reading the articles in their entirety as they appeared in journal form. The authors provide a wealth of information on innovative research methodologies and suggestions for further research. I also encourage you to pursue your own research in life-cycle developmental psychology from a multicultural perspective.

Give a man a fish and you feed him for a day. Teach a man to fish and you feed him for a lifetime.

Chinese Proverb

Praise the young and they will blossom.

Irish Proverb

Infancy

Questions for Reflection

- Do you believe parents should take an active role in helping their children develop gross and fine motor skills? Why or why not?
- Do you know infants who are smaller or larger than average for their age? What implications do you think their size will have for their social and emotional development throughout childhood?
- By what processes do you believe children learn to use language?
- How do you think infants influence the language that adults use to address them?
- Do you believe that there are temperamental differences among infants of different races? Between boys and girls?
- Do you believe it is healthier for infants to be physically separated from their parents while they sleep? Or do you believe it is healthier for them to be in the same room while they sleep?
- Do you believe that there are cultural differences in children's reactivity?
- Does culture influence the types of play in which infants engage? Why or why not?

OVERVIEW: CULTURAL INFLUENCES ON DEVELOPMENT IN INFANCY

The readings in this chapter deal with several popular areas of research in infancy: infant-directed speech, infants' sleeping arrangements, temperament, mother-infant attachment, and play during infancy. We begin with an overview of the physical changes that accompany the infancy period. Then we look at the focus of the research reported in the excerpted articles that have been selected to give students a broader grasp of the literature and the research context. Each of the dimensions of development discussed—the physical, cognitive, emotional, and social—reflects the others; there is a great deal of interdependence among the basic dimensions of human development over the entire life span.

PHYSICAL DEVELOPMENT IN INFANCY

The term *infancy* covers the life stage that extends from childbirth through toddlerhood, or the second year of life. Infancy is accompanied by tremendous changes in development (Bornstein, 1999; Rice, 1997). For example, at the end of this period, the average infant in the United States has grown from 20 to 36 inches in height and from 7 to approximately 27 pounds. Development for infants follows the cephalocaudal principle and the proximodistal principle: Growth progresses from the head region to the feet (cephalocaudal principle) and from the center of the body outward to the extremities (proximodistal principle). Sex comparisons have been noted in infancy. Infant girls are more mature at birth than are infant boys. Girls have more advanced skeletal and neurological systems (Rathus, 1988). Girls continue to mature between 2 and 2.5 years faster than boys, as we will discuss in more detail in the following sections.

Infants' fine and gross motor skills become more developed during this life stage (Williams & Abernathy, 2000). Infants learn to control the muscles of their head and neck, then their arms and abdomen, and finally their legs. Thus infants learn to hold their heads up before they can sit, and they learn to sit before they learn to walk. Their large muscle control develops before fine muscle control. Research has suggested that the development of motor skills reflects cultural differences. For example, Hopkins and Westra (1989) reported from their research with Jamaican, English, and Indian mothers that Jamaican mothers expected their infants to sit and to walk significantly earlier than did Indian and English mothers. The emergence of these activities in Jamaican infants was in line with their mothers' expectations. Jamaican mothers made their infants practice stepping early in infancy.

Furthermore, infants raised in Côte d'Ivoire (Ivory Coast), Africa, develop motor skills at an earlier age than infants reared in France (Dasen, Inhelder, Lavalee, & Retschitzki, 1978). Like Jamaican mothers, mothers in Ivory Coast emphasize motor skills more heavily than mothers in Western societies. These findings suggest that the time at which motor skills appear in infancy is partly determined by cultural factors: Parents teach activities that are an intrinsic part of their culture to their infants. This in turn leads to the potential for the earlier emergence of these activities (Nugent, Lester, & Brazelton, 1989). There is inconclusive data to date to indicate whether the differences in timing of motor activities in infancy have long-term effects on children's and adults' motor skill levels.

COGNITIVE DEVELOPMENT

Focus on Infant-Directed Speech

Infants communicate nonverbal body language, including facial expression, tense muscles, tears, shivering, quivering, and movement (McClure, 2000; Molfese & Molfese, 2000). Infants' early achievement of binocular vision allows sophisticated perception of depth and motion (McCarty & Ashmead, 1999). Infants' auditory perception is well developed, having begun growth in utero. Infants can localize sound, make fine sound discriminations, and discriminate tones and sound patterns. In fact, Marco Dondi and his colleagues (Dondi, Simon, & Caltran, 1999) found that newborns can discriminate between their own cry and the cry of another newborn infant. Furthermore, infants' senses of taste and smell are sophisticated. They react (as adults do, by smiling or crinkling their noses) to pleasant and unpleasant tastes and odors. Very young infants can even recognize their mothers' and fathers' scents (Porter, Bologh, & Makin, 1988).

Goodwyn and Acredolo (1993, reported in Rice, 1997) have found that gestural symbols appear before vocal symbols in infants. With respect to verbal communication, infants progress from cooing and babbling to the acquisition of a thousand-word vocabulary (Bornstein, 2000). Infants also acquire an understanding of grammar and syntax (Camaioni, Longobardi, Venuti, & Bornstein, 1998; D'Odorico, Salerni, Cassibba, & Jacob, 1999; Jusczyk, 1999). Burchinal et al. (2000) recently reported that quality of infant child care is correlated with language development and cognitive development for infants and toddlers. Infants' language development is a prime avenue of research for developmental psychologists. We will address this aspect of infants' cognitive development in more detail by focusing our attention on infant-directed speech.

Infants' speech is telegraphic, that is, infants communicate in short, simple sentences that have little formal structure. Parents and other adults speak to infants in this way as well: the pitch of their voice rises, their intonation has a singsong quality, they separate words carefully, and they utilize short, simple sentences. Thus adults shift in their language when speaking to infants; they engage in what developmental psychologists refer to as *infant-directed speech* or "motherese." Deaf mothers also use infant-directed speech. When using sign language with infants, deaf mothers sign at a significantly lower tempo than when they are signing with adults. Moreover, they repeat the signs (Masataka, 1993; Swanson, Leonard, & Grandour, 1992).

Infant-directed speech establishes ties of closeness and warmth between the infant and adult. This speech pattern is modified as children become older, usually when the child is 2 years old. Parents use longer sentences with children this age and vary vocal pitch to enhance important words. There have been clear-cut gender differences noted in the way adults speak to boys and girls (Gleason, 1987; Gleason, Perlmann, Ely, & Evans, 1991). For example, by 32 months, girls hear approximately twice as many diminutives as boys hear (e.g., *doggy, dolly, kitty* instead of *dog, doll,* and *cat*). Furthermore, parents respond to girls and boys differently in the use of their language (Perlmann & Gleason, 1990). For example, when refusing a son's request, parents are more likely to respond with a firm "No"; however, when refusing a daughter's request, they "soften" the response by making the refusal less direct. Thus, instead of saying "No—don't touch," parents are more likely to say "Why don't you play with this toy instead?"

Research has suggested that there are similarities across cultures in both mothers and fathers in the utilization *in* of high pitch, repetition, lowered volume, lengthened vowels, exaggerated intonation, and heavy stress on certain words (Fernald, 1989). Mothers, however, raise their pitch more than fathers when speaking to infants. Explanations for the cross-cultural similarities in infant-directed speech have centered on the way in which the characteristics of this form of speech activate innate responses in infants. Infants prefer infant-directed speech over adult-directed speech; thus their perceptual systems may be more responsive to such characteristics. In addition, infant-directed speech facilitates language development; that is, this type of speech provides cues to the meaning of speech before infants have developed the capacity for understanding what words mean (Fernald & Kuhl, 1987). The way in which adults speak to children plays an important role in the way children acquire language (Fernald, 1991). Extensive exposure to infant-directed speech is related to the early appearance of first words and other examples of linguistic competence. Further, infant-directed speech is a way to communicate the code of a culture to an infant.

In the excerpt from their article "Functional Analysis of the Contents of Maternal Speech to Infants of 5 and 13 Months in Four Cultures: Argentina, France, Japan, and the United States," in the readings section of this chapter (see p. 25–31), Marc H. Bornstein and his colleagues report on their naturalistic observations of maternal speech. They conclude that there is universality of maternal speech to infants. They also note no effects of infants' sex, maternal age, or educational status in the use of infant-directed speech by mothers in their sample.

In addition, Bornstein et al. report findings on how Argentinean, Japanese, French, and U.S. American mothers use affect-salient infant-directed speech with their 5-month-old infants and use more information-marked speech with their 13-month-old infants. Thus mothers from each of the cultures in the study expected their older infants to understand their questions more and to need an increasing amount of information about themselves and their environment. It is important to note that since infants begin to talk during this life stage, mothers may believe that they need to adjust their speech so it will take on more of an adultlike manner.

Differences in maternal speech were also observed by Bornstein et al. For example, Argentinean mothers made more direct statements to their infants than did mothers from the other three cultures in their sample. Bornstein and his colleagues discuss this finding by pointing to the traditional child-rearing orientation and pedagogical techniques in Argentina as fundamentally authoritative (Diaz Rossello, 1988). Thus, in this culture, infants are viewed as *needing* instruction.

In addition, Bornstein et al. found that American mothers questioned their infants more than did mothers from the other four cultures, suggesting that children participate in their own language development. French mothers placed less emphasis on achievement stimulation and more emphasis on emotional support and the use of language to establish warmth and closeness.

Bornstein et al. note the reciprocity of the impact of maternal speech on infants and the impact in turn of infants' behavior on maternal speech. They conclude:

> One of the ways infants become socialized into culture is through integrating maternal behavior and speech into their development, and one of the ways they do this is via mother–infant communication. . . . Universal aspects of infancy, such as the dramatic growth of competence over the 1st year, appear also to exert control over the contents of maternal speech. (p. 601; in this text, p. 29)

EMOTIONAL DEVELOPMENT

Focus on Infants' Sleeping Arrangements

Infants are able to express and experience emotions, even minutes after birth (Rice, 1997). Infants from different cultures use very similar facial expressions to reflect basic emotions such as being happy and sad. Initially, infants are not aware that they exist separately from the rest of their environment. This self-awareness usually develops after their first birthday (Rice, 1997). Also, by age 2 years, infants have developed a realization of a distinction between humans and inanimate objects and have begun to understand empathy and the ability to pretend.

For many theorists, one hallmark of "healthy" development is independence training—learning to separate from one's family of origin (Munroe, Munroe, & Whiting, 1981). In fact, among many child development experts in the United States, this independence training begins in infancy, with separate sleeping arrangements for infants and their caregivers (Brazelton, 1979; Ferber, 1986; Lozoff, Wolf, & Davis, 1984). Research has suggested that in the United States it is relatively rare for infants to sleep with their parents for part or all of a night on a regular basis (Crowell, Kenner, Ginsburg, & Anders, 1987; Lozoff et al., 1984; Valsiner & Hall, 1983). American theorists have cautioned parents about having their infants sleep with them at night, especially because of the difficulty in breaking this habit.

The value placed on this form of independence right from infancy appears to be unique to the United States. Whiting (1964) reported that in many cultures, it is considered customary for infants to sleep in the same room as their mothers or in the same beds with their mothers. A survey of the practice of infants sleeping with their parents in 100 societies indicated that only American parents have separate sleeping arrangements (McKenna, 1986). Studies that have focused on communities within the United States have found that distinct ethnic, economic, and demographic differences in infants sleeping with their parents are common. For example, Wolf and Lozoff (1989) reported less infant-mother sleeping arrangements when mothers had some college education, as opposed to those mothers who did not have some college education. Ward (1971) noted that African American children are more likely than white American children to fall asleep with a caregiver present and to have their beds in their parents' room. This is the general case; in a specific case, infants living in eastern Kentucky sleep near or with their parents throughout infancy (Abbott, 1992).

In another article, "Cultural Variation in Infants' Sleeping Arrangements: Questions of Independence," also excerpted in the readings section (see pp. 31–37), Gilda Morelli, Barbara Rogoff, David Oppenheim, and Denise Goldsmith report on their study of middle-class U.S. American and Highland Mayan parents' decisions about sleeping arrangements for their infants. Morelli and her colleagues found that all Mayan infants in their sample slept in their mothers' beds throughout the infancy period. None of the U.S. infants slept with their mothers on a regular basis as neonates, but the majority did sleep near their mother until they were between 3 and 6 months. How did the mothers explain their decisions for the infants' sleeping arrangements? Morelli et al. discuss Mayan mothers' value of closeness with their infants and the U.S. mothers' value of independence for their babies.

In addition, U.S. mothers relied on bedtime routines, such as reading bedtime stories or singing lullabies, as transitions to sleep. None of the Mayan mothers used these routines with their infants. Also, their infants typically did not use security objects or suck their thumbs. The majority of U.S. infants, however, did bring a favorite object with them to bed; those few infants who slept near another person did not use a security object.

Morelli and her colleagues note that when told of how U.S. mothers deal with their infants' sleeping arrangements, Mayan mothers responded to this distinction "... with shock, disapproval, and pity." As they comment:

> Another mother responded with shock and disbelief, asked whether the babies do not mind, and added with feeling that it would be very painful for her to have to do that. The responses of the Mayan parents gave the impression that they regarded the practice of having infants and toddlers sleep in separate rooms as tantamount to child neglect. (p. 608; in this text, p. 35)

Focus on Infant Temperament

Have you heard your parent(s) say that you were most active in infancy and toddlerhood, while a sibling or cousin was just the opposite—calm and passive? To what can we attribute such differences in infants? Developmental psychologists believe these differences can be explained by temperament. *Temperament* refers to patterns of arousal and emotionality that represent infants' consistent and enduring characteristics. Research has suggested that infants exhibit differences in temperament from birth. Genetic factors play a role in infants' temperament; prenatal factors and the nature of the child's birth influence an infant's temperament as well (Caspi, Henry, McGee, Moffitt, & Silva, 1995; Sanson, Smart, Prior, Oberklaid, & Pedlow, 1994). Research has also suggested that temperament is relatively stable from infancy through adolescence (Riese, 1990; Teerikangas, Aronen, Martin, & Huttumen, 1998).

Developmental psychologists use temperament as an umbrella term that encompasses many behaviors—for example, activity level or overall movement of infants, irritability, distraction, adaptability, attention span, and intensity of arousal (Thomas & Chess, 1977). This latter dimension, intensity of arousal, is sometimes referred to as "reactivity" or "ease of arousal" (Rothbart, 1989). Infants typically differ in behaviors that reflect their arousal level, including motor activity, fretting, crying, vocalization, and smiling. They also differ in the type of incentive that elicits their arousal (e.g., visual stimulation or auditory stimulation). Kagan and Snidman (1991) found that infants are more likely to respond more vigorously to moving objects than to speech. These researchers also noted that infants smile in response to speech more than to visual stimuli.

In their article, "Reactivity in Infants: A Cross-National Comparison," excerpted in the readings section (see pp. 37-41), Jerome Kagan, Doreen Arcus, Nancy Snidman, Wang Yu Feng, John Hendler, and Sheila Greene discuss research they conducted on reactivity with 4-month-old infants in Beijing, Dublin, and Boston. The research highlights temperamental differences among infants of different cultures in reactivity to stimulation. Specifically, Kagan et al. administered visual, auditory, and olfactory stimuli to infants and evaluated similarities and differences in their level of reactivity. This study poses the question, Do infants from different cultural backgrounds differ in ease of arousal? Kagan et al. found that Chinese infants were significantly less irritable, less active, and less vocal than infants in the Boston and Dublin samples. They also noted that American infants exhibited the highest level of reactivity.

With respect to sex comparisons, Kagan and his colleagues found no differences for fretting, crying, or motor activity. However, they noted a differential in vocalization and smiling: Male infants smiled more and vocalized more than female infants.

SOCIAL DEVELOPMENT

Focus on Mother-Infant Attachment

Attachment refers to a positive emotional bond that develops between an infant and another person. In fact, the types of attachments infants have during their first life stage has significant effects for how they relate to people throughout their lives

(Beckwith, Cohen, & Hamilton, 1999; Greenberg, Cicchetti, & Cummings, 1990). Attachment has been operationally defined as securely, avoidant, and ambivalent (Ainsworth, Blehar, Waters, & Wall, 1978). Infants described as *securely attached children* use their mothers as a kind of home base; they are at ease when their mothers are present and are upset when they leave. Upon their mothers' return, securely attached infants go to their mothers immediately.

Infants may also be described as avoidant children or as ambivalent children. *Avoidant children* do not seek proximity to their mothers and avoid their mothers when they return from being away. *Ambivalent children* respond positively and negatively to their mothers; while they show distress when their mothers leave, they exhibit close contact and aggression toward her (Cassidy & Berlin, 1994).

Egeland and Farber (1984) introduced a fourth category of attachment: disorganized-disoriented children. *Disorganized-disoriented children* exhibit inconsistent, contradictory behavior. A disorganized-disoriented child may approach his or her mother when she enters a room yet not look at her (Egeland & Farber, 1984).

Cross-cultural research on attachment suggests that German infants were more likely to be classified as avoidant children than attached or ambivalent (Grossman, Grossman, Huber, & Wartner, 1982) and Israeli and Japanese infants are less likely to be securely attached than infants in the United States (Sagi, 1990). In the excerpt of their article in the readings section (see pp. 41–44), "Sleeping Out of Home in a Kibbutz Communal Arrangement: It Makes a Difference for Infant-Mother Attachment," Abraham Sagi, Frank Donnell, Marinus H. van IJzendoorn, Ofra Mayseless, and Ora Aviezer describe research with two types of Israeli kibbutzim: settlements that have infants' houses with communal sleeping arrangements and others that have infants' houses with home-based sleeping arrangements. Sagi and his colleagues report that there were no differences in infants' temperament, mother-infant play interaction, quality of infants' daytime environment, or any of the maternal variables studied, such as age, education, profession, occupation, or background in child care.

Sagi et al. did find that among the home-based infants, 80% were securely attached to their mothers, whereas 48% of infants in communal sleeping arrangements were securely attached. The researchers also found that infants in the communal group cried on average 10 times a week, thus exhibiting distress. These infants encountered different women who looked after their needs. This arrangement does not permit infants to develop attachments. Their behavior is relatively inconsistent since they interact with their mothers during the day and different watchwomen at night.

It should be noted, however, that most of the data on attachment has been obtained by using Ainsworth's Strange Situation. This methodology consists of a sequence of staged episodes that illustrate the strength of attachment between children and parents. The staged episodes are a sequence of presences and absences, as follows: The parent and child enter an unfamiliar room. The parent sits down and leaves the baby free to explore. Next, an adult stranger enters the room and talks initially to the parent and then to the child. The parent then departs the room, leaving the infant alone with this stranger. The parent returns and comforts the baby, as the stranger now leaves the room. Again the parent exits, leaving the baby alone. In sequence, the stranger returns, and then finally, the parent returns and the stranger leaves (Ainsworth et al., 1978). This methodology was developed for use with United States infants. It has been used with infants from cultures other than the United States as well, raising another major theme of this book: that researchers have used methodologies normed on one cultural group on other cultural groups for which they are not appropriate (Sagi, van IJzendoorn, & Koren-Karie, 1991).

For example, in Japanese culture parents avoid separation experiences and independence training during infancy, as do parents in other cultures, including the United States. Japanese infants thus lack experience with separation situations. Consequently, they may experience a great deal of stress when placed in the Strange Situation. Their behavior may be mislabeled as avoidant or ambivalent or disorganized-disoriented (Nakagawa, Lamb, & Miyaki, 1992; Takahaski, 1990). In opposition to Bowlby's (1951) claim that attachment is universal, research suggests that attachment is not entirely biologically determined. Cultural norms and expectations play a major role in attachment.

Focus on Play

Marc H. Bornstein and his colleagues, O. Maurice Haynes, Liliana Pascual, Kathleen M. Painter, and Celia Galperín, in the excerpt from their article in the readings section (see pp. 45–50), "Play in Two Societies: Pervasiveness of Process, Specificity of Structure," also observe how culture is transmitted via mother-infant interaction—in this study, through play. Bornstein et al. note that play is engaged in by infants and children in most cultures and that play expresses unique concerns to specific cultures. Thus play, similar to infant-directed speech, provides a context for cultural learning. In some cultures (e.g., Italy, Indonesia, Guatemala), parents believe play does not require adult supervision: It is the purview of children themselves (New, 1994; Rogoff, Mistry, Göncü, & Mosier, 1993). In other cultures (e.g., Turkey), parents believe they are play partners for their children and take an active part in their child's play (Göncü & Mosier, 1991; Tamis-LeMonda, Bornstein, Cyphers, Toda, & Ogino, 1992).

Bornstein and his colleagues compared infants and their mothers from Argentina and the United States on different types of play, namely, exploratory, symbolic, and social play. *Exploratory play* includes actions directed toward a single object—for example, rolling a ball. In *symbolic play,* infants enact activities—for example, drinking from an empty cup. *Social play* in infancy is verbal and/or physical actions directed to the infant to draw out a social response, such as sounds to bring smiles. Bornstein et al. selected Argentinean infants and mothers to study because child-rearing values in this culture reflect an authoritarian style: obedience, reward and punishment, as well as mutual dependence with parents and children. Research has suggested that Argentinean mothers are self-critical and fearful of making mistakes in raising their children (Bornstein et al., 1998). Thus Bornstein and his colleagues hypothesized that these cultural beliefs would express themselves in Argentinean mothers' play with their children.

Similarly, Bornstein et al. believed that U.S. American mothers would express their cultural values toward child rearing in play with their children. Specifically, they would encourage individual achievement, self-actualization, and autonomy. Results suggested that U.S. mothers and their children engaged in more exploratory play and that Argentinean mothers and their children participated in more symbolic play. Argentinean mothers exceeded U.S. mothers in social play and verbal praise of their children.

An interesting gender comparison was observed in both Argentinean and U.S. children: Girls played more often in a symbolic mode and boys played more often in an exploratory mode. Moreover, results suggested that mothers of boys participated in more exploratory play and mothers of girls engaged in more symbolic play. How would you account for this gender comparison? Bornstein and his colleagues offer several interpretations related to differential socialization patterns that stress caregiving and nurturance in girls.

It should also be noted that children who participate in more symbolic play tend to exhibit more advanced language (Thal & Katich, 1996), more imaginative cognitions, and more skillful interpersonal actions (Burns & Brainard, 1979). Thus an interdependence among dimensions of development is evident. We return to the importance of play in children's cognitive and social development when we address the preschool stage of the life cycle in the next chapter. We will find that play for older children, similar to play for infants, reflects the cultures' child-rearing goals. As Bornstein and his colleagues conclude: "In play, processes may be pervasive, but emphases on different structures appear to be culture specific" (p. 328; in this text, p. 48).

Readings

Functional Analysis of the Contents of Maternal Speech to Infants of 5 and 13 Months in Four Cultures: Argentina, France, Japan, and the United States*

Marc H. Bornstein, Joseph Tal, Charles Rahn, Celia Z. Galperín, Marie-Germaine Pêcheux, Martine Lamour, Sueko Toda, Hiroshi Azuma, Misako Ogino, and Catherine S. Tamis-LeMonda

Maternal speech to infants serves several significant functions in development. First, verbal interactions establish ties of proximity, closeness, and warmth between mother and baby (e.g., Kaye, 1982; Stern, 1985). Second, although prelingual infants may not benefit from lexical as much as prosodic features of speech directed to them (Papoušek, Papoušek, & Bornstein, 1985), maternal speech is acknowledged to play a substantial role in the child's early language learning (e.g., Bornstein & Lamb, 1992; Garton, 1991; Harris, 1991; Rondal, 1985. Third, maternal speech begins the process of informing infants about themselves, about mother, and about the environment (e.g., Sachs, 1977). Last, but not least, to the extent that maternal speech reflects the communicational code of a culture, it plays a central role in socializing culturally appropriate communication style (e.g., Blount, 1990; Clancy, 1986; Givon, 1985; Ochs, 1986). These multiple functions elevate maternal speech to babies to the level of a central subject of psychological, linguistic, and cultural study.

Developmental psycholinguists have approached the analysis of maternal speech to babies with different aims. One has been to evaluate its functional aspects, as for example, to contrast categories of speech where the intent is social interaction from speech that is directed toward describing or discovering the environment. In this vein, Brown (1977, p. 6) divided the universe of maternal speech addressed to infants into contrasting "features concerned with affection (affection-inspiring, tenderness-inspiring, intimacy-inspiring) and features concerned with communicative competence (verbal production, verbal comprehension, and cognitive competence)." This basic division of maternal speech to infants into

*Bornstein et al. (1992). *Developmental Psychology, 28*(4), 593–603. Reprinted with permission.

affect-salient and information-salient contents has been widely adopted (e.g., de Villiers & de Villiers, 1978; Folger & Chapman, 1978; Penman, Cross, Milgrom-Friedman, & Meares, 1983; Sherrod, Crawley, Petersen, & Bennett, 1978; Toda, Fogel, & Kawai, 1990). The present study follows in this tradition.

In a related vein, investigators have long speculated that the contents of maternal speech to infants should also be influenced by characteristics of the baby, including age and developmental level (e.g., Bates, 1976; Bruner, 1974/1975; Cross, 1977; Philips, 1973; Sherrod, Friedman, Crawley, Drake, & Devieux, 1977). As infants grow over the 1st year, maternal speech patterns and actions toward them shift from feeling-oriented and self-marking content to object-oriented and environment-marking content in ways consistent with infants' increasing interest in their surroundings (Adamson & Bakeman, 1984; Bornstein & Tamis-LeMonda, 1990; Penman et al., 1983). In an exemplary longitudinal analysis, Snow (1977) observed that mothers changed emphasis from discussing their infants' internal states and feelings to discussing activities and events in the immediate surround. For this reason, in the present study we analyzed speech in mothers with babies of two ages, 5 months and 13 months. By the middle of the infant's 1st year, conversations with mothers have taken on many mature characteristics, such as turn taking (Bornstein & Tamis-LeMonda, 1990; Cohn & Tronick, 1987; Kaye & Fogel, 1980; Stevenson, Ver Hoeve, Roach, & Leavitt, 1986), but the infant is still almost exclusively preverbal. By the start of the 2nd year, infants comprehend considerable amounts of speech they hear, and many are even themselves beginning to talk (Bates, Bretherton, & Snyder, 1988; Tamis-LeMonda & Bornstein, 1990).

In this study, we also evaluated maternal speech to infants in different cultural settings. Argentina, France, Japan, and the United States comprise an attractive comparative set in which to investigate universal as well as culture-specific aspects of developmental change and continuity in maternal speech. There are several reasons why. In these countries, we specifically chose to study maternal speech in Porteños, Parisians, Tokyo people, and New Yorkers. These particular locales and samples are similar in terms of modernity, level of industrialization, urbanity, per capita income, education, and standard of living; in all four, infant caregiving is significant, the family is nuclear in organization, and mother is normally the primary caregiver in the family setting. So, locales and samples are roughly comparable in terms of sociodemographics. However, considerable differences exist among the four in terms of history, culture, beliefs, and values concerned with child rearing. Thus, the particular comparison set we assembled directly contrasts cultural conditions of child rearing and disentangles them (to the degree possible) from economic and educational, urban–rural, modern–traditional, as well as ecological and climatic factors (see Jahoda, 1980; Munroe & Munroe, 1980; Triandis, 1989). In comparing mothers from Argentina, France, Japan, and the United States, we are also contrasting four distinct language communities: Spanish, French, Japanese, and American English. Furthermore, this quartet of cultures contrasts three Western societies and one Eastern society and so presents the possibility for creating a wider comparison than is typical of cross-cultural research (see Bornstein, 1980, 1989, 1991; Brislin, 1983; Lewis & Ban, 1977; Piaget, 1966, 1974; Super, 1981; Whiting, 1981). To analyze maternal speech comprehensively, it is both desirable and necessary to approach the topic from cross-national and cross-language perspectives.

Our chief purposes in this study, then, were to analyze and compare the language environments directed to younger and older infants in terms of two prominent classes of speech—affect salient and information salient—and to assess the generality or specificity of infant-directed speech in Argentine, French, Japanese, and American mothers. We hypothesized significant main effects for age for both affect- and information-salient speech; presumably, mothers communicate verbally more with their 13-month-old infants than with their 5-month-olds. We also hypothesized that significant differences would emerge for culture; for example, previous work indicates that American mothers emphasize information, and Japanese mothers, affect, in their speech to babies. Finally, we expected Age × Culture interactions: that is, cultural differences in functional emphases in maternal speech should more likely be manifest with older than with younger babies (Azuma, 1986; Bornstein, 1989; Caudill & Weinstein, 1969; Clancy, 1986; Morsbach, 1973; Toda et al., 1990).

Method

Subjects

Primiparous mothers and their 5- and 13-month-old infants, recruited from patient populations of private obstetric and pediatric groups in Buenos Aires, Paris, Tokyo, and New York City, were observed interacting at home. There were 24 and 24 Argentine, 18 and 18 French, 22 and 22 Japanese, and 22 and 25 U.S. American mother–infant dyads with infants of 5 and 13 months, respectively. All infants were term at birth and healthy at the time of the study, with a mean weight of 3.25 kg and an average length of 49.8 cm. The samples were balanced for sex of baby and came from comparable middle-class to upper middle-class households. Babies in the Argentine, French, Japanese, and American samples were the same age at the time of the 5-month home visit ($M =$ 164 days, range of country means = 161–165) as well as the 13-month home visit ($M = 407$ days, range = 402–411). Mothers of babies in each of the two age groups were themselves approximately the same age ($M = 29.7$ years, range = 27.2–31.6, for mothers of 5-month-olds, and $M = 30.4$ years, range = 28.3–33.1, for mothers of 13-month-olds) and had similar educational histories (mean number of years of post-high-school education = 3.5, range = 2.8–4.5, for mothers of 5-month-olds, and $M = 3.6$, range = 2.1–6.3, for mothers of 13-month-olds).

. . .

Discussion

. . .

Mothers in these three Western cultures and one Eastern culture showed general similarity in certain aspects of speech to infants. These findings submit to cross-cultural evaluation the universality of developmental processes related to maternal speech. First, the consistency and face validity of findings resulting from the cross-cultural application of the present categorization scheme of maternal speech give evidence of its generalizability to culturally contrasting settings. Apparently, maternal language to infants nearly universally contains affect-salient as well as information-salient topics. Results of the present study also show that a functional perspective on maternal speech is applicable to infants of two ages in four different language communities across three Western cultures and one Eastern culture. It is likely that mothers everywhere intend to share feelings and contribute to emotional exchanges via their affect-salient speech to babies, just as they wish to impart or confirm cognitive information referential of infant perceptual experiences. Perhaps these are universal aspects of parenting (Papoušek & Papoušek, 1987; Vigilant, Stoneking, Harpending, Hawkes, & Wilson, 1991). Furthermore, no systematic sex effects or effects ascribable to maternal age or education emerged for maternal speech in these samples; but we limited variation in these dimensions, and these factors could be expected to influence maternal speech in other samples.

Mothers in the four cultures showed some similarity in the types and frequency of functional classes of speech they addressed to infants. Notably, predicted age effects emerged for affect- and information-salient speech. Mothers as a group increased the frequency with which they use both categories of speech as their infants approach their first birthdays. Provocatively, the age effect that emerged for affect was reversed when we analyzed proportions—between 5 and 13 months, the frequency of affect-salient speech climbs, but affect becomes a smaller proportion of total maternal speech. Penman et al. (1983) also found relatively greater increases in information-oriented versus affect-oriented classes of Australian mothers' speech to 3- and 6-month-old infants. Thus, independent of culture, mothers speak more to older infants, but "relatively speaking," information-salient versus affect-salient speech increases in emphasis with age in all cultures.

Argentine, French, Japanese, and U.S. American mothers also favored affect over information in speaking to their 5-month-old infants and information over affect in speaking to their 13-month-old infants. Examination of information subcategories showed that the mean frequency of the three approximately doubled with age. Apparently, over the second half of the 1st year of life, mothers tend to expect that their infants need to be directed more, expect that their infants know more or will perhaps better comprehend their questions, and expect that they can and should give their infants more information about the infants themselves, their mothers, and the environment. During this period, infants themselves are also of course beginning to talk, a fact that may encourage mothers to speak to them more in an increasingly adult-oriented conversational manner.

There were also exceptions to these generalities and variations in the speech of mothers in these four cultures that appear to reflect general cultural beliefs and values. Variation in affect-oriented speech appeared across the four cultures: Japanese mothers were highest in the use of affect-salient speech, meaning that they used the most grammatically incomplete utterances and that they played with sounds in speaking to their babies, using nonsense, onomatopoeia, song, and the like, more than did mothers of the other cultures. This result replicates and expands on the work of Toda et al. (1990), who found in the laboratory that Japanese mothers used nonsense, onomatopoeic utterances, and calling by name to their 3-month-olds more than did American mothers. The Japanese mother's goal in early child rearing is to empathize with her infant's needs—to meet her infant at the infant's level—as is well recognized, rather than to show authority as mother (Befu, 1986; Bornstein, Azuma, Tamis-LeMonda, & Ogino, 1990; Doi, 1973; Kojima, 1986a, 1986b). Reciprocally, the evidence that, relatively speaking, mothers from the three Western cultures favor information-salient speech and more often use grammatically complete utterances in speaking to babies—that is, speech more characteristic of adult–adult conversation—is consistent with the view that these mothers are more interested in supporting individual expression and imparting information to their children from an early age.

Variations in categories of information-oriented speech also emerged across these cultures. First, Argentine mothers displayed higher frequencies of direct statements than mothers in the three other cultures. In Argentina, the traditional child-rearing orientation is authoritative: that is, to direct a child's action is to behave positively toward the child and to express care and love in preparing the child for development (Aguinis, 1988; Diaz Rossello, 1988; Fillol, 1961). Blount (1990) noted that Spanish-speaking mothers rely comparatively more than English-speaking mothers on attentionals (utterances designed to attract the child's attention) and high volume in interactions with their 9- to 22-month-olds. Even in schooling, Argentines favor direct transmission of knowledge as, for example, by demonstration (Pascual, 1991; Petty, 1986). Perhaps the use of these features of speech stems from a view of infants and children as in need of instruction. The interaction effect showed that Argentine mothers more often directed their 13- than their 5-month-olds relative to mothers in the three other cultures, implying that as culture takes hold of language directed at the child, its effects may increase.

Second, U.S. American mothers tended to question their infants the most. It is unlikely that American mothers believe that their 5- or even 13-month-olds will answer their questions, or even need to, because many questions are asked about ongoing activities or about things in plain view. Rather, question asking of infants may be a way for American mothers to emphasize the information components of speech. After all, asking "What does that toy do?" goes beyond simply posing a question; it conveys information via labeling, for example, and at the same time does so in a most attention-getting way, as through the use of interrogative prosody (Bornstein & Lamb, 1992). Questions also emphasize the child's participation in his or her own language development in contrast to mothers' use of descriptions; this is a "distancing strategy" thought to promote cognitive development (Sigel, 1982).

Third, French mothers speak to their younger infants like other mothers, but they increased the frequency of their reports to older infants at a lower rate than mothers in the other three cultures. Reputedly, French mothers place less emphasis on achievement stimulation and more emphasis on emotional support and use language to establish closeness (Dion, 1989), an opinion consonant with their lower level of reporting to babies (found here) and their lower level of didactic activity and responsiveness overall (Bornstein et al., in press; Bornstein, Tamis-LeMonda, Pêcheux, & Rahn, 1991). It might also be that French mothers approach speech to their babies with a more egalitarian, adult–adult orientation.

. . .

One of the ways infants become socialized into culture is through integrating maternal behavior and speech into their development, and one of the ways they do this is via mother–infant communication. The general association between culture and development has been conceived in terms of several fundamentally different models. One traditional and influential paradigm suggests that cultural norms, convictions, images, and rules influence the development of parental beliefs about children, their abilities, character, needs, temperament, and so forth, and that in turn these parental beliefs (somehow) translate themselves into the verbal, enactive, and responsive practices that parents use to achieve their child-rearing goals (e.g., Bateson & Mead, 1942; Benedict, 1938; Caudill, 1973; Tapp, 1980; Whiting & Child, 1953). The present findings suggest that this model, at least in part, validly describes cultural forces that shape maternal speech to infants. At the same time, however, universal aspects of infancy, such as the dramatic growth of competence over the 1st year, appear also to exert control over the contents of maternal speech.

REFERENCES

Adamson, L. B., & Bakeman, R. (1984). Mothers' communicative acts: Changes during infancy. *Infant Behavior and Development, 7,* 467–478.

Aguinis, M. (1988). *Un pais de novela.* Buenos Aires, Argentina: Editorial Planeta.

Azuma, H. (1986). Why study child development in Japan? In H. W. Stevenson, H. Azuma, & K. Hakuta (Eds.), *Child development and education in Japan* (pp. 3–12). New York: W. H. Freeman.

Bates, E. (1976). *Language and context: The acquisition of pragmatics,* San Diego, CA: Academic Press.

Bates, E., Bretherton, I., & Snyder, L. (1988). *From first words to grammar.* New York: Cambridge University Press.

Bateson, G., & Mead, M. (1942). *Balinese character: A photographic analysis.* New York: New York Academy of Sciences.

Befu, H. (1986). Social and cultural background for child development in Japan and the United States. In H. W. Stevenson, H. Azuma, & K. Hakuta (Eds.), *Child development and education in Japan* (pp. 13–27). New York: W. H. Freeman.

Benedict, R. (1938). Continuities and discontinuities in cultural conditioning. *Psychiatry, 1,* 161–167.

Blount, B. G. (1990). Parental speech and language acquisition: An anthropological perspective. *Pre- and Peri-Natal Psychology, 4,* 319–337.

Bornstein, M. H. (1980). Cross-cultural developmental psychology. In M. H. Bornstein (Ed.), *Comparative methods in psychology* (pp. 231–281). Hillsdale, NJ: Erlbaum.

Bornstein, M. H. (1985). How infant and mother jointly contribute to developing cognitive competence in the child. *Proceedings of the National Academy of Sciences, 82,* 7470–7473.

Bornstein, M. H. (1989). Cross-cultural developmental comparisons: The case of Japanese–American infant and mother activities and interactions. What we know, what we need to know, and why we need to know. *Developmental Review, 9,* 171–204.

Bornstein, M. H. (1991). Approaches to parenting in culture. In M. H. Bornstein (Ed.), *Cultural approaches to parenting* (pp. 3–19). Hillsdale, NJ: Erlbaum.

Bornstein, M., Azuma, H., Tamis-LeMonda, C., & Ogino, M. (1990). Infant and mother activity and interaction in Japan and in the United States: I. A comparative macroanalysis of naturalistic exchanges. *International Journal of Behavioral Development, 13,* 267–287.

Bornstein, M. H., & Lamb, M. E. (1992). *Development in infancy: An introduction.* New York: McGraw-Hill.

Bornstein, M. H., & Tamis-LeMonda, C. S. (1990). Activities and interactions of mothers and their firstborn infants in the first six months of life: Covariation, stability, continuity, correspondence, and prediction. *Child Development, 61,* 1206–1217.

Bornstein, M. H., Tamis-LeMonda, C. S., Pêcheux, M.-G., & Rahn, C. W. (1991). Mother and infant activity and interaction in France and in the United States: A comparative study. *International Journal of Behavioral Development, 14,* 21–43.

Bornstein, M. H., Tamis-LeMonda, C. S., Tal, J., Ludemann, P., Toda, S., Rahn, C. W., Pêcheux, M.-G., Azuma, H., & Vardi, D. (in press). Maternal responsiveness to infants in three societies: The United States, France, and Japan. *Child Development.*

Brislin, R. W. (1983). Cross-cultural research in psychology. *Annual Review of Psychology, 34,* 363–400.

Brown, R. (1977). Introduction. In C. Snow & C. Ferguson (Eds.), *Talking to children* (pp. 1–27). New York: Cambridge University Press.

Bruner, J. S. (1974/1975). From communication to language: A psychological perspective. *Cognition, 3,* 255–287.

Caudill, W. (1973). The influence of social structure and culture on human behavior in modern Japan. *Journal of Nervous and Mental Disease, 157,* 240–257.

Caudill, W., & Weinstein, H. (1969). Maternal care and infant behavior in Japan and America. *Psychiatry, 32,* 12–43.

Clancy, P. (1986). The acquisition of communicative style in Japanese. In B. Schieffelin & B. Ochs (Eds.), *Language socialization across cultures* (pp. 213–250). Cambridge, England: Cambridge University Press.

Cohn, J. F., & Tronick, E. Z. (1987). Mother–infant face-to-face interaction: The sequence of dyadic states at 3, 6 and 9 months. *Developmental Psychology, 23,* 68–77.

Cross, T. G. (1977). Mothers' speech adjustments: The contribution of selected child listener variables. In C. Snow & C. Ferguson (Eds.), *Talking to children* (pp. 151–188). Cambridge, England: Cambridge University Press.

Della Corte, M., Benedict, H., & Klein, D. (1983). The relationship of pragmatic dimensions of mothers' speech to the referential–expressive distinction. *Journal of Child Language, 10,* 35–43.

de Villiers, J. G., & de Villiers, P. A. (1978). Semantics and syntax in the first two years: The output of form and function and the form and function of the input. In F. D. Minifie & L. L. Lloyd (Eds.), *Communicative and cognitive abilities: Early behavioral assessment* (pp. 309–348). Baltimore: University Park Press.

Diaz Rossello, J. L. (1988). La relacion madre-hijo en el periodo inicial. In M. Cusminsky, E. Moreno, & E. Suarez Ojeda (Eds.), *Crecimiento y desarrollo* (pp. 149–163). (Publicacion Cientifica No. 510). Buenos Aires, Argentina: Organizacion Panamericana de la Salud.

Dion, F. (1989). *Les représentations parentales du développement cognitif de leur bébé et de leur rôle dans ce développement.* Unpublished manuscript. Laboratoire de Psychologie du Développement et de l'Éducation de l'Énfant, Université Paris V.

Doi, T. (1973). [*The anatomy of dependence*] (J. Bester, Trans.). Tokyo: Kodansha International.

Fillol, T. R. (1961). *Social factors in economic development: The Argentine case.* Westport, CT: Greenwood Press.

Folger, J., & Chapman, R. (1978). A pragmatic analysis of spontaneous imitations. *Journal of Child Language, 5,* 25–38.

Garton, A. F. (1991). *Social interaction and the development of language and cognition.* Hillsdale, NJ: Erlbaum.

Givon, T. (1985). Function, structure, and language acquisition. In D. I. Slobin (Ed.), *The cross-linguistic study of language acquisition* (Vol. 2, pp. 1005–1027). Hillsdale, NJ: Erlbaum.

Harris, M. (1991). *Language experience and early language development: From input to uptake.* Hillsdale, NJ: Erlbaum.

Jahoda, G. (1980). Cross-cultural comparisons. In M. H. Bornstein (Eds.), *Comparative methods in psychology* (pp. 105–148). Hillsdale, NJ: Erlbaum.

Kaye, K. (1982). *The mental and social life of babies.* Chicago: University of Chicago Press.

Kaye, K., & Fogel, A. (1980). The temporal structure of face-to-face communication between mothers and infants. *Developmental Psychology, 16,* 454–464.

Keppel, G. (1982). *Design and analysis: A researcher's handbook.* Englewood Cliffs, NJ: Prentice Hall.

Kojima, H. (1986a). Child rearing concepts as a belief-value system of the society and the individual. In H. W. Stevenson, H. Azuma, & K. Hakuta (Eds.), *Child development and education in Japan* (pp. 39–54). New York: W. H. Freeman.

Kojima, H. (1986b). Japanese concepts of child development from the mid-17th to mid-19th century. *International Journal of Behavioral Development, 9,* 315–329.

Lewis, M., & Ban, P. (1977). Variance and invariance in the mother–infant interaction: A cross-cultural study. In P. H. Leiderman, S. R. Tulkin, & A. Rosenfeld (Eds.) *Culture and infancy: Variations in the human experience* (pp. 329–355). San Diego, CA: Academic Press.

Morikawa, H., Shand, N., & Kosawa, Y. (1988). Maternal speech to prelingual infants in Japan and the United States: Relationships among functions, forms, and referents. *Journal of Child Language, 15,* 237–256.

Morsbach, H. (1973). Aspects of nonverbal communication in Japan. *Journal of Nervous and Mental Disease, 157,* 262–277.

Munroe, R. L., & Munroe, R. H. (1980). Perspectives suggested by anthropological data. In H. C. Triandis & W. W. Lambert (Eds.), *Handbook of cross-cultural psychology: Perspectives* (Vol. 1, pp. 253–317). Boston: Allyn & Bacon.

Ochs, E. (1986). Introduction. In B. B. Schieffelin & E. Ochs (Eds.), *Language socialization across cultures* (pp. 1–13). Cambridge, England: Cambridge University Press.

Papoušek. H., & Papoušek, M. (1987). Intuitive parenting: A dialectic counterpart to the infant's integrative competence. In J. D. Osofsky (Ed.), *Handbook of infant development* (2nd ed., pp. 669–720). New York: Wiley.

Papoušek, M., Papoušek, H., & Bornstein, M. (1985). The naturalistic vocal environment of young infants: On the significance of homogeneity and variability in parental speech. In T. Field & N. Fox (Eds.), *Social perception in infants* (pp. 269–297). Norwood. NJ: Ablex.

Pascual, L. (1991). *Democracy and educational reforms in Argentina: Possibilities and limitations.* Paper presented at the Annual Conference of the Comparative and International Education Society, Pittsburgh, PA.

Penman, R., Cross, T., Milgrom-Friedman, J., & Meares, R. (1983). Mothers' speech to prelingual infants: A pragmatic analysis. *Journal of Child Language, 10,* 17–34.

Petty, M. (1986). *Autoritarismo y participación.* Buenos Aires, Argentina: Congreso Pedagógico.

Phillips, J. (1973). Syntax and vocabulary of mothers' speech to young children: Age and sex comparisons. *Child Development, 44,* 182–185.

Piaget, J. (1974). [Need and significance of cross-cultural studies in genetic psychology] (C. Dasen, Trans.). In J. W. Berry & P. R. Dasen (Eds.), *Culture and cognition* (pp. 299–309). London: Methuen. (Original work published 1966)

Rondal, J. (1985). *Adult–child interaction and the process of language acquisition.* New York: Praeger.

Sachs, J. (1977). The adaptive significance of linguistic input to prelinguistic infants. In C. Snow & C. Ferguson (Eds.), *Talking to children.* New York: Cambridge University Press.

Sherrod, K. B., Crawley, S., Petersen, G., & Bennett, P. (1978). Maternal language to prelinguistic infants: Semantic aspects. *Infant Behavior and Development, 1,* 335–345.

Sherrod, K. B., Friedman, S., Crawley, S., Drake, D., & Devieux, J. (1977). Maternal language to prelinguistic infants: Syntactic aspects. *Child Development, 48,* 1662–1665.

Sigel, I. E. (1982). The relationship between parental distancing strategies and the child's cognitive behavior. In L. M. Laosa & I. E. Sigel (Eds.), *Families as learning environments for children* (pp. 47–86). New York: Plenum Press.

Snow, C. (1977). The development of conversation between mothers and babies. *Journal of Child Language, 4,* 1–22.

Stern, D. N. (1985). *The interpersonal world of the infant.* New York: Basic Books.

Stevenson, M., Ver Hoeve, J., Roach, M., & Leavitt, L. (1986). The beginning of conversation: Early patterns of mother–infant vocal responsiveness. *Infant Behavior and Development, 9,* 423–440.

Super, C. M. (1981). Behavioral development in infancy. In R. H. Munroe, R. L. Munroe, & B. B. Whiting (Eds.), *Handbook of cross-cultural human development* (pp. 181–270). New York: Garland STPM Press.

Tamis-LeMonda, C. S., & Bornstein, M. H. (1990). Language, play, and attention at one year. *Infant Behavior and Development, 13,* 85–98.

Tapp, J. L. (1980). Studying personality development. In H. C. Triandis & A. Heron (Eds.), *Handbook of cross-cultural psychology: Developmental psychology* (Vol. 4, pp. 343–423). Boston: Allyn & Bacon.

Toda, S., Fogel, A., & Kawai, M. (1990). Maternal speech to three-month-old infants in the United States and Japan. *Journal of Child Language, 17,* 279–294.

Triandis, H. C. (1989). The self and social behavior in differing cultural contexts. *Psychological Review, 96,* 506–520.

Tukey, J. W. (1977). *Exploratory data analysis.* Menlo Park, CA: Addison-Wesley.

Vigilant, L., Stoneking, M., Harpending, H., Hawkes, K., & Wilson, A. C. (1991). African populations and the evolution of human mitochondrial DNA. *Science, 253,* 1503–1507.

Whiting, J. W. (1981). Environmental constraints on infant care practices. In R. H. Munroe, R. L. Munroe, & B. B. Whiting (Eds.), *Handbook of cross-cultural human development* (pp. 155–179). New York: Garland STPM Press.

Whiting, J. W. M., & Child, I. L. (1953). *Child training and personality: A cross-cultural study.* New Haven, CT: Yale University Press.

Woods, A., Fletcher, P., & Hughes, A. (1986). *Statistics in language studies.* Cambridge, England: Cambridge University Press.

Cultural Variation in Infants' Sleeping Arrangements: Questions of Independence*

Gilda A. Morelli, Barbara Rogoff, David Oppenheim, and Denise Goldsmith

> It was time to give him his own room . . . his own territory. That's the American way.
>
> Reflections of a middle-class U.S. mother

Among middle-class families and child-care experts in the United States, it is assumed that the proper sleeping arrangement for infants and parents is separate. The purpose of this article is to examine this assumption as a cultural practice. A sociocultural approach involves understanding how practices within a community relate to other aspects of the community's functioning, such as adult work roles, physical space arrangements, climate, and values

*Morelli et al. (1992). *Developmental Psychology, 28,* 604–613. Reprinted with permission.

and goals regarding desired characteristics of citizens. One of the most valuable aspects of comparisons across cultural communities is that they make us aware of the cultural basis for and the assumptions underlying our own practices, whoever we are (Cole, 1985; Munroe, Munroe, & Whiting, 1981; Rogoff, 1990; Rogoff & Morelli, 1989; B. B. Whiting & Edwards, 1988).

. . .

Folk wisdom in the United States considers the early nighttime separation of infants from their parents as essential for the infants' healthy psychological development. This widespread belief is reflected in the advice parents have received since the early 1900s from child-rearing experts regarding cosleeping. Spock (1945) wrote, "I think it's a sensible rule not to take a child into the parents' bed for any reason" (p. 101). Brazelton (1978, 1979) and Ferber (1986), pediatricians and writers nationally known as specialists on parenting, also warned parents of the dangers of sleeping with their infants. The concerns of such authors included possible smothering by a restless parent (Bundesen, 1944), the increased likelihood of catching a contagious illness (Holt, 1957), the difficulty of breaking the habit when the child grows older (Spock, 1945), and sexual overstimulation for the oedipal child (Spock, 1984). Although several accounts now acknowledge the value placed on cosleeping by some families (Brazelton, 1990), or advocate the practice (Thevinin, 1976), pediatricians generally advise parents to avoid cosleeping (Lozoff, Wolf, & Davis, 1984).

Research indicates that cosleeping is not commonly practiced by middle- to upper-class U.S. families. Lozoff et al. (1984) found that only 35% of urban Caucasian 6- to 48-month-olds slept with their parents for all or part of the night on a regular basis. Crowell, Keener, Ginsburg, and Anders (1987) reported even lower figures: A mere 11% of the 18- to 36-month-olds they studied shared a bed with their parents 3 or more nights a week, and only 15% shared a room with them. Valsiner and Hall (1983) found that 18 out of 19 infants from well-educated U.S. families slept in a room separate from their parents from before 3 months of age. Over half of the infants studied by Hong and Townes (1976) slept in their own rooms by 2 months of age. 75% by 3 months, and 98% by 6 months. Other researchers have noted that by 6 months, middle-class U.S. infants' designated sleeping place is in a room separated from their parents (Keener, Zeanah, & Anders, 1988; Richman, Miller, & Solomon, 1988; B. B. Whiting & Edwards, 1988). From these and other studies it appears that in the U.S. middle class, cosleeping is not a frequently occurring event in infancy and early childhood (Mandansky & Edelbrock, 1990; Rosenfeld, Wenegrat, Haavik, Wenegrat, & Smith, 1982).

In many non-U.S. communities it is customary for infants to sleep with their mothers for the first few years of life, at least in the same room and usually in the same bed. J. W. M. Whiting (1964) reported that infants sleep in bed with their mothers in approximately two thirds of the 136 societies he sampled around the world, and in the remainder the babies were generally in the same room with their mothers. Infants regularly slept with a parent until weaning in all but 1 (the United States) of the 12 communities studied by B. B. Whiting and Edwards (1988); in the U.S. community no cosleeping was observed. In a survey of 100 societies, American parents were the only ones to maintain separate quarters for their babies (Burton & Whiting, 1961; see also Barry & Paxson, 1971; McKenna, 1986). These findings are consistent with other work on sleeping arrangements in urban Korea (Hong & Townes, 1976) and urban and rural Italy (Gaddini & Gaddini, 1971; Gandini, 1990; New, 1984).

Communities that practice cosleeping include both highly technological and less technological communities. Japanese urban children usually sleep adjacent to their mothers in early childhood and generally continue to sleep with a parent or an extended family member until the age of 15 (Caudill & Plath, 1966; Takahashi, 1990). Parents often separate in order to provide all children with a parental sleeping partner when family size makes it difficult for parents and children to share a single room. Space considerations appear to play a minor role in cosleeping practices for Japanese families (Caudill & Plath, 1966).

. . .

In the present study, we examine differences between a U.S. middle-class community and a non-Western community in the sleeping arrangements of infants, including where the babies sleep and nighttime feeding and waking practices, as well as parents' rationales for and comfort with their infants' sleeping arrangements. We are particularly interested in the values expressed by parents regarding the consequences for children of cosleeping or sleeping apart. We also investigate practices that may be associated with sleeping arrangements, such as special activities occurring around bedtime. The transition to sleep may be a difficult process for young children that is eased by the presence of their caregivers or by substitute attachment objects or special bedtime activities (Albert, 1977; Wolf & Lozoff, 1989).

. . .

Results . . .

Sleeping Location

Mayan families. All 14 Mayan mothers slept in the same bed with their infants through the 1st year of life and into the 2nd year. A child had spent some time sleeping apart from her mother, on a cot in the same room, but was now sleeping with her mother again. In this case, the sleeping arrangement reflected changes in the presence of the father, from whom the mother was now separated.

Most of the Mayan toddlers (8 of them) also slept in the same bed with their fathers. Of the 6 who did not share a bed with their fathers, 3 had fathers sleeping in another bed in the same room (in 2 cases, father was sleeping with other young children), and the other 3 involved absent fathers. Four of the toddlers had a sibling (newborn to 4 years of age) in the same bed with them and their mothers, and of these, 2 also had the father in the same bed. Ten of the 14 toddlers had siblings sleeping in the same room with them, either in the same bed or another bed. Of the 4 toddlers who had no siblings sleeping in the same room, all were only children; one of these had paternal uncles sleeping in the same room.

U.S. families. In none of the 18 U.S. families did parents sleep with their newborns on a regular basis. Rather, most mothers and fathers (15 families) chose to share a room with their newborn infants, often placing them in a bassinet or crib near the parents' bed. This was a temporary arrangement; by 3 months of age 58% of the babies were already sleeping in separate rooms. This figure climbed to 80% by the 6th month of life. When the babies were moved to a room apart from their parents, firstborns were placed in a room of their own, but most second- and laterborns (89%) were moved into rooms with siblings. However, none of them shared a bed with a sibling.

In 3 of the 18 U.S. families, parents chose not to share a room with their babies from the time the babies were brought home from the hospital. These 3 newborn infants slept in their own rooms, despite the fact that 2 of them had siblings with whom they could have shared a room. For 1 family this meant keeping the infant in the living room.

Of the 15 families in which parents had slept near their newborn infants and then moved their babies to a separate room, 3 moved the infants back in the second half year of their baby's lives. Two babies were moved to cribs located in their parents' rooms; 1 baby was moved to her parents' bed. In addition, 1 family moved their child from a separate bed in the parents' room to the parents' bed when the child was 1 year old.

Night Feedings

Mayan families. The pattern of night feeding arrangements in the Mayan families was for the baby or toddler to sleep with the mother until shortly before the birth of another child (about age 2 or 3) and to nurse on demand. The mothers reported that they generally did not notice having to feed their babies in the night. Mothers said that they did not have to waken, just to turn and make the breast accessible. Hence night feedings were not an issue for the

Mayan mothers or for their infants and toddlers.

U.S. families. All but 1 of the 18 U.S. mothers reported having to stay awake during night feedings (which, for most mothers, lasted 6 months or so). Ten mothers chose not to feed their babies in their rooms, even though 7 of them had infants sleeping there and 8 of them were breastfeeding. Two mothers (both breastfeeding) fed infants in the parental room, but not in the parental bed; and 6 mothers (all breastfeeding) elected to feed their babies in the parental bed, but 5 of them regularly returned babies to their own beds when finished. The 1 mother whose infant regularly remained in bed with her following feedings was the only mother who said that nightly feedings did not bother her.

Bedtime Routines

Mayan families. The idea that sleeping arrangements were not an issue for the Mayan families is supported by the lack of bedtime routines carried out in the nightly transition to sleep. There was not a separate routine to coax the baby to sleep. Most of the babies simply fell asleep when sleepy, along with the rest of the family or before if they got tired. Seven of the babies fell asleep at the same time as their parents, and most of the rest fell asleep in someone's arms. Ten of them were nursed to sleep (as they are nursed on demand during the daytime as well). Of the 4 who were no longer nursing, 1 fell asleep alone with a bottle, 1 fell asleep with a bottle and his mother going to bed with him, and 2 who had been nursed to sleep until recently (and were being weaned) usually fell asleep on their own but were cuddled by their father or older brother on the occasions when they needed company at bedtime.

None of the babies received a bedtime story; there were no reports of bathtime or toothbrushing in preparation for bed; none of the babies sucked their thumbs; only 1 was reported to use a security object for falling asleep (a little doll—this belonged to the 1 child who had for a time had a bed by herself!). There was thus no focus on objects as comfort items for falling asleep.

None of the Mayan families sang special children's lullabies to the babies at bedtime; some laughed at the idea. However, 4 of the mothers admitted with embarrassment that they sometimes sang their babies church songs at bedtime. (One added that she does this when she feels badly about not having taken the baby out during the day.) The babies were not changed into pajamas in preparation for bed. (They do not have specialized nightclothes; nor do the parents.) However, 11 of them were changed into their oldest clothes for sleeping. The other 3 just slept in the clothes they had worn during the day. Thus it appears that no special preparations or coaxing are needed for these babies, whose sleeping occurs in the company of the same people with whom they spend the day.

U.S. families. Events surrounding bedtime for the U.S. families played a significant role in the organization of family evening activities. Besides the daily evening activity of putting on nightclothes and brushing teeth, 10 of the 18 parents engaged in additional routines such as storytelling. Routines varied in their degree of elaborateness, with some parents spending just a few minutes reading a story to their babies and other parents investing a fair amount of time getting their child ready for sleep. One mother jokingly said, "When my friends hear that it is time for my son to go to bed, they teasingly say 'See you in an hour."

Once infants were in bed, 11 were expected to fall asleep by themselves. It is interesting that 5 of the 8 infants who fell asleep alone took a favorite object such as a blanket to bed with them (data are missing for 3 children). By comparison, only 2 of the 6 infants who fell asleep in the company of another person (data are missing for 1 child) needed to do the same.

Reflections of Parents on Sleeping Arrangements

Mayan families. Most of the families regarded their sleeping arrangements as the only reasonable way for a baby and parents to sleep. In addition, in five interviews the subject of how U.S. families handle sleeping arrangements came up. Invariably, the idea that toddlers are put to sleep in a separate room was received with shock, disapproval, and pity. One mother responded, "But there's someone else with them there, isn't there?" When told that they are sometimes alone in the room the mother gasped and went on to express pity for the U.S. babies. Another mother responded with shock and disbelief, asked whether the babies do not mind, and added with feeling that it would be very painful for her to have to do that. The responses of the Mayan parents gave the impression that they regarded the practice of having infants and toddlers sleep in separate rooms as tantamount to child neglect. Their reactions and their accounts of their own sleeping arrangements seemed to indicate that their arrangements were a matter of commitment to a certain kind of relationship with their young children and not a result of practical limitations (such as number of rooms in the house).

In Mayan families, sleeping arrangements are not an issue until the child is displaced from the mother's side by a new baby. At the time or before the new baby is born, the toddler is weaned and may be moved to sleep beside the father in the same bed or in another bed in the same room. One mother and father told us that their little boy got very angry at his mother (when the next child arrived) and even cried when he was moved to his father's bed; he wanted to be the last born—he did not want someone else to take his place beside his mother. For most families, though, this transition is usually made without difficulty. Parents sometimes try to prevent any difficulties by getting the child accustomed to sleeping with another family member before the new baby is born.

The transition is sometimes difficult for Mayan mothers and fathers. Mothers may regret letting the child move from their care to that of another family member, and fathers may lose sleep as they often become responsible for the displaced child. One father of a toddler told us that his older son, whose wife was expecting a second child in 4 months, needed to move their 2-year-old firstborn to another bed soon, even though she did not want to move. The older man told us that the firstborn needed to become accustomed to sleeping apart from the mother or the father would have trouble later. "I know," said the older man, "because I went through this . . . If the first child doesn't sleep through the night, apart from the parents, when the new child comes, the father suffers. He has to get up in the night to give the child something."

If there are older siblings, they often take care of the displaced child if needed during the night, allowing the father to sleep. Of the 10 Mayan families with older siblings, in 5 of them the older siblings had moved to sleep with the father when our subjects were born (3 in the same bed with mother and the new baby, 2 with father in another bed in the same room), in 2 they had moved to sleep with a sibling in the same room, in 2 they had moved to a separate bed in the same room, and in 1 they slept with the mother and the new baby as father slept in a separate bed in the same room. It is noteworthy that even when the children are displaced from their mother's side, they still sleep in the same room with her, usually at someone else's side.

U.S. families. U.S. parents chose to sleep near their newborn infants for pragmatic reasons (mentioned by 78%, e.g., "Because I nurse them . . . it is sort of convenient to have them here") as well as for developmental and affectionate reasons (57% and 64% mentioned these). Of the parents who slept near their babies starting at birth, an overwhelming majority (92%) felt that sleeping near infants helped foster the development of an affectionate tie between them and their babies. . . .

The findings suggest that encouraging independence during infancy is an important goal for many U.S. families and that parents believe that sleeping apart helps train children to be independent. But the age at which parents think it is appropriate for infants to sleep apart is somewhat variable, ranging from 0 to usually 3 to 6 months. This range of variability is narrow compared with worldwide sleeping practices.

. . .

REFERENCES

Abbott, S. (1992). Holding on and pushing away: Comparative perspectives on an Eastern Kentucky child-rearing practice. *Ethos, 20,* 33–65.

Albert, S. (1977). *Rites of passage: Study of children's bedtime rituals.* Paper presented at the 85th Annual Convention of the American Psychological Association, San Francisco, CA.

Anders, T. (1979). Night-waking in infants during the first year of life. *Pediatrics, 63*(6), 860–864.

Barry, H., & Paxson, L. (1971). Infants and early childhood: Cross-cultural codes 2. *Ethnology, 10,* 466–508.

Benedict, R. (1955). Continuities and discontinuities in cultural conditioning. In M. Mead & M. Wolfenstein (Eds.), *Childhood in contemporary cultures* (pp. 21–30). Chicago: University of Chicago Press.

Brazelton, T. (1978, October). Why your baby won't sleep. *Redbook,* p. 82.

Brazelton, T. (1979, June). What parents told me about handling children's sleep problems. *Redbook,* pp. 51–54.

Brazelton, T. B. (1990). Parent–infant cosleeping revisited. *Ab Initio, 2*(1), pp. 1, 7.

Bundesen, H. (1944). *The baby manual.* New York: Simon & Schuster.

Burton, R., & Whiting, J. (1961). The absent father and cross-sex identity. *Merrill-Palmer Quarterly 7,* 85–95.

Caudill, W., & Plath, D. (1966). Who sleeps by whom? Parent–child involvement in urban Japanese families. *Psychiatry, 29,* 344–366.

Caudill, W., & Weinstein, H. (1969). Maternal care and infant behavior in Japan and America. *Psychiatry, 32,* 12–43.

Cole, M. (1985). The zone of proximal development. Where culture and cognition create each other. In J. V. Wertsch (Eds.), *Culture, communication, and cognition: Vygotskian perspectives* (pp. 146–161). Cambridge, England: Cambridge University Press.

Crowell, J., Keener, M., Ginsburg, N., & Anders, T. (1987). Sleep habits in toddlers 18 to 36 months old. *American Journal of Child and Adolescent Psychiatry, 26*(4), 510–515.

Edelman, G. N. (1983, November). When kids won't sleep. *Parents Magazine,* pp. 74–77.

Ferber, R. (1986). *Solve your child's sleep problems.* New York: Simon & Schuster.

Gaddini, R., & Gaddini, E. (1971). Transitional objects and the process of individuation. *Journal of the American Academy of Child Psychiatry, 9,* 347–365.

Gandini, L. (1986, September). *Parent–child interaction at bedtime: Strategies and rituals in families with young children.* Paper presented at the European Conference on Developmental Psychology, Rome, Italy.

Gandini, L. (1990). Children and parents at bedtime in two cultures. *Ab Initio, 2*(1), pp. 5, 7.

Hanks, C., & Rebelsky, F. (1977). Mommy and the midnight visitor: A study of occasional co-sleeping. *Psychiatry,* 40, 277–280.

Holt, E. (1957). *How children fail.* New York: Dell.

Hong, K., & Townes, B. (1976). Infants' attachment to inanimate objects: A cross-cultural study. *Journal of the American Academy of Child Psychiatry, 15,* 49–61.

Hoover, M. B. (1978, November). Does your bed belong to baby? *Parents Magazine,* p. 129.

Kawakami, K. (1987, July). *Comparison of mother–infant relationships in Japanese and American families.* Paper presented at the meeting of the International Society for the Study of Behavioral Development, Tokyo, Japan.

Keener, M. A., Zeanah, C. H., & Anders, T. F. (1988). Infant temperament, sleep organization, and parental interventions. *Pediatrics, 81*(6). 762–771.

Konner, M. J., & Super, C. M. (1987). Sudden Infant Death Syndrome: An anthropological hypothesis. In C. M. Super (Ed.), *The role of culture in developmental disorder* (pp. 95–108). San Diego, CA: Academic Press.

Kugelmass, N. (1959). *Complete child care.* New York: Holt, Rinehart, & Winston.

LeVine, R. (1980). A cross-cultural perspective on parenting. In M. D. Fantini & R. Cardenas (Eds.), *Parenting in a multicultural society* (pp. 17–26). San Diego, CA: Academic Press.

LeVine, R. (1990). Infant environments in psychoanalysis. In J. W. Stigler, R. A. Shweder, & G. Herdt (Eds.), *Cultural psychology: Essays on comparative human development* (pp. 454–474). Cambridge, England: Cambridge University Press.

Lozoff, B., Wolf, A., & Davis., N. (1984). Cosleeping in urban families with young children in the United States. *Pediatrics, 74*(2), 171–182.

Mandansky, D., & Edelbrock, C. (1990). Cosleeping in a community sample of 2- and 3-year-old children. *Pediatrics, 86,* 197–280.

McKenna, J. (1986). An anthropological perspective on the Sudden Infant Death Syndrome (SIDS): The role of parental breathing cues and speech breathing adaptations. *Medical Anthropology, 10*(1), 9–92.

Munroe, R. L., Munroe, R. H., & Whiting, J. W. M. (1981). Male sex-role resolutions. In R. H. Munroe, R. L. Munroe, & B. B. Whiting (Eds.), *Handbook of cross-cultural human development* (pp. 611–632). New York: Garland.

New, R. (1984). *Italian mothers and infants: Patterns of care and social development.* Unpublished doctoral dissertation. School of Education, Harvard University.

Richman, A. L., Miller, P. M., & Solomon, M. J. (1988). The socialization of infants in suburban Boston. In R. A. LeVine, P. M. Miller, & M. M. West (Eds.), *Parental behavior in diverse societies* (pp. 65–74). San Francisco: Jossey-Bass.

Rogoff, B. (1977). *A portrait of memory in cultural context.* Unpublished doctoral dissertation, Harvard University.

Rogoff, B. (1990). *Apprenticeship in thinking: Cognitive development in social context.* New York: Oxford University Press.

Rogoff, B., & Morelli, G. (1989). Perspectives on development from cultural psychology: *American Psychologist, 44,* 343–348.

Rogoff, B., Mosier, C., Mistry, J., & Göncü, A. (in press). Toddlers' guided participation with their caregivers in cultural activity. In E. Forman, N. Minick, & A. Stone (Eds.), *Contexts for learning: Sociocultural dynamics in children's development.* New York: Oxford University Press.

Rosenfeld, A., Wenegrat, A., Haavik, D., Wenegrat, B., & Smith, C. (1982). Sleeping patterns in upper-middle-class families when the child awakens ill or frightened. *Archives of General Psychiatry, 39,* 943–947.

Spock, B. J. (1945). *The common sense book of child and baby care.* New York: Duell, Sloan, & Pearce.

Spock, B. J. (1984, December). Mommy, can I sleep in your bed? *Parents Magazine,* p. 129.

Super, C. M., & Harkness, S. (1982). The infant's niche in rural Kenya and metropolitan America. In L. L. Adler (Ed.), *Cross-cultural research at issue* (pp. 47–55). San Diego, CA: Academic Press.

Takahashi, (1990). Are the key assumptions of the "Strange Situation" procedure universal? A view from Japanese research. *Human Development, 33,* 23–30.

Thevinin, T. (1976). *The family bed: An age old concept in childrearing.* Minneapolis, MN: Author.

Valsiner, J., & Hall, D. (1983). *Parents' strategies for the organization of child–environment relationships in home settings.* Paper presented at the Seventh Biennial Meeting of the International Society for the Study of Behavioural Development, Munchen, Bundesrepub, Germany.

Ward, M. C. (1971). *Them children.* New York: Holt, Rinehart, & Winston.

Whiting, B. B., & Edwards, C. (1988). *Children of different worlds: The formation of social behavior.* Cambridge, MA: Harvard University Press.

Whiting, J. W. M. (1964). The effects of climate on certain cultural practices. In W. H. Goodenough (Ed.), *Explorations in cultural anthropology: Essays in honor of George Peter Murdock* (pp. 511–544). New York: McGraw-Hill.

Wolf, A., & Lozoff, B. (1989). Object attachment, thumb-sucking, and the passage to sleep. *Journal of the American Academy of Child and Adolescent Psychiatry, 28,* 287–292.

Reactivity in Infants: A Cross-National Comparison*

Jerome Kagan, Doreen Arcus, Nancy Snidman, Wang Yu Feng, John Hendler, and Sheila Greene

Most developmentalists agree that ease and intensity of behavioral arousal to external stimulation is a salient temperamental quality of infants. Rothbart (1989), who calls this characteristic *reactivity,* regards it as one of the two basic temperamental dimensions, along with *self-regulation.* However, because *ease of arousal* is a general term, several issues arise. The first of these is the need to specify response mode and class of incentive. Infants differ with respect to the behaviors that reflect their level of arousal (e.g., motor activity, vocalization, smiling, fretting, or crying) as well as the type of incentive that most often elicits arousal (e.g., visual, auditory, or olfactory stimulation). Most infants show more vigorous motor activity to moving objects than to sounds or speech, but they smile more often to speech than to visual stimuli during the first few months of life (Kagan & Snidman, 1991a). A second issue is whether the early variation in arousal, specified by incentive and behavioral modality, predicts variation in other psychological qualities displayed in later infancy or childhood. A third, related question asks whether infants of different nationalities, differing in genetic or cultural backgrounds or both, differ in ease of arousal.

This article reports a difference between Chinese and Caucasian 4-month-old infants in the level of reactivity to stimulation. Anticipation of the major result can be found in earlier reports that suggested that Asian infants are at a lower level of arousal than Caucasian infants (Caudill & Weinstein, 1969; Freedman, 1974; Freedman & Freedman, 1969; Kagan, Kearsley, & Zelazo, 1978; Lewis, 1989). Over 20 years ago, Freedman and Freedman (1969) reported that newborn Asian-American infants, compared with European-Americans, were calmer, less labile, less likely to remove a cloth placed on their face, and more easily consoled when distressed. Kagan et al. (1978) found that Chinese-American infants living in Boston were less active, less vocal, and

*Kagan et al. (1994). *Developmental Psychology, 30,* 342–345. Reprinted with permission.

smiled less often to the presentation of visual and auditory events during the first year than did European-American infants.

Caudill and Weinstein (1969), who observed Japanese infants in their homes, reported them to be less easily aroused than European-American infants in the United States. More recently, Lewis (1989) and Lewis, Ramsay, and Kawakami (in press) reported that Japanese infants were less reactive than European-American infants during well baby examinations and were less likely to display intense distress to an inoculation.

These differences observed during the first year have some parallels in older children. The parents of school-age Thai children, compared with those of European-American children, were more concerned over low energy, low motivation, somatic problems, and forgetfulness; the parents of European-American children reported more concerns over disobedience, aggression, and hyperactivity (Weisz et al., 1987; Weisz et al., 1988). These differences have been viewed as reflecting only cultural variation in socialization values. However, assuming the validity of the parental descriptions, one might also regard the evidence as a result, in part, of differences in the temperaments of the children.

The aim of this article is to affirm, in a different experimental context, the possible differences in the level of reactivity between Asian and Caucasian infants. An additional incentive for the research was the recent discovery that 4-month-old European-American infants who showed very low levels of reactivity to the battery used in this study became outgoing and sociable in the second year, whereas infants with high reactivity became fearful to unfamiliar people and events (Kagan & Snidman, 1991a, 1991b). Green's (1969) observation that Chinese-American children in Chicago nursery schools were more subdued compared with European-American infants raises the possibility that the relation between reactivity in infancy and sociability in childhood is different in the two groups. Because the idea of ethnic differences in temperament is controversial, it is useful to examine its validity in varied experimental contexts.

. . .

There were two Caucasian samples of infants, one from the Boston metropolitan area and one from Dublin, Republic of Ireland. The Chinese sample lived in Beijing, People's Republic of China. There were 247 infants from the Boston area (48% male and 52% female). The Irish sample consisted of 106 infants (56% male and 44% female; Kagan, Snidman, Hendler, Greene, & Nugent, 1991). The Chinese sample consisted of 80 infants (59% male and 41% female).

The Dublin and Beijing samples were less heterogeneous in ethnic composition than the Boston sample because both parents and grandparents were born in each of those respective countries. By contrast, the parents of the Boston infants were ethnically more diverse and consisted of adults of both northern and southern European ancestries.

All three samples consisted of 4-month-old infants born at term with no pre- or perinatal complications to intact families who volunteered to participate. All the mothers in the three samples were married and between the ages of 20 and 40 years. All mothers in the American sample had college degrees or the equivalent. The Irish infants also came from predominantly middle-class families. Over half of the Irish parents—57%—either graduated from or had attended college, and 92% had completed their high school certificate. Seventy-six percent of the Chinese parents had attended or graduated college, and 99% had graduated high school. None of the American or Chinese infants has been in full-time day care before they were 4 months old; only 15% of the Irish infants had been in alternate care full time after 14 weeks (the length of paid maternity leave). It should be noted that the American sample, which was part of a larger study, was selected so that no infant was in full-time day care. Thus, there is comparability across the three samples with respect to the educational attainment of the mothers and daycare experience during the first 4 months of life.

. . .

The variables coded . . . were as follows:

1. *Motor activity:* A total score was a weighted sum of the frequency of movements of both arms, both legs, bursts of movement of either arms or legs (three or more movements in rapid succession), extensions of both arms or legs, and arches of the back. Each occurrence of a movement of both arms, both legs, or extensions was awarded 1 point; limb bursts and arches of the back were awarded 2 points. The rationale for this decision was based on the fact that bursts of activity and arches of the back reflected more intense motor activity.

2. *Vocalization:* Proportion of trials on which a vocalization that was neutral or happy in affective tone and not a fuss, fret, or protest was coded.

3. *Smiling:* Proportion of trials on which a smile occurred, where a smile was defined as a bilateral retraction and elevation of the lips.

4. *Fretting:* Proportion of trials on which the child fretted, where fretting was judged as a vocalization characterized by an increase in pitch in relation to a vocalization, a constrained quality, and audible negative affect.

5. *Crying:* Number of seconds the child cried. If an infant cried for more than 2 s on a particular trial, the examiner or the mother or both terminated the trial and attempted to soothe the infant.

For the infants who became irritable such that the session had to be terminated before the end of the battery, a prorated score was computed across the entire battery. For vocalization, smiling, and fretting, the variable was the proportion of trials administered during which the response occurred. The prorated motor and cry score was based on the formula: raw score + (trials missed × raw score)/trials completed. However, any infant who did not complete at least one half of the battery was eliminated from the analysis. All of the Chinese infants and 96% of the Irish infants completed the battery; 68% of the Boston sample completed the battery. The larger number of terminations in the Boston sample reflects the greater irritability in these infants.

We assessed the reliability of the scoring of behaviors from the videotapes by comparing each coder's judgments with those of the primary coder. This comparison was done both within and across the three ethnic groups. The within-group reliabilities (product-moment correlations) are based on 6% of the American sample, 8% of the Irish sample, and 9% of the Chinese sample. For motor activity, the average reliability was .75 for the American sample, .96 for the Irish sample, and .85 for the Chinese sample. For crying, reliability was .74 for the American sample, .70 for the Irish sample, and .99 for the Chinese sample. For fretting, the reliability was .93 for the American sample, .90 for the Irish sample, and .95 for the Chinese sample. For vocalizing, the reliability was .92 for the American sample, .63 for the Irish sample, and .79 for the Chinese sample. Finally, for smiling, the reliability was .79 for the American sample, .27 for the Irish sample, and .82 for the Chinese sample. Note the low reliability for smiling for the Irish sample. The coders of the Irish and Chinese samples also checked their reliability with tapes from the Boston sample to ensure that agreement was maintained across ethnic groups. The reliabilities of the coding for those observers who scored the Irish and Chinese infants with the primary coder using the videotapes of American infants were .79 and .95 for motor activity, .97 and .99 for crying, .87 and .92 for fretting, .81 and .89 for vocalizing, and .57 and .92 for smiling, respectively. These generally high reliabilities for coding across different samples indicate that there is minimal bias in the coding of each of the three ethnic groups.

. . .

The data indicate a significant difference in both level and variability of arousal to stimulation between Caucasian and Chinese infants, with the Chinese infants showing both lower levels of arousal as well as less variability. Although variation in experience during the first 4 months probably makes a contribution to this result, it is possible that temperamental factors are also of some influence. This claim rests on several arguments.

First, Freedman and Freedman (1969) reported very similar differences with infants who were less than 1-week-old; our results suggest that these differences are maintained beyond the neonatal period. A second reason for not attributing this result exclusively to prior experience rests on the presumption that infant smiling is unusually sensitive to differential reinforcement through social interactions with adults (Watson, 1972). However, the Chinese and Caucasian infants were minimally different on frequency of smiling and maximally different on motor activity, vocalization, and irritability. The latter three behaviors are more clearly indexes of degree of arousal to stimulation compared with smiling. In addition, the ethnic differences in vocalization and activity were also present in an independent sample of Chinese-American and European-American infants who attended the same experimental day-care center, 5 days a week, from early infancy to 2 years of age (Kagan et al., 1978).

Other investigators have reported biological differences between Asians and Caucasians. For example, Asian-American psychiatric patients require a lower dose of psychotropic drugs than do European-American patients (Lin, Poland, & Lesser, 1986), suggesting that Asian populations may be at a lower level of limbic arousal. Furthermore, there are known genetic differences between Asians and Europeans. For example, the proportion of Rh negative individuals is less than 1% in China but greater than 15% in Europe (Cavalli-Sforza, 1991). In addition, there is greater genetic diversity in many loci related to blood groups and proteins among Caucasians than Asians, a fact in accord with the greater variation in behavior discovered in this investigation (Latter, 1980). Even though all scientists agree that the genetic differences within an ethnic-geographic group is greater than the variation between groups, nonetheless, it is reasonable to at least entertain the hypothesis of genetically influenced behavioral differences in infants belonging to populations that have been reproductively isolated for a long time. Europeans and Asians have been reproductively isolated for about 30,000 years, or about 1,500 generations; it requires only 15 to 20 generations of selective breeding to produce obviously different behavioral profiles in many animal species (Mills & Faure, 1991; Plotkin, 1988).

Scientists should consider the ethnic composition of their samples when the psychological variables they quantify bear some relation to reactivity and ease of arousal. . . .

REFERENCES

Caudill, W., & Weinstein, H. (1969). Maternal care and infant behavior in Japan and America. *Psychiatry, 32,* 12–43.

Cavalli-Sforza, L. L. (1991). Genes, people and languages. *Scientific American, 265,* 104–111.

Freedman, D. G. (1974). *Human infancy: An evolutionary perspective.* Hillsdale, NJ: Erlbaum.

Freedman, D. G., & Freedman, M. (1969). Behavioral differences between Chinese-American and American newborns. *Nature, 224,* 1227.

Green, N. (1969). *An exploratory study of aggression and spacing behavior in two preschool nurseries: Chinese-American and European-American.* Unpublished master's thesis, University of Chicago.

Kagan, J., Kearsley, R. B., & Zelazo, P. R. (1978). *Infancy: Its place in human development.* Cambridge, MA: Harvard University Press.

Kagan, J., & Snidman, N. (1991a). Infant predictors of inhibited and uninhibited behavioral profiles. *Psychological Science, 2,* 40–44.

Kagan, J., & Snidman, N. (1991b). Temperamental factors in human development. *American Psychologist, 46,* 856–862.

Kagan, J., Snidman, N., Hendler, H., Greene, S. M., & Nugent, J. K. (1991). Predicting inhibited and uninhibited behavior. *Irish Journal of Psychology, 12,* 248–262.

Latter, B. D. H. (1980). Genetic differences within and between populations of the major human subgroups. *American Naturalist, 116,* 220–237.

Lewis, M. (1989). Culture and biology: The role of temperament. In P. R. Zelazo & R. G. Barr (Eds.), *Challenges to developmental paradigms: Implications for theory assessment and treatment* (pp. 203–223). Hillsdale, NJ: Erlbaum.

Lewis, M., Ramsay, D. S., & Kawakami, K. (in press). Affectivity and cortisol response differences between Japanese and American infants. *Child Development.*

Lin, K. M., Poland, R. E., & Lesser, I. M. (1986). Ethnicity and psychopharmacology. *Culture, Medicine and Psychiatry, 10,* 151–165.

Mills, A. D., & Faure, J. M. (1991). Diverse selection for duration of chronic immobility and social reinstatement behavior in Japanese quail. *Journal of Comparative Psychology, 105,* 25–38.

Plotkin, H. C. (1988). *The role of behavior in evolution.* Cambridge, MA: MIT Press.

Rothbart, M. K. (1989). Temperament in childhood: A framework. In G. A. Kohnstamm, J. E. Bates, & M. K. Rothbart (Eds.), *Temperament in childhood* (pp. 59–76). New York: Wiley.

Watson, J. S. (1972). Smiling, cooing, and "the game." *Merrill-Palmer Quarterly, 18,* 323–329.

Weisz, J. R., Suwanlert, S., Chaiyasit, W., Weiss, B., Achenbach, T. M., & Walter, B. A. (1987). Epidemiology of behavioral and emotional problems among Thai and American children: Parent reports for ages 6–11. *Journal of the American Academy of Child and Adolescent Psychiatry, 26,* 890–898.

Weisz, J. R., Suwanlert, S., Chaiyasit, W., Weiss, B., Walter, B. R., & Anderson, W. W. (1988). Thai and American perspectives on over- and undercontrolled child behavior problems. *Journal of Consulting and Clinical Psychology, 56,* 601–609.

Sleeping Out of Home in a Kibbutz Communal Arrangement: It Makes a Difference for Infant-Mother Attachment*

Abraham Sagi, Frank Donnell, Marinus H. van IJzendoorn, Ofra Mayseless, and Ora Aviezer

Bowlby (1984, p. 60) emphasized the importance of observing the development of children raised within settings that deviate considerably from the so-called environment of evolutionary adaptedness. In our first study on the development of attachment in infants raised in Israeli kibbutzim (Sagi et al., 1985), we examined the security of infant-mother attachment when infants were being raised in a traditional kibbutz communal sleeping arrangement. Infants in this setting are exposed to child-rearing practices that differ markedly from those that attachment theorists consider desirable, and consequently we expected to find an unusually high rate of insecure attachments among such infants. Employing the Strange Situation procedure (Ainsworth, Blehar, Waters, & Wall, 1978), we found that infants raised in this ecology were indeed classified as insecure-ambivalent to a greater extent than in most other cross-cultural samples (Sagi, 1990; van IJzendoorn & Kroonenberg, 1988).

In the ecology of a traditional kibbutz with communal sleeping arrangements, infants are moved into the infants' house at 6 weeks of age. There infants are cared for in small groups by professional caretakers, while their mothers visit regularly to feed and bathe them throughout the first year. During the night, two watchwomen are responsible for all the children under the age of 12 years on the kibbutz. The watchwomen are regular members of the kibbutz who contribute 1 week about every 6 months on a rotation basis, and they are responsible for monitoring via intercom a number of the children's houses from a central location, usually the infants' houses. Thus, at night the adults available to the infants (a total of about 50 women) are often unfamiliar and unable to respond promptly. Of necessity, then, infants are never able to establish a durable bond with the adults available to them at night.

. . .

The aim of the research design presented here was to compare two groups of infants who differed only in terms of their

*Sagi et al. (1994). *Child Development, 65,* 992–1004. Reprinted with permission.

sleeping arrangements: home-based as opposed to communal. . . .

Mothers' biographical characteristics, including age, number of children, education, professional training, and kibbutz experiences as a child, were considered background data. The data concerning potentially intervening variables consisted of appraisals of mothers' current job satisfaction, anxiety about separation from their infants, and attitudes toward their infants' houses, as well as observations of mother-infant interaction during a play session. Infants' background information and possible intervening variables included infants' age, sex, perceived temperament, and critical early life events such as illness and separation from parents. Another crucial comparison concerned the quality of care observed in each infants' house so we could examine the essential similarities in the daytime ecology of both groups of infants.

. . .

The subjects were 48 full-term, developmentally healthy infants aged 14 to 22 months (M = 18.29, SD = 2.25) from intact families. Thirteen boys and 10 girls were drawn randomly from 23 different kibbutz infants' houses with communal sleeping arrangements, and 13 boys and 12 girls were drawn randomly from 25 kibbutz infants' houses with home-based sleeping arrangements. An infants' house normally consists of six infants and two caregivers. The number of existing infants' houses in a given kibbutz depends on the annual birth rate, which changes from year to year and from one kibbutz to another (average is about 8–15 infants per year). We approached 50 kibbutz infants' houses through the official channels of the Institute of Research on Kibbutz Education, which monitors all research activities conducted with kibbutz children. One family had to leave the country unexpectedly after we obtained consent but before we visited, and one family withdrew its consent. Because this study is part of a larger project, we were unable to replace these two families. For communal versus home-based infants, mean ages were 18.74 (SD = 2.03) and 17.88 (SD = 2.40), respectively. There was no significant association between the type of sleeping arrangement and the sex of the infants.

. . .

More than half of the infants in communal sleeping arrangements developed insecure attachment relationships with their mothers. Only a fifth of home-based infants were found to be insecure. Other than the frequency and duration of infant-mother separations, all background characteristics of the two groups of mothers and infants were essentially the same. The quality of daily care in the infants' houses was also revealed to be equivalent across the two groups, demonstrating the hypothesis that apart from sleeping arrangements the two groups were equal. Lastly, the groups did not differ on quality of mother-infant interaction in a play session, suggesting that lack of contact at night time for the communal group did not secondarily change the interactions these mothers had with their infants during the day.

. . .

Every week infants in a communal sleeping arrangement encounter different watchwomen whose task is to look after their basic needs. Clearly, such an arrangement does not allow infants to develop attachment relationships to the watchwomen, who, in turn, cannot serve as a secure base for the infants whenever the infants wake up and require attention. Given that the infants in the communal group cried on average about 10 times per week (Donnell, 1991), these infants indeed experienced distress at night. Moreover, it is likely that any intervention by unfamiliar watchwomen in response to distress would elicit stranger anxiety in the infant (Bronson, 1986; Spitz, 1965; Tennes & Lample, 1964), which would further exacerbate the infant's distress. From the point of view of attachment theory, the continuous inaccessibility—without adequate replacement—of the mothers as primary attachment figures at night, combined with the mothers being available and responsive during the day, may constitute for the infants an inconsistently responsive interaction pattern.

This caretaking situation is likely to promote insecure-ambivalent relationships between mothers and their infants (Ainsworth et al., 1978), as was the case in more than half of the sample. It should be noted that because these infants experience inconsistency between the nature of interactions during the day and the nature of interactions during the night, their experience might be considered as different from the experience of infants with a parent who is continuously available physically and yet behaves inconsistently toward the infant.

. . .

It may seem surprising that the communal sleeping arrangement should alter attachment security so profoundly, whereas the long separations accompanying illness and hospitalization do not (van IJzendoorn et al., 1992). We suggest, however, that because the nightly separation in the communal sleeping arrangement recurs as an integral part of the child-care environment and is normative for all the children in the community, even sensitive parents may not think it necessary either to compensate for their absence during the night or to communicate the exceptional nature of the experience to the children (Lewin, 1990). On the other hand, parents of hospitalized infants may consider the nightly separations as unusual and perceive this regime to be stressful for the child; under these circumstances, parents often try to compensate for the child's hospital experiences, and often will sleep in the child's hospital room at night when possible. Because hospitalization is temporary, periods of intensive interaction at home may be effective in preventing the development of insecure attachment.

Mothers of home-based infants left them for longer and more frequent periods (e.g., for a short holiday without the child) than mothers of communal infants. We considered the number and duration of separations as potential intervening variables, because more separations of a longer duration may be associated with higher rates of attachment insecurity. Specifically, we were concerned that mothers of infants participating in a communal sleeping arrangement might be inclined to separate from their infants for longer periods than the mothers with infants in a home-based sleeping arrangement, because they might perceive such separations as less disruptive of their infants' daily routine, and therefore less stressful for the infants, than mothers of home-based infants. In fact, the results show the opposite pattern, suggesting that mothers who regularly care for their infants at night feel more comfortable in occasionally separating from them than mothers who do not. This is not to imply that infants who sleep at home are more exposed to strangers when their mothers are absent for more than 24 hours. In such cases infants are likely to be under the care of a familiar person (e.g., father, grandparents, or family friends) in the privacy of the family home (Gerson, 1978). . . .

REFERENCES

Ainsworth, M. D. S., Blehar, M. C., Waters, E., & Wall, S. (1978). *Patterns of attachment.* Hillsdale, NJ: Erlbaum.

Aviezer, O., Sagi, A., Donnell, F., Harel, Y., Joels, T., & Tuvia, M. (1989, April). *Mother-infant interaction observed during "love hour" in kibbutz infants' houses and the development of infant-mother attachment.* Paper presented at the biennial meeting of the Society for Research in Child Development, Kansas City, MO.

Barnard, K. E., Hammond, M. A., Booth, C. L., Bee, H. L., Mitchell, S. K., & Spieker, S. J. (1989). Measurement and meaning of parent-child interaction. In F. Morrison & J. Lord (Eds.), *Applied psychology* (Vol. 3, pp. 39–80). New York: Academic Press.

Bates, J. E., Freeland, C., & Lounsbury, M. (1979). Measurement of infant difficultness. *Child Development, 50,* 794–803.

Bayley, N. (1969). *Bayley Scales of Infant Development.* New York: Psychological Corp.

Belsky, J. (1988). The "effects" of infant daycare reconsidered. *Early Childhood Research Quarterly, 3,* 235–272.

Belsky, J., & Braungart, J. M. (1991). Are insecure-avoidant infants with extensive daycare experiences less stressed by and more independent in the Strange Situation? *Child Development, 62,* 567–571.

Belsky, J., & Walker, A. (1980). *Infant-Toddler Center Spot Observation System.* Unpublished manuscript, Pennsylvania State University, University Park.

Bowlby, J. (1973). *Attachment and loss: Vol. 2. Separation.* London: Penguin.

Bowlby, J. (1984). *Attachment and loss: Vol. 1. Attachment* (2d ed.). London: Pelican.

Brislin, R. W. (1980) Translation and content analysis of oral and written material. In H. C. Triandis & R. W Brislin

(Eds.), *Handbook of cross-cultural psychology/social psychology* (Vol. 2, pp. 389–444). Boston: Allyn & Bacon.

Bronfenbrenner, U. (1979). *The ecology of human development: Experiments by nature and design.* Cambridge, MA: Harvard University Press.

Bronson, G. W. (1968). The development of fear in man and other animals. *Child Development, 39,* 409–432.

Cook, T. D., & Campbell, D. T. (1979). *Quasi-experimentation: Design and analysis issues of field settings.* Chicago: Rand McNally.

Donnell, F. (1991). *The impact of family-based versus communal sleeping arrangements on the attachment relationships of kibbutz infants.* Unpublished master's thesis, School of Social Work, University of Haifa, Israel.

Gerson, M. (1978). *Family, women, and socialization in the kibbutz.* Lexington, MA: Lexington Books/Heath.

Hock, E. (1984). The transition to daycare: Effects of maternal separation anxiety on infant adjustment. In R. Ainslie (Ed.), *Quality variation in daycare: Implications for child development* (pp. 183–205). New York: Praeger.

Hock, E., & Clinger, J. B. (1981). Infant coping behaviors: Their assessment and their relation to maternal attributes. *Journal of Genetic Psychology, 138,* 231–243.

Hock, E., DeMeis, D. K., & McBride, S. L. (1988). Maternal separation anxiety: Its role in the balance of employment and motherhood in mothers of infants. In A. Gottfried & A. Gottfried (Eds.), *Maternal employment and children's development: Longitudinal research* (pp. 191–227). New York: Plenum.

Hock, E., McBride, S. L., & Gnezda, M. T. (1989). Maternal separation anxiety: Mother-infant separation from the maternal perspective. *Child Development, 60,* 793–802.

Lamb, M. E., Hwang, D., Bookstein, F. L., Broberg, A., Hult, G., & Frodi, M. (1988). Determinants of competence in Swedish preschoolers. *Developmental Psychology, 24,* 58–70.

Lavi, Z. (1982, April). *Correlates of sleeping arrangements of infants in kibbutzim.* Paper presented at the International Conference of Infant Studies, New York.

Lewin, G. (1990). Motherhood in the kibbutz. In Z. Lavi (Ed.), *Kibbutz members study kibbutz children* (pp. 34–39). New York: Greenwood.

Main, M., & Hess, E. (1990). The parents of insecure-disorganized/disoriented infants: Observations and speculations. In M. T. Greenberg, D. Cicchetti, & E. M. Cummings (Eds.), *Attachment in the preschool years: Theory, research and intervention* (pp. 161–184). Chicago: University of Chicago Press.

Main, M., & Solomon. J. (1990). Procedures for identifying infants as disorganized/disoriented during the Ainsworth Strange Situation. In M. T. Greenberg, D. Cicchetti, & E. M. Cummings (Eds.), *Attachment in the preschool years: Theory, research and intervention* (pp. 121–160). Chicago: University of Chicago Press.

Oppenheim, D., Sagi, A., & Lamb, M. E. (1988). Infant-adult attachments and their relation to socioemotional development four years later. *Developmental Psychology, 24,* 427–433.

Sagi, A. (1990). Attachment theory and research from a cross-cultural perspective. *Human Development, 33,* 10–22.

Sagi, A., & Koren-Karie, N. (in press). Day-care centers in Israel: An overview. In M. Cochran (Ed.), *International handbook of day-care policies and programs.* New York: Greenwood.

Sagi, A., Lamb, M. E., & Gardner, W. (1986). Relationships between Strange Situation behavior and stranger sociability among infants on Israeli kibbutzim. *Infant Behavior and Development, 9,* 271–282.

Sagi, A., Lamb, M. E., Lewkowicz, K., Shoham, R., Dvir, R., & Estes, E. (1985). Security of infant-mother, -father, and metapelet attachments among kibbutz-reared Israeli children. In I. Bretherton & E. Waters (Eds.), Growing points in attachment theory and research (pp. 257–275). *Monographs of the Society for Research in Child Development, 50*(1–2, Serial No. 209).

Sagi, A., van IJzendoorn, M. H., & Koren-Karie, N. (1991). Primary appraisal of the Strange Situation: A cross-cultural analysis of the preseparation episodes. *Developmental Psychology, 27,* 587–596.

Smith, P. B., & Pederson, D. R. (1988). Maternal sensitivity and patterns of infant-mother attachment. *Child Development, 59,* 1097–1101.

Spitz, R. A. (1965). *The first year of life: A psychoanalytic study of deviant object relations.* New York: International Universities Press.

Tennes, K. H., & Lample, E. E. (1964). Stranger and separation anxiety in infancy. *Journal of Nervous and Mental Disease, 139,* 247–254.

Tiger, L., & Shepher, J. (1975). *Women in the kibbutz.* New York: Harcourt Brace Jovanovich.

van IJzendoorn, M. H. (1990). Developments in cross-cultural research on attachment: Some methodological notes. *Human Development, 33,* 23–30.

van IJzendoorn, M. H. (1992). Intergenerational transmission of parenting: A review of studies in nonclinical populations. *Developmental Review, 12,* 76–99.

van IJzendoorn, M. H., Goldberg, S., Kroonenberg, P. M., & Frenkle, O. J. (1992). The relative effects of maternal and child problems on the quality of attachment: A meta-analysis of attachment in clinical samples. *Child Development, 63,* 840–858.

van IJzendoorn, M. H., & Kroonenberg, P. M. (1988). Cross-cultural patterns of attachment: A meta-analysis of the Strange Situation. *Child Development, 59,* 147–156.

Play in Two Societies: Pervasiveness of Process, Specificity of Structure*

Marc H. Bornstein, O. Maurice Haynes, Liliana Pascual, Kathleen M. Painter, and Celia Galperín

As the literature in children's object and representational play has matured since Piaget's (1962) homegrown observations of Jacqueline, Lucienne, and Laurent, two complementary currents have joined. One, flowing directly from Piaget, is that the growth of play in early childhood follows some pervasive developmental processes. A second, newer bearing is that specific structures associated with those general processes are modifiable in some degree with experience. One reason this new perspective has come into focus is cross-cultural investigation. Research regarding individual profiles and developmental milestones in children's play capacities, as well as mothers' play and styles of interaction, has in the past tended to concentrate geographically and culturally on Western family life. Although it subsidized considerable progress in describing the developmental phenomenon of play, monocultural research had the unintended consequence of restricting a broader understanding of play. Absent a comparative perspective, it is not possible to distinguish developmental characteristics which may be universal from those which may be specific to culture (e.g., Bornstein, 1980, 1991, 1995a; Kennedy, Scheirer, & Rogers, 1984; Moghaddam, 1987; Russell, 1984). The main purpose of the present study was to compare exploratory, representational, and social play and interaction styles in two contrasting groups of American children and mothers, one from Argentina and the other from the United States. These two societies were contrasted because of their differing social orientations related to childrearing.

. . .

Method

Samples

Participants were 39 Argentine and 43 U.S. primiparous mothers and their firstborn 20-month-old toddlers, 47 boys and 35 girls. Mothers in Buenos Aires were recruited from hospital birth notifications and patient lists of medical groups, and mothers in the Washington, DC, area responded to advertising in newspapers and to mailing lists. To avoid the potential complications of ethnically based differences in mothers' behavior, the Argentine sample was restricted to *Porteñas* of European background, and the U.S. sample was restricted to comparable women of European American heritage. The samples were also selected according to the following inclusive criteria: adult (20 years or older) and primiparous mothers by birth who were living with their husbands. U.S. mothers were slightly older, $M = 32.0$ years, $SD = 4.4$, than Argentine mothers, $M = 29.9$ years, $SD = 4.7$, $t(80) = -2.07$, $p \leq .05$. The Argentine and U.S. samples were selected to be as similar as possible on SES, with respect to the means and variances of the Hollingshead Four Factor Index of Social Status (Hollingshead, 1975; see, too, Gottfried, 1985), M Argentine SES = 46.1, $SD = 12.9$, and M U.S. SES = 48.6, $SD = 10.5$, $t(80) = .99$, $p \leq .33$; Levene's test for equality of variances, $F(1, 80) = 1.61$, $p \leq .21$. The validity of the Hollingshead as a measure of SES in Argentina is supported in the literature (Pascual, Galperín, & Bornstein, 1993). Both samples represented a range of SES (including occupation and education) from low to upper middle-class families. Mothers and

*Bornstein et al. (1999). *Child Development, 70,* 317–331. Reprinted with permission.

fathers in both samples showed a full range of occupational ratings from farm laborers and menial service workers to professionals (*medians* = 6 or 7, measured using the 9-point Hollingshead scale). The average educational level (measured from the 7-point Hollingshead scale) in the U.S. was also somewhat higher, $M = 5.7$, $SD = .9$, than in Argentina, $M = 5.0$, $SD = 1.2$, $t(80) = -2.88$, $p \leq .01$. Approximately 44% of U.S. mothers and 54% of Argentine mothers were working outside of the home when their child was 20 months of age, $\chi^2(1, N = 82) = .76$, *ns*.

All infants were born at term and had been healthy since birth, excluding minor illness. Argentine children averaged 20.6 months of age ($SD = .4$) and U.S. children averaged 20.1 months of age ($SD = .2$) at the time of the observation, $t(59.4) = 8.14$, $p \leq .001$. We recruited samples balanced with respect to sex of child so that potential differences between girls and boys, and between mothers of girls and mothers of boys, could be examined (Fagot, 1995; Maccoby & Jacklin, 1974).

Dyads were observed in the second year because this is typically a time when children still engage in exploratory play but also symbolically represent everyday experiences of self and others in their play. In the second year, children conceptualize abstract relations between symbols and their real-world referents, and play (along with language) has emerged as a significant mode of representation and basis of interaction, but children are thought to vary considerably among themselves in these abilities (e.g., Bornstein & Lamb, 1992; de Villiers & de Villiers, 1999; Edwards, 1995). The second-year child is also sensitive and responsive to maternal expressions of feelings and emotions, and by this age children demonstrate the cognitive capacity not only to interpret the physical and psychological states of others but also to experience those states affectively (e.g., Bronson, 1974; Clarke-Stewart & Hevey, 1981; Edwards, 1995; Zahn-Waxler, Radke-Yarrow, Wagner, & Chapman, 1992). We also wanted information from mothers who were settled in the maternal role and whose views of their own parenting had had ample opportunity to stabilize. In consequence, 2 years postpartum appeared to constitute an appropriate time to investigate cultural variation in child play and in associated parenting.

. . .

Discussion

. . .

Our findings provide evidence for both pervasive processes and different emphases on specific structures in cultural considerations of child-mother play and interaction. Twenty-month-olds growing up in and around Buenos Aires and around Washington, DC, observed under similar conditions of free play with their mothers at home with the same toys, engaged in similar play behaviors exploring constructively and pretending symbolically. Moreover, their mothers engaged in cognitive as well as affective types of interactions with them. These findings give evidence of species-general developmental processes, and this perspective provides support for the universalist, maturational tradition of play that has flowed from Piaget's own narrow data base. Furthermore, in both cultures, children and mothers were in tune with one another in terms of play: Children who engaged in more exploratory play had mothers who engaged in more exploratory play, and children who engaged in more symbolic play had mothers who engaged in more symbolic play. Although mothers' exploratory and symbolic play related to their children's exploratory and symbolic play in both places, mothers' expressions of social play, physical affection, and verbal praise toward their children did not relate to their children's exploratory or symbolic play in either culture. This pattern of results not only supports universalist views of mother-child object and representational play but also points to the existence of specific, rather than general, relations in mother and child interactions (see Bornstein, 1995b). Studies with other U.S. samples have shown that mothers who played more in pretense at 13 and 20 months had children who played more in pretense (Bornstein et al., 1996;

Tamis-LeMonda & Bornstein, 1994; Vibbert & Bornstein, 1989). The present findings broaden those results to exploratory play and across cultures. Maternal object play style is a notable factor in child object play style. Play requires time, energy, resources, and commitment on the part of parents, but parents' efforts appear to benefit their children. The finding that mothers are effective and influential play partners generally articulates with sequential analyses of mother-child play (Damast et al., 1996; Fiese, 1990) as well as multivariate analyses of the determinants of child play (Bornstein et al., 1996; Tamis-LeMonda & Bornstein, 1996). In addition, the findings show that instrumental and cognitive, rather than purely affective, components of mother-child interaction appear to be critical to the growth of exploratory and representational competencies as measured in child object play.

Finally concerning the universality of play, child gender emerged as a significant factor. Boys played more and more often in an exploratory mode, whereas girls played more and more often in a symbolic mode regardless of culture (see, too, Bornstein et al., 1996; Lytton & Romney, 1991). Similarly, mothers of boys engaged in more exploratory play, and mothers of girls engaged in more symbolic play across cultures. In attempting to understand these gender differences, it is well to consider that symbolic play tended to stress other-directed pretense. It could be that children who are more sensitive to others are more mature, as girls generally tend to be vis-à-vis boys in this age range. And, relatedly, it could be that these positive social characteristics are child effects, such that more socially aware children (girls) elicit more socially sensitive activities from their mothers and others. Or, it could be that girls, on average, experience more early caregiving socialization regarding interpersonal skills than do boys, or that girls are more susceptible to early caregiving socialization regarding interpersonal skills than are boys (e.g., Maccoby, 1988). . . .

Dyads in the two cultures we studied approached mother-child collaborative play in contrasting ways; and interactive play seemed to serve different functions and perhaps assume different meanings in the two (Bornstein, 1995b). In the U.S., the play session was the stage and the toys were typically the object of communication; in contrast, in Argentina, the play session and toys served predominantly to mediate dyadic interaction. This functional contrast is reflected prominently in the differential use of specific levels of object play and different emphases in social play by mothers and children in the two societies. Argentine mothers encouraged interactive, especially other-directed pretense (e.g., feeding or putting the doll to sleep), whereas U.S. mothers encouraged functional and combinatorial play (e.g., dialing the telephone or nesting the barrels). Argentine mothers displayed more positive affect and verbally praised their toddlers more. According to Romano Yalour (1986), "sharing with others" is one of the main goals of Argentine middle-class mothers for socialization of young children. Thus, children in these two cultures are provided by their mothers with opportunities to see and partake in all kinds of play but with different emphases. Not uninterestingly, these data echo our findings on Japanese and American mother-child play. Japan is an Eastern collectivist society (tied at 22/23 with Argentina in Hofstede's, 1991, ranking), possessing the same culturally divergent views of self from the U.S. (interdependent versus independent; see, e.g., Markus & Kitayama, 1991). We previously reported comparable cultural differences in mother-child communicative strategies and thematic content of pretend play between Japanese and Americans, both again consonant with the collectivist-individualist distinction (Tamis-LeMonda et al., 1992). . . .

Parent-child play has been linked to acquiring, refining, or extending a wide range of cognitive and social skills (Johnson et al., 1987; Singer & Singer, 1990). The cultural differences revealed in this study suggest that Argentine and U.S. children and mothers tend to engage in modes of exploration, representation, and social interaction differently, but in ways consonant with their larger cultural childrearing goals; such cultural emphases help to shape the course of child development (Bornstein, 1991; Bradley, 1995; Kessen, 1979). In play, processes may be pervasive, but emphases on different structures appear to be culture specific.

REFERENCES

Aguinis, M. (1988). *Un pais de novela* [A fictive country]. Buenos Aires, Argentina: Editorial Planeta.

Bellah, R. N., Madsen, R., Sullivan, W. M., Swindler, A., & Tipton, S. M. (1985). *Habits of the heart: Individualism and commitment in American life.* New York: Harper & Row.

Belsky, J., & Most, R. K. (1981). From exploration to play: A cross-sectional study of infant free play behavior. *Developmental Psychology, 17,* 630–639.

Bontempo, R., & Rivero, J. C. (1992, August). *Cultural variation in cognition: The role of self-concept in the attitude behavior link.* Paper presented at the meetings of the American Academy of Management, Las Vegas, Nevada.

Bornstein, M. H. (1980). Cross-cultural developmental psychology. In M. H. Bornstein (Ed.), *Comparative methods in psychology* (pp. 231–281). Hillsdale, NJ: Erlbaum.

Bornstein, M. H. (1991). Approaches to parenting in culture. In M. H. Bornstein (Ed.), *Cultural approaches to parenting* (pp. 3–19), Hillsdale, NJ: Erlbaum.

Bornstein, M. H. (1994), Cross-cultural perspectives on parenting. In G. d'Ydewalle, P. Eelen, & P. Bertelson (Eds.), *International perspectives on psychological science. Volume 2: State of the art lectures presented at the XXVth International Congress of Psychology, Brussels, 1992* (pp. 359–369). Hove, England: Erlbaum.

Bornstein, M. H. (1995a). Form and function: Implications for studies of culture and human development. *Culture & Psychology, 1,* 123–137.

Bornstein, M. H. (1995b). Parenting infants. In M. H. Bornstein (Ed.), *Handbook of parenting* (Vol. 1, pp. 3–39). Mahwah, NJ: Erlbaum.

Bornstein, M. H. (1999). Child play: Experimental and ecological considerations. In M. Kielar-Turska (Ed.), *Proceedings of the Second International Conference on Play.* Krakow, Poland: State Scientific Publishers PWN.

Bornstein, M. H., Haynes, O. M., Galperín, C., Maital, S., Ogino, M., Painter, K., Pascual, K., Pêcheux, M.-G., Rahn, C., Tanner, K., Toda, S., Vanuti, P., Vyt, A., & Wright, B. (1998). A cross-national study of self-perceptions and attributions about parenting: Argentina, Belgium, France, Israel, Italy, Japan, and the United States. *Developmental Psychology, 34,* 662–676.

Bornstein, M. H., Haynes, O. M., Legler, J. M., O'Reilly, A. W., & Painter, K. M. (1997). Symbolic play in childhood: Interpersonal and environmental context and stability. *Infant Behavior and Development, 20,* 197–207.

Bornstein, M. H., Haynes, O. M., O'Reilly, A. W., & Painter, K. (1996). Solitary and collaborative pretense play in early childhood: Sources of individual variation in the development of representational competence. *Child Development, 67,* 2910–2929.

Bornstein, M. H., & Lamb, M. E. (1992). *Development in Infancy: An Introduction* (3rd ed.). New York: McGraw-Hill.

Bornstein, M. H., & O'Reilly, A. W. (Eds.). (1993). *The role of play in the development of thought.* San Francisco: Jossey-Bass.

Bornstein, M. H., Tal, J., Rahn, C., Galperín, C. Z., Pêcheux, M.-G., Lamour, M., Azuma, H., Toda, S., Ogino, M., & Tamis-LeMonda, C. S. (1992). Functional analysis of the contents of maternal speech to infants of 5 and 13 months in four cultures: Argentina, France, Japan, and the United States. *Developmental Psychology, 28,* 593–603.

Bornstein, M. H., & Tamis-LeMonda, C. S. (1995). Parent-child symbolic play: Three stories in search of an effect. *Developmental Review, 15,* 382–400.

Bradley, R. H. (1995). Environment and parenting. In M. H. Bornstein (Ed.), *Handbook of parenting* (Vol. 2, pp. 235–261). Mahwah, NJ: Erlbaum.

Bradley, R. H., & Caldwell, B. M. (1995). Caregiving and the regulation of child growth and development: Describing proximal aspects of caregiving systems. *Developmental Review, 15,* 38–85.

Braedekamp, S. (1987). *Developmentally appropriate practice in early childhood programs serving children from birth through age 8.* Washington, DC: National Association for the Education of Young Children.

Bronson, W. C. (1974). Mother-toddler interaction: A perspective on studying the development of competence. *Merrill-Palmer Quarterly, 20,* 275–301.

Burns, S. M., & Brainard, C. J. (1979). Effects of constructive and dramatic play on perspective taking in very young children. *Developmental Psychology, 15,* 512–521.

Caldera, Y. M., Huston, A. C., & O'Brien, M. (1989). Social interactions and play patterns of parents and toddlers with feminine, masculine, and neutral toys. *Child Development, 60,* 70–76.

Christie, J. F. (Ed.). (1991). *Play and early literacy development.* Albany, NY: State University of New York Press.

Clarke-Stewart, K. A., & Hevey, C. M. (1981). Longitudinal relations in repeated observations of mother-child interaction from 1 to 2½ years. *Developmental Psychology, 17,* 127–145.

Connolly, J. A., & Doyle, A. B. (1984). Relations of social fantasy play to social competence in preschoolers. *Developmental Psychology, 20,* 797–806.

Damast, A. M., Tamis-LeMonda, C. S., & Bornstein, M. H. (1996). Mother-child play: Sequential interactions and the relation between maternal beliefs and behaviors. *Child Development, 67,* 1752–1766.

Danksy, J. L. (1980). Make-believe: A mediator of the relationship between play and associative fluency. *Child Development, 51,* 576–579.

Dempster, A. P., Laird, N. M., & Rubin, D. B. (1977). Maximum likelihood from incomplete data via the EM algorithm. *Journal of the Royal Statistical Society* (Ser. B), *39,* 1–38.

de Villiers, P. A., & de Villiers, J. G. (1999). Language development. In M. H. Bornstein & M. E. Lamb (Eds.), *Developmental psychology: An advanced textbook* (4th ed., pp. 313–373). Mahwah, NJ: Erlbaum.

Dunn, J., & Wooding, C. (1977). Play in the home and its implications for learning. In B. Tizard & D. Harvey

(Eds.), *The biology of play* (pp. 45–58). Philadelphia: Lippincott.

Edwards, C. P. (1995). Parenting toddlers. In M. H. Bornstein (Ed.), *Handbook of parenting* (Vol. 1, pp. 41–63). Mahwah, NJ: Erlbaum.

Eichelbaum de Babini, A. M. (1965). *Educatión familiar y status socioeconómico* [Socialization within the family and socioeconomic status]. Buenos Aires: Instituto de Sociologia.

Fagot, B. I. (1995). Parenting boys and girls. In M. H. Bornstein (Ed.), *Handbook of parenting* (Vol. 1, pp. 163–183). Mahwah, NJ: Erlbaum.

Farver, J. M. (1993). Cultural differences in scaffolding pretend play: A comparison of American and Mexican mother-child and sibling-child pairs. In K. MacDonald (Ed.), *Parent-child play: Descriptions and implications* (pp. 349–366). Albany, NY: State University of New York Press.

Farver, J. M., & Howes, C. (1993). Cultural differences in American and Mexican mother-child pretend play. *Merrill-Palmer Quarterly, 39,* 344–358.

Farver, J. M., & Wimbarti, S. (1995). Indonesian children's play with their mothers and older siblings. *Child Development, 66,* 1493–1503.

Fiese, B. H. (1990). Playful relationships: A contextual analysis of mother-toddler interaction and symbolic play. *Child Development, 61,* 1648–1656.

Fillol, T. R. (1961). *Social factors in economic development: The Argentine case.* Westport, CT: Greenwood Press.

Gaskins, S. (1996). How Mayan parental theories come into play. In S. Harkness & C. M. Super (Eds.), *Parents' cultural belief systems: Their origins, expressions, and consequences* (pp. 345–363). New York: Guilford Press.

Göncü, A., & Mosier, C. (1991, April). *Cultural variation in the play of toddlers.* Paper presented at the biennial meeting of the Society for Research in Child Development, Seattle, WA.

Gottfried, A. W. (1985). Measures of socioeconomic status in child development research: Data and recommendations. *Merrill-Palmer Quarterly, 31,* 85–92.

Haight, W. L., & Miller, P. J. (1992). The development of everyday pretend play: A longitudinal study of mothers' participation. *Merrill-Palmer Quarterly, 38,* 331–349.

Harwood, R. L., & Miller, J. G. (1991). Perceptions of attachment behavior: A comparison of Anglo and Puerto Rican mothers. *Merrill-Palmer Quarterly, 37,* 583–599.

Hofstede, G. (1980). *Culture's consequences: International differences in work-related values.* London: Sage.

Hofstede, G. (1991). *Cultures and organizations: Software of the mind.* London: McGraw-Hill.

Hollingshead, A. B. (1975). *The four factor index of social status.* Unpublished manuscript, Yale University.

Howes, C. (1992). *The collaborative construction of pretend: Social pretend play functions.* Albany, NY: State University of New York Press.

Johnson, J. E., Christie, J., & Yawkey, T. D. (1987). *Play and early childhood development.* Evanston, IL: Scott Foresman.

Johnson, R. A., & Wichern, D. W. (1988). *Applied multivariate statistical analysis* (2nd ed.). Englewood Cliffs, NJ: Prentice Hall.

Kağitçibaşi, C. (1994). A critical appraisal of individualism-collectivism: Toward a new formulation. In U. Kim, H. C. Triandis, C. Kağitçibaşi, C.-S. Choi, & G., Yoon, *Individualism and collectivism: Theory, method and applications* (pp. 52–65). Newbury Park, CA: Sage Publications.

Kağitçibaşi, C. (1997). Individualism and collectivism. In J. W. Berry, M. H. Segall, & C. Kağitçibaşi (Eds.), *Handbook of cross-cultural psychology* (2nd ed., Vol. 3, pp. 1–49). Boston: Allyn & Bacon.

Kennedy, S., Scheirer, J., & Rogers, A. (1984). The price of success: Our monocultural science. *American Psychologist, 39,* 996–997.

Kessen, W. (1979). The American child and other cultural inventions. *American Psychologist, 34,* 815–820.

Lasater, C., & Johnson, J. E. (1994). Culture, play, and early childhood education. In J. L. Roopnarine, J. E. Johnson, & F. H. Hooper (Eds.), *Children's play in diverse cultures* (pp. 210–220). Albany, NY: State University of New York Press.

Little, R. J. A. (1988). A test of missing completely at random for multivariate data with missing values. *Journal of the American Statistical Association, 83,* 1198–1202.

Lytton, H., & Romney, D. M. (1991). Parents' differential socialization of boys and girls: A meta-analysis. *Psychological Bulletin, 109,* 267–296.

Lyytinen, P., Poikkeus, A.-M., & Laakso, M.-L. (1997). Language and symbolic play in toddlers. *International Journal of Behavioral Development, 21,* 289–302.

Maccoby, E. E. (1988). Gender as a social category. *Developmental Psychology, 24,* 755–765.

Maccoby, E. E., & Jacklin, C. N. (1974). *The psychology of sex differences.* Stanford, CA: Stanford University Press.

MacDonald, K. (Ed.) (1993). *Parent-child play: Descriptions & implications.* Albany, NY: State University of New York Press.

Markus, H. R., & Kitayama, S. (1991). Culture and the self: Implications for cognition, emotion, and motivation. *Psychological Review, 98,* 224–253.

McCune-Nicolich, L. (1981). Toward symbolic functioning: Structure of early pretend games and potential parallels with language. *Child Development, 52,* 785–797.

McCune-Nicolich, L., & Fenson, L. (1984). Methodological issues in studying early pretend play. In T. D. Yawkey & A. D. Pelligrini (Eds.), *Child's play: Developmental and applied* (pp. 81–124). Hillsdale, NJ: Erlbaum.

Moghaddam, F. M. (1987). Psychology in three worlds. *American Psychologist, 42,* 912–920.

New, R. S. (1994). Child's play—*una cosa naturale:* An Italian perspective. In J. L. Roopnarine, J. E. Johnson, & F. H. Hooper (Eds.), *Children's play in diverse cultures* (pp. 123–147). Albany, NY: State University of New York Press.

O'Connell, B., & Bretherton, I. (1984). Toddler's play alone and with mother: The role of maternal guidance. In I. Bretherton (Ed.), *Symbolic play: The development of social understanding* (pp. 337–368). Orlando, FL: Academic Press.

Pascual, L., Galperín, C., & Bornstein, M. H. (1993). La medición del nivel socioeconómico y la psicología evolutiva: El caso Argentino [Measurement of socioeconomic status and developmental psychology: The

Argentine case]. *Revista Interamericana de Psicología/Interamerican Journal of Psychology, 27,* 59–74.

Pepler, D. J., & Ross, H. S. (1981). The effects of play on convergent and divergent problem solving. *Child Development, 52,* 1202–1210.

Pescatello, A. (Ed.). (1973). *Female and male in Latin America: Essays.* Pittsburgh, PA: University of Pittsburgh Press.

Piaget, J. (1962). *Play, dreams and imitation in childhood.* New York: Norton.

Rogoff, B., Mistry, J., Göncü, A., & Mosier, C. (1993). *Guided participation in cultural activity by toddlers and caregivers. Monographs of the Society for Research in Child Development, 58*(8), 179.

Rogoff, B., Mosier, C., Mistry, J., & Göncü, A. (1993). Toddlers' guided participation with their caregivers in cultural activity. In E. A. Forman, N. Minick, & C. A. Stone (Eds.), *Contexts for learning: Sociocultural dynamics in children's development* (pp. 230–253). New York: Oxford University Press.

Romano Yalour, M. (1986). *Como educan los argentinos a sus hijos* [How Argentines educate their children]. Buenos Aires: Ed. Sudamericana-Planeta.

Roopnarine, J. L., Johnson, J. E., & Hooper, F. H. (Eds.). (1994). *Children's play in diverse cultures.* Albany, NY: State University of New York Press.

Rubin, K. H., Fein, G. G., & Vandenberg, B. (1983). Play. In E. M. Hetherington (Ed.), P. H. Mussen (Series Ed.), *Handbook of child psychology: Vol. 4. Socialization, personality, and social development* (pp. 693–774). New York: Wiley.

Russell, R. (1984). Psychology in its world context. *American Psychologist, 39,* 1017–1025.

Schwartz, S. H. (1994). Beyond individualism and collectivism: New cultural dimensions of values. In U. Kim, H. C. Triandis, C. Kağitçibaşi, C.-S. Choi, & G. Yoon (Eds.), *Individualism and collectivism: Theory, method, and applications* (pp. 85–122), Newbury Park, CA: Sage Publications.

Schwartzman, H. (1978). *Transformations: The anthropology of children's play.* New York: Plenum.

Sigman, M., & Sena, R. (1993). Pretend play in high-risk and developmentally delayed children. In M. H. Bornstein & A. W. O'Reilly (Eds.), *The role of play in the development of thought* (pp. 29–42). San Francisco: Jossey-Bass.

Singer, D. G., & Singer, J. L. (1990). *The house of make-believe.* Cambridge, MA: Harvard University Press.

Slade, A. (1987a). A longitudinal study of maternal involvement and symbolic play during the toddler period. *Child Development, 58,* 367–375.

Slade, A. (1987b). Quality of attachment and early symbolic play. *Developmental Psychology, 23,* 78–85.

Smilansky, S., & Shefatya, L. (1991). *Facilitating play: A medium for promoting cognitive, socio-emotional and academic development in young children.* Gaithersburg, MD: Psychosocial & Educational Publications.

Smith, P. B., & Bond, M. H. (1994). *Social psychology across cultures.* Boston: Allyn & Bacon.

Stevenson, H. W., Stigler, J. W., Lee, S-y., Lucker, G. W., Kitamura, S., & Hsu, C.-c. (1985). Cognitive performance and academic achievement of Japanese, Chinese, and American children. *Child Development, 56,* 718–734.

Stevenson, M. B., Leavitt, L. A., Roach, M. A., Chapman, R. S., & Miller, J. F. (1986). Mothers' speech to their 1-year-old infants in home and laboratory settings. *Journal of Psycholinguistic Research, 15,* 451–461.

Super, C. M., & Harkness, S. (1986). The developmental niche: A conceptualization of the interface of child and culture. *International Journal of Behavioral Development, 9,* 546–569.

Tamis-LeMonda, C. S., & Bornstein, M. H. (1994). Specificity in mother-toddler language-play relations across the second year. *Developmental Psychology, 30,* 283–292.

Tamis-LeMonda, C. S., & Bornstein, M. H. (1996). Variation in children's exploratory, nonsymbolic, and symbolic play: An explanatory multidimensional framework. In C. R. Rovee-Collier & L. P. Lipsitt (Eds.), *Advances in infancy research* (Vol. 10, pp. 37–78). Norwood, NJ: Ablex.

Tamis-LeMonda, C. S., Bornstein, M. H., Cyphers, L., Toda, S., & Ogino, M. (1992). Language and play at one year: A comparison of toddlers and mothers in the United States and Japan. *International Journal of Behavioral Development, 15,* 19–42.

Tamis-LeMonda, C. S., Chen, L. A., & Bornstein, M. H. (1997). Mothers' knowledge about children's play and language development: Short-term stability and interrelations. *Developmental Psychology, 34,* 115–124.

Thal, D., & Katich, J. (1996). Predicaments in early identification of specific language impairment. Does the early bird always catch the worm? In K. N. Cole, P. S. Dale, & D. J. Thal (Eds.), *Assessment of communication and language* (Vol. 6, pp. 1–28). Baltimore: Paul H. Brookes.

Triandis, H. C. (1994). *Culture and social behavior.* New York: McGraw-Hill.

Triandis, H. C. (1995). *Individualism and collectivism.* Boulder, CO: Westview Press.

Tukey, V. W. (1977). *Exploratory data analysis.* Menlo Park, CA: Addison Wesley.

Ungerer, J. A., & Sigman, M. (1984). The relation of play and sensorimotor behavior to language in the second year. *Child Development, 55,* 1448–1455.

Užgiris, I. C., Benson, J. B., Kruper, J. C., & Vasek, M. E. (1989). Contextual influences on imitative interactions between mothers and infants. In J. Lockman & N. L. Hazen (Eds.), *Action in social context: Perspectives on early development* (pp. 103–127). New York: Plenum.

Užgiris, I. C., & Raeff, C. (1995). Play in parent-child interactions. In M. H. Bornstein (Ed.), *Handbook of parenting* (Vol. 4, pp. 353–376). Mahwah, NJ: Erlbaum.

Vibbert, M., & Bornstein, M. H. (1989). Specific associations between domains of mother-child interaction and toddler referential language and pretense play. *Infant Behavior and Development, 12,* 163–184.

Vygotsky, L. (1978). *Mind in society.* Cambridge, MA: Harvard University Press.

Whiting, J. W. M., & Child, I. L. (1953). *Child training and personality: A cross-cultural study.* New Haven, CT: Yale University Press.

Zahn-Waxler, C., Radke-Yarrow, M., Wagner, E., & Chapman, M. (1992). Development of concern for others. *Developmental Psychology, 28,* 126–136.

REVIEW QUESTIONS AND ACTIVITIES

1. Do infants from different cultures differ in ease of arousal?
2. Imagine you have been asked to speak to a group of parents-to-be about attachment during infancy. What information would you provide? Why this information?
3. Discuss the key research on the impact of culture on the emergence of motor skills in infancy.
4. You have been asked to be a consultant to a local parenting group. You are to summarize the literature on infants' sleeping arrangements and independence training. What research would you share with these parents? How would you answer their questions that challenge the research—especially those based on information they have read by Dr. Spock and other child-rearing experts?
5. What functions do infant-directed speech serve? Discuss the cultural similarities and differences in infant-directed speech.
6. Discuss the relationship between culture and play in infants. How would you integrate current research into designing a play area in infants' day care centers?
7. Critically reread one of the articles excerpted in this chapter, and then answer the following questions:
   a. Is the purpose of the research clear? Explain.
   b. Are studies contrary to the current hypothesis cited?
   c. Is the research hypothesis correctly derived from the literature and theory that has been cited? Or are there some important steps missing and/or left to the speculation of the reader?
   d. Are there possible experimenter biases? Explain.
   e. Were the conclusions drawn by the author consistent with the results obtained?
   f. What follow-up studies do you think are needed? Why these studies? Describe the methodology you would use in these follow-up studies.

SUGGESTIONS FOR FURTHER READING

Bornstein, M. H., Haynes, O., Galperín, C., Maital, S., Ogino, M., Painter, K., Pascual, K., Pêcheux, M. -G., Rahn, C., Tanner, K., Toda, S., Venuti, P., Vyt, A., & Wright, B. (1998). A cross-national study of self-perceptions and attributions about parenting: Argentina, Belgium, France, Israel, Italy, Japan, and the United States. *Developmental Psychology, 34,* 662–676.

LeVine, R., Miller, P., & West, M. (Eds.). (1988). *Parental behavior in diverse societies: New directions for child development,* No. 40. San Francisco: Jossey-Bass.

Richman, A., Miller, P., & LeVine, R. (1992). Cultural and educational variations in maternal responsiveness. *Developmental Psychology, 28,* 614–621.

Sagi, A., van IJzendoorn, M., & Koren-Karie, N. (1991). Primary appraisal of the Strange Situation: A cross-cultural analysis of preseparation episodes. *Developmental Psychology, 27,* 587–596.

Stevenson-Hinde, J. (1998). Parenting in different cultures: Time to focus. *Developmental Psychology, 34,* 698–700.

Younger, B., & Fearing, D. (1999). Parsing items into separate categories: Developmental change in infant categorization. *Child Development, 70,* 291–303.

God could not be everywhere and therefore he made mothers.

Jewish Proverb

One father is more than a hundred schoolmasters.

English Proverb

To teach is to learn.

Japanese Proverb

Preschool Years

Questions for Reflection

- What do you think is the influence of culture on preschoolers' development in social interaction and play?
- Identify what you believe is the impact of the father's role in child development, in terms of a child's cognitive skills, language competence, and behavior problems.
- What, in your view, is the relationship between socioeconomic class status and preschoolers' language development?
- What consequences can you hypothesize will come to children who have been exposed to long-term violence?
- In your opinion, what is the impact of quality child care on preschoolers' cognitive, social, and emotional development?

OVERVIEW: CULTURAL INFLUENCES ON DEVELOPMENT IN THE PRESCHOOL YEARS

The readings selected for this chapter deal with several topics in the study of development in preschoolers: language advances made during this life stage; peer relations and play; preschoolers' exposure to real violence in their communities; the impact of child care on preschoolers' cognitive, emotional, and social development; and the role of the father and mother in preschoolers' development. Several of the articles highlight continuity in development across the life cycle. Others revisit issues already discussed in the last chapter: language development, play, and emotional regulation.

We begin with an overview of the physical changes accompanying the preschool period, followed by a review of the literature that supports the focus of the research described in the readings. Although the readings are discussed under main headings, such as physical development or cognitive development, the topics are interdependent. For example, the article on the impact of fathers on preschoolers' development is included under the heading "Emotional Development," though it could have easily been discussed under the "Cognitive Development" or "Social Development" headings. Each dimension of development reflects the others. Keep this issue of interdependence among dimensions central in your mind as you read articles throughout this book.

PHYSICAL DEVELOPMENT IN THE PRESCHOOL YEARS

The *preschool period,* also known as *early childhood* by developmental psychologists, characterizes children 3 to 5 years of age. Have you observed children developing during the preschool years? It is amazing to watch their rapid growth—how they progress from looking like infants to taking on more adultlike physical proportions. For example, at the beginning of the preschool years, children weigh on average 25 to 30 pounds and are approximately 36 inches tall. By the end of the preschool period, children weigh on average 46 pounds and are approximately 46 inches tall (Feldman, 1998). Average differences in height and weight between girls and boys increase during the preschool period. On average, boys tend to be taller than, and weigh more than, preschool girls. It should be noted, however, that there is a tremendous overlap in these distributions for height and weight (Rice, 1997).

Differences in height and weight exist between children in economically less developed countries and those in more developed countries. Better health care and better nutrition are related to children weighing more and being taller. The United Nations (1990) has indicated that the average Swedish 4-year-old is as tall as the average 6-year-old in Bangladesh. Differences in height and weight also reflect economic factors in the United States (Barrett & Frank, 1987). Studies suggest that more than 10 percent of children in the United States whose family incomes are below the poverty level are among the shortest 5 percent of all preschool-age children (Sherry, Springer, Connell, & Garrett, 1992).

In addition to changes in weight and height, preschoolers' physiques take on a different form (Feldman, 1998). Preschoolers become less cherublike and more slender. Increased mobility and exercise helps preschoolers burn off the fat they have carried since infancy. Their arms and legs lengthen, and by the time children are at the end of this development stage, their proportions are similar to those of adults.

Muscle size increases in preschoolers; their bones become sturdier. Because the eustachian tube in the ear moves to an angular position at this point in development, preschoolers develop more earaches. Their brains grow at a faster rate than any other part of the body (Feldman, 1998); by the end of the preschool period, children's brains weigh 90 percent of the average adult brain weight (Rice, 1997). This rapid growth of the brain is due largely to an increase in cell interconnections and the amount of myelin in the brain. Children's senses improve during the preschool years as well, especially their vision and hearing (Rice, 1997).

Preschoolers are also progressing in their fine motor skills. They become increasingly better at folding paper into halves and quarters, drawing rectangles and triangles, stringing beads, building bridges with five blocks, pouring from various containers, copying letters and copying short words (Feldman, 1998).

Preschoolers' gross motor skills become more developed (Corbin, 1973; Feldman, 1998). Throughout this life stage, preschoolers become better at turning and stopping quickly, jumping, and hopping on one foot. Their activity level is high (Eaton & Yu, 1989). A sex difference has been noted in gross motor coordination: on average, boys have greater gross motor ability, as a result of their greater muscle strength. However, girls, on average, surpass boys in tasks that involve the coordination of their arms and legs (Cratty, 1979).

COGNITIVE DEVELOPMENT

Focus on Language Advances

During the preschool stage, language skills increase dramatically (Warner & Nelson, 2000). Preschoolers rapidly progress from two-word utterances (referred to as *duos*, e.g., *"Papa byebye," "Baby eat"*) to multiword sentences, exhibiting their growing vocabularies and understanding of grammar and syntax (e.g., "I would like some milk") (Warner & Nelson, 2000). Between the ages of 4 and 5 years, preschoolers' sentences average four to five words; between ages 5 and 6, they form sentences consisting of six to eight words, including prepositions, conjunctions, and articles (Bloom, Merkin, & Wooten, 1982). Their vocabulary grows to 8,000 to 14,000 words at age 5 (Feldman, 1998).

Preschoolers' language development also proceeds along a continuum from private speech to social speech. *Private speech* refers to spoken language that is not intended for others. In fact, between 20 and 60 percent of what children say is characterized by private speech (Berk, 1992). *Social speech,* on the other hand, is speech directed toward another person and is meant to be understood by that person. Preschoolers thus learn to adapt their speech to other children as well as to adults.

We learned in the last chapter that children's language skills are related to maternal interaction style. Marc Bornstein and his colleagues (1992; see pp. 25–31) reported that mothers from Argentina, France, Japan, and the United States speak more to older infants than to younger ones and that the quality of the language differs: Mothers give more information to older children than to younger ones. Bornstein et al. also noted that cultural values shape maternal speech to infants, which in turn reflects child-rearing goals. We learned that the more mothers (and others) talk and read to children, the more opportunities children have of learning new vocabulary (Wilson, 1985). Research also notes that when parents correct the morpheme usage of their children, the children are from 2 to 3 times more likely to use correct grammar (Farrar, 1992). Thus environmental influences—here in the form of maternal and paternal speech interaction—on language development in preschoolers are significant.

The impact of home environment on preschoolers' language acquisition and performance on cognitive tests has been studied in children who are being raised to be bilingual, that is, to speak more than one language. Romaine (1994), for example, reported that preschoolers who are bilingual exhibit greater cognitive flexibility; they have a wider range of linguistic possibilities from which to select as they assess a situation. They can solve problems with greater creativity as well. Bilingual preschoolers (and older children) also understand the rules of language more explicitly. Ricciardelli (1992) reported that French- and English-speaking children in Canada scored significantly higher on verbal and nonverbal tests of intelligence than children who spoke only one language.

Research has indicated that gender comparisons are common in children's development of language, with girls appearing to have more of an advantage in vocabulary acquisition during the preschool stage (Bee, Mitchell, Barnard, Eyres, & Hammond, 1984). There is also a positive correlation between preschoolers' language development and their socioeconomic status (Hart & Risley, 1995). Preschoolers who live in poverty tend to hear a smaller number of words and less variety of language from their caregivers than do preschoolers who live in more affluent homes. Hart and Risley (1995) found, for example, that by age 4, preschoolers in families that received welfare assistance were likely to have been exposed to approximately 13 million fewer words than those preschoolers in families considered professional. Preschoolers in families who received welfare assistance were also apt to hear prohibition words, such as *no* or *stop,* twice as frequently as those in families classified as professionals. This relationship between socioeconomic status and language development is further evidenced in later childhood: Preschoolers who live in poverty perform less well on standard measures of intelligence than their peers who do not live in poverty.

In addition to gender and socioeconomic class status, researchers have studied race influences on preschoolers' language development. In their article,

"Parents' Report of Vocabulary and Grammatical Development of African American Preschoolers: Child and Environmental Associations," excerpted in the readings section (see pp. 65–69), Joanne E. Roberts, Margaret Burchinal, and Meghan Durham report that African American preschoolers who lived in responsive and stimulating homes had larger vocabularies, used more irregular nouns and verbs, used longer utterances, and had more rapid rates of language acquisition than preschoolers from less responsive and less stimulating homes. Roberts and her colleagues also note gender comparisons. For example, girls in their sample used longer utterances and more irregular forms than boys.

Burchinal and her colleagues (2000) also found that preschoolers' cognitive and language development is related to the quality of center-based child care; higher quality child care was related to higher measures of language development, cognitive development, and communication skills among African American children. It is to this issue, child care for preschoolers, that we now turn.

Focus on Child Care

It may seem odd that a discussion devoted to development in preschoolers would take up school-related activities and settings. Indeed, you may believe the term "preschool period" is a misnomer. However, the majority of children ages 3 to 5 years are enrolled in child care settings or preschools outside of their homes (Clarke-Stewart, 1993). Most of these settings are designed to teach children skills that will enhance their cognitive and social abilities. Researchers have found that when compared with preschoolers who do not have formal educational involvement, those enrolled in quality preschools or child care exhibit cognitive and social benefits (Clarke-Stewart, 1993), including performing better on tests of language and cognitive skills.

What constitutes quality preschools or child care? As defined by the American Public Heath Association and the American Academy of Pediatrics, the standards of high quality include:

- Child–staff ratios of 3:1 for children under 25 months, 4:1 for children 25 to 30 months, and 7:1 for children 31 to 35 months.
- Group sizes of 6 for children under 25 months, 8 for children 25 to 30 months, and 14 for children 31 to 35 months.
- Child care providers who have formal, post-high-school training in child development, early childhood education, or a related field to work at all age levels.

Failure to meet these three standards undermines child development (Burchinal, Roberts, Nabors, & Bryant, 1996; Phillips, Voran, Kisker, Howes, & Whitebook, 1994). Low-quality care for preschoolers—whether in child care centers or homes—is associated with poorer school readiness and poorer performance on tests of expressive and receptive language skills. Bates et al. (1991)

found that preschoolers in high-quality programs are more confident and independent than those preschoolers who do not participate in quality child care programs.

There is a significant cultural distinction in the way preschools are valued. For example, in Belgium and France, access to preschool is a legal right. In Finland, preschoolers whose parents are employed have day care provided to them. In Russia, state-run *yasli-sads* (preschools) are attended by three quarters of all children ages 3 to 7 years. Thus in these countries, among others, there is a coordinated national policy on preschool education. However, in the United States we do not have such a coordinated policy. Rather, decisions about the education of preschoolers is left to the states and local school districts. We also do not have a formal curriculum for teaching preschoolers. Thus the value placed on children and early childhood education is reflected in whether countries have formal preschool programs or do not (Lamb, Ketterlinus, & Fracasso, 1992; Tobin, Wu, & Davidson, 1989).

In an article excerpted in the readings section (see pp. 70–73), "Child Care for Children in Poverty: Opportunity or Inequity?" Deborah A. Phillips, Miriam Voran, Ellen Kisker, Carollee Howes, and Marcy Whitebook describe their survey of nationally represented child care centers. They note that the quality of care in centers that serve predominantly low-income children was adequate, although highly variable. Centers who served children from predominantly upper-income families provided the highest quality of care. Phillips and her colleagues also found that centers that served children from middle-income homes provided the poorest quality of care. They further noted that since the status of preschoolers is low in the United States, salaries for preschool teachers have been correspondingly low as well. This creates a problem for attachment of children with teachers since the turnover rate among preschool and child care workers is high, reflecting the low salaries they earn compared to the enormous responsibility they have in educating and nurturing our young children.

A major finding of the Phillips et al. study should cause us to be alarmed: Preschoolers' education is affected by substantial class-based inequities. As the researchers conclude:

> If child care is to become a positive opportunity for all children, questions of equity need to become as salient a topic of study in the developmental field as do questions about quality. (p. 490)

According to Duncan and Brooks-Gunn (2000), in 1997, 13.4 million children were poor (living in families earning less than $13,000 per year). The impact of poverty on preschoolers—and on all children—is startling: 1.7 times higher chance of being a low-birth-weight baby, 3.5 times higher chance of lead poisoning, 1.7 times higher rate of child mortality, 2 times higher rate of grade repetition and school drop-outs, 1.4 times higher chance of having a learning disability, 1.3 times higher rate of emotional or behavioral problems, 6.8 times higher chance of child abuse, and 2.2 times higher likelihood of experiencing violent crime (Duncan & Brooks-

Gunn, 2000). Two of these statistics will be addressed in more detail in the sections below on emotional development and exposure to violent crime in neighborhoods.

EMOTIONAL DEVELOPMENT

Focus on the Role of the Mother

When we speak of preschoolers' emotional development, we are discussing the development of their feelings and the expression of their feelings in relation to themselves, their parents, their peers, and other individuals in their environment (Aksan et al., 1999). We learned in the last section that attachment is an important developmental process (Beckwith, Cohen, & Hamilton, 1999). Preschoolers' emotions, including attachment, are a means of communication with individuals (Fabes et al., 1999). There are a variety of influences on preschoolers' emotions, most notably their parents, as we discussed with respect to Sagi et al.'s research (1994; see pp. 41–44) on infant-mother attachment. Parents assist preschoolers in their development of trust and security (Volling & Elins, 1998).

In "Emotion Regulation in Early Childhood: A Cross-Cultural Comparison Between German and Japanese Toddlers," an article excerpted in the readings section (see pp. 74–79), Wolfgang Friedlmeier and Gisela Trommsdorff (1999) discuss their research on ways German and Japanese girls interacted with their mothers to regulate their emotions. Friedlmeier and Trommsdorff reported that the majority of girls from both cultures looked to their mother as the source of reference to regulate their negative emotions. In addition, these researchers found culture-specific distinctions; for example, Japanese girls stayed closer to their mothers than did German girls when interacting with peers. Japanese girls thus made their playmates come closer to them so they could continue playing. Moreover, Japanese girls exhibited a distress reaction more often than German girls. They didn't use eye contact as a way to express emotional reference; rather, they approached their mothers before a distress-inducing event occurred.

Friedlmeier and Trommsdorff also reported that German mothers raise their children so that the children feel their peers' sadness. However, German mothers emphasize the playmate's state. In contrast to the German mothers and their daughters, Japanese mothers expected their daughters to feel their peers' sadness and pain and react to them in an emotional way (distress or empathy). According to Friedlmeier and Trommsdorff:

> To the extent that the child turns to the mother for support . . . the mother's reaction is ambiguous. On one hand, she calms the child, and on the other hand, she makes the child more tense, because the mother represents the agent who most emphasizes the importance of empathy. (pp. 74–79; in this text, p.77)

Cultural definitions of parenting are highlighted in this article. This issue is addressed again when we discuss the importance of the father's role in preschoolers' emotional development.

Focus on the Role of the Father

Lamb (1997) and Lewis (1997) noted that the father becomes more involved as children progress from infancy to the preschool period and that their role is very important in helping preschoolers acquire a sense of self as well as a gender role identity. There are clear-cut differences in what mothers and fathers do with their children (Cabrera, Tamis-LeMonda, Bradley, Hofferth, & Lamb, 2000). Mothers spend the majority of their time nurturing children, feeding them, comforting them, and so forth. Fathers, on the other hand, spend most of their time with children in play. While fathers do contribute to child care (95% of fathers report that they participate in child care chores each day), they do less than mothers (Jacobsen & Edmondson, 1993). Fathers in two-parent families spend 67% as much time as mothers on weekdays and 87% as much time on weekends (Cabrera et al., 2000). Research has noted that 30% of fathers with wives who are employed do three or more hours of daily child care, while 74% of employed married mothers spend that amount of time in child care activities. Furthermore, fathers tend to spend more time with sons than with daughters (Ishii-Kuntz, 1994; Marsiglio, 1991). Research has found that when fathers do participate in the care of preschoolers, as well as children of other ages, the quality of parent-child relationships is enhanced (Amato & Rejac, 1994).

It should be noted, however, that only 31 to 40 percent of preschoolers live at one time or another with their fathers; the majority live in mother-headed single households. Mott (1994) reported that fathers are less likely to leave home if they have sons. In their article, "African American Fathers in Low Income, Urban Families: Development, Behavior, and Home Environment of Their Three-Year-Old Children," excerpted in the readings section (see pp. 80–84), Maureen M. Black, Howard Dubowitz, and Raymond H. Starr Jr. observed the contributions that low-income African American fathers make to their families and the corresponding impact on their preschoolers' cognitive development, competence, and behavior. They report that those homes that included a father were more child-centered. Preschoolers whose fathers contributed financially to the family were more nurturant during play and had better cognitive skills and receptive language skills. In addition, fathers who were satisfied with their parenting role had preschoolers with fewer behavioral problems. Black and her colleagues' research raises important issues about the importance of fathers in preschoolers' development. Their findings provide further evidence for more family-oriented policies that promote fathers' involvement with preschoolers as well as with children of all ages.

We note that Black et al. also highlight the importance of several maternal characteristics and preschoolers' cognitive, emotional, and social development. For example, they report that mothers who were more satisfied in their parenting role and who had higher levels of education had children who demonstrated more cognitive skills, had fewer behavioral problems, and lived in more child-centered homes.

Black et al. also point out the importance of studying factors other than fathers' economic role in parenting. They state:

> Although most attention has been directed toward the economic contributions that fathers make, the associations between children's cognition and paternal parenting satisfaction and between children's receptive language development and paternal nurturance during play, illustrate the importance of considering paternal roles beyond economic contributions. (p. 975; in this text, p. 82)

Black et al. also found that the biological relationship between children and fathers is not a significant factor. As they conclude: "Preschoolers understand nurturance and care, but not necessarily distinctions related to biological status." This finding is supported by Engle and Breaux (1998). Research on the role of fathers in preschoolers' development has benefited from a cultural perspective on fatherhood (Cabrera et al., 2000). For example, men other than biological fathers take on the parental role in many cultures (Engle & Breaux, 1998), including uncles and grandfathers. The important factor is the man's *engagement,* that is, his direct contact with, caregiving for, and shared interactions with the preschooler, not simply the man's *accessibility,* that is, his "presence" (Cabrera et al., 2000).

SOCIAL DEVELOPMENT

Focus on Play

The development of friendships with peers is one of the most important aspects of preschoolers' social development. They begin to participate in fewer solitary activities and become more involved in playing with their peers. The interdependence of dimensions of development is evident with play: Gains in language development make communication with peers possible in this second life stage, so that when they play together, preschool children talk about what they are doing—dressing up dolls or building bridges (Lim, 1998; Park, Lay, & Ramsay, 1993; Weissman, 1999). In their play, preschoolers share affection; they also offer approval and make demands on each other (Farber & Branstetter, 1994). In addition, preschoolers' play is related to their visual-spatial skills (Caldera et al., 1999). Play, therefore, is an excellent example of the interdependence among the dimensions of development.

Children's play has been categorized by researchers into several types: functional, constructive, parallel, onlooker, associative, and cooperative. *Functional play* refers to repetitive activities—for example, skipping, rolling and unrolling a piece of clay, moving cars. This type of play involves activity; it does not have a goal of creating some end result (Feldman, 1998). *Constructive play* involves children manipulating objects or toys in order to make something, such as a tower from blocks.

This type of play encourages children to practice their fine motor skills as well as cognitive skills—for example, how pieces fit together to make a tower or complete a puzzle.

Parallel play refers to actions in which preschoolers play with the same toys in the same manner yet do not interact with each other. This is a common play strategy of early preschoolers. Another type of play characteristic of the early preschool years is *onlooker play*. In this type of play, preschoolers simply watch others at play but do not participate in the activity themselves.

As they progress through this stage, preschoolers engage in *associative play*, in which two or more children interact with each other by sharing toys or materials, such as construction paper or crayons, but they do not work on the same task. In *cooperative play*, preschoolers interact with each other and take turns playing games.

Research has noted that children who have had experience with peers in child care settings are more likely to engage in more social forms of play, that is, in associative and cooperative play, at an earlier age during this life stage than their peers who have had less experience with other children (Roopnarine, Johnson, & Hooper, 1994). Play provides opportunities for preschool children to interact with children of the same age and from different backgrounds. They learn that some peers have one parent, others have two, and still others are being raised by grandparents. Through play, preschoolers learn that some peers have siblings, and some do not. These interactions lead preschoolers to begin asking questions about themselves, including why they don't have any siblings, why they can't have a dog or cat like their friend, why their peers don't live with their father or mother.

It is through play that preschoolers begin to expand their cognitive skills (Vygotsky, 1930/1978). They can practice activities that are unique to their culture. In their article, "Cultural Differences in Korean- and Anglo-American Preschoolers' Social Interaction and Play Behaviors," excerpted in the readings section (see pp. 84–88), Jo Ann M. Farver, Yonnie Kwak Kim, and Yoolim Lee note that Korean American preschoolers engage in a higher proportion of parallel play than Anglo American preschoolers. They also observe that Anglo American children engage in more pretend play than Korean American children. Farver et al. also reported that 47% of the Korean American mothers believed that the purpose of play is for amusement, to express curiosity, and to have their preschoolers relieve boredom. Only 10% of the Anglo American mothers believed play is for amusement, while 84% of them stated that play is for learning and is related to developmental outcomes. Thus the cultural backgrounds of preschoolers contribute to their different styles of play, just as infants' cultural backgrounds influence their play activities, as we saw in the last chapter.

Farver and her colleagues note that Korean American preschool settings had few or no materials available for pretend play. Thus toys such as dress-up clothes, cars, trucks, and dolls—all associated with pretend play—were absent from the Korean American preschool settings. In contrast, the Anglo American children had many toys that encouraged pretend play. Another finding of their study is that Anglo American preschoolers were more aggressive in interactions with peers than were the Korean American preschoolers. Farver and her colleagues note that

American culture fosters competitive relationships between children and thus tolerates aggressive behavior in children—two behaviors not valued in Korean culture.

Farver and her colleagues conclude that preschoolers' social interaction and pretend play are influenced by the culture-specific socialization practices that serve adaptive functions. They state:

> The Korean- and Anglo-American teachers shaped the preschool settings by emphasizing culturally valued skills and by using culturally appropriate methods that led to different developmental outcomes for children. (p. 87 in this text)

Specifically, cognitive functioning may be higher in Korean American preschoolers than in Anglo American preschoolers as a consequence of the emphasis placed on academic subjects by their preschool teachers. Furthermore, Anglo American preschoolers have higher social functioning than Korean American preschoolers as a consequence of being encouraged to interact with peers by their preschool teachers.

Focus on Preschoolers' Exposure to Real Violence

The finding that Korean American families typically do not socialize their children for aggression and competition asks us to reconsider America's focus on these values (Miedzian, 1991). During the preschool years, aggression is observed in children in their attempt to get a desired goal—for example, getting a toy away from a sibling or peer. The amount of aggression declines throughout the preschool period for most children. Instead of aggressive behavior, they learn to use language to negotiate what they want from other people (Cummings, Iannotti, & Zahn-Waxler, 1989). However, some children still exhibit aggressive behavior throughout this life stage—and, in fact, continue this behavior throughout childhood, as we will discuss in later chapters of this text. Aggressive behavior in the preschool years predicts conduct problems, delinquency, and antisocial disorders (Caspi & Silva, 1995; Crick, Casas, & Ku, 1999; Hay, Castle, & Davies, 2000).

A considerable amount of research has been conducted on the impact of televised violence on children (e.g., Attar, Guerra, & Tolan, 1994; Lorion & Saltzman, 1993). Results suggest that preschoolers' observation of televised aggression leads to subsequent aggression and an insensitivity to the suffering of victims (Attar et al., 1994). Research on televised violence has masked the fact that many children are exposed to real violence. For example, one third of children in urban neighborhoods have witnessed a homicide and two thirds of preschoolers have seen an assault (Bell & Jenkins, 1991; Osofsky, 1995). Osofsky and her colleagues (1993) reported that 91% of the children in their sample witnessed violence, 51% had been victimized themselves, and 72% reported seeing weapons used in violent attacks. What are the effects of real violence on preschoolers' cognitive, social, and emotional functioning?

In their article (also excerpted in the readings section; see pp. 88–91), "Effects of Community Violence on Inner-City Preschoolers and Their Families,"

Jo Ann M. Farver, Lucia X. Natera, and Dominick L. Frosch discuss research they conducted with preschoolers who are exposed to neighborhood violence. Farver et al. cite stress-related symptoms these preschoolers exhibit that prohibit them from doing well in preschool and elementary school. At least 50% of the mothers in their study reported that their family had been victimized by forced entry, muggings, and threats of physical harm. Participants in the study heard gunshots in their home; more than 60% reported witnessing drug deals, arrests, and people with guns in the neighborhood. More than half heard about serious violence in their neighborhood.

Mothers reported the following distress symptoms in their preschoolers from being exposed to neighborhood violence: worries about being safe, recurring memories, bad dreams, hypervigilance, tendency to be easily scared or upset, difficulty in paying attention, and jumpiness when hearing noises. Farver and her colleagues also note that there is a link between exposure to neighborhood violence and reduction in preschoolers' positive peer interaction and cognitive performance. They cite empirical evidence that exposure to real violence prohibits preschoolers from fully profiting from their education. For example, preschoolers who are exposed to real violence have memory impairments as a consequence of intrusive thoughts about the violence they have witnessed and/or experienced themselves (Osofsky, Wewers, Hann, & Flick, 1993).

Farver and her colleagues also note that the preschool period is an important life stage because of the fact that children are acquiring basic skills and ways of relating to people. Their research also dispels a myth about children who are exposed to real violence: that is, that they are always racially minority children. Farver's findings suggest that preschoolers' exposure to community violence is not related to race or ethnicity, although it is related to socioeconomic class, thus supporting a major theme of this book: namely, that race should not be used synonymously with class to explain individuals' behavior.

We will revisit many of the issues raised in this discussion of early childhood when we address middle childhood, in the next chapter.

Readings

Parents' Report of Vocabulary and Grammatical Development of African American Preschoolers: Child and Environmental Associations*

Joanne E. Roberts, Margaret Burchinal, and Meghan Durham

During the past two decades, there has been an increased recognition of the importance of individual variability in children's early acquisition of vocabulary and grammar (Bates et al., 1994; Fenson et al., 1994a; Goldfield & Reznick, 1990; Mervis & Bertrand, 1995). For example, Goldfield and Reznick (1990) described how some children had a prolonged period of increases in the rate of acquisition in vocabulary between 14 and 24 months, while other children had a more gradual word-learning rate. Bates, Bretherton, and Snyder (1988) described the rote nature of the earliest stages in lexical development, the change in composition of vocabulary, and the appearance of a vocabulary burst at 2 years of age, when children shift from single to multiword use. Methodology has varied considerably in these and other studies of early lexical and grammatical development. There are longitudinal studies that use parental diaries with a small number of children (Goldfield & Reznick, 1990; Nelson, 1973), cross-sectional studies that use parental reports of language development (Fenson et al., 1994a; Lieven, Pine, & Dresher-Barnes, 1992), and longitudinal observations of young children in naturalistic settings (Hart & Risley, 1995; Lieven et al., 1992). Most studies have focused on middle-class White children and their families. There has been insufficient research to date to determine whether developmental patterns differ by race (Huston, McLoyd, & Coll, 1994) and which methodologies are most useful with children from minority backgrounds.

The need to examine the context in which the child lives has been widely recognized in the developmental literature. A general systems view of developmental change (Sameroff, 1983) emphasizes the structure of the organism as well as the organization of the environment and the dynamic transactions between the child and environment. The child is seen as embedded in a number of hierarchically organized, inter-

*From Roberts et al. (1999, January/February). *Child Development, 70*(1), 92–106. Reprinted with permission.

related systems where changes that occur at one level of the hierarchy may have influences both within and across systems. A hierarchy of factors can facilitate or impair development, including characteristics of the child, caregivers, family, immediate environment, and the culture in general (Bronfenbrenner & Crouter, 1983; Raney, MacPhee, & Yeates, 1982; Sameroff, 1983). Such a model also describes a multitude of risk and protective factors both for children experiencing poverty and for children in general.

One of the most extensively studied factors that influences a child's development is the child's gender. Many studies (almost all of White children) have found that girls appear to have a slight advantage in vocabulary acquisition during early childhood based on standardized tests (Bee, Mitchell, Barnard, Eyres, & Hammond, 1984; Maccoby & Jacklin, 1974), observations (Huttenlocher, Haight, Bryk, Seltzer, & Lyons, 1991; Morisset, Barnard, & Booth, 1995), and parental report (Fenson, Pethick, & Cox, 1994b; Morisset et al., 1995), while a smaller number of studies have failed to find gender differences during infancy or the preschool years using standardized tests (Johnson, 1974; Morisset et al., 1995; Siegel, 1982), naturalistic observations (Barnes, Gutfreund, Satterly, & Wells, 1983), and parental report (Rescorla, 1989).

Family factors that have been studied in relation to children's language development include distal measures such as living in poverty and occupational status, as well as more proximal measures such as the quality of the home environment and maternal interaction style. Socioeconomic status (SES) has been shown to be related to children's language skills using standardized tests (Wells, 1985, 1986; Morisset et al., 1995; Siegel, 1982), observations (Hart & Risely, 1992, 1995), and parental report measures (Fenson et al., 1994a; Rescorla, 1989). Yet, other studies suggest that family income alone may not explain language differences. In a recent study, Hart and Risley (1995) found that overall mean scores for children with the most advanced language were from professional families (1 of 13 African American), children with the least advanced language were from welfare families (all six African American), and children from working class families (10 of 23 African American) fell between these two groups. However, the amount and variety of vocabulary children used at 3 years of age were more strongly related to the type of parents' utterances (e.g., use of modifiers, few imperatives) than to family income. A large body of literature (e.g., Hoff-Ginsberg, 1990; Vibbert & Bornsten, 1989) on primarily White middle-income children has also shown that children's language skills are related to maternal interaction style, while a smaller number of studies (Bee et al., 1984; Bradley et al., 1989; Siegel, 1981, 1982) have reported a similar relation for the quality of the home environment as measured by the Home Observation for the Measurement of the Environment (HOME; Caldwell & Bradley, 1984). Thus, these studies suggest that the relation between family factors and children's language development is complex with multiple factors affecting the relation.

Others contend that the effect of the home and childrearing environments of African American families on the development of children's early language skills may be different from that of White families. Ogbu (1988) and Heath (1983) describe the ways in which some minority cultures adopt different styles of childrearing in order to maintain a cultural identity. Bradley and colleagues (1989), in the collaborative study of the HOME, found that many correlations between background factors and language outcomes were greater in White children than African American children. At the same time, there is also evidence that some beliefs and practices of African American parents are different from those of the majority culture. For example, Kamii and Radin (1967) documented ways in which interaction patterns differ between African American middle-class mothers and African American lower-class mothers. Garcia-Coll (1990), in a recent review of the literature on factors contributing to developmental outcomes for minority infants, reported a failure to find strong associations between early patterns of family interactions and later cognitive development in African American children. She stated that the factors studied may not be sensitive to the variations in child development or that other factors not studied, such as the education of parents, may account for observed differences in parenting and developmental outcomes among minority groups.

. . .

As part of a longitudinal study of children's health and development (Roberts et al., 1995), 87 African American children participated as subjects. The children, recruited from nine community-based child care centers, were between the ages of 6 and 12 months with a mean entry age of 8.2 months. Enrollment occurred over a 24-month period, from February 1991 until February 1993. There were 47 females and 40 males. Sixty-nine of the children were full gestational age at birth (>37 weeks), while 18 were 37 weeks or less (nine were 37 weeks; four were 36 weeks; four were 35 weeks; and one was 32 weeks). At the children's birth, the mean maternal age was 24.2 years, 29 mothers were married (33%), 12 were separated or divorced (15%), and 45 were single (52%). Upon study entry, 60 (69%) of the families were from low-income households according to the federally defined poverty level. Mean maternal educational level was 12.4 years (*SD* = 2.3), with 31.8% of the mothers with less than a high school education, 28.2% who completed high school, and 40.0% with greater than a high school education. The mean IQ of the mothers was 87.1 (*SD* = 9.8) as measured by the Block Design and Vocabulary subtests of the Weschler Adult Intelligence Scale-Revised (WAIS-R). The mother's use of African American vernacular English (AAVE) was rated from videotapes, while mothers played with their 1-year-old children and taught them a task (Roberts, Jackson, Peebles, & Wolfram, in preparation). At this time, 21.8% of the mothers used standard American English, 31.5% used a few AAVE phonological features, 28.8% had 1–4 grammatical features of the same type and some phonological features of AAVE, and 18.0% used more than two different grammatical features and some phonological features of AAVE.

. . .

The results of this study showed that African American children's vocabulary and grammatical skills as reported by children's parents varied greatly and grew linearly over time between 18 and 30 months of age. Children from more stimulating and responsive homes were reported to have larger vocabularies, to use more irregular nouns and verbs, to use longer utterances, and to have more rapid rates of acquisition of irregular forms and longer utterances over time than children from less responsive and less stimulating homes. Girls used longer utterances and more irregular forms than boys. Girls also had larger vocabularies and quicker rates of acquisition of irregular nouns and verbs in a secondary analysis that eliminated children whose parent over- or underreported vocabulary. Whereas child and family predictors showed anticipated relations with patterns of development over time, comparisons of these parental reports and standardized language scores suggested that some of the parents underreported their children's vocabulary and grammatical skills. These results suggest that CDI percentile scores should be used cautiously with samples of African American children from predominately low-income families.

The home environment, as noted in previous studies (Bradley, 1994; Bradley et al., 1989; Elardo, Bradley, & Caldwell, 1977; Siegel, 1981, 1982), was one of the most important family and child variables related to children's language development. The measures of the home environment predicted all three measures of language: vocabulary, irregular forms, and mean sentence length. Children from more responsive and supportive homes had larger vocabularies, more irregular nouns and verbs, and longer utterances. This association was clear in the analysis of the entire sample and the subsample that omitted questionably low scores. This find provides further evidence that early language development in a primarily low-income African American sample is linked to the responsiveness and stimulation that the child receives within the family environment.

Findings also are consistent with a small number of studies on middle-class children (Bradley & Caldwell, 1984) and primarily low-income children (Elardo et al., 1977; Siegel, 1981, 1982) that measured language using standardized language tests.

In this study, we also found modest gender differences for the rate of increase in sentence length and number of irregular forms. Girls showed a more rapid increase in sentence length and more irregular forms between 18 and 30 months than boys. We also found gender differences for the rates of acquisition of vocabulary in this time period when we omitted the subsample with questionably underreported language scores. This finding of a gender effect for vocabulary and grammatical development over time is similar to several studies that used standardized tests (Bee et al., 1984; Maccoby & Jacklin, 1974), observations (Huttenlocher et al., 1991; Morisset et al., 1995), and parental report (Fenson et al., 1994a; Morisset et al., 1995). Our findings using a parental report instrument for primarily low-income African American children showed the developmental patterns by gender to be similar to results from studies using observational and other standardized measures of language development.

. . .

REFERENCES

Arriaga, R., Fenson, L., Cronan, T., & Pethick, S. (1998). Scores on the MacArthur Communicative Development Inventory of children from low and middle income families. *Applied Psycholinguistics, 19*(2), 209–223.

Barnes, S., Gutfreund, M., Satterly, D., & Wells, G. (1983). Characteristics of adult speech which predict children's language development. *Journal of Child Language, 10,* 65–84.

Bates, E., Bretherton, I., & Snyder, L. (1988). *From first words to grammar: Individual differences and dissociable mechanisms.* New York: C.U.P.

Bates, E., Marchman, V., Thal, D., Fenson, L., Dale, P., Reznick, J. S., Reilly, J., & Hartung, J. (1994). Developmental and stylistic variation in the composition of early vocabulary. *Journal of Child Language, 21,* 85–123.

Bee, H. L., Mitchell, S. K., Barnard, K. E., Eyres, S. J., & Hammond, M. A. (1984). Predicting intellectual outcomes: Sex differences in response to early environmental stimulation. *Sex Roles, 10*(9/10), 783–803.

Bradley, R. H. (1994). The HOME inventory: Review and reflections. *Advances in Child Development and Behavior, 25,* 241–288.

Bradley, R. H., & Caldwell, B. M. (1984). 174 children: A study of the relationship between home environment and cognitive development during the first 5 years. In A. W. Gottfried (Ed.), *Home Environment and Cognitive Development* (pp. 5–56). Orlando, FL: Academic Press.

Bradley, R. H., Caldwell, B. M., Rock, S. L., Barnard, K. E., Gray, C., Hammond, M. A., Mitchell, S., Siegel, L., Ramey, C. T., Gottfried, A. W., & Johnson, D. L. (1989). Home environment and cognitive development in the first 3 years of life: A collaborative study involving six sites and three ethnic groups in North America. *Developmental Psychology, 28,* 217–235.

Bronfenbrenner, U., & Crouter, A. C. (1983). The evolution of environmental models in developmental research. In P. H. Mussen (Ed.), *Handbook of Child Psychology.* New York: Wiley.

Bryk, A. S., & Raudenbush, S. W. (1987). Application of hierarchical linear models to assessing change. *Psychological Bulletin, 101,* 147–158.

Caldwell, B. M., & Bradley, R. H. (1984). *Home Observation for Measurement of the Environment* (Rev. ed.). Little Rock, AR: University of Arkansas at Little Rock.

Corkum, V., & Dunham, P. (1996). The Communicative Development Inventory—WORDS Short Form as an index of language production. *Journal of Child Language, 23*(3), 515–528.

Dale, P. S. (1991). The validity of a parent report measure of vocabulary and syntax at 24 months. *Journal of Speech and Hearing Research, 34,* 565–571.

Dale, P. S., Bates, E., Reznick, J. S., & Morisset, C. (1989). The validity of a parent report instrument of child language at twenty months. *Journal of Child Language, 16,* 239–249.

Dunn, L. M., & Dunn, L. M. (1981). *Peabody Picture Vocabulary Test-Revised.* Circle Pines, MN: American Guidance Service.

Elardo, R., Bradley, R., & Caldwell, B. M. (1977). A longitudinal study of the relation of infants' home environments to language development at age three. *Child Development, 48,* 595–603.

Fenson, L., Dale, P. S., Reznick, J. S., Bates, E., Thal, D., & Pethick, S. (1994a). Variability in early communicative development. *Monographs of the Society for Research in Child Development, 59* (Serial No. 242).

Fenson, L., Dale, P., Reznick, S., Thal, D., Bates, E., Hartung, J., Pethick, S., & Reilly, S. (1993). *MacArthur Communicative Development Inventories: User's guide and technical manual.* San Diego, CA: Singular Publishing Group.

Fenson, L., Pethick, S., & Cox, J. L. (1994b). *The MacArthur Communicative Development Inventories: Short form versions.* San Diego State University. San Diego, CA.

Garcia-Coll, C. T. (1990). Developmental outcome of minority infants: A process-oriented look into our beginnings. *Child Development, 61,* 270–289.

Goldfield, B. A., & Reznick, J. S. (1990). Early lexical acquisition: Rate, content, and the vocabulary spurt. *Journal of Child Language, 17,* 171–183.

Hart, B., & Risley, T. R. (1992). American parenting of language-learning children: Persisting differences in family-child interactions observed in natural home environments. *Developmental Psychology, 28*(6), 1096–1105.

Hart, B., & Risley, T. R. (Eds.). (1995). *Meaningful differences in the everyday experience of young American children.* Baltimore, MD: Paul H. Brookes Publishing Company.

Heath, S. B. (1983). *Ways with words: Language, life, and work in communities and classrooms.* England: Cambridge University Press.

Hedrick, D. L., Prather, E. M., & Tobin, A. R. (1984). *Sequenced Inventory of Communication Development—Revised.* Seattle, WA: University of Washington Press.

Hoff-Ginsberg, E. (1990). Maternal speech and the child's development of syntax: A further look. *Journal of Child Language 17,* 337–346.

Huston, A. C., McLoyd, V. C., & Garcia-Coll, C. (1994). Children and poverty: Issues in contemporary research. *Child Development, 65,* 275–282.

Huttenlocher, J., Haight, W., Bryk, A., Seltzer, M., & Lyons, T. (1991). Early vocabulary growth: Relation to language input and gender. *Developmental Psychology, 27*(2), 236–248.

Johnson, D. L. (1974). The influences of social class and race on language test performance and spontaneous speech of preschool children. *Child Development, 45,* 517–521.

Kamii, C., & Radin, N. (1967). Class differences in the socialization practices of Negro mothers. *Journal of Marriage and the Family, 29,* 302–310.

Lieven, E. V. M., Pine, J. M., & Dresher-Barnes, H. (1992). Individual differences in early vocabulary development: Redefining the referential-expressive distinction. *Journal of Child Language, 19,* 287–310.

Maccoby, E., & Jacklin, C. N. (1974). *The psychology of sex differences.* Stanford, CA: Stanford University Press.

Mervis, C. B., & Bertrand, J. (1995). Early lexical acquisition and the vocabulary spurt: A response to Goldfield & Reznick. *Journal of Child Language, 23,* 461–468.

Morisset, C. E., Barnard, K. E., & Booth, C. L. (1995). Toddlers' language development: Sex differences within social risk. *Developmental Psychology, 31*(5), 851–865.

Neisser, U., Boodoo, G., Bouchard, T. J., Boykin, A. W., Brody, N., Ceci, S. J., Halpern, D. F., Loehlin, J. C., Perloff, R., Sternberg, R. J., & Urbina, S. (1996). Intelligence: Knowns and unknowns. *American Psychologist, 51*(2), 77–101.

Nelson, K. (1973). Structure and strategy in learning to talk. *Monographs of the Society for Research in Child Development, 38* No. 149 (1–2).

Ogbu, J. U. (1988). Cultural diversity and human development. In D. T. Slaughter (Ed.), *Black children and poverty: A developmental perspective* (pp. 11–28). San Francisco: Jossey-Bass.

Pine, J. M., Lieven, E. V. M., & Rowland, C. (1996). Observational and checklist measures of vocabulary composition: What do they mean? *Journal of Child Language, 23,* 573–589.

Ramey, C. T., MacPhee, D., & Yeates, K. O. (1982). Preventing developmental retardation: A general systems model. In L. A. Bond & J. M. Joffe (Eds.), *Facilitating infant and early childhood development* (pp. 343–401). Hanover, NH: University Press of New England.

Rescorla, L. (1989). The Language Development Survey: A screening tool for delayed language in toddlers. *Journal of Speech and Hearing Disorders, 54,* 587–599.

Reznick, J. S., & Goldsmith, L. (1989). A multiple form word production checklist for assessing early language. *Journal of Child Language, 16,* 91–100.

Roberts, J. E., Burchinal, M. R., Medley, L. P., Zeisel, S. A., Mundy, M., Roush, J., Hooper, S., Bryant, D., & Henderson, F. W. (1995). Otitis media, hearing sensitivity, and maternal responsiveness in relation to language during infancy. *Journal of Pediatrics, 126*(3), 481–489.

Roberts, J. E., Jackson, S. C., Peebles, C. H., & Wolfram, W. (in preparation). Impact of family environment on mothers' and children's use of African American vernacular.

Roberts, J. E., Medley, L. P., Swartzfager, J. L., & Neebe, E. C. (1997). Assessing the communication of African American one-year-olds using the Communication and Symbolic Behavior Scales. *American Journal of Speech-Language Pathology, 6*(2), 59–65.

Sameroff, A. J. (1983). Developmental systems: Contexts and evolution. In W. Kessen (Ed.), *History, theories, and methods* (Vol. 1). New York: Wiley.

Siegel, L. S. (1981). Infant tests as predictors of cognitive and language development at two years. *Child Development, 52,* 545–557.

Siegel, L. S. (1982). Reproductive, perinatal, and environmental factors as predictors of the cognitive and language development of preterm and full-term infants. *Child Development, 53,* 963–973.

Snow, C. E., Barnes, W. S., Chandler, J., Goodman, I. F., & Hemphill, L. (1991). *Unfulfilled expectations: Home and school influences on literacy.* Cambridge, MA: Harvard University Press.

Vibbert, M., & Bornstein, M. H. (1989). Specific associations between domains of mother-child interaction and toddler language and pretense play. *Infant Behavior and Development, 12,* 163–184.

Wells, G. (Ed.). (1985). *Language development in the preschool years.* Cambridge: Cambridge University Press.

Wells, G. (Ed.). (1986). *The meaning makers: Children learning language and using language to learn.* Portsmouth, NH: Heinemann Educational Books, Inc.

Wetherby, A. M., & Prizant, B. M. (1993). *Manual of communication and symbolic behavior scales.* Chicago: Riverside Press.

Child Care for Children in Poverty: Opportunity or Inequity?*

Deborah A. Phillips, Miriam Voran, Ellen Kisker, Carollee Howes, and Marcy Whitebook

Reduction of poverty has provided the most long-standing rationale for child care policies in the United States. Within this context, two markedly different strategies have evolved—the welfare reform and the compensatory education approaches—each with important implications for the quality of care that children are likely to experience (Phillips, 1991; Wrigley, 1991). Child care that is funded in the context of welfare reform is approached as a necessary adjunct to policies whose central goal is to move families from income-maintenance programs to financial self-sufficiency, and thus to reduce welfare costs. This strategy for supporting child care is remedial in emphasis, targeted on adult goals, and focused on enhancing the supply of care at the expense of quality.

The alternative strategy provides child care to children in poverty with the intent of enriching these children's environments and improving their chances of success in school—the compensatory education approach. Rather than being primarily a convenience for working mothers or a mechanism for short-term reductions in welfare costs, child care cast as compensatory education constitutes an investment in human development (Steiner, 1976; Zigler & Valentine, 1979). In this equation, the approach is preventive, targeted on children, and supportive of quality "developmental" care.

. . .

This literature has further revealed that family social class and quality of care are confounded. Several studies have reported that lower-income families receive poorer quality care than families with greater financial and psychological resources (Anderson, Nagle, Roberts, & Smith, 1981; Goelman & Pence, 1987; Howes & Stewart, 1987; Kontos & Fiene, 1987). More recent studies have found a curvilinear relation between family income and quality of care (Voran & Whitebook, 1991; Waite, Leibowitz, & Witsberger, 1991; Whitebook, Howes, & Phillips, 1989; Zaslow, 1991), such that children from middle-income families receive the poorest quality child care. At a minimum, it appears that quality care is not equitably distributed among children from different social classes.

. . .

This study addresses these issues of quality and equity. It does so with two complementary data sets, one a national survey of a representative sample of center-based programs (Kisker, Hofferth, Phillips, & Farquhar, 1991) and the other an in-depth observational study of center-based care in five metropolitan areas (Whitebook et al., 1989).

. . .

Discussion

There is increasing agreement among both researchers and policy makers that high-quality early childhood programs can ameliorate some of the negative consequences of growing up in poverty. Yet we have only limited insights into the full spectrum of early care and education programs that children from low-income families actually experience. This study offers an extensive portrait of the quality of care that these children receive and the equity with which it is distributed in the United States.

Quality of Care in Subsidized Centers

The quality of care that is provided by child care centers that serve high proportions of low-income children is highly variable and, on many

*From Phillips et al. (1994). *Child Development, 65,* 472–492. Reprinted with permission.

key indices, barely adequate. Both the subsidized centers from the Profiles Survey and the low-income centers from the Staffing Study revealed substantial variation in quality such that, for example, approximately 60% of the toddler classrooms in both studies failed to meet recommended ratios and group sizes. In addition, a sizable minority of the classroom teachers had not received any education beyond high school, while many others had received college degrees. Turnover rates showed a disparate pattern whereby centers had either avoided turnover altogether or had experienced very high turnover among their teaching staff.

Perhaps most worrisome are the indications from the observations of classroom activities and interactions in the Staffing Study centers that only a minority of classrooms achieved a "good" level of quality, that "minimal" levels of quality were not uncommon, and that detachment and harshness were not entirely rare staff behaviors. These process indices of quality are of greatest interest to developmentalists and most strongly associated with child outcomes. Variation in the interactions and activities that children experience on a daily basis in their child care programs have been linked significantly and consistently to a wide range of developmental outcomes in studies not specifically focused on low-income children (Goelman & Pence, 1987; Hayes et al., 1990; Howes & Olenick, 1986; Phillips, 1987; Phillips et al., 1987; Zaslow, 1991). While one would expect that the wide range of quality that characterized the present sample of subsidized centers would be similarly associated with child outcomes, research that examines quality-outcome relations in programs that serve low-income families would fill an important knowledge gap. For example, while we know that high-quality settings can have beneficial short- and longer-term effects on children living in poverty (Lazar et al., 1982; Lee et al., 1990; Ramey & Campbell, 1991), we have very limited data on the effects of less than optimal care on these children (see Baydar & Brooks-Gunn, 1991).

Teacher turnover in child care has become the focus of much concern, given combined evidence that high turnover is endemic in child care and that it is detrimental to children (Howes, 1990; Whitebook et al., 1989). In prior reports, turnover rates have hovered around 40% (Phillips et al., 1993; Whitebook et al., 1989). The lower turnover rates from the Profiles Survey may be due, in part, to the exclusion of assistant teachers and aides from the sample. In addition, follow-up data from the Staffing Study (see Whitebook, Phillips, & Howes, 1993) suggested a relation between lower turnover rates and the tight job market that prevailed in 1989–1990—the period during which the Profiles data were collected. Perhaps most important is the evidence reported here that some child care centers experience no turnover, while those with turnover typically lose over one-third to over one-half of their teaching staff in just a year, depending on the database. Deciphering the factors that distinguish these two groups of centers is a fertile area for research aimed at providing guidance for efforts to improve child care quality.

. . .

Equity of Access to Quality Care across Social Classes

A central hypothesis of this study was that centers serving predominantly high-income families would provide higher quality care than centers serving less advantaged populations. This hypothesis was overwhelmingly supported. Children from upper-income families were more likely than either their middle- or low-income peers to be cared for by better trained and stable, better compensated, and more sensitive teachers in more developmentally appropriate settings.

The more intriguing finding with respect to class equity, however, is the curvilinear relation that was revealed between quality and family income. The most uniformly poor quality of care, ranging from teacher training to the appropriateness of the activities in preschool classrooms, was found in the predominantly middle-class centers. Middle-class families may be at a particular disadvantage because they have neither the financial resources to purchase high-quality care nor access to public subsidies that, at least in the case of government intervention programs, appear to provide some assurance of quality. A linear pattern was found, however, for the observations of teacher-child interaction, in which the low-income centers were either indistinguishable from or lower in quality than the middle- and upper-income centers. Given the particularly strong and consistent predictive role of teacher-child interactions for child outcomes in child care, noted above, these findings pose a serious challenge to any conclusions about the adequacy of low-income centers.

It is difficult to interpret this discrepancy in the conclusions about equity that can be drawn from the reported and classroom-level observational indices of quality, as compared to the observations of teacher-child interaction. The most straightforward implication is that centers serving low-income children show different profiles of quality depending on the type of quality measure that is examined. Perhaps "good things" do not always go together in child care. If true, this also raises an important caution for policy makers not to assume that the regulatable indices of ratio, group size, and training provide sufficient information about the quality of center-based care. From a different perspective, the relatively more negative ratings of teacher behavior in the low-income centers, in the context of care that was otherwise quite comparable to that offered by the upper-income centers, raises the possibility of measurement bias when observing individual teachers and highlights the importance of interpreting child-rearing behaviors within their cultural and socioeconomic milieu (McLoyd, 1990; Ogbu, 1981).

. . .

REFERENCES

Anderson, C. W., Nagle, R. J., Roberts, W. A., & Smith, J. W. (1981). Attachment to substitute caregivers as a function of center quality and caregiver involvement. *Child Development, 52,* 53–61.

Arnett, J. (1989). Caregivers in day care centers: Does training matter? *Journal of Applied Developmental Psychology, 10,* 541–552.

Barnett, W. S. (1985). Benefit-cost analysis of the Perry Preschool Programs and its long-term effects. *Educational Evaluation and Policy Analysis, 7,* 333–342.

Baydar, N., & Brooks-Gunn, J. (1991). Effects of maternal employment and child-care arrangements on preschoolers' cognitive and behavioral outcomes: Evidence from the children of the National Longitudinal Survey of Youth. *Developmental Psychology, 27,* 932–945.

Benasich, A. A., Brooks-Gunn, J., & Clewell, B. C. (in press). Who benefits from intervention programs begun in infancy? A review of maternal and child outcomes. *Journal of Applied Developmental Psychology.*

Berk, L. E. (1985). Relationship of caregiver education to child-oriented attitudes, job satisfaction, and behaviors toward children. *Child Care Quarterly, 14,* 103–129.

Brooks-Gunn, J., & Chase-Lansdale, P. L. (Eds.). (1991). Special section: Secondary data analyses in developmental psychology. *Developmental Psychology, 27,* 899–951.

Chase-Lansdale, P. L., Brooks-Gunn, J., Mott, F. L. & Phillips, D. A. (1991). Children of the National Longitudinal Survey of Youth: A unique research opportunity. *Developmental Psychology, 27,* 899–951.

Coelen, C., Glantz, F., & Calore, D. (1979). *Day care centers in the U.S.: A national profile, 1976–1977.* Cambridge, MA: Abt.

Duncan, G. J. (1991). Made in heaven: Secondary data analysis and interdisciplinary collaborators. *Developmental Psychology, 27,* 949–951.

Goelman, H., & Pence, A. R. (1987). Effects of child care, family, and individual characteristics on children's language development: The Victoria Day Care Research Project. In D. A. Phillips (Ed.), *Quality in child care: What does research tell us?* (pp. 89–104). Washington, DC: National Association for the Education of Young Children.

Gullo, D. F., & Burton, C. B. (1992). Age of entry, preschool experience, and sex as antecedents of academic readiness in kindergarten. *Early Childhood Research Quarterly, 7,* 175–186.

Harms, T., & Clifford, R. M. (1980). *The Early Childhood Environment Rating Scale.* New York: Teachers College Press.

Harms, T., Cryer, D., & Clifford, R. M. (1986). *Infant-Toddler Environment Rating Scale.* Unpublished document, University of North Carolina, Chapel Hill.

Hayes, C. D., Palmer, J. L., & Zaslow, J. J. (Eds.). (1990). *Who cares for America's children?* Child care policy for the 1990s (Report of the Panel of Child Care Policy, Committee on Child Development Research and Public Policy, Commission on Behavioral and Social Sciences and Education, National Research Council). Washington, DC: National Academy Press.

Howes, C. (1990). Can age of entry and the quality of care predict behaviors in kindergarten? *Developmental Psychology, 26,* 292–303.

Howes, C., & Olenick, M. (1986). Family and child influences on toddlers' compliance. *Child Development, 57,* 202–216.

Howes, C., Phillips, D., & Whitebook, M. (1991, September). *Supplemental findings from the National Child Care Staffing Study.* Technical paper prepared for a conference entitled "Advancing the debate about caregiver training," Child Care Employee Project, Berkeley, CA.

Howes, C., & Stewart, P. (1987). Child's play with adults, toys, and peers: An examination of family and child care influences. *Developmental Psychology, 23,* 423–430.

Kagan, S. L. (1991). Examining profit and nonprofit child care: An odyssey of quality and auspices. *Journal of Social Issues, 47,* 87–104.

Kisker, E. E., Hofferth, S. L., Phillips, D. A., & Farquhar, E. (1991). *A profile of child care settings: Early education and care in 1990* (Vol. 1). Princeton, NJ: Mathematica Policy Research, Inc.

Kontos, S., & Fiene, R. (1987). Child care quality, compliance with regulations, and children's development: The Pennsylvania study. In D. A. Phillips (Ed.), *Quality in child care: What does research tell us?* (pp. 57–80). Washington, DC: National Association for the Education of Young Children.

Kontos, S., & Stremmel, A. J. (1988). Caregivers' perceptions of working conditions in a child care environment. *Early Childhood Research Quarterly, 3,* 77–90.

Lazar, I., Darlington, R. B., Murray, H., Royce, J., & Snipper, A. (1982). Lasting effects of early education: A report of the Consortium for Longitudinal Studies. *Monographs of the Society for Research in Child Development, 47,* (2–3, Serial No. 195).

Lee, V. E., Brooks-Gunn, J., & Schnur, E. (1988). Does Head Start work? A 1 year follow-up comparison of disadvantaged children attending Head Start, no preschool, and other preschool programs. *Developmental Psychology, 24,* 210–222.

Lee, V. E., Brooks-Gunn, J., Schnur, E., & Liaw, F. (1990). Are Head Start effects sustained? A longitudinal follow-up comparison of disadvantaged children attending Head Start, no preschool, and other preschool programs. *Child Development, 61,* 495–507.

McCartney, K., Scarr, S., Phillips, D., & Grajek, S. (1985). Day care as intervention: Comparisons of varying quality programs. *Journal of Applied Developmental Psychology, 6,* 247–260.

McKey, R. H., Condelli, L., Granson, H., Barrett, B., McConkey, C., & Plantz, M. (1985, June). *The impact of Head Start on children, families, and communities* (Final Report of the Head Start Evaluation, Synthesis and Utilization Project). Washington, DC: CSR.

McLoyd, V. C. (1990). The impact of economic hardship on black families and children: Psychological distress, parenting, and socioemotional development. *Child Development, 61,* 311–346.

National Association for the Education of Young Children (1984). *Accreditation criteria and procedures of the National Academy of Early Childhood Programs.* Washington, DC: National Association for the Education of Young Children.

Ogbu, J. (1980). Origins of human competence: A cultural-ecological perspective. *Child Development, 52,* 413–429.

Phillips, D. (Ed.). (1987). *Quality in child care: What does research tell us?* Washington, DC: National Association for the Education of Young Children.

Phillips, D. (1991). With a little help: Children in poverty and child care. In A. Huston (Ed.), *Children in poverty: Child development and public policy* (pp. 158–189). New York: Cambridge University Press.

Phillips, D., & Howes, C. (1987). Indicators of quality in child care: Review of the research. In D. Phillips (Ed.), *Quality in child care: What does research tell us?* Research Monograph of the National Association for the Education of Young Children (Vol. 1). Washington, DC: National Association for the Education of Young Children.

Phillips, D., Howes, C., & Whitebook, M. (1991). Child care as an adult work environment. *Journal of Social Issues, 47,* 49–70.

Phillips, D., Howes, C., & Whitebook, M. (1992). The social policy context of child care: Effects on quality. *American Journal of Community Psychology, 20,* 25–51.

Phillips, D., McCartney, K., & Scarr, S. (1987). Child care quality and children's social development. *Developmental Psychology, 23,* 537–543.

Phillips, D., Mekos, D., Scarr, S., McCartney, K., & Abbott-Shim, M. (1993). *Paths to quality: Relations between structural and experiential measures.* Unpublished manuscript, University of Virginia.

Ramey, C. T., & Campbell, F. A. (1991). Poverty, early childhood education, and academic competence. In A. Huston (Ed.), *Children in poverty. Child development and public policy* (pp. 190–221). New York: Cambridge University Press.

Scarr, S., & Eisenberg, M. (1993). Child care research: Issues, perspectives, and results. *Annual Review of Psychology, 44,* 613–644.

Schweinhart, L. J., & Weikart, D. (1983). The effects of the Perry Preschool Program on youths through age 15—a summary. In Consortium for Longitudinal Studies (Ed.), *As the twig is bent: Lasting effects of preschool programs* (pp. 71–101). Hillsdale, NJ: Erlbaum

Steiner, G. Y. (1976). *The children's cause.* Washington, DC: Brookings.

Vaughn, B. E., Gove, F. L., & Egeland, B. (1980). The relationship between out-of-home care and the quality of infant-mother attachment in an economically disadvantaged population. *Child Development, 51,* 1203–1214.

Voran, M. J., & Whitebook, M. (1991, April). *Inequity begins early: The relationship between day care quality and family social class.* Paper presented at the meetings of the Society for Research in Child Development, Seattle, WA.

Waite, L. J., Leibowitz, A., & Witsberger, C. (1991). What parents pay for: Child care characteristics, quality, and costs. *Journal of Social Issues: Child Care Policy Research, 47,* 33–48.

Whitebook, M., Howes, C., & Phillips, D. (1989). *Who cares? Child care teachers and the quality of care in America.* Final Report of the National Child Care Staffing Study. Oakland, CA: Child Care Employee Project.

Whitebook, M., Phillips, D., & Howes, C. (1993). *National Child Care Staffing Study revisited: Four years in the life of centerbased child care.* Oakland, CA: Child Care Employee Project.

Wrigley, J. (1991). Different care for different kids: Social class and child care policy. In L. Weis, P. G. Altbach, G. P. Kelly, & G. Petrie (Eds.), *Critical perspectives on early childhood education* (pp. 189–209). New York: State University of New York Press.

Zaslow, M. J. (1991). Variation in child care quality and its implications for children. In D. Phillips & S. Hofferth (Eds.), *Journal of Social Issues: Child Care Policy Research, 47,* 125–138.

Zigler, E., & Valentine, J. (Eds.). (1979). *Project Head Start: A legacy of the war on poverty.* New York: Free Press.

Emotion Regulation in Early Childhood: A Cross-Cultural Comparison Between German and Japanese Toddlers*

Wolfgang Friedlmeier and Gisela Trommsdorff

In recent years, research on emotional development has shifted from a static to a process perspective and from a focus on person to a focus on interaction (cf. Campos, Campos, & Barrett, 1989; Dodge & Garber, 1991; Kopp, 1989).

The focus on process takes into account aspects of emotional response and regulation, especially the function of emotions for other psychological processes like cognitions, motives, and actions (Thompson, 1990). Emotions indicate the subjective meaning of a situation in regard to a person's needs by activating the appraisal system (cf. Lazarus, 1991). They are linked to instrumental behavior that may become habitual reactions or cognitively selected strategies (cf. Masters, 1991). Thereby, emotions encompass a regulation function in regard to the person's orientation in the environment. This raises the question of how children acquire competencies of emotion regulation.

The second shift refers to the assumption that emotion regulation in the first years of life is provided by some external regulator (e.g., caregivers), and emotional development emerges as a product of mutually influential interactions within a particular kind of social ecology (cf. Malatesta-Magai, 1991). In case of negative arousal, infants apply some strategies that reduce the emotional arousal, for example, gaze aversion, self-soothing, self-distraction, or contact- and proximity-seeking with the mother (cf. Mangelsdorf, Shapiro, & Marzolf, 1995). According to Kopp (1989), the necessity of external support is one principle of emotion regulation in childhood. Infants experiencing uncertainty actively seek contact with the caregiver and use their emotional expression or verbal information as guidance for their own emotional reaction and instrumental behavior; that is, they regulate their negative affect by referencing to others' (especially their mothers') reactions to events. Thereby, the basis for referencing is not only a cognitive analysis of meaning but also imitation, contagion, or modification of mood (cf. Walden, 1991). The children's motivation of referencing the mother is probably rooted in biologically based attachment processes (cf. Masters, 1991). Attachment theory also emphasizes the importance of caregivers as regulators for children's emotional development (cf. Greenspan & Greenspan, 1985). The need for care and protection provided by the caregivers is the beginning of the infant's socioemotional development (cf. Bowlby, 1982). This kind of regulation is an interactive and inherently cultural process because the caregivers interact with the infant according to their own subjective meaning system, which is socially and culturally transmitted (cf. Friedlmeier, 1995).

. . .

Culture provides meaning to intended and to actually demonstrated behavior and its consequences including emotional responses; these interpretations affect future behavior orientation (cf. Kâgitçibâsi, 1996). The main features of culture are a homogeneous set of shared values, norms, and beliefs. Cultural differences between Western and Eastern cultures are often explicated by using "relatedness-separatedness" (e.g., Kâgitçibâsi, 1996) or "individualism-collectivism" (e.g., Triandis, Bontempo, Villareal, Asai, & Lucca, 1988) as a basic dimension. For the purpose of this study, cultural values of children and related parental beliefs are central contextual features. In Western industrialized cultures, parents view their children as separate entities and consequently try to foster autonomy

*From Friedlmeir & Trommsdorff (1999, November). *Journal of Cross-Cultural Psychology, 30*(6), 684–711. Reprinted with permission.

and independence; in Eastern cultures, parents view their children as extensions of themselves—a strong emotional bonding and feeling of oneness characterize Japanese mothers (Azuma, 1984)—and accommodation to social expectations is an important child-rearing goal (Befu, 1986; Kornadt & Trommsdorff, 1990, 1997; Lebra, 1976; Trommsdorff, 1995a, 1995b, 1997; Trommsdorff & Friedlmeier, 1993). Consequently, Japanese (and Korean) mothers stress physical contact, whereas American and Canadian mothers encourage their children to express their needs (cf. Caudill & Schooler, 1973; Choi, 1992). Such culturally guided beliefs and child-rearing goals have consequences for the child's development, because mothers react to children's behavior in accordance to their beliefs and expectations. By this means, different dyadic patterns develop, and culture-specific differences in children's behavior can be explained primarily by the experience of different interaction patterns with the caregivers.

. . .

Method

Sample

Two-year-old German (n = 20) and Japanese (n = 20) girls and their mothers participated in this study carried out in Konstanz and Kobe. The dyads were recruited by phoning the families based on the birth register of the newspaper. There were no differences between the samples from both cultures with respect to socioeconomic status, child age, birth order, age of mother, or family size. The majority of the Japanese and German mothers had about the same educational level (BA or Abitur), and the majority of mothers in both cultures were homemakers. The original intention to get a sample of at least n = 25 dyads in each culture could not be realized due to organizational problems, and due to technical problems, the whole set of data was completely available for n = 17 German and n = 19 Japanese dyads. Gender differences are already documented for 14-month-old children in regard to expression of distress (e.g., Zahn-Waxler et al., 1992). The girls' presumably stronger emotional expressions facilitate the analyses of the observed emotional reactions. Therefore, we only included girls to get a homogeneous sample and to increase the validity of our observational methods.

Procedures

Observation of emotion regulation. The toddlers were observed during a quasi-experimental interaction with an adult playmate. The mother was sitting in a corner of the room; she was instructed to concentrate on reading some journals and not to initiate any actions toward her child; however, she could react if the child requested. The playmate introduced two teddy bears to the girl and both started to play with them. After a while, the playmate took off her teddy's clothes. By this action, one arm of the teddy bear broke. The playmate expressed her sadness (for about 2 minutes).

The emotional reactions of the child and the behavior toward the mother were videotaped. After 2 minutes, the playmate stopped her sadness; she gradually changed her behavior and adopted a relaxed expression. Then, she asked the child to continue to play together with the other remaining bear.

Observation of maternal sensitivity. The mother and her daughter were observed in two different interactions (task and disappointment situation). Instructions were given to the child while the mother was sitting nearer the child on the floor. If the mother asked about her role, she was informed that it was up to her to do whatever she wanted.

In the (a) task situation, the child was asked to build a tower. This task was too difficult for this age group. In the (b) disappointment situation, the child played with dolls and a dollhouse. These toys were suddenly taken away by a strange person who argued that she needed the toys for other children in another room. The interaction between mother and child during and after the task and disappointment situation were videotaped.

Order of series. The mother-child interaction was observed in the first session and the interaction with the playmate in the second session. The same female adult served as experimenter and as playmate. Following the mother-child interaction in the first session, the playmate and the child played together for about 30 minutes. This was a warming-up for the second session. Due to the necessity of guaranteeing a similar familiarity between the playmate and the child, the order of the sessions was not varied systematically.

. . .

Regarding the number of girls looking for support, it becomes clear that the overwhelming majority focused on the mother as a source of reference to regulate their negative emotions. This underlines the importance of the interactive process in emotion regulation in early childhood (cf. Friedlmeier, 1999; Malatesta-Magai, 1991; Parritz, 1996). Beyond this general result, several culture-specific differences occurred. Although the Japanese girls were only tendentially less distant from their mothers compared to the German girls, it should be noted that a different quality of distance regulation occurred that was not taken into account for the analyses of the interactions as reported here. A second analysis of the interactions showed that the German girls who displayed low distance from their mother moved back and forth between playmate and mother, whereas Japanese girls who displayed low distance approached and stayed closer to their mothers in a more continuous way. This way, the Japanese children made the playmate come closer to continue the play.

Also, the observation of the children in both cultures showed that the situation was apparently more stressful for the Japanese girls. This can be concluded from several results. As compared to the German toddlers, Japanese children displayed a distress reaction more often (Trommsdorff, 1995a); they also did not use eye contact as a means of emotional reference but rather approached their mothers, although they were already closer to their mothers before the distress-inducing event happened. Finally, they were markedly less relaxed at the end of the experimental situation.

The question of whether the experimental situation was functionally equivalent for both cultural groups cannot be answered definitely. The social constellation—playing with a nonfamily member (a less familiar person) in the presence of the mother—is realistic within both countries. However, the instruction given to the mothers not to intervene if the child does not ask may have reduced the functional equivalence of this situation in two ways: (a) If one assumes that Japanese as compared to German mothers protect their children more against negative emotions, Japanese mothers may have intervened earlier and thus have prevented the stronger distress reactions of their toddlers in a natural situation free from instructions. (b) The instruction to mothers not to intervene actively may have been interpreted in a more rigorous way by Japanese mothers (see Grossmann & Grossmann, 1996). These methodological limitations emphasize the necessity of taking into account this aspect in future research and possibly of complementing the laboratory studies by natural observations. . . .

The comparison of the distribution of regulation patterns yielded that German toddlers regulated the distress-evoking situation in a qualitatively different way as compared to Japanese toddlers. Apparently, Japanese children reacted to this situation in a more negative emotional way and were less relaxed at the end of the situation. This stronger negative experience can be explained neither by lack of instrumental reactions—they mostly looked for maternal support—nor by lack of support from their mothers. Japanese mothers reacted in a warm and prompt way to their children and did not differ in regard to those Japanese mothers whose girls displayed positive regulation. Japanese mothers displayed a contingent reaction more often than the German mothers did. In contrast to the Japanese sample, German toddlers' regulation depended more on the maternal reaction; that is, noncontingent maternal response was related to the child's negative regulation in the German sample. . . .

The result that Japanese mothers reacted more sensitively to their girls as compared to the German mothers is in line with other studies (cf. Azuma, 1986; Trommsdorff & Friedlmeier, 1993, 1999). Comparisons of mothers' sensitivity as compared to contingency yielded an analogous relationship: Low sensitivity was related to negative regulation and vice versa for the German dyads, whereas Japanese mothers' sensitivity had no impact on children's regulation. They were even somewhat more sensitive for toddlers with negative regulation as compared to toddlers with positive regulation. The lack of relationship for the Japanese sample has to be interpreted carefully because this could be an artifact due to the ceiling effect in regard to mothers' sensitivity.

Conclusions

The difference of toddlers' emotion regulation and the relationship to maternal reaction indicate that the results can be best interpreted as culture-specific interpersonal cycles.

Japanese mothers pursue the child-rearing goal that the child feels as one with another person in an in-group situation. In this sense, the child is expected to feel the pain and sadness of the playmate and consequently react in an emotional way—whether it be empathy or distress. At the same time, the feeling of oneness with the child encourages the mother to protect the child if he or she experiences negative emotional states. To the extent that the child turns to the mother for support in this situation, the mother's reaction is ambiguous. On one hand, she calms the child, and on the other hand, she makes the child more tense, because the mother represents the agent who most emphasizes the importance of empathy.

German mothers pursue the child-rearing goal that the child feels the partner's sadness. At the same time, the mother expects the child to regulate emotional experiences in a progressively autonomous way (e.g., the child should be able to comfort the partner). This expectation may induce the mother not to react to the child's emotional state but rather to emphasize the partner's state. The more the child turns to the mother for support in this situation and the more the mother perceives this reaction as immature, the more roughly she reacts by neglecting the child's emotional reaction.

Beyond the interactive process within the same situation, maternal sensitivity in the mother-child interaction was seen as a necessary condition for children's emotion regulation. These results indicate culture-specific implications for further development of emotion regulation. The significant relationship between low maternal sensitivity and toddlers' negative regulation may end in a distant relationship between mother and child with negative consequences for the development of emotion regulation. The generally more supportive interaction of Japanese mothers with their toddlers who showed negative emotion regulation does not allow a prediction of the same developmental trends but rather raises the question of whether their children will be more successful in regulating negative emotions later on. Some preliminary results support this line of reasoning (Trommsdorff & Friedlmeier, 1999). However, such questions can only be answered in cross-cultural longitudinal studies.

REFERENCES

Ainsworth, M. D. S. (1992). A consideration of social referencing in the context of attachment theory and research. In S. Feinman (Ed.), *Social referencing and the social construction of reality in infancy* (pp. 349–370). New York: Plenum.

Ainsworth, M. D. S., Bell, S. M., & Stayton, D. J. (1971). Individual differences in Strange Situation behavior of one-year-olds. In H. R. Schaffer (Ed.), *The origins of human relations* (pp. 17–57). London: Academic Press.

Ainsworth, M. D. S., Blehar, M. C., Waters, E., & Wall, S. (1978). *Patterns of attachment. A psychological study of the Strange Situation.* Hillsdale, NJ: Erlbaum.

Azuma, H. (1984). Secondary control as a heterogeneous category. *American Psychologist, 38,* 970–971.

Azuma, H. (1986). Why study child development in Japan? In H. Stevenson, H. Azuma, & K. Hakuta (Ed.), *Child development and education in Japan* (pp. 3–12). New York: Freeman.

Barratt, M. (1996, July 12–16). *Maternal responsiveness to infants' signals in Japan and the United States.* Paper presented at the ISSBD conference in Quebec, Canada.

Batson, C. D. (1990). How social an animal? *American Psychologist, 45,* 336–346.

Batson, C. D., Fultz, J., & Schoenrade, P. A. (1987). Distress and empathy: Two qualitatively distinct vicarious emotions with different motivational consequences. *Journal of Personality and Social Psychology, 55,* 19–40.

Befu, H. (1986). The social and cultural background of child development in Japan and the United States. In H. Stevenson, H. Azuma, & K. Hakuta (Eds.), *Child development and education in Japan* (pp. 13–27). New York: Freeman.

Bornstein, M. H. (1989). Cross-cultural developmental comparisons: The case of Japanese-American infant and mother activities and interactions. What we know, what we need to know, and why we need to know. *Developmental Review, 9,* 171–204.

Bowlby, J. (1982). *Attachment and loss, Vol. 1: Attachment (2nd ed.).* New York: Basic Books.

Campos, J. J., Campos, R. G., & Barrett, K. C. (1989). Emergent themes in the study of emotional development and emotion regulation. *Developmental Psychology, 25,* 394–402.

Caudill, W. A., & Schooler, C. (1973). Child behavior and child rearing in Japan and the United States: An interim report. *Journal of Nervous and Mental Disease, 157,* 323–338.

Choi, S. H. (1992). Communicative socialization processes: Korea and Canada. In S. Iwawaki, Y. Kashima, & K. Leung (Eds.), *Innovations in cross-cultural psychology* (pp. 103–122). Amsterdam, the Netherlands: Swets & Zeitlinger.

Dodge, K. A., & Garber, J. (1991). Domains of emotion regulation. In K. A. Dodge & J. Garber (Eds.), *The development of emotion regulation and dysregulation* (pp. 3–14). Cambridge, UK: Cambridge University Press.

Eisenberg, N. (1986). *Altruistic emotion, cognition, and behavior.* Hillsdale, NJ: Erlbaum.

Eisenberg, N., Fabes, R. A., Miller, P. A., Shell, R., Shea, C., & May-Plumlee, T. (1990). Preschoolers' vicarious emotional responding and their situational and dispositional prosocial behavior. *Merrill-Palmer Quarterly, 36,* 507–529.

Eisenberg, N., & Strayer, J. (1987). Critical issues in the study of empathy. In N. Eisenberg & J. Strayer (Eds.), *Empathy and its development* (pp. 3–14). New York: Cambridge University Press.

Feinman, S. (1992). What do we know and where shall we go? Conceptual and research directions in social referencing. In S. Feinman (Ed.), *Social referencing and the social construction of reality in infancy* (pp. 371–406). New York: Plenum.

Friedlmeier, W. (1993). *Entwicklung von Empathie, Selbstkonzept und prosozialem Handeln in der Kindheit* [Development of empathy, self-concept, and prosocial behavior in childhood]. Konstanz, Germany: Hartung-Gorre.

Friedlmeier, W. (1995). Subjektive Erziehungstheorien im Kulturvergleich [Subjective child-rearing theories in cultural perspective]. In G. Trommsdorff (Ed.), *Kindheit und Jugend im Kulturvergleich* (pp. 43–64). Weinheim, Germany: Juventa.

Friedlmeier, W. (1996). Entwicklung der Emotionsregulation aus soziokultureller Perspektive [Development of emotion regulation in sociocultural perspective]. In K. U. Ettrich & M. Fries (Eds.), *Lebenslange Entwicklung in sich wandelnden Zeiten* (pp. 31–37). Leipzig, Germany: Verlag Empirische Pädagogik.

Friedlmeier, W. (1999). Sozialisation der Emotionsregulation [Socialization of emotion regulation]. *Zeitschrift für Soziologie der Erziehung und Sozialisation, 1,* 35–51.

Friedlmeier, W., & Trommsdorff, G. (1998). Japanese and German mother-child interactions in early childhood. In G. Trommsdorff, W. Friedlmeier, & H-J. Kornadt (Eds.), *Japan in transition. Social and psychological aspects* (pp. 217–230). Lengerich, Germany: Pabst Science.

Greenspan, S., & Greenspan, T. (1985). *First feelings: Milestones in the emotional development of your baby and child.* New York: Viking.

Grossmann, K. & Grossmann, K. E. (1996). Kulturelle Perspektiven der Bindungsentwicklung in Japan and Deutschland [Cultural perspective about development of attachment in Japan and Germany]. In G. Trommsdorff & H. J. Kornadt (Eds.), *Gesellschaftliche und individuelle Entwicklung in Japan und Deutschland* (pp. 215–235). Konstanz, Germany: Universitätsverlag Konstanz.

Grossmann, K. E., & Grossmann, K. (1993). Emotional organization and concentration on reality from an attachment theory perspective. *International Journal of Educational Research, 19,* 541–554.

Grossmann, K. E., Grossmann, K., & Schwan, A. (1986). Capturing the wider view of attachment: A reanalysis of Ainsworth's Strange Situation. *International Journal of Behavioral Development, 4,* 157–181.

Hoffman, M. L. (1975). Developmental synthesis of affect and cognition and its interplay for altruistic motivation. *Developmental Psychology, 11,* 607–622.

Kâgitçibâsi, C. (1996). *Family and human development across cultures: A view from the other side.* Mahwah, NJ: Erlbaum.

Kopp, C. B. (1989). Regulation of distress and negative emotions: A developmental view. *Developmental Psychology, 25,* 343–354.

Kornadt, H. J., & Trommsdorff, G. (1990). Naive Erziehungstheorien Japanischer Mutter—Deutsch-Japanischer Kulturvergleich [Subjective child-rearing theories of Japanese mothers—A cross-cultural comparison between Japan and Germany]. *Zeitschrift für Sozialisationsforschung und Erziehungssoziologie, 2,* 357–376.

Kornadt, H. J., & Trommsdorff, G. (1997). Sozialisationsbedingungen von Aggressivitat in Japan und Deutschland [Conditions of socialization for aggressiveness in Japan and Germany]. In G. Foljante-Jost & D. Rössner (Eds.), *Gewalt unter Jugendlichen in Deutschland und Japan—Ursachen und Bekämpfung* (pp. 27–51). Baden-Baden, Germany: Nomos Verlag.

Lazarus, R. S. (1991). Progress on a cognitive-motivational-relational theory of emotions. *American Psychologist, 46,* 819–834.

Lebra, T. S. (1976). *Japanese patterns of behavior.* Honolulu: University of Hawaii Press.

Main, M., Kaplan, N., & Cassidy, J. (1985). Security in infancy, childhood, and adulthood: A move to the level of representation. In I. Bretherton & E. Waters (Eds.), Growing points of attachment theory and research. *Monographs of the Society for Research in Child Development, 50,* 66–106.

Malatesta-Magai, C. (1991). Development of emotional expression during infancy: General course and patterns of individual difference. In K. A. Dodge & J. Garber (Eds.), *The development of emotion regulation and dysregulation* (pp. 49–68). Cambridge, UK: Cambridge University Press.

Mangelsdorf, S. C., Shapiro, J. R., & Marzolf, D. (1995). Developmental and temperamental differences in emotion regulation in infancy. *Child Development, 66,* 1817–1828.

Masters, C. (1991). Strategies and mechanisms for the personal and social control of emotion. In K. A. Dodge & J. Garber (Eds.), *The development of emotion regulation and dysregulation* (pp. 182–207). Cambridge, UK: Cambridge University Press.

Mizuta, I., Zahn-Waxler, C., Cole, P. M., & Hiruma, N. (1996). A cross-cultural study of preschoolers' attachment: Security and sensitivity in Japanese and US dyads. *International Journal of Behavioral Development, 19,* 141–159.

Parritz, R. H. (1996). A descriptive analysis of toddler coping in challenging circumstances. *Infant Behavior and Development, 19,* 171–180.

Parritz, R. H., Mangelsdorf, S., & Gunnar, M. R. (1992). Control, social referencing, and the infant's appraisal of threat. In S. Feinman (Ed.), *Social referencing and the social construction of reality in infancy* (pp. 209–228). New York: Plenum.

Rothbart, M. K., Ziaie, H., & O'Boyle, C. G. (1992). Self-regulation and emotion in infancy. In N. Eisenberg & R. A. Fabes (Eds.), *Emotion and its regulation in early development. New Directions for Child Development* (Vol. 55, pp. 7–23). San Francisco: Jossey-Bass.

Rubin, K. H., Coplan, R. J., Fox, N. A., & Calkins, S. D. (1995). Emotionality, emotion regulation, and preschoolers' social adaptation. *Development and Psychopathology, 7,* 49–62.

Sroufe, A. (1983). Infant-caregiver attachment and patterns of adaptation in preschool: The roots of maladaptation and competence. In M. Perlmutter (Ed.), *Minnesota symposium on child psychology, Vol. 16: Development and policy concerning children with special needs* (pp. 41–83). Hillsdale, NJ: Erlbaum.

Sroufe, A., & Waters, E. (1977). Attachment as an organizational construct. *Child Development, 48,* 1184–1199.

Stenberg, C. R., & Campos, J. J. (1990). The development of anger expressions in infancy. In N. L. Stein, B. Leventhal, & T. Trabasso (Eds.), *Psychological and biological approaches to emotion* (pp. 247–282). Hillsdale, NJ: Erlbaum.

Thompson, R. A. (1990). Emotion and self-regulation. In R. A. Thompson (Ed.), *Nebraska Symposium on Motivation: Socioemotional development. Current theory and research in motivation* (Vol. 36, pp. 367–467). Lincoln: University of Nebraska Press.

Thompson, R. A. (1994). Emotion regulation: A theme in search of definition. *Monographs of the Society for Research in Child Development, 52,* 2–3.

Tinsley, H. E. A., & Weiss, D. J. (1976). Interrater reliability and agreement of subjective judgments. *Journal of Counseling Psychology, 22,* 358–376.

Triandis, H. C., Bontempo, R., Villareal, M. J., Asai, M., & Lucca, N. (1988). Individualism and collectivism: Cross-cultural perspectives on self-in-group relationships. *Journal of Personality and Social Psychology, 54,* 323–338.

Trommsdorff, G. (1995a). Empathy and prosocial action in cultural environments: A cross-cultural analysis. In T. Kindermann & J. Valsiner (Eds.), *Construction of self and social relationships* (pp. 112–146). Hillsdale, NJ: Erlbaum.

Trommsdorff, G. (1995b). Parent-adolescent relations in changing societies: A cross-cultural study. In P. Noack, M. Hofer, & J. Youniss (Eds.), *Psychological responses to social change: Human development in changing environments* (pp. 189–218). Berlin: De Gruyter.

Trommsdorff, G. (1997). Familie und Eltern-Kind-Beziehung in Japan [Family and parent-child relationship in Japan]. In B. Nauck & U. Schönpflug (Eds.), *Familie in verschiedenen Kulturen* (pp. 44–63). Stuttgart, Germany: Enke.

Trommsdorff, G., & Friedlmeier, W. (1993). Control and responsiveness in Japanese and German mother-child interactions. *Early Development and Parenting, 2,* 33.1–33.14.

Trommsdorff, G., & Friedlmeier, W. (1999). *Regulation of emotions and mother-child relationships: A comparison between Japanese and German preschoolers.* Manuscript submitted for publication.

Tronick, E. Z. (1989). Emotions and emotional communication in infants. *American Psychologist, 44,* 112–128.

Walden, T. A. (1991). Infant social referencing. In K. A. Dodge & J. Garber (Eds.), *The development of emotion regulation and dysregulation* (pp. 69–88). Cambridge, UK: Cambridge University Press.

Webster, M., & Foschi, M. (1992). Social referencing and theories of status and social interaction. In S. Feinman (Ed.), *Social referencing and the social construction of reality in infancy* (pp. 269–296). New York: Plenum.

Weinberg, M. K., & Tronick, E. Z. (1996). Affective reactions to the resumption of maternal interaction after the still-face. *Child Development, 67,* 905–914.

Zahn-Waxler, C., Radke-Yarrow, M., Wagner, E., & Chapman, M. (1992). Development of concern for others. *Developmental Psychology, 28,* 126–136.

African American Fathers in Low Income, Urban Families: Development, Behavior, and Home Environment of Their Three-Year-Old Children*

Maureen M. Black, Howard Dubowitz, and Raymond H. Starr Jr.

Changing family structures have resulted in many children being raised in households that do not include fathers. The percentage of American children living with their fathers has declined steadily since the 1960s (Hernandez, 1993), a trend that is not expected to change in the future as rates of divorce and nonmarital childbearing either plateau or continue to increase (Furstenberg & Cherlin, 1991), particularly in low income, African American communities where structural forces such as poverty, racism, and public policies undermine marriage and put women in control of the meager resources that are available (Bumpass & Sweet, 1989); Eggebeen, Crockett, & Hawkins, 1990; National Commission on Children, 1991).

Although many fathers express a desire to remain involved in the lives of their children (Elster & Lamb, 1986; Mott, 1990), a long-term follow-up study of fathers of children born to adolescent mothers in the mid-1960s, most of whom were African American, showed that by the time the children were teenagers only 14% were living with their biological fathers and almost half (46%) had no contact with them (Furstenberg & Harris, 1993). Almost half of the children (47%), however, spent part of their childhood living with a nonbiological father figure, a pattern that other investigators have noted, but few have investigated (Hawkins & Eggebeen, 1991). Much of the research on fathers has focused on the presence or absence of biological fathers, and little attention has been directed to the potentially important roles of nonbiological father figures.

. . .

Method

Participants

The 175 3-year-old African American children (M = 37.6 months, SD = 2.5) and families in this study were recruited from three pediatric clinics serving low income, urban families and are part of a larger investigation of child and family development. Approximately 26% of the children were recruited from a growth and nutrition clinic and had a history of nonorganic failure to thrive (FTT); 29% were recruited from a clinic that serves children at high risk for HIV infection, primarily through maternal drug abuse; and 45% were recruited from a general pediatric primary care clinic. The majority of the families received public assistance, including Medical Assistance (89%) and Aid for Families with Dependent Children (81%). Most of the mothers were in their 20s (M = 27.2 years, SD = 5.5), had limited education (M = 11.4 years of schooling, SD = 1.5), and were not married (92%).

Procedures

Mothers and children. Mothers agreed to participate in a longitudinal research project, using consent procedures approved by the Institutional Review Board at the University of Maryland at Baltimore. Laboratory and home evaluations were conducted involving the mother and child. The laboratory evaluation included an assessment of cognitive and receptive language skills, a videotaped observation of the mother and child, and a 1-hour interview in which standardized questionnaires were admin-

---

*From Black et al. (1999, July/August). *Child Development, 70,* 967–978. Reprinted with permission.

istered including demographic information and parent and family functioning. The assessments of cognitive and language skills were administered by a trained psychologist or graduate student. The mother and child were videotaped for 10 min in a clinic examining room that was furnished with a child's table and chairs, bright pictures, large plastic blocks, and a child's book with no words. Mothers and children were asked to play with the blocks and book and to behave as they did at home. The camera was visible in the room, but no operator was present. Questionnaires were administered orally to control for varying literacy levels. Mothers were compensated financially ($25) for their participation, time, and transportation.

Fathers. Mothers were asked how often the children had contact with their biological father. If fathers were involved at least monthly, we invited the father to participate in an evaluation that included an interview and a videotaped play observation with their child, conducted using procedures similar to those used with mothers. If the biological father was not involved, we asked about father figures—males who were "like a father" to the child. Father figures who had contact at least monthly were also invited to participate in the father evaluation. Unless otherwise stated, the term "father" refers to both biological fathers and father figures. Fathers were compensated financially ($25) for their participation, time, and transportation.

. . .

Among the 175 3-year-old children and families, 128 fathers were identified (73%) and 82 (64% of identified fathers) participated in the evaluation. Slightly over one quarter of the mothers (27%) reported that their child had no contact with the biological father or contact less than once per month, and that there was no other male who was "like a father" with at least monthly contact. Another quarter (26%) of the mothers reported that their child had a father or father figure who met the involvement criterion, but he did not participate in the interview. . . .

We examined differences in the four indices of children's well-being (cognition, receptive language, behavior, and child-centered quality of the home) as a function of father presence (regardless of interview status) or absence using analysis of variance. . . .

The 82 fathers who participated in the interview ranged in age from 21 to 51 years (M = 30.5, SD = 5.9). Over half (59%) were the child's biological father, 26% were the mother's partner, 7% were other relatives, and 7% were friends. The majority (72%) had daily contact with the child, 61% lived with the child (defined as living in the home at least 4 days per week), and 10% were married to the child's mother. Slightly over half (55%) had completed high school (or had a GED) and almost two thirds were employed (63%). The vast majority reported that they contributed financially to their child's household at least weekly (71%) or monthly (17%). The distribution of risk status among the children with participating fathers paralleled that within the larger sample (26% had a history of FTT, 31% were at risk for HIV infection, and 43% were from a general pediatric clinic).

. . .

Discussion

. . .

In the subset of families where the father was interviewed, fathers played significant, albeit modest, roles in the cognitive and language skills, behavior, and home environment of their 3-year-old children. At first glance, these findings appear to be at odds with those of Crockett and colleagues (1993). They also examined the relationship between African American fathers' involvement and the development, behavior, and home environment of their preschool children, but found no associations after controlling for maternal education and IQ. There are several important differences, however, between the two studies that may account for their discrepant findings. First, they studied biological fathers, not father figures. Second, their definition of involvement included fathers living in the household, rather than specific father roles regardless of living status. Finally, their sample (National Longitudinal Survey of Youth) was more heterogeneous in economic resources than the current sample.

The association between maternal characteristics and children's cognitive competence prominent among developmental theorists (Bronfenbrenner, 1993) was validated in this low income, African American sample of preschoolers. Maternal education was strongly associated with all measures of children's well-being, and maternal parenting satisfaction was associated with three of the four measures (with the exception of receptive language). These findings suggest that in spite of the overwhelming poverty characterizing most families, maternal characteristics and attitudes were directly related to children's well-being, whether measured by standardized test, observation, or maternal report. Mothers who had higher levels of education themselves and felt more satisfied and efficacious in their role as a parent had children who demonstrated more cognitive skills, fewer behavior problems, and lived in a more child-centered home.

The lack of association between maternal parenting satisfaction and father's roles suggests that factors other than paternal behavior contribute to maternal parenting satisfaction. In many low income communities there are few opportunities for males to assume the traditional fathering role of providing economic stability to the family (Furstenberg, 1995). In response, women adjust their expectations and look for other means to fulfill traditional male roles within the family (Lamb et al., 1987). Maternal parenting satisfaction may be less dependent on paternal roles because the mothers had few expectations of their child's father. Thus, it is not surprising that when paternal roles were significantly associated with children's well-being, they represented a "value added" component, rather than operating through maternal parenting satisfaction.

The relations between father's roles and children's cognitive and language competence, behavior, and home environment, above and beyond maternal characteristics (age and education) and maternal parenting satisfaction, document the role that African American fathers can play in the lives of their young children. Although most attention has been directed toward the economic contributions that fathers make, the associations between children's cognition and paternal parenting satisfaction, and between children's receptive language development and paternal nurturance during play, illustrate the importance of considering paternal roles beyond economic contributions. . . .

These findings highlight the need to consider father roles from functional and cultural perspectives, rather than relying solely on reports of father availability. Children do not benefit from the mere presence of fathers, probably because in their absence, traditional paternal roles are taken over by other family members. Given current economic and social conditions and the relatively high cost of maintaining a household, many children, particularly those in low income, African American families, are raised in multigenerational female-headed households where fathers are not necessarily well accepted. Nevertheless, households that do include a father are more child-centered, and children whose fathers (or father figures) contribute financially to the family, are nurturant during play, and are satisfied with their parenting role have better cognition, receptive language skills, and behavior. These findings validate ecological theories that emphasize the importance of father-child interaction to children's well-being and provide convincing evidence for more family-oriented social and economic policies that promote positive father involvement.

REFERENCES

Achenbach, T. M., Edelbrock, C., & Howell, C. T. (1987). Empirically based assessment of the behavioral/emotional problems of 2- and 3-year-old children. *Journal of Abnormal Psychology, 15,* 629–650.

Ahmeduzzaman, M., & Roopnarine, J. L. (1992). Sociodemographic factors, functioning style, social support, and fathers' involvement with preschoolers in African-

American families. *Journal of Marriage and the Family, 54,* 699–707.

Baron, R. M., & Kenny, D. (1986). The moderator/mediator variable distinction in social psychological research: Conceptual, strategic, and statistical considerations. *Journal of Personality and Social Psychology, 51,* 1173–1182.

Baumrind, D. (1971). Current theories of parental authority. *Developmental Psychology Monograph, 4*(1, part 2).

Belsky, J. (1984). The determinants of parenting. *Child Development, 55,* 83–96.

Black, M. M. & Jodorkovsky, R. (1994). Stress and family competence as predictors of pediatric contacts and behavior problems among toddlers. *Journal of Developmental and Behavioral Pediatrics, 15,* 198–203.

Bradley, R. H., & Caldwell, B. M. (1984). 174 children: A study of the relationship between home environment and cognitive development during the first 5 years. In A. W. Gottfried (Ed.), *Home environment and early cognitive development* (pp. 5–56). Orlando, FL: Academic Press.

Brody, G., Stoneman, Z., Flor, D., McCray, C., Hastings, L., & Conyers, O. (1994). Financial resources, parent psychological functioning, parent caregiving, and early adolescent competence in rural two-parent African American families. *Child Development, 65,* 590–605.

Bronfenbrenner, U. (1993). Ecological systems theory. In R. Wozniak & K. Fisher (Eds.), *Specific environments: Thinking in contexts* (pp. 3–44). Hillsdale, NJ: Erlbaum.

Bryan, D. L., & Ajo, A. A. (1992). The role perception of African American fathers. *Social Work Research and Abstracts, 28*(3), 17–21.

Bumpass, L. L., & Sweet, J. A. (1989). Children's experience in single-parent families: Implications of cohabitation and marital transitions. *Family Planning Perspectives, 21,* 256–260.

Caldwell, B. M., & Bradley, R. H. (1979). *Home observation for measurement of the environment.* Little Rock: University of Arkansas at Little Rock.

Chase-Lansdale, P. L. (1995). Whose responsibility? An historical analysis of the changing roles of mothers, fathers, and society. In P. L. Chase-Lansdale & J. Brooks-Gunn (Eds.), *Escape from poverty: What makes a difference for children?* (pp. 11–37). Cambridge, UK: Cambridge University Press.

Cowan, C. P., & Cowan, P. A. (1988). Who does what when partners become parents: Implications for men, women, and marriage. *Marriage and Family Review, 12,* 105–124.

Cowan, C. P., & Cowan, P. A. (1990). The "Who Does What?" In J. Touliatos, B. Perlmutter, & M. Strauss (Eds.), *Handbook of family measurement techniques.* Newbury Park, CA: Sage.

Crnic, K. A., Greenberg, M. T., Ragozin, A. S., Robinson, N. M., & Basham, R. B. (1983). Effects of stress and social support on mothers and premature and full-term infants. *Child Development, 54,* 209–217.

Crockett, L. J., Eggebeen, D. J., & Hawkins A. J. (1993). Fathers' presence and young children's behavioral and cognitive adjustment. *Journal of Family Issues, 14,* 355–377.

Dittus, P., Jaccard, J., & Gordon, V. V. (1997). The impact of African American fathers on adolescent sexual behavior. *Journal of Youth & Adolescence, 37,* 643–661.

Dornbusch, S. M., Carlsmith, J. M., Bushwall, S. J., Ritter, P. L., Leiderman, H., Hastorf, A. H., & Gross, R. T. (1985). Single parents, extended households, and the control of adolescents. *Child Development, 56,* 326–341.

Dunn, L., & Dunn, L. (1981). *PPVT-R manual.* Circle Pines, MN: American Guidance Service.

Eggebeen, D. J., Crockett, L. J., & Hawkins A. J. (1990). Patterns of male co-residence for children of adolescent mothers. *Family Planning Perspectives, 22,* 219–223.

Elder, G. H., Conger, R. D., Foster, E. M., & Ardelt, M. (1992). Families under economic pressure. *Journal of Family Issues, 13,* 5–37.

Elster, A., & Lamb, M. (1986). *Adolescent fatherhood.* Hillsdale, NJ: Erlbaum.

Fagan, J. (1996). A preliminary study of low income African American fathers' play interactions with preschool-age children. *Journal of Black Psychology, 22,* 7–19.

Furstenberg, F. F., Jr., (1995). Fathering in the inner city. In W. Marsiglio (Ed.), *Fatherhood: Contemporary theory.* Thousand Oaks, CA: Sage.

Furstenberg, F. F., Jr., & Cherlin, A. J. (1991). *Divided families: What happens to children when parents part.* Cambridge, MA: Harvard University Press.

Furstenberg, F. F., Jr., & Harris, K. M. (1993). When fathers matter/why fathers matter: The impact of paternal involvement on the offspring of adolescent mothers. In D. L. Rhode & A. Lawson (Eds.), *The politics of pregnancy* (pp. 189–215). New Haven, CT: Yale University Press.

Gibaud-Wallston, J., & Wandersman, L. P. (1978, August). *Development and utility of the Parenting Sense of Competence Scale.* Paper presented at the meeting of the American Psychological Association, Toronto.

Hawkins, A. J., & Eggebeen, D. J. (1991). Are fathers fungible? Patterns of co-resident adult men in maritally disrupted families and young children's well-being. *Journal of Marriage and the Family, 53,* 958–972.

Hernandez, D. J. (1993). *America's children: Resources from family, government, and the economy.* New York: Russell Sage Foundation.

Hetherington, E. M., & Henderson, S. H. (1997). The effects of divorce on fathers and their children. In M. E. Lamb (Ed.), *The role of the father in child development* (pp. 191–211). New York: Wiley.

Johnson, C., & Mash, E. J. (1989). A measure of parenting satisfaction and efficacy. *Journal of Clinical Child Psychology, 18,* 167–175.

Lamb, M. E. (1987). *The father's role: Cross cultural perspectives.* Hillsdale, NJ: Erlbaum.

Lamb, M. E. (1997). Fathers and child development: An introductory overview and guide. In M. E. Lamb (Ed.), *The role of the father in child development* (pp. 1–18). New York: Wiley.

Lamb, M. E., Pleck, J. H., Charnov, E. L., & Levine, J. A. (1987). A biosocial perspective on paternal behavior and involvement. In J. B. Lancaster, J. Altman, A. S. Rossi, & L. R. Sherrod (Eds.), *Parenting across the lifespan: Biosocial dimensions* (pp. 111–142). New York: Aldine de Gruyter.

Marsiglio, W. (1993). Adolescent males' orientation toward paternity and conception. *Family planning perspectives, 25,* 22–31.

Mason, C. A., Cauce, A. M., Gonzales, N., & Hiraga, Y. (1994). Adolescent problem behavior: The effect of peers and moderating role of father absence and mother-child relationship. *American Journal of Community Psychology, 22,* 723–743.

McAdoo, J. L. (1986). A black perspective on the father's role [in] child development. *Marriage and Family Review, 9,* 117–133.

McLanahan, S., & Sandefur, G. (1994). *Growing up with a single parent.* Cambridge, MA: Harvard University Press.

McLoyd, V. C., & Wilson, L. (1991). The strain of living poor: Parenting, social support, and child mental health. In A. C. Huston (Ed.), *Children in poverty* (pp. 105–135). Cambridge, UK: Cambridge University Press.

Mott, F. L. (1990). When is a father really gone? Paternal-child contact in father-absent homes. *Demography, 27,* 499–517.

Mott, F. L. (1993). Sons, daughters and fathers' absence: Differentials in father-leaving probabilities and in home environments. *Journal of Family Issues, 5,* 97–128.

National Commission on Children (1991). *Beyond rhetoric: A new American agenda for children and families.* Washington, DC: U.S. Government Printing Office.

Parke, R. D. (1996). *Fatherhood.* Cambridge, MA: Harvard University Press.

Parke, R. D., MacDonald, K. B., Burks, V. M., Bharnagri, N., Barth, J. M., & Beitel, A. (1989). Family and peer systems: In search of linkages. In N. Kreppner & R. M. Lerner (Eds.), *Family systems and life-span development* (pp. 65–92). Hillsdale, NJ: Erlbaum.

Pedersen, F. A., Rubenstein, J. L., & Yarrow, L. J. (1979). Infant development in father-absent families. *Journal of Genetic Psychology, 135,* 51–61.

Pleck, J. H. (1997). Paternal involvement: Levels, sources and consequences. In M. E. Lamb (Ed.), *The role of the father in child development* (pp. 66–103). New York: Wiley.

Pratt, M. W., Kerig, P., Cowan, P. A., & Cowan, C. P. (1988). Mothers and fathers teaching 3-year-olds: Authoritative parenting and adult scaffolding of children's learning. *Developmental Psychology, 24,* 832–839.

Radin, N. (1972). Father-child interaction and intellectual functioning of 4-year-old boys. *Developmental Psychology, 8,* 369–376.

Radin, N. (1981). The role of the father in cognitive, academic, and intellectual development. In M. E. Lamb (Ed.), *The role of the father in child development* (2nd ed., pp. 379–428). New York: Wiley.

Thorndike, R. L., Hagen, E. P., & Sattler, J. M. (1986). *The Stanford-Binet, 4th edition.* Chicago: Riverside.

Tolson, T. F., J., & Wilson, M. N. (1990). The impact of two- and three-generational black family structure on perceived family climate. *Child Development, 61,* 416–428.

Whitehurst, G. J. (1984). Interrater agreement for journal manuscript reviews. *American Psychologist, 39,* 22–28.

Woodworth, S., Belsky, J., & Crnic, K. (1996). The determinants of fathering during the child's second and third years of life: A developmental analysis. *Journal of Marriage and the Family, 58,* 679–692.

Yogman, M. W. (1987). Father-infant caregiving and play with preterm and full-term infants. In P. W. Berman & F. A. Pederson (Eds.), *Men's transitions to parenthood* (pp. 175–195). Hillsdale, NJ: Erlbaum.

Yogman, M. W., Kindlon, D., & Earls, F. (1995). Father involvement and cognitive/behavioral outcomes of preterm infants. *Journal of the American Academy of Child and Adolescent Psychiatry, 34,* 58–66.

Zill, N., Moore, K. A., Wolpow Smith, E., Stief, T., & Coiro, M. J. (1995). The life circumstances and development of children in welfare families: A profile based on national survey data. In P. L. Chase-Lansdale & J. Brooks-Gunn (Eds.), *Escape from poverty: What makes a difference for children?* (pp. 38–62). Cambridge, UK: Cambridge University Press.

Cultural Differences in Korean- and Anglo-American Preschoolers' Social Interaction and Play Behaviors*

Jo Ann M. Farver, Yonnie Kwak Kim, and Yoolim Lee

Although cross-cultural studies on children's social interaction and play behavior have recently increased, our theories continue to be based on studies of white, middle-class children who are raised in Western industrialized societies. Therefore, in attempting to generalize about what is typical of child behavior, researchers have frequently misinterpreted the cultural and ethnic differences observed in children's play as signs of deficiency rather than variation (Johnson, Christie, & Yawkey, 1987). Moreover, because of a focus on West-

*From Farver et al. (1995). *Child Development, 66,* 1088–1099. Reprinted with permission.

ern children Korean-American children have been particularly neglected by psychological research (Kitano, 1982). According to a 1990 U.S. census, the Korean-American population increased 124% from 357,000 to 798,849 in the past decade. Despite the fact that Korean-Americans are a rapidly growing and economically successful minority within the United States, very little is known about them.

Play is the predominant social activity of early childhood and has been related to young children's early cognitive growth, social development, and preparation for later formal schooling. Positive relations have been found between play and language acquisition and literacy, problem solving and creativity, friendliness, popularity, and social competence with peers, cooperative behavior, and perspective-taking skills (see Rubin, Fein, & Vandenberg, 1983, for a review of this literature).

While psychological research has been influential in fostering positive attitudes toward children's play and in developing preschool curriculums that provide American children with opportunities for daily play activity (Curry & Arnaud, 1984), there is considerable variation in children's social play in other cultures (Roopnarine, Johnson, & Hooper, 1994) and among minority populations in the United States (Johnson et al., 1987). In accounting for these variations, cultural-context models of child development stress the role of specific cultural practices in shaping and organizing the environment in which children's social interaction and play activities take place (Roopnarine et al., 1994).

Factors that have been shown to influence children's play behavior are time and space to play (Curry & Arnaud, 1984), access to objects and materials (Gottfried & Brown, 1986), adult behavior and attitudes (Curry & Arnaud, 1984), and the availability of play partners (Garvey, 1990; Rubin et al., 1983).

These contextual factors are interrelated and are influenced by culture. Children's social environments are structured by adult beliefs about play as well as the arrangements for play they think are necessary or desirable (Rubin et al., 1983). For example, research with American, Mexican, and Indonesian toddlers has shown that mothers who valued play for its educational and cognitive benefits were more likely to join their children's play activity and to provide props and suggestions that encouraged the expression of pretend play than mothers who viewed children's play as amusement or imitation of adult models (Farver & Howes, 1993; Farver & Wimbarti, 1995a). A comparable pattern has also been found for American father-toddler play. Fathers who believed play to be educational engaged their children in reading books, doing puzzles, and building with manipulatives. In contrast, fathers who believed that play is children's amusement, engaged in rough and tumble play in the home (Farver & Wimbarti, 1995b). Therefore, in settings where adults attribute little importance to play, they are unlikely to provide time, space, and play materials or to engage in children's play activity. When cultures emphasize different factors, children's play behavior can be expected to vary accordingly.

. . .

Consistent with their scripts for adult-child interaction and developmental goals, values, and beliefs, the Anglo-American teachers provided an environment that was conducive to independent thinking, problem solving, and active involvement in learning. Children had many opportunities for social interaction and play, and children were often involved in collaborative activities with teachers. Moreover, mothers' beliefs about the educational benefits of play for children were congruent with the play-oriented curriculum in the preschool settings.

In the Korean-American preschool, teachers organized their classrooms and lessons to encourage the development of academic skills, task perseverance, and passive involvement in learning. Children's social interaction and play were limited to periods of outdoor activity. Teachers and children rarely initiated or participated in collaborative play. Although the Korean-American teachers were born in the United States and were trained in American colleges, their teaching styles and academically oriented curriculum were reflective of the parents' (and possibly their own) traditional Korean values, expectations, and educational goals for children. Thus, the Korean-American teachers were acting more like Korean than American or Korean-American teachers.

The environmental differences in the two preschool settings may partially explain the differences found in children's social behaviors, pretend play, social competence, and cognitive functioning. The findings that Korean-American children were often unoccupied and engaged in more parallel and less pretend play than the Anglo-American children may be related to the way the Korean-American teachers arranged their preschool classrooms. During the observations it was noted that the Korean-American setting had few, if any materials available for pretend play. Research has shown that art and construction materials, blocks, and puzzles tend to be associated with nonsocial solitary and parallel play (Rubin, 1977), whereas open-ended relatively unstructured toys and objects such as dress-up clothes, dolls, cars, and trucks are associated with pretend play.

Moreover, the highly structured daily schedule in the Korean-American preschool, which centered primarily on academic-related activities, provided few opportunities for children to interact socially with peers. In contrast, the Anglo-American children had a wide variety of play materials and self-select activity centers which provided more opportunities for social interaction and play.

The low frequency of pretend play in the Korean-American setting may also be related to the collectivist orientation characteristic of Korean culture. Because pretend play requires children to abandon self-consciousness and to express their inner creativity, Korean values which deemphasize individuality and self-expression may have influenced children's expression of pretend in social play.

The findings that Korean-American children offered objects to initiate play and were more cooperative with peers than Anglo-American children may also be a reflection of the Korean culture's emphasis on group harmony and cooperation.

The finding that Korean-American children did not display shared positive affect as predicted seems to contradict the notion that positive affect is important in maintaining group harmony. However, in the Korean-American setting neutral affect may have been the more culturally appropriate way for children to express emotion in social contexts. In Korean culture, it is considered a virtue to hide one's feelings instead of outwardly displaying emotion (Chu, 1978). Therefore, the predominance of neutral affect may have been an influence of cultural values rather than an indication of uncooperative social behavior.

The finding that Anglo-American children were more aggressive and negative in their responses to peer initiations suggests that the American culture fosters more competitive relationships between children and tolerates a higher level of aggressive behavior than the Korean culture. . . .

The differences found in adult attitudes about play suggest that, although parents in both cultures have educational goals for their young children, their views about how to achieve them are different. Anglo-American children, whose mothers believed that play is important for children's learning and development, engaged in more pretend play in the home than Korean-American children, whose mothers considered play to be a way to escape boredom or to amuse children. These results are consistent with studies that have shown a relation between parental beliefs about play and the frequency with which it occurs (Farver & Howes, 1993; Farver & Wimbarti, 1995a, 1995b; Haight, 1991).

. . . We suggest here that the Korean-American children's cognitive functioning may be higher than the Anglo-American children due to the early emphasis in the Korean-American preschool on "school-like" tasks, the direct teaching of vocabulary words, and high parental expectations for academic achievement. The Anglo-American children's higher social functioning seems to be related to the frequent opportunities to learn social skills by interacting and playing with peers that were provided in their preschool programs.

However, in interpreting these results, it should be noted that the teachers' ratings of social competence was based on the teachers' perceptions. Therefore, this measure may be reflecting cultural differences in what teachers value in terms of social interaction, rather than children's actual social competence. . . .

While the children attended physically similar preschools in terms of the adult-child ratios, the group size, number and length of outdoor free play periods, and the differences in adult socialization practices were apparent. The preschool settings in both contexts were shaped by what adults believe children need to become productive and successful members of their society.

Therefore, consistent with other studies examining the influence of preschool environments on children's early socialization (Stevenson, 1991; Tobin et al., 1989), it is argued here that the differences observed in children's social interaction and play behavior are variations in socialization practices that serve adaptive functions. The Korean and Anglo-American teachers shaped the preschool settings by emphasizing culturally valued skills and by using culturally appropriate methods that led to different developmental outcomes for children.

Although this study is far from conclusive, its findings suggest that culture is an important influence on children's social behavior and their expression of pretend play. . . .

REFERENCES

Asher, S., Singleton, L., Tinsley, B., & Hymel, S. (1979). A reliable sociometric measure of preschool children. *Developmental Psychology, 15,* 443–444.

Ch'a, C. (1983). A prolegomenon to the revitalization of national character: A psychological approach. In *The ethical conceptions of the Korean people.* Seoul: Academy of Korean Studies.

Choy, B. (1979). *Koreans in America.* Chicago: Nelson-Hall.

Chu, H. (1978). The Korean learner in an American school. In *Teaching for cross-cultural understanding.* Arlington, VA: Arlington Public Schools.

Cuellar, I., Harris, L. C., & Jasso, R. (1980). An acculturation scale for normal Mexican-American and clinical populations. *Hispanic Journal of Behavioral Sciences, 20,* 199–217.

Curry, N. E., & Arnaud, S. (1984). Play in developmental settings. In T. Yawkey & A. Pellegrini (Eds.), *Child's play: Developmental and applied.* Hillsdale, NJ: Erlbaum.

Farver, J., & Howes, C. (1993). Cultural differences in American and Mexican mother-child pretend play. *Merrill-Palmer Quarterly, 39,* 344–358.

Farver, J., & Wimbarti, S. (1995a). Indonesian toddlers' social play with their mothers and older siblings. *Child Development, 66.*

Farver, J., & Wimbarti, S. (1995b). Paternal participation in toddlers' pretend play. *Social Development, 4,* 19–31.

Garvey, C. (1990). *Play.* Cambridge, MA: Harvard University Press.

Gottfried, A. E., & Brown, C. C. (1986). *Play interactions: The contribution of play materials and parental involvement to children's development.* Lexington, MA: Heath.

Haight, W. (1991, April). *Belief systems that frame and inform middle-class parents' participation in their young children's pretend play.* Symposium paper presented at the Society for Research in Child Development, Seattle.

Harkness, S., & Super, C. (1986). The cultural structuring of children's play in a rural African community. In K. Blanchard (Ed.), *The many faces of play.* Champaign, IL: Human Kinetics Publishing.

Hendrick, J. (1994). *Total learning: Developmental curriculum for the young child.* New York: Maxwell/Macmillan.

Hoffman, L. (1988). Cross-cultural differences in childrearing goals. In R. Levine, P. Miller, & M. Maxwell (Eds.), *Parenting behaviors in diverse societies: New directions for child development.* San Francisco: Freeman.

Hong, L. (1982). The Korean family in Los Angeles. In E. Yu, E. Phillips, & E. Yang (Eds.), *Koreans in Los Angeles.* Los Angeles: Koryo Research Institute.

Howe, R. W. (1988). *The Koreans.* New York: Harcourt, Brace & Jovanovich.

Howes, C. (1988). Peer interaction of young children. *Monographs for the Society of Research in Child Development,* 53(1, Serial No. 217).

Hymel, S. (1983). Preschool children's peer relations: Issues in sociometric assessment. *Merrill-Palmer Quarterly, 29,* 237–260.

Johnson, J. E., Christie, J. F., & Yawkey, T. D. (1987). *Play and early childhood development.* Glenview, IL: Scott, Foresman.

Kim, B. L. (1980a). *The future of Korean-American children and youth: Marginality, biculturality, and the role of the American public school.* (ERIC reproduction service, No. Ed 211 647)

Kim, B. L. (1980b). *The Korean child at school and at home: An analysis of interaction and intervention through groups* (Report for United States Department of Health, Education, and Welfare). Washington, DC: U.S. Government Printing Office.

Kim, J. U. (1991), *The Koreans: Their mind and behavior.* Seoul: Kyobo Centre Co.

Kitano, M. K. (1982). Early education for Asian American children. *Young Children, 35,* 13–26.

Levine, R. (1980). *Anthropology and child development: New directions for child development.* San Francisco: Jossey-Bass.

Roopnarine, J., Johnson, J., & Hooper, F. (1994). *Children's play in diverse cultures.* New York: State University of New York Press.

Rubin, K. H. (1977). The social and cognitive value of preschool toys and activities. *Canadian Journal of Behavioral Science, 9,* 382–385.

Rubin, K. H., Fein, G. G., & Vandenberg, B. (1983). Play. In E. M. Hetherington (Ed.), *Carmichael's manual of child psychology: Social development.* New York: Wiley.

Stevenson, H. (1984). American-Asian study: Reasons for academic difference. *Growing Child Research Review, 3,* 10–20.

Stevenson, H. (1991). The development of prosocial behavior in large scale societies: China and Japan. In R. Hinde (Ed.), *Cooperation and prosocial behavior* (pp. 89–105). Cambridge: Cambridge University Press.

Strom, R. (1981). *Growing through play: Readings for parents and teachers.* Monterey, CA: Brooks/Cole.

Strom, R., & Bernard, H. (1982). *Educational psychology.* Belmont, CA: Wadsworth.

Strom, R., Park, S. H., & Daniels, S. (1986). Adjustment of Korean immigrant families. *Educational and Psychological Research, 6,* 312–327.

Tobin, J., Wu, D., & Davidson, D. (1989). *Preschool in three cultures: Japan, China, and the United States.* New Haven, CT: Yale University Press.

Triandis, H. (1989). Cross-cultural studies of individualism and collectivism. *Nebraska symposium on motivation.* Lincoln: University of Nebraska Press.

Weisner, T., Gallimore, R., & Jordan, T. (1988). Unpackaging cultural effects on classroom learning: Hawaiian peer assistance and child generated activity. *Anthropology and Education Quarterly, 19,* 327–353.

Whiting, B., & Edwards, C. P. (1988). *Children of different worlds: The formation of social behavior.* Cambridge: MA: Harvard University Press.

Effects of Community Violence on Inner-City Preschoolers and Their Families*

Jo Ann M. Farver, Lucia X. Natera, and Dominick L. Frosch

Today, many young children are growing up in chronically violent inner-city neighborhoods. It is estimated that by age 5 most inner-city children have had firsthand encounters with shootings and gang activities in their communities (Bell & Jenkins, 1993). Despite the rise in neighborhood crime in American cities, there has been more research conducted on the effects of *televised* violence on young children than on the effects of *real* violence. Furthermore, apart from several studies on school-age children and adolescents (Attar, Guerra, & Tolan, 1994; Bell & Jenkins, 1993; Cooley-Quille, Turner, & Beidel, 1995a; Cooley, Turner, & Beidel, 1995b; Fitzpatrick, 1993; Fitzpatrick & Boldizar, 1993; Lorion & Saltzman, 1993; Osofsky, Wewers, Hann, & Flick, 1993; Richters & Martinez, 1993a; Schwab-Stone et al., 1995; Sharkoor & Chambers, 1991; Singer, Anglin, Song, & Lunghofer, 1995), at present we know little about the life experiences of very young children who are exposed to chronic violence. Accordingly, the current study was designed to examine the extent to which preschool children and their families are exposed to neighborhood violence and to explore the possible cognitive, social, and emotional impact of this exposure on young children.

. . .

Our results show that according to maternal reports, many of these inner-city families have been exposed to considerable violence in their communities. Although the prevalence rates reported by mothers may appear high, when the figures are compared with the crime statistics for this community, the numbers are not out of line. Moreover, the frequencies of neighborhood violence exposure and children's distress scores reported for the current study are similar to those revealed in current

*From Farver et al. (1999). *Journal of Applied Developmental Psychology, 20*(1), 143–158. Reprinted with permission.

research with older children and adolescents (Richters & Martinez, 1993a; Freeman et al., 1993; Osofsky et al., 1993; Pynoos, 1993; Taylor et al., 1994; Schwab-Stone et al., 1995) living in similar inner-city environments. This consistency across studies and populations lends support for our findings, and it provides evidence that very young children are also not "immune" to the effects of community violence. Because adults tend to deny that preschoolers are aware of what goes on around them and assume that young children do not understand or will forget what they have seen, they also assume that young children are unaffected by violence. The results reported here suggest that these "common sense" assumptions may be wrong.

Results . . . suggest a significant link between families' community violence exposure and a reduction in children's positive peer interaction and cognitive performance. These findings are supported by studies with older children and adolescents who have suffered from conduct disorders, peer-related aggression (Attar et al., 1994), varied distress symptoms (Marans & Adelman, 1997; Osofsky et al., 1993; Richters & Martinez, 1993a; Schwab-Stone et al., 1995), and social and emotional problems (Marans & Adelman, 1997; Pynoos, 1993; Pynoos & Eth, 1985) after exposure to acute and chronically violent circumstances. Moreover, in a recent study of violence exposure in young children, Scheeringa, Zeanah, Drell, and Larrieu (1995) reported that children under age 4 could evidence symptoms of PTSD [posttraumatic stress disorder].

Although we found a strong link between community violence exposure, children's distress, and their cognitive functioning, the partial mediation through distress found for positive peer interaction points to additional variables that were not measured in this study, which may be mediating the effects of community violence on positive peer interaction. Moreover, the effect of community violence on children's tendency to be hesitant socially with peers was comparatively weak, reflecting the lack of any direct relationship between the two variables. Thus, there may be alternative interpretations of these data. For example, it is quite possible that the methods parents use to protect their children from violence may be in effect contributing to their children's reduced social functioning with peers and diminished cognitive performance. During interviews with mothers the most common response to our question about how families cope with neighborhood violence was to keep children inside the house and to avoid going outdoors as much as possible. While these strategies may work in the short run, over time the necessity of keeping children at home may produce a conflict between children's needs for independence, autonomy, and social experiences with peers—and parents' worries about safety (Groves & Zuckerman, 1997).

. . . Exposure to community violence was not restricted to ethnicity per se, but seemed to be more a function of socioeconomic status. Taken together, these findings could help to dispel common stereotypes that minority - communities are domestically violent and are exposed to higher rates of neighborhood violence than nonminority communities.

. . .

REFERENCES

Asher, S. R., & Coie, J. D. (1990). *Peer rejection in childhood.* Cambridge, UK: Cambridge University Press.

Attar, B. K., Guerra, N. G., & Tolan, P. H. (1994). Neighborhood disadvantage, stressful life events, and adjustments in urban elementary school children. *Journal of Clinical and Child Psychology, 23,* 391–400.

Bandura, A. (1977). *Social learning theory.* Englewood Cliffs, NJ: Prentice Hall.

Bell, C., & Jenkins, E. (1991). Traumatic stress and children. *Journal of Health Care for the Poor and Underserved, 2,* 175–185.

Bell, C., & Jenkins, E. (1993). Community violence and children on Chicago's South Side. *Psychiatry, 56,* 46–53.

Bloch, D., Silber, E., & Perry, S. (1958). Some factors in the emotional reaction of children to disaster. *American Journal of Psychiatry, 133,* 416–422.

Cohen, J., & Cohen, P. (1983). *Applied multiple regression/correlation analysis for the behavioral sciences* (2nd ed.). Hillsdale, NJ: Erlbaum.

Cooley-Quile, M. R., Turner, S. M., & Beidel. D. C. (1995a) Emotional impact of children's exposure to community violence. *Journal of the American Academy of Child and Adolescent Psychiatry, 34,* 1362–1368.

Cooley, M. R., Turner, S. M., & Beidel, D. C. (1995b). Assessing community violence: The children's report of exposure to violence. *Journal of the American Academy of Child and Adolescent Psychiatry, 34,* 201–208.

Dodge, K. A., Bates, J. E., & Pettit, G. S. (1990). Mechanisms in the cycle of violence. *Science, 250,* 1678–1683.

Dodge, K. A., & Crick, N. R. (1990). Social information-processing of aggressive behavior in children. *Personality and Social Psychology Bulletin, 16,* 8–22.

Farver, J., & Frosch, D. (1996). L.A. stories: Aggression in preschoolers' spontaneous narratives after the riots of 1992. *Child Development, 67,* 29–42.

Fitzpatrick, K. M. (1993). Exposure to violence and the presence of depression among low-income African-American youth. *Journal of Consulting and Clinical Psychology, 61,* 528–531.

Fitzpatrick, K. M., & Boldizar, J. P. (1993). The prevalence and consequences of exposure to violence among African-American youth. *Journal of the American Academy of Child Psychiatry, 32,* 424–430.

Freeman, L., Mokros, H., & Pozanski, E. (1993). Violent events reported by normal urban school-aged children: Characteristics and depression correlates. *Journal of the American Academy of Child and Adolescent Psychiatry, 32,* 419–423.

Galante, R., & Foa, D. (1986). An epidemiological study of psychic trauma and treatment effectiveness for children after a natural disaster. *Journal of the American Academy of Child and Adolescent Psychiatry, 25,* 357–363.

Garbarino, J., Dubrow, N., Kostelny, K., & Pardo, C. (1992). *Children in danger: Coping with the consequences of community violence.* San Francisco: Jossey-Bass.

Garbarino, J., Kostelny, K., & Dubrow, N. (1991). *No place to be a child: Growing up in a war zone.* New York: Lexington Books.

Gardner, G. (1971). Aggression and violence—the enemies of precision learning in children. *American Journal of Psychiatry, 128,* 445–450.

Groves, B., & Zuckerman, B. (1997). Interventions with parents and caregivers of children who are exposed to violence. In J. D. Osofsky (Ed.), *Children in a violent society.* New York: Guilford Press.

Hollingshead, A. B. (1975). *The four-factor index of social class.* Unpublished manuscript, Yale University, New Haven, CT.

Howes, C. (1988). Peer interaction of young children. *Monographs for the Society of Research in Child Development, 53* (1, Serial No. 217).

Jenkins, E. J., & Bell, C. C. (1997). Exposure and response to community violence among children and adolescents. In J. D. Osofsky (Ed.), *Children in a violent society.* New York: Guilford Press.

Lorion, R., & Saltzman, W. (1993). Children's exposure to community violence: Following a path from concern to research action. *Psychiatry, 56,* 55–65.

Marans, S., & Adelman, A. (1997). Experiencing violence in a developmental context. In J. D. Osofsky (Ed.), *Children in a violent society.* New York: Guilford Press.

McFarlane, A. (1988). Recent life events and psychiatric disorder in children: The interaction with preceding extreme adversity. *Journal of Child Psychology and Psychiatry, 29,* 677–690.

McWhirter, L. (1982). Yoked by violence together: Stress and coping in children in Northern Ireland. *Community Care, 4,* 14–17.

McWhirter, L. (1983). Growing up in Northern Ireland: From aggression to the troubles. In A. P. Goldstein & M. H. Segall (Eds.), *Aggression in global perspective.* New York: Pergamon Press.

Newman, J. (1976). Children of disaster: Clinical observations at Buffalo Creek. *American Journal of Psychiatry, 133,* 306–312.

Osofsky, J., Wewers, S., Hann, D., & Flick, A. (1993). Chronic community violence: What is happening to our children? *Psychiatry, 58,* 36–45.

Parke, R., & Slaby, R. (1983). The development of aggression. In E. M. Hetherington (Ed.), *Handbook of child psychology: Vol. 4: Socialization, personality, and social development.* New York: Wiley.

Peterson, C., Luborsky, L., & Seligman, L. (1983). Attributions and depressive mood shifts: A case study using symptom-context method. *Journal of Abnormal Psychology, 92,* 96–103.

Pynoos, R. S. (1993). Traumatic stress and developmental psychopathology in children and adolescents. In J. M. Oldman, M. B. Biba, & A. Tasman (Eds.), *Review of psychiatry.* Washington, DC: American Psychiatric Press.

Pynoos, R., & Eth, S. (1985). Developmental perspective on psychic trauma in childhood. In C. R. Figley (Ed.), *Trauma and its wake.* New York: Brunner/Mazel.

Pynoos, R., & Nader, K. (1988). Case study: Children's memory and proximity to violence. *Journal of the American Academy of Child and Adolescent Psychiatry, 28,* 236–241.

Richters, J. E. (1990). *Survey of children's distress symptoms–Parent report.* Child and Adolescent Disorders Research, NIMH, Bethesda, MD.

Richters, J. E., & Martinez, P. (1993a). The NIMH community violence project: I. Children as victims and witnesses to violence. *Psychiatry 56,* 7–21.

Richters, J. E., & Martinez, P. (1993b). Violent communities, family choices, and children's chances: An algorithm for improving the odds. *Development and Psychopathology, 5,* 609–627.

Richters, J. E., & Saltzman, W. (1990). *Survey of exposure to community violence–parent report version.* Child and Adolescent Disorders Research, NIMH, Bethesda, MD.

Rosenblatt, R. (1983). *Children of war.* New York: Doubleday.

Sattler, J. M. (1979). Racial "experimenter effects" in experimentation, testing, interviewing, and psychotherapy. *Psychological Bulletin, 73,* 137–160.

Saylor, C., Swenson, C., & Powell, P. (1992). Hurricane Hugo blows down the broccoli: Preschoolers' post-disaster play and adjustment. *Child Psychiatry and Human Development, 22,* 139–149.

Scheeringa, M. S., Zeanah, C. H., Drell, M. J., & Larrieu, J. A. (1995). Two approaches to the diagnosis of posttraumatic stress disorder in infancy and early childhood. *Journal of the American Academy of Child and Adolescent Psychiatry, 34,* 191–200.

Schwab-Stone, M. E., Ayers, T. S., Kasprow, W., Voyce, C., Barone, C., Shriver, T., & Weissberg, R. P. (1995). No safe haven: A study of violence exposure in an urban community. *Journal of the American Academy of Child and Adolescent Psychiatry, 34,* 1343–1352.

Shakoor, B. H., & Chambers, D. (1991). Co-victimization of African-American children who witness violence and the theoretical implications of its effects on their cognitive, emotional, and behavioral development. *Journal of the American Medical Association, 83,* 233–238.

Singer, M. I., Anglin, T. M., Song, L. Y., & Lunghofer, L. (1995). Adolescents' exposure to violence and associated symptoms of psychological trauma. *Journal of the American Medical Association, 273,* 477–482.

Straus, M. (1979). Measuring intrafamily conflict and violence: The conflict tactics scales (CT). *Journal of Marriage and the Family, 41,* 75–88.

Taylor, L., Zuckerman, B., Harik, V., & Groves, B. (1994). Witnessing violence by young children and their mothers. *Developmental and Behavioral Pediatrics, 15,* 120–123.

Terr, L. (1985). Chowchilla revisited: The effects of psychic trauma four years after a schoolbus kidnapping. *American Journal of Psychiatry, 140,* 1543–1550.

Terr, L. (1990). *Too scared to cry.* New York: HarperCollins.

Wallach, L. B. (1994). Violence and children's development. Urbana, IL: University of Illinois Press.

Wechsler, D. (1989). *Wechsler preschool and primary scale of intelligence—revised.* San Antonio, TX: The Psychological Corporation.

REVIEW QUESTIONS AND ACTIVITIES

1. Discuss the ways language development and socioeconomic status are linked.
2. Identify some ways that an increased understanding of issues related to the physical development of preschoolers might assist parents in providing care to these children.
3. You have been asked to lobby your member of Congress from the House and your senators about the lack of a coordinated national policy on preschool education. What research would you share with your representatives? List some ways you will address how the status of preschoolers can be elevated in the United States.
4. What would be the advantages to a preschooler (and to an older child) if you were to become her or his "big sister" or "big brother" mentor? Identify the positive characteristics you would bring to the development of a preschooler in particular. Consider contacting your local Big Brothers and Big Sisters organization. Occasionally, there is a group you can join on your campus.
5. Write a letter to the local chief of police about your concerns that preschoolers may be witnessing violence in their neighborhoods. Ask for ways you can work toward helping these children. You may also want to contact your local domestic violence shelter (affiliated with the YWCA, for example) or other child service agencies for volunteer work.
6. Browse through a toy store or toy section in a department store. How are the toys arranged? By age of child? According to the sex of the child? What toys would be appropriate for preschoolers' play?
7. Critically reread one of the excerpted articles in this chapter, and then answer the following questions:
   a. Is the purpose of the research clear? Explain.
   b. Are studies contrary to the current hypothesis cited?
   c. Is the research hypothesis correctly derived from the literature and theory that has been cited? Or are there some important steps missing and left to the speculation of the reader?
   d. Were the conclusions drawn by the author consistent with the results obtained?
   e. What follow-up studies do you think are needed? Why these studies? Describe the methodology you would use in these follow-up studies.

SUGGESTIONS FOR FURTHER READING

Harris, S., & Handleman, J. (1994). *Preschool education programs for children with autism.* Austin, TX: Pro-Ed.

Lamb, M. (1987). *The father's role: Cross-cultural perspectives.* Hillsdale, NJ: Erlbaum.

Lee, V., Brooks-Gunn, J., Schnur, E., & Liaw, F.-R. (1990). Are Head Start effects sustained? A longitudinal follow-up comparison of disadvantaged children attending Head Start, no preschool, and other preschool programs. *Child Development, 61,* 495–507.

Nicoladis, E., Mayberry, R., & Genesee, F. (1999). Gesture and early bilingual development. *Developmental Psychology, 35*(2), 514–526.

Wallach, L. B. (1994). *Violence and children's development.* Urbana, IL: University of Illinois Press.

Listen or thy tongue will keep thee deaf.

Native American Proverb

A teacher is better than two books.

German Proverb

If you are planning for a year, sow rice; if you are planning for a decade, plant trees; if you are planning for a lifetime, educate people.

Chinese Proverb

Middle Childhood

Questions for Reflection

- During middle childhood, what did you learn from interacting with peers who were from different cultural backgrounds than you? How have you integrated these values into your own personality?
- What cognitive, physical, and social changes do you think characterize the middle childhood life stage?
- Do you believe divorce has only negative effects on children? Why or why not?
- In what ways did your views of yourself change during middle childhood?
- What sorts of relationships and friendships did you have during middle childhood?
- What kinds of classroom atmospheres do you think promote school success for racial and ethnic minority students?

OVERVIEW: CULTURAL INFLUENCES ON DEVELOPMENT IN MIDDLE CHILDHOOD

We saw in the last section that the preschool years are characterized by swift growth. Gross motor and fine motor skills development advances rapidly during the preschool years. Furthermore, during this life stage, the development of the self-concept becomes paramount. Preschool relationships begin to encompass genuine friendships; they develop from children's appreciation of other children whom they enjoy and in whom they can place their trust.

As in the preschool years, adolescence—the subject of the next chapter—is marked by a remarkable growth spurt and significant changes in cognitive development, especially the ability to think abstractly and hypothetically (Mueller, 1999; Rice, 1997). As we will see, the physical and cognitive changes in adolescence have psychological effects, including an increase in self-esteem and self-awareness (Adams, Montemayor, & Gullotta, 1996).

Between these two life stages is *middle childhood,* the life stage that encompasses ages 6 to 11. This stage is also referred to as the *school-age period* since advances are made in children's reading, writing, and mathematical skills. While the preschool years and adolescence are marked by rapid growth, middle childhood is characterized by its relative tranquility (Rice, 1997). Of course, development takes place during this stage, but it does so at a slower and steadier pace, as compared to the preschool years and adolescence.

The selections in the readings section deal with commonly discussed issues of the middle childhood stage of the life cycle: namely, phonetic awareness, afterschool care, adjustment within the family, children's social networks, and achievement striving and performance in school. The literature shows the continuity in development for many of the areas discussed in the previous two chapters: language development, peer relationships, and parent-child relationships. The interdependence among the dimensions of development throughout middle childhood will also be evident, in this overview and in the readings. We begin with a review of the physical changes in middle childhood.

PHYSICAL DEVELOPMENT IN MIDDLE CHILDHOOD

In the United States, elementary school children grow in height approximately 2 to 3 inches per year. By age 11, the average girl is 4 feet 10 inches tall and the average boy is 4 feet 9.5 inches tall. This is the only time during the life cycle when girls are, on average, taller than boys (Feldman, 1998). As we will see in the chapter on adolescence, this sex difference in height reflects the slightly more rapid physical development of girls, who typically begin their growth spurt at 10 years. Further, as discussed earlier, infant girls are more mature at birth than are infant boys: Infant girls have more advanced skeletal and neurological systems (Rice, 1997).

The pattern for weight gain during middle childhood is similar to that experienced for height (Feldman, 1998). Girls and boys gain approximately 5 to 7 pounds per year, and weight becomes redistributed. "Baby fat" generally disappears, and children's bodies become more muscular. Their strength increases as well. Girls continue to mature between 2 and 2.5 years faster than boys. While, as a group, boys are physically stronger and weigh more than girls after puberty, there is considerable overlap: Many girls are physically stronger and weigh more than the average boy (Feldman, 1998).

These average gains in height and weight are not universal. Girls and boys in other parts of the world do not follow this pattern for height and weight growth during middle childhood. Inadequate nutrition and disease contribute to this differential; these children are relatively shorter and weigh less than they would if they had better nutrition and less illness. Even children who live in poorer parts of cities such as Hong Kong and Calcutta are shorter and weigh less than their peers in more affluent areas of the same cities (Barrett & Frank, 1987).

In addition to differences in nutrition, variations in height and weight during middle childhood can be attributed to genetic factors relating to race and ethnicity. On average, children from Asian heritages tend to be shorter than children from northern and central European backgrounds. Note, however, that even within one race or ethnicity, there is significant variation as a consequence of differences in dietary customs and in affluence (Rice, 1997; Story et al., 2000).

Considerable research indicates that the level of nutrition children receive affects several areas of their functioning, including social and emotional development (Story et al., 2000). For example, Barrett and Frank (1987) found that Guatemalan children who received more nutrients were more self-confident, more alert in their activities at school, and more involved with their peers, and they experienced less anxiety, had more moderate activity levels, and exhibited more positive emotion than children who received less adequate nutrition.

It is also now recognized that the intake of too many calories—*overnutrition*—can also lead to cognitive, physical, and social difficulties (Brown & Pollitt, 1996; McDonald, Sigman, Espinosa, & Neumann, 1994). Since the 1960s, obesity among children in middle childhood has risen by 54 percent. Several factors contribute to obesity in middle childhood: Particular inherited genes are related to obesity and may predispose certain children to be overweight. Social characteristics also play a part, including lack of exercise (Gortmaker et al., 1996). Research has documented a general trend that during middle childhood, girls and boys engage in relatively little exercise and are not particularly fit. Results from school fitness surveys suggest that American children have shown little improvement in the amount of exercise they get, even with national efforts to increase the fitness level of girls and boys in middle childhood (Epstein, 1992; Ungrady, 1992).

One explanation for this failure to be more physically fit during middle childhood is suggested by a positive correlation between television viewing and obesity (Dietz, 1987). The more television children watch, the more likely they are to be overweight. Television viewing is a relatively passive activity; it also replaces social activity with friends that would involve some physical exercise. Moreover, while watching television, children frequently snack, thus increasing their caloric intake beyond their nutritional needs (Gortmaker et al., 1996).

In middle childhood, boys are overrepresented among children who have speech, behavior, and learning disorders (Feingold, 1993). Approximately twice as many boys as girls exhibit articulatory errors; 3 times as many boys as girls stutter. In addition, the incidence of reading problems is almost 5 times more prevalent in boys than in girls (Feingold, 1993). Mental retardation is higher among boys than girls. Further, more boys than girls are autistic and hyperactive (Chen & Siegler, 2000).

In middle childhood, girls and boys also master skills that they previously could not perform well—for example, riding a bicycle, ice-skating, swimming, and jumping rope (Rice, 1997). Fine motor skills also develop during this life stage; children's fine motor skills reach adult levels by the end of middle childhood, which is largely attributable to increases in the level of myelin in their brains (Rice, 1997). Several research studies have documented a sex difference in performance of motor tasks, and that advantage is for boys (Maccoby & Jacklin, 1974). This assignment of advantage contradicts the fact that girls have more accelerated physical development. It is illogical that biological acceleration may be given as an explanation of girls' rapid acquisition of language skills since their ability to excel in fine motor activity remains. Bem (1981) concluded that differences in motor performance appear to be influenced by both biological and environmental factors. The low expectations that parents and teachers have with respect to girls' motor performance, in addition to the lack of rewards given to girls for such activities, apparently combine to produce low motivation and low performance levels for girls in the behaviors that have been societally defined as appropriate for boys (Hyde, Fennema, Ryan, Frost, & Hopp, 1990).

Because of their more developed fine and gross motor skills, children are increasingly independent in this life stage. Consequently, they are increasingly likely to have accidents on such equipment as bicycles, skateboards, and roller-blades and during participation in sports. Of course, with proper gear (e.g., helmets), accidents are greatly reduced (Feldman, 1998).

COGNITIVE DEVELOPMENT

Focus on Academic Achievement and Adjustment

Cognitive development during middle childhood reaches the concrete operational stage (Piaget & Inhelder, 1958). This cognitive stage is characterized by the application of logical processes to concrete problems and by *decentering*, the ability to take multiple aspects of a situation into account. Children of this age range still experience a critical limitation in their thinking, however. They remain tied to a concrete, physical reality; they are unable to think hypothetically or abstractly (Mueller, 1999). This delimited level of cognitive maturity can be detrimental in some situations—for example, children can blame themselves for their parents' arguments and divorce, as we will subsequently discuss. We begin with a discussion of children's academic achievement during this period.

For the next few moments, think back to your classroom environment during your middle childhood. How were the seats arranged? In rows? In a circle? Did the classroom environment make it conducive to work cooperatively with your peers? Or did your teachers foster competition in the classroom? How did you feel when you were asked questions by teachers in front of your peers? Embarrassed? Confused? Were you in multiracial classrooms? Did you notice any similarities between you and peers of other races in your classes? Any differences?

The learning environments most United States children in middle childhood experience are not conducive to the value systems of many non–United States cultures (Slavin, 1997). For example, in a traditional U.S. classroom, school achievement is an individual endeavor; it is solitary (Feldman, 1998; Slavin, 1997). Students earn stickers, "smiley faces," praise, and high marks when they perform at a high level regardless of how their peers are performing. School achievement can also be competitive. Students are rank-ordered; an individual's performance is compared with the performance of peers (Rice, 1997; Slavin, 1997). Teachers commonly identify the best drawings in the class; others grade on a curve; still others rearrange the children's seats after each test, from highest scoring student to lowest scoring student.

However, individual pursuit and achievement through competition are not values accepted in all cultures (Landrine, 1995). For many children (and adults), group achievement is stressed over individual achievement. Native American, Southeast Asian, Mexican American, and Pacific Islander children are socialized to work cooperatively, not competitively. Their success is for the benefit of their community, not for themselves (Landrine, 1995). Thus students may not want to compete against their classmates and are confused when punished by the teacher for helping a peer. They may be labeled a "cheater," yet they perceive themselves as a good person, acting as they ought (Slavin, 1997).

In addition, in the traditional U.S. classroom, students are asked questions aloud. They may be asked to go to the chalkboard to solve arithmetic problems. While many of us learned in elementary school classrooms in this manner, this technique is not practiced in many cultures (Slavin, 1997). For example, children raised in the Yup'ik culture of Alaska learn by close observation of adults; they are not encouraged to ask questions when they do not understand. Children of Puerto Rican and Native American heritages have been taught that responding to adults' questions directly is rude and a sign of disrespect (Slavin, 1997). Children from Native American heritages also are accustomed to practicing skills privately first, before performing them in front of a classroom (LaFromboise, Choney, James, & Running Wolf, 1995). Children may become embarrassed and uncomfortable if they are asked to stand in front of their peers to demonstrate a skill that they have not fully mastered (Slavin, 1997).

Consider the following additional example of cultural distinctiveness in the classroom: You are in a class and have been asked a question by your teacher. How long does your teacher wait for your response? This pause or latency is referred to as *wait time.* When students are from non-English-speaking homes, they need longer than a second to respond to a question. They may have to translate the question back into their first language, answer in their first language to themselves, and then respond aloud in English. Moreover, a delayed response may indicate the student is respectful. In some cultures, such as the Northern Cheyenne, responding quickly to a question is a sign of disrespect; it shows that the question is not worth thinking about (Slavin, 1997).

Do you remember what kinds of questions your elementary school teachers commonly asked you? You may remember being asked about the color of an object, to identify an object, or to state your name. How did your teachers pose these questions to you? Very often, teachers ask questions in the following way: "What color is this crayon?" "What's this a picture of?" Yet, in many cultures other than the United States, children are not asked questions in this way. Parents and teachers in some cultures rarely ask children questions they themselves know the answer to; instead of asking a child "What's this?" a parent or teacher may ask the child "What is this like?" (Slavin, 1997). Furthermore, many children are taught not to answer questions that are personal or that deal with their home life, such as "What is your name?" and "Where do you live?" These children may remain silent when asked a question in this manner. While teachers may interpret this kind of response as a sign of being unprepared, antagonistic, bored, or unintelligent, the children are behaving according to their culture's expectations of them (Slavin, 1997). Thus there may exist a cultural "mismatch" between the family and the school cultures.

In the excerpt of their article, "Gender Effects in Children's Beliefs about School Performance: A Cross-Cultural Study," which follows in the readings section (see pp. 107–111), Anna Stetsenko, Todd D. Little, Tamara Gordeeva, Matthias Grasshof, and Gabriele Oettingen report on children's understanding of what behaviors contribute to their academic success. Children from seven cultural settings participated in their research: East Berlin, West Berlin, Moscow, Tokyo, Berne, Los Angeles, and Prague. Stetsenko et al. also investigated whether children's beliefs about their achievement were gendered. They report that both girls and boys from all cultural settings investigated held perceptions of their achievement potential that were similar when their academic performance was equal. Stetsenko et al. also report that boys and girls were realistic in their self-assessments about achievement potential; they take responsibility for their success, attributing it to effort and ability. As Stetsenko and her colleagues point out:

> Boys and girls appear to receive similar messages about what it takes to do well at school and these communicated contingencies are similar across the contexts we studied. (p. 524; in this text, p. 109)

Stetsenko et al. also report that unlike boys, girls discounted both their achievements and their ability to do well in school. This finding held regardless of the children's age, grade in school, achievement, or intelligence. This result supports previous research (Eccles, Adler, & Meece, 1984) on casual attributions girls and boys make for their academic success. Girls tend to attribute their success to external causes, for example, to luck, to the fact that the teacher likes them, or to an easy test; boys, on the other hand, attribute their success to internal causes, for example, to ability. Similarly, girls attribute their failure to internal causes, for example, to lack of ability, while boys attribute their failure to external causes, for example, to a poor exam or to an unfair allegation of cheating (Eccles et al., 1984; Yee & Eccles, 1988).

Focus on Language Development

During middle childhood, children's metalinguistic awareness improves. *Metalinguistic awareness* refers to our understanding of our own use of language (Kemper & Vernooy, 1994). In this stage, children understand that language is governed by a set of rules. They are also better able to self-monitor their communications. In addition, children in middle childhood are more likely to ask for clarification of information that they do not understand (Kemper & Vernooy, 1994).

Metalinguistic awareness allows children to converse with peers more successfully and to listen to and respond to another in a conversation (Kemper & Vernooy, 1994). During this stage, children are more likely to speak to themselves and sing to themselves. Consequently, most school-age children use language to help control their behavior (Feldman, 1998).

In this part of the life cycle, children also make gains in learning to read as well as in comprehending and retaining information they have read. They develop an understanding that reading involves deriving meaning from the printed word and that letters that make up the words represent *phonemes,* that is, speech sounds (Gough, Juel, & Griffith, 1992; Hansen & Bowey, 1994). Children learn to sound out the phonemes in the words they read and combine them so that the words are distinguished. Children come to understand that they cannot memorize sequences of letters by rote. Thus they learn to read words when they have correctly sounded out all of the letters of the words (Hatcher, Hulme, & Ellis, 1994; Thompson, Cottrell, & Fletcher-Flinn, 1996). Phonological awareness tasks are some of the best predictors of reading skill and are a distinction between learning-disabled and non-learning-disabled children (Lennox & Siegel, 1995).

In "Phonetic Awareness: Knowledge of Orthography–Phonology Relationships in the Character Acquisition of Chinese Children," excerpted in the readings section (see pp. 112–117), Hua Shu, Richard C. Anderson, and Ningning Wu address the role of phonological knowledge among children who learn to read Chinese, which is a nonalphabetic writing system (Ehri, 1993). In the Chinese language, there are no grapheme-to-phoneme correspondences in the pronunciation of the characters. As Ehri (1993) and Shu et al. point out, the correspondences in Chinese are character to syllable.

Shu et al. report that Chinese childrens' understanding of orthography–phonology relationships changes over time. As they state:

> The first step in phonetic awareness may be crude and simple, perhaps, if it could be articulated. "The part on the right tells the pronunciation." Later, the child making good progress in learning to read elaborates a more com-

> plicated theory that accommodates to facts such as that the phonetic component is not always on the right and that the pronunciation of a compound character may vary from the pronunciation of its phonetic in semipredictable ways. (p. 57; in this text, p. 114)

As Shu et al. point out with respect to the Chinese writing system, children will know how to pronounce characters they have been taught in school and will typically not know how to pronounce characters they have not been taught.

EMOTIONAL DEVELOPMENT

Focus on Children of Divorce

Research suggests that half of the children in the United States spend their entire childhoods living with both parents (Hetherington & Stanley-Hagan, 1999). The remainder live in single-parent homes, with stepparents, grandparents (discussed further in the chapter on adulthood), or other nonparental relatives. Other children live in foster care homes. Children whose parents are divorced typically respond with sleep disturbances, phobias, anxiety, and depression, especially from 6 months to 2 years following their parents' divorce (Chase-Lansdale, Cherlin, & Kiernan, 1995; Pedro-Carroll, Sutton, & Wyman, 1999).

During middle childhood, children of divorced parents often blame themselves for the marital problems that led to the divorce (Kaplan & Pruett, 2000). By age 10, children can feel pressure to choose sides, to take the position of either their father or their mother in the divorce and risk experiencing divided loyalty (Wallerstein & Blakeslee, 1989). After a low point at approximately one year following the divorce, most children begin to return to their predivorce state of psychological adjustment (Hetherington, Stanley-Hagan, & Anderson, 1989). Compared with peers whose parents have not divorced, however, twice as many children of divorced parents require psychological counseling (Chase-Lansdale et al., 1995; McConnell & Sim, 1999).

Certainly there are factors that relate to children's responses to divorce, including economic standing of the parent with whom the child is living. Since divorce brings a decline in both parents' standards of living, children may be living in poverty, which has a serious effect on their emotional and social development as well as sense of self-esteem and self-worth (Gottfried & Gottfried, 1994).

Furthermore, research has indicated that for many children, divorce reduces the anger in the home (Hetherington & Stanley-Hagan, 1999). If the child maintains a close, positive relationship with both the custodial and the noncustodial parent, he or she will experience fewer, if any, of the emotional responses characterized above (Gottfried & Gottfried, 1994; Lamb, 1999). Warshak (1992) outlined the following coping factors that can help maximize children's chances of dealing with divorce: (1) sufficient access to each parent to enable children to maintain high-quality relationships with both; (2) a cooperative, low-conflict relationship between the parents; (3) skilled and sensitive child-rearing practices; (4) minimal changes for children; and (5) good social-support systems for children and parents.

In their article, "A Prospective Study of the Effects of Marital Status and Family Relations on Young Children's Adjustment among African American and European American Families," excerpted in the readings section (see pp. 117–122), Daniel S. Shaw, Emily B. Winslow, and Clare Flanagan report on the moderating effects of ethnicity on children's adjustment in two-parent, to-be-divorced, already divorced, and always-single-parent families. Their findings indicated that to-be-divorced European American and African American families demonstrated higher rates of preschool-age behavior problems. Parental conflict accounted for predivorce differences in child behavior problems.

Ellwood and Stolberg (1993) reported similar findings in their study of three groups of children ages 8 to 11: those whose parents remained married, those whose parents were divorced, and those whose parents divorced and subsequently remarried. Higher levels of family functioning were associated with families in which parental hostility was low and parents displayed few rejection behaviors while practicing consistent and appropriate discipline. Pearson and Thoennes (1990) found that children in joint custody witness less tension and more cooperation between their parents than do children in traditional sole-custody arrangements. Joint custody in itself probably does not reduce the strain between ex-spouses; the parents were probably more cooperative to begin with. Their ability to maintain a collaborative relationship for their children eases the strain of divorce for their children. In their study, Pearson and Thoennes (1990) and Gindes (2000) identified basic rules for parents that help children of divorce avoid psychological problems: (1) cooperate with each other, (2) avoid physical violence in the home, (3) maintain children's regular access to each parent, and (4) minimize the number of changes in the children's lives (e.g., moving or changing schools).

Additionally, joint-custody arrangements are apt to inhibit one parent from kidnapping her or his child from the ex-spouse (Hatcher, Barton, & Brooks, 2000; Linder, 1999; Tedisco & Paludi, 1996). This is an important concern since it is estimated that between 300,000 and 600,000 children are abducted by their parents each year. Finkelhor and Dziuba-Leatherman (1994) reported that 81% of child victimizations involve a parental abduction. A child is most vulnerable to this form of victimization before either parent has been awarded custody. The prime targets for parental abductions are children ages 3 to 11, with those between 3 and 5 years the most likely victims (Hatcher et al., 2000). Children younger than 3 years are typically not abducted by a noncustodial parent because they create unique problems for the abductor: They need constant supervision and care. Similarly, adolescents are likely to telephone home, run away, or alert law-enforcement agencies (Tedisco & Paludi, 1996).

Abducted children frequently experience a split reality: Other people in their environment tell them how lucky they are to have such a wonderful parent. They themselves may come to reframe the victimization, perhaps blaming themselves, perhaps believing that all children have similar experiences. Children are driven into regression, alienation, powerlessness, shame, embarrassment, humiliation, self-blame, and self-hate (Linder, 1999; Tedisco & Paludi, 1996). Thus the psychological impact of being abducted by a parent and then living with this individual is stressful for children. Such children experience grief and fear over the loss of a parent, confusion about the divorce and their role in it, guilt for not calling the other parent, and hatred for their parents (Hatcher et al., 2000). Children often live under cruel circumstances, almost paralleling the life of a fugitive, with frequent changes of residences and names (Tedisco & Paludi, 1996).

Focus on Self-Care After School

The majority of mothers and fathers with children in middle childhood work outside the home. The rate of maternal employment for two-parent families with school-age children is more than 75 percent. African American women with school-age children are more likely to be employed than white or Latina women with children (Betz, 1993). The majority of American Indian women who are employed are in their peak childbearing years: 49% of American Indian women in their 20s and 55% of American Indian women in their 30s (LaFromboise et al., 1995). The reasons why women work outside the home are related primarily to financial needs and self-actualization (Caruso, 1996; Scarr, Phillips, & McCartney, 1989; Sinacore-Guinn, 1998). Because of the decline in family income from 1973 to 1988, families must have two incomes to support them at a level previously achieved by one wage earner. Single, widowed, and divorced women with children typically must work to avoid poverty. That is, employment may not always be a choice for women with school-age children: It is a necessity, as they must work outside the home or live in poverty (Etaugh, 1993).

Research on the impact of maternal employment on children has generally found no negative effects on the children (Hoffman, 1989; Sweeny, 1999). In fact, maternal employment appears to have a positive influence on adolescents, particularly daughters. Daughters of employed mothers are more likely to be self-confident, achieve better grades in school, and pursue careers themselves. Furthermore, employed mothers place more emphasis on independence training (Betz, 1993). Research with ethnic minority girls and boys has demonstrated consistently that maternal employment is positively associated with academic achievement (Betz, 1993).

As we have discussed, the nature and quality of the child care received are important factors in determining the children's adjustment to both parents working outside of the home. When children are in high-quality day care, there is no negative impact on their emotional adjustment or their relationships with their mothers (Caruso, 1996; Hoffman, 1989). Child care has also been found to have no negative effects on the intellectual development of children and it may have a positive impact on children from economically disadvantaged homes.

Most of the research, however, has focused on infant and preschool children's needs for child care, including day care centers. In their article, "Children of the National Longitudinal Survey of Youth: Choices in After-School Care and Child Development," excerpted in the readings section (see pp. 123–126), Deborah Lowe Vandell and Janaki Ramanan highlight the need for attention to child care for children in middle childhood. They cite studies that claim that children who care for themselves after school, *latchkey children,* are at risk for emotional, academic, and social problems, while other studies claim no difference between latchkey and nonlatchkey children. Vandell and Ramanan's sample included children in three racial classifications: Hispanic, black, and white American children. Their results indicated that contrary to a popular media claim that children are better off after school when they can come home to their mothers, this form of after-school care may not be ideal. Mothers, especially those who are single parents, may be stressed and not available to their children when they return home after school. Thus child care may be an important source of social support. Vandell and Ramanan conclude that the type of after-school care is not as important as the quality of children's experiences with their families.

Other research, supportive of Vandell and Ramanan's, suggests that what matters is how satisfied mothers are with the choices they have made about integrating work and family (Barnett & Rivers, 1992; Gilbert, 1994). Self-care or latchkey children may experience positive consequences, including the ability to develop an enhanced sense of independence and competence. These children's self-esteem may be higher because they feel they are contributing to the household in significant ways, including housecleaning and cooking (Hoffman, 1989).

Thus the consequences of being a self-care child are not always harmful. If they are at home rather than with friends in unsupervised activities, these children may avoid involvement in problematic situations, including gang activity and drug abuse (Rodman & Cole, 1987).

SOCIAL DEVELOPMENT

Focus on the Influence of a Peer Group

During middle childhood, children grow progressively more sensitive to the importance of their peer group (Van-Aken, 1999). The formation of friendships during this life stage influences children's development in several ways: Friends provide children with information about the world and other people; friends provide emotional support that allows children to respond more effectively to stress; friends teach children how to manage their emotions; and friends provide a mechanism for interacting with others (Bukowski, Newcomb, & Hartup, 1996).

Children's conception of friendship changes in middle childhood, from simply enjoying time spent together to a way of providing the rewards of friendship—intimacy and loyalty (Lloyd & Cohen, 1999). Friendships during middle childhood also display clear status hierarchies. High status in a peer group leads to a greater number of friendships. Children who are popular among their peers are those children who have traits that underlie social competence, such as cooperation, humor, adaptability, skill at social problem solving, and understanding (Bukowski et al., 1996). Moreover, children who are popular during middle childhood participate in activities that promote social development and skill (Feldman, 1998).

Children's closest friends during middle childhood are largely members of the same race and ethnicity, as well as of the same sex (Benenson, Apostoleris, & Pamass, 1998). Asher, Singleton, and Taylor (1982) found that when third graders from an integrated school were asked to name their best friend, approximately one quarter of white children and two thirds of African American children selected a child of another race. By the time these children reached tenth grade, however, less than 10% of white teens and 5% of African American teens chose a best friend of another race.

In schools that deal with breaking down stereotypes associated with members of racial and ethnic groups, children exhibit a high degree of mutual acceptance. Thus teachers who ask children of different races and ethnicities to work together on projects are helping to reduce prejudice and discrimination. Children learn there are many similarities between them, and they also learn to celebrate the differences (Gaertner, Mann, Dovidio, Morell, & Pomare, 1990).

Research indicates that sex is a significant factor in friendship formation and development in middle childhood (Paludi, M., Paludi, C., & Doyle, in press). Boys and girls increasingly prefer same-sex friendships. Male friendships are characterized by groups of more than two and by status hierarchies (Bakken & Romig, 1992); female friendships involve one or two close relationships, equal status among friends, and reliance on cooperation coupled with the avoidance of confrontation (Clark & Ayers, 1991; Collins & Miller, 1994; Fox, Gibbs, & Auerbach, 1985). Even the language girls use in friendships reflects their attempts to maintain equal-status relationships (Wood & Inman, 1993).

The majority of American Indian children, as well as adults, have a respect for the power of verbal communication. They are taught that words are used to talk to oneself, think, inform, and reconcile with other people. They are also taught that words can frighten, threaten, or insult others (Henley, 1995). Thus great care is taken when talking with others.

Libra (1987) noted that one of the basic values in Japanese culture is *omoiyari* (empathy). Given *omoiyari,* children and adults don't have to state an opinion explicitly because people should be able to understand or sense others' meanings intuitively. Libra also observed a related value, *enryo,* which refers to self-restraint required to avoid disagreeing with opinions held by the majority. Have you noticed this in your classrooms? Why do students remain silent? One possible explanation is that they do not want to challenge the opinion of the person in authority (i.e., the professor); they interpret this behavior as disrespectful. Thus, continuing with the Japanese example, contrary to American values that make directness ideal, Japanese hold in esteem individuals who communicate indirectly, subtly, nonverbally, and implicitly (Tannen, 1994). They trust their listeners' empathy to complete the meaning.

Friendship segregation by sex occurs in most cultures. Same-sex segregation may be a consequence of the types of activities in which children engage. Boys typically get assigned to activities girls do not, and vice versa. Thus segregation in chores and play activities leads to sex segregation in friendships (Gross, Downing, & d'Heurle, 1982; Whiting & Edwards, 1988). Melissa E. DeRosier and Janis B. Kupersmidt, in their article "Costa Rican Children's Perceptions of Their Social Networks," excerpted in the readings section (see pp. 126–129), report on fourth- and sixth-grade children in both Costa Rica and the United States whose relationships were assessed in terms of intimacy, conflict, companionship, affection, satisfaction, and instrumental aid. They observed the children's relationships with their same-sex best friend, as well as with their teacher, favorite grandparent, favorite sibling, mother, and father. Costa Rican children rated their relationships with most persons more positively than did children from the United States. Furthermore, for Costa Rican children, family members and teachers played a more important role in their lives than did their best friends.

DeRosier and Kupersmidt's research provides support for the fact that theoretical perspectives concerning children's friendship development are subject to cultural relativism. Gender comparisons were common in both cultures. Costa Rican and United States girls reported greater satisfaction in their relationships with their best friends than did boys, giving support for mutual dependence in girls' friendships.

We will address this theme once again in the next chapter on adolescence.

Readings

Gender Effects in Children's Beliefs About School Performance: A Cross-Cultural Study*

Anna Stetsenko, Todd D. Little, Tamara Gordeeva, Matthias Grasshof, and Gabriele Oettingen

Children's beliefs about their own academic potential and their perceptions of what leads to school performance outcomes are important factors affecting many aspects of their behavior—for example, how much they persist on a task and how well they achieve in school (e.g., Bandura, 1997; Skinner, 1995). Two general findings in this literature are that girls show lower perceptions of their competence and lower performance expectations than boys (see Frey & Ruble, 1987; Parsons & Ruble, 1977; Stipek, 1992). Girls are also (1) less likely to attribute success to their ability, (2) more likely to attribute failure to a lack of ability, and (3) less likely to believe that success can be achieved through effort (Dweck & Elliot, 1983; Nicholls, 1979; Stipek & Gralinski, 1991; Wittig, 1985). However, these effects are conditional in that they are (1) task specific (e.g., dependent on subjective task value, task difficulty, and sex typing of the task; see Deaux & Emswiller, 1974; Eccles, Adler, & Meece, 1984), (2) most consistent in mathematics (Ryckman & Peckham, 1987; Stipek & Gralinski, 1991), and (3) especially pronounced in adolescence (Phillips & Zimmerman, 1990). The nature and magnitude of these effects also appear to depend on the methods and measures that are used. For example, they are more pronounced when girls have just been exposed to a failure experience or when they must explain the failures of other females (Licht & Dweck, 1984; Frey & Ruble, 1987; Nemerowicz, 1979).

Even though these gender effects are rather conditional and sometimes inconsistent (for reviews of such inconsistencies, see Eccles, Wigfield, Harold, & Blumenfeld, 1993; Frey & Ruble, 1987; Stipek & Gralinski, 1991), they are often viewed as general and pervasive throughout school age (see Eccles et al., 1984, for a similar observation). A gap in the literature that may contribute to such a misconception is that similarities between boys and girls in these kinds of beliefs have received less attention than differences and, moreover, the similarities are often underreported (e.g., Golombok &

*From Stetsenko et al. (2000, April). *Child Development, 71*(2), 517–527. Reprinted with permission.

Fivush, 1994; for a similar critique, see Lott, 1995). Yet another gap is that cross-cultural comparisons have been only sparsely integrated into the study of gender differences in children's achievement-related beliefs (cf., Best & Williams, 1993; Lummis & Stevenson, 1990). Such gaps help propagate the stereotype of a pervasive difference between boys' and girls' beliefs. Given that such gender effects in school contexts have a variety of sociodevelopmental and school-policy implications, a further validation of findings in this field is clearly needed. . . .

We examined whether children's beliefs about school performance are gendered and whether they are gendered in the same way cross-culturally. We reasoned that a large-scale comparative approach would provide a broader picture of gender effects in such beliefs, thereby helping to further test their generality. Moreover, a comparative approach can suggest possible bases of gender effects because it varies (albeit quasi-experimentally) their possible antecedents and consequences (Edwards & Whiting, 1980). In addition, a comparative approach addresses an assumption of recent sociocognitive theories of gender, namely, that gender stereotyping practices and attitudes of a socializing community are mirrored in children's beliefs (e.g., Cross & Markus, 1993) and thus differentially (i.e., in culture-specific ways) shape gender effects in such beliefs. The samples in our study stem from diverse settings (Eastern and Western Europe, Russia, Japan, the United States) that vary along a number of sociocultural dimensions. Similarities and differences among these contexts allow one to draw comparisons along a number of naturally occurring combinations of various dimensions. For example, comparisons can be drawn (1) between the sociopolitically and culturally similar contexts of German-speaking Switzerland and West Germany, (2) among countries with different political, and hence schooling, systems (e.g., established democracies of Western Europe and the United States versus the transitioning systems of Eastern European countries), (3) among countries with the same Western-type political democratic institutions but differing cultural background (Western European countries and the United States versus Japan).

. . .

The data come from a large-scale study of children's beliefs about school performance across seven sociocultural settings (East Berlin, West Berlin, Moscow, Tokyo, Berne, Los Angeles, and Prague), with two longitudinal follow-ups in East Berlin, West Berlin, and Moscow. Given the crucial changes that occurred while the study was conducted (e.g., the demise of the Soviet Union, the fall of the Berlin Wall, and the implementation of democratic reforms), each measurement reflects a unique sociohistorical setting associated with the processes of transition and change. Because we had follow-ups in only three contexts, we do not focus on the longitudinal aspects but treat each time of measurement as a distinct context.

Over 3,000 boys and girls in grades 2 to 6 participated (22 to 179 children per grade level with approximately equal gender distributions and comparable average ages). The data were collected at the end of each school year (except for Moscow at Time 1, which was in the fall, and Tokyo, which was in the winter). As detailed in other reports on these samples (Karasawa, Little, Miyashita, Mashima, & Azuma, 1997; Little, Oettingen, Stetsenko, & Baltes, 1995; Little & Lopez, 1997; Oettingen et al., 1994; Stetsenko et al., 1995), each represented generally typical middle- to lower-middle-class settings. Supplemental analyses of between-school and ethnicity (when applicable) differences in each setting revealed nearly no differences (Little, Oettingen, & Baltes, 1995; Little, Oettingen, Stetsenko, & Baltes, 1995), indicating that our findings are consistent within each context and, therefore, are more readily interpretable.

. . .

We found a number of cross-cultural invariant trends and a few culture-specific variations in the gender patterning of children's achievement-related beliefs, indicating that (1) there are important regularities in how gender effects in beliefs come about across many different parts of the world, and (2) contextual influences can produce culturally unique profiles in some aspects of children's self-belief systems.

Cross-Culturally Consistent Gender Effects in Children's Beliefs

Boys and girls across the contexts were notably alike in that (1) when their performance was equal, their perceptions of their achievement potential were also equal; (2) better achieving students of both sexes had higher self-perceptions of their potential than lower achieving students; and (3) when girls had higher grades than boys, they also had higher beliefs than boys (with just a few exceptions) on several facets of their achievement potential (i.e., effort, luck, ability to access teachers' help), and on their general ability to achieve good grades (control expectancy). Finally, boys and girls around the world held similar views of what it generally takes to do well in school (means–ends beliefs).

These findings speak against a pervasive (across-the-board) bias in girls' beliefs about school performance and suggest that both boys and girls are, for the most part, realistic in their self-assessments (i.e., they are aware of their performance standing and credit themselves for it in one form or another). These important similarities are related to numerous aspects of formal schooling that are generally common across modern industrialized societies and appear to exclude overt gender typing. For example, boys and girls appear to receive similar messages about what it takes to do well at school and these communicated contingencies are similar across the contexts we studied. Moreover, many aspects of the individualized school-related experiences of children (e.g., feedback regarding effort and luck) also seem to be similar across these contexts and not pervaded by gender stereotyping.

However, one effect represents a significant exception to this general trend and suggests that one specific form of gender typing prevails in schooling contexts across many parts of the world. Specifically, notable evidence of biased self-perceptions was observed in girls' evaluations of how talented they are. In 9 of 10 contexts where girls actually achieved better than boys, their self-assessments of their own ability were only equal to those of boys, not higher. In these contexts, girls were generally as aware of their actual performance standing as were boys (i.e., the correlations between school grades and the personal agency beliefs were high and equal for boys and girls); however, girls did not credit themselves with being talented even though they performed better than the boys. Compared with boys, then, girls discounted their talent and showed no evidence of compensatory beliefs patterns (e.g., overly ascribing performance outcomes to factors such as effort or luck instead of talent).

This finding is in line with other work indicating that girls tend to downplay their own achievement potential and, specifically, to discount their own talent as a cause of their success at school (e.g., Eccles et al., 1984). The types of beliefs that we measured, however, are not overall self-perceptions of competence nor are they attributions about the causes of success or failure. Instead, they are self-assessments of specific facets of performance potential. Our findings, therefore, isolate one type of self-belief (i.e., self-perceptions of talent) in which the girls' bias is particularly pronounced even when they (1) actually perform better than boys, (2) are as aware as boys of their performance standing, (3) have veridically high beliefs in other aspects of their academic competence, and (4) share boys' views on the importance of factors that cause school performance, including the importance of talent. In addition, these findings are unique to the literature because they reveal quite remarkable cross-cultural consistency of the bias in girls' self-perceptions of their talent, suggesting that similar processes operate in many parts of the world.

Given the lack of gender differences in RAVEN intelligence, the equal correlations between RAVEN intelligence and achievement, and the absence of other interactive effects (i.e., age, achievement level), the nature of the expectations and feedback that the children receive (implicit or explicit) is a likely source for this effect. For example, prior research with U.S. samples indicates that teachers and parents are more likely to communicate to girls who are having difficulty at school tasks that their problem is related to a lack of ability, whereas they are more likely to communicate to boys that their problem results from a lack of effort (e.g., Phillips & Zimmerman, 1990; Yee & Eccles, 1988). Our findings suggest that gender stereotyping associated with girls' perceptions of their talent can be found in many parts of the world.

Culture-Specific Variations in Gender Patterning of School Performance-Related Beliefs

Gender effects were quite pronounced, but consistent, in Moscow, Los Angeles, East Berlin (at Times 1 and 3), and Tokyo, with girls showing higher mean levels than boys for achievement and for most or several of the self-belief dimensions (i.e., effort, teachers, and luck). In Prague and at Time 2 in East Berlin and West Berlin, on the other hand, girls and boys showed no differences on self-reported beliefs even though girls had higher school grades than boys. Perhaps even more strikingly, in several contexts (i.e., West Berlin at Times 1 and 3, and Berne) there were no gender differences in either performance or self-beliefs. The differentiated patterns are consistent with the idea that gender stereotyping practices and attitudes of a socializing community influence how boys and girls are treated in schooling contexts and thereby gender-type their beliefs about their achievement potential in culture-specific ways. Moreover, the variability suggests that gender stereotyping is more pronounced in some schooling contexts than in others.

Given the descriptive nature of this study, the exact reasons for why gender effects were more pronounced in some contexts than in others emerges as a central question for future research. We do not know, for example, when the gender patterns first emerge. Are girls better prepared for school than boys are in some contexts and thus achieve better from the start? Do some contexts operate to dampen girls' self-assessment or, alternatively, do these contexts simply sustain the initial levels of beliefs? To answer such questions, children's beliefs even at younger ages and the culture-specific characteristics of school contexts should be examined. . . .

REFERENCES

Bandura, A. (1997). *Self-efficacy: The exercise of control.* New York: Freeman.

Best, D. L., & Williams, J. E. (1993). A cross-cultural viewpoint. In A. E. Beall & R. J. Sternberg (Eds.), *The psychology of gender* (pp. 215–248). New York/London: Guilford Press.

Chapman, M., Skinner, E. A., & Baltes, P. B. (1990). Interpreting correlations between children's perceived control and cognitive performance: Control, agency, or means-ends beliefs? *Developmental Psychology, 53,* 1024–1037.

Cross, S. E., & Markus, H. R. (1993). Gender in thought, belief, and action: A cognitive approach. In A. E. Beall & R. J. Sternberg (Eds.), *The psychology of gender* (pp. 55–97). New York/London: Guilford Press.

Deaux, K., & Emswiller, E. (1974). Explanations of successful performance on sex-linked tasks: What is skill for the male is luck for the female. *Journal of Personality and Social Psychology, 29,* 80–85.

Dweck, C. S., & Elliot, E. S. (1983). Achievement motivation. In E. M. Hetherington (Ed.), P. H. Mussen (Series Ed.), *Handbook of child psychology: Vol. 4. Socialization, personality, and social development* (4th ed., pp. 643–691). New York: Wiley.

Eccles, J. S., Adler, T., & Meece, J. L. (1984). Sex differences in achievement: A test of alternative theories. *Journal of Personality and Social Psychology, 46,* 26–43.

Eccles, J. S., Jacobs, J. E., & Harold, R. D. (1990). Gender role stereotypes, expectancy effects, and parents' role in the socialization of gender differences in self-perceptions and skill acquisition. *Journal of Social Issues, 46,* 183–201.

Eccles, J. S., Wigfield, A., Harold, R. D., & Blumenfeld, P. (1993). Age and gender differences in children's self- and task perceptions during elementary school. *Child Development, 64,* 830–847.

Edwards, C. P., & Whiting, B. B. (1980). Differential socialization of girls and boys in light of cross-cultural research. *New Directions for Child Development, 8,* 625–643.

Frey, K. S., & Ruble, D. N. (1987). What children say about classroom performance: Sex and grade differences in perceived competence. *Child Development, 58,* 1066–1078.

Golombok, S., & Fivush, R. (1994). *Gender development.* Cambridge, UK: Cambridge University Press.

Greenwald, A. G., & Banaji, M. R. (1995). Implicit social cognition: Attitudes, self-esteem, and stereotypes. *Psychological Review, 102,* 1–27.

Hyde, J. S., Fennema, E., & Lamon, S. J. (1990). Gender differences in mathematics performance: A meta-analysis. *Psychological Bulletin, 107,* 139–155.

Jöreskog, K. G., & Sörbom, D. (1989). *LISREL 7: A guide to the program and applications* (2nd ed.) [Computer Software Manual]. Chicago: SPSS.

Karasawa, M., Little, T. D., Miyashita, T., Mashima, M., & Azuma, H. (1997). Japanese children's action-related perceived control of school performance. *International Journal of Behavioral Development, 20,* 405–423.

Licht, B. G., & Dweck, C. S. (1984). Determinants of academic achievement: The interaction of children's achievement orientations with skill area. *Developmental Psychology, 20,* 628–636.

Little, T. D. (1997). Mean and covariance structures (MACS) analyses of cross-cultural data: Practical and theoretical issues. *Multivariate Behavioral Research, 32,* 53–76.

Little, T. D. (1998). Sociocultural influences on the development of children's action-control beliefs. In J. Heckhausen & C. S. Dweck (Eds.), *Motivation and self-regulation across the life span* (pp. 281–315). New York: Cambridge University Press.

Little, T. D., & Lopez, D. F. (1997). Regularities in the development of children's causality beliefs about school performance in six sociocultural contexts. *Developmental Psychology, 33,* 165–175.

Little, T. D., Oettingen, G., & Baltes, P. B. (1995). *The revised control, agency, and means-ends interview (CAMI): A multicultural validity assessment using mean and covariance (MACS) analyses* (Materialen aus der Bildungsforschung, No. 49). Berlin: Max Planck Institute for Human Development and Education.

Little, T. D., Oettingen, G., Stetsenko, A., & Baltes, P. B. (1995). Children's action-control beliefs and school performance: How do American children compare with German and Russian children? *Journal of Personality and Social Psychology, 69,* 686–700.

Lott, B. (1995). Gender development or gender difference? *Contemporary Psychology, 40,* 1076–1077.

Lubinsky, D., & Humphreys, L. G. (1990). A broadly based analysis of mathematical giftedness. *Intelligence, 14,* 327–355.

Lummis, M., & Stevenson, H. W. (1990). Gender differences in beliefs and achievement: A cross-cultural study. *Developmental Psychology, 2,* 254–263.

Nemerowicz, G. M. (1979). *Children's perceptions of gender and work roles.* New York: Praeger.

Nicholls, J. G. (1979). Development of perception of own attainment and causal attributions for success and failure in reading. *Journal of Educational Psychology, 71,* 94–99.

Oettingen, G. (1995). Cross-cultural perspectives on self-efficacy. In A. Bandura (Ed.), *Self-efficacy in a changing society* (pp. 149–176). New York: Cambridge University Press.

Oettingen, G., Little, T. D., Lindenberger, U., & Baltes, P. B. (1994). Causality, agency, and control beliefs in East versus West Berlin children: A natural experiment on the role of context. *Journal of Personality and Social Psychology, 66,* 579–595.

Parsons, J. E., & Ruble, D. N. (1977). The development of achievement-related expectancies. *Child Development, 48,* 1075–1079.

Phillips, D. A., & Zimmerman, M. (1990). The developmental course of perceived competence and incompetence among competent children. In R. J. Sternberg & J. Kolligian, Jr. (Eds.), *Competence considered* (pp. 41–66). New Haven, CT: Yale University Press.

Raymond, C. L., & Benbow, C. P. (1986). Gender differences in mathematics: A function of parental support and student sex typing? *Developmental Psychology, 22,* 808–819.

Ryckman, D. B., & Peckham, P. (1987). Gender differences in attributions for success and failure. *Journal of Early Adolescence, 7,* 47–63.

Skinner, E. A. (1995). *Perceived control, motivation, and coping.* Thousand Oaks, CA: Sage.

Skinner, E. A., Chapman, M., & Baltes, P. B. (1988). Control, means-ends, and agency beliefs: A new conceptualization and its measurement during childhood. *Journal of Personality and Social Psychology, 54,* 117–133.

Stetsenko, A., Little, T. D., Oettingen, G., & Baltes, P. B. (1995). Control, agency and means-ends beliefs about school performance in Moscow children: How similar are they to beliefs of Western children? *Developmental Psychology, 31,* 285–299.

Stevenson, H. W., Stigler, J. W., Lee, S. Y., Lucker, G. W., Kitamura, S., & Hsu, C. C. (1985). Cognitive performance and academic achievement of Japanese, Chinese, and American children. *Child Development, 56,* 713–734.

Stipek, D. J. (1992). The child at school. In M. Bornstein & M. E. Lamb (Eds.), *Developmental psychology: An advanced textbook* (pp. 579–625). Hillsdale, NJ: Erlbaum.

Stipek, D. J., & Gralinski, J. H. (1991). Gender differences in children's achievement-related beliefs and emotional responses to success and failure in mathematics. *Journal of Educational Psychology, 83,* 361–371.

Stipek, D. J., & Hoffman, J. M. (1980). Children's performance-related expectancies as a function of academic performance histories and sex. *Journal of Educational Psychology, 72,* 861–865.

Wittig, M. A. (1985). Sex-role norms and gender-related attainment values: Their role in attributions of success and failure. *Sex Roles, 12,* 1–11.

Yee, D. K., & Eccles, J. S. (1988). Parent perceptions and attributions for children's mathematics achievement. *Sex Roles, 19,* 317–333.

Phonetic Awareness: Knowledge of Orthography–Phonology Relationships in the Character Acquisition of Chinese Children*

Hua Shu, Richard C. Anderson, and Ningning Wu

There is little doubt that phonological knowledge is crucial in learning to read alphabetic scripts. To become literate, children must realize that printed words are not arbitrary sequences of letters that can be memorized only by rote and, instead, learn and use systematic relationships between orthography and phonology (Gough, Juel, & Griffith, 1992; Goswami & Bryant, 1992; Thompson, Cottrell, & Fletcher-Flinn, 1996). The question we address in the present article is "What is the role of phonological knowledge when a child learns to read Chinese, a very different, nonalphabetic writing system?"

All writing systems represent information about the pronunciation of words (Perfetti, Zhang, & Berant, 1992), although systems vary in the directness and consistency with which they encode phonological information (Hung & Tzeng, 1981). Researchers have attempted to determine whether speech–orthography knowledge is actually used in reading. The often-replicated finding in alphabetic languages is that regular words, whose pronunciations can be generated by applying grapheme–phoneme correspondence rules (e.g., *gate*), are read faster and more accurately by both adults and children than irregular words, or exceptions, whose pronunciations cannot be derived using rules (e.g., *have;* Waters, Seidenberg, & Bruck, 1984; Backman, Bruck, Hebert, & Seidenberg, 1984). In addition to phonemes, larger phonological units and associated spelling patterns such as onset–rime also function as units of word recognition in alphabetic writing systems. The pronunciation of a word may be influenced by the pronunciation of its orthographic neighbors (Glushko, 1979; Jared, McRae, & Seidenberg, 1990). For instance, a child who knows *beak* could use this word as an analogy to read new words like *peak* and *bean* (Goswami, 1986).

Large individual differences in phonological knowledge and skill are found among children learning to read alphabetic languages. These differences can be observed at very early stages in learning to read. Although good and poor readers perform similarly when naming high-frequency words, poor readers make many more errors and are much slower when reading regular low-frequency words or pronounceable nonwords (Perfetti & Hogaboam, 1975). Poor readers make fewer phonetic spelling errors than their controls (Holligan & Johnston, 1991). Phonemic awareness has been reported to be the best predictor of later reading success for children learning alphabetic writing systems (Bradley & Bryant, 1983) and is also a good indicator for distinguishing learning-disabled and normal children (Lennox & Siegel, 1995).

There are no grapheme-to-phoneme correspondences in the pronunciation of Chinese characters. Rather, the correspondences in Chinese are character to syllable. It is important to note that these correspondences are not arbitrary. There is information in the internal structure of characters that gives at least partial information about the pronunciation of the majority of characters. In modern Chinese, 80% to 90% of the characters are semantic phonetic compounds. Such a compound consists of two parts: a semantic component called the *radical,* which provides information about meaning, and a phonetic component called simply the *phonetic,* which provides information

*From Shu et al. (2000). *Journal of Educational Psychology, 92*(1), 56–62. Reprinted with permission.

about pronunciation (Hoosain, 1991; Taylor, 1995; Wu, Li, & Anderson, 1999).

Unfortunately for Chinese children, the phonetics of semantic phonetic compound characters are neither entirely transparent nor completely reliable as a guide to pronunciation. Most phonetics, in addition to being components of compound characters, are themselves simple characters whose pronunciation is unambiguous. Regular compound characters are pronounced the same as the phonetic in isolation. For example, the compound 码 is pronounced /mǎ/, which is the same pronunciation as the phonetic when the phonetic functions as a simple character, 马 /mǎ/. However, there are many irregular compound characters that have a completely different pronunciation from the phonetic; for instance, the compound 租 is pronounced /zǔ/, whereas its phonetic 且 is pronounced /qiě/.

A smaller number of phonetics are bound forms; that is, they never appear alone but appear only as components of compound characters. The pronunciation of bound phonetics is not fixed, even for adults. However, the fact that, in many cases, characters sharing the same bound phonetic are related in pronunciation provides potentially useful information. For example, several characters sharing the bound phonetic 畐, such as 福, 幅, 福, 富, and 副, are pronounced /fu/. Presumably, the pronunciation of unfamiliar characters containing bound phonetics is resolved by analogy with a familiar character containing the same phonetic.

A great many compound characters are semiregular in the sense that the phonetic provides partial information about pronunciation. A character may be pronounced with the same syllable as its phonetic but with a different tone. Chinese is a tonal language. Every syllable in Mandarin Chinese is pronounced with one of four tones or voice inflections (five, if the neutral tone is counted). Tones distinguish syllables that otherwise would be homophones. For instance, the syllable /mā/ pronounced with first tone (high, steady inflection) means *mother,* whereas /mǎ/ pronounced with third tone (falling, then rising inflection) means *horse.* In another case of partial information, a character and its phonetic may be pronounced with a different onset (also called *initials* or *consonants*) but the same rime (also called *finals* or *vowels*). For example, the compound character 现 is pronounced /xiàn/, whereas the phonetic 见 is pronounced /jiàn/. Skilled readers of Chinese report that they can use the partial information from the phonetics in semiregular characters, but it is beyond the scope of the present research to determine whether children can do so.

The theoretical construct that guides the present research is the concept of *phonetic awareness,* in other words, insight into the structure and function of the phonetic component of semantic phonetic compound characters. We have chosen this expression to emphasize the parallel with *phonemic awareness* in alphabetic languages. A difference is that, strictly speaking, phonemic awareness has to do with paying attention to units of speech, whereas phonetic awareness is inextricably tied to orthographic units. This difference may be more apparent than real, however, inasmuch as phonemic awareness is facilitated by and goes hand in hand with learning to read in an alphabetic writing system (Ehri, 1993; Lazo, Pumfrey, & Peers, 1997; Scarborough, Ehri, Olson, & Fowler, 1998). This implies that in alphabetic languages, graphemes may serve as concrete markers for phonemes, which otherwise may be elusive linguistic abstractions (Ehri & Wilce, 1986).

We think of phonetic awareness as a child's working hypothesis about the relationship between speech and orthography in Chinese, a hypothesis that we suppose guides perceptual processing, strategies for learning and retrieving the pronunciations of characters, and attempts to forecast the pronunciations of unfamiliar characters. Thus, another parallel with a concept from scholarship on learning alphabetic languages is that children must come to the insight that their language is governed by the *alphabetic principle* (Ehri, 1993). We could say that Chinese children who are phonetically aware have insight into the principles that govern orthography–phonology relationships in Chinese.

Phonetic awareness should be distinguished from knowledge of myriad specific character-to-syllable associations. To be sure, phonetic awareness cannot be acquired in the abstract, apart from knowledge of specific associations. Presumably, quite a few specific associations must be known before phonetic awareness can emerge. Once it does emerge, we theorize that phonetic awareness serves to organize and rationalize the character-to-syllable associations already known and accelerate the learning of new associations. We suppose that there is a continuing reciprocal relationship between phonetic awareness and acquisition of specific associations (Nagy & Anderson, 1998).

Phonetic awareness should not be constructed as an all-or-none, once-and-for-always insight. Rather, we imagine that Chinese children progressively refine their theories of orthography–phonology relationships. The first step in phonetic awareness may be crude and simple, perhaps, if it could be articulated. "The part on the right tells the pronunciation." Later, the child making good progress in learning to read elaborates a more complicated theory that accommodates to facts such as that the phonetic component is not always on the right and that the pronunciation of a compound character may vary from the pronunciation of its phonetic in semipredictable ways.

The phonetically unaware child has no alternative but to learn character-to-syllable associations by rote. To learn by rote means to encode some arbitrary configuration of properties in the character; arbitrary in the sense that the configuration has no systemic status in the Chinese writing system. According to our theory, rote encodings are subject to continuing interference, as additional characters are learned, and lack generative value for assimilating new characters. Again, a parallel can be drawn with analyses of children learning to read alphabetic languages. Notably, in a well-known article, Gough and Hillinger (1980; see also Gough et al., 1992) have described the confusions of young children learning words in English when their encodings are not founded on the alphabetic principle. Regrettably, considering the present context, Gough and Hillinger called these children *logographic readers.* We assume that in any language, children unaware of the logic of the language will be inefficient learners, vulnerable to confusion and forgetting, and unable to cope well with the unfamiliar.

Phonetic awareness is one of several kinds and levels of metalinguistic awareness that we hypothesize are required to become a skillful reader of Chinese (see Nagy & Anderson, 1998). Another kind that is important in character acquisition is what we term *radical awareness,* that is, insight into the function of the semantic component of compound characters. By the third grade, Chinese children who are good readers are able to use the information in radicals as an aid to learning and remembering new characters (Shu & Anderson, 1997).

Although the Chinese orthography is thought to be relatively difficult to read because phonological information is represented less systematically than in other orthographies, among skilled adult readers, the factors that influence the pronunciation of Chinese have proved remarkably similar to the factors that influence pronunciation in alphabetic languages. Research has consistently shown that the naming latency for low-frequency regular characters is shorter than that for low-frequency irregular characters, whereas there is less influence of regularity on the naming latency of high-frequency characters (Fang, Horng, & Tzeng, 1986; Hue, 1992; Peng, Yang, & Chen, 1994; Seidenberg, 1985). This suggests that, just like readers in alphabetic writing systems, phonological information, or Chinese orthography–phonology correspondence rules (Ho & Bryant, 1997), is used in decoding at least some Chinese characters. The analogy process, which is described by Glushko (1979), has also been reported to apply to the pronunciation of Chinese characters. Adults' pronunciation errors on an unfamiliar compound character are influenced not only by its phonetic but also by its orthographic neighbors (other characters sharing the same phonetic). Analogy errors are more frequent when characters with bound phonetics are pronounced (Peng et al., 1994; Shu & Zhang, 1987). . . .

Extending previous studies, the purpose of the investigation reported in this article was to explore the development of phonetic awareness among Chinese children. We studied children in the second, fourth, and sixth grades, rated by their teachers as high, average, or low in Chinese reading ability. We examined the effects of the *familiarity* and the *regularity* of characters on the children's pronunciation. Familiarity was defined in terms of the school curriculum and was based on a comprehensive analysis of the approximately 3,000 characters prescribed by the Chinese Ministry of Education to be learned over the 6 years of elementary school (Shu, Anderson, Wu, Chenc, & Zheng, 2000). Familiar characters were those that had been taught during the previous school year; children had received drill, practice, and review of these characters and had read them numerous times (Wu, Li, & Anderson, 1999). Unfamiliar characters had not yet been taught in school. A few children may know some characters not yet taught in school, but in most cases, if children can pronounce these characters, it is because they are able to make productive use of orthography–phonology relationships.

. . .

The present study provides clear evidence for phonetic awareness among Chinese schoolchildren. Confirming the results of Ho and Bryant (1997), among others, children as young as second graders are better able to represent the pronunciations of regular characters than irregular characters or characters with bound phonetics. Phonetic awareness continues to develop over the elementary school years, as is shown by the increasing influence of phonetic regularity on the performance of children in higher grades and the increasing percentage of phonetic-related errors among older children.

The very strong influence of familiarity on pronunciation underlines an unavoidable fact about the Chinese writing system: The system does not offer pronunciation cues that are as reliable or consistent as those of many other writing systems. Thus, Chinese students are likely to know the pronunciations of characters that they have been taught in school and are unlikely to be able to forecast the pronunciations of characters that they have not been taught.

As we expected, regularity had more influence on the pronunciation of unfamiliar than familiar characters. Still, we wish to stress again that regularity did have a statistically reliable influence on the pronunciation of familiar characters. This fact is consistent with the theory that knowledge of orthography–phonology relationships provides the basis, or part of the basis, for nonarbitrary encoding of characters and that decomposition of compound characters into their phonetics and radicals provides the basis, or part of the basis, for successful retrieval of pronunciations and meanings.

Overall, characters with bound phonetics proved to be as difficult as irregular characters. One reason may be limited opportunities to learn. Of the 3,000 characters that Chinese children are supposed to learn in elementary school, about 2,000 are semantic phonetic compounds, but only 161 (8%) of the compounds contain a bound phonetic (Shu et al., 2000). Nonetheless, the increasing frequency of analogy errors over the elementary school years, as well as some correct pronunciations of unfamiliar characters with bound phonetics, indicates that many children are acquiring the analogy strategy.

By the time children reach the sixth grade (or earlier for those of high ability), they have a more sophisticated theory of Chinese orthography–phonology relationships than "The part on the right tells the pronunciation." The more sophisticated theory that emerges during the elementary school years incorporates insights into the information about pronunciation of characters with bound phonetics that can be found by analogy with neighbors sharing the same phonetic and presumably incorporates insights into the partial information about pronunciation available in semiregular characters.

REFERENCES

Backman, J., Bruck, M., Hebert, M., & Seidenberg, M. S. (1984). Acquisition and use of spelling–sound correspondences in reading. *Journal of Experimental Child Psychology, 38,* 114–133.

Bradley, L., & Bryant, P. E. (1983). Categorizing sounds and learning to read: A causal connection. *Nature, 303,* 419–421.

Chen, J., & Yuen, C. (1991). Effects of pinyin and script type on verbal processing: Comparisons of China, Taiwan, and Hong Kong experience. *International Journal of Behavioral Development, 14,* 429–448.

Ehri, L. C. (1993). How English orthography influences phonological knowledge as children learn to read and spell. In R. Scholes (Ed.), *Literacy and language analysis* (pp. 21–43). Hillsdale, NJ: Erlbaum.

Ehri, L., & Wilce, L. S. (1986). The influence of spellings on speech: Are alveolar flaps /d/ or /t/? In D. Yaden & S. Templeton (Eds.), *Metalinguistic awareness and beginning literacy* (pp. 101–114). Exeter, NH: Heinemann.

Fang, S. P., Horng, R. Y., & Treng, O. J. L. (1986). Consistency effects in the Chinese character and pseudo-character naming tasks. In H. S. R. Gao & Hoosain (Eds.), *Linguistics, psychology, and the Chinese language* (pp. 11–21). Hong Kong: University of Hong Kong, Center of Asian Studies.

Glushko, R. J. (1979). The organization and activation of orthographic knowledge in reading aloud. *Journal of Experimental Psychology: Human Perception & Performance, 5,* 674–691.

Goswami, U. (1986). Children's use of analogy in learning to read: A developmental study. *Journal of Experimental Child Psychology, 42,* 73–83.

Goswami, U., & Bryant, P. (1992). Rhyme, analogy, and children's reading. In P. Gough, L. Ehri, & R. Treiman (Eds.), *Reading acquisition* (pp. 49–63). Hillsdale, NJ: Erlbaum.

Gough, P. B., & Hillinger, M. L. (1980). Learning to read: An unnatural act. *Bulletin of the Orton Society, 30,* 180–196.

Gough, P. B., Juel, C., & Griffith, P. L. (1992). Reading, spelling, and the orthographic cipher. In P. Gough, L. Ehri, & R. Treiman (Eds.), *Reading acquisition* (pp. 35–48). Hillsdale, NJ: Erlbaum.

Ho, C.-H., & Bryant, P. (1997). Learning to read Chinese beyond the logographic phase. *Reading Research Quarterly, 32*(3), 276–289.

Holligan, C., & Johnston, R. S. (1991). Spelling errors and phonemic segmentation ability: The nature of the relationship. *Journal of Research Reading, 14*(1), 21–32.

Hoosain, R. (1991). *Psycholinguistic implications for linguistic relativity: A case study of Chinese.* Hillsdale, NJ: Erlbaum.

Hue, C. W. (1992). Recognition processing in character naming. In H. C. Chen & O. J. L. Tzeng (Eds.), *Language processing in Chinese* (pp. 93–107). Amsterdam: North-Holland.

Hung, D. L., & Tzeng, O. J. L. (1981). Orthographic variations and visual information processing. *Psychological Bulletin, 90,* 377–414.

Jared, D., McRae, K., & Seidenberg, M. S. (1990). The basis of consistency effects in word naming. *Journal of Memory and Language, 29,* 687–715.

Lazo, M. G., Pumfrey, P. D., & Peers, I. (1997). Metalinguistic awareness, reading, and spelling: Roots and branches of literacy. *Journal of Research in Reading, 20*(2), 85–104.

Lennox, C., & Siegel, L. S. (1995). Development of orthographic and phonological processes in normal and disabled reading. In V. W. Berninger (Ed.), *The varieties of orthographic knowledge II: Relationships to phonology, reading, and writing* (pp. 151–175). Norwell, MA: Kluwer Academic.

Meng, X., Shu, H., & Zhou, X. (in press). The relationship between tasks of Chinese reading developmental research. *Psychological Science.*

Nagy, W. E., & Anderson, R. C. (1998). Metalinguistic awareness and the acquisition of literacy in different languages. In D. Wagner, R. Venezky, & B. Street (Eds.), *Literacy: An international handbook* (pp. 155–160). Boulder, CO: Westview Press.

Peng, D. L., Yang, H., & Chen, Y. (1994). Consistency and phonetic independence effects in naming task of Chinese phonograms. In Q. C. Jing & H. C. Zhang (Eds.), *Information processing of Chinese language* (pp. 26–41). Beijing, China: Beijing Normal University Press.

Perfetti, C. A., & Hogaboam, T. (1975). Relationship between single word decoding and reading comprehension skill. *Journal of Educational Psychology, 67,* 461–469.

Perfetti, C. A., Zhang, S., & Berant, I. (1992). Reading in English and Chinese: Evidence for a "universal" phonological principle. In R. Frost & J. Katz (Eds.), *Orthography, phonology, morphology, and meaning* (pp. 227–248). Amsterdam: North-Holland.

Scarborough, H. S., Ehri, L. C., Olson, R. K., & Fowler, A. E. (1998). The fate of phonemic awareness beyond the elementary school years. *Scientific Studies of Reading, 2,* 115–142.

Seidenberg, M. S. (1985). The time course of phonological activation in two writing systems. *Cognition, 19,* 1–30.

Shu, H., & Anderson, R. C. (1997). Role of radical awareness in the character and word acquisition of Chinese children. *Reading Research Quarterly, 32*(1), 78–89.

Shu, H., Anderson, R. C., Wu, N.-N., Chenc, X., & Zheng, X. (2000). *Properties of school Chinese with implications for theory and practice.* Champaign, IL: Center for the Study of Reading.

Shu, H., & Zhang, H. (1987). The processing of pronunciation of Chinese characters by proficient mature readers. *Acta Psychologica Sinica, 3,* 282–290.

Taylor, I. (1995). *Writing and literacy in Chinese, Korean, and Japanese.* Philadelphia: John Benjamins Publishing.

Thompson, G. B., Cottrell, D. S., & Fletcher-Flinn, C. M. (1996). Sublexical orthographic–phonological relations early in the acquisition of reading: The knowledge sources account. *Journal of Experimental Child Psychology, 62,* 190–222.

Waters, G. S., Seidenberg, M. S., & Bruck, M. (1984). Children's and adults' use of spelling–sound information in three reading tasks. *Memory & Cognition, 12,* 293–305.

Wu, X., Li, W., & Anderson, R. C. (1999). Reading instruction in China. *Journal of Curriculum Studies, 31,* 571–586.

Yang, H., & Peng, D. L. (1997). The learning and naming of Chinese characters of elementary school children. In H. C. Chen (Ed.), *Cognitive processing of Chinese and related Asian languages* (pp. 323–346). Hong Kong: Chinese University Press.

A Prospective Study of the Effects of Marital Status and Family Relations on Young Children's Adjustment Among African American and European American Families*

Daniel S. Shaw, Emily B. Winslow, and Clare Flanagan

Within the last two decades, the divorce rate in the United States has increased substantially. Since 1958, when there were 2.1 divorces per 1,000 couples, a gradual increase in the number of divorces has occurred, peaking at 5.3 per 1,000 couples in 1979 and 1981 (Glick & Lin, 1986), and stabilizing at 4.7 as of 1990 (U.S. Department of Health and Human Services, 1990). According to projections based on 1990 census data, 40% of all U.S. children can expect to live in a single-parent household, because of divorce, before the age of 16 (Cherlin, 1992). Based on the increase in divorces over the last three decades and the prospect that a similarly high number will occur in the future, it remains imperative to understand the effects of divorce on children's adjustment.

As research on divorce and children's adaptation has accumulated, there has been a gradual shift in emphasis from family structure to family process (Emery, 1988; Emery, Hetherington, & DiLalla, 1984). That is, events that accompany marital dissolution, rather than the event of divorce per se, have been identified as potentially more salient correlates of children's adjustment (Amato & Rezac, 1994; Camara & Resnick, 1988; Emery, 1988; Fauber, Forehand, Thomas, & Wierson, 1990; Haurin, 1992). Longitudinal investigations of divorced families (Hetherington, Cox, & Cox, 1979, 1985; Wallerstein, 1991; Zill, Morrison, & Coiro, 1993) have provided particularly strong support for this focus on family process. However, in longitudinal studies in which data collection was begun following the parental separation, changes in family process may be attributed erroneously to the parental separation and are subject to the biasing errors of retrospective reporting. In such studies, parents may blame the child's problematic behavior on the divorce rather than circumstances that existed prior to the parental separation.

Prospective longitudinal studies begun prior to the parental separation therefore can be useful in addressing two issues. First, they allow researchers to examine if child adjustment problems were evident prior to parental separation. Second, if problematic child behavior began prior to the separation, factors that might be responsible for its development can be explored. Two family process factors consistently have been postulated to influence child behavior in both divorced and two-partner families: parent conflict and parenting.

. . .

Method

Participants

The source for participant recruitment was Allegheny County's Women, Infants, and Chil-

*From Shaw et al. (1999, May/June). *Child Development, 70*(3), 742–755. Reprinted with permission.

dren Program (WIC), which provides nutritional aid to low socioeconomic status (SES) families in the Pittsburgh metropolitan area. There were 310 participants, recruited from WIC sites throughout the Pittsburgh metropolitan area over the course of 2 years. The sample represents a second larger cohort of families recruited from WIC, with no overlap of participants from a smaller cohort of boys and girls (e.g., Shaw, Keenan, & Vondra, 1994). As the intent of the original investigation was to examine the developmental precursors of antisocial behavior, only boys were recruited, and all target children needed to have another sibling living in the home (because lack of family space also has been shown to increase risk for externalizing problems). Participants were recruited when target children were between 6 and 17 months of age. When infants were 18 months old, mothers ranged in age from 17 to 43 years, with a mean age of 28. Fifty-four percent of participants were European American, 40% were African American, and 6% were other (e.g., Hispanic American, Asian American, or biracial). Sampling of marital status was not restricted, due to the considerable relationship instability within the sample. At the 18-month visit, 64% were either married or living together, 8% were divorced, 28% were always single, and 1% were other (e.g., widowed, single when the child was born but living together with partner, widowed). Mean per capita family income was $242 per month ($2,892 per year, and $11,616 for a family of four), and the mean Hollingshead socioeconomic status (SES) score was 24.5, which is indicative of a working-class sample. Initially, 421 families were approached at WIC sites. Fourteen (3.3%) declined to participate at the time of recruitment, and an additional 97 declined before the first assessment. Thus, of the 421 families asked, 310 (71%) participated in the first assessment at 18 months. Of the 310 families seen at the 18-month assessment, data were available on 302 at the 24-month assessment, 282 at the 42-month assessment, and 291 at the age 5 assessment, an attrition rate of 6.1%. It is our belief that attrition was lower at the age 5 assessment, because these visits were carried out in families' homes as opposed to the laboratory.

Procedures

When children were 18 months old and 42 months old, they were seen for a 72-hour visit at the laboratory, during which time mothers and sons participated in a number of parent-child interaction tasks and mothers completed a series of questionnaires. At 24 months, a similar combined home-laboratory visit was conducted, lasting approximately 3½ hours. At 60 months, two separate home visits were conducted, both with the target child and his nearest age sibling—one assessment with the mother and one with the father. During these visits, observations of sibling and parent-child interaction occurred, at which time mothers, fathers, and alternative caregivers completed the Achenbach Child Behavior Checklist (CBCL; Achenbach, 1991, 1992). Mothers completed CBCLs at all assessment points, and alternative caregivers and fathers completed CBCLs at 60 months (available for 62% and 65% of cases, respectively). Alternative caregivers included family members who provided care for the target children on a regular basis, and included children's grandmothers (35%), aunts (19%), day care workers, babysitters, and teachers (25%), and family friends and other relatives (21%). Mothers were reimbursed for their participation at the end of each visit ($25 at all visits except $35 for the combined home-laboratory visit), as were fathers and alternative caregivers for completing questionnaires. ($10).

. . .

Discussion

The present study sought to extend our understanding of the effects of marital structure and transitions on young boys' behavioral adjustment using a predominantly low-income, ethnically diverse sample. When to-be-divorced and always two-parent families were compared, modest but significantly higher rates of CBCL problems were evident for boys in to-be-divorced families at 24 and 42 months. To-be-divorced parents also were found to have less satisfactory marital relationships at 18 months, higher rates of child-rearing disagreements at 24 months, higher rates of verbally aggressive conflict, and lower socioeconomic status at 42 months than always two-parent families. These predivorce differences appeared to hold true for both European American and African American families, whereas only to-be-divorced African American mothers demonstrated significantly higher levels of rejecting parenting and lower levels of per capita income. When family relations were used as covariates to account for group differences between to-be-divorced and always two-parent families, measures of marital adjustment/conflict accounted for differences on children's Internalizing but not Externalizing problems. The results suggest that for young children in families about to separate, parental conflict may play an important role in the development of early Internalizing symptoms. However, for boys' early externalizing problems, there appear to be other components of the predivorce environment, in addition to parental conflict, that contribute to disruptive behavior. One possible explanation involves changes in the stability of disruptive behavior, which has been found to increase from 24 months onward as the child is more able to express his/her feelings verbally and parents are likely to show less tolerance of children's aggressive behavior (Shaw & Bell, 1993). These developmental changes might help explain why group differences on Externalizing-type symptoms were not present among any marital structure groups at 18 months, but were present at 24 months and thereafter in several instances.

Group differences between to-be-divorced and always two-parent families were more consistently found for Internalizing symptoms, suggesting that young children may be more likely to respond to parental acrimony in the predivorce environment by demonstrating symptoms of distress and anxiety rather than acting in a disruptive manner. Unfortunately, there are few prospective studies of divorce that have been able to examine *Internalizing* symptoms in preschool-age children, although a number of studies have documented higher rates of Internalizing symptoms among school-age children and adolescents from divorced families (Forehand, McCombs, Wierson, Brody, & Fauber, 1990; Furstenberg & Allison, 1989; Hoyt, Cowan, Pedro-Carroll, & Alpert-Gillis, 1990). The differences in Internalizing symptoms may reflect young children's immature cognitive understanding of parental conflict (Brody & Neubaum, 1996; Hetherington, 1991; Wallerstein & Kelly, 1980). Parental conflict may be more anxiety inducing for young children given their greater dependence on the primary caregivers.

Results regarding differences in the predivorce adjustment of children are consistent with the studies of Block et al. (1986) and Cherlin (1992) showing that differences in adjustment patterns of to-be-divorced children are evident as early as 2 years of age. It should be noted that these effects were relatively modest, averaging .3–.4 standard deviations on CBCL factors, and more consistent for European Americans than African Americans. The results also are in accord with the Block et al. (1986) and Shaw et al. (1993) studies, which found that predivorce family environments were characterized by more dissatisfied and conflictual parental relations. . . .

In the course of comparing to-be-divorced, already divorced, and always two-parent families, we discovered several ethnic differences. The incomes of to-be-divorced and always two-parent European American families did not differ. However, African American mothers in our sample were less likely to be married or living with a partner at each age, and more likely to be always single, when compared to European American mothers. Moreover, among those married or living with a partner when the target child was 18 months old, African American mothers were more likely to divorce or separate by age 5 than European Americans. Interestingly, African American parents who were married or living together initially, but separated by the time the target child was age 5, had significantly less income than stable, two-parent African American families. However, the incomes of to-be-divorced and always two-parent European American families did not differ significantly. . . .

We also found some ethnic differences in parenting between mothers who would eventually separate from their partners versus those already divorced. Specifically, for European American mothers in the sample, levels of rejecting parenting at age 2 were higher among already divorced mothers than among to-be-separated mothers; whereas for African Americans, to-be-separated mothers were more rejecting than already separated mothers. On the other hand, to-be-separated European American and African American couples did not differ significantly with respect to levels of reported marital satisfaction or conflict prior to separation. Thus, although both subgroups of mothers experienced conflictual relations with their spouses prior to separation, African Americans seemed to exhibit higher levels of disrupted parenting before divorce than afterward, whereas European American mothers tended to show more disrupted parenting following the marital separation than before. These data point to the possibility that effects of family structure on the family system may vary for low-income European American and African American families. In order to understand these differences more clearly, it will be necessary to examine characteristics of the family context in more minute detail, such as investigating the specific reasons for parental separation as well as paternal psychological functioning prior to separation.

We found that rejecting parenting accounted for the higher levels of behavior problems found among boys from always single homes using maternal report of Externalizing and Internalizing problems. Many researchers have pointed to differences between the life circumstances of poor African American and European American families, which might explain why the always single-parent family structure seems to be associated with worse outcomes for low-income, African American boys than low-income, European American boys. Specifically, low-income African Americans tend to live in highly segregated neighborhoods characterized by a high proportion of unemployed and poverty-stricken residents, many female-headed households, and high rates of crime (Massey, Gross, & Shibuya, 1994; Sampson, 1987; South & Crowder, 1997; Wilson, 1996). (All of the aforementioned characteristics tend to co-occur in ghetto or underclass neighborhoods, although researchers often use the criterion of a poverty rate among residents greater than 40%.) In contrast, poverty-stricken European Americans rarely experience neighborhood conditions comparable to low-income African Americans. For example, in a high-risk sample of male adolescents recruited from the same city as our sample (Pittsburgh, PA), Peeples and Loeber (1994) discovered that they did not have enough European American participants living in underclass neighborhoods to permit statistical analyses on them. Only 2% of European Americans lived in underclass neighborhoods, compared to 41% of African Americans in their sample.

Living in underclass neighborhoods presents parents with stressors not experienced to the same degree by residents of working-class neighborhoods, where low-income European Americans typically live. For example, ghetto residents often believe they cannot trust their neighbors, due to high rates of crime and substance abuse among residents in the community. Many fear for the safety of themselves and their children to the extent that they may curtail activities outside the home, sometimes even preventing their children from participating in structured activities at school, church, or in neighborhood organizations (Furstenberg et al., 1993). Supportive characteristics of more organized communities, such as neighbors who watch over each others' property and assume responsibility for supervising the activities of children in the neighborhood, might be nonexistent in underclass neighborhoods (Sampson, 1987). Thus, single mothers in underclass neighborhoods may receive less caregiving support than other single mothers, hampering their ability to provide nurturant caregiving.

. . .

REFERENCES

Achenbach, T. M. (1991). *Manual for the Child Behavior Checklist/4–18 and 1991 profiles.* Burlington: University of Vermont, Department of Psychiatry.

Achenbach, T. M. (1992). *Manual for the Child Behavior Checklist 2/3 and 1992 profile.* Burlington: University of Vermont, Department of Psychiatry.

Amato, P., & Keith, B. (1991). Parental divorce and the well-being of children: A meta-analysis. *Psychological Bulletin, 110,* 26–46.

Amato, P. R., & Rezac, S. J. (1994). Contact with nonresident parents, interparental conflict, and children's behavior. *Journal of Family Issues, 15,* 191–207.

Bane, M. J. (1986). Household composition and poverty: Which comes first? In S. Danzinger & D. Weinberg (Eds.), *Fighting poverty: What works and what doesn't.* Cambridge, MA: Harvard University Press.

Baruch, D. W., & Wilcox, J. A. (1994). A study of sex differences in preschool children coexistent with interpersonal tensions. *Journal of Genetic Psychology, 64,* 281–303.

Baumrind, D. (1973). The development of instrumental competence through socialization. In A. Pick (Ed.), *Minnesota Symposia on Child Psychology* (Vol. 7, pp. 3–46). Minneapolis: University of Minnesota Press.

Block, J. H., Block, J., & Gjerde, P. F. (1986). The personality of children prior to divorce: A prospective study. *Child Development, 57,* 827–840.

Block, J. H., Block, J., & Gjerde, P. F. (1988). Parental functioning and the home environment in families of divorce: Prospective and concurrent analyses. *Journal of the American Academy of Child and Adolescent Psychiatry, 27,* 207–213.

Brody, G. H., & Neubaum, E. (1996). Family transitions as stressors in children and adolescents. In C. R. Pfeffer (Ed.), *Severe stress and mental disturbance in children* (pp. 559–590). Washington, DC: American Psychiatric Press.

Camara, K. A., & Resnick, G. (1988). Interparental conflict and cooperation: Factors moderating children's postdivorce adjustment. In E. M. Hetherington & J. Aratesh (Eds.), *Impact of divorce, single parenting, and step-parenting on children* (pp. 169–195). Hillsdale, NJ: Erlbaum.

Cherlin, A. J. (1992). *Marriage, divorce, & remarriage.* Cambridge, MA: Harvard University Press.

Cherlin, A. J., Furstenberg, F. F., Chase-Landsdale, P. L., Kiernan, K. E., Robins, P. K., Morrison, D. R., & Teitler, J. O. (1991). Longitudinal studies of effects of divorce on children in Great Britain and in the United States. *Science, 252,* 1386–1389.

Chess, S., & Thomas, A. (1984). *Origins and evolution of behavior disorders from infancy to early adult life.* New York: Brunner/Mazel.

Christopoulos, C., Cohn, D. A., Shaw, D. S., Joyce, S., Sullivan-Hanson, J., Kraft, S., & Emery, R. E. (1987). Children of abused women: I. Adjustment at time of shelter residence. *Journal of Marriage and the Family, 49,* 611–619.

Davies, P. T., & Cummings, E. M. (1994). Marital conflict and child adjustment: An emotional security hypothesis. *Psychological Bulletin, 116,* 387–411.

Dornbusch, S., Carlsmith, J., Bushwall, S., Ritter, P., Leiderman, H., Hastorf, A., & Gross, R. (1985). Single parents, extended households, and the control of adolescents. *Child Development, 56,* 326–341.

Duncan, G., Brooks-Gunn, J., & Klebanov, P. (1994). Economic deprivation and early childhood development. *Child Development, 65,* 296–318.

Emery, R. E. (1988). *Marriage, divorce, and children's adjustment.* Beverly Hills, CA: Sage.

Emery, R. E., Hetherington, E. M., & DiLalla, L. F. (1984). Divorce, children, and social policy. In H. W. Stevenson & A. E. Siegel (Eds.), *Child development research and social policy.* Chicago: University of Chicago Press.

Emery, R. E., & O'Leary, K. D. (1982). Children's perceptions of marital discord and behavior problems of boys and girls. *Journal of Abnormal Child Psychology, 10,* 11–24.

Erel, O., & Burman, B. (1995). Interrelatedness of marital relations and parent-child relations: A meta-analytic review. *Psychological Bulletin, 118,* 108–132.

Farnworth, M. (1984). Family structure, family attributes, and delinquency in a sample of low-income, minority males and females. *Journal of Youth and Adolescence, 13,* 349–364.

Fauber, R., Forehand, R., Thomas A., & Wierson, M. (1990). A mediational model of the impact of marital conflict on adolescent adjustment in intact and divorced families: The role of disrupted parenting. *Child Development, 61,* 1112–1123.

Forehand, R., Armistead, L., & David, C. (1997). Is adolescent adjustment following parental divorce a function of predivorce adjustment? *Journal of Abnormal Child Psychology, 25,* 157–164.

Forehand, R., McCombs, A. T., Wierson, M., Brody, G., & Fauber, R. (1990). Role of maternal functioning and parenting skills in adolescent functioning following parental divorce. *Journal of Abnormal Psychology, 99,* 278–283.

Furstenberg, F. F., & Allison, P. D. (1989). How marital dissolution affects children: Variations by age and sex. *Developmental Psychology, 25,* 540–549.

Furstenberg, F. F., Jr., Belzer, A., Davis, C., Levine, J., Morrow, K., & Washington, M. (1993). How families manage risk and opportunity in dangerous neighborhoods. In W. J. Wilson (Ed.), *Sociology and the public agenda* (pp. 231–258). Newbury Park, CA: Sage Publications.

Gardner, F. (1989). Inconsistent parenting: Is there evidence for a link with children's conduct problems? *Journal of Abnormal Child Psychology, 17,* 223–233.

Glick, P. C., & Lin, S. (1986). Recent changes in divorce and remarriage. *Journal of Marriage and the Family, 48,* 737–747.

Grych, J. H., & Fincham, F. D. (1990). Marital conflict and children's adjustment: A cognitive-contextual framework. *Psychological Bulletin, 108,* 267–290.

Haurin, R. J. (1992). Patterns of childhood residence and the relationship to young adult outcomes. *Journal of Marriage and the Family, 54,* 846–860.

Hetherington, E. M. (1991). Families, lies, and videotapes. Presidential address to the meeting of the Society for Research on Adolescence, Atlanta, GA, 1990. *Journal of Research on Adolescence, 1,* 323–348.

Hetherington, E. M., Cox, M., & Cox, R. (1979). Family interaction and the social, emotional, and cognitive development of children following divorce. In V. Vaughn & T. Brazelton (Eds.), *The family: Setting priorities* (pp. 89–128). New York: Science and Medicine.

Hetherington, E. M., Cox, M., & Cox, R. (1985). Long-term effects of divorce and remarriage on the adjustment of children. *Journal of the American Academy of Child Psychiatry, 24,* 518–530.

Hoyt, L. A., Cowen, E. L., Pedro-Carroll, J. L., & Alpert-Gillis, L. J. (1990). Anxiety and depression in young children of divorce. *Journal of Clinical Child Psychology, 19,* 26–32.

Jouriles, E. N., Murphy, C. M., Farris, A. M., Smith, D. A., Richters, J. E., & Waters, E. (1991). Marital adjustment, parental disagreements about child rearing, and behavior problems in boys: Increasing the specificity of the marital assessment. *Child Development, 62,* 1424–1433.

Larzelere, R. E., Martin, J. A., & Amberson, T. G. (1989). The toddler behavior checklist: A parent-completed assessment of social-emotional characteristics of young preschoolers. *Family Relations, 38,* 418–425.

Locke, H. J., & Wallace, K. M. (1959). Short marital-adjustment and prediction tests: Their reliability and validity. *Marriage and Family Living, 21,* 251–255.

Loeber, R., & Dishion, T. J. (1983). Early predictors of male delinquency: A review. *Psychological Bulletin, 94,* 68–99.

Massey, D. S., Gross, A. B., & Shibuya, K. (1994). Migration, segregation, and the geographic concentration of poverty. *American Sociological Review, 59,* 425–445.

McCord, W., McCord, J., & Zola, I. K. (1959). *Origins of crime.* New York: Columbia University Press.

McLeod, J., & Shanahan, M. (1993). Poverty, parenting, and children's mental health. *American Sociological Review, 58,* 351–366.

Minuchin, S. (1974). *Families and family therapy.* Cambridge, MA: Harvard University Press.

Montare, A., & Boone, S. (1980). Aggression and paternal absence: Racial-ethnic differences among inner-city boys. *Journal of Genetic Psychology, 137,* 223–232.

Offord, D. R., Sullivan, K., Allen, N., & Abrams, N. (1979). Delinquency and hyperactivity. *Journal of Nervous and Mental Disease, 167,* 734–741.

Patterson, G. (1982). *Coercive family processes* (Vol. 3). Eugene, OR: Castalia.

Peeples, F., & Loeber, R. (1994). Do individual factors and neighborhood context explain ethnic differences in juvenile delinquency? *Journal of Quantitative Criminology, 10,* 141–157.

Rothbaum, F., & Weisz, J. (1994). Parental caregiving and child externalizing behavior in nonclinical samples: A meta-analysis. *Psychological Bulletin, 116,* 55–74.

Sampson, R. J. (1987). Urban black violence: The effect of male joblessness and family disruption. *American Journal of Sociology, 93,* 348–382.

Shaw, D. S., & Bell, R. Q. (1993). Developmental theories of parental contributors to antisocial behavior. *Journal of Abnormal Child Psychology, 21,* 483–518.

Shaw, D. S., Emery, R. E., & Tuer, M. D. (1993). Parental functioning and children's adjustment in families of divorce: A prospective study. *Journal of Abnormal Child Psychology, 21,* 119–134.

Shaw, D. S., Keenan, K., & Vondra, J. I. (1994). The developmental precursors of antisocial behavior: Ages 1–3. *Developmental Psychology, 30,* 355–364.

Shaw, D. S., Winslow, E., Owens, E., Vondra, J., Cohn, J., & Bell, R. Q. (1998). The development of early externalizing problems among children from low-income families: A transformational perspective. *Journal of Abnormal Child Psychology, 26,* 95–107.

South, S. J., & Crowder, K. D. (1997). Escaping distressed neighborhoods: Individual, community, and metropolitan influences. *American Journal of Sociology, 102,* 1040–1084.

Strauss, M. (1979). Measuring intrafamily conflict and violence: The Conflict Tactics Scales. *Journal of Marriage and the Family, 41,* 75–88.

Thomas, A., & Chess, S. (1977). *Temperament and development.* New York: Brunner/Mazel.

U.S. Bureau of the Census. (1992). Current Population Reports, Series P-60, No. 181. *Poverty in the United States: 1991.* Washington, DC: U.S. Government Printing Office.

U.S. Department of Health and Human Services (1990). *Monthly vital statistics report, 13* (No. 13). Washington, DC: U.S. Government Printing Office.

Wallerstein, J. S. (1991). The long-term effects of divorce on children: A review. *Journal of the Academy of Child and Adolescent Psychiatry, 30,* 349–360.

Wallerstein, J. S., & Kelly, J. B. (1980). *Surviving the breakup.* New York: Basic Books.

Wilson, W. J. (1996). *When work disappears: The world of the urban poor.* New York: Alfred Knopf.

Wilson, W. J., & Neckerman, K. (1986). Poverty and family structure: The widening gap between evidence and public policy issues. In S. Danzinger & D. Weinberg (Eds.), *Fighting poverty: What works and what doesn't* (pp. 232–259). Cambridge, MA: Harvard University Press.

Winslow, E. B., Shaw, D. S., Bruns, H., & Kiebler, K. (1995, April). *Parenting as a mediator of child behavior problems and maternal stress, support, and adjustment.* Paper presented at the biennial meeting of the Society for Research in Child Development, Indianapolis, IN.

Zill, N., Morrison, D. R., & Coiro, M. J. (1993). Long-term effects of parental divorce on parent-child relationships, adjustment, and achievement in young adulthood. *Journal of Family Psychology, 7,* 91–103.

Zimmerman, M., Salem, D., & Maton, K. (1995). Family structure and psychological correlates among urban African-American adolescent males. *Child Development, 66,* 1598–1613.

Children of the National Longitudinal Survey of Youth: Choices in After-School Care and Child Development*

Deborah Lowe Vandell and Janaki Ramanan

In recent years, there has been increased public awareness that needs for child care are not restricted to families who have infants and preschoolers. Two thirds of the mothers of school-aged children are in the labor force, and this figure is expected to increase to 75% of the mothers of school-aged children by 1995 (Hofferth & Phillips, 1987). Many of these families must make some sort of child care arrangements for the times when their children are not attending elementary schools. These alternative arrangements include having children cared for by adults other than mothers, as well as having children caring for themselves, sometimes called latchkey arrangements.

There has been considerable interest in the popular press, Congress, and the scientific community about these different after-school arrangements. Two sets of questions have been raised: (a) what are the characteristics of families who use different types of after-school care, and (b) are some types of after-school care associated with increased social, emotional, or cognitive problems in children? Underlying the initial framing of these questions was a belief that families would use latchkey care only as a last resort (Cain & Hofferth, 1989) and that latchkey children were at risk for a wide range of problems (Long & Long, 1983).

Some recent research has contradicted these earlier beliefs. Although one early report (Long & Long, 1983) argued that latchkey children are at risk for emotional, social, and academic problems, others (Belle & Burr, 1989; Rodman, Pratto, & Nelson, 1985; Steinberg, 1986; Vandell & Corasaniti, 1988) have found no evidence of increased problems in latchkey children. Vandell and Corasaniti (1988), for example, found no differences in latchkey and mother-care children in terms of parent and teacher ratings of peer relationships and emotional well-being, the children's self-assessments, report card grades, standardized test scores, or ratings by peers. Surprisingly, within that suburban, middle-class sample, both latchkey and mother-care children appeared to be functioning better than children who went to after-school programs at local day-care centers. . . .

A primary purpose of this study was to examine further the associations between type of after-school care (latchkey, mother care, and other-adult care) and children's social, emotional, and cognitive development in a predominantly low-income, minority, urban sample. The question was whether latchkey care for these children was associated with increased behavior problems, lower self-concepts, or poorer academic performance as suggested by Woods (1972) and by Long and Long (1983).

This study also examined the characteristics of families who utilized latchkey as opposed to other types of after-school arrangements. . . .

In this study, children who were in three types of after-school care (mother care, latchkey, and other-adult care) were contrasted on a number of family characteristics including demographic variables like maternal age and education, family income, and race. In addition, the families were compared on more process-oriented measures like the extent to which they provided their children with emotional support and cognitive stimulation. In keeping with the need to consider possible confoundings of child care choices and family characteristics, we first determined whether there were differences between families using latchkey and other care. Then we controlled

*From Vandell & Ramanan (1991). *Developmental Psychology, 27*(4), 637–643. Reprinted with permission.

for these family differences when examining associations between child development and type of after-school care.

Associations between after-school care and family characteristics were examined in another context as well. One study (Steinberg, 1986) has suggested that the effects of after-school care are moderated by family characteristics. In that study, negative effects of latchkey arrangements were found in only a subsample of children and adolescents, those who lacked authoritative parenting. In this study, three possible moderators of after-school experience were studied: family poverty, family marital composition, and race. It was hypothesized that children from the economically poorest families, from single parent households, and from racial–ethnic minorities would be more vulnerable to different types of after-school care.

These questions were examined by using a national data set called the National Longitudinal Survey of Youth (NLSY). The NLSY was begun in 1979 as a survey of youth aged from 14 to 19 years. The original sample was selected with an overrepresentation of Blacks, Hispanics, and low-income Whites. Regular survey updates have been collected since 1979. In 1986, the survey was broadened to incorporate data from 4,953 children of the original female NLSY respondents. Children were directly assessed, and mothers were asked about their employment and child care uses, in addition to other demographic information.

This study focuses on the subset of third-, fourth-, and fifth-grade children within the larger NLSY data set. These were the youngest children in the data set who were using self-care in sufficient numbers for analysis.

. . .

This study contributes to the understanding of families and after-school care in several ways. First, within a sample of low-income children who have adolescent mothers, it illustrates links between families' financial and emotional resources and the types of after-school care that are used. Although one stereotypic model of an "ideal" after-school arrangement is for children to return home to their mothers after school (the Beaver Cleaver model), this study illustrates that this form of after-school care may be less than ideal for some families. In this study, when children returned home to their mothers after school, family incomes were only about 70% of those families using latchkey or other-adult care. And these mother-care families were significantly more likely to be living below the poverty line.

In addition to income differences, quality of emotional support provided to the children as measured by the HOME scale was poorer in those households using mother care after school. Although the focus of this study was not on determining how much living in poverty caused a poorer emotional environment, the repercussions of this association in this study were clear. Low-income children who were returning home to their mothers after school were spending more time in households that provided them with less emotional support. There were no significant differences in the emotional support provided by families using latchkey or other-adult care.

Although there were differences in the families in terms of emotional support and income, differences were not associated with other aspects of family functioning. In this study, type of after-school care was not related to children's sex, race, age, mothers' ages, family marital composition, or geographic area. Nor were differences found in the extent to which families provided cognitive stimulation. Thus, in many ways, the families using different types of after-school care were remarkably similar.

The next issue to be investigated concerned associations between type of after-school care and children's social and cognitive development. Within this area, the initial question was whether latchkey children demonstrated greater social, emotional, or cognitive problems in comparison with children in other forms of after-school care. In this socially disadvantaged sample, there were some indications that latchkey care was associated with more behavior problems. In contrast to the children who had other-adult supervised care after school, mothers reported that latchkey children were more hyperactive and headstrong. These results are consistent with Woods' (1972) findings with low-income children almost 20 years ago. An important issue is the source of these differences. Are they the result of the children's after-school experience per se, or are differences in the family environment actually major contributors to the apparent effects of different types of after-school care? In this study, when family income and family emotional support for the child were controlled, the apparent differences in child functioning associated with type of after-school care dissipated. This finding suggests that it was not latchkey care per se but the children's experiences within the family that were the critical contributors to development.

At the same time, there was a subgroup of latchkey children who displayed problematic functioning, even after we controlled for family emotional support. Children who were living below the poverty line *and* who were latchkey children were reported by their mothers to have significantly more antisocial behavior problems in comparison with children in supervised nonmaternal care. Although one must be cautious about overemphasizing a single difference, the report of increased antisocial behaviors in this subgroup of children does merit further study.

In the context of examining associations between after-school care and child functioning, it is also notable that this study found negative effects on those children who returned home to their mothers after school. In comparison with children who were supervised by other adults after school, children who returned home to their mothers were reported to have more problems related to antisocial behaviors, anxiety, and peer conflicts; also, their PPVT scores were lower. The subsequent interaction analyses that controlled for differences in family income and emotional support revealed that these effects were restricted to single-parent families. Although it is possible that the report of increased behavior problems was simply the result of single mothers having greater opportunities to observe such problems, the fact that mothers of latchkey children also reported elevated behavior problems suggests that opportunity is not the sole determinant of these reports.

Interestingly, these observations parallel other recent studies (Scarr, Lande, & McCartney, 1989; Vandell & Corasaniti, in press) that have found negative developmental outcomes associated with staying home with single mothers. One can speculate that alternative child care may be beneficial to these single-parent households. Vandell and Corasaniti (1990), for example, have argued that, in some single-parent families, mothers may be stressed and psychologically unavailable to their children. For these families, child care may be an important source of social support. Additional research should be directed at understanding children's and mother's experiences within these families and at determining whether increasing access to alternative child-care arrangements is of benefit.

This study has both strengths and limitations that should be explicitly acknowledged. One strength is that the study examined a nationally representative sample of children. Thus, we are able to make broader generalizations about the after-school care in a high-risk sample of chidden than is typically the case for research in developmental psychology. But the data set has a number of limitations. One is that the size of the data set is sometimes illusory. Although there were almost 5,000 children in the total data set, cell sizes relevant for particular focused interests are sometimes quite small. In this study, for instance, only 28 of the third, fourth, and fifth graders were in latchkey care. This relatively small sample resulted in limited statistical power, especially to detect interactions between type of after-school care and family functioning.

REFERENCES

Baker, P. C., & Mott, I. L. (1989). *NLSY child handbook: 1989.* Columbus, OH: Center for Human Resources Research, The Ohio State University.

Belle, D., & Burr, R. (1989, April). *Alone and with others: The context of children's after school experiences.* Paper presented at the biennial meeting of the Society for Research in Child Development, Kansas City, MO.

Bradley, R. H., & Caldwell, B. M. (1980). The relation of home environment, cognitive competence, and IQ among males and females. *Child Development, 51,* 1140–1148.

Cain, V. S., & Hofferth, S. L. (1989). Parental choice of self care for school age children. *Journal of Marriage and the Family, 51,* 65–77.

Harter, S. (1982). The perceived competence scale of children. *Child Development, 53,* 87–97.

Hofferth, S. L., & Phillips, D. A. (1987). Child care in the United States: 1970 to 1995. *Journal of Marriage and the Family, 49,* 559–571.

Long, T. J., & Long, L. (1983). *The handbook of latchkey children and their parents.* New York: Arbor House.

Peterson, J. L., & Zill, N. (1986). Marital disruption, parent–child relationship, and behavioral problems in children. *Journal of Marriage and the Family, 48,* 295–307.

Rodman, H., Pratto, D., & Nelson, R. (1985). Child care arrangements and children's functioning: A comparison of self-care and adult-care children. *Developmental Psychology, 21,* 413–418.

Scarr, S., Lande, J., & McCartney, K. (1989). Child care and the family: Cooperation and interaction. In J. Lande, S. Scarr, & N. Gunzenhauser (Eds.), *Caring for children: The future of child care in the United States* (pp. 1–21). Hillsdale, NJ: Erlbaum.

Steinberg, L. (1986). Latchkey children and susceptibility to peer pressure: An ecological analysis. *Developmental Psychology, 22,* 433–439.

Vandell, D. L., & Corasaniti, M. A. (1988). The relation between third graders' after school care and social, academic, and emotional functioning. *Child Development, 59,* 868–875.

Vandell, D. L., & Corasaniti, M. A. (1990). Child care and the family: Complex contributors to child development. In K. McCartney (Ed.), *New directions in child development.* San Francisco: Jossey-Bass.

Woods, M. B. (1972). The unsupervised child of the working mother. *Developmental Psychology, 6,* 14–25.

Costa Rican Children's Perceptions of Their Social Networks*

Melissa E. DeRosier and Janis B. Kupersmidt

Social support networks have been found to influence children's health, competence, and development (Cochran & Brassard, 1979; Garbarino, 1982; Sandler, Miller, Short, & Wolchik, 1989). Although both structural and functional characteristics of a social support network are associated with children's adjustment and development, functional characteristics may be more influential than structural ones (Sandler et al., 1989). Weiss (1974) has theorized that network members differ from one another in their functional characteristics both qualitatively and quantitatively. This theoretical position has been generally supported in studies of children's perceptions of their social networks (Buhrmester & Furman, 1987; Furman & Buhrmester, 1985).

. . .

Subjects

Costa Rican sample. The Hispanic subjects of this study were 148 children from a public school in Heredia, Costa Rica. The sample included 82 boys and 66 girls, of which 60 were fourth-grade students and 88 were sixth-grade students. According to school officials, most of the children were from working- and middle-class intact families. All of the children were White. At least one grandparent lived in 20% of the homes, and only 7% of the children had no siblings.

U.S. sample. Data from the U.S. children were obtained to allow for a direct comparison between North American and Hispanic cultures. To obtain an optimal match for the Costa Rican sample, the U.S. data came from two sources: Data on the sixth graders (n = 105)

*From DeRosier & Kupersmidt (1991). *Developmental Psychology, 27*(4), 656–662. Reprinted with permission.

were part of Furman and Buhrmester's (1985) original study, whereas data on the fourth graders ($n = 105$) were part of research that is still in progress (Furman & Buhrmester, 1990). The majority of the subjects were from Catholic parochial schools; however, some of the sample attended public school. The majority of the children came from middle- to upper-middle-class intact families, and they were predominantly White. There were 100 boys and 110 girls in the sample.

Procedure

The procedure for the U.S. sample was the same for both grades and was reported by Furman and Buhrmester (1985, 1990). The complete version of the Network of Relationships Inventory (NRI) was group administered in the classroom. The instructions to subjects, questionnaire format, and procedure for scale construction were the same as that discussed below for the Costa Rican sample.

The measure used to assess Costa Rican children's perceptions of their relationships with network members was a shortened version of the NRI developed by Furman and Buhrmester (1985). The measure was translated into Spanish and administered in written questionnaire form. One native Costa Rican psychologist and two Costa Rican graduate-level psychology students independently translated the NRI from English to Spanish and then back again, from Spanish to English. The few discrepancies among the three translators were discussed and resolved jointly. All three translators were bilingual in English and Spanish: the psychologist and one of the graduate students had lived in the United States. This procedure and use of Costa Rican translators were used to ensure that the subjects understood the language and content of the questions. The questionnaire was group administered in the classroom by a team of two or three Costa Ricans and one Anglo-American project staff member.

The version of the NRI used contained items that assessed children's perceptions of six qualities—instrumental aid, companionship, affection, intimacy, conflict, and satisfaction—for six relationships with important network members—mother or stepmother, father or stepfather, favorite sibling, favorite grandparent, best friend of the same sex, and teacher. We chose the qualities of instrumental aid, companionship, affection, and intimacy from the complete NRI because they represented the qualities of relationships in Weiss's theory (1974). We also chose conflict and satisfaction because previous research suggested that they were likely to be important constructs in a Hispanic culture. Children were asked to select their favorite sibling, favorite grandparent, and same-sex best friend as the targets for responding to the corresponding questions. Questions were answered on a 5-point Likert scale ranging from a low of 1 (*little or none*) to a high of 5 (*the most*). There were three separate questions for each quality that were then averaged to derive scale scores.

. . .

Our theories about social relationships tend to implicitly assume that network characteristics and development shifts are universally applicable. This study provided some support for this assumption; in Costa Rica, as was found in the United States (Furman & Buhrmester, 1985), the functional characteristics of children's social networks varied across network members, as Weiss's (1974) theory would suggest. However, this support was mitigated by the fact that children's perceptions of network members differed across the two cultures, suggesting that network characteristics are not universal among children. Thus, these findings provide support for the fact that theories concerning children's social development are subject to cultural relativism. In particular, to more completely understand children's social relationships, differences between cultures need to be examined.

In Tietjen's (1989) ecological view of support systems, the characteristics of social network members operate to promote children's competence. Children's competence is a relative term and is defined by the structure and goals of the particular ecological context.

Consistent with Tietjen's theoretical perspective, the cultural differences found between U.S. and Costa Rican children's perceptions of their social relationships reflected the areas of competence emphasized within each culture.

Costa Rican children consistently viewed their social relationships more positively than did U.S. children. In collectivistic cultures, competence involves the ability to cooperate with others to work toward the collective good. Thus, Costa Rican children's social relationships reflected the general prosocial and congenial social attitude found in this type of culture.

The prominence of family relationships compared with nonfamily relationships was evident in Costa Rica. Costa Rican parents were viewed as the two most important providers for all positive qualities, whereas in the United States best friends were often seen as more important than parents (Furman & Buhrmester, 1985). In addition, all positive qualities of relationships with siblings and grandparents in Costa Rica were significantly higher than those found in the United States. Because the family often serves an economic, as well as a social, function in collectivistic cultures, there is greater contact with and interdependence among immediate and extended family members. Therefore, competence may be much more closely tied to familial relationships than is the case in individualistic cultures.

Costa Rican teachers seemed to play a more important role in children's lives and were more highly regarded than U.S. teachers. Because Costa Rican children have a long-term relationship with their teacher, something which is not present in the United States, their competence would be expected to be more closely tied to this network member. However, despite the increased salience of this relationship, especially in the area of affection, teachers were still clearly viewed as less influential than family members on most social provisions.

Consistent with the greater importance of familial relationships in Costa Rica, the relationship with the best friend was found to be of lesser importance. In the United States, relationships with best friends were often viewed as more important than relationships with family members, especially siblings and grandparents (Furman & Buhrmester, 1985). Although there was evidence of a developmental shift toward greater importance of the best friend in terms of satisfaction, there was little evidence suggesting that family members in Costa Rica, especially mothers, became of lesser importance in any provision. One wonders whether this shift to the primacy of the peer group observed among U.S. children is delayed in a collectivistic culture or whether the shift occurs at all. Best friendships may function to promote the individual's goals rather than the group's goals, and therefore this network member may continually be seen as less significant in collectivistic cultures. These findings suggest that future developmental research on children's perceptions of network members in Hispanic cultures needs to examine social relationships over an extended developmental period to clarify these results.

The gender differences for best friends in Costa Rica supports previous research suggesting that girls' best friendships mature at an earlier developmental stage than do boys' (Furman & Buhrmester, 1985; Sharabany, Gershoni, & Hofman, 1981). Costa Rican girls reported greater satisfaction in their relationships with their best friends than did boys, which may reflect research findings that intensive and interdependent relationships are preferred by girls (Tietjen, 1989). However, both boys and girls in Costa Rica perceived equally high levels of affection in all relationships, suggesting that affection is a quality that is highly regarded across network members in collectivistic cultures regardless of gender.

Many similarities in how children from the United States and Costa Rica perceived their relationships with network members were evident, but there were important differences as well. These differences reflected the influence of the culture on children's perceptions. Overall, this study provided evidence for the importance of considering cultural relativism in the study of children's social development. To further advance theories of social relationships and understanding of contextual effects on social development, future research efforts might examine the influence of multiple ecological contexts on children's perceptions of their social relationships.

REFERENCES

Biesanz, R., Biesanz, K. Z., & Biesanz, M. H. (1982). *The Costa Ricans.* Englewood Cliffs, NJ: Prentice Hall.

Block, J., & Funder, D. C. (1986). Social roles and social perception: Individual differences in attribution and error. *Journal of Personality and Social Psychology, 51,* 1200–1207.

Buhrmester, D., & Furman, W. (1987). The development of companionship and intimacy. *Child Development, 58,* 1101–1113.

Cochran, M. M., & Brassard, J. A. (1979). Child development and personal social networks. *Child Development, 50,* 601–616.

Furman, W., & Buhrmester, D. (1985). Children's perceptions of the personal relationships in their social networks. *Developmental Psychology, 21,* 1016–1024.

Furman, W., & Buhrmester, D. (1990). *Age differences in perceptions of networks of personal relationships.* Unpublished manuscript.

Garbarino, J. (1982). *Children and families in the social environment.* New York: Aldine de Gruyter.

Hunter, F. T., & Youniss, J. (1982). Changes in functions of three relations during adolescence. *Developmental Psychology, 18,* 806–811.

Kagan, S. (1977). Social motives and behaviors of Mexican-American and Anglo-American children. In J. L. Martinez (Ed.), *Chicano psychology* (pp. 45–86). San Diego, CA: Academic Press.

Kim, J. O., & Mueller, C. W. (1978). *Factor analysis: Statistical methods and practical issues.* Sage University Papers series on Quantitative applications in the social sciences (Series No. 07–014). Beverly Hills, CA: Sage.

Murillo, N. (1971). The Mexican-American family. In C. A. Hernandez, M. J. Haug, & N. N. Wagner (Eds.), *Chicanos: Social and psychological perspectives* (pp. 97–108). St. Louis, MO: C. V. Mosby.

Penalosa, P. (1968). Mexican family roles. *Journal of Marriage and the Family, 30*(4), 680–689.

Raymond, J., Rhoads, D., & Raymond, R. (1980). The relative impact of family and social involvement on Chicano mental health. *American Journal of Community Psychology, 8,* 557–569.

Sandler, I. N., Miller, P., Short, J., & Wolchik, S. A. (1989). Social support as a protective factor for children in stress. In D. Belle (Ed.), *Children's social networks and social support* (pp. 277–307). New York: Wiley.

Sharabany, R., Gershoni, R., & Hofman, J. E. (1981). Girlfriend, boyfriend: Age and sex differences in intimate friendship. *Developmental Psychology, 17,* 800–808.

Sullivan, H. S. (1953). *The interpersonal theory of psychiatry.* New York: Norton.

Tietjen, A. M. (1989). The ecology of children's social support networks. In D. Belle (Ed.), *Children's social networks and social support* (pp. 37–69). New York: Wiley.

Triandis, H. C., Marin, G., Hui, C. H., Lisansky, J., & O'Hati, V. (1984). Role perceptions of Hispanic young adults. *Journal of Cross-Cultural Psychology, 15,* 297–320.

Weiss, R. S. (1974). The provisions of social relationships. In Z. Rubin (Ed.), *Doing unto others* (pp. 17–26). Englewood Cliffs, NJ: Prentice Hall.

Whiting, B. B., & Edwards, C. D. (1988). *Children of different worlds.* Cambridge, MA: Harvard University Press.

Whiting, J. W. M., & Whiting, B. B. (1973). Altruistic and egoistic behavior in six cultures. In D. H. Maybury Lewis (Ed.), *Anthropological studies* (pp. 918–944). Washington, DC: American Anthropological Association.

REVIEW QUESTIONS AND ACTIVITIES

1. Summarize the research on the impact of employed mothers on children's cognitive, emotional, and social development.
2. Do you believe that friendship development in middle childhood is unique to that life stage, or do you believe adolescents and adults display similar friendship behaviors?
3. Describe the ways individuals from cultures different from your own influenced your identity in middle childhood.
4. You have been asked to be a consultant to a local school district. The superintendent wants you to suggest ways teachers can foster multicultural learning in the classrooms. What suggestions would you make? Cite empirical research to support your suggestions.
5. Browse through some children's books. Look at the illustrations as well as the content. Are ethnic and racial minority boys and girls represented throughout the text? Do the authors describe cross-race friendships between characters? Cross-sex friendships? Cross-socioeconomic status friendships?
6. Critically reread one of the excerpted articles in the readings section, and then answer the following questions:
   a. Is the purpose of the research clear? Explain.
   b. Are studies contrary to the current hypothesis cited?
   c. Is the research hypothesis correctly derived from the literature and theory that have been cited? Or are there some important steps missing and left to the speculation of the reader?
   d. Are there possible experimenter biases? Explain.
   e. Were the conclusions drawn by the author consistent with the results obtained?
   f. What follow-up studies do you think are needed? Why these studies? Describe the methodology you would use in these follow-up studies.

SUGGESTIONS FOR FURTHER READING

Banks, J., & Banks, C. (Eds.). (1995). *Handbook of research on multicultural education.* New York: Simon & Schuster Macmillan.

Laosa, L. M. (1999). Intercultural transitions in human development and education. *Journal of Applied Developmental Psychology, 20,* 355–406.

McLoyd, V. (1990). The impact of economic hardship on black families and children: Psychological distress, parenting, and socioemotional development. *Child Development, 61,* 311–346.

Sleeter, C. (1992). Restructuring schools for multicultural education. *Journal of Teacher Education, 43,* 141–148.

4

Don't look where you fall, but where you slipped.
African Proverb

A friend's eye is a good mirror.
Irish Proverb

Adolescence

Questions for Reflection

- Do you believe your adolescence was a period of psychic conflict for you? Why or why not?
- Do you know of anyone who has a negative body image? What problems do they suffer because of this negative image? What do you believe can help an individual overcome a negative body image?
- What sorts of things made you the happiest during adolescence? Most afraid? The unhappiest? Did you ever feel depressed during adolescence? How do you account for these emotions?
- List the names of your friends during adolescence. Do you still consider these individuals to be your friends today? Why or why not? What activities did you engage in with your friends during adolescence? What activities did you avoid? Why?
- From whom did you learn about sexuality? Did this instruction include the emotional aspects of sexuality? Did it include taking responsibility for one's sexuality?

OVERVIEW: CULTURAL INFLUENCES ON DEVELOPMENT IN ADOLESCENCE

The word *adolescence* comes from the Latin verb *adolescere,* which translates "to grow to maturity" or "to grow up." In the life cycle, adolescence is a transitional stage or bridge between childhood and adulthood. The age at which this transition begins, and its duration or length in time, varies from one person to another. Look at a photo from your junior high school yearbook. All of the students are approximately the same age, yet they do not look like they are at all. Notice how some of your peers were taller than most, others shorter than most, those who were "developed" for their age, and those peers who resembled much younger children. Would you claim that all of the people in this photo were in adolescence? Why or why not? What sort of markers would you use to indicate when adolescence begins and ends?

In some cultures, elaborate ceremonies are held to celebrate the passage from childhood to adulthood to announce to the community that a child is now a member of adult society. For example, many cultures require that girls who begin menstruating must be prepared for adult womanhood by undergoing a process of instruction in domestic and parental duties, sexuality, and modes of dress (Rice, 1997). Boys in one South Pacific culture leap headfirst from a platform built 100 feet high in a tree, with 90-foot-long vines tied to their ankles. The vines catch them up short, just before they hit the ground. It is believed that if a boy is brave enough to go through this rite, he is worthy to be an adult (Rice, 1997).

These events are called *rites of passage* or *initiation rites.* While you or your peers may not have participated in such a rite of passage, there are other rites that usher in the stage of adolescence. For example, those who participate in an organized religion are initiated through ceremonies such as confirmation or bar or bat mitzvahs. What sorts of initiation rites do you recall from your and your peers' adolescence? Were these rites associated with physical changes taking place in your body? With chronological age? Or with some other event?

When do you believe you entered adolescence? Do you believe your adolescence began at age 13, when you first entered the "teen years"? Or do you believe you entered adolescence when you entered middle school? Perhaps you attribute the beginning of your adolescence to menarche or spermarche, the signals of sexual maturation for females and males, respectively. You may, on the other hand, set the onset of adolescence as we already mentioned, when you participated in a religious ceremony marking your maturity. Or, in fact, you may have no markers to highlight when adolescence began for you.

When do you believe adolescence ends? Perhaps at 19, the end of the "teen years"? Perhaps when you complete high school? When you move out of your parents' home? When you graduate from college? When you get your driver's license? When you become eligible to vote?

Unlike the other stages of the life cycle we have discussed, adolescence (and, as we will see in the next chapter, adulthood) does not have a fixed age range associated with it. In addition, issues that individuals in their later teens must master (e.g., developing a vocational identity) are qualitatively different from those tasks younger adolescents face. Thus, as some theorists have suggested (e.g., Newman & Newman, 1975), adolescence consists principally of two stages, early adolescence (ages 13–17) and late adolescence (ages 18–22).

In this chapter, we will address issues common to both early and late adolescence. Specifically, we will discuss identity development, friendships and membership in a peer group, body image, depression, sexual activity and risk-taking behavior. We begin with a discussion of the physical changes that take place during adolescence.

PHYSICAL DEVELOPMENT DURING ADOLESCENCE

Adolescence is marked by changes in physical development. These physical changes occur during the stage of development referred to as *pubescence,* which is the period of rapid growth that culminates in *puberty,* or sexual maturation and reproductive capacity. Pubescence technically begins when the hypothalamus (part of the upper brain stem) signals the pituitary gland to release the hormones known as gonadotrophins. This occurs during girls' and boys' sleep a year or so before any of the physical changes associated with pubescence appear (Schowalter & Anyan, 1981). Look back at the photo of your junior high class. The obvious physical differences among adolescents of identical chronological age underscore an endocrinological issue: The hypothalamus does not signal the pituitary to release gonadotrophins at the same time in every adolescent. The factors that activate the hypothalamus have not yet been determined. However, researchers (e.g., Frisch, 1984) have argued that the hypothalamus monitors adolescents' body weight and releases the necessary hormones when the body is of sufficient weight.

In the United States, the age at which puberty is reached has declined, with the trend now leveling off (Adams, Montemayor, & Gullotta, 1996). Most adolescent girls in the United States begin pubescence at approximately 11 years of age and reach the end of their growth by age 17. Their growth spurt starts between 9.5 and 14.5 years. Girls grow fastest in height and weight at approximately 12 years of age. They reach 98% of their adult height at 16.25 years. Girls typically mature, on the average, two years earlier than boys. As a group, boys are physically stronger, are taller, and weigh more than girls after puberty (Rice, 1997).

During adolescence, girls and boys undergo common physical changes. For example, their lymphatic tissues decrease in size, they lose vision due to rapid changes in eyes between the ages of 11 and 14, and their facial structures change during pubescence (Steinberg, 1999). Also, their hairline recedes and the facial bones mature in such a way that the chin and nose become prominent (Steinberg, 1999). Adolescents' weight nearly doubles during pubescence; on average, girls weigh 25 pounds less than boys, as a result of their lower proportion of muscle to fat tissue (Hyde & DeLamater, 1999; Reid & Paludi, 1993); however, there is considerable overlap in the distributions (Petersen & Taylor, 1980). By the time they are 15, adolescents have lost 20 deciduous teeth, and during pubescence, the number of bone masses drops as well, from approximately 350 to less than 220, as a result of epiphyseal unions (Petersen & Taylor, 1980).

The sequence of events in the maturation of sexual and reproductive anatomy in adolescent girls is not universally predictable, but maturation does proceed in distinct developmental stages (Hyde & DeLamater, 1999; Katchadorian, 1977) as follows:

Growth of breasts
Growth of pubic hair
Body growth
Menarche
Growth of underarm hair
Increased output of oil- and sweat-producing glands

For adolescent boys, the sequence of development also proceeds by general pattern (Hyde & DeLamater, 1999; Katchadorian, 1977), as follows:

Growth of testes, scrotal sac
Growth of pubic hair
Body growth
Growth of penis, prostate gland, seminal vesicles
Change in voice
First ejaculation of semen
Growth of facial and underarm hair
Increased output of oil- and sweat-producing glands

Further, children who are better nourished mature earlier. Menarche is reached later in less developed countries than in more developed countries (Hyde & DeLamater, 1999).

The age at which puberty is reached for boys and girls has a considerable impact on their behavior during adolescence. The impact of *early* or *late puberty* for girls is not favorable (Ge, Conger, & Elder, 1996; Gunn & Petersen, 1984; Swar & Richards, 1996) and generally poses an added source of anxiety and embarrassment, concerns that affect girls' identity development. For example, adolescent girls who mature earlier than average begin dating earlier and will more often express less self-confidence than girls who reach puberty at a later age. Early maturing girls also express dissatisfaction with their bodies, feel isolated from other girls their own age who haven't reached puberty, and earn lower grades in school (Blyth, Simmins, & Zakin, 1985). In addition, early maturing girls have imposed on them sexual responsibilities that they are not ready to accept, given that their intellectual, social, and emotional maturity lag behind their physical maturity. Longitudinal studies have reported that by adulthood, early maturing girls exhibit a high level of cognitive mastery and coping skills because of their role-taking experiences throughout adolescence (Livson & Peskin, 1980).

Adolescent girls who mature later tend to be more tense, have low self-esteem, and more actively seek attention than non–later-maturing girls. Once menarche is reached, however, these feelings of low self-esteem diminish (Brooks-Gunn, Newman, & Holerness, 1994; Lackovic-Grgin, Dekovic, & Opacic, 1994; Livson & Peskin, 1980; Spencer, Dupree, & Swanson, 1998).

Early maturing boys, because they are tall for their age, more muscular, and better coordinated, enjoy athletic and social advantages. They are more likely to participate in extracurricular activities in school, receive greater social recognition by peers who appoint them to positions of leadership, and are more popular with girls because of their "adultlike" appearance and skills. Early puberty for boys is typically associated with early sexual experiences (Spencer et al., 1998).

Later maturing boys suffer several social disadvantages and report feelings of inferiority as a result (Apter, Galatzer, Beth-Halachmi, & Laron, 1981). At age 15, later maturing boys are approximately 8 inches shorter and 30 pounds lighter than early maturing boys. Consequently, they exhibit less strength and poorer motor performance, coordination, and reaction time than early maturing boys. Since coordination and physical size are important for peer acceptance among adolescent boys, later maturing boys may have a negative self-concept and identity (Spencer et al., 1998).

The physical changes that take place during adolescence take on psychological importance in adolescents' lives, including various critical aspects of cognitive, emotional, and social development. We will discuss first the impact of changing physiques on body image and dating behavior for adolescent girls, which illustrates this interdependency among the physical, cognitive, emotional, and social processes of development.

COGNITIVE DEVELOPMENT

Focus on Body Image

Most adolescent girls in North American culture do not view the normal developmental process of adolescence positively. During adolescence, girls normally accumulate body fat. Girls interpret this accumulation of fat as "gaining weight" and thus begin dieting and engaging in weight-related concerns (O'Dea & Abraham, 1999). Pipher (1994), after examining the adjustment problems faced by adolescent girls searching for beauty, concluded that adolescent girls suffer psychologically from negative body image, lowered self-esteem, and achievement conflicts—all as a consequence of the culture's messages about young women's bodies needing to be protected, made more beautiful, and preserved.

Approximately 1% of women between the ages of 12 and 25 years suffer from *anorexia nervosa,* in which almost all food is refused (Smith, 1996). The most likely age for the onset of anorexia is 12 to 18 years. Anorexia is considered a serious eating disorder because 15% of anorexics die (Smith, 1996; vanBuskirk, 1977). *Bulimia,* or the "binge-purge" syndrome in which the individual eats and then rids herself of the food by vomiting or by using laxatives, is a fairly common problem. Surveys of college populations, not clinical populations, have found a high incidence (13% to 67%) of women who engage in bulimic behaviors. These percentages underreport this eating disorder because of the extreme secrecy bulimics maintain surrounding the complex behavior. Unlike anorexics, the eating habits of bulimics in social situations appear "normal."

Very often, eating disorders begin in response to a new situation in which adolescent girls may be judged by masculine-biased standards—for example, in dating, starting high school or college, and achievement situations. Eating disorders are becoming widespread problems in North American culture. In recent years, there has been empirical support for minority adolescent girls developing a higher incidence of eating disorders as they assimilate into the majority white culture (Henriques, Calhoun, & Cann, 1996), in which many adolescent girls associate gaining weight with rejection by their friends, especially male friends and boyfriends.

It seems that as long as our society stresses thinness as a major criterion of beauty, we will have many women jeopardizing their physical well-being and having poor self-concepts. As Christine Smith (1996) concluded:

> Beliefs about what is attractive or erotic vary from one culture to another and from one historical period to another. What is beautiful? In some cultures facial scarring is attractive; in others, drooping breasts. What is currently beautiful for women in Western culture? If one looks at the media . . . one sees models who are tall and very thin; they are wrinkle-free, and have small hips and waists, medium to large breasts, and European features. Women in Western cultures are constantly bombarded with images of this unrealistically slim, eternally young, ideal woman. (p. 91)

Carolyn Tucker Halpern, J. Richard Udry, Benjamin Campbell, and Chirayath Suchindran, in their article, "Effects of Body Fat on Weight Concerns, Dating, and Sexual Activity: A Longitudinal Analysis of Black and White Adolescent Girls," excerpted in the readings section (see pp. 147–154), report that the majority of adolescent girls in their sample indicated that having a boyfriend was important to them and that slimness is an important factor in dating and popularity with boys. Halpern and her colleagues also report that for both black and white adolescent girls, more body fat was associated with a lower probability of dating. Approximately one third of black adolescent girls and one half of white adolescent girls indicated they dieted. Approximately 25% of white and 20% of black girls reported more than two weight-loss attempts within the six-month period of the study. Methods of weight-loss attempt included counting calories, exercising, eating diet foods, fasting, attending a weight-loss clinic, using laxatives or diet pills, and vomiting.

Ferron's (1997) research offers us another view of the impact of culture on developmental processes. Ferron studied French adolescent and American adolescent girls' experiences with body image. She reported that the majority (75%) of American girls in her sample refused to believe any predisposition for physique; rather, they believed that there are personal characteristics that will enable them to achieve a body that represents an image of perfection. Examples of these personal characteristics include willpower, self-confidence, adherence to rules, and courage. Ferron also reported that American adolescent girls were more likely than French girls to engage in behaviors that are harmful to their health, including eating unbalanced diets. American girls were more likely than French girls to be dissatisfied with their bodies.

Ferron's French adolescent girls, on the other hand, believed that an ideal body was not possible to attain. Seventy-five percent of these girls reported that their bodily limitations, as well as their physical appearance, were predetermined and could not be modified through willpower or courage.

Ferron also interviewed adolescent boys and found that 80% of American boys (compared with 90% of American girls) believed in special diets and exercise programs; less than half of French boys and girls gave similar answers. Ferron reported that in both the French and American samples, the majority of boys were satisfied with their height and weight. American boys were more likely than French boys to believe that they have a good physique in general.

Ferron further reported that approximately 75% of the American sample, as compared with less than 25% of the French sample, believed they would be considerably happier in their lives if they had a "flawless" body. Happiness was operationally translated into having more friends, having an easier life, being accepted by a peer group, and finding love.

Both Halpern et al. and Ferron offer suggestions for teachers, parents, and therapists in helping adolescent girls and boys incorporate a positive body image into their identity, an important developmental task of the adolescent stage of the life cycle.

EMOTIONAL DEVELOPMENT

Focus on Identity Development

Erik Erikson (1963) theorized that adolescence is the life stage during which we acquire an identity. The term *identity* has many components, including psychological, sexual, physical, social, moral, ideological, religious, and vocational elements that make up the total self (Kroger, 2000; Vartanian, 1998). During adolescence, according to Erikson, we may be identified by our physical characteristics, appearance, or physique or by our skills in social interaction with members of our peer group. We may also be identified by our commitment to a career, our political party or religious affiliation, and our ethnic or racial identity. Erikson theorized that adolescents who accept themselves and have developed what he termed a positive identity are more likely to be psychologically healthy than adolescents who have a so-called negative identity, that is, an identity based on dislike of the self.

Erikson termed the time during which we are developing an identity a "psychological moratorium." He theorized that the length of the adolescence period, and the degree of emotional conflict experienced by adolescents, will vary among different cultures. Individuals who do not achieve an identity during this stage are filled with self-doubt and role confusion. Some adolescents may withdraw from their parents, school, and friends (Greenberger, Chen, Tally, & Dong, 2000). Others may abuse alcohol and other drugs to relieve the anxiety associated with not knowing who they are (French & Picthall-French, 1998; Hussong, 2000; Litterick, 1998; Vik & Brown, 1998). Still others may be delinquent and/or engage in violent behavior toward themselves and/or others, including eating disorders, murder, and suicide (Brown, 1999; Erkut, Szalacha, Alarcon, & Coll, 1999; Wagner, Aiken, Mullaley, & Tobin, 2000; Wichstrom, 1999; Zayas, Kaplan, Turner, Romano, & Gonzalez-Ramos, 2000).

Erikson's theory has been extended in more recent years to include ethnic identity membership. *Ethnic identity* refers to the total of group members' feelings about the values, symbols, and common histories that identify them as a distinct group (Yeh & Huang, 1996). Ethnic identity provides us with a sense of belonging as well as with a sense of historical continuity. The culture into which some adolescents are born is typically not valued or appreciated by the culture in which they are raised (White & Burke, 1987). Minority adolescents must relate the minority group to the dominant culture (Atkinson, Morten, & Sue, 1983). They can accomplish this task through *assimilation,* which occurs when ethnic group members choose to identify with the culture of the dominant society and thus relinquish essential ties to their natal ethnic culture.

Alternatively, some adolescents accomplish this identity development through *integration,* which occurs when there is strong identification and involvement with both the dominant culture and the ethnic culture. Still other adolescents may *separate,* that is, focus exclusively on their cultural values, with little or no interaction with the dominant society; or they may engage in *marginality,* in which there is an absence of attachment or attention to one's culture of origin as well as a lack of involvement with the dominant society.

Thus, in addition to the identity concerns of adolescents in general, minority adolescents must also establish an ethnic identity. Empirical research suggests that adolescents who engage in integration are better adjusted psychologically and have higher self-esteem than those adolescents who participate through assimilation, separation, or marginality (White & Burke, 1987). Hence, giving up one's ethnic culture has a negative impact on adolescents' self-esteem and self-concept.

Furthermore, research has suggested that African American adolescents encounter barriers to racial identity (Landrine, 1995). For gifted African American adolescents, the development of a racial identity may be especially difficult (Miller, 1999). In developing a racial identity, they typically confront conflicting values which they must choose between. Gifted African American adolescents may choose to be underachievers academically so they will not be perceived as "acting white" (Miller, 1999).

Dien (1983) highlighted the distinction in Chinese culture between the "big me" (referring to the group) and the "little me" (referring to the individual). This distinction illustrates the subordination of an individual identity to the collective identity: The "little me" is sacrificed to complete the "big me." Thus in Chinese culture, an individual's successful development of the self is measured by his or her ability to maintain interdependence between the "little me" and the "big me." This process is different from Western psychological theories of identity development, which maintain that separation and individuation from the group is a successful resolution of this process. Doi (1973) also pointed out that *amae* (dependence on and connection to others) is the central part of the Japanese conception of identity. Guneri, Sumer, and Yildirim (1999) described how adolescents in Turkey are expected to demonstrate cultural and familial allegiance and to be modest about personal qualities.

In "The Collectivistic Nature of Ethnic Identity Development Among Asian-American College Students," which is excerpted in the readings section (see pp. 154–158), Christine J. Yeh and Karen Huang discuss Asian American college students' ethnic identity development. They report that traditional theories of ethnic identification are inappropriate for Asians and Asian Americans. Traditionally, these theories have discussed individuals as being motivated by internal forces—for example, by frustration. Yeh and Huang, however, report that Asian Americans are influenced by relationships and external forces (e.g., social context or geographic location). Further, Yeh and Huang report that contrary to previous research, Asian Americans have their ethnic identity forced upon them by people in their environment. They also found that shame was a strong influence on Asian American students' identity development. As Yeh and Huang discuss:

> Subjects reported that they conformed to "white society" in order to avoid the embarrassment of being different, or identified with their own culture when it was expected, in order to avoid shame in the family or among other Asians. (p. 656; in this text, pp. 156–157)

Yeh and Huang's research suggests that ethnic identity development influences emotional state, cognitive development, and social relations. We will now turn our attention to issues related to adolescents' emotional development.

Focus on Adolescent Depression

Adolescence was not recognized as a stage in human development until the twentieth century. The study of adolescence as a scientific field of study is credited to G. Stanley Hall, whose book, *Adolescence: Its Psychology and Its Relation to Physiology, Anthropology, Sociology, Sex, Crime, Religion, and Education,* was published in 1904. Hall theorized that the major physical changes of adolescence cause major psychological changes. He believed that young people's efforts to adjust to their changing bodies usher in a period of *"sturm und drang"* (storm and stress), from which adolescents can emerge stronger. Hall described adolescence as a time of emotional upset and instability in which adolescents' moods oscillate between energy and lethargy, joy and depression, and egotism and self-deprecation. Hall, as well as some contemporary theorists and researchers (e.g., Arnett, 1999; Buchanan et al., 1990), viewed adolescence as more difficult than other life stages because of three major issues: (1) conflict with parents, (2) mood disruptions, and (3) risk behavior that may potentially cause adolescents to harm themselves and/or others. We can see Hall's image of adolescence played out in such popular television programs and movies of the 1990s as *Beverly Hills 90210, Melrose Place,* and *Stepmom.* Classic books such as *Catcher in the Rye* and *Lord of the Flies* also portray Hall's *sturm und drang* view of adolescence.

Apart from the media attention to Hall's views about the inevitable storm and stress of adolescence, his theory is no longer universally accepted by scholars (see Arnett, 1999, for a review of Hall's theory). Adolescence is now seen as much more differentiated. In addition, while Hall believed adolescents would outgrow the turmoil, the evidence is clear that psychological difficulties that appear in adolescence persist and should be treated; they seldom disappear by themselves. Moreover, the more adolescents experience negative life events associated with adolescence (e.g., low popularity with a peer group, poor school performance, marital discord in their family), the more they will experience mood disruptions (Brooks-Gunn & Warren, 1989; Crystal et al., 1994).

Added to this, lesbian and gay adolescents have a two- to threefold risk of suicide and are at greater risk for depression because of homophobia, violence directed at them, and a culture that typically does not value their sexual orientation (Saewyc, Bearinger, Heinz, Blum, & Resnick, 1998). Adolescents who live in rural areas are also at greater risk for depression than adolescents who live in urban or suburban areas (Sarigiani, Wilson, Petersen, & Vicary, 1990).

The article by Anne Petersen and her colleagues, "Depression in Adolescence," which is excerpted in the readings section (see pp. 158–170), clearly identifies adolescence as an important stage of the life cycle for understanding depression. Their review of the empirical research ". . . demonstrated the inappropriateness of the belief that difficulties such as depression were normal manifestations of adolescence and pointed toward the need for assessment, diagnosis, prevention, and treatment at this age" (p. 155; in this text, p. 159).

Petersen and her colleagues discuss the finding that rates of depression are higher among minority adolescents than in majority adolescents. For example, high rates of depression have been found among American Indian adolescents (LaFromboise et al., 1995). Adolescent American Indian girls are especially vulnerable; they are 6 times as likely as boys to be sexually abused (LaFromboise et al., 1995; U.S. Congress, 1990). According to LaFromboise and her colleagues:

> The impact of the welfare culture and . . . losses can be identified at the individual level by feelings of victimization attributable to racism and stereotyping, value conflicts, or confusion, isolation, and oppression. (p. 201)

Latina adolescents also are at high risk for depression attributable to discrimination, cultural role conflicts, immigration trauma, language barriers, and a lowered level of financial, educational, and medical resources (Ginorio, Gutierrez, Cauce, & Acosta, 1995). Root (1995) also identified depression as a major issue for Asian adolescent girls, especially those who are immigrants and refugees, who feel constrained in their new environment by language barriers and lack of social networks.

Despite the high incidence of depression among ethnic minority adolescents, they are not likely to utilize mental health services (Ginorio et al., 1995). Several factors contribute to this underutilization, including lack of culturally relevant therapeutic treatment, language barriers, lack of transportation to mental health facilities, and the perception that mental health services are only for seriously impaired individuals. There is also the belief that problems should not be discussed with individuals outside of the family (McGoldrick, Giordano, & Pearce, 1996).

SOCIAL DEVELOPMENT

Focus on Friendships and Membership in a Peer Group

During your adolescence, how did you define a close personal friend?

During adolescence did you have cross-race friendships? Why or why not?

What did you talk about with your adolescent friends? What did you not talk about?

Did you have friendships with people who had chronic illnesses and/or disabilities? Why or why not?

As we have seen in previous chapters, research has identified the critical importance of friendship in life cycle development. For example, during adolescence the peer group becomes more structured and organized than it was during childhood (Adams et al., 1996; Hartup & Stevens, 1999).

The functions of a peer group for adolescents include social support, emotional intimacy, companionship, fun, and understanding (Adams et al., 1996; Connolly & Goldberg, 1999; Hartup & Stevens, 1999; Steinberg, 1999). Adolescents who have close friendships with peers show better academic performance, are more likely to stay in school, and have lower rates of juvenile delinquency and adult psychopathology (Hartup & Stevens, 1999; Steinberg, 1999). Furthermore, in peer groups, adolescents learn how to buffer stress due to family discord, relationship problems, and academic problems (Hartup & Stevens, 1999). In adolescence, friendships with peers provide part of the emotional support formerly provided by parents (Cotterell, 1992). While friendships are important to us at all ages, it is during adolescence that friendships take the form of intimate relationships built on trust and loyalty (Connolly & Goldberg, 1999). This development in friendship patterns results from the normative cognitive changes—especially the ability to take others' perspectives—that occur during adolescence (Adams et al., 1996). This new ability increases adolescents' capacity for empathy and helpfulness (Hartup & Stevens, 1999).

There is empirical research to suggest gender comparisons in friendship development in adolescence. Adolescent girls, as compared with boys, prefer to have a *clique*—a few close friendships (all girls, typically)—rather than many less-intimate friends (Rose, 1995). Because adolescent girls are trying to resolve, simultaneously, identity issues in vocational development, sexual development, and gender-role development, they seek out another girl, or two girls, in whom they can confide the intimate details of their life and from whom they can obtain emotional support.

In American Indian cultures, the central theme for adolescent girls and adult women is caring for others. Red Horse (1980) described the cycle of this three-stage theme: being cared for, preparing to care for, and caring for. As American Indians have recognized, respected, and encouraged, many adolescent girls, in general, are socialized to have a capacity for intimacy in relationships. This intimacy is expressed verbally by discussing intimate issues such as love interests, career plans, concerns about appearance, and fear of gaining weight; it is expressed nonverbally through body posture, eye contact, and touch (Mayo & Henley, 1981). Podrouzek and Furrow (1988) found this capacity for expressing intimacy in girls as young as 2 and 4 years of age.

Friendships for adolescent boys differ from those of adolescent girls in a number of ways. For example, boys are less likely to participate in a clique; rather, they tend to participate in a *crowd*—a large group of boys recognized by a few characteristics, such as orientation toward academics or involvement in athletics (Adams et al., 1996; Way & Pahl, 1999). Conversations in crowds are typically less intimate than those in cliques (Steinberg, 1999).

During adolescence, in-school contact with friends occurs in student government and service clubs. However, the organization of such extracurricular activities provides little opportunity for students to interact with peers of a variety of ethnic backgrounds. Consequently, interracial friendships are less common than same-race friendships during adolescence (Rose, 1996). According to Suzanna Rose (1996):

> Is it possible for Black and white women to be friends? The analysis of racism, racial identity, and cross-race friendship presented here suggests that mutually satisfying and fully reciprocal cross-race friendships are rare. Moreover, the desire and ability to establish them may depend not only on the individual women's racial identity but the match between the two. . . . It appears that Black and white women can indeed be friends, but only if the right combination of people and circumstances is present. Otherwise, as one Black woman asserted, the friendships will be held together "by a very weak glue." (p. 224)

Cami K. McBride and Tiffany Field, in their article, "Adolescent Same-Sex and Opposite-Sex Best Friend Interactions," excerpted in the readings section (see pp. 170–173), report that adolescent girls feel more comfortable during interactions with other girls than with boys. They report that adolescent boys in their sample were also more comfortable interacting with girls, not with other boys. McBride and Field's findings support the theory that girls encourage intimacy and comfortableness in conversations. Boys may feel more likely to open up and discuss their feelings about issues with girls than with boys since intimacy and sharing are perceived to be more "feminine" behaviors than ones associated with "masculinity" in most cultures. To be more accepted by their male peer group, adolescent boys may inhibit their desire to self-disclose (i.e., to share personal or intimate information about oneself with others; Jourard, 1964). In conversations with girls, however, boys are reinforced for self-disclosure (Tannen, 1995). This discussion of peer group behaviors continues in the following section, which addresses adolescents' risk-taking behavior and its effects on the development of sexual responsibility.

Focus on Sexual Activity and Risk-Taking Behavior

The age at which first sexual intercourse occurs has steadily declined over the years (Conley, 1999; Michael, Gagnon, Laumann, & Kolata, 1994). Recent research suggests that approximately half of all black men have had intercourse by age 15, half of all Latinos by age 16.5, and half of all white men by 17 years. The age of first sexual intercourse for women is slightly older: half of all black women have had intercourse by 17, and half of white women and Latinas have had intercourse by 18 years (Michael et al., 1994).

Researchers (e.g., Michael et al., 1994) have also interviewed adolescents and young adults about the reasons why they decided to have sexual intercourse for the first time. The majority of the men (51%) attributed it to readiness and curiosity; 25% indicated they had affection for their partner. For women, the reverse was true: Approximately half indicated the reason for engaging in sexual intercourse was affection for their partner and about one fourth reported curiosity and readiness for sexual intercourse. Michael and his colleagues (1994) reported that most of the women in their sample indicated they were in love with their first sexual partner; by contrast, most of the men said they were not in love with their first sexual partner.

One explanation for the increase in early sexual activity among adolescents is that it is an expression of cultural norms (Miller & Benson, 1999; Slonin-Nevo, 1992). Adolescents in North American culture, especially boys, perceive sexual activity as normative and abstinence as nonnormative. Adolescent girls may engage in sexual intercourse as a way to establish intimate relationships (Stanton, Black, Kaljee, & Ricardo, 1993). Since establishing intimate relationships is perceived as normative for adolescents, especially adolescent girls, girls may feel a sense of urgency in engaging in sexual activity so that intimacy may be reached. Research also indicates that adolescent girls who do not have supportive parental relationships frequently try to establish intimate relationships outside of the family (Whitbeck, Hoyt, Miller, & Kao, 1992).

Although the majority of adolescents are engaging in sexual intercourse, they are not using contraceptives (Davis & Bibace, 1999; DiBliasio & Benda, 1990; Lagana, 1999). Approximately 35% of young people ages 15 to 19 used any methods of contraceptives (Forrest & Singh, 1990). Research with adolescent boys 15 to 19 years indicated that of these boys, 23% reported that they or their partners used no contraceptive method or used an ineffective one (i.e., withdrawal, douching, or rhythm) at their last sexual intercourse (Sonnenstein, Pleck, & Ku, 1991). Those adolescents who do use contraception are more likely to use birth control pills or condoms (Amaro, 1995). Many adolescent women who have conceived say they knew about birth control and chose not to use it. In the United States, adolescent women are placed in a double bind when it comes to sex and sexuality. They are encouraged by the media, peers, and family members to be sexy, yet they are also given the clear message to be "not sexual." Using contraception is a clear signal that one is sexually active. Adolescent women may not be able to face their family with this marker of adult status. When they do not use contraception, being "swept off their feet" in passionate romance may be one way to not take total responsibility for their actions in a culture that condemns women's sexuality (Amaro, 1995).

Because adolescents fail to or decline to use contraception, 1 out of every 8 women ages 15 to 19 (most of them unmarried) becomes pregnant each year in the United States (Hyde & DeLamater, 1999). Adolescents account for a third of all out-of-wedlock births each year nationwide (Hyde & DeLamater, 1999). Approximately 30% of these unplanned pregnancies are terminated by abortion, 50% result in live births, and the remainder end in miscarriage (Hyde & DeLamater, 1999).

For many adolescents, sexuality is a socially scripted activity. The expression of sexuality is governed less by biological drives per se than by the expectations and social significance associated with certain patterns of sexual activity. This scripting is further governed by the adolescents' and adults' ethnic backgrounds. For example, discussing sex is usually not appropriate behavior, especially for women, in many Latin American communities (Amaro & Gornemann, 1992; Brooks-Gunn, Boyer, & Hein, 1988).

Typically, women and men do not share information about past or current sexual partners or practices. This is especially true with regard to the use of birth control methods and the prevention of sexually transmitted diseases (Amaro & Gornemann, 1992). Worth and Rodriguez (1987) suggested that traditional beliefs about gender roles continue to have a major influence on how women and men interact as well as on their attitudes about sex. Their observations of the interplay between *marianismo* and *machismo* in Latin American communities suggested that marianismo demands that women defer to men:

> Attractiveness is seen as being synonymous with sexual inexperience or purity. The males are seen as the seducers of the inexperienced (sexually uneducated) women. A woman prepared for sex (e.g., carrying condoms) is perceived to be experienced, loose, and therefore unattractive. (p. 6)

Consequently, women may feel unable to assert themselves by suggesting that their partners wear condoms. They and their partners then are at risk for sexually transmitted diseases as well as for pregnancy. Moreover, if men suggest they use condoms, women may perceive men as wanting sex for pleasure—not for love or with the intention of marriage. Cunningham and Boult (1996) reported that black teenage pregnancy as well as sexually transmitted diseases in South Africa have reached a threatening level. Black adolescent girls in South Africa are especially vulnerable because they reach menarche early and engage in coitus early. LaFromboise and her colleagues (1995) noted that adolescent American Indian girls are a vulnerable population: Those who are sexually active use contraception at one half the rate of their white European American peers. Consequently, the pregnancy rate among American Indian adolescent girls is higher than it is for white adolescents.

Adolescents may view the use of condoms only as a form of birth control, not as a means of protection against sexually transmitted diseases. Use of birth control indicates deliberate sexuality—something that many cultures disapprove of in adolescent girls but encourage and praise in adolescent boys. Adolescent boys assume birth control responsibility significantly less often than do adolescent girls (Jacobs, 1978; McDermott & Gold, 1985). Furthermore, adolescents who feel comfortable in discussing contraception were more likely to use them than those adolescents who are uncomfortable with such self-disclosure (Cunningham & Boult, 1996).

In addition, the majority of women diagnosed with AIDS (acquired immunodeficiency syndrome) are ethnic minority women. Amaro (1988) reported that Hispanic women and children are overrepresented among individuals diagnosed with AIDS. The highest risk factors for adolescents are intravenous (IV) drug use and sexual contact with an individual at risk for AIDS (Suffet & Lifshitz, 1991). Sexual contact includes contact with heterosexual men, gay men, bisexual men, and men having sex with multiple partners.

Research has indicated that the risk of HIV (human immunodeficiency virus) transmission and AIDS infection in adolescent girls is quite great. Risks to adolescent girls result from the increasing rate of unprotected sexual activity, IV drug use, and/or sexual relations with IV drug users (Amaro, 1995; Brooks-Gunn et al., 1988; Dancy, 1996). Girls represent the majority (91.5%) of AIDS cases known to have occurred through heterosexual transmission among adolescents (Amaro, 1995).

Flora and Thoresen (1988) reported that there is a disproportionately high risk of AIDS for adolescent girls who reside in economically deprived communities. Add to this risk the notable misunderstanding of the causes, prevention, and treatment of the AIDS virus among adolescents (DiClemente, Boyer, & Morales, 1988). Adolescent girls and boys may engage in risk behaviors because of developmental limitations in their cognitive abilities. Their thinking is concrete, egocentric, and not future-oriented. They may have a "personal fable" (Elkind, 1984) about their own vulnerability to AIDS. They tell themselves that they are unique, that they are special persons to whom no harm will come, that *they* will not be infected, or that their relationships are different. This personal fable is often supported by a long latency between HIV transmission and the emergence of AIDS symptoms, a period that may last 8 to 10 years. As many as 20% of HIV-positive adults contracted the virus during adolescence (Amaro, 1995). Adolescence is a vulnerable period because risk-taking behavior that can lead to HIV infection and AIDS is a part of this stage of the life cycle. Even when accurate information about AIDS is shared with adolescents, most do not modify their behavior (Travis, 1993).

Flora and Thoresen (1988), as well as others (e.g., Boyer, Shafer, & Tschann, 1997; Brooks-Gunn et al., 1988), recommend that AIDS education programs include information about stereotypes of women and men, sexuality, and lesbian and gay sexual orientations. This "attitudes training" is necessary because many adolescents (as well as many adults) still believe that AIDS is a punishment inflicted on ethnic minority and gay individuals for their lifestyles. Researchers have also noted that individuals who have negative attitudes toward lesbians and gay men are more likely to be poorly informed about AIDS and therefore more likely to stigmatize people with AIDS (Herek & Glunt, 1988). Education must strive to reduce antigay and antiminority prejudice (Amaro, 1995). Flora and Thoresen (1988) recommend training programs that are tailored to gender and ethnic differences among students.

In their excerpted article in the readings section (see pp. 173–177), "Searching for the Magic Johnson Effect: AIDS, Adolescents, and Celebrity Disclosure," Bruce R. Brown Jr., Marc D. Baranowski, John W. Kulig, John N. Stephenson, and Barbara Perry describe their research with adolescent boys' and girls' attitudes toward HIV and AIDS following Magic Johnson's disclosure that he was HIV positive. Sixty percent of adolescents in their study reported that Mr. Johnson's announcement had increased their awareness of AIDS. However, only a small percentage of the adolescents reported an increase in personal threat from the disease. Brown and his colleagues offer suggestions for a comprehensive AIDS-prevention curriculum. Such a curriculum would include cognitive approaches (e.g., gaining knowledge about sexually transmitted diseases, including HIV), behavioral approaches (e.g., learning how to resist peer pressure for sex), and environmental approaches (e.g., having parents talk with adolescents about intimacy in relationships and how and why it is broader than engaging in sexual activity).

In the next chapter on adulthood, the final stage of the life cycle, we will revisit many of the issues addressed in this chapter.

Readings

Effects of Body Fat on Weight Concerns, Dating, and Sexual Activity: A Longitudinal Analysis of Black and White Adolescent Girls*

Carolyn Tucker Halpern, J. Richard Udry, Benjamin Campbell, and Chirayath Suchindran

Pubertal development entails a significant accumulation of body fat for adolescent girls and marks a turning point in weight-related concerns and behavior. Although dieting, eating concerns, and problem eating are relatively rare before adolescence, dieting is common among normal-weight adolescent girls (Attie, Brooks-Gunn, & Warren, 1985; Hawkins, Turell, & Jackson, 1983; Nylander, 1971; Rosen & Gross, 1987), and there is evidence that eating disorders begin during the adolescent years (Crisp, 1984; Johnson, Lewis, Love, Lewis, & Stuckey, 1984; Johnson, Stuckey, Lewis, & Schwartz, 1982; Pyle, Mitchell, & Eckert, 1981). Even when weight control behavior is not pathological, studies have commonly found that many pubertal and postpubertal girls are dissatisfied with their weight, almost always desiring to be slimmer, even when their weight is within the normal range for their height (Casper & Offer, 1990; Dornbusch et al., 1984; Drenowski & Yee, 1987; Fisher, Schneider, Pegler, & Napolitano, 1991; Tobin-Richards, Boxer, & Petersen, 1983; Wardle & Beales, 1986).

Accommodation to the physical transformations of puberty constitutes one of the key developmental challenges during the adolescent period. Attie and Brooks-Gunn (1989) proposed that dieting and problem eating during adolescence may reflect attempts to accommodate "to the physical changes of the pubertal period within a cultural milieu that values the prepubertal over the mature female body" (p. 70). They offered support for this position by pointing to documentation of increasing cultural emphasis on thinness (Bennett & Gurin, 1982; Garner, Garfinkel, Schwartz, & Thompson, 1980) and to demonstrations of links among body fat, abnormal eating attitudes, and eating problems in their own and others' samples of normal-weight adolescent

*From Halpern et al. (1999). *Developmental Psychology, 35*(3), 721–736. Reprinted with permission.

girls (Attie & Brooks-Gunn, 1987, 1989; Rosen & Gross, 1987).

Pubertal maturation is the physical manifestation of the beginning transition to adulthood, and accommodation to the physical changes of puberty therefore provides the context and impetus for other significant transitions in adolescents' interests, expectations, and behavior. One fundamental and linked aspect of these changes is heightened romantic and sexual interest, as well as the increasing concern with physical appearance that accompanies these interests (Simmons & Blyth, 1987). As Attie and Brooks-Gunn suggested (1989), pubertal girls may begin to feel that their changing bodies are diverging from the idealized, slim, but nevertheless "adult," female form that is proffered to them in multiple media. Thus, the convergence of pubertal fat accumulation and increasing romantic interest can result in a struggle with weight that is fueled primarily by concerns about physical attractiveness rather than health. In ethnographic interviews with eighth- and ninth-grade girls, Nichter and Vuckovic (1994) asked whether "a girl has to be thin to be popular with boys" (p. 121); almost half thought that thinness was a requirement for popularity with boys. Similarly, Koff and Rierdan (1991) found that when asked to name the "worst thing about being fat" (p. 309), the most frequent response among their sample of White sixth-grade girls was "feeling unattractive." Paxton et al. (1991) also reported that adolescent girls believe that being slimmer would make them more successful in dating. Recent data on adolescents' perceptions of health norms also indicate that weight is an appearance, rather than health, issue (Evans, Gilpin, Farkas, Shenassa, & Pierce, 1995) and that adolescent girls may worry about fat gains largely because they want to feel and look attractive, not because they worry about diabetes or hypertension.

Ironically, data on perceptions of the "ideal" female figure suggest that adolescent girls' and women's ideals about slimness and physical attractiveness can be somewhat extreme and may diverge from what is seen as attractive by men. Fallon and Rozin (1985) found, for example, that college women's image of the female figure preferred by men was significantly thinner than the preferences actually expressed by college men. Other studies that were based on high school seniors (Dwyer, Feldman, Seltzer, & Mayer, 1969) and middle-school students (Cohn et al., 1987) have also found that girls choose thinner female figures as an ideal body image than boys do, suggesting that adolescent girls may try to adhere to rigid standards of conformity and attractiveness. On the other hand, Fallon and Rozin did find that men "desire women who are thinner than what women currently perceive themselves to be" (p. 104), suggesting that the significant differences between women's ratings of their current and ideal figures are grounded, at least to some extent, in what men actually find attractive.

The coincidence of increases in body fat and increasing heterosocial interest and activity may be particularly problematic for early-maturing girls. Early-maturing girls accumulate body fat earlier and tend to be heavier for their height than later maturers (Faust, 1977). For a time, they are "out of phase" with both their female and male peers and thus face the departure from the slim female form they may idealize earlier than other girls do, and without the reassurances and knowledge that may come from observing similar physical processes in others. When these early physical changes coincide with school transitions, early dating, and attention from older peers, accommodation to increases in body fat may be especially challenging (Caspi & Moffitt, 1991; Simmons & Blyth, 1987; Smolak, Levine, & Gralen, 1993). Earlier maturing girls have more negative attitudes about their bodies and weight and are at higher risk for the development of eating problems and a variety of problem behaviors and norm violations, such as early sexual activity and substance use (Graber, Brooks-Gunn, Paikoff, & Warren, 1994; Stattin & Magnusson, 1990; Tobin-Richards et al., 1983).

Much of what is known about adolescent dieting and weight concerns is based on studies of middle- or upper-middle-class White samples, the group that is most likely to be focused on thinness and that is thought to be most at risk for the development of eating problems. There is relatively little information about dieting and weight attitudes among Black adolescents, despite the facts that Black female adolescents are among the demographic groups most likely to be overweight (U.S. Department of Health and Human Services, 1997; Popkin & Udry, 1998) and that it is during adolescence when a significantly higher overweight prevalence among Blacks versus Whites first appears (Kumanyika, 1987). The implications of socioeconomic differences for weight concerns during adolescence are also unclear. Among both Black and White adult women there is a clear, inverse relationship between socioeconomic status (SES) and obesity (Sobal & Stunkard, 1989) and between social class and weight concerns (Dornbush et al., 1984; Stunkard, 1975), with higher SES girls being thinner and more concerned about weight. Because of the disproportionate representation of Blacks in lower income groups, it has been assumed that a preoccupation with weight is less common among Black adolescent girls (Attie & Brooks-Gunn, 1987).

There is some empirical support for the assumption that Black adolescent girls are less concerned about weight. Studies of high school and college students have found that Blacks are more satisfied with their weight and figures, are less likely to think they are fat, and have a heavier ideal weight than their White peers (Desmond, Price, Hallinan, & Smith, 1989; Huenemann, Shapiro, Hampton, & Mitchell, 1966; Rucker & Cash, 1992). Black girls also are reported to be less preoccupied with weight and dieting than Whites and to diet less often (Abrams, Allen, & Gray, 1993; Casper & Offer, 1990; Desmond et al., 1989; Emmons, 1992; Rosen & Gross, 1987). Race differences in self-satisfaction and in perceptions of ideal weight suggest that there are race-based cultural differences in the "standards" presented and, therefore, in the development of body image and body ideals. Thomas and James (1988) argued that Blacks develop a less strict body-image ideal than Whites. Blacks may be less likely to internalize the thin standards of beauty that are so common in majority media and be more likely to rely on family and community standards that are less "fat phobic" (Allan, Mayo, & Michel, 1993; Rucker & Cash, 1992). These ideas are consistent with ethnographic interview data from adolescents. White girls are more likely to hold a narrow, fixed ideal of attractiveness, which assumes that thinness is a prerequisite for popularity and romance; whereas Blacks report greater reliance on interpersonal feedback and admiration of unique personal styles (Parker et al., 1995). Recently reported longitudinal data from the National Heart, Lung, and Blood Institute Growth and Health Study also indicate that Black adolescent girls are significantly less likely to desire to be thin and are more likely to endorse statements equating greater body fat with feeling "healthier," "prettier," and "more like a girl"; these differences are evident at ages 9 and 10 and continue into adulthood (Schreiber, 1998).

. . .

We address these questions by using data from a 2-year longitudinal study of biosocial factors in adolescent development. The project included repeated measurements of physical, attitudinal, and behavioral variables for 200 Black and White adolescent girls of varying economic backgrounds.

. . .

Most girls in our sample reported that having a boyfriend was either somewhat or very important to them, and virtually all girls saw physical attractiveness as important. As adolescent girls experience the weight and fat gains that accompany and follow puberty, they must reconcile these gains with their belief that slimness is an important factor in dating and popularity with boys. One of our purposes was to examine the implications that individual differences in body fat actually have for dating and sexual activity among female adolescents. For White girls and Black girls with college-educated mothers, more body fat, even among nonobese girls, strongly lowered the probability of dating. What is particularly striking about this finding is that not only were above average levels of body fat a disadvantage in terms of dating but below average levels of body fat actually conferred a significant advantage over average body fat levels. The 5 ft 3 in. girl who weighed 110 pounds was twice as likely to date as a girl of the same height and level of pubertal maturity who weighed 126 pounds. Differences in body fat also had indirect implications for sexual activity; slimmer girls, because they were more likely to date, were also likely to have higher levels of noncoital and coital activity. Obviously these adolescent girls had not carried out the sort of probability calculations that we have presented here, but adolescents, White adolescents in particular, believe that slimness is important to the likelihood of dating (Paxton et al., 1991). Our data indicate that they are right. . . .

In our repeated measures of analyses covering a 2-year period from early to middle adolescence, we found no evidence that dating or sexual activity contributes to or exacerbates dieting and weight concerns. The absence of an association held for both Blacks and Whites, across mother education groups, for both early and on-time maturers, and for girls who reached menarche in the 6-month period before study entry. We also found no support for a reverse causal path, that weight concerns may prompt girls to seek out sexual encounters. Unfortunately, our data did not allow us to sequence precisely the initiation of dating in relation to early manifestations of pubertal maturation and fat accumulation. If there are exacerbating effects of dating or sexual activity on weight concerns that go beyond individual differences in body fat, then the effects may be specific to the joint occurrence of multiple developmental transitions. For example, in their analysis of 79 White adolescent girls followed from sixth to eighth grade, Smolak et al. (1993) concluded that long-term differences in weight concerns and weight management were only evident if dating was synchronous with early menarche and a move to middle school. These latter findings suggest that synchronous transitions may be critical. However, no measures of weight or body fat were included in these analyses, and therefore their importance as mediators in this process cannot be determined. . . .

We did not find a significant relationship between age at menarche and indicators of weight and eating concerns. This may be partly a function of the fact that very late-maturing girls were not included in our sample. We did find significant relationships between pubertal development and each indicator of weight and eating concerns when body fat was not included as a predictor (analyses not shown). However, when body fat was added to the models, the effect of pubertal development was reduced and became nonsignificant for weight dissatisfaction and dieting. This pattern suggests that body fat is a mediator, or mechanism, through which this pubertal process operates (Baron & Kenny, 1986). Early pubertal maturation, and more advanced pubertal status, have been linked to more dieting and an increased risk of eating problems. The present findings, and those of other researchers who have simultaneously examined the effects of pubertal timing and weight or body fat (e.g., Attie & Brooks-Gunn, 1989), suggest that pubertal timing and status effects on body dissatisfaction and eating concerns are partly a function of the fact that early maturers, on average, are heavier than on-time and late maturers. This conclusion underscores the utility of distinguishing the specific attributes and processes that mediate the link between a multifaceted construct such as pubertal timing and the variety of outcome variables with which it may be associated. In the specific case of outcomes such as weight dissatisfaction and dieting, differences in body fat appear to be an important operative factor. Cairns and Cairns (1996) made similar arguments about the mediational role that body mass index may serve in the relationship between pubertal timing and social outcomes such as dropping out of school among adolescent girls. We are not suggesting that body fat can account for all of the links between pubertal timing and social or psychological outcomes. However, studies that fail to consider weight or body fat when examining the effects of pubertal timing or status on weight concerns may be missing key dynamics underlying the relationship because there is no physical context in which to evaluate the appropriateness of the levels of dieting and weight concern that are observed.

In the present sample, weight concerns were strongly tied to individual levels of body fat for both Black and White adolescent girls. Regardless of maternal education, race, absence of obesity, and timing of puberty, girls with more body fat were more likely to report dieting, to diet more frequently and for longer time periods, to be more dissatisfied with their weight, and to have greater eating concerns. These results are consistent with those of Schreiber et al. (1996), who found that a higher body mass index was strongly associated with efforts to lose weight for both Black and White adolescent girls, and they concluded that the degree of being overweight was the main determinant of weight loss efforts for each race. However, even though body fat was strongly linked to indicators of weight concern for both Blacks and Whites, weight issues were more salient to White girls. When we controlled for mother's education, and for race differences in body fat and obesity, White girls were significantly more dissatisfied with their weight, were more likely to diet, and had higher eating concerns than Black girls. These findings are consistent with proposals that there are race-based cultural differences in body ideals. At early adolescence, and continuing into middle adolescence, Black girls are more comfortable with higher levels of body fat.

All adolescent girls value physical attractiveness. However, given the race-based differences in cultural standards of attractiveness, the implications of accumulations of body fat also vary by race, and for Blacks, by SES. In any given sample of White girls, reported levels of dieting and weight concern are likely to be out of proportion to levels of overweight and obesity. It is clear that many White girls have internalized a slim female form that is biologically unrealistic, and because of this, they struggle with normal fat gains. However, the present data indicate that these weight concerns are grounded in measurable experiential differences. Individual differences in body fat, even among normal-weight girls, have significant implications for dating—an activity that is highly valued. For White adolescents, the implications of differences in body fat are consistent across outcomes, and for the socioeconomic range reflected in the present sample, they did not vary by mother's education. Parents and other agents who are concerned about high, yet nonclinical, levels of weight concern and management among adolescents must approach the issue with the understanding that messages about weight control will not be credible if they do not take the experiential implications of weight differences into account. Furthermore, if the goal is to convince normal-weight girls to worry less about their weight, then adults must also convince girls' male peers about the attractiveness of a broader range of body types.

Among Black girls, mother's education was a moderator of dating outcomes but not of weight concerns. For the daughters of college-educated mothers, more body fat was associated with a lower probability of dating. In contrast, for Black girls in the noncollege group, fat had no significant implications for dating probability. Although we could not examine this possibility directly in our data, these differential implications suggest that there may be differences in the potential partners, and their perceptions of what is attractive, of Black girls who fall into these two economic categories. We know relatively little about the homogamy of adolescent couples, and pursuit of this issue would be an interesting expansion of research on weight concerns. Of further interest is the finding that the different implications of body fat for dating for low- and high-SES Black adolescents did not translate into differential weight concern across economic groups. Black girls with college-educated mothers reported the same (lower) levels of dieting and weight concern as their peers whose mothers were not college educated. This pattern may be partly a function of the race differences observed in the importance placed on having a boyfriend. Black girls were less likely than White girls to think that having a boyfriend was important, a difference that was not moderated by mother's education. Thus, it appears that higher levels of body fat are viewed as acceptable and attractive by Black adolescent girls, regardless of their economic status or the implications body fat may have for dating outcomes.

In one sense, these patterns reflect a healthy acceptance of normal female physical maturation patterns and suggest that Black adolescent girls are likely to accommodate more easily to fat gains. However, just as a rigid adherence to an impossibly slim body ideal can set the stage for problematic eating attitudes, a blanket acceptance of very high levels of body fat has negative implications for long-term social adjustment and health. . . .

REFERENCES

Abrams, K. K., Allen, L. R., & Gray, J. J. (1993). Disordered eating attitudes and behaviors, psychological adjustment, and ethnic identity: A comparison of black and white female college students. *International Journal of Eating Disorders, 14,* 49–57.

Allan, J. D., Mayo, K., & Michel, Y. (1993). Body size values of white and black women. *Research in Nursing and Health, 16,* 323–333.

Attie, I., & Brooks-Gunn, J. (1987). Weight concerns as chronic stressors in women. In R. C. Barnett, L. Biener, & G. K. Baruch (Eds.), *Gender and stress* (pp. 218–254). New York: Free Press.

Attie, I., & Brooks-Gunn, J. (1989). Development of eating problems in adolescent girls: A longitudinal study. *Developmental Psychology, 25,* 70–79.

Attie, L., Brooks-Gunn, J., & Warren, M. P. (1985). *Developmental antecedents of restrained eating: The impact of pubertal change.* Paper presented at the biennial meeting of the Society for Research in Child Development, Toronto, Ontario, Canada.

Bachrach, C. A., Horn, M. C., Mosher, W. D., & Shimizu, I. (1985). *National Survey of Family Growth, Cycle III: Sample design, weighting and variance estimation* (Vital and Health Statistics, Series 2, No. 98, DHHS Publication No. PHS85-1372). Hyattsville, MD: U.S. National Center for Health Statistics.

Baron, R. M., & Kenny, D. A. (1986). The moderator—mediator variable distinction in social psychological research: Conceptual, strategic and statistical considerations. *Journal of Personality and Social Psychology, 41,* 1173–1182.

Bearman, P. S., Jones, J., & Udry, J. R. (1997). *The National Longitudinal Study of Adolescent Health: Research Design* [On-line]. Available: http://www.cpc.unc.edu/projects/addhealth/design.html

Bennett, W., & Gurin, J. (1982). *The dieter's dilemma: Eating less and weighing more.* New York: Basic Books.

Bentler, P. M. (1968a). Heterosexual behavior assessment: I. Males. *Behavior Research and Therapy, 6,* 21–25.

Bentler, P. M. (1968b). Heterosexual behavior assessment: II. Females. *Behavior Research and Therapy, 6,* 27–30.

Blair, D., Habicht, J. P., Sims, E. A. H., Sylwester, D., & Abraham, S. (1984). Evidence for an increased risk for hypertension with centrally located body fat and the effect of race and sex on this risk. *American Journal of Epidemiology, 119,* 526–540.

Cairns, R. B., & Cairns, B. D. (1996. March). *An attractive proposal on early maturation.* Paper presented at the biennial meeting of the Society for Research on Adolescence, Boston.

Casper, R. C., & Offer, D. (1990). Weight and dieting concerns in adolescents, fashion or symptom? *Pediatrics, 86,* 384–390.

Caspi, A., & Moffitt, T. E. (1991). Individual differences are accentuated during periods of social change: The sample case of girls at puberty. *Journal of Personality and Social Psychology, 61,* 157–168.

Caufman, E., & Steinberg, L. (1996). Interactive effects of menarcheal status and dating on dieting and disordered eating among adolescent girls. *Developmental Psychology, 32,* 631–635.

Cohn, L. D., Adler, A. E., Irwin, C. E., Jr., Millstein, S. G., Kegeles, S. M., & Stone, G. (1987). Body figure preferences in male and female adolescents. *Journal of Abnormal Psychology, 96,* 276–279.

Crisp, A. H. (1984). The psychopathology of anorexia nervosa: Getting the "heat" out of the system. In A. J. Stunkard & E. Stellarm (Eds.,), *Eating and its disorders* (pp. 209–234). New York: Raven Press.

Desmond, S. M., Price, J. H., Hallinan, C., & Smith D. (1989). Black and white adolescents' perceptions of their ideal weight. *Journal of School Health, 59,* 353–358.

Dornbusch, S. M., Carlsmith, J. M., Duncan, P. D., Gross, R. T., Martin, J. A., Ritter, P. L., & Siegel-Gorelick, B. (1984). Sexual maturation, social class, and the desire to be thinner among adolescent females. *Developmental and Behavioral Pediatrics, 5,* 308–314.

Drenowski, A., & Yee, D. K. (1987). Men and body image: Are males satisfied with their body weight? *Psychosomatic Medicine, 49,* 626–634.

Dwyer, J. T., Feldman, J. J., Seltzer, C. C., & Mayer, J. (1969). Adolescent attitudes toward weight and appearance. *Journal of Nutrition Education, 1,* 14–19.

Emmons, L. (1992). Dieting and purging behavior in black and white high school students. *Journal of the American Dietetic Association, 92,* 306–312.

Evans, N., Gilpin, E., Farkas, A. J., Shenassa, E., & Pierce, J. P. (1995). Adolescents' perceptions of their peers' health norms. *American Journal of Public Health, 85,* 1064–1069.

Fallon, A. E., & Rozin, P. (1985). Sex differences in perceptions of desirable body shape. *Journal of Abnormal Psychology, 94,* 102–105.

Faust, M. (1977). Somatic development of adolescent girls. *Monograph of the Society for Research in Child Development, 42*(1, Serial No. 169).

Fisher, M., Schneider, M., Pegler, C., & Napolitano, B. (1991). Eating attitudes, health-risk behaviors, self-esteem, and anxiety among adolescent females in a suburban high school. *Journal of Adolescent Health, 12,* 377–384.

Forbes, G. B., & Amirhakimi, G. H. (1970). Skinfold thickness and body fat in children. *Human Biology, 42,* 401–418.

Frisancho, A. R., & Flegel, P. N. (1982). Relative merits of old and new indices of body mass with reference to skinfold thickness. *American Journal of Clinical Nutrition, 36,* 697–699.

Garn, S. M., & Clark, D. C. (1976). Trends in fatness and the origins of obesity. *Pediatrics, 57,* 443–456.

Garner, D. M., & Garfinkel, P. E. (1979). The Eating Attitudes Test: An index of the symptoms of anorexia nervosa. *Psychological Medicine, 9,* 1–7.

Garner, D. M., Garfinkel, P. E., Schwartz, D., & Thompson, M. (1980). Cultural expectations of thinness in women. *Psychological Reports, 47,* 483–491.

Gillum, R. F. (1987). Overweight and obesity in black women: A review of published data from the National Center for Health Statistics. *Journal of the National Medical Association, 79,* 865–871.

Gortmaker, S. L., Dietz, W. H., Sobol, A. M., & Wehler, C. A. (1987). Increasing pediatric obesity in the United States. *American Journal of Diseases of Children, 141,* 535–540.

Gortmaker, S. L., Must, A., Perrin, J. M., Sobol, A. M., & Dietz, W. H. (1993). Social and economic consequences of overweight in adolescence and young adulthood. *New England Journal of Medicine, 329,* 1008–1012.

Graber, J. A., Brooks-Gunn, J., Paikoff, R. L., & Warren, M. P. (1994). Prediction of eating problems: An 8-year study of adolescent girls. *Developmental Psychology, 30,* 823–834.

Halpern, C. T., Udry, J. R., Campbell, B., & Suchindran, C. (1993). Testosterone and pubertal development as predictors of sexual activity: A panel analysis of adolescent males. *Psychomatic Medicine, 55,* 436–447.

Halpern, C. T., Udry, J. R., & Suchindran, C. (1997). Testosterone predicts initiation of coitus in adolescent females. *Psychosomatic Medicine, 59,* 161–171.

Hanan, W. R., Harlan, E. A., & Grillo, C. P. (1980). Secondary sex characteristics of girls 12 to 17 years of age: The U.S. Health Examination Survey. *Journal of Pediatrics, 96,* 1074–1078.

Hawkins, R. C., Turell, S., & Jackson, L. J. (1983). Desirable and undesirable masculine and feminine traits in relation to students' dieting tendencies and body image dissatisfaction. *Sex Roles, 9,* 705–718.

Herman-Giddens, M. E., Slora, E. J., Wasserman, R. C., Bourdony, C. J., Bhapkar, M. V., Koch, G. G., & Hasemeier, C. M. (1997). Secondary sex characteristics and menses in young girls seen in office practice: A study from the Pediatric Research in Office Settings Network. *Pediatrics, 99,* 505–512.

Huenemann, R. L., Shapiro, L. R., Hampton, M. C., & Mitchell, B. W. (1966). A longitudinal study of gross body composition and body conformation and their association with food and activity in a teen-age population. *American Journal of Clinical Nutrition, 18,* 325–338.

Johnson, C., Lewis, C., Love, S., Lewis, L., & Stuckey, M. (1984). Incidence and correlates of bulimic behavior in a female high school population. *Journal of Youth and Adolescence, 13,* 15–26.

Johnson, C. L., Stuckey, M. K., Lewis, L. D., & Schwartz, D. M. (1982). Bulimia: A descriptive survey of 316 cases. *International Journal of Eating Disorders, 2,* 3–16.

Johnston, F. E., Hamill, P. V. V., & Lemeshow, S. (1974). Skinfold thickness of youths 12–17 years, United States (Vital and Health Statistics Series 11, No. 132, HRA 74-1614). Hyattsville, MD: National Center for Health Statistics.

Kahn, J. R., Kalsbeek, W. D., & Hofferth, S. L. (1988). National estimates of teenage sexual activity: Evaluating the comparability of three national surveys. *Demography, 25,* 189–204.

Koff, E., & Rierdan, J. (1991). Perceptions of weight and attitudes toward eating in early adolescent girls. *Journal of Adolescent Health, 12,* 307–312.

Kumanyika, S. (1987). Obesity in black women. *Epidemiologic Reviews, 9,* 31–50.

Morris, N. M., & Udry, J. R. (1980). Validation of a self-administered instrument to assess stage of adolescent development. *Journal of Youth and Adolescence, 9,* 271–280.

Mueller, W. H. (1982). The changes with age of the anatomical distribution of fat. *Social Science Medicine, 16,* 191–196.

National Center for Health Statistics. (1979). *Plan and operation of the Health and Nutrition Examination Survey, United States, 1971–1973* (Vital and Health Statistics Series 1, No. 10, HRA 75-1310). Hyattsville, MD: Author.

Nichter, M., & Vuckovic, N. (1994). Fat talk: Body image among adolescent girls. In N. Sault (Ed.), *Many mirrors: Body image and social relations* (pp. 109–131). New Brunswick, NJ: Rutgers University Press.

Nylander, I. (1971). The feeling of being fat and dieting in a school population: An epidemiologic interview investigation. *Acta SocioMedica Scandinavica, 3,* 17–26.

Parker, S., Nichter, M., Nichter, M., Vuckovic, N., Sims, C., & Ritenbaugh, C. (1995). Body image and weight concerns among African American and white adolescent females: Differences which make a difference. *Human Organization, 54,* 103–114.

Paxton, S., Wertheim, E., Gibbons, K., Szmukler, G., Hiller, L., & Petrovich, J. (1991). Body image satisfaction, dieting beliefs, and weight loss behaviors in adolescent girls and boys. *Journal of Youth and Adolescence, 20,* 361–379.

Popkin, B. M., & Udry, J. R. (1998). Adolescent obesity increases significantly for second and third generation U.S. immigrants: The National Longitudinal Study of Adolescent Health. *Journal of Nutrition, 128,* 701–706.

Pyle, R. L., Mitchell, J. E., & Eckert, E. D. (1981). Bulimia: A report of 34 cases. *Journal of Clinical Psychiatry, 42,* 60–64.

Robson, J. R. K., Bazin, M., & Soderstrom, R. (1971). Ethnic differences in skin-fold thickness. *American Journal of Clinical Nutrition, 24,* 864–868.

Rosen, J. C., & Gross, J. (1987). Prevalence of weight reducing and weight gaining in adolescent girls and boys. *Health Psychology 6,* 131–147.

Rucker, C. E., III, & Cash, T. F. (1992). Body images, body-size perceptions, and eating behaviors among African-American and white college women. *International Journal of Eating Disorders, 12,* 291–299.

SAS Institute, Inc. (1997). *SAS/STAT software: Changes and enhancements through Release 6.12.* Cary, NC: Author.

Schreiber, G. B. (1998, February). *Black–white differences in perceptions of body shape and attitudes toward being fat: Desire or destiny?* Paper presented at the biennial meeting of the Society for Research on Adolescence, San Diego, CA.

Schreiber, G. B., Robins, M., Striegel-Moore, R., Obarzanek, E., Morrison, J. A., & Wright, D. J. (1996). Weight modification efforts reported by black and white preadolescent girls: National Heart, Lung, and Blood Institute Growth and Health Study. *Pediatrics, 98,* 63–70.

Seltzer, C. C., & Mayer, J. (1965). A simple criterion of obesity. *Postgraduate Medicine, 38,* A101–A107.

Simmons, R. G., & Blyth, D. A. (1987). *Moving into adolescence: The impact of pubertal change and school context.* Hawthorne, NJ: Aldine de Gruyter.

Smith, E. A., & Udry, J. R. (1985). Coital and non-coital sexual behaviors of white and black adolescents. *American Journal of Public Health, 75,* 1200–1203.

Smolak, L., Levine, M. P., & Gralen, S. (1993). The impact of puberty and dating on eating problems among middle school girls. *Journal of Youth and Adolescence, 22,* 355–368.

Sobal, J., & Stunkard, A. J. (1989). Socioeconomic status and obesity: A review of the literature. *Psychological Bulletin, 105,* 260–275.

Stattin, H., & Magnusson, D. (1990). *Pubertal maturation in female development.* Hillsdale, NJ: Erlbaum.

Stevens, J. (1986). *Applied multivariate statistics for the social sciences.* Hillsdale, NJ: Erlbaum.

Stunkard, A. J. (1975). From explanation to action in psychosomatic medicine: The case of obesity. *Psychosomatic Medicine, 37,* 195–236.

Swarr, A. E., & Richards, M. H. (1966). Longitudinal effects of adolescent girls' pubertal development, perceptions of pubertal timing, and parental relations on eating problems. *Developmental Psychology, 32,* 636–646.

Tanner, J. M. (1962). *Growth at adolescence.* Oxford, England: Blackwell.

Thomas, V. G., & James, M. D. (1988). Body image, dieting tendencies, and sex role traits in urban black women. *Sex Roles, 18,* 523–529.

Tobin-Richards, M. H., Boxer, A. M., & Petersen, A. C. (1983). The psychological significance of pubertal change: Sex differences in perceptions of self during early adolescence. In J. Brooks-Gunn & A. C. Petersen (Eds.), *Girls at puberty* (pp. 127–154). New York: Plenum.

Udry, J. R., Talbert, L. M., & Morris, N. M. (1986). Biosocial foundations for adolescent female sexuality. *Demography, 23,* 217–230.

U.S. Department of Health and Human Services. (1997). Update: Prevalence of overweight among children, adolescents, and adults—United States, 1988–94. *Morbidity and Mortality Weekly Report, 46,* 199–202.

Wardle, J., & Beales, S. (1986). Restraint, body image and food attitudes in children from 12 to 18 years. *Appetite, 7,* 209–217.

Weiner, J. S., & Lourie, J. A. (1969). *Human biology: A guide to field methods.* Philadelphia: F. A. Davis.

Zeger, S. L., & Liang, K. Y. (1986). Longitudinal data analysis for discrete and continuous outcomes. *Biometrics, 42,* 121–130.

Zelnik, M., & Kantner, J. F. (1980). Sexual activity, contraceptive use and pregnancy among metropolitan-area teenagers: 1971–1979. *Family Planning Perspectives, 125,* 230–237.

Zelnik, M., & Shah, J. K. (1983). First intercourse among young Americans. *Family Planning Perspectives, 152,* 64–70.

The Collectivistic Nature of Ethnic Identity Development Among Asian-American College Students*

Christine J. Yeh and Karen Huang

Phinney and Alipuria (1987) define ethnic identity as "an individual's sense of self as a member of an ethnic group and the attitudes and behaviors associated with that sense" (p. 36). They further state that ethnic identity development is "the process of development from an unexamined ethnic identity through a period of exploration, to arrive at an achieved ethnic identity" (p. 38). According to Sotomayor (1977), ethnic identification refers to identification or feeling of membership with others regarding the character, the spirit of a culture or the cultural ethos based on a sense of commonality of origin, beliefs, values, customs or practices of a specific group of people. Thus, unlike the concept of race, which pertains to specific physical traits, the concept of ethnicity connotes cultural group membership.

For Asian-Americans, questions arise as to how they develop an integrated sense of self inclusive of their past and present cultural contexts. Since an integrated ethnic identity is believed to precede bicultural competence (Zuniga, 1988), understanding the process and

*From Yeh & Huang (1996). *Adolescence, 31*(123), 645–661. Reprinted with permission.

components of ethnic identification is valuable; in addition, it may also help to prevent numerous psychological dysfunctions related to identity confusion (Sommers, 1960; Wong-Rieger & Taylor, 1981).

The construct of ethnic identity has been under considerable scrutiny in recent decades. In her literature review of ethnic identity, Phinney (1990) describes three theoretical frameworks of research: identity formation, social identity, and acculturation. While these frameworks overlap in their general conceptualizations of ethnic identity, they differ in the specific aspects they emphasize. As a result, the range of inquiry and focus of ethnic identity research has been broad, including self-identification, group membership, attitudes toward one's ethnic group, ethnic involvement, and cultural values and beliefs (Phinney, 1990).

Theories of identity formation parallel those of ego identity development, investigating the psychological states through which the individual progresses in establishing an ethnic identity.

Acculturation theories focus on how an individual relates to the dominant or host society, arguing that a unified ethnic identity results from the individual's commitment to, or separation from, his or her ethnic ties (Makabe, 1979; Ullah, 1985). Such research typically investigates the extent to which ethnic identity persists over time within a dominant majority group context.

Finally, social identity theory asserts that ethnic identity is influenced by the social context and that the ethnic individual develops an identity from his or her own group as well as from the "countergroup" (White & Burke, 1987). The majority of ethnic identity studies in this framework investigate how ethnic group membership contributes to self-hatred or self-concept, as well as the solutions that "minority group" members employ to improve their social status (e.g., "passing" as a dominant group member; establishing a bicultural identity).

Very few studies of ethnic identity include social context as part of their empirical examinations. However, ethnic identity must be considered within a specific social context since the contrast an individual experiences between his or her culture of origin and the dominant culture will significantly affect the self. Further, an individual's ethnic identity may vary according to the influence of other individuals and the social context (Rosenthal & Hrynevich, 1985).

. . .

There were three main goals for the present study: first, to gather more descriptive information on the influences, experiences, and other factors involved in Asian-American ethnic identification; second, to determine the patterns or commonalities in the process of their ethnic identity development; third, to understand the collectivistic nature of Asian cultures in relation to the process of Asian-American ethnic identification.

The question asked in order to address these research goals was: *How do Asian-American adolescents conceptualize the concept of ethnic identity both visually and verbally, and which factors do they identify as influential in the development of their ethnic identity?*

. . .

Participants were 78 college students from a prestigious California university (41 males and 46 females with a mean age of 19.3 years). The sample reflected 30 academic majors. Only students of self-identified Asian ancestry who were at the undergraduate level were included; 30% identified their ethnic background as Chinese, 33% as Taiwanese, 14% as Korean, 7% as Japanese, 3% as Filipino, 2% as Vietnamese, 1% as Indian, and 7% as mixed Asian.

. . . In order to investigate the specific research question and goals, the authors developed the Ethnic Identity Development Exercise (EIDE), a projective assessment that obtains detailed and descriptive information about ethnic identity development. The first section includes several demographic items to be completed by the subject. The second section is open-ended; subjects are instructed to describe (write, draw) the process of their ethnic identity development, including anything that they believe to be significant in this process. The instructions were intended to give subjects the freedom to explore and describe their ethnic identity development without specific cues or leads.

Research in developmental psychology and projective techniques indicates that the use of drawings (visual representations) in psychological assessment is a valuable and effective means of soliciting information about various intrapsychic structures, wishes, and fantasies (Brandell, 1986), behaviors and emotions (Koppitz, 1968), body image concerns (Fisher, 1959), interpersonal relationships (Burns & Kaufman, 1972), personality characteristics and identity conflicts (Ellis, 1989), and experiences (Schildkrout & Schenker, 1972; Howe, Burgess, & McCormack, 1987). Historically, drawings have been used to identify personality factors and intellectual capacities (Goodenough, 1926; Hammer, 1958; Koppitz, 1968; Machover, 1949). This method is particularly relevant with children and adolescents who may not yet have the vocabulary or verbal skills required for adequate self-expression (Gardner, 1973).

The drawing process has also been utilized in psychological research because its indirect and task-oriented nature often provides a nonthreatening, anxiety-reducing means of expressing feelings and potential distress for adolescents (Burgess, Hartman, McCausland, & Powers, 1984; Kelley, 1984; Pynoos & Eth, 1985). This method may be particularly relevant for research with Asian-Americans, where concern over shame, embarrassment, and emotional expressiveness may inhibit their willingness and ability to articulate their experiences. Therefore, psychological research utilizing methodologies that encourage projective self-expression (e.g., the drawing process) may be successful in uncovering descriptive factors, processes, and conflicts related to ethnic identity development.

. . .

The data from the sample support our contention that the present theories and stages models of ethnic identification are inappropriate for Asians and Asian-Americans. These models describe a process that is linear, intrapersonal, and individualistic; the individual is typically motivated by internal forces such as anger and frustration. For instance, Sotomayor (1977) noted that "The meaning of ethnicity is highly subjective and concerned with the sentiment felt by the individual." Our results, however, describe ethnic identification as a dynamic and complex process, emphasizing collectivism, the impact of external forces in defining one's sense of self, and the power of shame as a motivating force in ethnic identity development.

. . .

The subjects made numerous and consistent references to the impact of "white society" in our results. Many subjects believed that the standards and beliefs of, and their alienation from, the dominant white culture were very strong factors in shaping their ethnic identity. . . .

The results of this study clearly indicate that our sample of Asian-Americans was strongly motivated by external forces, such as relationships and social context, in the ethnic identification process. Thus, theories of ethnic identity development should consider and incorporate the collectivistic nature of Asian culture. The variety and number of external, relational and situational influences suggest a model of ethnic identity formation that is dynamic, malleable, and situation-specific. Current models of ethnic identity development are individuocentric and fail to acknowledge the importance of social interactions and context. Moreover, they oversimplify and overgeneralize the complex process of ethnic identity development by failing to recognize the range of factors and experiences unique to Asian-Americans.

. . . We found that shame strongly influenced the subjects, the results indicating that 40% of the sample described shame as an important factor in ethnic identity development. Subjects reported that they conformed to "white society" in order to avoid the embarrassment of being different, or identified with their own culture when it was expected, in order to avoid shame in the family or among other

Asians. However, previous theories on ethnic identification argue that individuals are motivated by internal anger and resentment toward the dominant culture. Interestingly, our sample reported low rates of anger in their completed EIDE forms; only 6% mentioned anger as a motivating force in their ethnic identification. Therefore, we believe that the process of ethnic identification is unique for Asian-Americans in that shame, not anger, is a culturally powerful motivating force in defining oneself.

. . .

In conclusion, theories of ethnic identity development must acknowledge the collectivistic nature of ethnic identity development among Asian-Americans. Future investigative efforts in this area should focus on creating a model of ethnic identity development that includes collectivistic considerations.

REFERENCES

Alba, R. (1985). *Ethnicity and race in the U.S.A.* London: Routledge & Kegan Paul.

Arce, C. (1981). A reconsideration of Chicano culture and identity. *Daedalus, 110*(2), 177–192.

Atkinson, D. R., Morten, G., & Sue, D. W. (1983). *Counseling American minorities: A cross-cultural perspective.* Dubuque, IA: Wm. C. Brown.

Betancourt, H., & Lopez, S. R. (1992). The study of culture, ethnicity, and race in American psychology. *American Psychologist, 48,* 629–637.

Brandell, J. R. (1986). Autogenic stories and projective drawings: Tools for the clinical assessment and treatment of severely disturbed and at-risk children. *Journal of Independent Social Work, 1*(2), 19–32.

Burgess, A. W., Hartman, C. R., McCausland, M. P., & Powers, P. A. (1984). Response patterns in children and adolescents exploited through sex rings and pornography. *American Journal of Psychiatry, 141*(5), 656–662.

Burns, R. C., & Kaufman, S. H. (1972). *Actions, styles and symbols in kinetic family drawings (K-F-D): An interpretive manual.* New York: Brunner/Mazel.

Cooley, C. H. (1902). *Human nature and the social order.* New York: Scribner.

Dashefesky, A. (1976). *Ethnic identity in society.* Chicago: Rand McNally.

DeVos, G., & Rommanucci-Ross, L. (1975). *Ethnic identity: Cultural continuities and change.* Palo Alto: Mayfield.

Dien, D. S. (1983). Big me and little me: A Chinese perspective on self. *Psychiatry, 46,* 281–286.

Doi, T. (1973). *The anatomy of dependence.* New York: Harper & Row.

Ellis, M. L. (1989). Women: The mirage of the perfect image. *Arts in Psychotherapy, 16*(4), 263–276.

Erickson, E. (1968). Identity: Youth and crisis. New York: Norton.

Fisher, S. (1959). Body reactivity gradients and figure drawing variables. *Journal of Consulting Psychology, 23,* 54–59.

Frideres, J., & Goldenberg, S. (1982). Myth and reality in western Canada. *International Journal of Intercultural Relations, 6,* 137–151.

Gardner, H. (1975). *The shattered mind.* New York: Random House.

Gay, G. (1985). Implications of the selected models of ethnic identity development for educators. *Journal of Negro Education, 54,* 43–55.

Goodenough, F. L. (1926). *Measuring of intelligence by drawings.* New York: World Book.

Gurin, P., & Epps, E. (1975). *Black consciousness, identity and achievement.* New York: Wiley.

Hammer, E. (1958). *The clinical applications of projective drawings.* Springfield, IL: C. C. Thomas.

Hayano, D. (1981). Ethnic identification and disidentification: Japanese-American views of Chinese-Americans. *Ethnic Groups, 3,* 157–171.

Helms, J. E. (1986). Expanding racial identity theory to cover counseling process. *Journal of Counseling Psychology, 33, 62–64.*

Higgins, E. T., & King, G. (1981). Accessibility of social constructs: Information-processing consequences of individual and contextual variability. In N. Cantor & J. F. Kihlstrom (Eds.), *Personality, cognition and social interaction* (pp. 69–121). Hillsdale, NJ: Erlbaum.

Howe, J. W., Burgess, A. W., & McCormack, A. (1987). Adolescent runaways and their drawings. *Arts in Psychotherapy, 14*(1), 35–40.

Hu, H. C. (1975). The Chinese concepts of face. In D. G. Haring (Ed.), *Personal character and cultural milieu* (p. 452). Syracuse: Syracuse University Press.

Jeffres, L. W. (1983). Communication, social class, and culture. *Communication Research, 10*(2), 220–246.

Jones, W. T. (1990). Perspectives in ethnicity. In L. Moore (Ed.), *Evolving theoretical perspectives on students. New directions for student services, no. 51* (pp. 59–72). San Francisco: Jossey-Bass.

Kelley, S. J. (1984). The use of art therapy for sexually abused children. *Journal of Psychosocial Nursing, 22*(12), 12–18.

Koppitz, E. M. (1968). *Psychological evaluation of children's human figure drawings.* New York: Grune & Stratton.

LaFromboise, T., Coleman, H. L. K., & Gerton, J. (1993). Psychological impact of biculturalism: Evidence and theory. *Psychological Bulletin, 114*(3), 395–412.

Lee, Y. T. (1994). Why does American psychology have cultural limitations? *American Psychologist, 49*(6), 524.

Machover, K. (1949). *Personality projection in the drawing of a human figure.* Springfield, IL: C. C. Thomas.

Makabe, T. (1979). Ethnic identity scale and social mobility: The case of Nisei in Toronto. *The Canadian Review of Sociology and Anthropology, 16,* 136–145.

Maldonado, D., Jr. (1975). Ethnic self-identity and self-understanding. *Social Casework, 56,* 618–622.

Markus, H. R., & Kitayama, S. (1991). Culture and self: Implications for cognition, emotion, and motivation. *Psychological Review, 98*(2), 224–253.

Markus, H., & Kunda, Z. (1986). Stability and malleability of the self-concept. *Journal of Personality and Social Psychology, 51*(4), 858–866.

Mendelberg, H. (1986). Identity conflict in Mexican-American adolescents. *Adolescence, 21,* 215–222.

Noda, K. E. (1989). Growing up Asian in America. In Asian Women United of California (Ed.), *Making waves: Anthology of writing by and about Asian-American women* (p. 243). Boston: Beacon Press.

Ostrow, M. (1977). The psychological determinants of Jewish identity. *Israel Annals of Psychiatry and Related Disciplines, 15,* 313–335.

Phinney, J., & Alipuria, L. (1987). *Ethnic identity in older adolescents from four ethnic groups.* Paper presented at the biennial meeting of the Society for Research in Child Development, Baltimore. (ERIC Document Reproduction Service No. ED 283 058)

Phinney, J. S. (1990). Ethnic identity in adolescents and adults: Review of research. *Psychological Bulletin, 108*(3), 499–514.

Pye, L. (1968). *The spirit of Chinese politics: A study of authority crisis in political development.* Cambridge, MA: MIT Press.

Pynoos, R. S., & Eth, S. (1985). Children traumatized by witnessing acts of personal violence: Homicide, rape, or suicide behavior. In S. Eth & R. S. Pynoos (Eds.), *Post-traumatic stress disorder in children.* Washington: American Psychiatric Press.

Rosenthal, D., & Hrynevich, C. (1985). Ethnicity and ethnic identity: A comparative study of Greek-, Italian-, and Anglo-Australian adolescents. *International Journal of Psychology, 20,* 723–742.

Schildkrout, M., & Shenker, I. (1972). *Human figure drawings in adolescence.* New York: Brunner/Mazel.

Shon, S., & Ja, D. (1982). Asian-American families. In M. McGoldrick, K. Pearce, & J. Giordano (Eds.), *Ethnicity and family therapy* (p. 452). New York: Guilford.

Sommers, V. S. (1960). Identity conflict and acculturation problems in Oriental-Americans. *Journal of Orthopsychiatry, 30*(3), 368–644.

Sotomayor, M. (1977). Language, culture, and ethnicity in developing self-concept. *Social Casework, 58,* 195–203.

Staiano, K. (1980). Ethnicity as process: The creation of an Afro-American identity. *Ethnicity, 7,* 27–33.

Sue, S., & Sue, D. W. (1971). Chinese-American personality and mental health. *Amerasia Journal, 1,* 36–49.

Tajfel, H. (1978). *The social psychology of minorities.* New York: Minority Rights Group.

Tajfel, H. (1981). *Human groups and social categories.* Cambridge, UK: Cambridge University Press.

Tajfel, H., & Turner, J. (1979). An integrative theory of intergroup conflict. In W. Austin & S. Worchel (Eds.), *The social psychology of intergroup relations* (pp. 33–47). Monterey, CA: Brooks/Cole.

Toupin, E. A. (1980). Counseling Asians: Psychotherapy in the context of racism and Asian-American history. *American Journal of Orthopsychiatry, 50*(1), 76–86.

Triandis, H. C. (1989). The self and social behavior in differing cultural contexts. *Psychological Review, 96*(3), 506–520.

Ullah, P. (1985). Second generation Irish youth: Identity and ethnicity. *New Community, 12,* 310–320.

White, C., & Burke, P. (1987). Ethnic role identity among black and white college students: An interactionist approach. *Sociological Perspectives, 30,* 310–331.

Wong-Rieger, D., & Taylor, D. M. (1981). Multiple group membership and self-identity. *Journal of Cross-Cultural Psychology, 12*(4), 61–79.

Yancey, W., Ericksen, E., & Juliana, R. (1976). Emergent ethnicity: A review and reformulation. *American Sociological Review, 41,* 391–403.

Zinn, M. (1980). Gender and ethnic identity among Chicanos. *Frontiers, 5,* 18–24.

Zuniga, M. E. (1988). Assessment issues with Chicanas: Practice implications. *Psychotherapy, 25,* 288–293.

Depression in Adolescence*

Anne C. Petersen, Bruce E. Compas, Jeanne Brooks-Gunn, Mark Stemmler, Sydney Ey, and Kathryn E. Grant

The image of adolescence as a time of storm and stress, intense moodiness, and preoccupation with the self has permeated both professional and lay perspectives on this developmental period. The belief that significant difficulties, including depression, during adolescence represent normal development has had two major effects on research and practice: (a) Difficulties during adolescence were not considered as an important developmental variation, and (b) adolescent problems were often not treated because of the belief that the adolescent would grow out of them.

*From Petersen et al. (1993, February). *American Psychologist, 48*(2), 155–168. Reprinted with permission.

Although this view of adolescence is the one commonly reflected in the media and many professional descriptions of adolescence, it is not supported by research on this period (Petersen, 1988a). In the late 1960s, there were reports showing that many adolescents traverse this period of life without significant psychological difficulties (Douvan & Adelson, 1966; Offer, 1969). It is now known that the majority of adolescents of both genders successfully negotiate this developmental period without any major psychological or emotional disorder, develop a positive sense of personal identity, and manage to forge adaptive peer relationships at the same time they maintain close relationships with their families (Powers, Hauser, & Kilner, 1989). Conversely, research in the 1970s focusing on those youth with problems demonstrated that psychological difficulties in adolescence frequently developed into serious psychiatric disorder in adulthood (Rutter, Graham, Chadwick, & Yule, 1976; Weiner & DelGaudio, 1976). These and other studies demonstrated the inappropriateness of the belief that difficulties such as depression were normal manifestations of adolescence and pointed toward the need for assessment, diagnosis, prevention, and treatment at this age. These studies also highlighted the need for more research on the development of depression in adolescence.

What Is Adolescent Depression?

Three approaches to the assessment and classification of adolescent psychopathology have been reflected in the literature on adolescent depression: (a) depressed mood, (b) depressive syndromes, and (c) clinical depression. Each approach reflects different assumptions about the nature of psychopathology, serves different purposes, and reflects a different level of depressive phenomena (e.g., Angold, 1988; Cantwell & Baker, 1991; Compas, Ey, & Grant, 1992; Kazdin, 1988; Kovacs, 1989). For example, the study of depressed mood during adolescence has emerged from developmental research in which depressive emotions are studied along with other features of adolescent development. The depressive syndrome approach assumes that depression and other syndromes reflect the co-occurrence of behaviors and emotions as quantitative deviations from the norm. The clinical approach is based on assumptions of a disease or disorder model of psychopathology.

Depressed Mood

Everyone experiences periods of sadness or unhappy mood at various points in his or her life. These periods of depressed mood may occur in response to many situations, such as the loss of a significant relationship or failure on an important task. They may last for a brief or an extended period of time; they may be associated with no other problems or many problems. Research on depressed mood has been concerned with depression as a symptom and refers to the presence of sadness, unhappiness, or blue feelings for an unspecified period of time. No assumptions are made about the presence or absence of other symptoms. Depressed mood is typically measured through adolescents' self-reports of their emotions, either through measures specifically concerned with mood (e.g., Petersen, Schulenberg, Abramowitz, Offer, & Jarcho, 1984) or through items included in checklists of depressive symptoms (e.g., Kovacs, 1980). Sad or depressed mood is usually experienced with other negative emotions, such as fear, guilt, anger, contempt, or disgust (Watson & Kendall, 1989) and is frequently present during adolescence when any of these other negative emotions are present (Saylor, Finch, Spirito, & Bennett, 1984). Depressed mood is also likely to be linked with other problems, such as anxiety and social withdrawal. Although anxiety and depressed mood frequently occur at the same time, anxiety may or may not be related to positive moods; in contrast, depressed mood is not present when one feels happy, or, conversely, happy mood does not occur at the same time as depressed mood (Watson & Clark, 1984; Watson & Kendall, 1989). Moreover, the presence of depressed mood, based on parents' or adolescents' reports, has been found to be the single most powerful symptom in differentiating clinically referred and nonreferred youth (Achenbach, 1991b, 1991d).

Depressive Syndromes

Multivariate empirical approaches to the assessment of adolescent psychopathology, including depression, have shown that aspects of depression are associated with many other problems (Achenbach, 1991a). Depression is viewed as a constellation of behaviors and emotions that have been found statistically to occur together in an interpretable pattern at a rate that exceeds chance, without implying any particular model for the nature or cause of these associated symptoms. This approach has identified a syndrome of complaints that include both anxiety and depression and is based on symptoms such as feels lonely; cries; fears doing bad things; feels the need to be perfect; feels unloved; believes others are out to get him or her; feels worthless, nervous, fearful, guilty, self-conscious, suspicious, or sad; and worries (Achenbach, 1991a, 1991b, 1991c). This constellation of symptoms has been reliably identified in reports of adolescents, their parents, and their teachers. Scores on this syndrome are strongly related (average $r = .51$) to seven other problem syndromes identified by this approach: withdrawn, somatic complaints, social problems, thought problems, attention problems, delinquent behavior, self-destructive, and aggressive behavior (Achenbach, 1991a).

Clinical Depression

There are two major diagnostic models typically used to diagnose clinical depression: the categorization of mental disorders developed by the American Psychiatric Association (1987) and the method developed by the World Health Organization (1990). The American Psychiatric Association method is the one most widely used in the United States and abroad (Maser, Kaelber, & Weise, 1991). It bases the diagnosis of disorders on a review of the presence, duration, and severity of sets of symptoms. This approach not only assumes that depression includes the presence of an identifiable syndrome of associated symptoms but also assumes that these symptoms are associated with significant levels of current distress or disability and with increased risk for impairment in the individual's current functioning. Under depressive disorders, adolescents may be diagnosed as experiencing major depressive disorder (MDD) or dysthymic disorder, or both. To meet the criteria for MDD, the adolescent must have experienced five or more of the following symptoms for at least a two-week period at a level that differs from previous functioning: (a) depressed mood or irritable mood most of the day, (b) decreased interest in pleasurable activities, (c) changes in weight or perhaps failure to make necessary weight gains in adolescence, (d) sleep problems, (e) psychomotor agitation or retardation, (f) fatigue or loss of energy, (g) feelings of worthlessness or abnormal amounts of guilt, (h) reduced concentration and decision-making ability, and (i) repeated suicidal ideation, attempts, or plans of suicide.

A dysthymic disorder is diagnosed when the adolescent has had a period of at least one year in which he or she has shown depressed or irritable mood every day without more than two symptom-free months. In addition, dysthymic disorder requires the presence of at least two of the following symptoms: (a) eating problems, (b) sleeping problems, (c) lack of energy, (d) low self-esteem, (e) reduced concentration or decision-making ability, and (f) feelings of hopelessness. There cannot be an episode of MDD during the first year of dysthymic disorder. Primary dysthymia (DY) is unrelated to non-mood disorders such as eating disorders, substance abuse disorders, or anxiety disorders; any of these would classify the disorder as a secondary DY. . . .

Variations by Gender, Ethnic Group, and Cohort

All the evidence suggests that increases in depressive disorders and mood are greater for girls than for boys during adolescence (e.g., Kandel & Davies, 1982; Kashani et al., 1987; Petersen, Kennedy, & Sullivan, 1991). The gender difference that emerges by age 14–15 years appears to persist into adulthood. Many scholars have considered whether the gender difference is a true difference in depression or whether it can be explained by artifacts such as different styles of responding to questions and differences in openness. These examinations have concluded that the gender difference appears to be a true difference in the experience of depression (Gove & Tudor, 1973; Nolen-Hoeksema, 1987; Nolen-Hoeksema, Girgus, & Seligman, 1991; Weissman & Klerman, 1977). Men and women may have different response styles in which men distract themselves, whereas women ruminate on their depressed mood and therefore amplify it (Nolen-Hoeksema, 1987). Sex role socialization in early adolescence, related to the biological changes of puberty that heighten an identity with one's gender, is thought to produce the observed change in these gender differences by midadolescence. Another explanation for increased experience of depression among girls is that girls experience more challenges in early adolescence (Petersen, Sarigiani, & Kennedy, 1991). For example, girls are more likely than boys to go through puberty before or during the transition to secondary school (Petersen, Kennedy, & Sullivan, 1991; Simmons & Blyth, 1987). In addition, several studies have reported that parental divorce is more likely for girls than for boys in early adolescence (e.g., J. H. Block, Block, & Gjerde, 1986; Petersen, Sarigiani, & Kennedy, 1991). Both less effective coping styles and more challenges may increase the likelihood of depression among girls. Studies are needed that simultaneously test these and other hypotheses.

Rates of depression and depressed mood may be higher among adolescents in some ethnic groups or other subgroups. For example, in a review of community studies of adolescent depression, Fleming and Offord (1990) reported that in two of five studies where race was examined, African-American adolescents had higher rates of depression and depressed mood than Whites. On the other hand, Nettles and Pleck (in press) reviewed several studies and concluded that although African-American youth are at greater risk for many negative behavioral and health outcomes, rates of depressive symptoms in African-American samples are typically lower than in Caucasian youth. In a study of one of the largest multiethnic samples of adolescents, Dornbusch, Mont-Reynand, Ritter, Chen, and Steinberg (1991) reported that Caucasian and Asian-American youth reported more depressive symptoms than African-American or Hispanic-American adolescents, even after controlling for levels of stressful life events. Given other findings (e.g., Fitzpatrick et al., 1990), it is probably wise to note Hammen's (1991) conclusion that there is no evidence for Black–White differences in depression among adults. Rates among Native-American adolescents appear to be elevated (Beiser & Attneave, 1982; May, 1983); high rates have been reported especially among Native Americans in boarding schools (Kleinfeld & Bloom, 1977; Kursh, Bjork, Sindell, & Nelle, 1966; Manson, Ackerson, Dick, Baron, & Fleming, 1990). Furthermore, adolescents living in rural areas may be at a greater risk for depression compared with those in urban or suburban areas (Sarigiani, Wilson, Petersen, & Vicary, 1990; Petersen, 1991; Petersen, Bingham, Stemmler, & Crockett, 1991), although Hammen (1991) concluded that there are no urbanicity variations among adults. Gay and lesbian youth have a two- to threefold risk of suicide, and they are probably at greater risk for depression.

The National Institute of Mental Health Epidemiological Catchment Area studies have suggested historical increases in depression (Weissman, Leaf, Holzer, Myers, & Tischler, 1984). Rates of depression have increased significantly since World War II (Klerman, 1988). These historical changes in rates of depression may have had an especially strong impact on the adolescent population. This was supported by a recent study by Ryan et al. (1992), who found similar increases in depressive disorders in more recently born cohorts of prepubertal siblings of depressive probands. Although it has been speculated that these increases were baby boom effects (Klerman, 1988), recent cohorts continue to show higher rates of most of these problems, suggesting that it is not simply due to a larger cohort of youth (Gans, Blyth, Elsby, &

Gaveras, 1990). In summary, although much more work is needed on the epidemiology of depression in adolescence, existing evidence suggests increased risk of depression in recent decades. Girls and other groups—such as Native Americans and homosexual youth—may have increased risk of depression, but too few studies have considered subgroup variations, with the exception of gender, to permit inferences about depression in subgroups of adolescents.

. . .

Approaches to Intervention: Treatment and Prevention of Adolescent Depression

Treatment

Pharmacotherapy. Building on research with adults, several varieties of psychoactive medications have been evaluated as treatments for adolescent depression. The results of the initial controlled studies have failed to support the efficacy of pharmacotherapy for adolescent depression (Petersen, Compas, & Brooks-Gunn, 1991; Strober et al., 1988). For example, two double-blind placebo studies of tricyclic antidepressants with adolescents found no differences between treated and control subjects (Boulos et al., 1991; Geller, Cooper, Graham, Marsteller, & Bryant, 1990), and open trial studies report improvement rates of much less than 50% (e.g., Strober, Freeman, & Rigali, 1990). Given the efficacy of these treatments with adults, researchers have speculated on the reasons for the lack of results and perhaps negative effects. The possibilities range from the different biological substrate of adolescents to the possibility that adolescent depressives have more serious forms of depressive disorders because of earlier onset and higher rates of comorbid disorders such as anxiety.

Psychosocial and psychotherapeutic treatments. Psychosocial and psychotherapeutic interventions in the treatment of adolescent depression include cognitive–behavioral therapy (Lewinsohn, Clarke, Hops, & Andrews, 1990), psychodynamically oriented therapy (Bemporad, 1988), family therapy (Lantz, 1986), social skills training (Fine, Forth, Gilbert, & Haley, 1991), and supportive group therapy (Fine et al., 1991). The three studies that included random assignment to treatment and no-treatment control groups all provide some confirmation that depressed mood, or, in one case, depressive disorders, can be significantly reduced through treatment (Kahn, Kehle, Jenson, & Clark, 1990; Lewinsohn et al., 1990; Reynolds & Coats, 1986). Improvement was found on self-report measures of depressive symptoms, with effect sizes of one standard deviation on the Beck Depression Inventory (BDI) and Center for Epidemiologic Studies of Depression scale (Lewinsohn et al., 1990), two standard deviations on the BDI (Reynolds & Coats, 1986), and three standard deviations on the Children's Depression Inventory (Kahn et al., 1990). Furthermore, Lewinsohn et al. found a 50% reduction in the rate of MDD in the treated versus untreated groups in their study. There was also some evidence that reductions in depressive symptoms and disorders were maintained over longer periods of time ranging from five weeks to six months posttreatment. These studies also suggest that treatment effects are not limited to depressive symptoms; significant reductions have also been found in anxiety symptoms (Lewinsohn et al., Reynolds & Coats). Studies comparing the efficacy of different types of psychosocial interventions have been rare and the findings inconclusive.

No research has yet compared or integrated the effects of pharmacotherapy and psychotherapy for depressed adolescents. Attention to individual differences in response to treatments as well as to the overall effectiveness rates of these interventions appears to be a more productive avenue for research. It is important to discover whether there are subgroups who show different responsiveness to pharmacologic versus psychosocial treatment.

Prevention of Adolescent Depression

On the basis of the high rates of depressed mood, depressive syndromes, and depressive disorders that occur during adolescence, it is clear that treatment efforts will never be sufficient to meet the full needs of the population. Professional resources are inadequate to meet these needs, both in terms of the limited number of trained professionals who are available and in terms of barriers to access to treatment that are confronted by adolescents, especially adolescents living in poverty. Therefore, prevention of the entire spectrum of depressive problems experienced by adolescents is of paramount importance if the needs of the largest number of adolescents are to be met.

Prevention of adolescent depression can take two forms. First, preventive services can be delivered to entire populations of adolescents on the basis of the assumption that all adolescents are at some risk of experiencing at least depressed mood, if not for the development of depressive disorders. The assumption behind such programs is that all adolescents are exposed to factors that place them at risk for depression and that enhancing their ability to respond adaptively to these risk factors will reduce the incidence of depression in the population. This approach further assumes that depressive symptoms exist on a continuum and that subclinical levels of depressed mood or negative affect may serve as markers of increased risk for the development of depressive disorders. By reducing depressed mood in the population, the overall risk for depressive disorders may also be reduced. Second, adolescents who have been exposed to an identifiable risk factor can be selectively targeted for preventive efforts. For example, adolescents whose parents are clinically depressed are known to be at increased risk of suffering from depressive disorders, as well as other problems, compared with the population at large. Services can be delivered selectively to those at greatest risk and in greatest need.

Populationwide prevention programs. In spite of the promise that broad-based preventive intervention could contribute to reduction in the incidence of depression, no controlled evaluations of such programs have been published. The ongoing research of Petersen and colleagues (cf. Petersen, 1988b, 1991) promises to provide the first such data concerning the effects of a preventive intervention targeting depression for early adolescents.

Broadly focused programs designed to promote social competence and teach problem-solving skills also have relevance for the prevention of depressive mood and symptoms at the population level (e.g., Weissberg, Caplan, & Harwood, 1991). This general family of interventions has been designed to teach the social competencies and life skills needed by adolescents to foster positive social, emotional, and academic development. Although problem-solving interventions have been found to influence a wide variety of outcomes, measures of depressed mood, syndromes, or disorders have not been included in evaluations of these programs. Assessment of depression will be an important criterion to include in future evaluations of social competence promotion programs.

Prevention programs for adolescents at risk for depression. Although populationwide interventions may provide some level of protection against sources of risk for depression for many adolescents, others may be exposed to conditions and circumstances that present a more profound risk for the development of depressive syndromes and disorders. The basic skills that can be taught in broadly focused programs such as those described above may not be sufficient for individuals faced with heightened risk for depression. Secondary preventive services can be directed to those groups who are identified on the basis of a marker of their increased risk.

Compelling evidence has been summarized above indicating that the single most powerful source of risk for adolescent depression is the presence of a depressive disorder in a parent (Downey & Coyne, 1990; Fendrich, Warner, & Weissman, 1990; Phares & Compas, 1992). The diagnosis of depression in parents serves as a distinct marker of the need for either a prevention- or treatment-oriented intervention for the offspring of these individuals. It would not be an overstatement to say that the need for services for children of depressed parents as closely approximates a *prescriptive* recommendation as can be found in the mental health professions. Furthermore, the incidence of MDD in offspring of depressed parents increases substantially during adolescence, indicating that young adolescents whose parents suffer from depression are a group in particularly high need of services (Beardslee, 1990).

Initial steps have been taken in the development of preventive interventions for depressed parents and their families by Beardslee and colleagues (Beardslee, 1990; Beardslee et al., 1992; Beardslee & Podorefsky, 1988). The intervention is guided by research on the characteristics of adolescents who have displayed resilience in the face of depressive disorders in their parents. Parents and children participate in a psychoeducational intervention that focuses on providing family members the information needed to enhance their understanding of and ways of coping with the parent's depression.

Although there are few prevention programs targeting depression specifically, a number of preventive interventions have been developed to address stressors and problems that may be linked to depression. For example, several programs have been developed to assist adolescents in coping with the stress of divorce (see Grych & Fincham, 1992, for a review). Although the effects of these programs have been reported with regard to anxiety symptoms and other internalizing problems, measures of depressed affect or symptoms have not been, but should be, included in reports of their effectiveness.

Integrating Treatment and Prevention Efforts

It is an unfortunate reality that the resources to support mental health services in the United States fall far short of the economic and human resources needed to address mental health problems. It is even more unfortunate that limits on these resources have contributed to conflict among mental health professionals about the best way to expend these limited resources. In particular, battle lines have been drawn between proponents of prevention and those who favor treatment (e.g., Albee, 1982, 1990).

With regard to adolescent depression, the battle between proponents of prevention and treatment is one that we cannot afford to fight. Services aimed at alleviating the pain and misfortune associated with depression during adolescence must reflect a broad effort to provide coordinated prevention and treatment programs. This position is based on the assumption that no one approach to providing services for adolescent depression will be sufficient to address the problem. Although we fully expect that primary prevention programs will be able to reduce levels of depressed mood and perhaps deter the development of some forms of depressive syndromes and disorders, they will not provide a sufficient dose to interrupt the development of depression in a substantial portion of the population.

The addition of secondary prevention programs aimed at high-risk groups should provide a second net to catch and help many adolescents who, because of exposure to high-risk circumstances such as parental depression, conflict, or divorce, were not helped by the resources they gained through primary preventive efforts. Finally, treatment programs will remain a necessity because many adolescents who are exposed to conditions of profound risk will not be able to gain access to secondary prevention services in order to prevent the onset of more serious depressive disorders. Moreover, the majority of adolescents may have insufficient access to treatment services (Keller, Lavori, Beardslee, Wunder, & Ryan, 1991).

Primary prevention programs at the population level, secondary prevention services for high-risk groups, and treatment for adolescents who manifest severe forms of depressive disorders must be delivered in a coordinated, sequential fashion (Compas, in press). Evidence is accumulating to indicate that interventions at all three of these levels need to address dysfunctional cognitive processes, skills for coping with acute and chronic stress, and strategies to deal with interpersonal relationships and problems. If these themes were addressed in primary and secondary prevention programs as well as in treatment, they would contribute to the development of a core set of competencies for all adolescents. The groundwork for these skills would be laid in a preventive intervention delivered at the population level (Petersen, 1988b). Further development of these competencies could then be pursued in secondary prevention programs for adolescents whose parents are suffering from clinical depression or other sources of risk (Beardslee, 1990). Finally, for those adolescents who warrant further intervention, these same skills would continue to be the target in psychotherapeutic interventions (Lewinsohn et al., 1990). Continuity of this type across interventions could enhance the effects of our efforts to alleviate adolescent depression at the levels of both prevention and treatment.

. . .

REFERENCES

Achenbach, T. M. (1991a). *Integrative guide for the 1991 CBCL/4–18, YSR, and TRF Profiles.* Burlington: University of Vermont, Department of Psychiatry.

Achenbach, T. M. (1991b). *Manual for the Child Behavior Checklist and 1991 Profile.* Burlington: University of Vermont, Department of Psychiatry.

Achenbach, T. M. (1991c). *Manual for the Teacher's Report Form and 1991 Profile.* Burlington: University of Vermont, Department of Psychiatry.

Achenbach, T. M. (1991d). *Manual for the Youth Self-Report and 1991 Profile.* Burlington: University of Vermont, Department of Psychiatry.

Akiskal, H. S., & McKinney, W. T., Jr. (1973). Depressive disorders: Toward a unified hypothesis. *Science, 182,* 20–29.

Albee, G. W. (1982). Preventing psychopathology and promoting human potential. *American Psychologist, 37,* 1043–1050.

Albee, G. W. (1990). The futility of psychotherapy. *Journal of Mind and Behavior, 11,* 369–384.

Allgood-Merten, B., Lewinsohn, P. M., & Hops, H. (1990). Sex differences and adolescent depression. *Journal of Abnormal Psychology, 99,* 55–63.

American Psychiatric Association. (1987). *Diagnostic and statistical manual of mental disorders* (3rd ed., rev.). Washington, DC: Author.

Andreasen, N. C., Endicott, J., Spitzer, R. L., & Winokur, G. (1977). Family history method using diagnostic criteria. *Archives of General Psychiatry, 34,* 1223–1229.

Angold, A. (1988). Childhood and adolescent depression: 1. Epidemiological and aetiological aspects. *British Journal of Psychiatry, 152,* 601–617.

Asarmov, J. R., & Horton, A. A. (1990). Coping and stress in families of child psychiatric inpatients: Parents of children with depressive and schizophrenia spectrum disorders. *Child Psychiatry and Human Development, 21,* 145–157.

Asnis, G. M., Halbreich, U., Rabinovich, H., Ryan, N., Sachar, E. J., Nelson, B., Puig-Antich, J., & Novacenko, H. (1985). Cortisol response to desipramine in endogenous depressives and normal controls: Preliminary findings. *Psychiatry Research, 14,* 225–233.

Attie, I., & Brooks-Gunn, J. (1992). Development issues in the study of eating problems and disorders. In J. H. Crowther, S. E. Hobfoll, M. A. P. Stephens, & D. L. Tennenbaum (Eds.), *The etiology of bulimia: The individual and familial context* (pp. 35–40). Washington, DC: Hemisphere.

Attie, I., Brooks-Gunn, J., & Petersen, A. C. (1990). A developmental perspective on eating disorders and eating problems. In M. Lewis & S. Miller (Eds.), *Handbook of developmental psychopathology* (pp. 409–420). New York: Plenum Press.

Beardslee, W. R. (1990). Development of a clinician-based preventive intervention for families with affective disorders. *Journal of Preventive Psychiatry and Allied Disciplines, 4,* 39–61.

Beardslee, W. R., Hoke, L., Wheelock, I., Rothberg, P., van de Velde, P., & Swatling, S. (1992). Initial findings on preventive interventions for families with parental affective disorders. *American Journal of Psychiatry, 149,* 1335–1340.

Beardslee, W. R., & Podorefsky, D. (1988). Resilient adolescents whose parents have serious affective and other psychiatric disorders: The importance of self-understanding and relationships. *American Journal of Psychiatry, 145,* 67–69.

Beiser, M., & Attneave, C. M. (1982). Mental disorders among Native American children: Rate and risk periods for entering treatment. *American Journal of Psychiatry, 139,* 193–198.

Bemporad, J. R. (1988). Psychodynamic treatment of depressed adolescents. *Journal of Clinical Psychiatry, 49,* 26–31.

Block, J. (1991, April). *Self-esteem through time: Gender similarities and differences.* Paper presented at the 1991 biennial meeting of the Society for Research in Child Development, Seattle, WA.

Block, J., & Gjerde, P. F. (1990). Depressive symptomatology in late adolescence: A longitudinal perspective on personality antecedents. In J. E. Rolf, A. Masten, D. Cicchetti, K. Nuechterlein, & S. Weintraub (Eds.), *Risk and protective factors in the development of psychopathology* (pp. 334–360). New York: Cambridge University Press.

Block, J. H., Block, J., & Gjerde, P. F. (1986). The personality of children prior to divorce: A prospective study. *Child Development, 57,* 827–840.

Boulos, C., Kutcher, S., Marton, P., Simeon, J., Ferguson, B., & Roberts, N. (1991). Response to desipramine treatment in adolescent major depression. *Psychopharmacology Bulletin, 27,* 59–65.

Burge, D., & Hammen, C. (1991). Maternal communication: Predictors of outcome at follow-up in a sample of children at high and low risk for depression. *Journal of Abnormal Psychology, 100,* 174–180.

Camarena, P., Sarigiani, P., & Petersen, A. C., (1990). Gender specific pathways to intimacy in early adolescence. *Journal of Youth and Adolescence, 19,* 19–32.

Cantwell, D. P., & Baker, L. (1991). Manifestations of depressive affect in adolescence. *Journal of Youth and Adolescence, 20,* 121–133.

Carlton-Ford, S., Paikoff, R. L., & Brooks-Gunn, J. (1991). Methodological issues in the study of divergent views of the family. In R. L. Paikoff (Ed.), *New directions for child development: Shared views in the family during adolescence* (pp. 87–102). San Francisco: Jossey-Bass.

Caron, C., & Rutter, M. (1991). Comorbidity in child psychopathology: Concepts, issues and research strategies. *Journal of Child Psychology and Psychiatry, 32,* 1063–1080.

Cavanaugh, S. V. (1986). Depression in the hospitalized inpatient with various medical illnesses. *Journal of Psychotherapy and Psychosomatics, 45,* 97–104.

Cherlin, A. J., Furstenberg, F. F., Jr., Chase-Lansdale, P. L., Kiernan, K. E., Robins, P. K., Morrison, D. R., & Teitler, J. O. (1991). Longitudinal studies of effects of divorce on children in Great Britain and the United States. *Science, 252,* 1386–1389.

Clarkin, J. F., Friedman, R. C., Hurt, S. W., Corn, R., & Aronoff, M. (1984). Affective and character pathology of suicidal adolescent and young adult inpatients. *Journal of Clinical Psychiatry, 45,* 19–22.

Compas, B. E. (in press). Promoting successful coping during adolescence. In M. Rutter (Ed.), *Youth in the year 2000.*

Compas, B. E., Ey, S., & Grant, K. E. (1992). *Depression during adolescence: Issues of taxonomy, assessment and diagnosis.* Manuscript under review.

Compas, B. E., Grant, K. E., & Ey, S. (in press). Psychosocial stress and child/adolescent depression: Can we be more specific? In W. M. Reynolds & H. F. Johnston (Eds.), *Handbook of depression in children and adolescents.* New York: Plenum.

Compas, B. E., & Hammen, C. L. (in press). Depression in childhood and adolescence: Convariation and comorbidity in development. In R. J. Haggerty, N. Garmezy, M. Rutter, & L. Sherrod (Eds.), *Risk and resilience in children: Developmental issues.* New York: Cambridge University Press.

Compas, B. E., Howell, D. C., Phares, V., Williams, R., & Ledoux, N. (1989). Parent and child stress and symptoms: An integrative analysis. *Developmental Psychology, 25,* 550–559.

Dahl, R. E., Ryan, N. D., Puig-Antich, J., Nguyen, N. A., Al-Shabbout, M., Meyer, V. A., & Perel, J. (1991). 24-hour cortisol measures in adolescents with major depression: A controlled study. *Biological Psychiatry, 30,* 25–36.

Dahl, R. E., Ryan, N. D., Williamson, D. E., Ambrosini, P. J., Rabinovich, H., Novacenko, H., Nelson, B., & Puig-Antich, J. (1992). Regulation of sleep and growth hormone in adolescent depression. *Journal of the American Academy of Child and Adolescent Psychiatry, 31,* 615–621.

Daniels, D., & Moos, R. H. (1990). Assessing life stressors and social resources among adolescents: Applications to depressed youth. *Journal of Adolescent Research, 5,* 268–289.

Dornbusch, S. M., Mont-Reynand, R., Ritter, P. L., Chen, Z., & Steinberg, L. (1991). Stressful events and their correlates among adolescents of diverse backgrounds. In M. E. Colten & S. Gore (Eds.), *Adolescent stress: Causes and consequences* (pp. 111–130). New York: Aldine de Gruyter.

Douvan, E. A., & Adelson, J. (1966). *The adolescent experience.* New York: Wiley.

Downey, G., & Coyne, J. C. (1990). Children of depressed parents: An integrative review. *Psychological Bulletin, 108,* 50–76.

Ebata, A. T., & Petersen, A. C. (1992). *Pattern of adjustment during early adolescence: Gender differences in depression and achievement.*

Edelbrock, C., & Costello, A. J. (1988). Convergence between statistically derived behavior problem syndromes and child psychiatric diagnoses. *Journal of Abnormal Child Psychology, 16,* 219–231.

Ehlers, C. L., Frank, E., & Kupfer, D. J. (1988). Social zeitgebers and biological rhythms: A unified approach to understanding the etiology of depression. *Archives of General Psychiatry, 45,* 948–952.

Feldman, S., S., & Elliott, G. R. (Eds.). (1990). *At the threshold: The developing adolescent.* Cambridge, MA: Harvard University Press.

Fendrich, M., Warner, V., & Weissman, M. M. (1990). Family risk factors, parental depression, and psychopathology in offspring. *Developmental Psychology, 26,* 40–50.

Finch, A. J., Lipovsky, J. A., & Casat, C. D. (1989). Anxiety and depression in children and adolescents: Negative affectivity or separate constructs? In P. C. Kendall & D. Watson (Eds.), *Anxiety & depression: Distinctive & overlapping features* (pp. 171–202). San Diego, CA: Academic Press.

Fine, S., Forth, A., Gilbert, M., & Haley, G. (1991). Group therapy for adolescent depressive disorder: A comparison of social skills and therapeutic support. *Journal of the American Academy of Child and Adolescent Psychiatry, 30,* 79–85.

Fitzpatrick, S. B., Fujii, C., Shragg, G. P., Rice, L., Morgan, M., & Felice, M. E. (1990). Do health care needs of indigent Mexican-American, Black and White adolescents differ? *Journal of Adolescent Health Care, 11,* 128–132.

Fleming, J. E., & Offord, D. R. (1990). Epidemiology of childhood depressive disorders: A critical review. *Journal of the American Academy of Child and Adolescent Psychiatry, 29,* 571–580.

Friedrich, W. N., Reams, R., & Jacobs, J. (1982). Depression and suicidal ideation in early adolescents. *Journal of Youth and Adolescence, 11,* 403–407.

Gans, J. E., Blyth, D. A., Elsby, A. B., & Gaveras, C. C. (1990). America's adolescents: How healthy are they? *AMA profiles of adolescent health series* (Vol. 1). Chicago, IL: American Medical Association.

Garber, J., Kriss, M. R., Koch, M., & Lindholm, L. (1988). Recurrent depression in adolescents: A follow-up study. *Journal of the American Academy of Child and Adolescent Psychiatry, 27,* 49–54.

Garrison, C. Z., Addy, C. L., Jackson, K. L., McKeown, R. E., & Waller, J. L. (1991). The CES-D as a screen for depression and other psychiatric disorders in adolescents. *Journal of the American Academy of Child and Adolescent Psychiatry, 30,* 636–641.

Geller, B., Cooper, T. B., Graham, D. L., Marsteller, F. A., & Bryant, D. M. (1990). Double-blind placebo-controlled study of nortriptyline in depressed adolescents using a "fixed plasma level" design. *Psychopharmacology Bulletin, 26,* 85–90.

Gershon, E. S., Hamovit, J., Guroff, J. J., Dibble, E., Leckman, J., Sceery, W., Targum, S., Nurnberger, J., Goldin, L., & Bunney, N. (1982). A family study of schizoaffective, bipolar I, bipolar II, unipolar, and normal control probands. *Archives of General Psychiatry, 39,* 1157–1167.

Gibson, P. (1989). Gay male and lesbian youth suicide. In M. R. Feinleib (Ed.), *Report of the Secretary's Task Force on Youth Suicide* (Vol. 3, DHHS Publication No. ADM 89-1623). Rockville, MD: U.S. Department of Health and Human Services, Alcohol, Drug Abuse, and Mental Health Administration.

Gove, W. R., & Tudor, J. F. (1973). Adult sex roles and mental illness. *American Journal of Sociology, 78,* 812–835.

Graber, J. A., & Petersen, A. C. (1991). Cognitive changes at adolescence: Biological perspectives. In K. R. Gibson & A. C. Petersen (Eds.), *Brain maturation and cognitive development: Comparative cross-cultural perspectives* (pp. 253–279). Hawthorne, NY: Aldine de Gruyter.

Grych, J. H., & Fincham, F. D. (1992). Interventions for children of divorce: Toward greater integration of research and action. *Psychological Bulletin, 111,* 434–454.

Hammen, C. (1990). Cognitive approaches to depression in children: Current findings and new directions. In B. B. Lahey & A. E. Kazdin (Eds.), *Advances in clinical child psychology* (Vol. 13, pp. 139–173). New York: Plenum.

Hammen, C. (1991). *Depression runs in families.* New York: Springer-Verlag.

Harrington, R., Fudge, H., Rutter, M., & Pickles, A. (1990). Adult outcomes of childhood and adolescent depression: 1. Psychiatric status. *Archives of General Psychiatry, 47,* 465–473.

Harter, S. (1990). Causes, correlates and the functional role of global self-worth: A life-span perspective. In R. Sternberg & J. Kolligian (Eds.), *Competence considered* (pp. 68–97). New Haven, CT: Yale University Press.

Horwitz, S. M., Klerman, L. V., Sungkuo, H., & Jekel, J. F. (1991). Intergenerational transmission of school age parenthood. *Family Planning Perspective, 23,* 168–177.

Jacobsen, R. H., Lahey, B. B., & Strauss, C. C. (1983). Correlates of depressed mood in normal children. *Journal of Abnormal Child Psychology, 11,* 29–39.

Kahn, J. S., Kehle, T. J., Jenson, W. R., & Clark, E. (1990). Comparison of cognitive–behavioral, relaxation, and self-modeling interventions for depression among middle-school students. *School Psychology Review, 19,* 196–211.

Kandel, D. B., & Davies, M. (1982). Epidemiology of depressive mood in adolescents. *Archives of General Psychiatry, 39,* 1205–1212.

Kandel, D. B., Raveis, V. H., & Davies, M. (1991). Suicidal ideation in adolescence: Depression, substance use, and other risk factors. *Journal of Youth and Adolescence, 20,* 289–309.

Kashani, J. H., Carlson, G. A., Beck, N. C., Hoeper, E. W., Corcoran, C. M., McAllister, J. A., Fallahi, C., Rosenberg, T. K., & Reid, J. C. (1987). Depression, depressive symptoms, and depressed mood among a community sample of adolescents. *American Journal of Psychiatry, 144,* 931–934.

Kashani, J. H., Reid, J., & Rosenberg, T. (1989). Levels of hoplessness in children and adolescents: A developmental perspective. *Journal of Consulting and Clinical Psychology, 57,* 496–499

Kaslow, N. J., Rehm, L. P., & Siegel, A. W. (1984). Social-cognitive and cognitive correlates of depression in children. *Journal of Abnormal Psychology, 12,* 605–620.

Katon, W., Kleinman, A., & Rosen, G. (1982). Depression and somatization: A review: Part 1. *American Journal of Medicine, 71,* 127–135.

Kazdin, A. E. (1988). Childhood depression. In E. J. Mash & L. G. Terdal (Eds.), *Behavioral assessment of childhood disorders* (2nd ed., pp. 157–195). New York: Guilford Press.

Keating, D. (1990). Adolescent thinking. In S. S. Feldman & G. R. Elliott (Eds.). *At the threshold: The developing adolescent* (pp. 54–89). Cambridge, MA: Harvard University Press.

Keller, M. B., Lavori, P. W., Beardslee, W. R., Wunder, J., & Ryan, N. (1991). Depression in children and adolescents: New data on "undertreatment" and a literature review on the efficacy of available treatments. *Journal of Affective Disorders, 21,* 163–171.

Kendler, K. S., Heath, A., Martin, N. G., & Eaves, L. J. (1986). Symptoms of anxiety and depression in a volunteer twin population. *Archives of General Psychiatry, 43,* 213–221.

Kleinfeld, J., & Bloom, J. D. (1977). Boarding schools: Effects on the mental health of Eskimo adolescents. *American Journal of Psychiatry, 134,* 411–417.

Klerman, G. L. (1988). The current age of youthful melancholia. Evidence for increase in depression among adolescents and young adults. *British Journal of Psychiatry, 152,* 4–14.

Kovacs, M. (1980). Rating scales to assess depression in school-aged children. *Acta Paedopsychiatry, 46,* 305–315.

Kovacs, M. (1989). Affective disorders in children and adolescents. *American Psychologist, 44,* 209–215.

Kovacs, M. (1990). Comorbid anxiety disorders in childhood-onset depressions. In J. D. Maser & C. R. Cloniger (Eds.), *Comorbidity of mood and anxiety disorders* (pp. 272–281). Washington, DC: American Psychiatric Press.

Kovacs, M., Feinberg, T. L., Crouse-Novak, M. A., Paulauskas, S., & Finkelstein, R. (1984). Depressive disorders in childhood: 1. A longitudinal prospective study of characteristics and recovery. *Archives of General Psychiatry, 41,* 219–239.

Kovacs, M., Feinberg, T. L., Crouse-Novak, M. A., Paulauskas, S. L., Pollack, M., & Finkelstein, R. (1984). Depressive disorders in childhood: 2. A longitudinal study of the risk for a subsequent major depression. *Archives of General Psychiatry, 41,* 643–649.

Kovacs, M., Paulauskas, S., Gatsonis, C., & Richards, C. (1988). Depressive disorders in childhood: 3. A longitudinal study of comorbidity with and risk for conduct disorders. *Journal of Affective Disorders, 15,* 205–217.

Kursh, T. P., Bjork, J., Sindell, P. S., & Nelie, J. (1966). Some thoughts on the formation of personality disorder: Study of an Indian boarding school. *American Journal of Psychiatry, 122,* 868–876.

Kutcher, S. P., & Marton, P. (1989). Parameters of adolescent depression: A review. *Psychiatric Clinics of North America, 12,* 895–918.

Lantz, J. (1986). Depression movement in family therapy with depressed adolescents. *Child and Adolescent Social Work, 3,* 123–128.

Larsson, B., & Melin, L. (1990). Depressive symptoms in Swedish adolescents. *Journal of Abnormal Psychology, 18,* 91–102.

Lee, C. M., & Gotlib, I. H. (1991). Family disruption, parental availability and child adjustment. In R. Prinz (Ed.), *Advances in behavioral assessment of children and families.* (Vol. 5, pp. 173–202). New York: Kingsley.

Lempers, J. D., & Clark-Lempers, D. (1990). Family economic stress, maternal and paternal support and adolescent distress. *Journal of Adolescence, 13,* 217–229.

Lester, D., & Miller, C. (1990). Depression and suicidal preoccupation in teenagers. *Journal of Personality and Individual Differences, 11,* 421–422.

Levy, J. C., & Deykin, E. Y. (1989). Suicidality, depression, and substance use in adolescence. *American Journal of Psychiatry, 146,* 1462–1467.

Lewinsohn, P. M., Clarke, G. N., Hops, H., & Andrews, J. (1990). Cognitive–behavioral treatment for depressed adolescents. *Behavior Therapy, 21,* 385–401.

Manson, S. M., Ackerson, L. M., Dick, R. W., Baron, A. E., & Fleming, C. M. (1990). Depressive symptoms among American Indian adolescents: Psychometric characteristics of the Center for Epidemiologic Studies Depression Scale (CES-D). *Psychological Assessment, 2,* 231–237.

Maser, J. D., Kaelber, C., & Weise, R. W. (1991). International use and attitudes toward *DSM-III* and *DSM-III-R:* Growing consensus in psychiatric classification. *Journal of Abnormal Psychology, 100,* 271–279.

May, P. (1983). *A survey of the existing data on mental health and the Albuquerque area.* Unpublished manuscript.

Nettles, S. M., & Pleck, J. H. (in press). Risk, resilience, and development: The multiple ecologies of Black adolescents. In R. J. Haggerty, N. Garmezy, M. Rutter, & L. Sherrod (Eds.), *Risk and resilience in children: Developmental approaches.* New York: Cambridge University Press.

Nolen-Hoeksema, S. (1987). Sex differences in unipolar depression: Evidence and theory. *Psychological Bulletin, 101,* 259–282.

Nolen-Hoeksema, S., Girgus, J. S., & Seligman, M. E. P. (1991). Sex differences in depression and explanatory style in children. *Journal of Youth and Adolescence, 20,* 233–246.

Nolen-Hoeksema, S., Girgus, J. S., & Seligman, M. E. P. (1992). Predictors and consequences of childhood depressive symptoms: A 5-year longitudinal study. *Journal of Abnormal Psychology, 101,* 405–422.

Offer, D. (1969). *The psychological world of the teenager: A study of normal adolescent boys.* New York: Basic Books.

Petersen, A. C. (1988a). Adolescent development. In M. R. Rosenzweig (Ed.), *Annual review of psychology* (pp. 583–607). Palo Alto, CA: Annual Reviews, Inc.

Petersen, A. C. (1988b). *Coping with early adolescent challenge: Gender-related mental health outcomes.* Proposal funded by the W. T. Grant Foundation.

Petersen, A. C. (1991). *Coping with early adolescent challenge: Second year progress report.* Unpublished manuscript.

Petersen, A. C., Bingham, R., Stemmler, M., & Crockett, L. J. (1991, July). *Subcultural variations in development of depressed affect.* Poster presented at the biennial meeting of the International Society for the Study of Behavioral Development, Minneapolis, MN.

Petersen, A. C., Compas, B., & Brooks-Gunn, J. (1991). *Depression in adolescence: Implications of current research for programs and policy.* Report prepared for the Carnegie Council on Adolescent Development, Washington, DC.

Petersen, A. C., Kennedy, R. E., & Sullivan, P. (1991). Coping with adolescence. In M. E. Colten & S. Gore (Eds.), *Adolescent stress: Causes and consequences* (pp. 93–110). New York: Aldine de Gruyter.

Petersen, A. C., Sarigiani, P. A., & Kennedy, R. E. (1991). Adolescent depression: Why more girls? *Journal of Youth and Adolescence, 20,* 247–271.

Petersen, A. C., Schulenberg, J. E., Abramowitz, R. H., Offer, D., & Jarcho, H. D. (1984). A Self-Image Questionnaire for Young Adolescents (SIQYA): Reliability and validity studies. *Journal of Youth and Adolescence, 13,* 93–111.

Petersen, A. C., White, N., & Stemmler, M. (1991, April). *Familial risk and protective factors influencing adolescent mental health.* Paper presented at the biennial meeting of the Society for Research in Child Development, Seattle, WA.

Phares, V., & Compas, B. E. (1992). The role of fathers in child and adolescent psychopathology: Make room for daddy. *Psychological Bulletin, 111,* 387–412.

Post, G., & Crowther, J. H. (1985). Variables that discriminate bulimic from nonbulimic adolescent females. *Journal of Youth and Adolescence, 14,* 85–98.

Powers, S. I., Hauser, S. T., & Kilner, L. A. (1989). Adolescent mental health. [Special issue: Children and their development: Knowledge base, research agenda, and social policy application]. *American Psychologist, 44,* 200–208.

Puig-Antich, J. (1987). Sleep and neuroendocrine correlates of affective illness in childhood and adolescence. *Journal of Adolescent Health Care, 8,* 505–529.

Radloff, L. S. (1991). The use of the Center for Epidemiological Studies Depression Scale in adolescents and young adults [Special issue: The emergence of depressive symptoms during adolescence]. *Journal of Youth and Adolescence, 20,* 149–166.

Reinherz, H. Z., Stewart-Berghauer, G., Pakiz, B., Frost, A. K., & Moeykens, B. A. (1989). The relationship of early risk and current mediators to depressive symptomatology in adolescence. *Journal of the American Academy of Child and Adolescent Psychiatry, 28,* 942–947.

Renouf, A. G., & Harter, S. (1990). Low self-worth and anger as components of the depressive experience in young adolescents. *Development and Psychopathology, 2,* 293–310.

Rey, J. M., & Morris-Yates, A. (1991). Adolescent depression and the Child Behavior Checklist. *Journal of the American Academy of Child and Adolescent Psychiatry, 30,* 423–427.

Reynolds, W. M., & Coats, K. I. (1986). A comparison of cognitive–behavioral therapy and relaxation training for the treatment of depression in adolescents. *Journal of Consulting and Clinical Psychology, 54,* 633–660.

Richards, M. H., Boxer, A. M., Petersen, A. C., & Albrecht, R. (1990). Relation of weight to body image in pubertal girls and boys from two communities. *Developmental Psychology, 26,* 313–321.

Rivinus, T. M., Biederman, J., Herzog, D., Kemper, K., Harper, G., Harmatz, G., & Houseworth, S. (1984). Anorexia nervosa and affective disorder: A controlled family history study. *American Journal of Psychiatry, 14,* 1414–1418.

Roberts, R. E., Lewinsohn, P. M., & Seeley, J. R. (1991). Screening for adolescent depression: A comparison of depression scales. *Journal of the American Academy of Child and Adolescent Psychiatry, 30,* 58–66.

Rohde, P., Lewinsohn, P. M., & Seeley, J. R. (1991). Comorbidity of unipolar depression: 2. Comorbidity with other mental disorders in adolescents and adults. *Journal of Abnormal Psychology, 100,* 214–222.

Rosen, J. C., Gross, J., & Vara, L. (1987). Psychological adjustment of adolescents attempting to lose or gain weight. *Journal of Consulting and Clinical Psychology, 55,* 742–747.

Rotheram-Borus, M. J., & Trautman, P. D. (1988). Hopelessness, depression, and suicidal intent among adolescent suicide attempters. *Journal of the American Academy of Child and Adolescent Psychiatry, 27,* 700–704.

Rutter, M. (1986). The developmental psychopathology of depression: Issues and perspectives. In M. Rutter, C. E. Izard, & P. B. Read (Eds.), *Depression in young people: Developmental and clinical perspectives* (pp. 3–32). New York: Guilford Press.

Rutter, M., Graham, P., Chadwick, O. F. D., & Yule, W. (1976). Adolescent turmoil: Fact or fiction? *Journal of Child Psychology and Psychiatry, 17,* 35–36.

Rutter, M., Tizard, J., & Whitmore, E. (Eds.). (1970). *Education, health and behavior.* London: Longman.

Ryan, N. D., Williamson, D. E., Iyengar, S., Orvaschel, H., Reich, T., Dahl, R. E., & Puig-Antich, J. A. (1992). A secular increase in child and adolescent onset affective disorder. *Journal of the American Academy of Child and Adolescent Psychiatry, 31,* 600–605.

Sachar, E., Puig-Antich, J., & Ryan, N. (1985). Three tests of cortisol secretion in adult endogenous depressives. *Acta Psychiatrica Scandinavica, 71,* 1–8.

Sarigiani, P. A. (1990). *A longitudinal study of relationship adjustment of young adults from divorced and nondivorced families.* Unpublished doctoral dissertation, Pennsylvania State University, University Park.

Sarigiani, P. A., Wilson, J. L., Petersen, A. C., & Vicary, J. R. (1990). Self-image and educational plans for adolescence from two contrasting communities. *Journal of Early Adolescence, 10,* 37–55.

Saylor, C. F., Finch, A. J., Spirito, A., & Bennett, E. (1984). The Children's Depression Inventory: A systematic evaluation of psychometric properties. *Journal of Consulting & Clinical Psychology, 52,* 955–967.

Schulenberg, J. E., Asp, C. E., & Petersen, A. C. (1984). School from the young adolescent's perspective: A descriptive report. *Journal of Early Adolescence, 4,* 107–130.

Shelton, R. C., Hollon, S. D., Purdon, S. E., & Loosen, P. T. (1991). Biological and psychological aspects of depression. *Behavior Therapy, 22, 201–228.*

Simmons, R. G., & Blyth, D. A. (1987). *Moving into adolescence: The impact of pubertal change and school context.* Hawthorne, NY: Aldine de Gruyter.

Spirito, A., Overholser, J., Ashworth, S., Morgan, J., & Benedict-Drew, C. (1988). Evaluation of a suicide awareness curriculum for high school students. *Journal of the American Academy of Child and Adolescent Psychiatry, 27,* 705–711.

Sroufe, A., & Rutter, M. (1984). The domain of developmental psychopathology. *Journal of Child Development, 55,* 17–29.

Strober, M. (1983, May). *Follow-up of affective disorder patients.* Paper presented at the annual meeting of the American Psychiatric Association, New York.

Strober, M., Freeman, R., & Rigali, J. (1990). The pharmacotherapy of depressive illness in adolescence: 1. An open label trial of imipramine. *Psychopharmacology Bulletin, 26,* 80–84.

Strober, M., Morrell, W., Burroughs, J., Lampert, C., Danforth, H., & Freeman, R. (1988). A family study of bipolar I disorder in adolescence: Early onset of symptoms linked to increased familial loading and lithium resistance. *Journal of Affective Disorders, 15,* 255–268.

Suomi, S. J. (1991). Primate separation models of affective disorders. In J. Madden (Ed.), *Neurobiology of Learning, Emotion, and Affect* (pp. 195–214). New York: Raven Press.

U.S. Congress, Office of Technology Assessment. (1991). *Adolescent health: Vol. 1. Summary and policy options.* Washington, DC: Author

Vernberg, E. M. (1990). Psychological adjustment and experiences with peers during early adolescence: Reciprocal, incidental, or unidirectional relationships? *Journal of Abnormal Child Psychology, 18,* 187–198.

Wagner, B. M., Compas, B. E., & Howell, D. C. (1988). Daily and major life events: A test of an integrative model of psychosocial stress. *American Journal of Community Psychology, 16,* 189–205.

Watson, D., & Clark, L. (1984). Negative affectivity: The disposition to experience aversive emotional states. *Psychological Bulletin, 96,* 465–490.

Watson, D., & Kendall, P. C. (1989). Common and differentiating features of anxiety and depression: Current findings and future directions. In P. C. Kendall & D. Watson (Eds.), *Anxiety and depression: Distinctive and overlapping features* (pp. 493–508). San Diego, CA: Academic Press.

Weiner, I. B., & DelGaudio, A. (1976). Psychopathology in adolescence. *Archives of General Psychiatry, 34,* 98–111.

Weinstein, S. R., Noam, G. G., Grimes, K., Stone, K., & Schwab-Stone, M. (1990). Convergence of *DSM-III* diagnoses and self-reported symptoms in child and adolescent inpatients. *Journal of the American Academy of Child and Adolescent Psychiatry, 29,* 627–634.

Weissberg, R. P., Caplan, M. Z., & Harwood, R. L. (1991). Promoting competent young people in competence-enhancing environments: A systems-based perspective on primary prevention. *Journal of Consulting and Clinical Psychology, 59,* 830–841.

Weissman, M. M. (1990). Evidence for comorbidity of anxiety and depression: Family and genetic studies of children. In J. D. Maser & C. R. Cloninger (Eds.), *Comorbidity of mood and anxiety disorders* (pp. 349–365). Washington, DC: American Psychiatric Press.

Weissman, M. M., & Klerman, G. L. (1977). Sex differences and the epidemiology of depression. *Archives of General Psychiatry, 35,* 1304–1311.

Weissman, M. M., Leaf, P. J., Holzer, C. E., III, Myers, J. K., & Tischler, G. L. (1984). The epidemiology of depression: An update on sex differences in rates. *Journal of Affective Disorders, 7,* 179–188.

Wender, P. H., Kety, S. S., Rosenthal, D., Schulsinger, F., Ortmann, J., & Lunde, I. (1986). Psychiatric disorders in the biological and adoptive families of adopted individuals with affective disorders. *Archives of General Psychiatry, 43,* 923–929.

Whybrow, P., Akiskal, H., & McKinney, W. (1984). *Mood disorders: Toward a new psychobiology.* New York: Plenum.

World Health Organization. (1990). *International classification of diseases and related health problems* (10th revision). Geneva: Author.

Yanchyshyn, G., Kutcher, S., & Cohen, C. (1986). Diagnosis of borderline personality disorder in adolescents: Use of the diagnostic interview for borderlines. *Journal of the American Academy of Child and Adolescent Psychiatry, 25,* 427–429.

Adolescent Same-Sex and Opposite-Sex Best Friend Interactions*

Cami K. McBride and Tiffany Field

Several studies have highlighted the critical importance of friendship in human development (Goldstein, Field, & Healy, 1989; Greenberg, Siegel, & Leitch, 1983). A recent review of the literature on friendship revealed that children with close friends showed better academic performance, were less likely to drop out of school, and had lower rates of juvenile delinquency and adult psychopathology (Parker & Asher, 1987). Another review emphasized that the DSM-III-R uses lack of close peer relationships as a criterion for a number of psychiatric disorders of childhood (Reisman, 1985).

Intimate friendship seems to be one of the most salient characteristics of adolescence, more so than in previous developmental stages (Buhrmester, 1990). A study that compared preadolescents with adolescents found that intimate friendship is more important to adolescents (Buhrmester, 1990). The study also noted that competence in peer relationship skills is a greater concern for adolescents than for preadolescents.

The present study examined the interactions of adolescent best friend pairs in the same manner as a study by Field, Greenwald, Morrow, Healy, Foster, Guthertz, and Frost (1992) on preadolescents. In that research preadolescent best friends, as compared with acquaintances, showed more matching of positive behavioral states and lower stress as evidenced by lower cortisol levels. The present study used the same paradigm to determine whether adolescent best friend pairs show similar matching of behavior states during interactions and whether there are differences across same-sex and opposite-sex interactions at a time when opposite-sex friendships are developing. The opposite-sex friendship assessment was new to this study.

Few studies have compared same-sex friendships with opposite-sex friendships in adolescents. A discontinuity in opposite-sex friendship might be expected because of the erotic element (Sharbany, Gershoni, & Hoffman, 1981). Opposite-sex friendship is considered a learning stage for mature sexual relations and has been considered a more intimate form of friendship than same-sex friendship in adolescence (Sharbany et al., 1981). However, because of the relative novelty, opposite-sex interactions may not be as relaxed.

Questions addressed in this study were whether personality characteristics, such as self-esteem and extraversion, would be important factors in opposite-sex friendships versus same-sex friendships. Would opposite-sex friends be more matched in their behavior states than would same-sex friends, or would they be less matched because high school juniors have less

*From McBride & Field (1997). *Adolescence, 32*(127), 515–522. Reprinted with permission.

experience with opposite-sex friends? Opposite-sex friends might engage in more polite turn-taking rather than being in similar behavior states of animation and playfulness. Also, cortisol levels may be higher in opposite-sex friends than in same-sex friends because the erotic element may elicit more stress during the interaction (Sharbany et al., 1981).

To examine these questions, adolescents were videotaped in same-sex and opposite-sex best friend pairs during a conversation on any topic. The videotapes were later rated for concordance of behavior states. In addition, saliva samples were collected to determine the subjects' cortisol levels before and after the interaction. The subjects also completed questionnaires in which they rated their interaction and the likability and characteristics of their partner. They were also asked to complete self-esteem, peer intimacy, depression, and anxiety scales.

Method

Subjects and Procedures

Forty-eight high school juniors (24 males and 24 females) were asked to participate in the study and to name their best same-sex friend and best opposite-sex friend who attended the same high school. Their best friends were then invited to participate with them. The average age of the adolescents was 16.3 years (range = 15–17). Their ethnic distribution was 35% Hispanic, 33% white, 18% African American, and 14% other, consistent with the high school distribution. Fifty-seven percent of their parents were married, 89% had at least some college, and over 49% had a graduate school degree. Eighty-two percent of their parents earned more than $30,000, and the sample averaged 2.3 (middle to upper middle SES) on the Hollingshead Index.

Selection of best friend pairs. The students were asked to provide demographic information (age, sex, race) and the names of their best same-sex friend and best opposite-sex friend within the same high school grade. The questions used to ascertain best friends were: "I spend the most time with _____"; "I know _____ the best"; and "I have lunch with _____ the most." The students named as best friends were then asked to participate and to answer the same questions. The students who designated one another on two out of three of the above questions were matched in pairs.

Same-sex and opposite-sex best friend interactions. The best friend pairs were seated face-to-face across a table and asked to have a conversation on any topic. The interaction lasted 10 minutes and was videotaped. A mirror was propped next to one friend so that the image on the video screen showed the dyad side by side. Immediately after the conversation, an observer rated each adolescent on interaction behavior.

Instruments

Adolescent questionnaires. The questionnaires were administered after the interactions so as not to influence students' mood state. The self-esteem, peer intimacy, depression, and anxiety scales were administered only after the first session, and the same-sex/opposite-sex interaction order was counterbalanced. Feelings about the interaction and partner ratings were obtained after both same-sex and opposite-sex interactions.

Feelings scale. Conversation comfort, or how the adolescents felt during the interaction, was tapped using a 5-point Likert scale that included the following positive bipolar ratings: relaxed, friendly, interested, calm, self-conscious, enthusiastic, confident, involved, happy, in charge of the situation, natural, and pleasant. The scale was the same as that used in the Field et al. (1992) study, with items generated on a face validity basis in a study by Warner et al. (1987).

Partner rating. The students were asked to rate how much they liked their conversation partner on a 5-point Likert scale. The 12 items were the same as those used in the study by Field et al. (1992): (a) the way he/she looks, (b) his/her personality, (c) the things he/she said, (d) the way he/she talks, (e) the way he/she smiles/laughs, (f) his/her ideas, (g) the way he/she listens, (h) the way he/she laughs at things, (i) the way we share ideas, (j) the way he/she looks at me, (k) the way we take turns talking, and (1) the way we have fun together talking.

Self-esteem scale. This scale asked the students to compare themselves with their peers on a variety of descriptors, including confident, independent, angry, and moody. Students responded to questions that began: "Compared to my peers I would say that I am in general . . . (e.g., happy: *less, the same,* or *more*)."

Peer intimacy scale. This scale measured students' level of intimacy with best friend. There were eight questions (e.g., "How much do you share your inner feelings or secrets with your best friend?"), with answers ranging from *not at all* to *very much* and higher scores signifying greater intimacy.

Center for Epidemiological Studies Depression Scale (CES-D) (Radloff, 1977). This scale assesses depression levels by asking subjects to compare their feelings during the preceding week on items representing the primary symptoms of depression. A 4-point Likert scale (*rarely or none of the time, some or little of the time, a lot of the time,* and *most or all of the time*) measures subjects' feelings.

State-Trait Anxiety Inventory (STAI) (Spielberger, Gorsuch, & Lushene, 1970). This questionnaire assesses level of current situational anxiety. It consists of 40 items rated on a 4-point Likert scale (*not at all, somewhat, moderately,* and *very much so*).

Extraversion Scale (Buck, 1975). Buck's internalizer-externalizer scale was used to determine the adolescents' extraversion-introversion. Items are rated on a 5-point Likert scale, from *not at all characteristic* to *always characteristic.* Examples of items are: "I am warm and friendly to others," "I am shy," and "I have many friends."

. . .

The most comfortable, playful interactions in this study on high school juniors appeared to be those between females. Females rated their same-sex interactions as more comfortable and their female partners more likable, and they engaged in more playful behavior together than did male-male or opposite-sex dyads. This could be due to females' having more experience with face-to-face interactions. Anecdotal observations suggest that adolescent females spend more time talking about relationships while males spend more time roughhousing. It is interesting in this regard that males were more playful during their interactions with females than with other males, as if learning how to be playful in face-to-face interactions with the more experienced females. Although we had anticipated that by their junior year these adolescents would be spending more time in heterosexual relationships and therefore rating them more optimally and showing more playful behavior, that did not appear to be true for this sample.

Because of assortative mating theories for selection of adult relationships, we expected within-dyad similarities on at least some mood state or personality variables. However, like the results of Field et al. (1992) for a sixth-grade sample, there did not appear to be any similarity between partners within any of the dyads for mood states (depression and anxiety) or for the two personality variables (extraversion and self-esteem). Anecdotally, we noticed no other physical or personality variables that might have been criteria for friend selection. The members of the pairs seemed extremely different at first glance.

The adolescents did, however, receive similar peer intimacy and partner ratings following opposite-sex interactions. And behaviorally, they spent similar amounts of time together in an interested state, and in an animated state in the case of male-male dyads and in a playful state in the case of female-female dyads. Basically, then, although there was very little similarity within dyads on self-ratings for mood and personality factors, the adolescents were often in the same behavior state as their partner during interactions, suggesting behavior matching or synchrony. These findings highlight the probability that the adolescents were in fact interacting with their best friends. In a previous study (Field et al., 1992), matching of behavior states, particularly optimal ones, was noted only among best friend pairs.

Further research is needed on how these friendships evolve. Determining whether a "comfort level" similar to that of female-female interactions in a face-to-face situation develops for males, and whether females come to experience that level of comfort and matching of playful behavior in their interactions with males, will require additional study even later in adolescent development than we had anticipated.

REFERENCES

Buck, R. (1975). Nonverbal communication of affecting children. *Journal of Personality and Social Psychology, 31*(4), 644–653.

Buhrmester, D. (1990). Intimacy of friendship, interpersonal competence, and adjustment, during preadolescence and adolescence. *Child Development, 61*(4), 1101–1111.

Field, T., Greenwald, P., Morrow, C., Healy, B., Foster, T., Guthertz, M., & Frost, P. (1992). Behavior state matching during interactions of preadolescent friends versus acquaintances. *Developmental Psychology, 28,* 242–250.

Goldstein, S., Field, T., & Healy, B. (1989). Concordance of play behavior and physiology in preschool friends. *Journal of Applied Developmental Psychology, 28,* 242–250.

Greenberg, M. T., Siegel, J. M., & Leitch, C. J. (1983). The nature and importance of attachment relationships to parents and peers during adolescence. *Journal of Youth and Adolescence, 12,* 373–386.

Parker, J. G., & Asher, S. R. (1987). Peer relations and later adjustment: Are low-accepted children at risks? *Psychological Bulletin, 102,* 357–389.

Radloff, L. S. (1977). The CES-D Scale: A self-report depression scale for research in the general population. *Applied Psychological Measurement, 1,* 385–401.

Reisman, J. M. (1985). Friendship and its implications for mental health or social competence. *Journal of Early Adolescence, 5,* 383–391.

Sharbany, R., Gershoni, R., & Hoffman, J. E. (1981). Girlfriend, boyfriend: Age and sex differences in intimate friendship. *Developmental Psychology, 17,* 800–808.

Spielberger, C. D., Gorsuch, R. C., & Lushene, R. E. (1970). *The State-Trait Anxiety Inventory.* Palo Alto, CA: Consulting Psychologists Press.

Warner, R., Malloy, D., Schneider, K., Knoth, R., et al. (1987). Rhythmic organization of social interaction and observer ratings of positive affect and involvement. *Journal of Nonverbal Behavior, 11*(2), 57–74.

Searching for the Magic Johnson Effect: AIDS, Adolescents, and Celebrity Disclosure*

Bruce R. Brown Jr., Marc D. Baranowski, John W. Kulig, John N. Stephenson, and Barbara Perry

Efforts at AIDS prevention have included adolescents as a particularly vulnerable group. Since as many as 20% of HIV-positive adults (Hein, 1989a) are estimated to have contracted the virus in adolescence, this effort seems to be appropriately focused. Research has attempted to identify the teens at risk (Hingson, Strunin, & Berlin, 1990; Sugerman, Hergenroeder, Chacko, & Parcel, 1991; Zimet et al., 1992), characterize those behaviors or attitudes which define risk (Goodman & Cohall, 1989; Nader, Wexler, Patterson, McKusick, & Coates, 1989), and develop prevention programs which modify high-risk behaviors (Centers for Disease Control, 1988; DiClemente, Boyer, & Mills, 1987; Nader et al., 1989; Zimet et al., 1992). Although there have been modest improvements in information (Hingson et al., 1990), a decrease in substance use (Johnston, O'Malley, & Backman, 1992), and an increase in condom use (Hernandez, 1990; Rotherdam-Borus, Koopman, Haignere, & Davies, 1991), adoles-

*From Brown et al. (1996). *Adolescence, 31*(122), 253–264. Reprinted with permission.

cents as a subpopulation continue to remain at great risk for contracting HIV through sexual contact and needle sharing (Hein, 1989a; Sugerman et al., 1991). To many observers, adolescents appear immune to the messages intended to modify those behaviors which place them at risk for contracting the virus.

It was within this public health context that the events of November 7, 1991 came to offer promise to the youth of the nation. On that date, Earvin "Magic" Johnson, a premier professional basketball player with the Los Angeles Lakers, announced that he had contracted the human immunodeficiency virus (HIV). His announcement was reported widely in the print, radio, and television media and generated an immediate reaction from many adolescents (Shen, 1991; Specter, 1991). This coverage was accompanied by a flood of hopeful speculation in the lay press that this personal tragedy might modify the rate at which adolescents contract the virus (Gerstenzang & Cimons, 1991; Litvin, 1991). It was predicted that males generally and black males in particular would be positively affected by Magic's announcement. The lay press was not without dissenting opinions, however (Rabinowitz, 1991; Raeburn, 1992). Speaking of inner-city youth, one commentator groused: "Lets be realistic. . . . Those are the kids that'll kill you for a dime. . . . Wear condoms? Forget it!" (Berkow, 1991).

Both the medical (Hein, 1991; Shafer & Boyer, 1991) and the social science (Andre & Bormann, 1991; Metzler, Noell, & Biglan, 1992) literature have proposed methods of measuring AIDS risk in teens. These include a quantitation of recent and remote sexual behavior, focusing on anal or vaginal intercourse and condom use, as well as determining the frequency and sterility of intravenous drug abuse. Using these variables, it has been possible to separate teens into low-risk and at-risk groups (Hein, 1989b; Novello, Wise, Willoughby, & Pizzo, 1989). In addition, attitudes and beliefs have been assessed (Goodman & Cohall, 1989; Joffe & Radius, 1993; Nader et al., 1989; Strunin, 1991; Sugerman et al., 1991; Walter & Vaughn, 1993; Zimet et al., 1991, 1992), especially those which involve self-perceived risk for contracting HIV, resistance to peer pressure with respect to activities which would place the teen at increased risk, and self-efficacy, the teen's ability to insist on condom use during sexual intercourse.

In designing this study it was felt that if Magic Johnson's announcement did influence teens' thoughts or behavior about AIDS, then special subgroups of adolescents might be identifiable based on the presence of AIDS-related behaviors. In addition, it was anticipated that the impact of his announcement would be measurable by assessing current perceived risk, resistance to peer pressure, and self-efficacy.

The present study explored adolescents' perceptions of the influence of Magic Johnson by examining the following questions:

1. Do adolescents perceive that their AIDS-related attitudes and behaviors have changed as a result of Magic Johnson's announcement?
2. Are adolescents in the at-risk category for AIDS more likely than those in the low-risk category to perceive that their AIDS-related attitudes and behaviors have changed as a result of Magic Johnson's announcement?
3. What are the influences of adolescents' gender, race, age, number of sexual partners, pre-existing self-efficacy, resistance to peer pressure, and frequency of condom use on the perceived impact of Magic Johnson's announcement?

. . .

Beginning in March 1992, a consecutive convenience sample of adolescents attending four adolescent clinics (Bangor, ME, Portland, ME, Boston, MA, Madison, WI) was invited to participate in the study. Subjects at each site were limited to the first 25 males and 25 females aged 12–19 who consented to participate and did so prior to December 22, 1992. A total of 181 adolescents completed usable surveys. Each subject was judged by clinic staff to be cognitively capable of answering the questionnaire. Consent was obtained according to the method specified by the Human Subjects Committee of the institution where the subject received medical care. In all cases, participation was voluntary and the responses entirely anonymous, requiring neither names nor identification codes other than clinic site. . . .

A 23-question instrument was developed by extracting seminal questions on demographics and AIDS-related behaviors and attitudes from the Secondary School Student Health Risk Survey (SSSHRS) (Kann, Nelson, Jones, & Kolbe, 1989). The limitations of the SSSHRS have been described elsewhere (DiClemente, 1991). DiClemente (personal communication) expanded the SSSHRS by adding questions that measured perceived risk for contracting HIV, resistance to peer pressure, and self-efficacy. To the abridged questionnaire drawn from these two sources were added questions which identified Magic Johnson and queried changes in attitudes and behaviors since his announcement. . . .

General demographic information was assessed using questions from the SSSHRS as modified by DiClemente, Lanier, Horan, & Lodico (1991). Behaviors assessed included whether subjects had injected illegal drugs or shared needles, number of sexual partners in the last year and lifetime, age of first sexual intercourse, and how often a condom was used ("always" to "never"). Pre-existing resistance to peer pressure to engage in sexual intercourse and pre-existing self-efficacy (the confidence to insist on condom use) were also measured.

The adolescents' perceptions of changes in their AIDS-related attitudes and behaviors as a result of Magic Johnson's announcement were assessed, inquiring specifically about changes in perceived risk, increased awareness of AIDS, increased resistance to peer pressure to engage in sexual intercourse, and increased ability to insist that a condom be used during sexual encounters.

The low-risk group was defined as the presence of all of the following: never having had sexual intercourse or always using a condom, absence of IV drug use, ability (by self-report) to insist on condom usage during sexual intercourse. All other combinations of responses resulted in the subject being placed in the at-risk category.

. . .

While there were modest increases in AIDS awareness and intention to use condoms in future intercourse, only a minority of our sample of adolescents described an increase in personal threat from the disease following Johnson's revelation that he was HIV positive. Of the teens who did report being affected by his announcement, those who were most influenced were at lowest risk. Despite the concern that changes in AIDS-related attitudes and behaviors might not be measurable in this group, the low-risk subject proved to be capable of change: improvements in self-efficacy and resistance to peer pressure as a result of Johnson's announcement were reported by significantly more low-risk than at-risk subjects and were found even in virgins.

We were surprised that females reported greater AIDS awareness and resistance to intercourse-related peer pressure since the announcement. However, as the receptive partner in an epidemic which places them at special risk, the female adolescents' failure to perceive their increased vulnerability or to develop the ability to insist on condom use limits whatever benefits may accrue from gains in awareness or resistance to peer pressure.

Age was shown to have no effect on positive change in any of the attitudinal or behavioral measures of this study, despite the expectation that with greater age comes an increase in ability to process information, measure outcomes, and make responsible choices.

Although the virgins in the low-risk group were younger than their nonvirgin counterparts, sexual experience did not substantially alter that group's attitudinal or behavioral response to Johnson's announcement, suggesting that their shared attitudes justifies combining them within the low-risk group.

The relationships between pre-existing behaviors and attitudes and reported changes in our study population since the announcement remained complex. With the exception of those respondents (37% of sample) whose increased self-perceived risk for contracting the virus predicted increased self-efficacy, AIDS awareness, and resistance to peer pressure, few other clusters of responses were apparent. Reported positive changes in a single attitude or behavior, such as with the more sexually experienced group who reported increased vulnerability as a result of the announcement, appear to be minimized by teens' failure to generalize to other sexual attitudes or behaviors which present equal risk.

There are several possible explanations for the widespread persistence of risk-taking behavior in the face of the AIDS epidemic. One offered by Elkind is the powerful "personal fable" (Elkind, 1984). Although adolescents may know that it is indeed possible for people to acquire AIDS through unprotected sex, their feelings of personal uniqueness may prevent them from applying this knowledge to their own lives. Thus, they may become convinced that AIDS might happen to others but not to them. The fact that Magic Johnson is far more famous and wealthy than most adolescents may further influence them to cognitively distance his experience from their own despite the theory (Bandura & Walters, 1963) that Johnson represents an attractive role model for many teens. Of all the variables measured in our study, perceived risk (Janz & Becker, 1984) appeared to be the necessary prerequisite for the development of other behavior and attitudinal changes which lower a teen's risk for contracting HIV.

. . .

REFERENCES

Andre, T., & Bormann, L. (1991). Knowledge of acquired immune deficiency syndrome and sexual responsibility among high school students. *Youth and Society, 22,* 339–361.

Bandura, A., & Walters, R. (1963). *Social learning and personality development.* New York: Holt, Rinehart and Winston.

Berkow, I. (1991, November 21). Magic, Quayle and the message. *New York Times,* p. B17.

Centers for Disease Control. (1988). Guidelines for effective school health education to prevent the spread of AIDS. *Morbidity and Mortality Weekly Report, 37,* 1–14.

Centers for Disease Control. (1990). HIV-related knowledge and behaviors among high school students—Selected U.S. Sites 1989. *Morbidity and Mortality Weekly Reports, 39,* 385–389, 396–397.

DiClemente, R. (1991). Predictors of HIV-preventive sexual behavior in a high-risk adolescent population: The influence of perceived peer norms and sexual communication on incarcerated adolescents' consistent use of condoms. *Journal of Adolescent Health, 12,* 385–390.

DiClemente, R., Boyer, C., & Mills, S. (1987). Prevention of AIDS among adolescents: Strategies for the development of comprehensive risk-reduction health education programs. *Health Education Research, 2,* 287–291.

DiClemente, R., Lanier, M., Horan, P., & Lodico, M. (1991). Comparison of AIDS knowledge, attitudes, and behaviors among incarcerated adolescents and a public school sample in San Francisco. *American Journal of Public Health, 81,* 628–630.

Elkind, D. (1984). *All grown up and no place to go: Teenagers in crisis.* Reading, MA: Addison Wesley.

Gerstenzang, J., & Cimons, M. (1991, November 9). Bush calls Johnson a hero, defends administration's policy on AIDS. *Los Angeles Times,* p. A26.

Goodman, E., & Cohall, A. (1989). Acquired immunodeficiency syndrome and adolescents: Knowledge, attitudes, beliefs, and behaviors in a New York City adolescent minority population. *Pediatrics, 84,* 36–42.

Hein, K. (1989a). AIDS in adolescence: Exploring the challenge. *Journal of Adolescent Health Care, 10,* 10S–35S.

Hein, K. (1989b). Commentary on adolescent acquired immunodeficiency syndrome: The next wave of the human immunodeficiency virus epidemic? *Journal of Pediatrics, 114,* 144–149.

Hein, K. (1991). Risky business: Adolescents and human immunodeficiency virus. *Pediatrics, 88,* 1052–1054.

Hernandez, P. (1990, November 8). More teenagers engage in sex, use condoms, study says. *Boston Globe,* p. 66.

Hingson, R., Strunin, L., & Berlin, B. (1990). Acquired immunodeficiency syndrome transmission. Changes in knowledge and behaviors among teenagers, Massachusetts statewide surveys, 1986–1988. *Pediatrics, 85,* 24–29.

Janz, N., & Becker, M. (1984). The health belief model: A decade later. *Health Education Quarterly, 11,* 1–47.

Joffe, A., & Radius, S. (1993). Self-efficacy and intent to use condoms among entering college freshmen. *Journal of Adolescent Health, 14,* 262–268.

Johnston, L., O'Malley, P., & Backman, J. (1992). *Smoking, drinking, and illicit drug use among American secondary school students, college students, and young adults, 1975–1991 (Vols. 1 and 2)* (NIH Publication #93-3480). Rockville, MD: National Institute on Drug Abuse.

Kalichman, S., & Hunter, T. (1992). The disclosure of celebrity HIV infection: Its effects on public attitudes. *American Journal of Public Health, 82,* 1374–1376.

Kann, L., Nelson, G., Jones, J., & Kolbe, L. (1989). Establishing a system of complementary school-based surveys to annually assess HIV-related knowledge, beliefs, and behaviors among adolescents. *Journal of School Health, 59,* 55–58.

Litvin, T. (1991, November 17). Can Magic breach the wall of denial students built around AIDS? *Los Angeles Times,* p. M3.

Metzler, C., Noell, J., & Biglan, A. (1992). The validation of a construct of high-risk sexual behavior in heterosexual adolescents. *Journal of Adolescent Research, 7,* 233–249.

Nader, P., Wexler, D., Patterson, T., McKusick, L., Coates, T. (1989). Comparison of beliefs about AIDS among urban, suburban, incarcerated, and gay adolescents. *Journal of Adolescent Health Care, 10,* 413–418.

Novello, A., Wise, P., Willoughby, A., & Pizzo, P. (1989). Final report of the United States Department of Health and Human Services secretary's work group on pediatric human immunodeficiency virus infection and disease: Content and implications. *Pediatrics, 84,* 547–555.

Rabinowitz, D. (1991, November 18). Television: The magic circus. *Wall Street Journal,* p. A14.

Raeburn, P. (1992, May 27). Peers, not role models, seen as influencing black youth. *Boston Globe,* p. 15.

Rotherdam-Borus, M., Koopman, C., Haignere, C., & Davies, M. (1991). Reducing HIV sexual risk behaviors among runaway adolescents. *Journal of the American Medical Association, 66,* 1237–1241.

Shafer, M., & Boyer, C. (1991). Psychosocial and behavioral factors associated with risk of sexually transmitted disease, including human immunodeficiency virus infection, among urban high school students. *Journal of Pediatrics, 119,* 826–833.

Shen, F. (1991, November 9). Hero's shocker leaves teens grasping for answers. *Washington Post,* p. 1.

Spector, M. (1991, November 9). When AIDS taps a hero, his "children" feel pain. *New York Times,* pp. 1, 32.

Stiffman, A., Cunningham, R., & Dore, P. (1993). Magic Johnson (letter). *Journal of Adolescent Health, 14,* 427.

Strunin, L. (1991). Adolescents' perceptions of risk for HIV infection: Implications for future research. *Social Science and Medicine, 32,* 221–228.

Sugerman, S., Hergenroeder, A., Chacko, M., & Parcel, G. (1991). Acquired immunodeficiency syndrome and adolescents. *American Journal of Diseases of Children, 145,* 431–436.

Walter, H., & Vaughn, R. (1993). AIDS risk reduction among a multiethnic sample of urban high school students. *Journal of the American Medical Association, 270,* 725–730.

Zimet, G., Bunch, D., Anglin, T., Lazebnik, R., Williams, P., & Krowchuk, D. (1992). Relationship of AIDS-related attitudes to sexual behavior changes in adolescents. *Journal of Adolescent Health, 13,* 493–498.

Zimet, G., Hillier, S., Anglin, T., & Ellick, E., Krowchuk, D., & Williams, P. (1991). Knowing someone with AIDS: The impact on adolescents. *Journal of Pediatric Psychology, 16,* 287–294.

Zimet, G., Lazebnik, R., DiClemente, R., Anglin, T., Williams, P., & Ellick, E. (1993). The relationship of Magic Johnson's announcement of HIV infection to the AIDS attitudes of junior high school students. *Journal of Sex Research, 30,* 129–134.

REVIEW QUESTIONS AND ACTIVITIES

1. Ask friends to state how they plan to teach their children about contraception. How do they feel about discussing this topic with their children? Note religious themes in their responses. Share with your friends the research and theories presented in this chapter.
2. How does an adolescent's changing self-concept relate to changes in his or her cognitive development?
3. What dangers do adolescents face as they deal with the stresses of adolescence?
4. On a piece of paper, list three things about your body that you dislike. Then answer these questions:
   a. Why do you dislike these characteristics?
   b. Do you believe you are just the right weight? Underweight? Overweight?
   c. How many pounds do you believe you should gain or lose? (Check with your physician about the weight that's right for you.)
5. How are the themes of this chapter—for example, identity development, friendships and membership in a peer group, and sexuality—intertwined during adolescence?
6. Offer some examples of ways teachers can instruct adolescents about cultural similarities and differences.
7. Discuss ways in which the perception of a body change, such as weight loss or body fat accumulation, is magnified by cultural factors.
8. Look through the latest issue of magazines marketed primarily to female adolescents—for example, *Teen* and *YM*. What percentage of the adolescent girls featured would be considered overweight? Underweight? Of average weight? Are there adolescent girls of color represented in these magazines? If so, are they similar in physique to the white girls portrayed? What suggestions would you offer to these magazines for helping to increase adolescent girls' self-concept?
9. Critically reread one of the excerpted articles in this chapter, and then answer the following questions:
   a. Is the purpose of the research clear? Explain.
   b. Are studies contrary to the current hypothesis cited?
   c. Is the research hypothesis correctly derived from the literature and theory that have been cited? Or are there some important steps missing and left to the speculation of the reader.
   d. Were the conclusions drawn by the author consistent with the results obtained?
   e. What follow-up studies do you think are needed? Why these studies? Describe the methodology you would use in these follow-up studies.

SUGGESTIONS FOR FURTHER READING

Alasker, F., & Flammer, A. (Eds.). (1999). *The adolescent experience: European and American adolescents in the 1990s.* Mahwah, NJ: Erlbaum.

Feldman, S., & Elliott, G. (Eds.). (1990). *At the threshold: The developing adolescent.* Cambridge, MA: Harvard University Press.

Gullotta, T., Adams, G., & Markstrom, C. (2000). *The adolescent experience.* San Diego, CA: Academic Press.

Lagana, L. (1999). Psychosocial correlates of contraceptive practices during late adolescence. *Adolescence, 34,* 463–482.

Smith, C. (1996). Women, weight, and body image. In J. Chrisler, C. Golden, & P. Rozee (Eds.), *Lectures on the psychology of women.* New York: McGraw-Hill.

A people without history is like wind on the buffalo grass.

Lakota Proverb

Those who lose dreaming are lost.

Australian Proverb

The beginning of wisdom is to call things by their right names.

Chinese Proverb

When you were born, you cried and the world rejoiced. Live your life so that when you die, the world cries and you rejoice.

Indian Proverb

Adulthood

Questions for Reflection

- In your opinion, is there change or continuity within an individual with respect to personality?
- How do cultural and familial contexts interact with developmental contexts in explaining women's body consciousness?
- How do you think cultural values impact domestic violence, in terms of attitudes and help-seeking behavior?
- How do grandparents impact their grandchildren? Is this relationship bidirectional, that is, do grandchildren impact the work life, life satisfaction, and relationships of their grandparents?
- Why do you believe women are more depressed than men? Why are older people of color more depressed than older white individuals?
- What is the impact of biculturalism on children's identity development, social development, and emotional development?
- What personality factors do you believe contribute to older adults' fear of death?

OVERVIEW: CULTURAL INFLUENCES ON DEVELOPMENT IN ADULTHOOD

When does adulthood begin? Unlike most of the previous life stages discussed in this text, there is no clearly identifiable age at which we leave adolescence and enter adulthood (Arnett, 2000). Most developmental psychologists would agree that adulthood describes events that occur after age 20 until death. In fact, this life stage of adulthood has been organized by some developmental psychologists into early or young adulthood (20–40 years), middle adulthood (40–65 years), older adulthood (65–85 years), and the old old or very old (85 years and older). Levinson (1986) theorized that adulthood can be defined in terms of distinct stages: for example, the period from 17 to 22 years was defined as a bridge between pre-adulthood and early adulthood; the period from age 22 to 28 as a time for building and maintaining an adult life style; or the period from age 40 to 45 as a time of midlife transition. It should be noted, however, that there is no empirical research to support universally applicable stages of adult development (Hoyer, Rybash, & Roodin, 1999).

Longevity has increased considerably in the United States as a consequence of better living conditions. The average life span for individuals during prehistoric times was probably 18 years (Shultz, 1978). Today we now have more than 23 million individuals age 65 and older (Bee, 1996). We even have more than 100,000 people age 100 years and older (referred to as "the graying of America"; Bee, 1996). The increase in the number of elderly individuals is not unique to the United States. In fact, the United States has the world's third largest population of adults age 65 and older and the largest old old population (age 85 and older). The highest concentration of adults 65 and older is found in Sweden. Some countries have recorded a higher concentration of adults 65 and older than the United States: the United Kingdom, the former West Germany, Italy, and France (U.S. Bureau of the Census, 1993). As a consequence of medical advances, many developing countries (e.g., China, India, Mexico) will have an older population. It is estimated that within 25 years, the percentage of elderly adults in these countries will begin to approximate the number of elderly adults in developed countries (Bee, 1996).

The life expectancy for white women in the United States is 79.2 years; for white men, 73.0 years (U.S. Bureau of the Census, 1993). Life expectancy in the United States is approximately six years longer for whites than for people of color. For example, the equivalent life expectancy figures for African American women and men are 74.3 years and 65.5 years, respectively. The U.S. Bureau of the Census (1993) reported that life expectancies are shorter for both Mexican Americans and Native Americans. Note, however, that the racial difference in life expectancy is significantly smaller for adults who live to be 65 years old. Moreover, among the very old (e.g., those 85 years and older), people of color have longer life expectancies than white individuals, supporting the theory that people of color who live to this advanced age exhibit hardiness (Clark, Maddox, & Steinhauser, 1993). Demographic trends indicate that the number of elderly of color is growing at a faster rate than white elderly (Ralston, 1991).

In this chapter, we will discuss the impact of multiculturalism in several areas of adult development: physical functioning, bicultural identification, utilization of long-term care services, depression, personality development, grandparenting, family violence, body consciousness, and fear of death. Since adulthood spans many years, there are more readings included in this chapter that deal with each of the dimensions of development than in previous chapters. These selections will provide further support for the interdependence among dimensions of development. You will also see continuity in development into adulthood for several issues we have discussed throughout this text, including violence. We begin with an overview of physical development throughout adulthood.

PHYSICAL DEVELOPMENT IN ADULTHOOD

Focus on Physical Functioning

A major textbook on adult development and aging (Bee, 1996) is entitled *The Journey of Adulthood.* The word *journey* is an apt term for the process of development, which indeed continues throughout the life cycle. The word *journey* also counters the once prevalent belief among scientists (but still reinforced by laypersons; e.g., see Pennington, 1999) that adulthood is identified only by decline, not by growth (Bee, 1996). Considerable development has been noted throughout adulthood in education, work roles, and relationships, to name a few (Doering, Rhodes, & Schuster, 1983; Freedman & Martin, 1999; Matthews, 1986).

We may believe that physiological changes only decline as we enter later adulthood, but in fact, the empirical evidence suggests that the majority of our bodily functions reach their maximum capacity either prior to or during early adulthood, after which they gradually decline (Bee, 1996). Thus physiological changes are taking place years before we enter older adulthood, but we may not realize this fact since we tell ourselves we are still "young."

During adulthood there is some loss in perceptual ability (e.g., dark adaptation becomes less rapid and effective; hearing becomes less acute) (Ahmed, 1998; Fozard, 1990; Hunt & Hertzog, 1981), changes in physical functioning (Ferrucci et al., 1998), and changes in long-term and short-term memory (Craik, 2000; Hultsch & Dixon, 1990). However, there are large differences in the timing and extent of loss. For example, adults who maintain higher levels of mental and physical activity exhibit slower rates of intellectual decline in older adulthood (Dixon & Hultsch, 1999; Schwarz & Knaeuper, 2000). Poor health is almost always implicated in declines in intellectual functioning (Bee, 1996; Gill, 1999; Schaie & Willis, 1998). There is thus a large amount of empirical research that counters the stereotype that adulthood is synonymous only with decline (Helson, 1999; Wheatley, 2000).

Furthermore, while there are physiological changes associated with growing older, these changes do not necessarily translate into any direct effect on our health or daily functioning (Ausman & Russell, 1990; Bee, 1996; Kligman, Grove, & Balin, 1985). Such changes include the outward signs of aging. For example, we develop lines in our foreheads and around our eyes; our skin becomes less elastic, more spread out, stiffer, and less uniform in color. In addition, our cranial hair becomes thinner and turns gray and then white. Weight increases from young adulthood to middle adulthood and then tends to decline throughout the remainder of adulthood. Height decreases 1 to 2 inches, as a consequence of dealing with the effects of gravity (Hayflick, 1994).

In addition to these changes, our muscle tissue slowly declines in tone, flexibility, and strength. Our pulmonary, cardiovascular, and excretory systems become less efficient. Furthermore, our joints become less flexible and more brittle. These changes are not necessarily incapacitating (Hayflick, 1994).

There is a positive relationship between growing older and vulnerability to diseases, chronic disorders, accidents, and fatal illnesses (Hayflick, 1994). In adulthood, for example, the mortality rates for men exceed those of women for most disorders, especially heart disease, malignancy, accidents, and chronic pulmonary disease (Hoyer et al., 1999; Strickland, 1988). Lung cancer surpasses breast cancer as the leading cause of cancer death for women. While more men than women die from pulmonary causes, there has been a leveling off in deaths of white men, whereas for white and African American women and African American men there has been an increase (Klonoff, Landrine, & Scott, 1995). Women have a higher death rate than men for strokes since they live longer and are thus more likely to suffer cerebral accidents. Breast cancer is the second leading cause of cancer deaths among women between ages 35 and 55 years (George, 2000; McKenna et al., 1999). Cancer of the prostate accounts for 10 percent of the malignancies that occur for men (Kunkel, Bakker, Myers, Oyesanmi, & Gomella, 2000).

In adulthood, the number of women with Alzheimer's disease is twofold to threefold that of afflicted men (Laakso, Hallikainen, Haenninen, Partanen, & Soininen, 2000; Ott, Lapane, & Gambassi, 2000). In addition, women are more likely than men to be subject to chronic and disabling diseases, such as arthritis, rheumatism, hypertension, and diabetes (Hayflick, 1994). The highest male-to-female ratios occur for AIDS (approximately eight times more men than women; Amaro, 1995), suicide (four times more men; Leenaars, 1999), homicide (three times more men; Bee, 1996), accidents (twice as many men; Hayflick, 1994), and chronic liver disease (twice as many men; Bennett, McCrady, Johnson, & Pandina, 1999; Hayflick, 1994).

In addition to race and ethnic group differences in various areas of functioning in adulthood, social class variations are noted as well. For example, compared with working-class adults, middle-class adults are less likely to experience unemployment, are healthier, live longer, are more likely to retain a higher level of intellectual functioning into their elderly years, and in general are more satisfied with their lives (Adler et al., 1994; George, 1990; Launer, Dinkgreve, Jonker, Hooijer, & Lindeboom, 1993). Working-class occupations are predominantly more dangerous and physically strenuous than most middle-class occupations, which can contribute to working-class adults having shorter life expectancies. Certainly differences in income level directly impact life satisfaction if emphasis is placed on money among adults (Bee, 1996).

In their article, "Constant Hierarchic Patterns of Physical Functioning Across Seven Populations in Five Countries," excerpted in the readings section (see pp. 196–199), Luigi Ferrucci and his colleagues review chronic diseases and physical impairments as they relate to disability in older adulthood. They identified stages in the decline in physical function that accompanies aging. Ferrucci and his colleagues studied individuals who were 60 years old and older from Italy, Finland, Germany, Ukraine, and the Republic of Serbia. Ferrucci and his co-researchers assessed disability in the following areas of daily living activities: cutting one's own toenails, doing heavy housework, moving around outdoors, walking at least 400 meters, shopping daily for basic necessities, doing one's own cooking, doing light housework, bathing or showering, using stairs, walking between rooms, using the lavatory, dressing and undressing, getting in and out of bed, feeding oneself, and washing one's arms and face.

Ferrucci et al. identified four domains of disability: the ability to perform complex manual dexterity activities; good balance on slippery or steep surfaces and capacity to walk long distances; capacity to maintain static balance and mobility at home; and ability in activities that are performed with the use of one's upper extremities. Results suggest the stages of disability were similar among five different European countries. In addition, disabilities among the individuals exhibited a consistent increase with increasing age for women and for men. In older individuals, the disabling process follows a general pattern of progression. The most common disability for individuals related to balance problems. Ferrucci et al.'s methodology has implications for " . . . delaying the deterioration of functional status in older persons who are already disabled (p. 198 in this text)."

COGNITIVE DEVELOPMENT

Focus on Awareness and Utilization of Long-Term Care Services

As is suggested by the results from the research by Ferrucci et al., there is an interdependence among physical and cognitive aspects in adulthood (as well as throughout the other stages of the life cycle already discussed). How do older individuals deal with disabilities that are a consequence of the aging process? From whom do they seek support for their physical functioning? Burr and Mutchler (1993) reported that Hispanic and Asian American widowed older women are significantly more likely to live with relatives than are white widowed women, who are more likely to live alone. In addition, Hispanic, African American, and Asian American elderly individuals are less likely to be institutionalized than white Americans (Belgrave, Wykle, & Choi, 1993). These findings highlight the emphasis placed on family interaction and solidarity in these cultures.

In some cultures, the incidence of specific diseases is significantly higher: For example, among American Indians, diabetes is 5 times the rate among white Americans (Indian Health Service, 1991). In addition, American Indian and Alaska Native women experience a much higher rate of cervical cancer—more than double the rate of women of all other ethnic groups (Joe & Justice, 1992). Cervical cancer is diagnosed in later stages for American Indian women, and therefore, survival rates are lower for them than for women in any other ethnic group. LaFromboise et al. (1995) explained these culturally related differences in terms of the emphasis placed on enduring, which means self-care is given a low priority among these women.

Thus, despite these higher prevalence rates of illnesses among racial and ethnic minority individuals, the utilization of health services by them is significantly less than among individuals from the white majority culture (Spence & Atherton, 1991; Wallace, Andersen, & Levy-Storms, 1993). In addition, ethnic elderly individuals typically have less knowledge about long-term care services. In their article, "Awareness and Utilization of Community Long-Term Care Services by Elderly Korean and Non-Hispanic White Americans," excerpted in the readings section (see pp. 200–204), Ailee Moon, James E. Lubben, and Valentine Villa discuss their comparative study of the level of awareness and utilization of long-term care services by elderly Korean and non-Hispanic white men and women. Moon et al. reported that Korean American elderly individuals prefer a more independent living arrangement rather than living with their extended family. In addition, Korean American elderly individuals are less likely to get assistance from formal support services than from informal ones. Some explanations offered for this finding include their lack of knowledge about available assistance, cultural norms of shame, face-saving, and language barriers between themselves and practitioners.

Moon et al. interviewed elderly individuals about whether they were knowledgeable about community-based long-term care services and whether they had utilized such services. The care services included a senior citizen center, adult day care or elderly day care, hospice for the terminally ill, mental health services, home health aide services, Meals on Wheels or similar programs, and visiting nurse services, among others. Results suggest that Korean American elderly individuals had little knowledge of these services as compared with white American elders. In addition, Korean Americans in this study did not utilize the services to the same degree as their white peers.

Moon et al. offer suggestions for ways to inform Korean Americans (as well as all minority individuals) about community services to assist them in their daily functioning. As they conclude:

> Given that minority and immigrant elderly populations will continue to grow over the next century, this study suggests the importance of continued research on such populations because they may have low levels of awareness and utilization of health and social services. (pp. 202–203 in this text)

Focus on Objectified Body Consciousness

Cultural values surrounding long-term health care are reflected in Moon and her colleagues' research. Cultural values also play an important role in individuals' perceptions of their bodies and in how individuals harm their bodies in order to meet their culture's value on and image of "beauty." In the previous chapter, we discussed eating disorders in the context of cultures stressing thinness as a major criterion of beauty. We noted that anorexia and bulimia commonly begin in adolescence or in young adulthood. We should point out, however, that both anorexia and bulimia need to be considered as eating disorders affecting women of all ages.

For women in middle adulthood, for example, the culture's narrow standard of beauty and femininity can lead to mourning over the loss of important years of youth (Martin, 1987). As women grow older, many gain weight. Women's metabolism slows as they age; consequently, they require fewer calories (Paludi, 1997). Women usually consume the same amount of food as before, however. Gaining weight in midlife and beyond may be especially hard to accept when women must deal simultaneously with a host of other bodily changes contributing to menopause. Health problems too can lead to body changes, including weight gain (Paludi, 1997). Women taking steroids (e.g., prednisone) for asthma, rheumatoid arthritis, or lupus typically gain weight; their faces become more rounded and puffy.

Do older women view their bodies as negatively as adolescent and younger women do? Against whom do older women compare their bodies? Do they compare themselves with other older women? Perhaps older women feel better about their bodies than do younger women and have more self-esteem related to their body. In other words, is body consciousness continuous throughout the life span, or are there changes in reported self-esteem and satisfaction with women's bodies? In her article, "Women and Objectified Body Consciousness: Mothers' and Daughters' Body Experience in Cultural, Developmental, and Familial Context," excerpted in the readings section (see pp. 205–212), Nita Mary McKinley discusses her research with middle-aged mothers and their young adult daughters. She hypothesized that daughters' and mothers' feelings about their appearances are bidirectional:

> A daughter's appearance may affect the messages her parents give her about her body. At the same time, a daughter's experience of her body—both how she feels about her body and the types of behaviors she exhibits—is also likely to be affected not only by what her family tells her directly, but also by how her mother feels about her own body and how her mother's partner feels about her mother's body. (p. 761; in this text, p. 207)

McKinley reviewed the following variables for mothers and daughters: body shame (feeling one is a bad person when appearance does not meet cultural standards) and surveillance (watching the body as an outside observer) of their bodies, weight satisfaction, body esteem, length of intimate relationships, and approval of appearance by partners. Her results suggest that mothers had lower levels of surveillance and body shame than daughters. In addition, mothers weighed more and were less satisfied with their weight than daughters. McKinley also noted that both mothers and daughters internalized the cultural body standards. In addition, perceptions of partner approval were positively related to body esteem for daughters and mothers. Mothers also objectify their bodies less than daughters do.

Restricted eating showed no age differences. Middle-aged women restricted their eating because of a fear of aging (Gupta, 1995; Rabinor, 1994). Thus restricted eating is common for women in both age groups and is an expression of many anxieties related to female socialization practices. McKinley also reported that among the mothers in her sample, those whose partners disapproved had the lowest body esteem compared with those middle-aged women with no partners or with partners who approved of their appearance. McKinley concludes:

> As parents, we need to do more than reassure our daughters that they are attractive; we need to encourage them to evaluate themselves on other dimensions altogether. . . . As long as women and society continue to evaluate women's worth in terms of how well they meet some arbitrary appearance standard, the lives of women of all ages will be negatively affected. (p. 769; in this text, p. 210)

EMOTIONAL DEVELOPMENT

Focus on Continuity in Personality Across the Life Cycle

McKinley's research emphasizes the continuity in development across the life cycle. This issue of continuity in development is also found with personality traits. In 1993, the American Psychological Association's Commission on Violence and Youth documented cultural values among various racial groups. The Commission listed the following values associated with African Americans: harmony and interrelatedness with nature, spirituality and strong religious orientation, communalism rather than individualism, child-centeredness, and flexibility of roles. The Commission also identified the following values associated with Native Americans: harmony with and respect for nature, emphasis on family and tradition, and emphasis on group cooperation instead of individual achievement.

Those values identified by the Commission as common among Hispanics include: preference for participating in groups, strong adherence to family, avoidance of interpersonal conflict, and deference to and respect for authority systems. Asian and Pacific Island Americans reported the following values as central to their culture: strong cultural affiliation, strong family ties, a link to ancestors and expected obedience of the young to their elders, a social order of hierarchy of interpersonal relations, and pacifism.

These values have a direct effect on the shape of adult life. In their article "Age Differences in Personality Across the Adult Life Span: Parallels in Five Cultures," excerpted in the readings section (see pp. 212–216), Robert R. McCrae and his colleagues discuss consistency and changes in personality across adulthood. In earlier work, McCrae and Costa (1987) had proposed five basic personality dimensions: neuroticism, extraversion, openness, agreeableness, and conscientiousness. Previous research with white adults indicated that these five dimensions show stability over relatively long periods of adulthood. As Costa and McCrae (1994) conclude:

> We now know that in many fundamental ways, adults remain the same over periods of many years and that their adaptation to life is profoundly shaped

> by their personality. People surely grow and change, but they do so on the foundation of enduring dispositions. (pp. 35–36)

In order to determine whether consistency in personality is universal, McCrae and his colleagues studied women and men in Germany, Italy, Portugal, Croatia, and South Korea. Their findings suggest that despite the widely varying languages and cultures included in their study, the data were consistent. Older adults from all cultures sampled in the study were less emotionally volatile and more responsive to social demands placed on them. Researchers have interpreted this finding among older adults as an indication that they are more mature. Younger individuals typically respond with impulsiveness, vulnerability, depression, anxiety, and low self-discipline. More mature ways of responding apparently are associated with growing older.

The results reported by McCrae and his colleagues are important to consider in light of the fact that each of the five cultures they studied have different historical experiences, from economic decline and wars to differences in approaches to parental discipline methods. Yet, despite the vast differences in historical as well as cultural experiences, there is no corresponding impact on the pattern of age differences in personality traits.

McCrae and his colleagues thus found support for the universality of personality, especially for the openness to experience. Their data affirm theoretical positions that as we enter adulthood and make commitments to careers and relationships, we need to accommodate and consequently become more mature in personality. McCrae and his colleagues discuss their results in terms of both hereditary factors and social factors. Their findings suggest the need for longitudinal studies of personality in a variety of cultures.

Focus on Depressive Psychopathology in Older Adults

In the previous chapter, we discussed depression in adolescence, placing it in the context of the cognitive, physical, and interpersonal changes taking place in individuals during that life stage. Research suggests a U-shaped curve with respect to rates of depression in adulthood: high rates in young adulthood and then again among the old and old old (Turnbull & Mui, 1995). This distribution is found to hold for African Americans as well as for white Americans (Turnbull & Mui, 1995). Furthermore, African Americans have higher levels of depressive symptomatology than whites (McBarnette, 1996). We should point out, however, that the majority of research on depression in adulthood is cross-sectional in nature. This poses a methodological bias in the research, namely, cohort effects. Weissman and Klerman (1992) found that the rate of depression has risen for each succeeding cohort of young adults over several decades. Consequently, young adults may appear worse off in comparison to older adults in a cross-sectional study of depressive symptomatology.

Depression has been found to be the most common emotional health problem in the elderly population (Burns & Taube, 1990). Gender comparisons have been noted. Young adult and older adult women are more likely to be depressed than men (Perlin, 1989; Russo & Green, 1993). Ginorio, Gutierrez, Cauce, & Acosta (1995) reported a high risk of depression among Latinas, especially because of race discrimination and the conflicts between cultural expectations and achievement as minorities. LaFromboise et al. (1995) cited depression as a major clinical problem of American Indian women.

Several theories have been suggested to account for the greater incidence of depression among women than among men. One general view is that women are more likely to admit to depressive symptoms, whereas men are not. Other theories suggest that because women suffer greater discrimination and a relative lack of power in society as compared with men, the consequence is "legal and economic helplessness, dependency on others, chronically low self-esteem, low aspiration, and ultimately, clinical depression" (Weissman & Klerman, 1977, p. 106).

Belle (1990) noted the impact of low income and ethnic minority membership on women's depressive symptomatology. For example, Belle (1984) found that in a sample of 42 urban low-income mothers, the subjects had personally experienced 37 violent events and witnessed 35 stressful events among family and friends during the preceding two years. Inadequate housing, dangerous neighborhoods, and financial concerns are more serious stressors than acute crises. Belle (1990) also noted that women are likely to experience a contagion of stress: stressful events occurring to others they care for or about are added to the stressors in their own lives. This fact contributes to the greater risk for depression among low-income women. As Belle stated:

> Women's coping strategies are constrained by poverty. To be poor generally means that one is frighteningly dependent on bureaucratic institutions such as the welfare system, the public housing authority, the health care system, and the courts. Poor women who must seek assistance from such systems often experience repeated failure that reflects no lack of imagination or effort on the women's part, merely the fact that a powerful institution declined to respond. Repeated instances of such failure, however, may lead to the (often veridical) perception that one is indeed powerless to remove the major stressors from one's life. (p. 387)

Maria E. Fernandez, Elizabeth J. Mutran, Donald C. Reitzes, and S. Sudha, in their article "Ethnicity, Gender, and Depressive Symptoms in Older Workers" that is excerpted in the readings section (see pp. 216–220), report on their study of depressive symptomatology among African American men, African American women, white American men, and white American women. Statistically significant group differences were obtained. Specifically, work stressors had long-term effects on African American men, whose levels of depressive symptomatology were elevated by retirement or poor health. In addition, white men were more vulnerable to social network losses at work than were white women. African American women had significantly more depressive symptomatology than did white men and white women. Fernandez et al. found that income had a major impact on depressive symptoms among African Americans, more than for white individuals, with African American women showing the greatest impact, even above African American men.

Fernandez and her colleagues' research highlights the need to look at minority men's and women's experiences with stressors, especially with the loss of work roles, pay inequity, and the discrimination they face in seeking other employment.

Focus on Fear of Death

How would you answer the following questions?

> How disturbed or anxious are you about dying? About never thinking or experiencing anything again? About your lack of control over dying?

These questions are adapted from Lester's (1990) questionnaire that measures fear of death.

Lester and others (e.g., Thorson & Powell, 1992) have reported that among young, middle, and older adults, individuals in middle adulthood exhibit the greatest fear of death. Older adults report more anxiety about the process of dying but fear death the least of the three age groups. Young adults' fear of death are in-between these two extremes. In an early study of adults' fear of death, Bengtson, Cuellar, and Ragan (1977) found that middle-aged African American, Mexican American, and white American individuals all exhibit more fear than other age groups in adulthood.

Middle adulthood appears to be a prime period for experiencing fear of death since it is during this stage of the life cycle that the death of one's parents typically occurs. As Bee (1996) pointed out: "the death of one's parents may be especially shocking and disturbing, not only because of the specific loss to be mourned but because you must now face the realization that you are now the oldest generation in the family lineage and thus 'next in line' for death" (p. 411).

In addition to stage in the life cycle, the following factors in particular contribute to individuals' fear of death: intensity of religiosity, social support, and sense of worth and competence. Individuals who describe themselves as deeply religious report less fear of death than those who are less religious (Kaufman, 1998; Thorson & Powell, 1992). Individuals who have stronger social supports fear death less than those individuals who are alone (Kalish, 1985). In addition, adults who believe they have led their life to the fullest, that is, accomplished the goals they set out for themselves in their family relationships and career, report being less fearful of death than individuals who are disappointed in the way they led their life (Neimeyer & Chapman, 1981).

In his article, "Personality and Demographic Factors in Older Adults' Fear of Death," excerpted in the readings section (see pp. 220–225), Victor Cicirelli studied fear of death in African American and white American elderly individuals (operationally defined as being between 60 and 100 years old). Cicirelli found that African Americans reported less fear of death than white individuals in his sample.

He also found that greater fear of dying was correlated with the following variables: being younger, being a woman, being white, having a more external locus of control, having less religiosity, and being of a lower socioeconomic class. Cicirelli also reported that fear of death was better supported by individuals' fear of the unknown than by their fear of dying, including fear of nonexistence and a fear of an unknown afterlife. Thus Cicirelli's methodological advances to the study of death and dying have helped us understand the distinctions among fear of death, fear of dying, and fear of the unknown.

Cicirelli's research is, in many ways, an extension of the work by Moon et al. He notes that while there has been increased attention paid to long-term care for the elderly, most elderly individuals experience constant pain, with little or no medication to help relieve the pain. Cicirelli further notes that it is the oldest patients and the racial and ethnic minority patients who are not provided adequate medication.

SOCIAL DEVELOPMENT

Focus on Family Violence

The research cited in this chapter overview on the stability of various aspects of personality across adulthood brings into focus the continuity of aggressiveness throughout the life cycle. We have seen in this text that violence in the middle-school-age period and later adolescence is common, especially violence against other individuals. Statistics suggest (see Paludi, 1999 for a review) that 30% of all women are battered at least once in their adult lives. Elder abuse among American Indians is high as a consequence of changes in status and the role of older adults in American Indian cultures (LaFromboise et al., 1995).

Mollica, Wyshak, and Lavelle (1987) found that among Asian refugee women living in Boston, the prevalence of sexual violence approximated 100%. They also reported that the majority of these victimized women feared reporting their abuse to authorities since in their country of origin, it was the authorities who committed many war atrocities, including murder and rape. Rimonte (1989) also noted that battering is a huge problem in many Asian American communities.

Sexual victimization is more common in cultures that are characterized by male dominance and by a high degree of violence in general. Also, it should be noted that most sexual victimization remains a secret, especially within ethnic and racial minority groups (Browne, 1993; Graham & Rawlings, 1999; Ryan, Frieze, & Sinclair, 1999).

Walker (1999) discussed the interaction among gender, religious beliefs, political structure, attitudes toward violence, actual violence toward women, and state-sponsored violence (e.g., wars) that determine women's vulnerability and safety. Walker noted that the Fourth United Nations International Conference on Women (1996) identified no country that had an absence of domestic violence.

Walker also noted that law enforcement in many countries will not intervene in family violence despite the fact that empirical evidence suggests that without any intervention, abusers will not stop their battering. Furthermore, violence is a learned behavior (Walker, 1999) and is passed from one generation to the next.

Walker summarized advocacy programs and intervention programs several countries have established to deal with domestic violence. She noted that strategies to end family violence must deal with eliminating the social causes that maintain the violence, including renegotiating the balance of power between men and women. The goals of these programs in Chile, Japan, Russia, Greece, Mexico, Nicaragua, and Argentina are to assist women in recognizing and disclosing abuse and to encourage less victim-blaming in the attitudes of family members and friends of the victim.

One of the intervention programs reviewed by Walker is presented in one of the selections in the readings (see pp. 226–231), "Changing Community Responses to Wife Abuse: A Research and Demonstration Project in Iztacalco, Mexico," by Gillian M. Fawcett, Lori L. Heise, Leticia Isita-Espejel, and Susan Pick. Fawcett and her colleagues note that myths about why violence occurs are common in the Iztacalco community as is resistance to intervening in family violence. A common phrase reported by women in their research was "El que mete paz, saca más" (Whoever tries to make peace, gets more than [s]he bargained for). Fawcett et al. learned that women respondents were unaware of what levels of violence were acceptable and thus of when to intervene. Their research indicated that 66% of women in a peri-urban neighborhood in Mexico City had reported being physically abused, 76% psychologically abused, and 21% sexually abused. Romero and Tolbert (1995) reported similar incidence rates: 61% of women attending an outpatient clinic in San Miguel de Allende experienced physical abuse in adulthood. Fawcett et al.'s intervention program involved peer and community outreach using posters and other media and a 12-session workshop to train women as agents of community change. Issues covered in the workshops included:

Family violence as a community problem
Family violence legislation
Forms of violence
Gender role expectations and violence against women
Female socialization and violence against women
Male socialization and violence against women
The cycle of violence
The personal and social consequences of violence against women
Alternatives available for abused women
Crisis-intervention skills
Institutions that support victims of violence
Community intervention

Psychologically based treatment for batterers has also shown to be helpful (Waldo, 1987). Such treatment includes training men in basic anger management, teaching methods for improving personal adjustment, and focusing on the development of relationship skills. Evaluation studies of such treatment programs has indicated a range from 64% to 85% for nonviolent behavior by participants. It should be noted, however, that treatment programs only reach a small percentage of batterers.

Focus on Grandparenting

Family violence may precipitate the children's being taken care of by another relative, including a grandparent. Research has estimated that each year, approximately 3.3 million children in the United States between the ages of 3 and 17 years are at risk of exposure to one parent being battered by their other parent (Browne, 1993). Children may be neglected by their parents, who may be too emotionally and physically abused to help even themselves (Browne, 1993; Graham & Rawlings, 1999).

Approximately 3.5% of all homes in the United States include a grandparent and grandchild under 18 years of age (Casper & Bryson, 1998). The majority of adults in the United States become grandparents before they are 65 years old, with the median age for becoming a grandparent between 42 and 45 (Mills, 1999; Sprey & Matthews, 1982). Researchers have predicted that as longevity increases for our older Americans, individuals will live to see their grandchildren become adults (Hagestad, 1988).

Cherlin and Furstenberg (1986) identified three basic styles of grandparenting: remote, companionate, and involved. Those identified as *remote* grandparents see their grandchildren infrequently, primarily as a consequence of living far apart from each other. *Companionate* grandparents share a warm, comforting relationship that is pleasing to both grandparents and grandchildren. *Involved* grandparents have a more intense involvement with their grandchildren. Most involved grandparents see their grandchildren every day and are responsible for the majority of child care. The role of the grandmother appears to be distinct from the role of the grandfather. For example, Hagestad (1985) reported that grandmothers primarily give advice about personal relationships; grandfathers provide advice about work or the world in general, especially to their grandsons.

Cultural distinctions have been noted in this research. Both African American and Hispanic American grandparents report closer and more frequent interactions with their grandchildren than do white grandparents (Kivett, 1991). In fact, African American homes are more likely than white American homes to include a grandparent and grandchild (Bryson, 1998). Some grandparents are acting as parents to their grandchildren because the grandparents' children have emotional problems, are drug abusers, have died, are incarcerated, or are teen parents. Minkler and Roe (1993) estimated that the percentage of children being cared for primarily by their grandparents was between 30% and 50% in inner cities.

In the selection from her article in the readings section (see pp. 231–236), "Raising Grandchildren: The Experiences of Black and White Grandmothers," Rachel Pruchno discusses her research with grandmothers raising their grandchildren in the absence of the middle generation. Pruchno reported that African American grandmothers were more likely than white American grandmothers to have peers who also live with their grandchildren. White grandmothers reported experiencing more burden from their caregiving role than did African American grandmothers. Most of the women reported that they were living with their grandchildren because their own children were drug addicted or had physically or emotionally neglected the children. Analyzing these responses for race, Pruchno found that white grandmothers were more likely than African American grandmothers to indicate they were the caretakers of the children because their own children were mentally ill, emotionally abusive, physically neglectful, or emotionally neglectful. African American grandmothers reported that their grandchild's mother was drug addicted and the father's living arrangements were not known.

Pruchno also reported that African American and white grandmothers indicated that their caregiving responsibilities took a toll on their work lives, including instances of absenteeism, tardiness, and leaving work to care for sick children and to take the children to their appointments. African American grandmothers were more likely to arrive to work late, while white grandmothers were more likely to change jobs. This finding may reflect economic factors as well as the difficulty, due to both race and age discrimination, for African American older women to obtain new employment.

Results from this research suggested that African American and white grandmothers were similar in their experiences in raising their grandchildren. They began their caregiving roles at similar times in their life cycles and were raising children of similar ages. Despite the impact on their work roles, both African American and white grandmothers reported high levels of satisfaction with their grandparenting role.

Focus on the Experience of Bicultural Identity

The results of Pruchno's research have great applicability for state and federal legislators. The term *family* must be redefined to include grandmothers and grandfathers who are primary caretakers of their grandchildren. Financial assistance for grandparents who are primary caretakers would greatly affect their ability to cope with their caregiving responsibilities.

The term *family* must also include adoptive parents (Friedlander et al., 2000). The majority of individuals who adopt children are white American couples with middle and upper incomes who have undergone treatments for infertility (Simon & Alstein, 1991). There is an increasingly large percentage of these couples seeking international adoptions (Adoptive Families, 1999). In their article, "Bicultural Identification: Experiences of Internationally Adopted Children and Their Parents," excerpted in the readings section (see pp. 237–241), Myrna L. Friedlander and her colleagues note that little research has been conducted on the psychosocial experiences of white parents and their internationally adopted children of color.

Friedlander et al. studied bicultural identity development in families who had adopted children; the children had Korean and Latin American (from Brazil, Mexico, Paraguay, and Peru) heritages. Bicultural identity refers to the maintenance of one's original cultural identity while one is becoming integrated into the dominant culture (LaFromboise, Coleman, & Gerton, 1993). Friedlander et al. found that the majority of the parents in their study expected their children to continue to identify with their birth culture as they matured. In addition, parents took an active role in promoting diversity within their children's schools. Moreover, parents of Korean children sent their children to a Korean culture camp. A majority of the families studied participated in a support group that celebrated multiculturalism. Families in this research reported educating themselves about the history of their children's birth country as well as becoming familiar with ethnic food, music, and traditions.

Friedlander et al. also report that the children in their sample were doing well in integrating their birth culture into the culture of their adoptive parents. One issue for the children that was highlighted in this research concerned a "sense of being different."

Parents in this study helped their children cope with racial slurs, racial bias, and discriminatory treatment. Friedlander et al. report that families in their study had "an openness to human diversity that may have contributed to their children's psychosocial well-being." This important research suggests that individuals can and do cross race and ethnic lines and put into action what is suggested by Mary Catherine Bateson's sentiment (presented at the beginning of this book of readings and now at the end):

> What would it be like to have not only color vision but culture vision, the ability to see the multiple worlds of others?

Readings

Constant Hierarchic Patterns of Physical Functioning Across Seven Populations in Five Countries*

Luigi Ferrucci, Jack M. Guralnik, Francesca Cecchi, Niccoló Marchionni, Bernardo Salani, Judith Kasper, Romano Celli, Sante Giardini, Eino Heikkinen, Marja Jylhä, and Alberto Baroni

Chronic diseases and physical impairments are major causes of disability in old age (Ettinger, Fried, Harris, Shemanski, Schulz, & Robbins, 1994; Fried, Herdman, Kuhn, Rubin, & Turano, 1991). Over the life span persons may become disabled through a variety of mechanisms. In young and middle age, disability is usually the consequence of an isolated event such as a single disease or trauma. The resulting profile of disability is strongly disease-specific. When disability affects an older person, however, it is often the consequence of multiple causes (Guralnik & Simonsick, 1993; Fried et al., 1991), such as co-occurring pathologic conditions, physiological changes directly attributable to the aging process, and disuse and deconditioning. Several lines of research indicate that this age-related, multifactorial decline in function follows a general pattern; disability in some specific activities typically appears in the early, less severe stages of the process, while disability in other activities develops in the more advanced, more severe stages. This stereotyped pattern is, at least in part, independent of the underlying pathological causes (Katz & Akpom, 1976; Katz, Ford, & Moskowitz, 1963; Kempen, Myers, & Powell, 1995; Kempen & Suurmeijer, 1990; Lammi, Kivela, Nissinen, Punsar, Puska, & Karvonen, 1989; Rosow & Breslau, 1966; Spector, Katz, Murphy, & Fulton, 1987; Tesi, Antonini, Ferrucci, Maggino, & Baroni, 1990; Verbrugge, Lepkowski, & Imanaka, 1989; Verbrugge & Jette, 1994). Katz and Apkom (1976) described this phenomenon for basic activities of daily living (ADLs). More recently, Spector et al. (1987) and Kempen and Suurmeijer (1990) showed such a hierarchic structure for a more complex scale including both basic and instrumental ADLs, and Wolinsky and Johnson (1991) suggested a three-dimensional hierarchic structure for ADL disability. Considered together, these studies point out that the inability to perform specific ADLs tends to follow a typical sequence with

*From Ferrucci et al. (1998). *The Gerontologist, 38*(3), 286–294. Reprinted with permission.

progressing disability. Furthermore, such a process tends to involve groups of activities rather than single activities, suggesting that, at a population level, physical functioning declines following a typical pattern that implies progressive deterioration of the specific motor abilities required for each cluster of activities (Fried, Ettinger, Hermanson, Newman, & Gardin, 1994; Guralnik et al., 1994; Nagi, 1964). For example, it has been demonstrated that poor performances in balance and mobility are not only cross-sectionally associated with ADL disability but also provide information on the risk of future disability in persons who are not disabled (Briggs, Gossman, Drews, & Shaddeau, 1993; Guralnik et al., 1994; Guralnik, Ferrucci, Simonsick, Salive, & Wallace, 1995; Kelly-Hayes, Jette, Wolf, D'Agostino, & Odell, 1992).

. . .

A panel of 10 health professionals (5 geriatricians and 5 physical therapists) experienced in the field of geriatrics was randomly selected among those working at the Instituto Nazionale di Ricovero e Cura degli Anziani (INRCA) Geriatric Department (Florence, Italy). The panel was asked to identify within the ELSA instrument at least three groups of activities for which disability is usually caused by similar type and severity of underlying impairments (for example, poor manual dexterity is expected to cause disability both in *eating* and in *washing arms and face*). Each member created his or her own classification scheme. Nine out of the 10 schemes provided were based on four domains of disability, but the assignment of certain activities—namely, cutting toenails, shopping, and bathing—to specific domains differed somewhat between the members of the panel. These schemes were compared during a one-day meeting. After extensive discussion, a consensus was reached on four domains of disability which were defined as:

1. Ability to perform complex manual dexterity activities while being in unstable postures (cutting own toenails; doing heavy housework);
2. Good balance on slippery or steep surfaces and capacity to walk long distances and overcome obstacles or steps (moving around outdoors; walking at least 400 meters; shopping daily for basic necessities; doing own cooking; doing light housework; washing and bathing self; using stairs);
3. Capacity to maintain static balance, mobility in the home environment, and good upper extremity control (walking between rooms; using the lavatory; dressing and undressing; getting in and out of bed);
4. Ability in activities that can be performed using the upper extremities even in a seated position (feeding self; washing arms and face).

. . .

This study uses data from three separate epidemiologic surveys on elderly populations: the Lugo study, the Dicomano study, and the ELSA study. Detailed descriptions of these studies have been reported elsewhere (Benvenuti, Ferrucci, Guralnik, Gangemi, & Baroni, 1995; Ferrucci et al., 1993; Ferrucci et al., 1995); a brief description of each follows:

The Lugo study is an epidemiologic survey performed in 1991 in Lugo di Romagna, Italy. The study population included 1,531 subjects randomly selected from the local registry of those age 70 years and older.

The Dicomano study was performed in 1989 and includes interviews with all 658 consenting persons age 65 years or older living in Dicomano, a small town in the surroundings of Florence, Italy.

The European Longitudinal Study on Aging (ELSA) is an epidemiologic survey involving 11 different countries. The project was started in 1979 under the supervision of the World Health Organization Regional Office for Europe. Each country selected an age- (5-year age groups, from 60–64 to 85+) and gender-stratified random sample from the electoral lists or the central registry. The analyses presented here used baseline data collected over the period 1979–80 from five sites: Florence, Italy (n = 1,026); Tampere,

Finland (n = 1,061); Berlin, Germany (n = 1,515); Kiev, Ukraine (n = 1,364); and Belgrade, Republic of Serbia, Federation of Yugoslavia (n = 1,914).

. . .

The purpose of this research was to define critical steps in the progression of disability in old age. Based on clinical experience and on existing literature, we postulated the existence of four conceptually well-differentiated states of disability. These four states may be viewed both as degrees of severity of disability and as subsequent stages of the disablement process. Each state is defined by severity and specific types of underlying physical impairments.

The validity of this model was verified by proving that, in seven populations across five different European countries, these states of disability have an almost perfect hierarchic structure and by comparing levels of disability with objective measures of impairments.

Although the relationship between specific impairments and the capacity to perform ADLs has not been thoroughly established, many studies have shown a strong association between decline in physical capacities and disability (Benvenuti et al., 1995; Ensrud et al., 1994; Ferrucci et al., 1996; Fried et al., 1994; Gill, Williams & Tinetti, 1995; Guralnik, 1994; Guralnik et al., 1994; Hochberg, Kasper, Williamson, Skinner, & Fried, 1995). Jette and Branch (1984) used performance-based tests to assess the distribution of musculoskeletal impairment in a noninstitutionalized elderly population. The frequency of impairments showed a clear and consistent increase with increasing age both in men and in women; "balance problems" were the most prevalent condition. Moreover, factorial analysis revealed four meaningful impairment dimensions: wrist, hand, upper extremity, and lower extremity. Greene, Williams, Marcera, & Carter (1993) studied the dimensionality and construct validity of physical function within the context of performance-based measures. Using a factor analytic approach, they identified six meaningful dimensions (muscular strength, unimanual dexterity, mobility/agility, static balance, general upper extremity control, movement planning speed) that are implicated in the deterioration of physical functioning in elderly people. Jette, Branch, and Berlin (1990), using a longitudinal approach, found that changes in musculoskeletal function relative to hand, upper extremity, and lower extremity functions were predictors of change in self-reported disability.

. . .

Our picture of the disabling process should not be regarded as a new method for measuring disability, but rather as a first step in understanding the pathophysiology of the progressive deterioration of physical function that often parallels the aging process. The strength of this scaling approach might open a new perspective in the field of research on the causal pathways leading to disability, allowing us to examine how specific diseases and functional limitations map to different domains and to generate new hypotheses concerning the most effective way of delaying the deterioration of functional status in older persons who are already disabled.

REFERENCES

Benvenuti, F., Ferrucci, L., Guralnik, J. M., Gangemi, S., & Baroni, A. (1995). Foot pain and disability in older persons: An epidemiologic survey. *Journal of the American Geriatrics Society, 43,* 479–484.

Briggs, R. C., Gossman, M. R., Drews, J. E., & Shaddeau, S. A. (1993). Balance performance among noninstitutionalized elderly women. *Physical Therapy, 70,* 410–415.

Ensrud, K. E., Nevitt, M. C., Yunis, C., Cauley, J. A., Seeley, D. G., Fox, K. M., & Cummings, S. R. (1994). Correlates of impaired function in older women. *Journal of the American Geriatrics Society, 42,* 481–489.

Ettinger, W. H., Jr., Fried, L. P., Harris, T., Shemanski, L., Schulz, R., & Robbins, J. (1994). Self-reported causes of physical disability in older people: The Cardiovascular Health Study. CHS Collaborative Research Group. *Journal of the American Geriatrics Society, 42,* 1035–1044.

Ferrucci, L., Guralnik, J. M., Bandeen-Roche, K. J., Lafferty, M. E., Pahor, M., & Fried, L. P. (1996). Physical performance measures. In J. M. Guralnik, L. P. Fried, E. M. Simonsick, J. D. Kasper, & M. E. Lafferty (Eds.), *The Women's Health and Aging Study: Health and social characteristics of older women with disability* (pp. 35–49). Bethesda, MD: National Institutes of Health.

Ferrucci, L., Guralnik, J. M., Baroni, A., Tesi, G., Antonini, E., & Marchionni, N. (1991). Value of combined assessment of physical health and functional status in community-dwelling aged: A prospective study in Florence, Italy. *Journal of Gerontology, 46,* M52–M56.

Ferrucci, L., Heikkinen, E., Waters, W. E., & Baroni, A. (1995). *Pendulum. Health and quality of life in older Europeans.* Florence, Italy: Editrice Giuntina.

Ferrucci, L., Salani, B., Costanzo, S., Lamponi, M., Cecchi, S., De Benedetti, A., Flisi, E., & Baroni, A. (1993, June). Disability as a major priority in the allocation of health and social services [Abstract]. *Proceedings of the International Conference on Chronic Diseases and Changing Care Patterns in an Ageing Society.* Amsterdam.

Fried, L. P., Ettinger, W. H., Hermanson, B., Newman, A. B., & Gardin, J. (1994). Physical disability in older adults: A physiological approach. *Journal of Clinical Epidemiology, 47,* 747–760.

Fried, L. P., Herdman, S. J., Kuhn, K. E., Rubin, G., & Turano, K. (1991). Preclinical disability: Hypothesis about the bottom of the iceberg. *Journal of Aging and Health, 3,* 285–300.

Gill, T. M., Williams, C. S., & Tinetti, M. E. (1995). Assessing risk for the onset of functional dependence among older adults: The role of physical performance. *Journal of the American Geriatrics Society, 43,* 603–609.

Greene, L. S., Williams, H. G., Macera, C. A., & Carter, J. S. (1993). Identifying dimensions of physical (motor) functional capacity in healthy older adults. *Journal of Aging and Health, 5,* 163–178.

Guralnik, J. M. (1994). Understanding the relationship between disease and disability. *Journal of the American Geriatrics Society, 42,* 1128–1129.

Guralnik, J. M., Ferrucci, L., Simonsick, E. M., Salive, M. E., & Wallace, R. B. (1995). Lower-extremity function in persons over the age of 70 years as a predictor of subsequent disability. *New England Journal of Medicine, 332,* 556–561.

Guralnik, J. M., & Simonsick, E. M. (1993). Physical disability in older Americans. *Journal of Gerontology, 48* Spec No, 3–10.

Guralnik, J. M., Simonsick, E. M., Ferrucci, L., Glynn, R. J., Berkman, L. F., Blazer, D. G., Scherr, P. A., & Wallace, R. B. (1994). A short physical performance battery assessing lower extremity function: Association with self-reported disability and prediction of mortality and nursing home admission. *Journal of Gerontology, 49,* M85–M94.

Guttman, L. (1944). A basis for scaling qualitative data. *American Society Reviews, 9,* 139–150.

Guttman, L. (1950). The basis of scalogram analysis. In S. A. Stouffer (Ed.), *Measurement and prediction.* New York: Princeton University Press.

Hochberg, M. C., Kasper, J., Williamson, I., Skinner, A., & Fried, L. P. (1995). The contribution of osteoarthritis to disability: Preliminary data from the women's health and aging study. *Journal of Rheumatology, 22,* 16–18.

Jette, A. M., & Branch, L. G. (1984). *Musculoskeletal impairment among the noninstitutionalized aged.* International Rehabilitation Medicine, *6*(4), 157–161.

Jette, A. M., Branch, L. G., & Berlin, J. (1980). Musculoskeletal impairments and physical disablement among the aged. *Journal of Gerontology, 45,* 203–208.

Katz, S., & Akpom, C. A. (1976). A measure of primary sociobiological function. *International Journal of Health Services, 6,* 493–507.

Katz, S., Ford, A. B., & Moskowitz, R. W. (1963). Studies of illness in the aged: The index of ADL: A standardized measure of biological and psychological function. *Journal of the American Medical Association, 185,* 914–921.

Kelly-Hayes, M., Jette, A. M., Wolf, P. A., D'Agostino, R. B., & Odell, P. M. (1992). Functional limitations and disability among elders in the Framingham Study. *American Journal of Public Health, 82,* 841–845.

Kempen, G. I., Myers, A. M., & Powell, L. E. (1995). Hierarchical structure in ADL and IADL: Analytical assumptions and applications for clinicians and researchers. *Journal of Clinical Epidemiology, 48,* 1299–1305.

Kempen, G. I., & Suurmeijer, T. P. (1990). The development of a hierarchical polychotomous ADL–IADL scale for noninstitutionalized elders. *The Gerontologist, 30,* 497–502.

Lammi, U., Kivela, S., Nissinen, A., Punsar, S., Puska, P., & Karvonen, M. (1989). Predictors of disability in elderly Finnish men—A longitudinal study. *Journal of Clinical Epidemiology, 42,* 1215–1225.

Lawton, M. P., & Brody, E. M. (1969). Assessment of older people: Self-maintaining and instrumental activities of daily living. *The Gerontologist, 9,* 179–186.

Lazaridis, E. N., Rudberg, M. A., Furner, S. E., & Cassel, C. K. (1994). Do activities of daily living have a hierarchical structure? An analysis using the longitudinal study of aging. *Journal of Gerontology, 49,* M47–M51.

McIver, J. P., & Carmines, E. G. (1981). *Unidimensional scaling.* Beverly Hills, CA: Sage.

Menzel, H. (1953). A new coefficient for program analysis. *Public Opinion Quarterly, 17,* 269–280.

Nagi, S. Z. (1964). A study in the evaluation of disability and rehabilitation potential: Concepts, methods, and procedures. *American Journal of Public Health, 54,* 1568–1579.

Rosow, I., & Breslau, M. (1966). A Guttman health scale for the aged. *Journal of Gerontology, 21,* 556–559.

SAS Institute Inc. (1993). *SAS procedures guide, Version 6* (4th ed.). Cary, NC: Author.

Spector, W. D., Katz, S., Murphy, J. B., & Fulton, J. P. (1987). The hierarchical relationship between activities of daily living and instrumental activities of daily living. *Journal of Chronic Diseases, 40,* 481–489.

Tesi, G., Antonini, E., Ferrucci, L., Maggino, F., & Baroni, A. (1990). La misura dell'autosufficienza nell'anziano [Assessment of disability in the elderly]. *Giornale Italiano di Gerontologia, 38,* 381–385.

Torgerson, W. S. (1958). *Theory and methods of scaling.* New York: Wiley.

Verbrugge, L. M., & Jette, A. M. (1994). The disablement process. *Social Science and Medicine, 38,* 1–14.

Verbrugge, L. M., Lepkowski, J. M., & Imanaka, Y. (1989). Comorbidity and its impact on disability. *Milbank Memorial Fund Quarterly, 67,* 454–484.

Wolinsky, F. D., & Johnson, R. J. (1991). The use of health services by older adults. *Journal of Gerontology, 46,* 5345–5357.

Awareness and Utilization of Community Long-Term Care Services by Elderly Korean and Non-Hispanic White Americans*

Ailee Moon, James E. Lubben, and Valentine Villa

Although a considerable amount of research has examined the patterns and predictors of health and social service utilization among elderly populations, there are few studies among minority and immigrant elderly populations. Studies among nonminority elders consistently find that a client's awareness or knowledge of existing services is an important prediction of service use (Chapleski, 1989; Downing & Copeland, 1980; Fujii, 1976; Gallagher, 1988; Garcia, 1985; Gelfand, 1982; Harel, McKinney, & Williams, 1987; Holmes, Teresi, & Holmes, 1983; Krout, 1984; Kulys, 1990; McCaslin, 1988; Newton, 1980; Ralston, 1982; Rao & Rao, 1983; Starrett, Wright, Mindel, & Tran, 1989). Using the Andersen model of service utilization (Andersen, 1968; Andersen & Newman, 1973), Starrett and colleagues (1989) also reported that awareness of social services is an important enabling factor for service use. Similarly, Mindel and Wright (1982) indicate that the Anderson model enabling factor of "number of services perceived available" has a direct effect on service use other than perceived need.

Accordingly, McCaslin (1989) concluded that while demographic and functional capacity variables traditionally studied are relatively poor predictors of service use, knowledge of and orientation to the formal service system are salient determinants of use, especially among programs for healthy elderly adults. More recently, Calsyn and Roades (1993) also attributed much of the variance in service utilization to greater awareness.

Given the importance of service knowledge for utilization, a number of studies also have sought the predictors of such knowledge and consistently implicate higher educational levels (Calsyn & Roades, 1993; Chapleski, 1989; Krout, 1983, 1984; Kushman & Freeman, 1986). In contrast, findings on other variables such as age, gender, marital status, income, and informal support are mixed (Calsyn & Roades, 1993; Krout, 1983, 1985, 1988; Kushman & Freeman, 1986; Mindel & Wright, 1982; Ward, Sherman, & LaGory, 1984; Chapleski, 1989).

Some studies have addressed the relevance of race/ethnicity to differentials in the utilization and knowledge of health and social services among the elderly (Bass & Noelker, 1987; Cantor & Mayer, 1975; Coulton & Frost, 1982; Harel, 1987; Holmes, Teresi, & Holmes, 1983; Mindel & Wright, 1982; Spence & Atherton, 1991; Wolinsky et al., 1983). However, increasing diversity of minority populations and limited research on minority elders in general, combined with variations in research methods and types of services investigated, render available knowledge too limited and inconsistent for conclusive generalizations.

Nevertheless, a number of studies indicate that minority elders in general tend to utilize services less than White elders. For example, African Americans tended to use formal in-home services less than Whites (Wallace, Andersen, & Levy-Storms, 1993), Latinos tended to use fewer services than non-Latino Whites (Greene & Monahan, 1984), and significantly fewer Asian Americans use social services than Latinos and Blacks (Guttmann & Cuellar, 1982). In contrast, some health service researchers observe that African Americans exercise greater utilization than Whites (Bass & Noelker, 1987; Calsyn & Roades, 1993). Further, some studies suggest race exerts no significant effect on health and social service utilization (Coulton & Frost, 1982; Wallace,

*From Moon et al. (1998). *The Gerontologist, 38*(3), 309–316. Reprinted with permission.

Levy-Storms, & Ferguson, 1995; Wolinsky et al., 1983).

Comparing four ethnic elderly groups' knowledge and utilization of community-based long-term care services, Holmes, Teresi, and Holmes (1983) found significantly less knowledge and utilization among African Americans and Puerto Ricans than among Whites or Mexican Americans. They also reported that knowledge of community resources and activity limitation were the most important predictors of service use. Other studies (Harel, 1987; Lee & Yee, 1988; Spence & Atherton, 1991) suggest lack of knowledge about community services as central to ethnic elders' low utilization rates. Lee (1987) further attributes Asian American elders' underutilization of formal social services to five factors: culturally inappropriate services, Asian values, historical discrimination, organizational barriers, and social alienation.

Research on service utilization by minorities has tended to focus on African Americans and, to a lesser extent, Latinos, while generally neglecting other minority elderly populations, such as Korean Americans. However, because ethnic groups differ greatly in language, culture, demographics, and behavior, Barresi and Stull (1993) argue that practitioners and policy makers need to know more regarding, specifically, how ethnicity affects service needs, knowledge, and utilization in order to plan and implement culturally sensitive and effective programs.

Addressing the need for more knowledge about specific minority elders, this study focuses on Korean American elders, whose service needs, knowledge, and utilization have received relatively little attention from gerontological researchers and practitioners alike. It should be noted that Korean Americans are one of the fastest growing ethnic populations in the U.S. The 1990 Census counted 798,847 Korean Americans, a 125% increase since 1980 (U.S. Bureau of the Census, 1990). This growth continues such that the Korean Embassy estimates the actual number exceeded 1.3 million by 1995 (The Los Angeles Consulate of the Republic of Korea, 1996). The population of Korean Americans 65 years of age or older increased at an even faster rate (309%), rising from 8,613 in 1980 to 35,247 in 1990 (U.S. Bureau of the Census, 1990). Continued U.S. immigration of Koreans and family reunification under current immigration policy, combined with aging among many immigrants who came to the U.S. in the 1960s and 1970s, is likely to continue to increase their numbers significantly.

Unlike some other Asian American groups, such as Chinese, Japanese, and Filipinos, who have a relatively long immigration history, it was not until the mid-1970s that Koreans began to immigrate to the U.S. in large numbers. Many Korean immigrants have subsequently sponsored their parents' immigration to the U.S. In fact, the Immigration and Naturalization Service reported that Koreans were more likely than other groups to sponsor their parents' immigration to America (U.S. Department of Justice, 1990). Consequently, many Korean American elders have aged in Korea and face multiple adjustment problems in the U.S., such as language barriers, cultural differences, lack of employment opportunities, and unfamiliarity with the social service systems (Kim & Kim, 1988; Koh & Bell, 1987; Moon & Pearl, 1990, 1991; Wallace, Villa, Moon, & Lubben, 1996).

Korean American elders are different from those in Korea in several ways, including religious affiliation, availability of and dependency on public assistance, and living arrangement preference. While the majority of elders in Korea are Buddhist, over two thirds of Korean American elders are Christian (Park, 1989). Nearly half (47%) of Korean American elders receive public assistance, mainly Supplemental Security Income (SSI), whereas less than 5% of those in Korea depend on similar public assistance programs (Kim & Kim, 1988; Lee, 1992). This largely reflects the sharp difference in social welfare systems between the two countries. Whereas the U.S. has various social services and public income support programs to help elders maintain independent living, such programs in Korea are very limited in number and coverage, generally targeting childless elders because of the social expectation in Korea that adult children will provide for their parents.

Research on elderly Korean Americans, though sparse, suggests further changes may be taking place. For example, Korean American elderly adults are less apt to prefer traditional extended family living arrangements and more apt to seek a more independent living situation (Koh & Bell, 1987). A national survey reported that in 1988, 55% of the elderly population in Korea preferred to live with children, whereas only 30% of Korean American elders expressed such a residential preference (Koh & Bell, 1987; Korean Population and Health Research Institute, 1989). Similarly, there may be a decrease in family support and filial piety. Also, there appear to be increased reports of low morale and poor mental health (Kiefer, Kim, Choi, Kim, & Kim, 1985; Moon, 1996; Yamamoto, Rhee, & Chang, 1994).

. . .

This study found extremely low levels of awareness and utilization of community-based long-term health and social services among Korean Americans, suggesting that from a practical standpoint most of these services hardly exist for them. Also evident is that accessibility, as measured in terms of service-awareness and utilization of services, are unequal between Korean Americans and non-Hispanic Whites. This finding supports previous studies reporting that health and social services are generally more accessible to and utilized by White elders, who are often more socioeconomically advantaged than their minority counterparts. The findings challenge the success of the Older Americans Act, an important funding source for those services, at meeting its stated objective to increase service availability and delivery to minority elders and socioeconomically disadvantaged elders. Based on the premise that awareness is crucial to use of services, this study raises concern that Korean American elders' service needs remain unmet, even though needed services exist and may be desired.

The present study suggests that Korean American elderly adults do use services known to them. Therefore, efforts must be made to inform Korean American elders about the availability of services and how to use them, and to encourage service use. Considering that most Korean American elders in the U.S. only speak Korean, use of the Korean American ethnic media, churches, social clubs, and service agencies is crucial for effective outreach and public education efforts. Furthermore, because most Korean American elders are unfamiliar with the complex American social welfare system, including its long-term care services, a resource information handbook in the Korean language would be extremely useful. The handbook should contain practical information about various service areas for the elderly (e.g., nutrition, transportation, in-home supportive services), including descriptions of services and eligibility, where and how to receive services, and names and telephone numbers of Korean-speaking representatives, if any, of all agencies providing the specific services in different locations. Funding of these efforts, we believe, will be very cost effective.

At the same time, for these services to be truly accessible, they must be culturally sensitive to the needs of Korean Americans. In fact, although more than half of Korean American respondents were aware of senior citizen centers, which provide a wide range of health, social, and recreational programs and services, only 17.9% of the aware had ever used such a center (34.1% of the aware for non-Hispanic Whites), primarily due to language and cultural barriers. Having a Korean-speaking worker, providing Korean food, and offering more culturally diverse activities (e.g., Korean dance, Korean traditional games), for example, would attract more Korean American elders to such centers and increase knowledge and potential use of other valuable community services as well. Again, meaningful Korean American access to long-term care health and social services requires not only policy makers' recognition of the service gap and resource need, but also service providers' cultural knowledge and responsiveness.

Finally, given that minority and immigrant elderly populations will continue to grow over the next century, this study suggests the importance of continued research on such populations because they may have low levels of awareness and utilization of health and social services. It would be particularly useful to replicate this study with other specific Asian American elderly populations for whom no similar empirical data is currently available. Also useful would be a study assessing the need for community long-term care services and other special service needs among minority and immigrant elderly populations. Study results would enable us to measure the service gap and the relationships among the need, awareness, and utilization of community long-term care services by such populations. Another potentially important area of investigation concerns informal services or "traditional" support available to and utilized by the elderly populations in an attempt to satisfy the service need not met by formal professional services. With continued research exploring ways in which to increase the minority population's access to services, policy makers and service providers will need to make informed and conscientious decisions in allocating scarce resources to promote the equity, efficiency, and well-being of the elderly population.

REFERENCES

Andersen, R. (1968). *A behavioral model of families' use of health services.* Research Series No. 25. Chicago: Center for Health Administration Studies, University of Chicago.

Barresi, C. M., & Stull, D. E. (1993). Ethnicity and long-term care: An overview. In C. M. Barresi & D. E. Stull (Eds.), *Ethnic elderly and long-term care.* New York: Springer.

Bass, D. M., & Noelker, L. S. (1987). The influence of family caregivers on elders' use of in-home services: An expanded conceptual framework. *Journal of Health and Social Behavior, 28,* 184–196.

Calsyn, R. F., & Roades, L. A. (1993). Predicting perceived service need, service awareness, and service utilization. *Journal of Gerontological Social Work, 21,* 59–76.

Cantor, M., & Mayer, M. (1975). Factors in differential utilization of services by urban elderly. *The Gerontologist, 15,* 97–98.

Chang, J., & Moon, A. (1997). Korean American elderly's knowledge and perceptions of elder abuse: A qualitative analysis of cultural factors. *Journal of Multicultural Social Work, 11,* 139–154.

Chapleski, E. E. (1989). Determinants of knowledge of services to the elderly: Are strong ties enabling or inhibiting? *The Gerontologist, 29,* 539–545.

Coulton, C., & Frost, A. K. (1982). Use of social and health services by the elderly. *Journal of Health and Social Behavior, 23,* 330–339.

Downing, R., & Copeland, E. (1980). Services for the Black elderly: National or local problems? *Journal of Gerontological Social Work, 2,* 289–303.

Fujii, S. M. (1976, March). Elderly Asian Americans and use of public services. *Social Casework,* 202–207.

Gallagher, K. (1988). *Methods to increase the participation of minority elderly in programs funded under the Older Americans Act.* Denver, CO: Aging and Adult Services, Colorado Department of Social Services.

Gelfand, D. E. (1982). *Aging: The ethnic factor.* Boston: Little, Brown.

Greene, V. L., & Monahan, D. (1984). Comparative utilization of community-based long-term care services by Hispanic and Anglo elderly in a case management system. *Journal of Gerontology, 39,* 730–735.

Guttmann, D., & Cuellar, J. (1982). Barriers to equitable services. *Generations, 6,* 31–33.

Harel, Z. (1987). Older Americans Act related to homebound aged: What difference does racial background make. *Ethnicity & Gerontological Social Work, 9,* 133–143.

Harel, Z., McKinney, E., & Williams, M. (1987). Aging, ethnicity, and services: Empirical and theoretical perspectives. In D. E. Gelfand & C. M. Barresi (Eds), *Ethnic dimensions of aging.* New York: Springer.

Holmes, D. J., Teresi, J., & Holmes, M. (1983). Differences among Black, Hispanic, and White people in knowledge about long-term care services. *Health Care Financing Review, 5,* 51–67.

Kiefer, C. W., Kim, S., Choi, C., Kim, L., & Kim, B. L. (1985). Adjustment problems of Korean American elderly. *The Gerontologist, 25,* 477–482.

Kim, S. S., & Kim, P. K. (1988). Korean-American urban elderly. *Journal of Korean Gerontological Society, 7,* 77–91.

Koh, J. Y., & Bell, W. G. (1987). Korean elders in the United States: Intergenerational relations and living arrangements. *The Gerontologist, 27,* 66–71.

Korean Population and Health Research Institute. (1989). *Research for future welfare policy development for the elderly.* Seoul, South Korea: KPHRI.

Krout, J. A. (1983). Knowledge and use of services by the elderly: A critical review of the literature. *International Journal of Aging & Human Development, 17,* 153–167.

Krout, J. A. (1984). Notes on policy and practice: Utilization of services by the elderly. *Social Service Review, 58,* 281–290.

Krout, J. A. (1985). Service awareness among the elderly. *Journal of Gerontological Social Work, 9,* 7–19.

Krout, J. A. (1988). Community size differences in service awareness among elderly adults. *Journal of Gerontology, 43,* 528–530.

Kulys, R. (1990). The ethnic factor in the delivery of social services. In A. Monk (Ed.), *Handbook of gerontological services.* New York: Columbia University Press.

Kushman, J. E., & Freeman, B. K. (1986). Service consciousness and service knowledge among older Americans. *International Journal of Aging and Human Development, 23,* 217–237.

Lee, J. (1987). Asian American elderly: A neglected minority group. *Ethnicity and Gerontological Social Work, 9,* 103–117.

Lee, K. (1992). *Korean Americans.* Seoul, South Korea: Il-chokak.

Lee, S. S., & Yee, A. K. (1988). The development of community-based health services for minority elderly in Boston's Chinatown. *Pride Institute Journal of Long Term Care Home Health Care, 7,* 3–9.

McCaslin, R. (1988). Reframing research on service use among the elderly: An analysis of recent findings. *The Gerontologist, 28,* 512–522.

McCaslin, R. (1989). Service utilization by the elderly: The importance of orientation to the formal system. *Journal of Gerontological Social Work, 14,* 153–174.

Mindel, C. H., & Wright, R., Jr. (1982). The use of social services by Black and White elderly: The role of social support systems. *Journal of Gerontological Social Work, 4,* 107–125.

Moon, A. (1986). Morale among Korean American elders living alone or with a spouse only and its correlates. *Journal of Korean Gerontological Society, 16,* 96–109.

Moon, A., & Williams, O. (1993). Perceptions of elder abuse and help-seeking patterns among African American, Caucasian American, and Korean American elderly women. *The Gerontologist, 33,* 386–395.

Moon, J., & Pearl, H. (1990). Sources of alienation among elderly Korean-American immigrants: Subjective reports. *Journal of Minority Aging, 12,* 1–16.

Moon, J., & Pearl, H. (1991). Alienation of elderly Korean American immigrants as related to place of residence, gender, age, years of education, time in the U.S., living with or without children, and living with or without a spouse. *International Journal of Aging and Human Development, 32,* 115–124.

Newton, F. (1980). Issues in research and service delivery among Mexican-American elderly: A concise statement with recommendations. *The Gerontologist, 20,* 208–212.

Park, K. (1989). *Korean Elderly in Queens.* Paper presented at the 6th Annual Conference of the Asian-American Studies. Hunter College, City University of New York.

Ralston, R. A. (1982). Perception of senior centers by the Black elderly: A comparative study. *Journal of Gerontological Social Work, 4,* 127–137.

Rao, V. P., & Rao, V. N. (1983). Factors related to the knowledge and use of social services among the Black elderly. *Journal of Minority Aging, 8,* 26–35.

Spence, S. A., & Atherton, C. R. (1991). The Black elderly and the social service delivery system: A study of factors influencing the use of community-based services. *Journal of Gerontological Social Work, 16,* 19–35.

Starrett, R. A., Wright, R., Jr., Mindel, C. H., & Tran, T. V. (1989). The use of social services by Hispanic elderly: A comparison of Mexican American, Puerto Rican and Cuban elderly. *Journal of Social Service Research, 13,* 1–25.

The Los Angeles Consulate of the Republic of Korea. (1996). Personal interview with Consul Jung Keun Han on January 12, 1996.

U.S. Bureau of the Census. (1990). *Census and you* (Press Release CB91–100). Washington, DC: U.S. Government Printing Office.

U.S. Department of Justice, Immigration and Naturalization Service. (1990). *Report on U.S. Immigration in 1989.* Washington, DC: U.S. Government Printing Office.

Wallace, S. P., Villa, V., Moon, A., & Lubben, J. E. (1996). Health practice of Korean elderly people: National health promotion priorities and minority community needs. *Family and Community Health, 19,* 29–42.

Wallace, S. P., Levy-Storms, L., & Ferguson, L. R. (1995). Access to paid in-home assistance among disabled elderly people: Do Latinos differ from non-Latino Whites? *American Journal of Public Health, 85,* 970–975.

Wallace, S. P., Levy-Storms, L. (1993, November). *Access to long-term care by minority elderly: Implications of health care reform.* Paper presented at the Gerontological Society of America Annual Meeting, New Orleans, LA.

Ward, R. A., Sherman, S. R., & LaGory, M. (1984). Informal networks and knowledge of services for older persons. *Journal of Gerontology, 39,* 216–223.

Wolinsky, F. D., Coe, R. M., Miller, D. K., Prendergast, J. M., Creel, M. J., & Chavez, M. N. (1983). Health services utilization among the noninstitutionalized elderly. *Journal of Health and Social Behavior, 24,* 325–337.

Yamamoto, J., Rhee, S., & Chang, D. (1994). Psychiatric disorders among elderly Koreans in the United States. *Community Mental Health Journal, 30,* 17–27.

Women and Objectified Body Consciousness: Mothers' and Daughters' Body Experience in Cultural, Developmental, and Familial Context*

Nita Mary McKinley

Life span developmental contextual theories examine the dynamic interaction between biological–maturational processes and sociocultural–historical change (Lerner, Skinner, & Sorell, 1980). The purpose of this article was to place women's body experience within this developmental and cultural context and to present some data collected from a sample of undergraduate women and their middle-aged mothers to test hypotheses developed from this contextual perspective.

Psychological research suggests that there may be both similarities and differences in the body experience of younger and older women. Many studies have found no age differences in body satisfaction (Ben-Tovim & Walker, 1994; Davis & Cowles, 1991; Garner, 1997; Rozin & Fallon, 1988) and weight-related behaviors (Cash & Henry, 1995; Rand & Kuldau, 1991). A few large-scale studies, however, have found that middle-aged women place less importance on their appearance and feel better about their appearance than young women (Cash, Winstead, & Janda, 1986; Pliner, Chaiken, & Flett, 1990), and a few studies have found young women to feel better about their appearance (Cash & Henry, 1995). Additional data clarifying these age differences would be important. The similarities and differences in young and middle-aged women's body experience are likely related to the cultural context, which defines women in terms of their bodies, and the developmental context, which includes age-related differences in life tasks, the interaction of biological changes with cultural standards of appearance, and cohort differences. Likewise, the familial context, which includes bidirectional influences between a daughter's body experience and the messages she receives from her family, is likely to be important in understanding women's experience.

The Cultural Context: Objectified Body Consciousness

Although researchers have pointed to the importance of culture in shaping women's body experience, the psychological measurement of body image has focused primarily on individual variables, such as affective variables (e.g., body esteem; Franzoi & Shields, 1984), perceptual accuracy in size estimation (e.g., Thompson & Spana, 1988), and cognitive variables (e.g., importance of appearance; Brown, Cash, & Mikulka, 1990). To provide a way to study women's body experience with attention to cultural context, I have used the construct of objectified body consciousness (OBC), which is based on feminist theory about how women are taught to view their bodies in U.S. culture (McKinley, 1995; McKinley & Hyde, 1996). OBC consists of three components, the first of which is surveillance, that is, viewing one's body as an outside observer. Girls learn quite early that they are evaluated for how they look, and they come to experience their own bodies in terms of how they look to others, rather than, for example, how they feel or what they can do (Spitzack, 1990). When people focus attention on themselves as they appear to others and are aware of standards for their behavior, they feel bad if they cannot reduce any discrepancy (Carver & Scheier, 1981). I found higher surveillance to be related to lowered body esteem and increased restricted eating and disordered eating in young women (McKinley & Hyde, 1996).

. . .

*From McKinley, N. M. (1999). *Developmental Psychology, 35*(3), 760–769. Reprinted with permission.

The Developmental Context

Life Span Tasks

Life span tasks "derive from the interplay between age-graded, history-graded, and non-normative influences and events" (Baltes, Reese, & Lipsitt, 1980, p. 81). Life cycle theorists, such as Erikson (1959) and, more recently, Levinson (1986), have contrasted young adulthood as a time of establishing intimacy and individual achievement, with middle age as a time of generativity, that is, contributing to the next generation. These differing tasks may account for some differences in women's body experience across the life span. For example, for young women, appearance may be especially important because a woman's appearance is important during the establishment of heterosexual relationships (Feingold, 1990). Also, theorists have connected objectification and appearance standards to individual achievement for women (e.g., Bartky, 1988). Research similarly suggests that competitiveness, achievement orientation, nontraditional role preference, and the importance of professional success are related to body issues for women (Silverstein, Carpman, Perlick, & Perdue, 1990; Silverstein & Perdue, 1988; Silverstein, Perdue, Peterson, Vogel, & Fantini, 1986; Silverstein, Perdue, Wolf, & Pizzolo, 1988; Striegel-Moore, Silberstein, Grunberg, & Rodin, 1990).

In addition, the tasks of intimacy and individual achievement may conflict for young women, insofar as they must be "feminine" (which culture defines as being passive) to have intimate relationships, and they must be instrumental to succeed in individual achievement. Working to achieve a body that is consistent with cultural ideals may allow a woman to work on both these goals in a culturally acceptable way (Rodin, Silberstein, & Striegel-Moore, 1985). Therefore, the tasks of intimacy and achievement and the conflict between the two make young adulthood the time when body experience and psychological well-being (PWB) are most strongly connected and the age when women may most objectify their bodies and feel the least satisfied with their bodies.

In contrast, at middle age, long-term relationships may have been established in which appearance may not be so important for women as during the initiation of relationships (although not all middle-aged women are in established relationships, and appearance may continue to be important even in long-term relationships; Blumstein & Schwartz, 1983). Also, appearance may not be as important in the middle-aged task of generativity. For this reason, in middle age, women may objectify their bodies less and feel more satisfied with their bodies, and their appearance may be less strongly related to their PWB.

The Interaction of Biology and Culture

Young women are likely to come as close to the culturally ideal feminine body as they ever will in their lifetime, which should make them more satisfied with their bodies. However, Spitzack (1990) argued that having a body that conforms to cultural standards makes women more visible as objects and more subject to surveillance and judgment. Therefore, young women are likely to be high on OBC, and OBC's relationship to their body esteem, behavior, and PWB is likely to be important.

As women age, their bodies change, growing fatter and less toned as a function of middle age as well as passages such as childbirth and menopause. At the same time, these changes are often socially constructed as degenerative (Martin, 1987). Although these physical changes and the attached cultural meanings may make achieving the ideal feminine body more difficult for middle-aged women, cultural constructions of the older woman as less sexual make women less visible at this age and, presumably, less subject to the intense body objectification of young adulthood. Middle-aged women may also compare themselves with other middle-aged women, and this different reference group may lessen pressures to attain an idealized body type. Thus, older woman may feel better about their bodies than young women and their appearance may be less strongly related to their PWB.

Historical Change: Cohort Differences

Each successive cohort of women since 1959 has faced standards of thinness that are increasingly more difficult to attain (Garner, Garfinkel, Schwartz, & Thompson, 1980; Wiseman, Gray, Mosimann, & Ahrens, 1992), and so even though they conform less to cultural standards than young women, middle-aged women may feel better about their bodies. Lamb, Jackson, Cassiday, and Priest (1993) found that young women preferred a thinner ideal than older women, which may make younger women feel pressured to be thinner and thus have lower body esteem. On the other hand, the current cohort of middle-aged women has had to face intensified visibility as the media portrays them as capable of attractiveness also. This seeming admiration for older women appreciates them only insofar as they do not *look* old and extends the requirement for objectification through middle age (Spitzack, 1990). Thus, middle-aged women may feel more satisfied with their bodies, but some older women may continue to watch their bodies and connect their appearance to their PWB.

The Familial Context

The relationship between daughters' body experience and family messages is likely to be bidirectional. A daughter's appearance may affect the messages her parents give her about her body. At the same time, a daughter's experience of her body—both how she feels about her body and the types of behaviors she exhibits—is also likely to be affected not only by what her family tells her directly, but also by how her mother feels about her own body and how her mother's partner feels about her mother's body. Daughters may learn the acceptability of the adult female body through these latter two types of messages. Positive messages, both direct and indirect, may make a woman feel better about her body but may have little effect on objectification because the standard of judgment for attractiveness has not been challenged. Daughters' body experience, and especially eating problems, have been shown to be related to positive relations with both mothers and fathers (Swarr & Richards, 1996), parental attitudes toward female achievement (Silverstein et al., 1988), and mothers' eating concerns and problems (Steiger, Stotland, Trottier, & Ghadirian, 1966).

. . .

Discussion

. . .

Development in Cultural Context

The cultural context that encourages women to view their bodies as outside observers presumably puts women of all ages at risk for negative body experience. However, young women and middle-aged women differed in their body experience in ways that were consistent with differences in life tasks and the interaction of biological aging with cultural standards of appearance, although these differences may also be explained by cohort differences. Surveillance was related to body esteem in young women but not in middle-aged women. Surveillance was also related to most measures of PWB for young women but only to autonomy for middle-aged women, and these relationships for young women were significantly stronger than those of middle-aged women. When older women watch their bodies, they may apply a less strenuous set of standards than young women do because of life span tasks, the interaction between culture and biology, and cohort differences, and thus their body esteem and PWB may not be negatively affected. On the other hand, it may be for younger women that when they like their appearance more and have greater PWB, they engage in less surveillance, whereas older women's PWB or how much they like their appearance does not affect their surveillance.

Internalization of cultural body standards as measured by body shame appears to be pervasively related to body esteem and PWB in both young and middle-aged women, and there was no difference in the strength of these relationships for the two ages. The evaluation of the self in terms of achievement of cultural body standards is apparently related negatively to multiple dimensions of psychological functioning for women in both age groups. The difficulty of achieving many cultural body standards, both for weight and for youth, may make this attitude particularly problematic for women.

Believing the appearance can be controlled was unrelated to young women's body esteem, but it was positively related to middle-aged women's body esteem. Middle-aged women may feel better about their bodies when they feel in control, or it may be that women who feel better about their bodies (perhaps because their bodies conform to some standard) believe they control their bodies more. Control beliefs were positively related to some measures of PWB for young and middle-aged women, and there were no age differences in the strength of these relationships. It is interesting that there was only a small (for young women) or nonsignificant (for middle-aged women) relationship between appearance control beliefs and environmental mastery. Thus, appearance control beliefs represent a dimension distinct from more generalized feelings of control.

Middle-aged women had lower levels of body surveillance and body shame than young women, and this may account for the fact that there were no differences in body esteem for these two groups even though the older women weighed more than the younger women, were less satisfied with their weight, and presumably conformed less to cultural body standards of youth. These findings (a) suggest that middle-aged women objectify their bodies less than do young women and (b) are consistent with previous research that found no differences in body esteem for these two age groups (Ben-Tovim & Walker, 1994; Davis & Cowles, 1991; Garner, 1997; Rozin & Fallon, 1988). These findings are also consistent with Spitzack's (1990) notion that having a body that conforms to cultural standards may encourage young women to objectify their bodies even more than middle-aged women. This latter hypothesis is also consistent with the finding that the closer middle-aged women were to cultural weight ideals, the more they engaged in surveillance, although it may also be that those who engage in surveillance work more at controlling their weight. That BMI was unrelated to surveillance for young women suggests that either this hypothesis was not supported for young women or that standards other than body weight contribute more importantly to increased objectification at this age.

Body esteem was an important predictor of all six domains of PWB for both groups of women. This finding is consistent with previous research that found satisfaction with appearance was related to a variety of measures for young women, including self-esteem (e.g., Jackson, Sullivan, & Rostker, 1988; McCauley, Mintz, & Glenn, 1988; Silberstein, Striegel-Moore, Timko, & Rodin, 1988; Thomas & Freeman, 1990), social well-being (Hesse-Biber, Clayton-Matthews, & Downey, 1987), and depression (McCauley et al., 1988; Noles, Cash, & Winstead, 1985; Thompson & Psaltis, 1988), and in mixed-age studies (ages 10 to 79), body esteem has been shown to be related to self-esteem (Pliner et al., 1990). Body esteem was more strongly connected with young women's autonomy, environmental mastery, positive relations with others, and self-acceptance than with those measures for middle-aged women. This finding suggests that appearance issues may vary because of differences in the developmental context or cohort differences and that appearance is more importantly related to PWB for young women.

The finding that there were no age differences in restricted eating and dieting is consistent with previous research where there were no age differences in weight-related behaviors, such as restrained eating (Rand & Kuldau, 1991), dieting (Rozin & Fallon, 1988), and weight concern (Ben-Tovim & Walker, 1994; Cash & Henry, 1995; Davis & Cowles, 1991; Pliner et al., 1990; Rozin & Fallon, 1988). This result occurred even though the older women weighed more and were less satisfied with their weight, and it provides interesting support for the hypothesis that weight control behaviors are likely to be related to something more than simple weight dissatisfaction. For example, in middle-aged women, restricted eating may be related to fear of aging (see Gupta, 1995). Other research has linked problem eating with other types of concerns in young women, such as gender role conflict (Silverstein et al., 1988). Restricted eating may be an expression of a variety of anxieties for women of all ages.

The length of intimate relationships was not related to body esteem for young women or for middle-aged women when BMI was controlled, so it is not likely this variable accounts for the finding that body esteem is not lowered in middle age. Perceptions of partner approval, however, were positively related to body esteem for both young and middle-aged women. Among the middle-aged women, those whose partners disapproved had the lowest body esteem compared with those who had no partners and those whose partners approved of their appearance. Although women whose partners approved had the lowest BMI, there were no differences in BMI for women whose partners disapproved and those who had no partners. For women whose body size conforms less to cultural standards, having a disapproving partner may place them at risk for lowered body esteem.

The Familial Context

The positive relationship between mothers' and daughters' body esteem and surveillance and the negative relationship between mothers' body shame and daughters' body esteem suggests that mothers' body experience may influence their daughters. When a mother watches her body, she may model this behavior for her daughter. When she feels good about her body, she may be teaching her daughter that an adult woman's body is acceptable. When she demonstrates low levels of body shame, her daughter may feel better about her own appearance. In interpreting these findings, however, it is important to remember that the mother also lives in the same cultural context as the daughter and may encourage these behaviors either unintentionally or with the expectation that she is helping her daughter. Another interpretation of these data is that mothers' and daughters' appearance are related and this accounts for similarities in body esteem and surveillance. The fact that mothers' and daughters' BMI were moderately correlated provides some support for this second explanation. On the other hand, body shame, control beliefs, weight dissatisfaction, dieting, and restricted eating were not related for mothers and daughters. These measures may reflect the effects of the women's life span tasks, the interaction of biology and culture, or cohort differences rather than intergenerational variables or biological similarities.

Daughters' perceptions of family approval of her appearance were important predictors of higher body esteem. Mothers' own reports of their approval of their daughters' appearance were not significantly related to daughters' body esteem. Daughters may interpret their mother's feelings as consistent with the daughter's own feelings about her body. On the other hand, mothers' reports of approval and daughters' perceptions were correlated, so daughters' perceptions do not appear to be independent of mothers' approval. Also, the relationship between approval and body esteem does not appear to be merely a function of daughters who more closely approximate certain weight standards, although there may be other standards to which daughters conform that elicit approval from their families.

The relationship of family approval to OBC told a different story. As predicted, for the most part, daughters' perceptions of family approval were not significantly related to measures of OBC. When a daughter perceives her parents as approving of her appearance, the understanding that appearance is an important dimension of evaluation is not disrupted.

Conclusions

These data demonstrate that understanding the cultural, developmental, and familial contexts of young adulthood and middle age can contribute to an understanding of some of the cross-sectional age differences in women's body experience. However, these data are limited in several ways. First of all, the sample of mothers and daughters, although allowing for matched groups on variables such as socioeconomic status (SES), is limited in that physical similarities may account for many of the relationships between variables. In addition, the sample consisted primarily of European American, presumably relatively high-SES heterosexual women. Much of the research has been conducted on samples with similar demographics, and it would be important to determine whether OBC is a meaningful construct for lesbians, women of color, and working-class women. The body experience of women of nondominant groups may be simultaneously shaped by their own group and by dominant culture. Finally, this research is limited in that cross-sectional data are unable to distinguish between effects related to maturation and those related to chort. Longitudinal studies are needed to understand how individual women's body experience changes over her life span.

Understanding how the cultural context interacts with developmental and familial context to shape women's experience is important to understanding both why body dissatisfaction has become a "normative discontent" (Rodin et al., 1985) for women across the life span and how body experience may differ for women of different ages. These data also suggest important issues to address in helping women overcome this dissatisfaction and its negative effects, such as problem eating and lowered PWB. One might ask in what other ways might women experience their bodies, for example, in terms of what they can do or how they feel, rather than how they look to others. As parents, we need to do more than reassure our daughters that they are attractive; we need to encourage them to evaluate themselves on other dimensions altogether. In addition, addressing body issues from a developmental perspective requires that one take into account both the similarities and differences in women's body experience across the life span. Finally, one needs to understand that as long as women and society continue to evaluate women's worth in terms of how well they meet some arbitrary appearance standard, the lives of women of all ages will be negatively affected.

REFERENCES

Baltes, P. B., Reese, H. W., & Lipsitt, L. P. (1980). Life-span developmental psychology. *Annual Review of Psychology, 31,* 65–110.

Bartky, S. L. (1988). Foucault, femininity, and the modernization of patriarchal power. In I. Diamond & L. Quinby (Eds.), *Feminism and Foucault: Reflections on resistance* (pp. 61–86). Boston: Northeastern University Press.

Ben-Tovim, D. I., & Walker, M. K. (1994). The influence of age and weight on women's body attitudes as measured by the Body Attitudes Questionnaire (BAQ). *Journal of Psychosomatic Research, 38,* 477–481.

Blumstein, P., & Schwartz, P. (1983). *American couples: Money, work, and sex.* New York: William Morrow.

Bordo, S. R. (1993). *Unbearable weight: Feminism, Western culture, and the body.* Berkeley: University of California Press.

Bradburn, N. M. (1969). *The structure of psychological well-being.* Chicago: Aldine de Gruyter.

Brown, T. A., Cash T. F., & Mikulka, P. J. (1990). Attitudinal body-image assessment: Factor analysis of the Body–Self Relations Questionnaire. *Journal of Personality Assessment, 55,* 135–144.

Brownell, K. D., & Rodin, J. (1994). The dieting maelstrom: Is it possible and advisable to lose weight? *American Psychologist, 49,* 781–791.

Carver, C. S., & Scheier, M. F. (1981). *Attention and self-regulation: A control theory approach to human behavior.* New York: Springer-Verlag.

Cash, T. F., & Henry, P. E. (1995). Women's body images: The results of a national survey in the U.S.A. *Sex Roles, 33,* 19–28.

Cash, T. J., Winstead, B. A., & Janda, L. H. (1986, April). The great American shape-up. *Psychology Today, 20,* 30–37.

Davis, C., & Cowles, M. (1991). Body image and exercise: A study of relationships and comparisons between physically active men and women. *Sex Roles, 25,* 33–44.

Erikson, E. (1959). Growth and crises of the healthy personality [Monograph No. 1]. *Psychological Issues, 1,* 50–100.

Ernsberger, P., & Haskew, P. (1987). Rethinking obesity: An alternative view of its health implications. *Journal of Obesity and Weight Reduction, 6,* 58–137.

Etaugh, C., & Hall, P. (1989). Restrained eating: Mediator of gender differences on cognitive restructuring tasks? *Sex Roles, 20,* 465–471.

Feingold, A. (1990). Gender differences in effects of physical attractiveness on romantic attraction: A comparison across five research paradigms. *Journal of Personality and Social Psychology, 59,* 981–993.

Franzoi, S., & Shields, S. (1984). The Body Esteem Scale: Multidimensional structure and sex differences in a college population. *Journal of Personality Assessment, 48,* 173–178.

Fredrickson, B. L., Roberts, T., Noll, S. M., Quinn, D. M., & Twenge, J. M. (1998). The swimsuit becomes you: Sex differences in self-objectification, restrained eating, and math performance. *Journal of Personality and Social Psychology, 75,* 269–284.

Garner, D. M. (1997, February). The 1997 body image survey results. *Psychology Today, 30,* 30–44.

Garner, D. M., Garfinkel, P. E., Schwartz, D., & Thompson, M. (1980). Cultural expectations of thinness in women. *Psychological Reports, 47,* 483–491.

Gupta, M. A. (1995). Concerns about aging and a drive for thinness: A factor in the biopsychosocial model of eating disorders? *International Journal of Eating Disorders, 18,* 351–357.

Hesse-Biber, S., Clayton-Matthews, A., & Downey, J. (1987). The differential importance of weight and body image among college men and women. *Genetic, Social, and General Psychology Monographs, 113,* 509–528.

Jackson, L. A., Sullivan, L. A., & Rostker, R. (1988). Gender, gender role, and body image. *Sex Roles, 19,* 429–443.

Lamb, C. S., Jackson, L. A., Cassiday, P. B., & Priest, D. J. (1993). Body figure preferences of men and women: A comparison of two generations. *Sex Roles, 28,* 345–359.

Lawton, M. P. (1975). The Philadelphia Geriatric Center Morale Scale: A revision. *Journal of Gerontology, 30,* 85–89.

Lerner, R. M., Skinner, E. A., & Sorell, G. T. (1980). Methodological implications of contextual/dialective theories of development. *Human Development, 23,* 225–235.

Levinson, D. J. (1986). A conception of adult development. *American Psychologist, 41,* 3–13.

Martin, E. (1987). *The woman in the body: A cultural analysis of reproduction.* Boston: Beacon Press.

McCauley, M., Mintz, L., & Glenn, A. A. (1988). Body image, self-esteem, and depression-proneness: Closing the gender gap. *Sex Roles, 18,* 381–391.

McKinley, N. M. (1995). Women and objectified body consciousness: A feminist psychological analysis. *Dissertation Abstracts International, 56,* 05B. (University Microfilms No. 9527111)

McKinley, N. M., & Hyde, J. S. (1996). The Objectified Body Consciousness Scale: Development and validation. *Psychology of Women Quarterly, 20,* 181–215.

National Institutes of Health. (1992). *Methods for voluntary weight loss and control: Technological assessment conference statement.* Bethesda, MD: National Institutes of Health, Office of Medical Applications of Research.

Neugarten, B. L., Havighurst, R., & Tobin, S. (1961). The measurement of life satisfaction. *Journal of Gerontology, 16,* 134–143.

Noles, S. W., Cash, T. F., & Winstead, B. A. (1985). Body image, physical attractiveness, and depression. *Journal of Consulting and Clinical Psychology, 53,* 88–94.

Pliner, P., Chaiken, S., & Flett, G. L. (1990). Gender differences in concern with body weight and physical appearance over the life span. *Personality and Social Psychology Bulletin, 16,* 263–273.

Rand, C. S., & Kuldau, J. M. (1991). Restrained eating (weight concerns) in the general population and among students. *International Journal of Eating Disorders, 10,* 699–708.

Rodin, J., Silberstein, L., & Striegel-Moore, R. (1985). Women and weight: A normative discontent. In T. Sonderegger (Ed.), *Psychology and gender: Nebraska symposium on motivation* (pp. 265–306). Lincoln: University of Nebraska Press.

Rosenberg, M. (1965). *Society and adolescent self-image.* Princeton, NJ: Princeton University Press.

Rozin, P., & Fallon, A. (1988). Body image, attitudes to weight, and misperceptions of figure preferences of the opposite sex: A comparison of men and women in two generations. *Journal of Abnormal Psychology, 97,* 342–345.

Ryff, C. D. (1989a). Beyond Ponce de Leon and life satisfaction: New directions in the quest of successful aging. *International Journal of Behavioral Development, 12,* 35–55.

Ryff, C. D. (1989b). Happiness is everything, or is it? Explorations on the meaning of psychological well-being. *Journal of Personality and Social Psychology, 57,* 1069–1081.

Ryff, C. D. (1993). *Scales of Psychological Well-Being (short forms).* Unpublished scale.

Silberstein, L., Striegel-Moore, R., Timko, C., & Rodin, J. (1988). Behavioral and psychological implications of body dissatisfaction: Do men and women differ? *Sex Roles, 19,* 219–232.

Silverstein, B., Carpman, S., Perlick, D., & Perdue, L. (1990). Nontraditional sex role aspirations, gender identity conflict, and disordered eating among college women. *Sex Roles, 23,* 687–695.

Silverstein, B., & Perdue, L. (1988). The relationship of role concerns and preferences for slimness, and symptoms of eating problems among college women. *Sex Roles, 18,* 101–106.

Silverstein, B., Perdue, L., Peterson, B., Vogel, L., & Fantini, D. A. (1986). Possible causes of the thin standard of bodily attractiveness for women. *International Journal of Eating Disorders, 5,* 907–916.

Silverstein, B., Perdue, L., Wolf, C., & Pizzolo, C. (1988). Bingeing, purging, and estimates of parental attitudes regarding female achievement. *Sex Roles, 19,* 723–733.

Spitzack, C. (1990). *Confessing excess: Women and the politics of body reduction.* Albany: State University of New York Press.

Steiger, H., Stotland, S., Trottier, J., & Ghadirian, A. M. (1996). Familial eating concerns and psychopathological traits: Causal implications of transgenerational effects. *International Journal of Eating Disorders, 19,* 147–157.

Steiger, J. H. (1980). Tests for comparing elements of a correlation matrix. *Psychological Bulletin, 87,* 245–251.

Striegel-Moore, R. H., Silberstein, L. R., Grunberg, N. W., & Rodin, J. (1990). Competing on all fronts: Achievement orientation and disordered eating. *Sex Roles, 23,* 697–702.

Swarr, A. E., & Richards, M. H. (1996). Longitudinal effects of adolescent girls' pubertal development, perceptions of pubertal timing, and parental relations on eating problems. *Developmental Psychology, 32,* 636–646.

Taylor, S. E. (1989). *Positive illusions: Creative self-deception and the healthy mind.* New York: Basic Books.

Thomas, C. D., & Freeman, R. J. (1990). The Body Esteem Scale: Construct validity of the female subscales. *Journal of Personality Assessment, 54,* 204–212.

Thompson, J. K., & Psaltis, K. (1988). Multiple aspects and correlates of body figure ratings: A replication and extension of Fallon and Rozin (1985). *International Journal of Eating Disorders, 7,* 813–817.

Thompson, J. K., & Spana, R. E. (1988). The adjustable light beam method for the assessment of size estimation accuracy: Description, psychometrics, and normative data. *International Journal of Eating Disorders, 7,* 521–526.

Wiseman, C. V., Gray, J. J., Mosimann, J. E., & Ahrens, A. H. (1992). Cultural expectations of thinness in women: An update. *International Journal of Eating Disorders, 11,* 85–89.

Wolf, N. (1991). *The beauty myth: How images of beauty are used against women.* New York: Anchor Press.

Age Differences in Personality Across the Adult Life Span: Parallels in Five Cultures*

Robert R. McCrae, Paul T. Costa Jr., Margarida Pedroso de Lima, António Simões, Fritz Ostendorf, Alois Angleitner, Iris Marušić, Denis Bratko, Gian Vittorio Caprara, Claudio Barbaranelli, Joon-Ho Chae, and Ralph L. Piedmont

Although some research on adult personality development has been theoretically guided (e.g., Whitbourne, Zuschlag, Elliot, & Waterman, 1992), most has been exploratory and descriptive, seeking to identify age trends in a variety of traits (McCrae & Costa, 1990). Findings from studies in American samples show consistent patterns; the present study asks whether these patterns can be generalized to other cultures. At the same time, these cross-cultural comparisons offer insight into the origins of adult age differences in personality that may advance description toward explanation.

At the broadest conceptual level, age differences or changes may be attributed to nature or to nurture: They may be due either to intrinsic, biologically based, and universal maturational processes or to environmental influences that are likely to vary across time and place (Cohler, 1985). Most personality theories have linked personality formation and change to features in the environment, including child-rearing practices (Whiting & Child, 1953), the cultural ethos (Fromm, 1941), and major historical events (Elder, 1974). However, evidence that personality traits are substantially heritable (Loehlin, 1992) makes it reasonable to postulate that there are biological bases for personality development, and a recent theoretical formulation of trait psychology has postulated that traits are endogenous dispositions whose maturation is minimally affected by environmental influences (McCrae & Costa, 1996). Of course, both genetic and environmental causes may play a role.

Cross-cultural comparisons are informative here because culture represents a powerful and pervasive set of environmental influences that shape the expression, and perhaps the development, of personality traits. There is as yet no articulated theory systematically linking culture-level variables to adult personality development, but environmental perspectives support the general hypothesis that different cultures would be likely to produce different patterns of age changes and differences. By contrast, intrinsic maturational perspectives would suggest that even widely different cultures would show similar age trends.

Cross-cultural studies are also particularly useful in interpreting cross-sectional data. All cross-sectional studies confound intrinsic maturation with generational differences that result from growing up in a particular historical period. To the extent that personality is shaped by earlier life experience, different birth cohorts may show different personality profiles at a given point in time even if there are no age-related changes in personality. For example, older Americans today may score higher in

*From McCrae et al. (1999). *Developmental Psychology, 35*(2), 466–477. Reprinted with permission.

Conscientiousness than American teenagers because children were better disciplined in the 1930s and 1940s than in the 1970s and 1980s.

Within any single culture, generational and maturational confounds are usually unavoidable in cross-sectional studies. But cross-cultural comparisons offer an interpretive tool because, as Riley, Johnson, and Foner (1972) noted, when cohort effects are considered, "our concern is not with dates themselves, but with the particular sociocultural and environmental events, conditions, and changes to which the individual is exposed at particular periods" (pp. 419–420). In other words, the same historical period may be different in its psychological effects in different countries.

That fact greatly complicates the interpretation of cross-cultural differences in age effects: Any such differences might be due either to culture or to differing historical influences on personality development. However, to the extent that similar patterns of age differences emerge in different cultures, the variation in histories strengthens the case for interpreting them as intrinsic maturational processes. One might argue, for example, that American college students today score low in Conscientiousness because they grew up spoiled by the affluence of the 1980s. However, the argument would not explain a similar finding in Croatian samples, because the 1980s were a period of economic decline in Yugoslavia. If Americans and Croatians were to show similar patterns of age differences in Conscientiousness, a common biological trend might offer a better explanation.

The present article reports secondary analyses of data from five societies—Germany, Italy, Portugal, Croatia, and South Korea—that differ substantially in both culture and recent history. By examining cross-sectional associations with age, we tested the generalizability of findings on adult personality development derived chiefly from American samples. Wide generalizability would suggest that intrinsic maturational processes are important influences; substantial cross-cultural divergence would point to the importance of environmental influences on development.

. . .

These data, from five samples with widely different languages and cultures, are remarkably consistent. Older men and women in each case were lower in E [Extraversion] and O [Openness to Experience] and higher in A [Agreeableness] and C [Conscientiousness] than were younger adults. Although less consistent (cf. Eysenck, 1979), there was also a tendency for younger individuals to score higher on N [Neuroticism]. Similar patterns across cultures were also seen at the level of facet traits, and even in analyses of the specific variance in facet scales. All these age differences are consistent with previous cross-sectional and longitudinal findings in American samples. Older adults in all these cultures appear to be less emotionally volatile and more attuned to social demands, together amounting to an increase in what Whitbourne and Waterman (1979) called "psychosocial maturity."

Because these studies were cross-sectional, it is possible that age differences reflect birth cohort effects rather than intrinsic maturation. Perhaps cultural changes common to all five countries over the past century explain the similar patterns of generational differences. The younger generation worldwide has experienced better health care and nutrition than their grandparents' generation, but they have also been exposed to mass media that sometimes conflict with traditional values. Conceivably, such influences might account for their relatively higher levels of E and O and lower levels of A and C.

But in many respects, the historical experience of the five societies has been very different and contrasts even more with the experience of Americans; yet these different experiences seem to have had little effect on the pattern of age differences in personality traits. Respondents who grew up during the totalitarian regimes of Hitler, Mussolini, and Salazar showed the same personality profiles relative to their children as Americans who grew up in the era of Franklin Roosevelt. Late adolescents from prosperous Germany and the United States resembled late adolescents from less affluent Portugal and Croatia. Even decades of occupation and oppression by the Japanese, a civil war, and military tension that continues to this day do not seem to have produced a different pattern of age differences in Koreans.

Evidence for universality is strongest for O, in which equivalent slopes were found in all five cultures, and weakest for N, in which only two cultures replicated the American pattern. It is likely that the observed trends reflect some combination of maturational, cultural, cohort, and sampling effects but that maturational effects are strong enough to emerge in most cases. Their explanation might involve either social or biological factors (cf. Light, Grigsby, & Bligh, 1996). Haan, Millsap, and Hartka (1986) argued that personality changes between adolescence and young adulthood serve adaptive functions: "When people enter the adult world, they expose themselves to the binding, consequential claims of career, marriage, and parenthood. As a result, they must accommodate" (p. 229). Their argument suggests that personality traits change in response to social tasks, a hypothesis that is testable by comparing personality development in societies that impose very different tasks on the same age group. A fair test might require study of third-world nations, in which the experience of adolescence is dramatically different from that seen in the more highly developed countries studied here.

. . .

The cross-cultural findings reported here suggest a reinterpretation of some American findings. In previous research, longitudinal studies of age changes typically showed little consistent evidence of change (e.g., Costa & McCrae, 1988). In view of those findings, the small cross-sectional age differences frequently reported (e.g., Costa et al., 1986) could plausibly be interpreted as cohort effects. That argument is now less persuasive; the cross-cultural replication of adult age differences suggests that the small age differences in American samples probably reflect very slow maturational processes continuing after age 30. . . . Rates of change may differ in other cultures, even if the direction of change is the same (cf. Tarnowski et al., 1996); it would be of interest to determine what cultural influences may accelerate or retard mean-level changes in personality traits in adulthood.

The studies reported here were not originally designed to examine age differences and were less than optimal with respect to sampling procedures, age range, and information gathered (such as educational level). Certainly, however, they offer strong hypotheses that could be better tested in further research. In particular, it would be useful to begin longitudinal studies of personality in non-English-speaking countries. Such studies could reduce the possible effects of sampling bias and selective mortality in estimating mean-level changes in personality traits. More important, they would also offer the possibility of studying the stability of individual differences in personality. In the United States, personality traits show high stability coefficients, especially after age 30 (McCrae & Costa, 1990). Longitudinal studies are needed to determine whether similar patterns of stability are seen in other cultures.

. . .

Like all human beings, personality psychologists are prisoners of the time in which they live. All the development they study, whether cross-sectionally or longitudinally, occurs in a particular historical era, and in principle they cannot replicate their studies in other eras to assess directly the generalizability of their conclusions. Unless they are prepared to abandon the quest for a cumulative science of psychology (Gergen, 1977), they must turn to indirect methods. The study of personality development in cultures with different recent histories provides one such method, and the evidence so far suggests that there are lawful patterns of adult personality development that are likely to hold in all times and places.

REFERENCES

Aldwin, C. M., & Levenson, M. R. (1994). Aging and personality assessment. In M. P. Lawton & J. A. Teresi (Eds.), *Annual review of gerontology and geriatrics* (Vol. 14, pp. 182–209). New York: Springer.

Angleitner, A. (1974). Changes of personality in older people over a 5-year period of observation. *Gerontologia, 20,* 179–185.

Angleitner, A., Riemann, R., Spinath, F. M., Hempel, S., Thiel, W., & Strelau, J. (1995, July). *The Bielefeld–Warsaw Twin Project: First report on the Bielefeld samples.* Paper presented at the Workshop on Genetic Studies on Temperament and Personality, Warsaw–Pultusk, Poland.

Angleitner, A., Schmitz-Scherzer, R., & Rudinger, G. (1971). Die Altersabhängigkeit der Persönlichkeit im Sinne von R. B. Cattell [The age dependency of personality in the sense of R. B. Cattell]. *Actuelle Gerontologie, 1,* 721–729.

Baltes, M. M., & Schmid, U. (1987). Psychological gerontology. *German Journal of Psychology, 11,* 87–123.

Baum, A., O'Keefe, M. K., & Davidson, L. M. (1990). Acute stressors and chronic response: The case of traumatic stress. *Journal of Applied Social Psychology, 20,* 1643–1654.

Buss, D. M. (1991). Evolutionary personality psychology. *Annual Review of Psychology, 42,* 459–491.

Caprara, G. V., Barbaranelli, C., Borgogni, L., & Perugini, M. (1993). The "Big Five Questionnaire": A new questionnaire to assess the five-factor model. *Personality and Individual Differences, 15,* 281–288.

Caprara, G. V., Gentilomo, A., Barbaranelli, C., & Giorgi, P. (1993). Profili di personalita nell'arco vitale [Personality profiles in the life span]. *Archivio di Psicologia, Neurologia e Psichiatria, 54,* 25–39.

Cattell, R. B. (1973). *Personality and mood by questionnaire.* San Francisco: Jossey-Bass.

Cohen, J., & Cohen, P. (1975). *Applied multiple regression/correlation analysis for the behavioral sciences.* Hillsdale, NJ: Erlbaum.

Cohler, B. J. (1985). Aging in the Old and New World: Variations in the peasant tradition. *Contributions to Human Development, 14,* 65–79.

Costa, P. T., Jr., & McCrae, R. R. (1988). Personality in adulthood: A six-year longitudinal study of self-reports and spouse ratings on the NEO Personality Inventory. *Journal of Personality and Social Psychology, 54,* 853–863.

Costa, P. T., Jr., & McCrae, R. R. (1992). *Revised NEO Personality Inventory (NEO-PI–R) and NEO Five-Factor Inventory (NEO-FFI) professional manual.* Odessa, FL: Psychological Assessment Resources.

Costa, P. T., Jr., & McCrae, R. R. (1994). Stability and change in personality from adolescence through adulthood. In C. F. Halverson, G. A. Kohnstamm, & R. P. Martin (Eds.), *The developing structure of temperament and personality from infancy to adulthood* (pp. 139–150). Hillsdale, NJ: Erlbaum.

Costa, P. T., Jr., & McCrae, R. R. (in press). A theoretical context for adult temperament. In T. Wachs & D. Kohnstamm (Eds.), *Temperament in context.* Hillsdale, NJ: Erlbaum.

Costa, P. T., Jr., McCrae, R. R., Zonderman, A. B., Barbano, H. E., Lebowitz, B., & Larson, D. M. (1986). Cross-sectional studies of personality in a national sample: 2. Stability in Neuroticism, Extraversion, and Openness. *Psychology and Aging, 1,* 144–149.

Digman, J. M. (1990). Personality structure: Emergence of the five-factor model. *Annual Review of Psychology, 41,* 417–440.

Dyce, J., & O'Connor, B. P. (1998). Personality disorders and the five-factor model: A test of facet-level predictions. *Journal of Personality Disorders, 12,* 31–45.

Elder, G. H. (1974). *Children of the Great Depression.* Chicago: University of Chicago Press.

Eley, T., & Plomin, R. (1997). Genetic analyses of emotionality. *Current Opinion in Neurobiology, 7,* 279–284.

Eysenck, H. J. (1979). Personality factors in a random sample of the population. *Psychological Reports, 44,* 1023–1027.

Fromm, E. (1941). *Escape from freedom.* New York: Farrar & Rinehart.

Gergen, K. J. (1977). Stability, change, and chance in understanding human development. In N. Datan & H. W. Reese (Eds.), *Life-span developmental psychology: Dialectical perspectives on experimental research* (pp. 135–158). New York: Academic Press.

Goldberg, L. R. (1993). The structure of phenotypic personality traits. *American Psychologist, 48,* 26–34.

Gough, H. G. (1987). *California Psychological Inventory administrators' guide.* Palo Alto, CA: Consulting Psychologists Press.

Haan, N., Millsap, R., & Hartka, E. (1986). As time goes by: Change and stability in personality over fifty years. *Psychology and Aging, 1,* 220–232.

Helson, R., & Klohnen, E. C. (1998). Affective coloring of personality from young adulthood to midlife. *Personality and Social Psychology Bulletin, 24,* 241–252.

Jang, K. L., McCrae, R. R., Angleitner, A., Riemann, R., & Livesley, W. J. (1998). Heritability of facet-level traits in a cross-cultural twin sample: Support for a hierarchical model of personality. *Journal of Personality and Social Psychology, 74,* 1556–1565.

Jessor, R. (1983). The stability of change: Psychosocial development from adolescence to young adulthood. In D. Magnusson & V. L. Allen (Eds.), *Human development: An interactional perspective* (pp. 321–341). New York: Academic Press.

Krueger, J., & Heckhausen, J. (1993). Personality development across the adult life span: Subjective conceptions vs. cross-sectional contrasts. *Journal of Gerontology, 48,* P100–P108.

Light, J. M., Grigsby, J. S., & Bligh, M. C. (1996). Aging and heterogeneity: Genetics, social structure, and personality. *The Gerontologist, 36,* 165–173.

Loehlin, J. C. (1992). *Genes and environment in personality development.* Newbury Park, CA: Sage.

MacDonald, K. (1995). Evolution, the five-factor model, and levels of personality. *Journal of Personality, 63,* 523–567.

Marušić, I., Bratko, D., & Eterović, H. (1996). A contribution to the cross-cultural replicability of the five-factor personality model. *Review of Psychology, 3,* 23–35.

McCrae, R. R., & Costa, P. T., Jr. (1990). *Personality in adulthood.* New York: Guilford Press.

McCrae, R. R., & Costa, P. T., Jr. (1992). Discriminant validity of NEO-PI-R facets. *Educational and Psychological Measurement, 52,* 229–237.

McCrae, R. R., & Costa, P. T., Jr. (1996). Toward a new generation of personality theories: Theoretical contexts for the five-factor model. In J. S. Wiggins (Ed.), *The five-factor model of personality: Theoretical perspectives* (pp. 51–87). New York: Guilford Press.

McCrae, R. R., & Costa, P. T., Jr. (1997a). Conceptions and correlates of Openness to Experience. In R. Hogan, J. A. Johnson, & S. R. Briggs (Eds.), *Handbook of personality psychology* (pp. 269–290). Orlando, FL: Academic Press.

McCrae, R. R., & Costa, P. T., Jr. (1997b). Personality trait structure as a human universal. *American Psychologist, 52,* 509–516.

McCrae, R. R., Costa, P. T., Jr., Piedmont, R. L., Chae, J. H., Caprara, G. V., Barbaranelli, C., Marušić, I., & Bratko, D. (1996, November). *Personality development from college to midlife: A cross-cultural comparison.* Paper presented at the 49th Annual Scientific Meeting of the Gerontological Society of America, Washington, DC.

McCrae, R. R., Yik, M. S. M., Trapnell, P. D., Bond, M. H., & Paulhus, D. L. (1998). Interpreting personality profiles across cultures: Bilingual, acculturation, and peer rating studies of Chinese undergraduates. *Journal of Personality and Social Psychology, 74,* 1041–1055.

McGue, M., Bacon, S., & Lykken, D. T. (1993). Personality stability and change in early adulthood: A behavioral genetic analysis. *Developmental Psychology, 29,* 96–109.

McHenry, R. (Ed.). (1993). *The new Encyclopedia Britannica.* Chicago: Encyclopedia Britannica.

Mortimer, J. T., Finch, M. D., & Kumka, D. (1982). Persistence and change in development: The multidimensional self-concept. In P. B. Baltes & O. G. Brim, Jr. (Eds.), *Life-span development and behavior* (Vol. 4, pp. 264–315). New York: Academic Press.

Piedmont, R. L., & Chae, J.-H. (1997). Cross-cultural generalizability of the five-factor model of personality: Development and validation of the NEO-PI-R for Koreans. *Journal of Cross-Cultural Psychology, 28,* 131–155.

Riemann, R., Angleitner, A., & Strelau, J. (1997). Genetic and environmental influences on personality: A study of twins reared together using the self- and peer report NEO-FFI scales. *Journal of Personality, 65,* 449–475.

Riley, M. W., Johnson, M., & Foner, A. (1972). *Aging and society: Vol. 3. A sociology of age stratification.* New York: Russell Sage Foundation.

Schneider, A., & Gibbins, K. (1982). The EPI in research with the aged. *Australian Psychologist, 17,* 41–46.

Shimonaka, Y., & Nakazato, K. (1986). The development of personality characteristics of Japanese adults. *Journal of Genetic Psychology, 147,* 37–46.

Siegler, I. C., George, L. K., & Okun, M. A. (1979). Cross-sequential analysis of adult personality. *Developmental Psychology, 15,* 350–351.

Tarnowski, A., Shen, J., Diehl, M., & Labouvie-Vief, G. (1996, November). *Adult age differences in personality: Similarity of U.S. and Chinese patterns.* Paper presented at the 49th Annual Scientific Meeting of the Gerontological Society of America, Washington, DC.

Watson, D., & Walker, L. M. (1996). The long-term stability and predictive validity of trait measures of affect. *Journal of Personality and Social Psychology, 70,* 567–577.

Whitbourne, S. K., & Waterman, A. S. (1979). Psychosocial development during the adult years: Age and cohort comparisons. *Developmental Psychology, 15,* 373–378.

Whitbourne, S. K., Zuschlag, M. K., Elliot, L. B., & Waterman, A. S. (1992). Psychosocial development in adulthood: A 22-year sequential study. *Journal of Personality and Social Psychology, 63,* 260–271.

Whiting, J. W. M., & Child, I. L. (1953). *Child training and personality: A cross-cultural study.* New Haven, CT: Yale University Press.

Ethnicity, Gender, and Depressive Symptoms in Older Workers*

Maria E. Fernandez, Elizabeth J. Mutran, Donald C. Reitzes, and S. Sudha

Depression is the most common mental health problem in the elderly population (Burns & Taube, 1990). Whether conceptualized as a psychiatric disorder based on criteria set in the Diagnostic and Statistical Manual of Mental Disorders (American Psychiatric Association, 1987) or as a continuum of depressive symptoms, depression compromises functioning and quality of life particularly for those experiencing age-related physiological declines and the waning of social and economic resources. Findings from Epidemiologic Catchment Area studies indicate the six-month prevalences of depression based on diagnostic criteria to be lower in the population aged 65 years and over, ranging from 0.5% to .95%, in comparison to those younger than 65, with estimates ranging from 1.5% to 3.1% (George, 1993). On the other hand, levels of depressive symptoms have been found to be high in younger populations,

*From Fernandez et al. (1998). *The Gerontologist, 38*(1), 71–79. Reprinted with permission.

to be lowest in middle age (around 45 years old), and to increase at subsequent ages (Mirowsky & Ross, 1992), a finding that holds for African Americans as well (Turnbull & Mui, 1995).

Depression varies by gender and ethnicity, key identifiers of an individual's locus in the social structure which, in turn, determines the individual's access to the resources that are available in the society. Women tend to be more depressed than men on measures based on diagnostic criteria and depressive symptoms (Blazer, Burchett, Service, & George, 1991; Pearlin, 1989). Minority status exhibits a similar effect on depressive symptoms. African Americans, the largest minority group in the United States, are reported to have higher levels of depressive symptomatology in contrast to Whites (McBarnette, 1996; Ulbrich, Warheit, & Zimmerman, 1989). These differences may be exacerbated as individuals age. Data from the 1984 National Alcohol Survey indicate that African Americans aged 50 years and older had a higher proportion of individuals scoring at or above the cut-off point for clinical depression on the Center for Epidemiological Studies Depression Scale than Whites in the same age range (Jones-Webb & Snowden, 1993). Two large population-based studies, however, failed to show differences in the rates of psychiatric disorders between African Americans and Whites (Kessler et al., 1994; Robins and Regier, 1991).

Though research on gender and ethnic differences in depression has proliferated, there are few studies that contrast older men and women of majority and minority ethnic groups. One of the more unfortunate consequences of the paucity of research in this area is that it leaves unanswered the question of whether differences are leveled off or exacerbated as people age. Moreover, findings from available studies are inconsistent. For instance, Murrel, Himmelfarb, and Wright (1983) found depressive symptoms to be highest among older African American women followed by White women, African American men, and White men, whereas Reskin and Coverman (1985) found levels of depressive symptoms among African Americans to be lower than those of same-sex Whites although the difference was significant only among women. But Brown, Milburn, and Gary (1992) found no gender differences in depressive scores in a community-based sample of 148 African Americans 65 years and older, a finding that they attribute to the similarities of the subgroups in their exposure to stressful life events and number of social roles, factors that were hypothesized to be associated with depressive symptomatology. There is also some indication that gender differences level off with increasing age among African Americans (Antonucci, Jackson, Gibson, & Herzog, 1994).

Variations in the prevalence and levels of depression are commonly attributed to the differential distribution of stressors and resources in society. Using a longitudinal data set derived from a sample of men and women who were 58–64 years old and who were all fully employed when they were recruited into the study, we examine whether depressive symptomatology levels measured two years after baseline, are distributed differentially by ethnicity and gender and whether these differences may be accounted for by the differential distribution of stressors and resources. Findings on whether differences exist, where these differences lie, and which factors are responsible for them will assist in determining whether policies should be universally applicable or should accommodate the needs of more vulnerable subgroups of the older population. Our dependent variable, it should be noted, refers to symptoms of depression. . . .

Our analyses were based on a group of fully employed men and women residing in a North Carolina metropolitan area who were 58–64 years old at baseline and 60–66 years old at Wave 2. Our choice of sample may therefore limit the generalizability of our findings to younger cohorts of workers and other regions. The sample size that we had for African American men was small. Despite the low power associated with small sample size, we had significant findings for this group. However, our comparison of the characteristics of respondents who remained in the sample and those who were lost to follow-up indicates the need for caution in generalizing our findings, particularly for African American men. Considering the longitudinal nature of our data and the paucity of comparative investigations of groups that differ by ethnicity and gender, our findings contribute to the body of empirical findings on how the relationships between stressors, resources, and mental health vary for different groups, particularly for African American men, about whom very little is known.

In comparing depressive symptoms and their potential determinants among four groups that varied by ethnicity and gender, we found that White women and African American men did not have significantly higher levels of depressive symptomatology than White men. However, we did find African American women to have significantly more depressive symptoms than White men and White women. Our attempts to identify potential determinants for depressive symptomatology revealed that African American women derived the same degree of satisfaction in their relationships with spouses or partners, friends and offsprings as those in other groups. But despite educational levels that were comparable to those of White women and African American men, they had levels of household income that were lower than those of White men, White women, and African American men. These resources, however, are also associated with marital status. We had relatively larger proportions of women who were in the not-married category, which is to be expected because our initial sample consisted of fully employed men and women. With no spouses to depend on, single women are more compelled to work, drawing household incomes that are lower compared to men and to married, employed counterparts whose spouses may also be employed. African American women constitute the largest segment of the single elderly. In 1990, 75% of African American women fell into the married-spouse absent, widowed, divorced, and never married categories as opposed to 59% of White women, 46% of African American men, and 26% of White men among those over 64 years old (U.S. Bureau of the Census, 1991). The proportion of elderly single women will continue to increase in the future. Thus, efforts to equalize the work place should continue and programs such as those that allow women to take extended leaves of absence for family exigencies should be encouraged to make this segment of the population less economically vulnerable.

Our model for depressive symptomatology was confirmed for all groups. All baseline explanatory variables affected depressive symptoms assessed two years later, either directly, or indirectly, through baseline depressive symptoms. The more work stressors and losses in the social network one had, the more depressive symptoms one tended to have. More satisfying relationships, higher incomes, higher educational levels, and better health decreased depressive symptoms. Retirement status was also associated with fewer depressive symptoms. However, there were significant group differences in the effects of certain variables. Losses in the social network had more persistent effects on White men than White women. Work stressors influenced concurrent depressive symptomatology but its direct effects wore off over time for all groups, except for African American men, whose levels of depressive symptomatology were still elevated by work stressors two years after their occurrence. Poor health had a larger effect on African American men than other groups. Where retirement decreased depressive symptoms in other groups, it increased depressive symptoms in African American men. With the decline of job opportunities in manufacturing industries, the traditional sources of stable and high-paying jobs for African American men (Wilson, 1996), the benefits that African American men expect to have at retirement are likely to be low in comparison to other groups (Gibson, 1991). Thus, it is not surprising that African American men are more disturbed by retirement than other groups. Income had a dominant influence on depressive symptoms among African Americans compared to Whites. Its effect was greater for African American women than African American men.

These findings suggest that intervention strategies on depressive symptoms may be more effective when they take group differences into account. There is a need to recognize that men also experience difficulties in dealing with separations and deaths and that African American men are not impervious to the loss of the work role through disability, a threat that is more real to them than to any other group. And finally, the dominance of the influence of income on depressive symptoms among African Americans, particularly for African American women who also lag behind all other groups in income, suggests that the effects of federal programs and legislation that address discrimination have not been equal for all groups. These differences are going to be exacerbated in older age. Jackson, Lockery, and Juster (1996) warn that without significant policy interventions and the maintenance of programs that are their main sources of support, future cohorts of the elderly in minority groups will be even more disadvantaged in comparison to Whites, and even to current minority elders.

REFERENCES

American Psychiatric Association. (1987). *Diagnostic and statistical manual of mental disorders* (3rd ed., revised). Washington, DC: Author.

Aneshensel, C. S. (1992). Social stress: Theory and research. *Annual Review of Sociology, 18,* 15–38.

Antonucci, T. C. (1991). Social supports and social relationships. In R. H. Binstock & L. K. George (Eds.), *Handbook of aging and the social sciences* (3rd ed., pp. 205–227). San Diego, CA: Academic Press.

Antonucci, T. C., Jackson, J. S., Gibson, R. C., & Herzog, A. R. (1994). Age, gender, race, and productive activities across the life span. In M. Stevenson (Ed.), *Gender roles through the life span* (pp. 259–282). Muncie, IN: Ball State University Press.

Bayne-Smith, M., & McBarnette, L. S. (1996). Redefining health in the 21st century. In M. Bayne Smith (Ed.), *Race, gender, and health* (pp. 172–193). Newbury Park, CA: Sage.

Berkman, L. F., & Syme, S. L. (1979). Social networks, host resistance, and mortality: A nine-year follow-up study of Alameda County residents. *American Journal of Epidemiology, 109,* 186–204.

Blazer, D. G., Burchett, B. B., Service, C., & George, L. K. (1991). The association of age and depression among the elderly: An epidemiologic exploration. *Journal of Gerontology: Medical Sciences, 46,* M210–M215.

Brown, G. W., & Harris, T. (1978). *Social origins of depression: A study of psychiatric disorder in women.* New York: Free Press.

Brown, D. R., Milburn, N. G., & Gary, L. E. (1992). Symptoms of depression among African Americans: An analysis of gender differences. *The Gerontologist, 32,* 789–795.

Burns, B. J., & Taube, C. (1990). Mental health services in general medical care and in nursing homes. In B. S. Fogel, A. Furino, & G. L. Gottlieb (Eds.), *Mental health policy for older Americans: Protecting minds at risk* (pp. 63–83). Washington, DC: American Psychiatric Press.

Burton, L. M. (1992). Black grandparents rearing children of drug-addicted parents: Stressors, outcomes, and social service needs. *The Gerontologist, 32,* 744–751.

Cassel, J. (1976). The contribution of the social environment to host resistance. *American Journal of Epidemiology, 104,* 107–123.

Chatters, L. M. (1993). Health disability and its consequences for subjective stress. In J. S. Jackson, L. M. Chatters, & R. J. Taylor (Eds.), *Aging in black America* (pp. 167–184). Newbury Park, CA: Sage.

Cohen, S., & Willis, T. A. (1985). Stress, social support and the buffering hypothesis. *Psychological Bulletin, 98,* 310–357.

Conger, R. D., Elder, G. H., Jr., Simons, R. L., & Ge, X. (1993). Husband and wife differences in response to undesirable life events. *Journal of Health and Social Behavior, 34,* 71–88.

Durkheim, E. (1951). *Suicide* (J. A. Spaulding & G. Simpson, Trans.). Glencoe, IL: Free Press.

George, L. K. (1993). Depressive disorders and symptoms in later life. In M. A. Syer (Ed.), *Mental health and aging* (pp. 65–73). New York: Springer.

Gibson, R. (1991). Retirement in Black America. In J. S. Jackson (Ed.), *Life in Black America* (pp. 179–198). Newbury Park, CA: Sage.

Gove, W. R., Hughes, M. M., & Style, C. B. (1983). Does marriage have positive effects on the psychological well-being of the individual? *Journal of Health and Social Behavior, 24,* 122–131.

Jackson, J. S., Lockery, S. A., & Juster, F. T. (1996). Introduction: Health and retirement among ethnic and racial minority groups. *The Gerontologist, 36,* 282–286.

Jöreskog, K. G., & Sorbom, D. (1989). *LISREL 7: A guide to the program and applications.* Chicago: SPSS, Inc.

Jones-Webb, R. J., & Snowden, L. R. (1993). Symptoms of depression among Blacks and Whites. *American Journal of Public Health, 82,* 240–244.

Kessler, R. C., McGonagle, K. A., Zhao, S., Nelson, C. B., Hughes, M., Eshleman, S., Wittchen, H.-U., & Kendler, K. S. (1994). Lifetime and 12-month prevalence of DSM-III-R psychiatric disorders in the United States. *Archives of General Psychiatry, 51,* 8–19.

McBarnette, L. S. (1996). African American women. In M. Bayne-Smith (Ed.), *Race, gender, and health* (pp. 43–67). Newbury Park, CA: Sage.

McLeod, J. D., & Kessler, R. C. (1990). Socioeconomic status differences in vulnerability to undesirable life events. *Journal of Health and Social Behavior, 31,* 162–172.

Mirowsky, I., & Ross, C. E. (1992). Age and depression. *Journal of Health and Social Behavior, 33,* 187–205.

Murrell, S. A., Himmelfarb, S., & Wright, K. (1983). Prevalence of depression and its correlates in older adults. *American Journal of Epidemiology, 117,* 183–185.

Mutran, E. J., Reitzes, D. C., Bratton, K. A., & Fernandez, M. E. (1997). Self-esteem and subjective responses to work among mature workers: Similarities and differences by gender. *Journal of Gerontology: Social Sciences, 52B,* S89–S96.

Parnes, H. S., & Less, L. J. (1985). Introduction and overview. In H. S. Parnes, J. E. Crowley, R. J. Haurin, L. J. Less, W. R. Morgan, F. L. Mort. & G. Nestel, *Retirement among American men* (pp. 1–29). Lexington, MA: Heath.

Pearlin, L. I. (1989). The sociological study of stress. *Journal of Health and Social Behavior, 30,* 241–256.

Radloff, L. (1977). The CES-D scale: A self-report depression scale for research in the general population. *Applied Psychological Measurement, 1,* 385–401.

Rahe, R. (1989). Recent life change stress and psychological depression in T. W. Miller (Ed.), *Stressful life events* (pp. 5–11). Madison, CT: International Universities Press.

Reskin, B. F., & Coverman, S. (1985). Sex and race in the determinants of psychophysical distress: A reappraisal of the sex-role hypothesis. *Social Forces, 63,* 1038–1059.

Robins, L., & Regier, D. (Eds.). (1991). *Psychiatric disorders in America: Epidemiologic Catchment Area Study.* New York: Free Press.

Taylor, R. J., Chatters, L. M., Tucker, B. M., & Lewis, E. (1990). Developments in research on Black families: A decade review. *Journal of Marriage and the Family, 52,* 993–1014.

Thoits, P. A. (1995). Stress, coping, and social support processes: Where are we? What next? *Journal of Health and Social Behavior (Extra Issue),* 53–79.

Turnbull, J. E., & Mui, A. C. (1995). Mental health status and needs of Black and White elderly: Differences in depression. In D. K. Padgett (Ed.), *Handbook on ethnicity, aging, and mental health* (pp. 73–112). Westport, CT: Greenwood Press.

Ulbrich, P. M., Warheit, G. J., & Zimmerman, R. S. (1989). Race, socioeconomic status, and psychological distress: An examination of differential vulnerability. *Journal of Health and Social Behavior, 30,* 131–146.

U.S. Bureau of the Census. (1991). Marital status and living arrangements: March 1990. *Current Population Reports.* Series P-20, No. 450. Washington, DC: U.S. Government Printing Office.

U.S. Bureau of the Census (1992). *Statistical abstract of the United States: 1992.* Washington, DC: U.S. Government Printing Office.

Wilson, W. J. (1996). *When work disappears: The world of the new urban poor.* New York: Knopf.

Personality and Demographic Factors in Older Adults' Fear of Death*

Victor G. Cicirelli

Fear of death can be defined as the anxiety experienced in daily life caused by the anticipation of the state in which one is dead (Tomer, 1994). It is regarded as an ongoing state in everyday life, in contrast to a more acute fear elicited by an immediate threat to one's life.

Although fear of death may not be a universal phenomenon, it has certainly been an important influence in many cultures throughout the world. It has been a more conscious concern in Western cultures in recent times, manifested in the death awareness movement of the 1950s and in the great number of writings on fear of death during the past few decades (Neimeyer & Van Brunt, 1995).

. . .

Global versus Specific Fears of Death

Fear of death was originally regarded as a single global concept, assessed by summing responses to a wide variety of death-related items. More recent research has advanced the study of fear of death by establishing it as a multidimensional concept involving many specific fears. Viewing fear of death as multidimensional provided some clarification of the former global concept. However, this approach also has difficulties in that investigators have not agreed on the specific dimensions involved (Lester, 1994; Neimeyer & Moore, 1994; Wong, Reker, & Gesser, 1994), and findings remain inconsistent.

*From Cicirelli, V. G. (1999). *The Gerontologist, 39*(5), 569–579. Reprinted with permission.

The present study focuses on two specific death fears identified in Hoelter's Multidimensional Fear of Death Scale (MFODS; Hoelter, 1979; Neimeyer & Moore, 1994). The first, fear of the unknown, deals with the fear of nonexistence and an unknown afterlife (a possibility of either no afterlife or a threatening one). This fear is regarded as more fundamental than others, having been at the core of death fear in many cultures for centuries (Becker, 1973). Also, themes dealing with nonexistence and the afterlife have been pervasive concerns in studies of adults' personal meanings of death (Cicirelli, 1998; Durlak, Horn, & Kass, 1990; Holcomb, Neimeyer, & Moore, 1993; Neimeyer, Fontana, & Gold, 1984).

The second, fear of dying, deals with the fear of undergoing a painful and/or violent death. This fear also seems to be rather fundamental, as dying is a prerequisite for the occurrence of death itself. Because dying and death constitute an inevitable sequence, it seems important to study them together if one is to understand the fears they generate. Additionally, fear of dying has been identified as a major concern of the very old (Johnson & Barer, 1997; Tobin, 1996), and as such is highly relevant to the study of fear of death in older adults.

. . .

Review of Previous Studies

. . .

Demographic Background Factors: Age

Advancing age implies increased likelihood of death, but whether this increased threat of death is accompanied by increased or decreased fear is unclear. Among studies investigating the relationship of age to fear of death, some researchers have found that fear of death tends to be lower for older people (Bengtson, Cuellar, & Ragan, 1977; Gesser, Wong, & Reker, 1987–1988; Kastenbaum, 1992; Lonetto & Templer, 1986; Neimeyer, 1988). This view is supported by recent studies of the oldest old (those aged 85 and over) using unstructured interview techniques (Johnson & Barer, 1997; Tobin, 1996). These authors concluded that most of the oldest old had reached an acceptance of death and felt that they could face it without fear, but they also appeared to have a heightened awareness of impending death and expressed fears about the dying process. The opposing view, that fear of death becomes greater as older people get closer to death, has also found some support (Kureshi & Husain, 1981; Mullins & Lopez, 1982; Viney, 1984). An intermediate position, based on the conceptualization of fear of death as a multidimensional construct, is that some dimensions of fear of death increase with age and other dimensions decrease. Using Hoelter's (1979) MFODS, Neimeyer and Moore (1994) found that scores on six of the eight MFODS subscales (including Fear of Dying) declined with age, one (Fear of the Unknown) increased with age, and one was unrelated. However, if other antecedent variables were included in a path model, age might have indirect as well as direct effects on fear of death, with the resultant effect greater than that due to the direct effect of age alone.

Ethnicity

The limited existing research on ethnicity and fear of death yielded mixed results. Some studies (Cole, 1978; Dodd & Mills, 1985; Myers, Wass, & Murphy, 1980; Sanders, Poole, & Rivero, 1980; Young & Daniels, 1980) reported that African Americans had greater fear of death than Whites; others (Davis, Martin, Wilee, & Voorhees, 1978; Pandy & Templer, 1972; Thorson & Powell, 1994) reported the opposite. On the one hand, minority group members may feel that death is a greater threat because they have less access to the society's rewards and services, for example, less job opportunity, poorer housing, less safety, poorer health care, and so on (Markides & Black, 1996). Given this possibility, we hypothesized that older African Americans would have a greater fear of death than Whites. On the other hand, African Americans who are well integrated into their cultural subsystem are more tightly bound to their own norms and values than to those of the larger society and have close relationships with family, friends, and church (Johnson, 1995; Taylor & Chatters, 1986); these arguments suggest that fear of death might be lower for African Americans.

Gender

Gender has also been investigated in relation to fear of death. Most previous studies have reported that women have greater fear of death than men (e.g., Davis, Bremer, Anderson, & Tramill, 1983; Young & Daniels, 1980), although others (e.g., Conte, Weiner, & Plutchik, 1982) have found no gender difference. On the MFODS, women had more fear of death than men on most subscales, but they had less fear of the unknown than did men (Neimeyer & Moore, 1994).

Socioeconomic Status

SES may also be hypothesized to be related to less fear of death, in that those of higher status have a more secure place in society, with more goods and services available to them (good food, shelter, health care, safety, etc.), which would make them feel less vulnerable to death in their immediate future. One would expect them to have less fear of nonexistence (fear of the unknown) as well as less fear of dying. Existing studies have found that higher educational and occupational levels (components of most SES measures) are related to less fear of death (Aday, 1984–1985; Kinlaw & Dixon, 1980–1981; Schulz, 1978).

Conclusions from Existing Research

Findings of existing research tend to be inconsistent and inconclusive. Obviously, this could be partially due to the variety of age ranges, samples, and instruments used, with global measures used in most earlier research and multivariate instruments used in later research. All these factors make it difficult to compare findings.

Additionally, the previous studies examined effects of antecedent variables one at a time, without considering their combined direct and indirect effects on the specific fears of death.

. . .

The sample of 388 study participants was obtained from two sites, a medium-sized midwestern city (Greater Lafayette, Indiana, with approximately 100,000 residents) and a large urban area (Indianapolis, Indiana, with a population of approximately 1,250,000). Study participants were at least 60 years of age, were living in private homes or apartments in the community, and were alert, oriented, and of sufficient cognitive ability to respond to the interview questionnaire (as judged by the interviewer or the senior center director).

Elders were sampled through seniors' organizations, by first securing a representation of such organizations in each site and then interviewing elders within organizations. Data were collected at 20 different centers, 16 in Indianapolis and 4 in Lafayette, selected to represent different geographic areas of the two cities and thus to represent a wide range of SES levels. The Indianapolis site included 12 senior programs in community centers and 4 multidenominational church-operated centers; 11 of the 16 centers served both African American and White seniors. The Lafayette site included 1 community-operated senior center serving the entire city, 1 interdenominational church-operated center, and 2 programs serving retirement housing complexes. The investigator visited each center during a regularly scheduled group meeting, explained the study, and asked for participants. All who consented were scheduled to be interviewed at the center at a convenient time. Participation rates ranged from 40% to 85%.

Of the people who consented to participate in the study, 447 were interviewed. The sample used for the analyses reported here consisted of 388 older people for whom all data were complete, ranging in age from 60 to 100. There were 285 women and 103 men, 265 Whites and 123 African Americans, and 293 from Indianapolis and 95 from Lafayette. All of the African Americans in the sample were from Indianapolis.

. . .

Perhaps fear of dying may be better predicted by contextual variables, such as respondents' perceptions and beliefs about dying (likelihood of pain, loss of dignity, duration, nature of symptoms, etc.) as well as personal experiences regarding the deaths of family members and friends.

The finding that a more external locus-of-control orientation was related to both greater fear of dying and fear of the unknown was in agreement with previous literature linking externality to greater fear of death (e.g., Hayslip & Stewart-Bussey, 1986–1987; Hunt et al., 1988; Schulz, 1978).

The finding that greater subjective (or intrinsic) religiosity was related to less fear of the unknown and fear of dying is consonant with the earlier research of Thorson and Powell (1990). The substantial effect of religiosity on fear of the unknown is not surprising, in that study participants represented primarily adherents to various Protestant faiths and Catholicism. These religions offer a positive picture of the afterlife and the comfort to be gained from religious faith and prayer as one approaches death.

The indirect effects of SES on fear of dying and fear of the unknown were weak but in the predicted direction, indicating that those with higher SES had less fear of death. This effect is in agreement with previous studies (Aday, 1984–1985; Kinlaw & Dixon, 1980–1981; Schulz, 1978).

Earlier findings that African Americans reported less fear of death than Whites (Davis et al., 1978; Pandy & Templer, 1972; Thorson & Powell, 1994) were supported by the study findings of the direct effect of ethnicity on fear of dying and its indirect effect on fear of the unknown. This finding was explained in earlier studies by the strong extended family ties and high involvement in the church. However, this explanation is only partially satisfactory in the present study. When one looks at the possible indirect paths for the effects of ethnicity on fear of the unknown, the major contribution to the overall indirect effect is the path from ethnicity via religiosity, whereas the contribution of path of ethnicity via social support is negligible. In the case of fear of dying, the contribution of the indirect path of ethnicity via religiosity is small compared with its direct effect and the indirect path via social support does not exist. Some other explanation for African Americans' lesser fear of dying as compared with Whites needs to be found.

The effect of gender on fear of death is interesting in that its effects are in different directions for the two fear of death subscores. Women have more fear of dying than men, but less fear of the unknown, a finding that is in agreement with results reported by Neimeyer and Moore (1994). When one examines the possible indirect paths for the effect of gender on fear of the unknown, the path via religiosity is the major contributor to the net effect of gender. The greater religiosity of women is well-known. No such explanation is available for the direct effect of gender on fear of dying, although a greater sensitivity to pain may be one possibility.

Study findings were that greater age is associated with less fear of dying (a direct effect) but with greater fear of the unknown (a weak indirect effect). The finding regarding fear of dying is in agreement with its correlation with age reported by Neimeyer and Moore (1994), whereas the finding regarding fear of the unknown is in agreement with findings of others that fear of death is greater among those closer to death (Kureshi & Husain, 1981; Mullins & Lopez, 1982; Viney, 1984). Another point that needs to be considered when comparing the effects of age with studies in the literature is that studies carried out in the 1970s and early 1980s generally found that fear of death increased with age, whereas more recent studies have reported the opposite effect. One cannot explain these differences after the fact; however, increases in longevity over time may enter in: Elders of a given age in 1970 may have perceived themselves as much closer to death than elders of the same age in 1990. Another possibility is that the nature of dying itself has changed over time, with advanced technologies available to sustain life for longer periods (although perhaps with a lower quality of life) along with more options about when and how to die.

The small positive effect of age on fear of the unknown (i.e., fears of nonexistence and the afterlife) does not appear to support the statements of Johnson and Barer (1997) and Tobin (1996) that the very old accept death itself and do not fear it. The negative effect of age on fear of dying also seems at odds with these researchers' additional assertion that the very old are more afraid of the dying process than of death itself. However, if one compares the relative strength of the two fear-of-death subscores, the conclusions of Johnson and Barer and Tobin have some support. Comparing average item means to adjust for differing number of items in the two subscales, the item mean for fear of dying ($M = 3.00$) was significantly greater than that for fear of the unknown ($M = 2.06$).

. . .

REFERENCES

Aday, R. H. (1984–1985). Belief in afterlife and death anxiety: Correlates and comparisons. *Omega, 15,* 67–75.

Antonucci, T. C., & Akiyama, H. (1987). Social networks in adult life and a preliminary examination of the convoy model. *Journal of Gerontology, 42,* 519–527.

Becker, E. (1973). *The denial of death.* New York: Free Press.

Bengtson, V. L., Cuellar, J. B., & Ragan, P. K. (1977). Stratum contrasts and similarities in attitudes toward death. *Journal of Gerontology, 32,* 76–88.

Bernabel, R., Gambassi, R., Lapane, K., Landi, F., Gatsonis, C., Dunlop, R., Lipsitz, L., Steele, K., & Mor, V. (1988). Management of pain in elderly patients with cancer. *Journal of the American Medical Association, 279,* 1877–1882.

Cicirelli, V. G. (1997). Relationship of psychosocial and background variables to elders' end-of-life decisions. *Psychology and Aging, 12,* 77–83.

Cicirelli, V. G. (1998). Personal meanings of death in relation to fear of death. *Death Studies, 22,* 713–733.

Cole, M. A. (1978). Sex and marital status differences in death anxiety. *Omega, 9,* 139–147.

Conte, H.R., Weiner, M. B., & Plutchik, R. (1982). Measuring death anxiety: Conceptual, psychometric, and factor analytic aspects. *Journal of Personality and Social Psychology, 43,* 775–785.

Davis, S. F., Bremer, S. A., Anderson, B. J., & Tramill, J. L. (1983). The interrelationships of ego strength, self-esteem, death anxiety, and gender in undergraduate college students. *Journal of General Psychology, 108,* 55–59.

Davis, S. F., Martin, D. A., Wilee, C. T., & Voorhees, J. W. (1978). Relationship of fear of death and level of self-esteem in college students. *Psychological Reports, 42,* 419–422.

Dodd, D. K., & Mills, L. L. (1985). FADIS: A measure of the fear of accidental death and injury. *Psychological Record, 35,* 269–275.

Durlak, J. A., Horn, W., & Kass, R. A. (1990). A self-administering assessment of personal meanings of death: Report on the revised Twenty Statement Test. *Omega, 21,* 301–309.

Emanuel, E. J., & Emanuel, L. L. (1998). The promise of a good death. *Lancet, 351*(Suppl. 2), 21–29.

Florian, V., & Kravitz, S. (1983). Fear of personal death: Attribution, structure, and relation to religious belief. *Journal of Personality and Social Psychology, 44,* 600–607.

Fukuyama, F. (1999). *The great disruption: Human nature and the reconstitution of social order.* New York: Free Press.

Gesser, G., Wong, P. T. P., & Reker, G. T. (1987–1988). Death attitudes across the life span: The development and validation of the death attitude profile (DAP). *Omega, 18,* 113–128.

Hayslip, B., & Stewart-Bussey, D. (1986–1987). Locus of control-levels of death anxiety relationships. *Omega, 17,* 41–50.

Hoelter, J. W. (1979). Multidimensional treatment of fear of death. *Journal of Consulting and Clinical Psychology, 47,* 996–999.

Holcomb, L. E., Neimeyer, R. A., & Moore, M. K. (1993). Personal meanings of death: A content analysis of free response narratives. *Death Studies, 17,* 299–318.

Hollingshead, A. B. (1957). *Two-factor index of social position.* New Haven, CT: Author.

Hunt, D. M., Lester, D., & Ashton, N. (1988). Fear of death, locus of control, and occupation. *Psychological Reports, 53,* 1022.

Johnson, C. L. (1995). Determinants of adaptation of oldest-old Black Americans. *Journal of Aging Studies, 9,* 231–244.

Johnson, C. L., & Barer, B. M. (1997). *Life beyond 85 years: The aura of survivorship.* New York: Springer.

Kalish, R. A. (1985). *Death, grief, and caring relationships* (2nd ed.). Monterey, CA: Brooks/Cole.

Kastenbaum, R. J. (1992). *The psychology of death* (2nd ed.). New York: Springer.

Krause, N. (1993). Measuring religiosity in later life. *Research on Aging, 2,* 170–197.

Kinlaw, B. J. R., & Dixon, R. D. (1980–1981). Fear of death and fertility reconsidered. *Omega, 11,* 119–137.

Kureshi, A., & Husain, A. (1981). Death anxiety in intrapunitiveness among smokers and nonsmokers: A comparative study. *Journal of Psychological Research, 25,* 42–45.

Lester, D. (1994). The Collett-Lester Fear of Death Scale. In R. A. Neimeyer (Ed.), *The death anxiety handbook: Research, instrumentation, and application* (pp. 45–60). Washington, DC: Taylor & Francis.

Levenson, H. (1981). Differentiating among internality, powerful others, and chance. In H. M. Lefcourt (Ed.), *Research with the locus of control construct* (Vol. 1, pp. 15–63). New York: Academic Press.

Lonetto, R., & Templer, D. I. (1986). *Death anxiety.* Washington, DC: Hemisphere.

Lynn, J., Teno, J. M., Phillips, R. S. (1997). Perceptions by family members of the dying experience of older and seriously ill patients. *Annals of Internal Medicine, 126,* 97–106.

Markides, K. S. (1983). Aging, religiosity, and adjustment: A longitudinal analysis. *Journal of Gerontology, 38,* 621–625.

Markides, K. S., & Black, S. A. (1996). Race, ethnicity, and aging: The impact of inequality. In R. H. Binstock & L. K. George (Eds.), *Handbook of aging and the social sciences* (4th ed., pp. 153–170). San Diego, CA: Academic Press.

Mullins, L. C., & Lopez, M. A. (1982). Death anxiety among nursing home residents: A comparison of the young-old and the old-old. *Death Education, 6,* 75–86.

Myers, J. E., Wass, H., & Murphy, M. (1980). Ethnic differences in death anxiety among the elderly. *Death Education, 4,* 237–244.

Neimeyer, R. A. (1988). Death anxiety. In H. Wass, R. Berardo, & R. A. Neimeyer (Eds.), *Dying: Facing the facts* (2nd ed., pp. 97–136). Washington, DC: Hemisphere.

Neimeyer, R. A., Fontana, D. J., & Gold, K. (1984). A manual for content analysis of death constructs. In F. R. Epting & R. A. Neimeyer (Eds.), *Personal meanings of death* (pp. 213–234). Washington, DC: Hemisphere.

Neimeyer, R. A., & Moore, M. K. (1994). Validity and reliability of the Multidimensional Fear of Death Scale. In R. A. Neimeyer (Ed.), *Death anxiety handbook: Research, instrumentation, and application* (pp. 103–119). Washington: DC: Taylor & Francis.

Neimeyer, R. A., & Van Brunt, D. (1995). Death anxiety. In H. Wass & R. A. Neimeyer (Eds.), *Dying: Facing the facts* (3rd ed., pp. 49–88). Washington, DC: Taylor & Francis.

Pandy, R. E., & Templer, D. I. (1972). Use of the Death Anxiety Scale in an inter-racial setting. *Omega, 3,* 127–130.

Pollak, J. M. (1979). Correlates of death anxiety: A review of empirical studies. *Omega, 10,* 427–488.

Rigdon, M. A., & Epting, F. R. (1985). Reduction in death threat as a basis for optimal functioning. *Death Studies, 9,* 427–448.

Rodin, J., & Langer, E. (1977). Long-term effects of a control-relevant intervention with the institutionalized aged. *Journal of Personality and Social Psychology, 35,* 897–902.

Sanders, J. F., Poole, T. P., & Rivero, W. T. (1980). Death anxiety among the elderly. *Psychological Reports, 46,* 53–56.

Schulz, R. (1978). *The psychology of death, dying, and bereavement.* Reading, MA: Addison-Wesley.

Schulz, R. (1986). Successful aging: Balancing primary and secondary control. *Adult Development and Aging News, 13*(3), 2–4.

Shapiro, D. H., Jr., Schwartz, C. E., & Astin, J. A. (1996). Controlling ourselves, controlling our world: Psychology's role in understanding positive and negative consequences of seeking and gaining control. *American Psychologist, 51,* 1213–1230.

Siegler, I. C., & Gatz, M. (1985). Age patterns in locus of control. In E. Palmore, E. W. Busse, G. L. Maddox, J. B. Nowlin, & I. E. Siegler (Eds.), *Normal aging III* (pp. 138–143). Durham, NC: Duke University Press.

Singer, P. A., Martin, D. K., & Kelner, M. (1999). Quality end-of-life care: Patients' perspectives. *Journal of the American Medical Association, 281*(2), 163–168.

Taylor, R. J., & Chatters, L. M. (1986). Church-based informal support among elderly Blacks. *The Gerontologist, 26,* 637–642.

Thorson, J. A., & Powell, F. C. (1990). Meanings of death and intrinsic religiosity. *Journal of Clinical Psychology, 46,* 379–391.

Thorson, J. A., & Powell, F. C. (1994). A Revised Death Anxiety Scale. In R. A. Neimeyer (Ed.), *Death anxiety handbook: Research, instrumentation, and application* (pp. 31–43). Washington, DC: Taylor & Francis.

Tobin, S. S. (1996). A non-normative old age contrast. Elderly parents caring for offspring with mental retardation. In V. L. Bengston (Ed.), *Adulthood and aging: Research on continuities and discontinuities* (pp. 124–142). New York: Springer.

Tomer, A. (1994). Death anxiety in adult life: Theoretical perspectives. In R. A. Neimeyer (Ed.), *Death anxiety handbook: Research, instrumentation, and application* (pp. 3–28). Washington, DC: Taylor & Francis.

Viney, L. L. (1984). Concerns about death among severely ill people. In F. R. Epting & R. A. Neimeyer (Eds.), *Personal meanings of death* (pp. 143–158). Washington, DC: Hemisphere.

Vygotsky, L. S. (1978). *Mind in society.* Cambridge, MA: Harvard University Press.

Wong, P. T. P., Reker, G. T., & Gesser, G. (1994). Death Attitude Profile–Revised: A multidimensional measure of attitudes toward death. In R. A. Neimeyer (Ed.), *Death anxiety handbook: Research, instrumentation, and application* (pp. 121–148). Washington, DC: Taylor & Francis.

Young, M., & Daniels, S. (1980). Born again status as a factor in death anxiety. *Psychological Reports, 47,* 367–370.

Changing Community Responses to Wife Abuse: A Research and Demonstration Project in Iztacalco, Mexico*

Gillian M. Fawcett, Lori L. Heise, Leticia Isita-Espejel, and Susan Pick

The Setting

The setting of our research and demonstration project is a peri-urban community in the Iztacalco district of Mexico City. Central to community life in this neighborhood is Centro Felipe Carrillo Puerto (CFCP), a community center that has served low-income women and their families for over 23 years. CFCP trains community promoters, holds workshops on infant development and sexual and reproductive health, and has recently opened a bakery to train women in microenterprise development. Nevertheless, the community is suffering economic hardship and severe social problems, especially among its youth. A needs assessment conducted in 1995 found that members of the community identified alcoholism and violence as priority concerns, with drug abuse and drug dealing as significant threats on the horizon. With little institutional support besides CFCP, the community lacks a formal means of addressing the issue of domestic violence. Therefore, the proposal to develop a community-based response to wife abuse provides not only an ideal opportunity to test a new approach to violence prevention but also a means to address a felt local need.

. . .

In this project, we intended to design an intervention specifically linked to the dominant beliefs and concerns of community members, - incorporating, where appropriate, insights suggested from theory and other research. We therefore undertook an extensive program of formative research that included participant observation, eight focus groups with a total of 45 people recruited from the community in question, and five in-depth interviews with abused women.

Focus Groups

The goal of the focus groups was to explore community norms, attitudes, and beliefs around the following themes: (a) origins of violence against women, (b) responsibility for violence against women, (c) strategies available to women living with a violent partner, and (d) intervention of others in cases of domestic violence.

. . .

Two exercises were developed to encourage the open expression of norms, attitudes, and beliefs around the four identified themes. The first part of the focus group session was based on a story-completion exercise, for which we developed a short description of the life of Rosita, a woman who suffered abuse from her partner, Victor. Four scenarios were also created, each with a separate set of questions to elicit participants' responses to the different choices that Rosita could make. After listening to the description of Rosita's life, members of the focus groups were paired. Each pair was given one of these scenarios to discuss, before sharing their opinion with the rest of the group.

The second part of the session was an exercise adapted from the concept of the Venn Diagram to depict the interaction between abused women and various sources of support (Ellsberg et al., 1997). A circle representing the abused woman (Rosita) was placed on the wall, and participants were asked to think about potential forms of support available for her. They were then asked to place circles representing these sources of support around the original circle to show their accessibility for Rosita (close representing accessible, far representing inaccessible).

Both of these exercises formed the basis of all the focus group discussions. However, dif-

*From Fawcett et al. (1999). *American Psychologist, 54,* 41–49. Reprinted with permission.

ficulty in recruiting male participants for these sessions led us to interview three groups of young men on the street, which made it necessary to adapt the exercises to an outdoor setting. Due to these circumstances, it was only possible to tape one of these three sessions, and field notes were made for the other two.

In-Depth Interviews

Because the very nature of focus groups limits the depth of information that can be obtained by the researcher, we decided to conduct additional in-depth interviews with women from the community who had revealed that they had lived with or were currently living with a violent partner. Five women were invited to take part in the interview by the person to whom they had revealed their experience of abuse, and all five agreed to be interviewed.

The in-depth interviews took place after the focus group sessions had been analyzed and had the purpose of (a) clarifying some of the findings from the focus groups, (b) exploring the perceptions of abused women about the violence they experienced and the support available to them, and (c) determining strategies adopted by these women to survive and/or end the abuse.

Results of Formative Research

Perceived Origins of Violence Against Women

Research participants described violence in general as being related to a lack of education and to economic hardship. They did not identify unequal power relations between men and women as an origin of violence against women. Among focus group members, alcoholism, work pressure, and the threat of unemployment were the most commonly named reasons for Victor's violence toward Rosita. Given the high levels of unemployment and alcoholism in the community in question, it is not surprising that these factors were far more tangible to participants than the concept of gender inequality. Some individuals also observed that violent men have either witnessed violence between their parents during childhood or been victims of violence themselves. Abused women specifically mentioned the following as sources of their partners' aggression: alcohol, money problems, jealousy, unfaithfulness, criticisms about family, their children's education, pregnancy, and the birth of a child of the "wrong" sex.

Perceived Responsibility for Violence Against Women

Some adult and teenage women in the focus groups suggested that violence was an expected consequence of women not having complied with their (gender) roles, thus implying a sense of responsibility on their part. Male participants blamed men's violence on external factors such as being "under pressure" as family breadwinners, being "under the influence" of alcohol, or being "driven to" it by their wives. Male denial of responsibility has been documented in research from other countries (Bograd, 1988; Hydèn, 1994; Ptacek, 1988) and is closely related to the self-blame that many battered women suffer. Our fictitious character, Rosita, was therefore not only considered responsible for provoking violence but also for not setting limits, not being able to communicate with her partner, and not being able to "make him behave." Three of the abused women described the violence as first occurring while they were dating their partners. In these instances, women noted that they had hoped their partner would change or assumed that they would be able to make this change come about.

Abused Women's Perceptions of Violence and Their Violent Partner

Women in the in-depth interviews who discussed current relationships also tended to minimize the violence they experienced and to emphasize the good points of their partner, as a father or as a responsible provider for the family. Two women who were interviewed and who no longer lived with their violent partners were unable to describe any positive qualities in their ex-partners. It is not clear if this perception helped precipitate the separation or was the result of the separation. However, minimization or neutralization of violent acts has been documented as a strategy used by both men and women for preserving the relationship (Hydèn, 1994; Kelly, 1988).

Separation as a Strategy for Ending the Violence

Focus group participants were aware of the many emotional and practical obstacles that Rosita faced if she wished to leave Victor. Among those mentioned were low self-esteem, insecurity, fear of reprisals or further violence, the hope that her partner would change, lack of support from her family and friends, and lack of income. The children's needs were focused on primarily, because participants were concerned that they would lose a father figure (see Finkler, 1997). These factors have also been documented in extensive research carried out in several Latin American countries to determine what inhibits or facilitates help seeking by women affected by family violence (Shrader, 1998). Despite understanding why a woman might remain with her husband, respondents insisted that she should separate and expressed little support for Rosita in the scenario in which she returns to Victor. Thus, participants were unable to appreciate that temporary separation may be part of a longer process of change (Brown, 1997). Abused women seem to face a catch-22 situation: They are judged if they leave for breaking up their family, and they are judged if they stay for remaining with an abuser.

Factors mentioned as potential catalysts in the abused women's decision to leave their partners were the realization that their partner would not change, not being able to accept his promises and forget the violence, seeing that the situation was affecting their children, starting to work, and having a home of their own. Some women in the focus groups suggested that meeting a more caring man would also enable a woman to leave her violent partner. Nevertheless, separation was clearly problematic for these women due to the obstacles described above.

Protective Strategies Used by Women in the Face of Violence

In order to diffuse potentially violent situations, the abused women described adopting certain strategies such as patience, tolerance, remaining silent, hiding from their partner, ignoring him, having sex with him, or doing exactly as he asked. None of them had thought of developing an emergency plan in case their own life or those of their children were at risk. One woman described how she used to defend herself both verbally and physically from her partner with some degree of success, although she described always fearing for her life. Although some of the women recognized that they too were aggressive toward their partners, they considered this to be a response to their partners' behavior. The forms of aggression that they acknowledged using were withholding sex, insulting their partner or criticizing his sexual ability and his ability to support the family, not serving him his meals, and locking him out of the family home.

Help Seeking Behavior and Perceived Support

Of the few formal institutions known to women, the CFCP community center was seen as a possible source of support that would enable women to confront their situation. Abused women expressed feeling embarrassment and shame at disclosing their situation, preferring to try to solve their problems on their own, rather than create more problems for their family or friends. Nevertheless, both women in the focus groups and the abused women themselves said they would feel more comfortable turning to other women for help, particularly their mother or a mother figure, rather than formal support services. For example, in the Venn Diagram exercises, individuals tended to place formal institutions, such as the police, very far from the central character representing Rosita, indicating that these sources of support were perceived as inaccessible. By contrast, the family, and particularly mothers, were consistently located close to the center of the diagram, indicating that, in Iztacalco as in many other studies (Hanmer, 1995; McGibbon,

Cooper, & Kelly, 1989; Mooney, 1994), women perceived family, close friends, and other informal sources of support as more accessible.

The attitudes of family and friends, however, were not uniformly supportive and in some cases were very judgmental and blaming. It was felt that friends in particular were likely to gossip, whereas mothers frequently responded that daughters should tolerate the situation because "tú te lo buscaste" [you asked for it] or advised them to try to keep the family together. The image of the woman as a self-sacrificing martyr is one that holds considerable emotional currency in Mexican gender ideology (Finkler, 1997). When the abused women were asked how they would like someone to intervene, they responded that they wanted someone to stop their partner while he was hitting them or to talk to him and "make him understand."

. . .

The Intervention

In keeping with sound theory on community action (Bracht, 1990; Piotrow, Kincaid, Rimon, & Rinehart, 1997), we designed a multifaceted intervention that involves peer outreach, small-scale media, popular theater, and other special events to reach abused women and members of the community at large.

The intervention has two main parts: (a) a 12-session intensive consciousness-raising and skills-developing workshop for women and (b) a large-scale community campaign.

The Workshop

. . .

Specifically, the objectives of the workshop are (a) To create a cadre of nonjudgmental community women (especially mothers) who could provide support and information to abused women, thus encouraging them to move from precontemplation, to contemplation, preparation, and action; and (b) To help those abused women who participate to recognize abuse, realize that they are not to blame, and identify different sources of support (thus helping them move through stages of change toward preparation and action).

The workshop covered many of the points that arose in the formative research, as well as other issues that have been addressed by theory and research on domestic violence, including

1. Family violence as an important community problem
2. Family violence legislation
3. Forms of violence and their objectives
4. Gender role expectations and violence against women
5. Female socialization and violence against women
6. Male socialization and violence against women
7. The cycle of violence
8. The personal and social consequences of violence against women
9. Alternatives available for abused women
10. Crisis-intervention skills
11. Institutions that support victims of violence
12. Community-intervention

. . .

The Community Campaign

. . .

The objectives of this community campaign are (a) To shift the community perception of domestic violence from a private problem that should not be interfered with to a community issue that is the responsibility of all, (b) To reduce victim-blaming of women and encourage more useful, supportive responses on the part of family and friends to women living in violent relationships, and (c) To help individual women in the community to move from precontemplation to contemplation, preparation, and action by advertising the types of violence, the elements of the new domestic violence laws, and where to go for help.

In keeping with these goals, the project has adopted key slogans that have been incorporated into posters, buttons, and community events. The campaign slogan aims at attacking the dominant norm that says it is inappropriate to intervene into the private sphere of the family. The slogan transforms the commonly used phrase "El que mete paz, saca más" (Whoever tries to make peace gets more than [s]he bargained for) into "El que mete paz, *gana* más," in order to emphasize what can be *gained* from getting involved.

The poster message aims at encouraging more constructive, less victim-blaming responses on the part of community members to women living in abusive situations. The phrase "La mujer maltrada te necesita" (The abused woman needs you) precedes a list of four phrases that give step by step guidance about how to help an abused woman. Each phrase begins with the letter "A," to help members of the community remember the four steps. The poster concludes with a list of local services available for family violence.

. . .

REFERENCES

Bograd, M. (1988). How battered women and abusive men account for domestic violence: Excuses, justifications, or explanations? In G. T. Hotaling, D. Finkelhor, J. T. Kirkpatrick, & M. A. Shaw (Eds.), *Coping with family violence: Research and policy perspectives* (pp. 60–77). Newbury Park, CA: Sage.

Bracht, N. (Ed.). (1990). *Health promotion at the community level.* Newbury Park, CA: Sage.

Brown, J. (1997). Working toward freedom from violence. *Journal of Violence Against Women, 3,* 5–26.

Ellsberg, M., Winkvist, A., & Liljestrand, J. (1997). The Nicaraguan network of women against violence: Using research and action for change. *Reproductive Health Matters, 10,* 82–92.

Finkler, K. (1997). Gender, domestic violence and sickness in Mexico. *Social Science and Medicine, 45,* 1147–1160.

Hanmer, J. (1995, January). *Women's coping strategies.* Keynote address presented at the National Organization of Battered Women in Sweden (ROKS) conference, Stockholm, Sweden.

Heise, L. (1996). Violence against women: Global organizing for change. In J. L. Edelson & Z. C. Eisikovits (Eds.), *Future interventions with battered women and their families* (pp. 7–33). Thousand Oaks, CA: Sage.

Heise, L. (1998). Violence against women: An integrated, ecological framework. *Journal of Violence Against Women, 4,* 262–290.

Hydèn, M. (1994). Woman battering as a marital act: Interviewing and analysis in context. In K. K. Riessman (Ed.), *Qualitative studies in social work research* (pp. 95–111). Thousand Oaks, CA: Sage.

Kelly, L. (1988). How women define their experiences of violence. In K. Yllo & M. Bograd (Eds.), *Feminist perspectives on wife abuse* (pp. 133–157). Newbury Park, CA: Sage.

Kelly, L. (1996). Tensions and possibilities: Enhancing informal responses to domestic violence. In J. L. Edelson & Z. C. Eisikovits (Eds.), *Future interventions with battered women and their families* (pp. 67–86). Thousand Oaks, CA: Sage.

McGibbon, A., Cooper, L., & Kelly, L. (1989). *"What support?": An exploratory study of council policy and practice and local support services in the area of domestic violence within Hammersmith and Fulham.* London: Hammersmith and Fulham Council.

Mooney, J. (1994). *The hidden figure: Domestic violence in North London.* London: Islington Police and Crime Prevention Unit.

Panamerican Health Organization (PAHO). (1998). *Ruta crítica que siguen las mujeres víctimas de violencia intrafamiliar: Analisis y resultados de investigación* [Help seeking by victims of family violence: Analysis and research results]. Panama City, Panama: Organización Panamericana de la Salud en Panamá.

Piotrow, P., Kincaid, D. L., Rimon II, J. G., & Rinehart, W. (1997). *Health communication: Lessons from family planning and reproductive health.* Westport, CT: Praeger.

Prochaska, J. O., & DiClemente, C. C. (1982). Transtheoretical therapy: Toward a more intergrative model of change. *Psychotherapy: Theory, Research, and Practice, 19,* 276–288.

Procuraduría General de Justicia del Distrito Federal. (1997). *Violencia intrafamiliar: Un modelo de atención* [Intrafamily violence: A model of attention]. Mexico City, Mexico: Author.

Ptacek, J. (1988). Why do men batter their wives? In K. Yllo & M. Bograd (Eds.), *Feminist perspectives on wife abuse* (pp. 133–157). Newbury Park, CA: Sage.

Ramirez, J. C., & Uribe, G. (1993). Mujer y violencia: Un hecho cotidiano [Women and violence: A daily occurrence]. *Salud Pública de México, 35,* 148–160.

Riquer, F., Saucedo, I., & Bedolla, P. (1996). Agresión y violencia contra el género femenino: Un asunto de salud pública [Aggression and violence against the feminine gender: A public health issue]. In A. Langer & K. Tolbert (Eds.), *Mujer: Sexualidad y salad reproductiva en México* [Woman, sexuality and reproductive health in Mexico] (pp. 247–288). Mexico City, Mexico: Population Council.

Romero, M., & Tolbert, K. (1995, June). *La consulta externa como oportunidad de detección de la violencia doméstica* [Outpatient consultation as a means of detection of domestic violence]. Paper presented at the National Council of International Health Conference, Crystal City, VA.

Shepard, M. F., & Campbell, J. A. (1992). The abusive behavior inventory: A measure of psychological and physical abuse. *Journal of Interpersonal Violence, 7,* 291–305.

Shrader, E. (1998, November). *La ruta crítica: An evaluation of institutional responses to domestic violence.* Paper presented at the 126th annual meeting of the American Public Health Association, Washington, DC.

Shrader, E., & Valdez, R. (1992). *Violencia hacia la mujer mexicana como problema de salud pública: La incidencia de la violencia doméstica en una microregión de Ciudad Nezahualcóyotl* [Violence against Mexican women as a public health problem: The prevalence of domestic violence in a microregion of Nezahualcóyotl City]. Mexico City, Mexico: CECOVID.

Straus, M. A. (1979). Measuring intrafamily conflict and violence: The Conflict Tactics Scales. *Journal of Marriage and the Family, 41,* 75–88.

Tolman, R., & Edleson, J. (1995). Intervention for men who batter: A review of research. In S. R. Stith & M. A. Straus (Eds.), *Understanding partner violence: Prevalence, causes, consequences and solutions* (pp. 262–273). Minneapolis, MN: National Council on Family Relations.

Raising Grandchildren: The Experiences of Black and White Grandmothers*

Rachel Pruchno

A total of 2,444,000 households, or 3.5% of all households in the United States, include a grandparent and a grandchild under the age of 18 (Casper & Bryson, 1998). Between 1970 and 1994, the percentage of grandchildren living with a grandparent increased from 3.2% to 5.4% (Saluter, 1996). In 1997, 5.6% of children in the United States, or approximately 4.0 million children, were living with 3.7 million grandparents (Lugaila, 1998). Although Black households are more likely than White households to include both a grandparent and a grandchild (9.2% vs 2.3%; Bryson, 1998), the past decade has witnessed exponential growth in the number of both Black and White children living with a grandparent (increases of 24% and 54%, respectively, since 1980; Saluter, 1992). Analyzing data from Wave 2 of the National Survey of Families and Households (NSFH), Szinovacz (1998) concludes that when data are gathered from the perspective of grandparents, the prevalence of grandparents living with grandchildren is substantially higher than that represented in the Census data. According to Szinovacz's analysis, 8.3% of all grandparents (26.0% of Black grandmothers and 7.3% of White grandmothers) live in households with their grandchildren. Thus, coresidence among grandparents and grandchildren has become increasingly common, yet there is a dearth of information about how these living arrangements affect the mental and physical well-being of the grandparents.

The majority of households that include both a grandparent and a grandchild also include at least one of the grandchild's parents. However, since 1990 the fastest growing type of household that includes both grandparent and grandchild is that in which grandchildren and their grandparents reside together with neither of the grandchild's parents present (Casper & Bryson, 1998). In 1997, 780,000 homes in the United States included a grandparent and grandchild and neither of the grandchild's parents. Close to half of these households (47.3%) were White; 35.9% were African American; and 15.1% were Hispanic (Bryson, 1998). Data from the NSFH (Fuller-Thomson, Minkler, & Driver, 1997) revealed that 10.9% of grandparents who have at least one grandchild report having had primary responsibility for raising a grandchild for a period of six months or more at some point in the child's life. As described by Fuller-Thomson and colleagues (1997), "a variety of factors, including substance abuse, teen pregnancy, AIDS, incarceration, emotional problems, and parental death" (p. 406) contribute to the significant number of grandparents who find themselves in the role of parent to their grandchildren. In many inner cities, hit hard by multiple social epidemics, health and social service providers estimate that between

From Pruchno. (1999). *The Gerontologist, 39,* 209–221. Reprinted with permission.

30% and 50% of children younger than 18 years of age live in the care of their grandparents (Minkler & Roe, 1993).

In their review of the literature, Fuller-Thomson and colleagues (1997) find that the early to mid-1990s witnessed increasing research attention to the phenomenon of grandparent caregiving (Burton, 1992; Dowdell, 1995; Dressel & Barnhill, 1994; Jendrek, 1994; Joslin & Brouard, 1995; Minkler & Roe, 1993; Shore & Hayslip, 1994). Fuller-Thomson and colleagues suggest that "these studies provided useful information including initial explorations of the special problems and challenges faced by grandparents raising grandchildren of imprisoned mothers (Dressel & Barnhill, 1994) and of drug-involved parents (Burton, 1992; Minkler & Roe, 1993)" (p. 406). However, as they conclude, because most of the research to date has been based on small samples in particular geographic areas, their findings cannot be generalized to the growing national population of custodial grandparents. This article describes the experience of Black and White grandparents in the United States who are living with their grandchildren in households that do not include the grandchildren's parents.

Becoming a Custodial Grandparent

Numerous studies have shown that the most common reason children are in the care of their grandparents is child maltreatment, typically associated with substance abuse by one or both of their parents (Dowdell, 1995); Jendrek, 1994; Kelley, 1993; Kelley, Yorker, & Whitley, 1997). Other reasons for grandparents raising grandchildren, although much less common than child maltreatment, include parental death (Kelley & Yorker, 1997; Schable et al., 1995), incarceration (Dowdell, 1995; Dressel & Barnhill, 1994; Gaudin & Sutphen, 1993; Kelley, 1993), and mental illness (Dowdell, 1995; Kelley, 1993). Although custodial grandparenting cuts across gender, class, and ethnicity, analysis of the NSFH data by Fuller-Thomson and colleagues (1997) revealed that women, recently bereaved parents, and African Americans had approximately twice the odds of becoming caregiving grandparents. Furthermore, these data document the long-term, labor-intensive commitment involved in being a custodial grandparent. More than half (56%) of custodial grandparents had provided care to a grandchild for a period of at least three years; one in five grandparent caregivers took care of a grandchild for 10 or more years.

Although a great deal of attention has been paid to the pathways by which custodial grandparenting develops in families where the middle generation is addicted to cocaine, little is known about the pathways that emerge in other circumstances. For example, in their study of 71 African American custodial grandmothers of grandchildren whose parents were involved with crack cocaine, Minkler and Roe (1993) found several patterns emerged with respect to the assumption of care. The first involved a small minority of women for whom becoming a full-time caregiver happened quickly and without warning. In such families, the middle generation may have abandoned the children or become imprisoned. A second, more frequent pattern was for a grandmother to negotiate informally with her crack-involved daughter to have her children stay with the grandmother temporarily while the substance-abusing individual went into treatment. The third, and by far most prevalent, route to caregiving described by Minkler and Roe (1993) typically began with a

> grandmother's growing awareness of and concern over the extent of an adult child's drug involvement and the toll it was taking on the grandchildren. For grandparents fitting this pattern, assumption of the caregiver role often came after a difficult and sometimes protracted period of trying in vain to help the crack-abusing child, checking up on the grandchildren, and providing more and increasingly lengthy informal care to ensure their well-being. This period usually came to a head when the grandparent felt forced either to take the children directly or to call the police and have them removed from the parent's home. (p. 56)

The Lives of Custodial Grandparents

Studies of the ways in which becoming a custodial grandparent affects the lives of individuals have generally included either Blacks or Whites and have involved either Blacks or Whites and have involved small samples. One of the first research studies to focus on the lives of custodial grandparents was that of Burton (1992). Data from two qualitative studies of 60 Black grandparents and great-grandparents who had assumed a surrogate parent role to their grandchildren as a result of drug addiction by the children's parents, identified three types of stressors. These included the contextual, familial, and individual. Contextual stressors involved dangers associated with the neighborhood drug trade. A majority of the respondents (93%) expressed concern and fear about burglaries, drive-by shootings, and drug trafficking in their neighborhoods. Familial stressors included having to provide care for multiple kin and to cope with the drains on family income related to the drug-addicted adult child's behavior. With regard to caring for grandchildren, grandparents were concerned about long-term and permanent child care responsibilities and their own ability to keep up with the school, social, and physical activities of their grandchildren. The individual stressors included balancing work and family life, and tremendous demands on personal time. The data also suggested that grandparents experienced both costs and rewards in their roles as surrogate parents. A majority of the grandparents (86%) reported feeling "depressed or anxious most of the time"; 61% said that they were smoking more than they ever had in their lives; and 36% complained of heightened medical problems, especially diabetes and arthritis. Yet, in spite of these health costs, the majority of grandparents indicated that they experienced tremendous rewards from raising their grandchildren.

In a related study of African American grandmothers raising their grandchildren as a result of the crack-cocaine involvement of the children's parents, Minkler and Roe (1993) found that for the majority of women, surrogate parenthood involved a major and abrupt disruption of mid- or late-life activities, as well as their plans and hopes for the future. Many working women had to quit their jobs in order to become full-time caregivers. For some of the elderly women who had long awaited leisure time and the prospects of economic security in later life, dreams were shattered by the demands of their child care responsibilities. For a small minority of women, the assumption of caregiving, although tragic in what it stood for in terms of an adult child's crack involvement, was nevertheless a very positive life change. However, even among grandmothers for whom the assumption of caregiving represented a positive life change, the long-term consequences of taking this step were overwhelming.

In her study of 36 White custodial grandparents, Jendrek (1993) reports that at least half experienced a decline in privacy, time for themselves, time with a spouse, contact with friends, time spent doing things for fun, and money. The majority of grandparents reported increases in need to alter routines and plans, feeling physically tired, having a purpose for living, being emotionally drained, and worrying. In a similar study of 41 White, middle-class custodial grandparents, Kelley (1993) reports that respondents experienced greater psychological distress in terms of depression, interpersonal sensitivity, hostility, paranoia, obsessive-compulsiveness, and somatization than did grandparents in a normative group. When Jendrek contrasted custodial grandparents with noncustodial grandparents, she found that the former group reported significantly more disruptions to their lives. Similarly, Shore and Hayslip (1994) found that custodial grandparents had lower well-being scores, less satisfaction with the grandparent role, and poorer perception of the grandparent-grandchild relationship than did a contrast group of grandparents whose grandchildren were in the custody of their own parents.

Although these studies hint at the strains involved in the lives of custodial grandparents, the small sample sizes and tendency to include either Blacks or Whites limit generalizability. The analyses that follow describe the experiences of custodial grandparents for a sample of Black and White grandparents living in the United States. It is important to contrast the experience of White and Black grandparents for a number of reasons. First, Black and White grandparents historically have played different roles within families; older Black grandparents have traditionally played more pivotal roles in the family structure and in holding kin networks together (Burton & Dilworth-Anderson, 1991; Hagestad & Burton, 1986). Second, at all ages, Blacks are more likely than Whites to live in extended family households (Allen, 1979; Angel & Tienda, 1982; Hofferth, 1984; Tate, 1983; Taylor, 1988), yet it is unclear how this experience affects the grandparent experience. Third, research indicates that Black grandparents are less likely than White grandparents to embrace norms of noninterference, especially when the middle generation is comprised of single parents (Cherlin & Furstenberg, 1986; Kornhaber & Woodward, 1981). Finally, contrasts of the grandparent experience for custodial Black and White grandparents are intriguing because the broader caregiving literature, which has contrasted the experiences of Black and White people responsible for a variety of care recipients, is inconsistent regarding the effects of race on the caregiving experience.

. . .

Grandmothers who live with and are responsible for the care of their grandchildren provide society with a vital service. Were it not for these women, the majority of their grandchildren would most likely become wards of the state. These data, for the first time, provide the opportunity to describe the experiences of grandmothers living in the United States who are providing care for their grandchildren. It is also the first large-scale study to include both Black and White grandmothers.

The similarities of the caregiving experience for Black and White grandmothers are striking. Black and White grandmothers come to the role at similar times in their lives, with similar levels of education, have similar familial relationships with their grandchildren, and are raising grandchildren whose ages are similar. Many of the reasons that Black and White grandmothers become responsible for their grandchildren (e.g., a middle generation lost to death, imprisonment, drug and alcohol addiction, and child abandonment) are similar. The grandchildren for whom these grandmothers provide care exhibit a number of very difficult behaviors, including sudden mood changes, nervous behavior, trouble paying attention, hyperactive behavior, stubbornness, and temper tantrums. The lack of support both Black and White grandmothers receive from the grandchild's parents is clear; the overwhelming majority of these grandmothers have little or no support from the grandchild's parents.

Black and White grandmothers who raise a grandchild and also work outside the home experience severe impacts on their work lives. Missing work, having to leave work for doctor appointments for their grandchild, coming to work late, and having to leave work suddenly because of a grandchild take a tremendous toll. These data suggest that educating employers to the needs of grandparents raising grandchildren must become a priority if these women are to be able to continue effectively in both their work and family roles.

On the positive side, both Black and White grandparents report high levels of satisfaction with themselves as a function of their grandparent role. Furthermore, the marriages of both Black and White grandmothers do not seem to be affected detrimentally by their caregiving roles. Of course, it is possible that married women who assume this role have strong, intact marriages and supportive husbands, although this study cannot directly disentangle these variables.

Equally striking are the differences in the experiences of Black and White grandmothers. According to these data, White grandmothers are more likely to be married than are Black grandmothers, whereas Black grandmothers are more likely to be widowed and divorced than are White grandmothers. Black grandmothers are more likely than their White counterparts to be employed outside the home and to have lower per capita incomes. They also tend to have more grandchildren in their households.

Black and White grandmothers differ from one another in terms of their experience with the grandparent role, both among their peers and within their own families. Black grandmothers are more likely to have friends who also live with their grandchildren, to report that it was not unusual for multiple generations to live together in their family, to have lived at one of their grandparent's homes when they themselves were young, and to report having a grandparent who helped raise them. The effects of this important experiential difference between Black and White grandmothers needs to be understood as it is likely that it will have an important impact on the way in which Black and White grandmothers embrace the role of custodial grandparent.

Likewise, the extent of help received from the formal system differs between Black and White grandmothers. Black grandmothers are more likely to be receiving AFDC, food stamps, Medicaid, WIC, and SSI, and their grandchildren are more likely to be participants in programs such as Head Start than are White grandmothers. Most likely this difference in service is a function of difference in income between Black and White grandmothers, yet the extent to which it affects the experience must be explored further.

Finally, the differences in degree of burden reported by Black and White grandparents are noteworthy. White grandmothers were more likely than Black to feel trapped in their role, tired, isolated, and alone, and to feel that they do not have enough time for themselves, that their social life has suffered because of their grandchild, that caring for their grandchild affects relationships with other family members in a negative way, that caring for their grandchild does not allow them as much privacy as they would like, that other family members have had to do without because of their grandchild, and that caring for their grandchild has interfered with use of space in their home. Although these findings are consistent with results reported in studies of caregivers of older people (Hinrichsen & Ramirez, 1992; Lawton, Rajagopal, Brody, & Kleban, 1992; Macera, Eaker, Jannarone, Davis, & Stoskopf, 1993; Mintzer & Macera, 1992; Mui, 1992; Young & Kahana, 1995) and in a study of women providing care to adult children with chronic disabilities (Pruchno, Patrick, & Burant, 1997), they beg for more complete explanation.

In summary, Black and White grandmothers who live with and have primary responsibility for their grandchildren have experiences that are both similar to and different from one another. Although identification of these similarities and differences is important, examination of the mechanisms linking race to the way in which the grandparent role is experienced represents the next important step. Unraveling the intricate relationship between race and the grandparent caregiving role will provide important knowledge about how the role of custodial grandparent is embraced and how it affects both individuals and families.

. . .

REFERENCES

Achenbach, T. M. (1991). *Manual for the child behavior checklist/4–18 and 1991 profile.* Burlington, VT: University of Vermont Department of Psychiatry.

Allen, W. R. (1979). Class, culture, and family organization: The effects of class and race on family structure in urban America. *Journal of Comparative Family Studies, 10,* 301–313.

Angel, R., & Tienda, M. (1982). Determinants of extended household structure: Cultural pattern or economic model? *American Journal of Sociology, 87,* 1360–1383.

Bryson, K. R. (1998, March). Census Bureau table. Washington, DC: U.S. Bureau of the Census, Population Division, Fertility & Family Statistics Branch. Unpublished raw data.

Burton, L. M. (1992). Black grandparents rearing children of drug-addicted parents: Stressors, outcomes, and social service needs. *The Gerontologist, 32,* 744–751.

Burton, L. M., & Dilworth-Anderson, P. (1991). The intergenerational family roles of aged Black Americans. *Marriage & Family Review, 16,* 311–330.

Casper, L. M., & Bryson, K. R. (1998). *Coresident grandparents and their grandchildren: Grandparent-maintained families.* Population Division Working Paper No. 26. Washington, DC: U.S. Bureau of the Census.

Cherlin, A. J., & Furstenberg, F. F. (1986). *The new American grandparent: A place in the family, a life apart.* New York: Basic Books.

Cohler, B. J., & Grunebaum, H. V. (1981). *Mothers, grandmothers, and daughters: Personality and child care in three-generation families.* New York: Wiley.

Dowdell, E. B. (1995). Caregiver burden: Grandmothers raising their high risk grandchildren. *Journal of Psychosocial Nursing, 33*(3), 27–30.

Dressel, P. L., & Barnhill, S. K. (1994). Reframing gerontological thought and practice: The case of grandmothers with daughters in prison. *The Gerontologist, 34,* 685–691.

Fuller-Thomson, E., Minkler, M., & Driver, D. (1997). A profile of grandparents raising grandchildren in the United States. *The Gerontologist, 37,* 406–111.

Gaudin, J. M., & Sutphen, R. (1993). Foster care vs extended family care for children of incarcerated mothers. *Journal of Offender Rehabilitation, 19,* 129–147.

Hagestad, G. O. (1985). Community and connectedness. In V. L. Bengston & J. F. Robertson (Eds.), *Grandparenthood.* Beverly Hills, CA: Sage.

Hagestad, G. O., & Burton, L. M. (1986). Grandparenthood, life context, and family development. *American Behavioral Scientist, 29,* 471–484.

Hagestad, G. O., & Smyer, M. A. (1982). Dissolving long-term relationships: Patterns of divorce in middle age. In S. Duck (Ed.), *Dissolving personal relationships* (pp. 155–196). London: Academic Press.

Hinrichsen, G. A., & Ramirez, M. (1992). Black and White dementia caregivers: A comparison of their adaptation, adjustment, and service utilization. *The Gerontologist, 32,* 375–381.

Hofferth, S. L. (1984). Kin networks, race, and family structure. *Journal of Marriage and the Family, 46,* 791–806.

Jendrek, M. P. (1993). Grandparents who parent their grandchildren: Effects on lifestyle. *Journal of Marriage and the Family, 55,* 609–621.

Jendrek, M. P. (1994). Grandparents who parent their grandchildren: Circumstances and decision. *The Gerontologist, 34,* 206–216.

Joslin, D., & Brouard, A. (1995). The prevalence of grandmothers as primary caregivers in a poor pediatric population. *Journal of Community Health, 20,* 383–401.

Kelley, S. J. (1993). Caregiver stress in grandparents raising grandchildren. *IMAGE: Journal of Nursing Scholarship, 25,* 331–337.

Kelley, S. J., Yorker, B. C., & Whitley, D. (1997). To grandmother's house we go . . . and stay: Children raised in intergenerational families. *Journal of Gerontological Nursing, 23*(9), 12–20.

Kornhaber, A., & Woodward, R. (1981). *Grandparents/ grandchildren: The vital connection.* New York: Doubleday.

Lawton, M. P., Kleban, M. H., Moss, M., Rovine, M., & Glicksman, A. (1989). Measuring caregiving appraisal. *Journal of Gerontology: Psychological Sciences, 44,* P61–P71.

Lawton, M. P., Rajagopal, D., Brody, E. M., & Kleban, M. H. (1992). The dynamics of caregiving for a demented elder among Black and White families. *Journal of Gerontology: Social Sciences, 47,* S156–S164.

Lugaila, T. (1998). *Marital status and living arrangements: March 1997.* Current Population Reports, P 20-514. Washington, DC: U.S. Bureau of the Census.

Macera, C. A., Eaker, E. D., Jannarone, R. J., Davis, D. R., & Stoskopf, C. H. (1993). The association of positive and negative events with depressive symptomatology among caregivers. *International Journal on Aging and Human Development, 36*(1), 75–80.

Minkler, M., & Roe, K. M. (1993). *Grandmothers as caregivers: Raising children of the crack cocaine epidemic.* Newbury Park, CA: Sage.

Mintzer, J. E., & Macera, C. A. (1992). Prevalence of depressive symptoms among White and African American caregivers of demented patients. *American Journal of Psychiatry, 149,* 575–576.

Mui, A. C. (1992). Caregiver strain among Black and White daughter caregivers: A role theory perspective. *The Gerontologist, 32,* 203–212.

Pruchno, R. A., Patrick, J. H., & Burant, C. J. (1997). African American and White mothers of adults with chronic disabilities: Caregiving burden and satisfaction. *Family Relations, 46,* 335–346.

Saluter, A. F. (1992). *Marital status and living arrangements: March 1991.* (Report No. 461, Current Population Reports, Population Characteristics, Series P-20). Washington, DC: U.S. Government Printing Office.

Saluter, A. (1996). *Marital status and living arrangements: March 1994.* (Report No. 484, Current Population Reports, Series P-20). Washington, DC: U.S. Bureau of the Census, U.S. Government Printing Office.

Schable, B., Diaz, T., Chu, S. Y., Caldwell, M. B., Conti, L., Alston, O. M., Sorvillo, F., Checko, P. J., Hermann, P., Davidson, A. J., Boyd, D., Fann, S. A., Herr, M., & Frederick, M. (1995). Who are the primary caretakers of children born to HIV-infected mothers? Results of a multistate surveillance project. *Pediatrics, 95,* 511–515.

Shore, R. J., & Hayslip, B., Jr. (1994). Custodial grandparenting: Implications for children's development. In A. E. Gottfried & A. W. Gottfried (Eds.), *Redefining families: Implications for children's development* (pp. 171–218). New York: Plenum.

Szinovacz, M. E. (1998). Grandparents today: A demographic profile. *The Gerontologist, 38,* 37–52.

Tate, N. (1983). The Black aging experience. In R. L. McNeeley & J. L. Colen (Eds.), *Aging in minority groups* (pp. 95–107). Beverly Hills, CA: Sage.

Taylor, R. J. (1988). Aging and supportive relationships among Black Americans. In J. S. Jackson (Ed.), *The Black American elderly: Research on physical and psychosocial health* (pp. 259–281). New York: Springer.

Young, R. F., & Kahana, E. (1995). The context of caregiving and well-being outcomes among African and Caucasian Americans. *The Gerontologist, 35,* 225–232.

Bicultural Identification: Experiences of Internationally Adopted Children and Their Parents*

Myrna L. Friedlander, Lucille C. Larney, Marianne Skau, Marcus Hotaling, Marsha L. Cutting, and Michelle Schwam

Whereas U.S. children adopted in the early part of the century were orphaned or relinquished by their birth parents because of age, marital status, illness, or poverty, in the past 25 years the predominant reasons for relinquishment have changed dramatically, as have the psychosocial characteristics of adoptive families. In contrast to the 1950s, there are now many more older children whose birth parents' rights were terminated because of child abuse or neglect. Furthermore, there are fewer healthy infants who need homes because of the increased acceptance of single parenthood and the availability of abortion and birth control. Currently, the majority of those who adopt infants are middle- and upper-income White couples, most of whom have undergone stressful medical treatments for infertility (Simon & Altstein, 1991). Although many infertile couples choose to adopt domestically through organizations or private attorneys, increasing numbers of couples and single adults seek children abroad. In the fiscal year 1998 alone, 15,774 children were adopted internationally (Adoptive Families, 1999).

Little is known about the psychosocial experiences of White parents with international adopted children of color. On reflection, one can see that their experiences differ from same-race adoptive families because the child's adoptive status is immediately visible. Knowledge of the adoption cannot be kept from the very young child or remain a private family matter when physiognomic differences regularly prompt questions and comments from strangers.

Adoption is also visible for Native American and African American children adopted by White couples, but children in these transracial families are faced with somewhat different identity concerns. Although many of them struggle with issues of racial and cultural identification, as well as with stigmatization, their birth culture is in the United States and is thus available to them. Internationally adopted children, on the other hand, have little exposure to the culture of Peru, Nepal, Brazil, or Sierra Leone, for example. Indeed, a Peruvian child may grow up without ever having met another Peruvian person. Coming to terms with being a minority and an immigrant is only part of the picture. By adolescence, these children understand that not only their identity but also their personality, social status, and experience of the world would have been vastly different in their birth countries (Friedlander, 1999). They would have spoken another language, dressed differently, and observed different customs. In most cases, they would have been impoverished—parentless, homeless, and unable to attend school, find employment, or receive medical care. Indeed, many children may not have survived in their birth country.

Little is known about how adopted children come to terms with issues like these or develop a cohesive personal identity (Grotevant, 1992). Although several studies have concluded that, on average, adopted children fare well psychologically (e.g., Borders, Black, & Pasley, 1998; Sharma, McGue, & Benson, 1998), they tend to be overrepresented in the clinical population (Brodzinsky, Schecter, & Henig, 1992). Often the reason given for this is the trauma of adoption, although there are a number of alternative explanations (Borders et al., 1998). Many adopted children were neglected or maltreated in their birth families or suffer from medical problems (e.g., fetal alcohol syn-

*From Friedlander et al. (2000). *Journal of Counseling Psychology, 47*(2), 187–198. Reprinted with permission.

drome), attachment disorders, and learning disabilities that are due to institutionalization or prenatal conditions (Friedlander, 1999). Adoptive parents, who tend to be educated professionals, readily seek help for children with these kinds of difficulties, as well as for healthy children who are struggling with identity concerns. Parents often turn to counselors when their children have problems that they themselves have not experienced.

There is little, however, in either the clinical adoption literature or the empirical literature to guide counselors working with internationally adopted children (Friedlander, 1999). Most of the available research considers only the self-esteem or psychological adjustment of these children, not the process by which they achieve an understanding and acceptance of their history and identity. There are many studies suggesting that self-esteem is closely tied to ethnic pride for children of color (Phinney, 1991), but to what extent do adopted children identify with their country of origin? Is cultural identification more desirable than assimilation? Indeed, can a bicultural identity be achieved when there is minimal exposure to the birth culture?

The literature on biracial identity formation, although scant, provides a context for these questions. To a large extent, the formation of a healthy biracial identity is compromised by society's stigmatization of the minority group (Pinderhughes, 1995). Some early authors emphasized the difficulties associated with trying to meet the expectations of two cultures simultaneously (e.g., Stonequist, 1935) and urged Black/White biracial families to identify their children as Black. More recently, LaFromboise, Coleman, and Gerton (1993) suggested that identity confusion only occurs when the individual internalizes the conflict between the two cultures. Supporting this argument, Kerwin, Ponterotto, Jackson, and Harris (1993) found in their qualitative study of Black/White families that a cohesive biracial identity is possible and that young children naturally view themselves as biracial if they are exposed to both cultures and their parents foster an open dialogue on the topic. By age 13 or 14, however, these youth often feel peer pressure to choose a single racial designation (Kerwin et al., 1993). In a review of the literature, Brown (1990) concluded that biracial individuals tend to be more comfortable with the minority group, but their social acceptance depends on how closely their appearance, speech, and behavior match those of the group.

Of course, adopted children of color raised by White parents are less likely than biracial children to develop the behavioral characteristics of the minority culture. Children who live in predominantly White communities may have limited exposure to any minority culture. Under these conditions, it is not surprising that some children are confused about race and ethnicity. A survey of international adoption in Canada (Westhues & Cohen, 1994) found that roughly 14% of adoptees could not identify their race, and 10% thought of themselves as White, although their countries of origin were Korea, Bangaladesh, and Haiti.

The first extensive U.S. investigation of internationally adopted children was conducted over 20 years ago. In this research, Kim (1977) reported good psychosocial adjustment by 406 Korean adolescents (mean age = 14.1 years) in terms of self-reported family life, self-esteem scores, and educational achievement. Whereas those who were adopted at a younger age had somewhat better adjustment scores than those who were adopted later, there were no differences in self-concept. Although self-concept was not related to ethnic identity, the major problem reported by these teens was discomfort with their appearance. Overall, these adoptees had "little 'Korean' identity" (Kim, 1977, p. 5). Most identified themselves as American or, more frequently, as Korean American.

In their longitudinal study of adoptive families, Simon and Altstein (1992) concluded that young transracially adopted children tend to have a stronger sense of ethnicity than either nonadopted children of color or adopted children in same-race families. However, despite being proud of their birth heritage, many adopted children are uncertain about their race (Westhues & Cohen, 1994). Indeed, they tend to have more concerns about race than about their adoption (Benson, Shama, & Roehlkepartain, 1994). These concerns often become pronounced in adolescence, when they find themselves ill equipped to handle bias, discrimination, and racial insults (Triseliotis, 1993). In general, adopted children's psychosocial adjustment seems to depend on age at time of placement, exposure to positive role models from the country of origin, and parental nurturance (Friedlander, 1999).

A number of adoption studies indicate that ethnic self-identification and pride are related to family attitudes and to the child's exposure to the birth culture (Andujo, 1988; Benson et al., 1994; Feigelman & Silverman, 1983; Kim, 1977). It is not clear, however, if and how bicultural identification develops or whether it is necessary for healthy adjustment (Friedlander, 1999). Research suggests that ethnic identification seems to be important for some internationally adopted children but not for others (Textor, 1991). Even those who are adopted abroad at an older age rapidly become assimilated (Feigelman & Silverman, 1983), and a strong identification with mainstream culture is the norm for these children (Textor, 1991).

Knowledge of their adoption comes at an early age for children of color with White parents because of the visible physical differences. The child's cognitive understanding of being adopted, being an immigrant, and being an ethnic minority develop simultaneously, and the feelings that are aroused as this awareness unfolds can be overwhelming (Friedlander, 1999).

The purpose of the present study was to further our knowledge of the cognitive, emotional, and familial experiences of internationally adopted children of color. The specific questions we addressed were as follows: In what psychosocial contexts are these families raising their children? How do the parents and children identify themselves? Do the parents encourage biculturalism? How do the children understand and feel about adoption and racial/ethnic issues? What is the family's experience of racial or prejudicial incidents? How do the parents recognize and try to ease these concerns for their children? An important aspect of the study concerned the developmental progression of children's cultural identification as they gained an understanding of international adoption.

. . .

The present results were consistent with both the theoretical and empirical literature. A number of authors have pointed out that the psychosocial adjustment of adopted children is maximized when parents acknowledge their children's physical differences but emphasize their psychological similarities (Benson et al., 1994; Kaye, 1990). The parents we interviewed seemed to be doing just that, as well as attempting to promote their children's cultural identification. As recommended by various authors (Andujo, 1988; Benson et al., 1994; Kim, 1977), the present parents consider it important for their children to be knowledgeable about and feel pride in their birth heritage. Consistent with Kerwin et al.'s (1993) findings about biracial identity, the children's identity development is taking place in caring environments with parents who discuss the issues and provide the children with opportunities to become acquainted with their heritage. A major theme was the parents construing the family as a whole multiculturally (e.g., "We are a Brazilian American family"), a construction that not only reflects the family's cultural transition but also serves to reduce the children's sense of isolation or differentness.

The existing literature provides little information about the attitudes of White adoptive parents toward multiculturalism. Our findings contribute to theory in this regard. First, most of the parents in our sample had had some experience with racial/ethnic or religious differences in their families of origin prior to adopting. This experience suggests an openness to human diversity that may have contributed to their children's psychosocial well-being. Second, although the parents were similar in how they promote cultural pride (educating themselves about the birth country's history, traditions, music, and food; attending cultural events; socializing with people from the same heritage; etc.), they differed markedly in their views of race and ethnicity. Indeed, the perspectives on diversity domain had the greatest number of minor themes. Parents' approaches to the issue ranged from wanting their children to learn about and appreciate people from many different cultures (the sensitivity-to-diversity perspective) to minimizing group differences, denigrating the use of "labels," and emphasizing individual self-worth and shared humanity (the universalist perspective). Not only did these perspectives differ across families but also between parents in the same family. More importantly, perhaps, parents from both perspectives anticipated that providing their children with their particular set of lenses on the world would bolster their children's self-esteem and help them cope with any racial insults, bias, or discrimination that came their way. These data suggest that although bicultural identification is important for children in multiethnic families, there is no one preferred approach to educating them about multiculturalism.

By all accounts (parents, kinetic family drawings, and the children themselves), the children in our sample were faring exceptionally well. They felt connected with and similar to their adoptive parents. Although a few children expressed sadness and loss, by and large they described their adoption in positive terms. Even the two drawings that suggested self-esteem difficulties had markers of attachment and integration, and the sense of isolation conveyed in one of the drawings could reflect the artist's medical condition rather than adoption-related concerns.

Overall, the major psychosocial hurdle for these children seemed to be a sense of being different. How, then, does a cohesive personal identity develop for children like these? The variations in our sample's understanding of international adoption were clearly developmental, reflecting changes in a growing child's cognitions, values, and sense of personal identity. Furthermore, the results were consistent with developmental theories on children's understanding of adoption (Brodzinsky et al., 1992). From a young age, all of the children in this study noticed physical differences from family members and could tell their adoption story in simple terms, that is, that they look different because they came from another country. Those in elementary school were generally aware of the reasons for their adoption and could identify ways in which their birth country differs from the United States. Preteens had a greater understanding of ethnic and cultural differences, their birth parents' reasons for relinquishment, and what it means to be an immigrant in the United States. The adolescents in the sample were well aware that their way of life and standard of living would have been very different had they remained in their birth countries. It is notable that the two oldest teens had strikingly different attitudes about their ethnicity, although both identified themselves as Korean American. Although one teen was clearly interested in learning more about Korea, the other indicated feeling uncomfortable around other Koreans.

How can counselors best help adopted children come to terms with their history and identity? First, a careful assessment needs to be done, because other personal, physical, or family problems may overshadow adoption or race-related concerns. Second, parents as well as children should be encouraged to identify themselves biculturally, to gain knowledge of the children's birth culture, and to associate with others from that culture. Third, counselors working with adopted children need to approach the issues of adoption and race/ethnicity developmentally so as not to provide their clients with more information than they can handle cognitively or emotionally. Fourth, counselors need to emphasize the family's strong pyschosocial bonds and help parents understand that their children's sadness and sense of loss is normal under the circumstances. The parents' nondefensiveness and openness to the child's full range of feelings on the topic seem to be particularly important. Indeed, in some cases counselors may do better to coach parents how to handle the issues sensitively rather than to recommend individual counseling (Friedlander, 1999). For a child who is suffering in this area but doing well in other areas of life, seeing a counselor may unwittingly foster his or her sense of differentness.

. . .

REFERENCES

Adoptive Families. (1999). International adoption statistics released. *Adoptive Families, 32*(1), 6.

Andujo, E. (1988). Ethnic identity of transethnically adopted Hispanic adolescents. *Social Work, 33,* 531–535.

Benson, P. L., Sharma, A. R., & Roehlkepartain, E. C. (1994). *Growing up adopted: A portrait of adolescents and their families.* Minneapolis, MN: Search Institute.

Borders, L. D., Black, L. K., & Pasley, B. K. (1998). Are adopted children and their parents at greater risk for negative outcomes? *Family Relations, 47,* 237–241.

Brodzinsky, D. M., Schechter, M. D., & Henig, R. M. (1992). *Being adopted: The lifelong search for self.* New York: Doubleday.

Brown, P. M. (1990). Biracial identity and social marginality. *Child and Adolescent Social Work, 7,* 319–337.

Burns, R. C. (1982). *Self-growth in families: Kinetic Family Drawings (K-F-D) research and application.* New York: Brunner/Mazel.

Burns, R. C., & Kaufman, S. H. (1970). *Kinetic Family Drawings (K-F-D): An introduction to understanding children through kinetic drawings.* New York: Brunner/Mazel.

Burns, R. C., & Kaufman, S. H. (1972). *Actions, styles and symbols in kinetic family drawings (K-F-D): An interpretive manual.* New York: Brunner/Mazel.

DiLeo, J. H. (1983). *Interpreting children's drawings.* New York: Brunner/Mazel.

Feigelman, W., & Silverman, A. R. (1983). *Chosen children: New patterns of adoptive relationships.* New York: Praeger.

Friedlander, M. L. (1999). Ethnic identity development among internationally adopted children: Implications for family therapists. *Journal of Marital and Family Therapy, 25,* 43–60.

Grotevant, H. D. (1992). Assigned and chosen identity components: A process perspective on their integration. In G. Adams, T. Gullota, & R. Montemayor (Eds.), *Adolescent identity formation* (pp. 73–90). Newbury Park, CA: Sage.

Handler, L., & Habenicht, D. (1994). The kinetic family drawing technique: A review of literature. *Journal of Personality Assessment, 62,* 440–464.

Hill, C. E., Thompson, B. J., & Williams, E. N. (1997). A guide to conducting consensual qualitative research. *The Counseling Psychologist, 25,* 517–572.

Kaye, K. (1990). Acknowledgment or rejection of differences? In D. M. Brodzinksy & M. D. Schechter (Eds.), *The psychology of adoption* (pp. 121–143). New York: Oxford University Press.

Kerwin, C., Ponterotto, J. G., Jackson, B. L., & Harris, A. (1993). Racial identity in biracial children: A qualitative investigation. *Journal of Counseling Psychology, 40,* 221–231.

Kim, D. S. (1977). How they fared: A follow-up study of adoption. *Children Today, 6,* 2–6, 36.

Kramer, E. (1971). *Art as therapy with children.* New York: Schocken Books.

LaFromboise, T., Coleman, H. L. K., & Gerton, J. (1993). Psychological impact of biculturalism: Evidence and theory. *Psychological Bulletin, 114,* 395–412.

Levick, M. F. (1983). *They could not talk and so they drew—Children's styles of coping and thinking.* Springfield, IL: Charles C. Thomas.

Lincoln, Y. S., & Guba, E. G. (1985). *Naturalistic inquiry.* Beverly Hills, CA: Sage.

Phinney, J. S. (1990). Ethnic identity in adolescents and adults: Review of research. *Psychological Bulletin, 108,* 499–514.

Phinney, J. S. (1991). Ethnic identity and self-esteem: A review and integration. *Hispanic Journal of Behavioral Sciences, 13,* 193–208.

Pinderhughes, E. (1995). Biracial identity—asset or handicap? In H. W. Harris, H. C. Blue, & E. Griffith (Eds.), *Racial and ethnic identity: Psychological development and creative expression* (pp. 73–114). New York: Routledge.

Ryskamp, A. M. (1999). You light up my life. *Adoptive Families, 32*(1), 21–23.

Sharma, A. R., McGue, M. K., & Benson, P. L. (1998). The psychological adjustment of United States adopted adolescents and their nonadopted siblings. *Child Development, 69,* 791–802.

Simon, R. J., & Altstein, H. (1991). Intercountry adoptions: Experiences of families in the United States. In H. Altstein & R. J. Simon (Eds.). *Intercountry adoption: A multinational perspective* (pp. 23–54). New York: Praeger.

Simon, R. J., & Altstein, H. (1992). *Adoption, race, and identity: From infancy through adolescence.* New York: Praeger.

Stiles, W. B. (1993). Quality control in qualitative research. *Clinical Psychology Review, 13,* 593–618.

Stonequist, E. V. (1935). The problem of marginal man. *American Journal of Sociology, 7,* 1–12.

Strauss, A., & Corbin, J. (1990). *Basics of qualitative research: Grounded theory procedures and techniques.* Newbury Park, CA: Sage.

Textor, W. M. R. (1991). Auslandsadoptionen: Forschungsstand und Folgerungen [Foreign adoption: State of the Research and Implications]. *Praxis der Kinderpsychologie and Kinderpsychiatrie, 40,* 42–49.

Triseliotis, J. (1993). Inter-country adoption: In whose best interest? In M. Humphrey & H. Humphrey (Eds.), *Inter-country adoption: Practical experiences* (pp. 129–137). London: Routledge.

Westhues, A., & Cohen, J. S. (1994). *Intercountry adoption in Canada.* Unpublished manuscript, University of Toronto, Toronto, Ontario, Canada.

REVIEW QUESTIONS AND ACTIVITIES

1. Call or write your state senator and/or assemblymember about bills that have been introduced in the legislature that deal with domestic violence. Provide an overview of the research you have read about domestic violence in general and of the interface of violence and race in particular. Inquire about the kinds of support representatives might need from constituents pending the passage or defeat of particular bills.
2. Discuss the information presented in this chapter with your parent(s) and/or grandparent(s). Do their experiences fit with the research findings described in the chapter? Why or why not? What interpretations can you offer for any differences you have found?
3. Are there universal patterns of adult personality development? If so, what are they specifically? Have you observed any universal patterns among your peers from different cultures?
4. Imagine you have been asked to develop a training program for mothers and daughters that is informed by research on body consciousness and eating disorders. Using McKinley's study as a base, how would you design this program? Provide the rationale for your work.
5. Write an overview of the empirical evidence on the interface of sex, race, and depressive symptomatology.
6. Critically reread one of the selections in the readings section, and then answer the following questions:
   a. Is the purpose of the research clear? Explain.
   b. Are studies contrary to the current hypothesis cited?
   c. Is the research hypothesis correctly derived from the literature and theory that have been cited? Or are there some important steps missing and left to the speculation of the reader?
   d. Were the conclusions drawn by the author consistent with the results obtained?
   e. What follow-up studies do you think are needed? Why these studies? Describe the methodology you would use in these follow-up studies.

SUGGESTIONS FOR FURTHER READING

Cohen, C. (1999). Aging and homelessness. *The Gerontologist, 39,* 5–14.

Hashimoto, A. (1996). *The gift of generations: Japanese and American perspectives.* New York: Cambridge University Press.

Phinney, J., Ong, A., & Madden, T. (2000). Cultural values and intergenerational value discrepancies in immigrant and non-immigrant families. *Child Development, 71,* 528–539.

Willis, S., & Reid, J. (Eds.). (1999). *Life in the middle: Psychological and social development in middle age.* San Diego, CA: Academic Press.

References

Abbott, S. (1992). Holding on and pushing away: Comparative perspectives on an Eastern Kentucky child-rearing practice. *Ethos, 20,* 33–65.

Adams, G., Montemayor, R., & Gullotta, T. (Eds.). (1996). *Psychosocial development during adolescence.* Thousand Oaks, CA: Sage.

Adler, N., Boyce, T., Chesney, M., Cohen, S., Folkman, S., Kahn, R., & Syme, S. (1994). Socioeconomic status and health. The challenge of the gradient. *American Psychologist, 49,* 15–24.

Adoptive Families. (1999). International adoption statistics released. *Adoptive Families, 32,* 6.

Ahmed, R. (1998). Psychology of aging. In R. Ahmed & U. Gielen (Eds.), *Psychology in the Arab countries.* Menoulfia, Egypt: Menoulfia University Press.

Ainsworth, M., & Bell, M. (1970). Attachment, exploration, and separation: Illustrated by the behavior of one-year-olds in a Strange Situation. *Child Development, 41,* 49–67.

Ainsworth, M., Blehar, M., Waters, E., & Wall, S. (1978). *Patterns of attachment.* Hillsdale, NJ: Erlbaum.

Aksan, N., Goldsmith, H., Smider, N., Essex, M., Clark, R., Hyde, J., Klein, M., & Vandell, D. (1999). Derivation and prediction of temperamental types among preschoolers. *Developmental Psychology, 35,* 958–971.

Albert, R. (1988). The place of culture in modern psychology. In P. Bronstein & K. Quina (Eds.), *Teaching a psychology of people: Resources for gender and sociocultural awareness.* Washington, DC: American Psychology Association.

Amaro, H. (1988). Considerations for prevention of HIV infection among Hispanic women. *Psychology of Women Quarterly, 12,* 429–444.

Amaro, H. (1995). Love, sex, and power: Considering women's realities in HIV prevention. *American Psychologist, 50,* 437–447.

Amaro, H., & Gornemann, I. (1992). HIV/AIDS. Reported in Amaro, H. (1995), Love, sex, and power: Considering women's realities in HIV prevention. *American Psychologist, 50,* 437–447.

Amato, P., & Rejac, S. (1994). Contact with non-resident parents, interparental conflict, and children's behavior. *Journal of Family Issues, 15,* 191–207.

American Psychological Association (1993). *Violence and youth: Psychology's response. Vol. 1.* Summary report of the American Psychological Association Commission on violence and youth. Washington, DC: Author.

Apter, A., Galatzer, A., Beth-Halachmi, N., & Laron, Z. (1981). Self-image in adolescents with delayed puberty and growth retardation. *Journal of Youth and Adolescence, 10,* 501–505.

Arnett, J. J. (1999). Adolescent storm and stress, reconsidered. *American Psychologist, 54,* 317–326.

Arnett, J. (2000). Emerging adulthood: A theory of development from the late teens through the twenties. *American Psychologist, 55,* 469–480.

Asher, S., Singleton, L., & Taylor, A. (1982). *Acceptance vs. friendship.* Paper presented at the Meeting of the American Research Association, New York.

Atkinson, D., Morten, G., & Sue, D. (1983). *Counseling American minorities: A cross-cultural perspective.* Dubuque, IA: Brown.

Attar, B., Guerra, N., & Tolan, P. (1994). Neighborhood disadvantage, stressful life events, and adjustment in urban elementary school children. *Journal of Clinical and Child Psychology, 23,* 391–400.

Ausman, L., & Russell, R. (1990). Nutrition and aging. In E. Schneider & J. Rowe (Eds.), *Handbook of the biology of aging.* New York: Academic Press.

Azibo, D. (1988). Understanding the proper and improper usage of the comparative research framework. *Journal of Black Psychology, 15,* 81–91.

Bakken, L., & Romig, C. (1992). Interpersonal needs in middle adolescents: Companionship, leadership, and intimacy. *Journal of Adolescence, 15,* 301–316.

Barnett, R., & Rivers, C. (1992, February). The myth of the miserable working woman. *Working Woman, 2,* 62–65, 83–85.

Barrett, D., & Frank, D. (1987). *The effects of undernutrition on children's behavior.* New York: Gordon & Breach.

Bates, J., Marvinney, D., Bennett, D., Dodge, K., Kelly, T., & Pettit, G. (1991). *Children's daycare history and kindergarten adjustment.* Paper presented at the biennial meeting of the Society for Research in Child Development, Seattle, WA.

Beckwith, L., Cohen, S., & Hamilton, C. (1999). Maternal sensitivity during infancy and subsequent life events relate to attachment representation at early adulthood. *Developmental Psychology, 35,* 693–700.

Bee, H. (1996). *The journey of adulthood.* Englewood Cliffs, NJ: Prentice Hall.

Bee, H., Mitchell, S., Barnard, K., Eyres, S., & Hammond, M. (1984). Predicting intellectual outcomes: Sex differences in response to early environmental stimulation. *Sex Roles, 10,* 783–803.

Belgrave, L., Wykle, M., & Choi, J. (1993). Health, double jeopardy, and culture: The use of institutionalization by African-Americans. *The Gerontologist, 33,* 379–385.

Bell, C., & Jenkins, E. (1991). Traumatic stress and children. *Journal of Health Care for the Poor and Underserved, 2,* 175–185.

Belle, D. (1984). Inequality and mental health: Low income and minority women. In L. Walker (Ed.), *Women and mental health policy.* Newbury Park, CA: Sage.

Belle, D. (1990). Poverty and women's mental health. *American Psychologist, 45,* 385–389.

Bem, S. (1981). Gender schema theory: A cognitive account of sex typing. *Psychological Review, 88,* 354–364.

Benenson, J., Apostoleris, N., & Pamass, J. (1998). The organization of children's same-sex peer relationships. In W. Bukowski & A. Cillessen (Eds.), *Sociometry then and now: Building on six decades of measuring children's experiences with the peer group. New directions for child development.* San Francisco: Jossey-Bass.

Bengtson, V., Cuellar, J., & Ragan, P. (1977). Stratum contrasts and similarities in attitudes toward death. *Journal of Gerontology, 32,* 76–88.

Bennett, M., McCrady, B., Johnson, V., & Pandina, R. (1999). Problem drinking from young adulthood to adulthood: Patterns, predictors, and outcomes. *Journal of Studies on Alcohol, 60,* 605–614.

Berk, L. (1992). Children's private speech: An overview of the theory and the status of research. In R. Diaz & L. Berk (Eds.), *Private speech: From social interaction to self-regulation.* Hillsdale, NJ: Erlbaum.

Betancourt, H., & Lopez, S. (1993). The study of culture, ethnicity, and race in American psychology. *American Psychologist, 48,* 629–637.

Betz, N. (1993). Women's career development. In F. Denmark & M. Paludi (Eds.), *The psychology of women: A handbook of issues and theories.* Westport, CT: Greenwood Press.

Bloom, L., Merkin, S., & Wooten, J. (1982). Wh-questions: Linguistic factors that contribute to the sequence of acquisition. *Child Development, 53,* 1084–1092.

Blyth, D., Simmins, R., & Zakin, D. (1985). Satisfaction with body image for early adolescent females: The impact of pubertal timing within different school environments. Time of maturation and psychosocial functioning in adolescence: I [Special Issue]. *Journal of Youth and Adolescence, 14,* 207–225.

Bornstein, M. H. (1999). Human infancy: Past, present, future. In M. Bennett (Ed.), *Developmental psychology: Achievements and prospects.* Philadelphia: Psychology Press.

Bornstein, M. H. (2000). Infant into conversant: Language and nonlanguage processes in developing early communication. In N. Budwig & I. Uzgiris (Eds.), *Communication: An arena of development.* Stamford, CT: Ablex.

Bornstein, M. H., Haynes, O., Galperín, C., Maital, S., Ogino, M., Painter, K., Pascual, K., Pêcheux, M. G., Rahn, C., Tanner, K., Toda, S., Venuti, P., Vyt, A., & Wright, B. (1998). A cross-national study of self-perceptions and attributions about parenting: Argentina, Belgium, France, Israel, Italy, Japan, and the United States. *Developmental Psychology, 34,* 662–676.

Bowlby, J. (1951). Maternal care and mental health. *Bulletin of the World Health Organization, 3,* 355–534.

Boyer, C., Shafer, M., & Tschann, J. (1997). Evaluation of a knowledge and cognitive-behavioral skills-building intervention to prevent STDs and HIV infection in high school students. *Adolescence, 32,* 25–42.

Brazelton, T. B. (1979, June). What parents told me about handling children's sleep problems. *Redbook,* 51–54.

Brooks-Gunn, J., Boyer, C., & Hein, K. (1988). Preventing HIV infection and AIDS in children and adolescents. *American Psychologist, 43,* 958–964.

Brooks-Gunn, J., Newman, D., & Holerness, C. (1994). The experience of breast development and girls' stories about the purchase of a bra. *Journal of Youth and Adolescence, 23,* 539–565.

Brooks-Gunn, J., & Warren, M. (1989). Biological and social contributions to negative affect in young adolescent girls. *Child Development, 60,* 40–55.

Brown, J., & Pollitt, E. (1996, February). Malnutrition, poverty, and intellectual development. *Scientific American,* 38–43.

Brown, R. (1999). Assessing attitudes and behaviors of high-risk adolescents: An evaluation of the self-report method. *Adolescence, 34,* 25–32.

Browne, A. (1993). Violence against women by male partners: Prevalence, outcomes, and policy implications. *American Psychologist, 48,* 1077–1087.

Bryson, K. (1998, March). *Census Bureau table.* Washington, DC: U.S. Bureau of the Census, Population Division. Fertility and Family Statistics Branch.

Buchanan, C. M., Eccles, J., Flanagan, C., Midgley, C., Feldlaufer, H., & Harold, R. (1990). Parents' and teachers' beliefs about adolescents: Effects of sex and experience. *Journal of Youth and Adolescence, 19,* 363–394.

Bukowski, W., Newcomb, A., & Hartup, W. (Eds.). (1996). *The company they keep: Friendships in childhood and adolescence.* New York: Cambridge University Press.

Burchinal, M., Roberts, J., Nabors, L., & Bryant, D. (1996). Quality of center child care and infant cognitive and language development. *Child Development, 67,* 606–620.

Burchinal, M., Roberts, J., Riggins, R., Zeisel, S., Neebe, E., & Bryant, D. (2000). Relating quality of center-based child care to early cognitive and language development longitudinally. *Child Development, 71,* 339–357.

Burns, B., & Taube, C. (1990). Mental health services in general medical care and in nursing homes. In B. Fogel, A. Furino, & C. Gottlieb (Eds.), *Mental health policy for older Americans: Protecting minds at risk.* Washington, DC: American Psychiatric Press.

Burns, S., & Brainard, C. (1979). Effects of constructive and dramatic play on perspective taking in very young children. *Merrill-Palmer Quarterly, 20,* 275–301.

Burr, J., & Mutchler, J. (1993). Nativity, acculturation, and economic status: Explanations of Asian American living arrangements in later life. *Journal of Gerontology, 48,* S55–S63.

Cabrera, N., Tamis-LeMonda, C., Bradley, R., Hofferth, S., & Lamb, M. (2000). Fatherhood in the twenty-first century. *Child Development, 71,* 127–136.

Caldera, Y., McDonald-Culp, A., O'Brien, M., Truglio, R., Alvarex, M., & Huston, A. (1999). Children's play preferences, construction play with blocks, and visual-spatial skills: Are they related? *International Journal of Behavioral Development, 23,* 855–872.

Camaioni, L., Longobardi, E., Venuti, P., & Bornstein, M. H. (1998). Maternal speech to 1-year-old children in two Italian cultural contexts. *Early Development and Parenting, 7,* 9–18.

Campbell, D. (1967). Stereotypes and the perception of group differences. *American Psychologist, 22,* 817–829.

Caruso, D. (1996). Maternal employment status, mother-infant interaction, and infant development. *Child and Youth Care Forum, 25,* 125–134.

Casper, L., & Bryson, K. (1998). *Coresident grandparents and their grandchildren: Grandparent-maintained families.* Population Division. Working Paper. Washington, DC: U.S. Bureau of the Census.

Caspi, A., Henry, B., McGee, R., Moffitt, T., & Silva, P. (1995). Temperamental origins of child and adolescent behavior problems: From age three to age fifteen. *Child Development, 66,* 55–68.

Caspi, A., & Silva, P. (1995). Temperamental qualities at age 3 predict personality traits in young adulthood: Longitudinal evidence from a birth cohort. *Child Development, 66,* 486–498.

Cassidy, J., & Berlin, L. (1994). The insecure/ambivalent pattern of attachment: Theory and research. *Child Development, 65,* 971–991.

Chase-Lansdale, P., Cherlin, A., & Kiernan, K. (1995). The long-term effects of parental divorce on the mental health of young adults: A developmental perspective. *Child Development, 66,* 1514–1634.

Chen, Z., & Siegler, R. (2000). Intellectual development in childhood. In R. Sternberg (Ed.), *Handbook of intelligence.* New York: Cambridge University Press.

Cherlin, A., & Furstenberg, F., Jr. (1986). *The new American grandparent.* New York: Basic Books.

Clark, D., Maddox, G., & Steinhauser, K. (1993). Race, aging, and functional health. *Journal of Aging and Health, 5,* 536–539.

Clark, M., & Ayers, M. (1991). Friendship similarity during early adolescence: Gender and racial patterns. *Journal of Psychology, 126,* 393–405.

Clarke-Stewart, A. (1993). *Daycare.* Cambridge, MA: Harvard University Press.

Cole, P., & Tamang, B. (1998). Nepali children's ideas about emotional displays in hypothetical challenges. *Developmental Psychology, 34,* 640–646.

Collins, N., & Miller, L. (1994). Self-disclosure and liking: A meta-analytic review. *Psychological Bulletin, 116,* 457–475.

Conley, O. (1999). Early sexual onset: A study of the relationship between social and psychological factors in the National Longitudinal Survey of Adolescent Health. *Dissertation Abstracts International, 59,* 2369.

Connolly, J., & Goldberg, A. (1999). Romantic relationships in adolescence: The role of friends and peers in their emergence and development. In W. Furman & B. Brown (Eds.), *The development of romantic relationships in adolescence.* New York: Cambridge University Press.

Corbin, C. (1973). *A textbook of motor development.* Dubuque, IA: Brown.

Costa, P., & McCrae, R. (1994). Stability and change in personality from adolescence through adulthood. In C. Halverson, G. Kohnstamm, & R. Martin (Eds.), *The developing structure of temperament and personality from infancy to adulthood.* Hillsdale, NJ: Erlbaum.

Cotterell, J. (1992). The relation of attachments and supports to adolescent well-being and school adjustment. *Journal of Adolescent Research, 7,* 28–42.

Craik, F. (2000). Age-related changes in human memory. In D. Park & N. Schwarz (Eds.), *Cognitive aging: A primer.* Philadelphia, PA: Psychology Press.

Cratty, B. (1979). *Perceptual and motor development in infants and children.* Englewood Cliffs, NJ: Prentice Hall.

Crick, N., Casas, J., & Ku, H.C. (1999). Relational and physical forms of peer victimization in preschool. *Developmental Psychology, 35,* 376–385.

Crowell, J., Kenner, M., Ginsburg, N., & Anders, T. (1987). Sleep habits in toddlers 18 to 36 months old. *American Journal of Child and Adolescent Psychiatry, 26,* 510–515.

Crystal, D., Chen, C., Fuligni, A., Stevenson, H., Hsu, C., Ko, H., Kitamura, S., & Kimura, S. (1994). Psychological maladjustment and academic achievement: A cross-cultural study of Japanese, Chinese, and American high school students. *Child Development, 65,* 738–753.

Cummings, E., Iannotti, R., & Zahn-Waxler, C. (1989). Aggression between peers in early childhood: Individual continuity and developmental change. *Child Development, 60,* 887–895.

Cunningham, P., & Boult, B. (1996). Black teenage pregnancy in South Africa: Some considerations. *Adolescence, 31,* 691–700.

Cushner, K. (1987). Teaching cross-cultural psychology: Providing the missing link. *Teaching of Psychology, 14,* 220–224.

Dancy, B. (1996). What African American women know, do, and feel about AIDS: A function of age and education. *AIDS Education and Prevention, 8,* 26–36.

Dasen, P., Inhelder, B., Lavalee, M., & Retschitzki, J. (1978). *Naissance de l'intelligence chez l'enfant Baoule de Cote d'Ivoire.* Bern, Switzerland: Hans Huber.

Davis, M., & Bibace, R. (1999). Dating couples and their relationships: Intimacy and contraceptive use. *Adolescence, 34,* 1–7.

DeFour, D. C., & Paludi, M. (1988, March). *Integrating the scholarship on ethnicity into the psychology of women course.* Paper presented at the meeting of the Association for Women in Psychology, Bethesda, MD.

Denmark, F., Russo, N., Frieze, I., & Sechzer, J. (1988). Guidelines for avoiding sexism in psychological research: A report of the ad hoc committee on nonsexist research. *American Psychologist, 43,* 582–585.

Diaz Rossello, J. (1988). La relacion madre-hijo en el periodo inicial. In M. Cusminsky, E. Moreno, & E. Suarez Ojeda (Eds.), *Crecimiento y desarrollo.* Buenos Aires, Argentina: Organizacio Panamericana de la Salud.

DiBliasio, F., & Benda, B. (1990). Adolescent sexual behavior: Multivariate analysis of a social learning model. *Journal of Adolescent Research, 5,* 449–466.

DiClemente, R., Boyer, C., & Morales, E. (1998). Minorities and AIDS: Knowledge, attitude, and misconceptions among Black and Latino adolescents. *American Journal of Public Health, 78,* 55–57.

Dien, D. (1983). Big me and little me: A Chinese perspective on self. *Psychiatry, 46,* 281–286.

Dietz, W. (1987). Childhood obesity. *Annals of the New York Academy of Sciences, 499,* 47–54.

Dixon, R., & Hultsch, D. (1999). Intelligence and cognitive potential in late life. In J. Cavanaugh & S. Whitbourne (Eds.), *Gerontology: An interdisciplinary perspective.* New York: Oxford University Press.

D'Odorico, L., Salerni, N., Cassibba, R., & Jacob, V. (1999). Stability and change of maternal speech to Italian infants from 7 to 21 months of age: A longitudinal study of its influence on early stages of language acquisition. *First Language, 19,* 313–346.

Doering, M., Rhodes, S., & Schuster, M. (1983). The aging worker: Research and recommendations. Beverly Hills, CA: Sage.

Dondi, M., Simon, F., & Caltran, G. (1999). Can newborns discriminate between their own cry and the cry of another newborn infant? *Developmental Psychology, 35,* 418–426.

Doi, T. (1973). *The anatomy of dependence.* New York: Norton.

Doyle, J., & Paludi, M. (1997). *Sex and gender.* New York: McGraw-Hill.

Duncan, G., & Brooks-Gunn, J. (2000). Family poverty, welfare reform, and child development. *Child Development, 71,* 188–196.

Eaton, W., & Yu, A. (1989). Are sex differences in child motor activity level a function of sex differences in maturational status? *Child Development, 60,* 1005–1011.

Eccles, J., Adler, T., & Meece, J. (1984). Sex differences in achievement: A test of alternative theories. *Journal of Personality and Social Psychology, 46,* 26–43.

Egeland, B., & Farber, E. (1984). Infant-mother attachment: Factors related to its development and changes over time. *Child Development, 55,* 753–771.

Ehri, L. (1993). How English orthography influences phonological knowledge as children learn to read and spell. In R. Scholes (Ed.), *Literacy and language analysis.* Hillsdale, NJ: Erlbaum.

Elkind, D. (1984). *All grown up and no place to go.* Reading, MA: Addison-Wesley.

Ellwood, M., & Stolberg, A. (1993). The effects of family composition, family health, parenting behavior and environmental stress on children's divorce adjustment. *Journal of Child and Family Studies, 2,* 23–36.

Engle, P., & Breaux, C. (1998). Fathers' involvement with children: Perspectives from developing countries. *Social policy report,* Society for Research in Child Development, XII, 2–21.

Epstein, L. (1992). Exercise and obesity in children. *Journal of Applied Sport Psychology, 4,* 120–133.

Erikson, E. (1963). *Childhood and society.* New York: Norton.

Erkut, S., Szalacha, L., Alarcon, O., & Coll, C. (1999). Stereotyped perceptions of adolescents' health risk behaviors. *Cultural Diversity and Ethnic Minority Psychology, 5,* 340–349.

Etaugh, C. (1993). Women in the middle and later years. In F. Denmark & M. Paludi (Eds.), *Psychology of women: A handbook of issues and theories.* Westport, CT: Greenwood Press.

Eveleth, P., & Tanner, J. (1976). *Worldwide variation in human growth.* New York: Cambridge University Press.

Fabes, R., Eisenberg, N., Jones, S., Smith, M., Guthrie, I., Poulin, R., Shepard, S., Friedman, J. (1999). Regulation, emotionality, and preschoolers' socially competent peer interactions. *Child Development, 70,* 432–442.

Farber, J., & Branstetter, W. (1994). Preschoolers' prosocial responses to their peers' distress. *Developmental Psychology, 30,* 334–341.

Farrar, M. (1992). Negative evidence and grammatical morpheme acquisition. *Developmental Psychology, 28,* 90–98.

Feingold, A. (1993). Cognitive gender differences: A developmental perspective. *Sex Roles, 29,* 91–112.

Feldman, R. (1998). *Child development.* Upper Saddle River, NJ: Prentice Hall.

Ferber, R. (1986). *Solve your child's sleep problems.* New York: Simon & Schuster.

Fernald, A. (1989). Intonation and communicative intent in mothers' speech to infants: Is the melody the message? *Child Development, 60,* 1497–1510.

Fernald, A. (1991). Prosody in speech to children: Prelinguistic and linguistic functions. In R. Vasta (Ed.), *Annals of child development* (Vol. 8). London: Jessica Kingsley.

Fernald, A., & Kuhl, P. (1987). Acoustic determinants of infant preference for motherese speech. *Infant Behavior and Development, 10,* 279–293.

Ferron, C. (1997). Body image in adolescence: Cross-cultural research—Results of the preliminary phase of a quantitative survey. *Adolescence, 32,* 735–744.

Ferrucci, L., Guralnik, J., Cecchi, F., Marchionni, N., Salani, B., Kasper, J., Celli, R., Giardini, S., Heikkinen, E., Jylha, M., & Baroni, A. (1998). Constant hierarchic patterns of physical functioning across seven populations in five countries. *The Gerontologist, 38,* 286–294.

Finkelhor, D., & Dziuba-Leatherman, J. (1994). Victimization of children. *American Psychologist, 49,* 173–183.

Flora, J., & Thoresen, C. (1988). Reducing the risk of AIDS in adolescents. *American Psychologist, 43,* 965–970.

Forrest, J., & Singh, S. (1990). The sexual and reproductive behavior of American women, 1982–1988. *Family Planning Perspectives, 22,* 206–214.

Fox, M., Gibbs, M., & Auerbach, D. (1985). Age and gender dimensions of friendship. *Psychology of Women Quarterly, 9,* 489–502.

Fozard, J. (1990). Vision and hearing. In J. Birren & K. W. Schaie (Ed.), *Handbook of the psychology of aging.* New York: Academic Press.

Freedman, V., & Martin, L. (1999). The role of education in explaining and forecasting trends in functional limitations among older Americans. *Demography, 36,* 461–473.

French, L., & Picthall-French, N. (1998). The role of substance abuse among rural youth by race, culture, and gender. *Alcoholism Treatment Quarterly, 16,* 101–108.

Friedlander, M., Larney, L., Skau, M., Hotaling, M., Cutting, M., & Schwam, M. (2000). Bicultural identification: Experiences of internationally adopted children and their parents. *Journal of Counseling Psychology, 47,* 187–198.

Frisch, R. (1984). Fatness, puberty, and fertility. In B. Gunn & A. Petersen (Eds.), *Girls at puberty: Biological, psychological, and social perspectives.* New York: Plenum.

Gaertner, S., Mann, J., Dovidio, J., Morell, A., & Pomare, M. (1990). How does cooperation reduce intergroup bias? *Journal of Personality and Social Psychology, 66,* 692–704.

Ge, X., Conger, R., & Elder, G. (1996). Coming of age too early: Pubertal influences on girls' vulnerability to psychological distress. *Child development, 67,* 3386–4000.

Geer, C., & Shields, S. (1996). Women and emotion: Stereotypes and the double bind. In J. Chrisler, C. Golden, & P. Rozee (Eds.), *Lectures on the psychology of women.* New York: McGraw-Hill.

George, L. (1990). Social structure, social processes, and social-psychological states. In R. Binstock & L. George (Eds.), *Handbook of aging and the social sciences.* San Diego, CA: Academic Press.

George, S. (2000). Barriers to breast cancer screening: An integrative review. *Health Care for Women International, 21,* 53–65.

Gilbert, L. (1994). Current perspectives on dual-career families. *Current Directions in Psychological Science, 3,* 101–105.

Gill, N. (1999). Internalized shame: Challenges to self and parenting: A cross-generational narrative study. *Dissertation Abstracts International, 60,* 0864.

Gindes, M. (2000). Child custody. In F. Kaslow (Ed.), *Handbook of couple and family forensics: A sourcebook for mental health and legal professionals.* New York: Wiley.

Ginorio, A., Gutierrez, L., Cauce, A., & Acosta, M. (1995). Psychological issues for Latinas. In H. Landrine (Ed.), *Bringing cultural diversity to feminist psychology: Theory, research, and practice.* Washington, DC: American Psychological Association.

Gleason, J. B. (1987). Sex differences in parent-child interaction. In S. Philips, S. Steele, & C. Tanz (Eds.), *Language, gender, and sex in comparative perspective.* New York: Cambridge University Press.

Gleason, J. B., Perlmann, R., Ely, R., & Evans, D. (1991). The babytalk register: Parents' use of diminutives. In J. Sokolov & C. Snow (Eds.), *Handbook of research in language development using CHILDES.* Hillsdale, NJ: Erlbaum.

Göncü, A., & Mosier, C. (1991, April). *Cultural variation in the play of toddlers.* Paper presented at the biennial meeting of the Society for Research in Child Development, Seattle, WA.

Gortmaker, S., Must, A., Sobol, A., Peterson, K., Coditz, G., & Dietz, W. (1996). Television viewing as a cause of increasing obesity among children in the United States, 1986–1990. *Archives of Pediatrics & Adolescent Medicine, 150,* 356–362.

Gottfried, A., & Gottfried, A. (Eds.). (1994). *Redefining families.* New York: Plenum.

Gough, P., Juel, C., & Griffith, P. (1992). Reading, spelling, and the orthographic cipher. In P. Gough, L. Ehri, & R. Treiman (Ed.), *Reading acquisition.* Hillsdale, NJ: Erlbaum.

Graham, D., & Rawlings, E. (1999). Observers' blaming of battered wives: Who, what, where and why? In M. Paludi (Ed.), *Psychology of sexual victimization: A handbook.* Westport, CT: Greenwood Press.

Graham, S. (1992). "Most of the subjects were white and middle class": Trends in published research on African Americans in selected APA Journals, 1970–1989. *American Psychologist, 47,* 629–639.

Greenberg, M., Cicchetti, D., & Cummings, E. (Eds.). (1990). *Attachment in the preschool years: Theory, research, and intervention.* Chicago: University of Chicago Press.

Greenberger, E., Chen, C., Tally, S., & Dong, Q. (2000). Family, peer, and individual correlates of depressive symptomatology among U.S. and Chinese adolescents. *Journal of Consulting and Clinical Psychology, 68,* 209–219.

Gross, I., Downing, J., & d'Heurle, A. (1982). *Sex role attitudes and cultural change.* Boston: Reidel Publishing.

Grossman, K., Grossman, K., Huber, F., & Wartner, U. (1982). German children's behavior towards their mothers at 12 months and their fathers at 18 months in Ainsworth's Strange Situation. *International Journal of Behavioral Development, 4,* 157–181.

Guneri, O., Sumer, Z., & Yildirim, A. (1999). Sources of self-identity among Turkish adolescents. *Adolescence, 34,* 535–547.

Gunn, B., & Petersen, A. (Eds.). (1984). *Girls at puberty: Biological, psychological, and social perspectives.* New York: Plenum.

Gupta, M. (1995). Concerns about aging and a drive for thinness: A factor in the biopsychosocial model of eating disorders? *International Journal of Eating Disorders, 18,* 351–357.

Hagestad, G. (1985). Community and connectedness. In V. Bengston & J. Robertson (Eds.), *Grandparenthood.* Beverly Hills, CA: Sage.

Hagestad, G. (1988). Demographic change and the life course: Some emerging trends in the family realm. *Family Relations, 37,* 405–410.

Hall, G. S. (1904). *Adolescence: Its psychology and its relation to physiology, anthropology, sociology, sex, crime, religion, and education.* Englewood Cliffs, NJ: Prentice Hall.

Halpern, D. (1995). Cognitive gender differences: Why diversity is a critical research issue. In H. Landrine (Ed.), *Bringing cultural diversity to feminist psychology.* Washington, DC: American Psychological Association.

Hansen, J., & Bowey, J. (1994). Phonological analysis skills, verbal working memory, and reading ability in second-grade children. *Child Development, 65,* 938–950.

Hart, B., & Risley, T. (1995). *Meaningful differences in the everyday experience of young American children.* Baltimore: Brookes.

Hartup, W., & Stevens, N. (1999). Friendships and adaptation across the life span. *Current directions in Psychological Science, 8,* 76–79.

Hatcher, C., Barton, C., & Brooks, L. (2000). Parental abduction. In F. Kaslow (Ed.), *Handbook of couple and family forensics: A sourcebook for mental health and legal professionals.* New York: Wiley.

Hatcher, P., Hulme, C., & Ellis, A. (1994). Ameliorating early reading failure by integrating the teaching of reading and phonological skills: The phonological linkage hypothesis. *Child Development, 65,* 41–57.

Hay, D., Castle, J., & Davies, L. (2000). Toddlers' use of force against familiar peers: A precursor of serious aggression? *Child Development, 71,* 457–467.

Hayflick, L. (1994). *How and why we age.* New York: Ballantine Books.

Helson, R. (1999). A longitudinal study of creative personality in women. *Creativity Research Journal, 12,* 89–101.

Henley, N. (1995). Ethnicity and gender issues in language. In H. Landrine (Ed.), *Bringing cultural diversity to feminist psychology: Theory, research, and practice.* Washington, DC: American Psychological Association.

Henriques, G., Calhoun, L., & Cann, A. (1996). Ethnic differences in women's body satisfaction: An experimental investigation. *Journal of Social Psychology, 136,* 689–697.

Herek, G., & Glunt, E. (1988). An epidemic of stigma: Public reactions to AIDS. *American Psychologist, 43,* 886–891.

Hetherington, E. M., & Stanley-Hagan, M. (1999). The adjustment of children with divorced parents: A risk and resiliency perspective. *Journal of Child Psychology and Psychiatry and Allied Disciplines, 40,* 129–140.

Hetherington, E. M., Stanley-Hagan, M., & Anderson, E. (1989). Marital transitions: A child's perspective. *American Psychologist, 44,* 303–312.

Hoffman, L. W. (1989). Effects of maternal employment in the two-parent family. *American Psychologist, 44,* 283–292.

Hopkins, B., & Westra, T. (1989). Maternal expectations of their infants' development: An intracultural study. *Genetic Psychology Monographs, 114,* 377–420.

Hoyer, W., Rybash, J., & Roodin, P. (1999). *Adult development and aging.* New York: McGraw-Hill.

Hultsch, D., & Dixon, R. (1990). Learning and memory in aging. In J. Birren & K. W. Schaie (Eds.), *Handbook on the psychology of aging.* New York: Academic Press.

Hunt, E., & Hertzog, C. (1981). *Age-related changes in cognition during the working years.* Arlington, VA: Office of Naval Research.

Hussong, A. (2000). The settings of adolescent alcohol and drug use. *Journal of Youth and Adolescence, 29,* 107–119.

Hyde, J., Fennema, E., Ryan, M., Frost, L., & Hopp, C. (1990). Gender differences in verbal ability: A meta-analysis. *Psychological Bulletin, 104,* 53–69.

Hyde, J. S., & DeLamater, J. (1999). *Understanding human sexuality.* New York: McGraw-Hill.

Indian Health Service (1991). *Indian women's health care: Consensus statement.* Rockville, MD: U.S. Department of Health and Human Services.

Ishii-Kuntz, M. (1994). Parental involvement and perception toward fathers' roles: A comparison between Japan and the United States. *Journal of Family Issues, 15,* 30–48.

Jacobs, K. (1978). *Responsibility for birth control: Sex differences and personality correlates.* Paper presented at the annual convention of the Southeastern Psychological Association, Atlanta, GA.

Jacobsen, L., & Edmondson, B. (1993, August). *American Demographics,* 22–27.

Jacobson, N. (1987). Family type, visiting patterns, and children's behavior in the stepfamily: A linked family system. In K. Pasley & M. Ihinger-Tallman (Eds.), *Remarriage and stepparenting.* New York: Guilford Press.

Joe, J., & Justice, J. (1992). Introduction: Proceedings of the first national conference on cancer in Native Americans. *American Indian Culture and Research Journal, 16,* 9–20.

Jourard, S. (1964). *The transparent self.* Princeton, NJ: Van Nostrand.

Jusczyk, P. (1999). Narrowing the distance to language: One step at a time. *Journal of Communications Disorders, 32,* 207–222.

Kagan, J. (1984). *The nature of the child.* New York: Basic Books.

Kagan, J., & Snidman, N. (1991). Temperamental factors in human development. *American Psychologist, 46,* 856–862.

Kalish, R. (1985). The social context of death and dying. In R. Binstock & E. Shanas (Eds.), *Handbook of aging and the social sciences.* New York: Van Nostrand-Reinhold.

Kaplan, M., & Pruett, K. (2000). Divorce and custody: Developmental implications. In C. Zeanah (Ed.), *Handbook of infant mental health.* New York: Guilford Press.

Katchadorian, H. (1977). *The biology of adolescence.* San Francisco: Freeman.

Kaufman, S. (1998). Intensive care, old age, and the problem of death in America. *The Gerontologist, 38,* 715–725.

Kemper, R., & Vernooy, A. (1994). Metalinguistic awareness in first graders: A qualitative perspective. *Journal of Psycholinguistic Research, 22,* 41–57.

Kessler, R., McGonagle, K., Zhao, S., Nelson, C., Hughes, M., Eshleman, S., Wittchen, H., & Kendler, K. (1994). Lifetime and 12-month prevalence of DSM-III-R psychiatric disorders in the United States. *Archives of General Psychiatry, 51,* 8–19.

Kivett, V. (1991). Centrality of the grandfather role among older rural black and white men. *Journal of Gerontology, 46,* S250–S258.

Kligman, A., Grove, A., & Balin, A. (1985). Aging of human skin. In C. Finch & E. Schneider (Eds.), *Handbook on the biology of aging.* New York: Van Nostrand-Reinhold.

Klonoff, E., Landrine, H., & Scott, J. (1995). Double jeopardy: Ethnicity and gender in health research. In H. Landrine (Ed.), *Bringing cultural diversity to feminist psychology: Theory, research and practice.* Washington, DC: American Psychological Association.

Kroger, J. (2000). *Identity development: Adolescence through adulthood.* Thousand Oaks, CA: Sage.

Kunkel, E., Bakker, J., Myers, R., Oyesanmi, O., & Gomella, L. (2000). Biopsychosocial aspects of prostate cancer. *Psychosomatics, 4,* 85–94.

Laakso, M., Hallikainen, J., Haenninen, T., Partanen, K., & Soininen, H. (2000). Diagnosis of Alzheimer's disease: MRI of the hippocampus vs. delayed recall. *Neuropsychologia, 38,* 579–584.

Lackovic-Grgin, K., Dekovic, M., & Opacic, G. (1994). Pubertal status, interaction with significant others, and self-esteem of adolescent girls. *Adolescence, 29,* 691–700.

LaFromboise, T., Choney, S., James, A., & Running Wolf, P. (1995). American Indian women and psychology. In H. Landrine (Ed.), *Bringing cultural diversity to feminist psychology.* Washington, DC: American Psychological Association.

LaFromboise, T., Coleman, H., & Gerton, J. (1993). Psychological impact of biculturalism: Evidence and theory. *Psychological Bulletin, 114,* 395–412.

Lagana, L. (1999). Psychosocial correlates of contraceptive practices during late adolescence. *Adolescence, 34,* 463–482.

Lamb, M. (Ed.). (1997). *The role of the father in child development.* New York: Wiley.

Lamb, M. (1999). Noncustodial fathers and their impact on the children of divorce. In R. Thompson and P. Amato (Eds.), *The postdivorce family: Children, parenting, and society.* Thousand Oaks, CA: Sage.

Lamb, M., Ketterlinus, R., & Fracasso, M. (1992). Parent-child relationships. In M. H. Bornstein & M. Lamb (Eds.), *Developmental psychology: An advanced textbook.* Hillsdale, NJ: Erlbaum.

Landrine, H. (Ed.). (1995). *Bringing cultural diversity to feminist psychology.* Washington, DC: American Psychological Association.

Landrine, H., Klonoff, E., & Brown-Collins, A. (1995). Cultural diversity and methodology in feminist psychology: Critique, proposal, empirical example. In H. Landrine (Ed.), *Bringing cultural diversity to feminist psychology.* Washington, DC: American Psychological Association.

Launer, L., Dinkgreve, M., Jonker, C., Hooijer, C., & Lindeboom, J. (1993). Are age and education independent correlates of the mini-mental state exam performance of community-swelling elderly? *Journal of Gerontololgy, 48,* P271–P277.

Leenaars, A. (1999). Suicide across the adult life span: Replications and failures. *Archives of Suicide Research, 5,* 261–274.

Lefkowitz, E., Romo, L., Corona, R., Au, T., & Sigman, M. (2000). How Latino Americans and European American adolescents discuss conflicts, sexuality, and AIDS with their mothers. *Developmental Psychology, 36,* 315–325.

Lennox, C., & Siegel, L. (1995). Development of orthographic and phonological processes in normal and disabled reading. In V. W. Berninger (Ed.), *The varieties of orthographic knowledge II: Relationships to phonology, reading, and writing.* Norwell, MA: Kluwer Academic.

Lester, D. (1990). The Collett-Lester fear of death scale: The original version and a revision. *Death Studies, 14,* 451–468.

Levinson, D. (1986). A conception of adult development. *American Psychologist, 41,* 3–13.

Lewis, C. (1997). Fathers and preschoolers. In M. Lamb (Ed.), *The role of the father in child development.* New York: Wiley.

Libra, T. (1987). The cultural significance of silence in Japanese communication. *Multilingua, 6,* 343–357.

Lim, S. (1998). Linking play and language in Singapore preschool settings. *Early Child Development and Care, 144,* 21–36.

Linder, D. (1999). Parental kidnapping and child abuse: What is the appropriate intervention? In M. A. Paludi (Ed.), *The psychology of sexual victimization: A handbook.* Westport, CT: Greenwood Press.

Litterick, J. (1998). Family factors associated with levels of adolescent substance abuse. *Dissertation Abstracts International, 59,* 1370.

Livson, N., & Peskin, H. (1980). Perspectives on adolescence from longitudinal research. In J. Adelson (Ed.), *Handbook of adolescent psychology.* New York: Wiley.

Lloyd, P., & Cohen, E. (1999). Peer status in the middle school: A natural treatment for unequal participation. *Social Psychology of Education, 3,* 193–216.

Lorion, R., & Saltzman, W. (1993). Children's exposure to community violence: Following a path from concern to research action. *Psychiatry, 56,* 55–65.

Lozoff, B., Wolf, A., & Davis, N. (1984). Cosleeping in urban families with young children in the United States. *Pediatrics, 74,* 171–182.

Maccoby, E. E., & Jacklin, C. N. (1974). *The psychology of sex differences.* Stanford, CA: Stanford University Press.

MacPhee, D., Kreutzer, J., & Fritz, J. (1994). Infusing a diversity perspective into human development courses. *Child Development, 65,* 699–715.

Marsiglio, W. (1991). Paternal engagement activities with minor children. *Journal of Marriage and the Family, 53,* 973–986.

Martin, E. (1987). *The woman in the body: A cultural analysis of reproduction.* Boston: Beacon Press.

Masataka, N. (1993). Motherese in a language. *Infant Behavior and Development, 15,* 453–460.

Matthews, S. (1986). *Friendships through the life course.* Newbury Park, CA: Sage.

Mayo, C., & Henley, N. (Eds.). (1981). *Gender and nonverbal behavior.* New York: Springer-Verlag.

McBarnette, L. (1996). African American women. In M. Bayne-Smith (Ed.), *Race, gender and health.* Newbury Park, CA: Sage.

McCarty, M., & Ashmead, D. (1999). Visual control of reaching and grasping in infants. *Developmental Psychology, 35,* 620–631.

McClure, E. (2000). A meta-analytic review of sex differences in facial expression processing and their development in infants, children, and adolescents. *Psychological Bulletin, 126,* 424–453.

McConnell, R., & Sim, A. (1999). Adjustment to parental divorce: An examination of the differences between counselled and non-counselled children. *British Journal of Guidance and Counselling, 27,* 245–257.

McCrae, R., & Costa, P. (1987). Validation of the five-factor model of personality across instruments and observers. *Journal of Personality and Social Psychology, 52,* 81–90.

McDermott, R., & Gold, R. (1985). *Gender differences in perception of contraception alternatives by never-married college students.* Paper presented at the national convention of the American Alliance for Health, Physical Education, Recreation, and Dance, Atlanta, GA.

McDonald, M., Sigman, M., Espinosa, M., & Neumann, C. (1994). Impact of a temporary food shortage on children and their mothers. *Child Development, 65,* 404–415.

McGoldrick, M., Giordano, J., & Pearce, J. (Eds.). (1996). *Ethnicity and family therapy.* New York: Guilford Press.

McHugh, M., Koeske, R., & Frieze, I. (1986). Issues to consider in conducting nonsexist psychological research: A guide for researchers. *American Psychologist, 41,* 879–890.

McKenna, J. (1986). An anthropological perspective on the Sudden Infant Death Syndrome: The role of parental breathing cues and speech breathing adaptations. *Medical Anthropology, 10,* 9–92.

McKenna, M., Zevon, M., Corn, B., & Rounds, J. (1999). Psychosocial factors and the development of breast cancer: A meta-analysis. *Health Psychology, 18,* 520–531.

Michael, R., Gagnon, J., Laumann, E., & Kolata, G. (1994). *Sex in America: A definitive survey.* Boston: Little, Brown.

Miedzian, M. (1991). *Boys will be boys: Breaking the link between masculinity and violence.* New York: Doubleday.

Miller, B., & Benson, B. (1999). Romantic and sexual relationship development during adolescence. In W. Furman and B. Brown (Eds.), *The development of romantic relationships in adolescence.* New York: Cambridge University Press.

Miller, D. (1999). Racial socialization and racial identity: Can they promote resiliency for African American adolescents? *Adolescence, 34,* 493–501.

Mills, T. (1999). When grandchildren grow up: Role transition and family solidarity among baby boomer grandchildren and their grandparents. *Journal of Aging Studies, 13,* 219–239.

Minkler, M., & Roe, K. (1993). *Grandmothers as caregivers: Raising children of the crack cocaine epidemic.* Newbury Park, CA: Sage.

Molfese, D., & Molfese, V. (2000). The continuum of language development during infancy and early childhood: Electrophysiological correlates. In C. Rovee-Collier & L. Lipsett (Eds.), *Progress in infancy research.* Mahwah, NJ: Erlbaum.

Mollica, R., Wyshak, G., & Lavelle, J. (1987). The psychological impact of war trauma and torture on Southeast Asian refugees. *American Journal of Psychiatry, 144,* 1567–1571.

Mott, F. (1994). Sons, daughters, and fathers' absence: Differentials in father-leaving probabilities and in-home environments. *Journal of Family Issues, 15,* 97–128.

Mueller, U. (1999). Structure and content of formal operational thought: An interpretation in context. *Archives de Psychologie, 67,* 21–35.

Munroe, R., Munroe, R., & Whiting, J. (1981). Male sex-role resolutions. In R. Munroe, R. Munroe, & B. Whiting (Eds.), *Handbook of cross-cultural human development.* New York: Garland.

Nakagawa, M., Lamb, M., & Miyaki, K. (1992). Antecedents and correlates of the Strange Situation behavior of Japanese infants. *Journal of Cross Cultural Psychology, 23,* 300–310.

Neimeyer, R., & Chapman, K. (1981). Self/ideal discrepancy and fear of death: The test of an existential hypothesis. *Omega, 11,* 233–239.

New, R. (1994). Child's play–una cosa naturale: An Italian perspective. In J. Roopnarine, J. Johnson, & F. Hopper (Eds.), *Children's play in diverse cultures.* Albany: State University of New York Press.

Newman, B., & Newman, P. (1975). *Development through life.* Homewood, IL: Dorsey.

Nugent, J., Lester, B., & Brazelton, T. (Eds.). (1989). *The cultural context of infancy: Vol. 1. Biology, culture, and infant development.* Norwood, NJ: Ablex.

O'Dea, J., & Abraham, S. (1999). Onset of disordered eating attitudes and behaviors in early adolescence: Interplay of pubertal status, gender, weight, and age. *Adolescence, 34,* 671–679.

Old Dog Cross, P. (1982). Sexual abuse: A new threat to the Native American woman: An overview. *Listening Post, 6,* 18.

Osofsky, J. (1995). The effects of exposure to violence on young children. *American Psychologist, 50,* 782–788.

Osofsky, J., Wewers, S., Hann, D., & Flick, A. (1993). Chronic community violence: What is happening to our children? *Psychiatry, 58,* 36–45.

Ott, B., Lapane, K., & Gambassi, G. (2000). Gender differences in the treatment of behavior problems in Alzheimer's disease. *Neurology, 54,* 427–432.

Paludi, M. (1997). *The psychology of women.* Upper Saddle River, NJ: Prentice Hall.

Paludi, M. (Ed.). (1999). *The psychology of sexual victimization: A handbook.* Westport, CT: Greenwood Press.

Paludi, M., Paludi, C., & Doyle, J. (in press). *Sex and gender: The human experience* (5th ed.). New York: McGraw-Hill.

Park, K., Lay, K., & Ramsay, L. (1993). Individual differences and developmental changes in preschoolers' friendships. *Developmental Psychology, 29,* 264–270.

Pearson, J., & Thoennes, N. (1990). Custody after divorce: Demographic and attitudinal patterns. *American Journal of Orthopsychiatry, 60,* 233–249.

Pedro-Carroll, J., Sutton, S., & Wyman, P. (1999). A two-year follow-up evaluation of a preventive intervention for young children of divorce. *School Psychology Review, 28,* 467–476.

Pennington, H. (1999). Cognitive aspects of ageing as portrayed in introductory psychology texts. *New Zealand Journal of Psychology, 28,* 48–50.

Perlin, L. (1989). The sociological study of stress. *Journal of Health and Social Behavior, 30,* 241–256.

Perlmann, R., & Gleason, J. (1990, July). *Patterns of prohibition in mothers' speech to children.* Paper presented at the Fifth International Congress for the Study of Child Language, Budapest, Hungary.

Petersen, A., Bingham, R., Stemmler, M., & Crockett, L. (1991, July). *Subcultural variations in development of depressed affect.* Poster presented at the biennial meeting of the International Society for the Study of Behavioral Development, Minneapolis, MN.

Petersen, A., & Taylor, B. (1980). The biological approach to adolescence. In J. Adelson (Ed.), *Handbook of adolescent psychology.* New York: Wiley.

Phillips, D., Voran, M., Kisker, E., Howes, C., & Whitebook, M. (1994). Child care for children in poverty: Opportunity or inequity? *Child Development, 65,* 472–492.

Piaget, J., & Inhelder, B. (1958). *The growth of logical thinking from childhood to adolescence* (A. Parsons & S. Seagrin, Trans.). New York: Basic Books.

Pipher, M. (1994). *Reviving Ophelia: Saving the selves of adolescent girls.* New York: Ballantine.

Podrouzek, W., & Furrow, D. (1988). Preschoolers' use of eye contact while speaking: The influence of sex, age, and conversational pattern. *Psycholinguistic Research, 17,* 89–98.

Porter, R., Bologh, R., & Makin, J. (1988). Olfactory influences on mother-infant interactions. In C. Rovee-Collier & L. Lipsitt (Eds.), *Advances in infancy research* (Vol. 5). Norwood, NJ: Ablex.

Rabinor, J. (1994). Mothers, daughters, and eating disorders: Honoring the mother-daughter relationship. In P. Fallon, M. Katzman, & S. Wooley (Eds.), *Feminist perspectives on eating disorders.* New York: Guilford Press.

Ralston, P. (1991). Senior centers and minority elders: A critical review. *The Gerontologist, 31,* 325–331.

Rathus, S. (1988). *Human sexuality.* New York: Holt, Rinehart, & Winston.

Red Horse, J. (1980). Family structure and value orientation in American Indians. *Social Casework, 61,* 462–467.

Reid, P., & Paludi, M. (1993). The psychology of women: Conception to adolescence. In F. Denmark & M. Paludi (Eds.), *Psychology of women: A handbook of issues and theories.* Westport, CT: Greenwood Press.

Ricciardelli, L. (1992). Bilingualism and cognitive development in relation to threshold theory. *Journal of Psycholinguistic Research, 21,* 301–316.

Rice, F. P. (1997). *Child and adolescent development.* Upper Saddle River, NJ: Prentice Hall.

Riese, M. (1990). Neonatal temperament in monozygotic and dizygotic twin pairs. *Child Development, 61,* 1230–1237.

Rimonte, N. (1989). Domestic violence among Pacific Asians. In Asian Women United (Eds.), *Making waves: An anthology of writings by and about Asian American women.* Boston: Beacon Press.

Rodman, H., & Cole, C. (1987). Latchkey children: A review of policy and resources. *Family Relations, 36,* 101–105.

Rogoff, B., Mistry, J., Göncü, A., & Mosier, C. (1993). Guided participation in cultural activity by toddlers and caregivers. *Monographs of the Society for Research in Child Development, 58,* 179.

Romaine, S. (1994). *Bilingualism.* London: Blackwell.

Romero, M., & Tolbert, K. (1995, June). *La consulta externa como oportunidad de deteccion de la vilencia domestica.* Paper presented at the National Council of International Health Conference, Crystal City, VA.

Roopnarine, J., Johnson, J., & Hooper, F. (Eds.). (1994). *Children's play in diverse cultures.* Albany: State University of New York Press.

Root, M. (1995). Psychology of Asian American women. In H. Landrine (Ed.), *Bringing cultural diversity to feminist psychology*. Washington, DC: American Psychological Association.

Rose, S. (1995). Friendships and women. In J. Chrisler, C. Golden, & P. Rozee (Eds.), *Lectures on the psychology of women*. New York: McGraw-Hill.

Rothbart, M. K. (1989). Temperament in childhood: A framework. In G. Kohnstamm, J. Bates, & M. Rothbart (Eds.), *Temperament in childhood*. New York: Wiley.

Rubin, K. (1998). Social and emotional development from a cultural perspective. *Developmental Psychology, 34,* 611–615.

Russell, G., & Radojevic, M. (1992). The changing role of fathers? Current understandings and future directions for research and practice. Special Section, Australian Regional Meeting: Attachment and the relationship of infant and caregivers. *Infant Mental Health Journal, 13,* 296–311.

Russo, N., & Green, B. (1993). Women and mental health. In F. Denmark & M. Paludi (Eds.), *Psychology of women: A handbook of issues and theories*. Westport, CT: Greenwood Press.

Ryan, K., Frieze, I. H., & Sinclair, H. C. (1999). Physical violence in dating relationships. In M. A. Paludi (Ed.). *The psychology of sexual victimization: A handbook*. Westport, CT: Greenwood Press.

Saarni, C. (1998). Issues of cultural meaningfulness in emotional development. *Developmental Psychology, 34,* 647–652.

Saewyc, E., Bearinger, L., Heinz, P., Blum, R., & Resnick, M. (1998). Gender differences in health and risk behaviors among bisexual and homosexual adolescents. *Journal of Adolescent Health, 23,* 181–188.

Sagi, A. (1990). Attachment theory and research from a cross-cultural perspective. *Human Development, 33,* 10–23.

Sagi, A., van IJzendoorn, M., & Koren-Karie, N. (1991). Primary appraisal of the Strange Situation: A cross-cultural analysis of preseparation episodes. *Developmental Psychology, 27,* 587–596.

Sanson, A., Smart, D., Prior, M., Oberklaid, F., & Pedlow, R. (1994). The structure of temperament from age 3 to 7 years: Age, sex, and sociodemographic influences. *Merrill-Palmer Quarterly, 40,* 233–252.

Sarigiani, P. A., Wilson, J., Petersen, A., & Vicary, J. (1990). Self-image and educational plans for adolescence from two contrasting communities. *Journal of Early Adolescence, 10,* 37–55.

Scarr, S., Phillips, D., & McCartney, K. (1989). Working mothers and their families. *American Psychologist, 44,* 1402–1409.

Schaie, K. W., & Willis, S. (1998). Can decline in adult intellectual functioning be reversed? In M. Lawton & T. Salthouse (Eds.), *Essential papers on the psychology of aging*. New York: New York University Press.

Schowalter, J., & Anyan, W. (1981). *Family handbook of adolescence*. New York: Knopf.

Schulz, R. (1978). *The psychology of death, dying, and bereavement*. Reading, MA: Addison-Wesley.

Schwarz, N., & Knaeuper, B. (2000). Cognition, aging, and self-reports. In D. Park & N. Schwarz (Eds.), *Cognitive aging: A primer*. Philadelphia, PA: Psychology Press.

Sherry, B., Springer, D., Connell, F., & Garrett, S. (1992). Short, thin, or obese? Comparing growth indexes of children from high- and low-poverty areas. *Journal of the American Dietetic Association, 92,* 1092–1095.

Simon, R., & Alstein, H. (1991). Intercountry adoptions: Experiences of families in the United States. In H. Alstein & R. Simon (Eds.), *Intercountry adoption: A multinational perspective*. New York: Praeger.

Sinacore-Guinn, A. (1998). Employed mothers: Job satisfaction and self-esteem. *Canadian Journal of Counseling, 32,* 242–258.

Slavin, R. (1997). *Educational psychology: Theories and practice* (5th ed.).

Slonin-Nevo, B. (1992). First premarital intercourse among Mexican-American and Anglo-American adolescent women. Interpreting ethnic differences. *Journal of Adolescent Research, 7,* 332–351.

Smith, C. (1996). Women and weight. In J. Chrisler, C. Golden, & P. Rozee (Eds.), *Lectures on the psychology of women*. New York: McGraw-Hill.

Sonnenstein, F., Pleck, J., & Ku, L. (1991). Levels of sexual activity among adolescent males in the United States. *Family Planning Perspectives, 23,* 162–167.

Spence, S., & Atherton, C. (1991). The Black elderly and the social service delivery system: A study of factors influencing the use of community-based services. *Journal of Gerontological Social Work, 16,* 19–35.

Spencer, M., Dupree, D., & Swanson, D. (1998). The influence of physical maturation and hassles on African American adolescents' learning behaviors. *Journal of Comparative Family Studies, 29,* 189–200.

Sprey, J., & Matthews, S. (1982). Contemporary grandparenthood: A systematic transition. *Annals of the American Academy of Political Science, 464,* 91–103.

Stanton, B., Black, M., Kaljee, L., & Ricardo, I. (1993). Perceptions of sexual behavior among urban early adolescents: Translating theory through focus groups. *Journal of Early Adolescence, 13,* 44–66.

Steinberg, L. (1999). *Adolescence.* New York: McGraw-Hill.

Story, M., Mays, R., Bishop, D., Perry, B., Taylor, G., Smyth, M., & Gray, C. (2000). 5-a-Day Power Plus: Process evaluation of a multicomponent elementary school program to increase fruit and vegetable consumption. *Health Education and Behavior, 27,* 187–200.

Strickland, B. (1988). Sex-related differences in health and illness. *Psychology of Women Quarterly, 12,* 382–399.

Suffet, F., & Lifshitz, M. (1991). Women addicts and the threat of AIDS. *Qualitative Health Research, 1,* 51–79.

Swanson, L., Leonard, L., & Grandour, J. (1992). Vowel duration in mothers' speech to young children. *Journal of Speech and Hearing Research, 35,* 617–625.

Swar, A., & Richards, M. (1996). Longitudinal effects of adolescent girls' pubertal development, perceptions of pubertal timing, and parental relations on eating disorders. *Developmental Psychology, 32,* 636–646.

Sweeny, Y. (1999). The evolution of motherhood: Balancing family and work roles during children's school-age years. *Dissertation Abstracts International, 59,* 3674.

Takahashi, K. (1990). Are the key assumptions of the "Strange Situation" procedure universal? A view from Japanese research. *Human Development, 33,* 23–30.

Tamis-LeMonda, C., Bornstein, M. H., Cyphers, L., Toda, S., & Ogino, M. (1992). Language and play at one year: A comparison of toddlers and mothers in the United States and Japan. *International Journal of Behavioral Development, 15,* 19–42.

Tannen, D. (1994). *Talking from 9 to 5.* New York: Morrow.

Tedisco, J., & Paludi, M. (1996). *Missing children: A psychological approach to understanding the causes and consequences of stranger and non-stranger abduction of children.* Albany: State University of New York Press.

Teerikangas, O., Aronen, E., Martin, R., & Huttunen, M. (1998). Effects of infant temperament and early intervention on the psychiatric symptoms of adolescents. *Journal of the American Academy of Child and Adolescent Psychiatry, 37,* 1070–1076.

Thal, D., & Katich, J. (1996). Predicaments in early identification of specific language impairment. Does the early bird always catch the worm? In K. Cole, P. Dale, & D. Thal (Eds.), *Assessment of communication and language.* Baltimore: Brookes.

Thomas, A., & Chess, S. (1977). *Temperament and development.* New York: Brunner-Mazel.

Thompson, G., Cottrell, D., & Fletcher-Flinn, C. (1996). Sublexical orthographic-phonological relations early in the acquisition of reading: The knowledge sources account. *Journal of Experimental Child Psychology, 62,* 190–222.

Thorson, J., & Powell, F. (1992). A revised death anxiety scale. *Death Studies, 16,* 507–521.

Tobin, J., Wu, D., & Davidson, D. (1989). *Preschool in three cultures: Japan, China, and the United States.* New Haven, CT: Yale University Press.

Travis, C. (1993). Women and health. In F. Denmark & M. Paludi (Eds.), *Psychology of women: A handbook of issues and theories.* Westport, CT: Greenwood Press.

Turnbull, J., & Mui, A. (1995). Mental health status and needs of Black and White elderly: Difference in depression. In D. Padgett (Ed.), *Handbook on ethnicity, aging, and mental health.* Westport, CT: Greenwood Press.

Ungrady, D. (1992, October 19). Getting physical: Fitness experts are helping shape up young America. *Washington Post,* p. B5.

United Nations. (1990). *Declaration of the world summit for children.* New York.

U.S. Bureau of the Census (1993). *Statistical Abstract of the United States: 1993.* Washington, DC: U.S. Government Printing Office.

U.S. Congress (1990). *Indian adolescent mental health.* (Tech. Rep. No. OTA-H-446). Washington, DC: U.S. Government Printing Office.

Valsiner, J., & Hall, D. (1983). *Parents' strategies for the organization of child-environment relationships in home settings.* Paper presented at the Seventh Biennial Meeting of the International Society for the Study of Behavioral Development, Munchen, Bundersrub, Germany.

Van-Aken, D. (1999). Exploration of sibling relationships in middle childhood. *Dissertation Abstracts International, 59,* 5623.

vanBuskirk, S. (1977). A two-phase perspective on the treatment of anorexia nervosa. *Psychological Bulletin, 84,* 529–538.

Vartanian, L. (1998). Concern over social evaluation during adolescence: Sensitivity to an "imaginary" audience. *Dissertation Abstracts International, 58,* 4495.

Vik, P., & Brown, S. (1998). Life events and substance abuse during adolescence. In T. Miller (Ed.), *Children of trauma: Stressful life events and their effects on children and adolescents.* Madison, CT: International Universities Press.

Volling, B., & Elins, J. (1998). Family relationships and children's emotional adjustment as correlates of maternal and paternal differential treatment: A replication with toddler and preschool siblings. *Child Development, 69,* 1640–1656.

Vygotsky, L. (1930/1978), *Mind in society: The development of higher psychological processes.* Cambridge, MA: Harvard University Press.

Wagner, B., Aiken, C., Mullaley, P., Tobin, J. (2000). Parents' reactions to adolescents' suicide attempts. *Journal of the American Academy of Child and Adolescent Psychiatry, 39,* 429–436.

Waldo, M. (1987). Also victims: Understanding and treating men arrested for spouse abuse. *Journal of Counseling and Development, 65,* 385–388.

Walker, L. (1999). Psychology and domestic violence around the world. *American Psychologist, 54,* 21–29.

Wallace, S., Andersen, R., & Levy-Storms, L. (1993, November). *Access to long-term care by minority elderly: Implications of health care reform.* Paper presented at the Gerontological Society of America Annual Meeting, New Orleans, LA.

Wallerstein, J., & Blakeslee, S. (1989). *Second chances.* New York: Ticknor & Fields.

Ward, M. (1971). *Them children.* New York: Holt, Rinehart, & Winston.

Warner, C., & Nelson, N. (2000). Assessment of communication, language, and speech: questions of "what to do next?" In B. Bracken (Ed.), *The psychoeducational assessment of preschool children.* Boston: Allyn & Bacon.

Warshak, R. (1992). *The custody revolution.* New York: Poseidon Press.

Way, N., & Pahl, K. (1999). Friendship patterns among urban adolescent boys: A qualitative account. In M. Kopala & L. Suziki. (Eds.), *Using qualitative methods in psychology.* Thousand Oaks, CA: Sage.

Weissman, D. (1999). Gender of preschoolers' preferred play partners: Children's perspectives. *Dissertation Abstracts International, 59*(12-B), 6518.

Weissman, M., & Klerman, G. (1977). Sex differences in the epidemiology of depression. *Archives of General Psychiatry, 34,* 98–111.

Weissman, M., & Klerman, G. (1992). Depression: Current understanding and changing trends. *Annual Review of Public Health, 13,* 319–339.

Wheatley, J. (2000). Psychological development in adult life. In D. Gupta & R. Gupta (Eds.), *Psychology for psychiatrists.* London: Whurr Publishers.

Whitbeck, L., Hoyt, D., Miller, M., & Kao, M. (1992). Parental support, depressed affect, and sexual experience among adolescents. *Youth and Society,* 24, 166–177.

White, C., & Burke, P. (1987). Ethnic role identity among black and white college students: An interactionist approach. *Sociological Perspectives, 30,* 310–331.

Whiting, B., & Edwards, C. (1988). *Children of different worlds: The formation of social behavior.* Cambridge, MA: Harvard University Press.

Whiting, J. (1964). The effects of climate on certain cultural practices. In W. H. Goodenough (Ed.), *Explorations in cultural anthropology: Essays in honor of George Peter Murdock.* New York: McGraw-Hill.

Wichstrom, L. (1999). The emergence of gender difference in depressed mood during adolescence: The role of intensified gender socialization. *Developmental Psychology, 35,* 232–245.

Williams, H., & Abernathy, D. (2000). Assessment of gross motor development. In B. Bracken (Ed.), *The psychoeducational assessment of preschool children.* Boston: Allyn & Bacon.

Wilson, P. (1985). *Amount of reading, reading instruction, and reading achievement.* Paper presented at the Annual Meeting of the National Reading Conference.

Wolf, A., & Lozoff, B. (1989). Object attachment, thumbsucking, and the passage to sleep. *Journal of the American Academy of Child and Adolescent Psychiatry, 28,* 287–292.

Wood, J., & Inman, C. (1993). In a different mode: Masculine styles of communicating closeness. *Journal of Applied Communication Research, 21,* 279–295.

Worell, J. (1990). Images of women in psychology. In M. Paludi & G. Steuernagel (Eds.), *Foundations for a feminist restructuring of the academic disciplines.* New York: Haworth.

Worth, D., & Rodriguez, R. (1987, January–February). Latina women and AIDS. *SIECUS Report,* pp. 5–7.

Yee, D., & Eccles, J. (1988). Parent perceptions and attributions for children's mathematics achievement. *Sex Roles, 19,* 317–333.

Yeh, C., & Huang, K. (1996). The collectivistic nature of ethnic identity development among Asian-American college students. *Adolescence, 31,* 645–661.

Zayas, L., Kaplan, C., Turner, S., Romano, K., & Gozalez-Ramos, G. (2000). Understanding suicide attempts by adolescent Hispanic females. *Social Work, 45,* 53–63.

Credits

"Functional Analysis of the Contents of Maternal Speech to Infants of 5 and 13 Months in Four Cultures: Argentina, France, Japan, and the United States" by Marc H. Bornstein, Joseph Tal, Charles Rahn, Celia Z. Galperín, Marie-Germaine Pêcheux, Martine Lamour, Sueko Toda, Hiroshi Azuma, Misako Ogino, and Catherine S. Tamis-LeMonda, *Developmental Psychology,* 1992, vol. 28.

"Cultural Variations in Infants' Sleeping Arrangements: Questions of Independence" by Gilda A. Morelli, Barbara Rogoff, David Oppenheim, and Denise Goldsmith, *Developmental Psychology,* 1992, vol. 28. Copyright © 1992 by American Psychological Association. Reprinted with permission.

"Reactivity in Infants: A Cross-Cultural Comparison" by Jerome Kagan, Doreen Arcus, Nancy Snidman, Wang Yu Feng, John Hendler, and Sheila Greene, *Developmental Psychology,* 1994, vol. 30. Copyright © 1994 by American Psychological Association. Reprinted with permission.

"Sleeping Out of Home in a Kibbutz Communal Arrangement: It Makes a Difference for Infant-Mother Attachment" by Abraham Sagi, Frank Donnell, Marinus H. van IJzendoorn, Ofra Mayseless, and Ora Aviezer, *Child Development,* 1994, vol. 65. Copyright © 1994 by The Society for Research in Child Development. Reprinted with permission.

"Play in Two Societies: Pervasiveness of Process, Specificity of Structure" by Marc H. Bornstein, O. Maurice Haynes, Liliana Pascual, Kathleen M. Painter, and Celia Galperín, *Child Development,* 1999, vol. 70. Copyright © 1999 by The Society for Research in Child Development. Reprinted with permission.

"Parents' Report of Vocabulary and Grammatical Development of African American Preschoolers: Child and Environmental Associations" by Joanne E. Roberts, Margaret Burchinal, and Meghan Durham, *Child Development,* 1999, vol. 70. Copyright © 1999 by The Society for Research in Child Development. Reprinted with permission.

"Child Care for Children in Poverty: Opportunity or Inequity?" by Deborah A. Phillips, Miriam Voran, Ellen Kisker, Carollee Howes, and Marcy Whitebook, *Child Development,* 1994, vol. 65. Copyright © 1994 by The Society for Research in Child Development. Reprinted with permission.

"Emotion Regulation in Early Childhood: A Cross-Cultural Comparison Between German and Japanese Toddlers" by Wolfgang Friedlmeier and Gisela Trommsdorff, *Journal of Cross-Cultural Psychology,* 1999, vol. 30. Copyright © 1999 by Sage Publications, Inc. Reprinted with permission.

"African American Fathers in Low Income, Urban Families: Development, Behavior, and Home Environment of Their Three-Year-Old Children" by Maureen M. Black, Howard Dubowitz, and Raymond H. Starr Jr., *Child Development,* 1999, vol. 70. Copyright © 1999 by The Society for Research in Child Development. Reprinted with permission.

"Cultural Differences in Korean- and Anglo-American Preschoolers' Social Interaction and Play Behaviors" by Jo Ann M. Farver, Yonnie Kwak Kim, and Yoolim Lee, *Child Development,* 1995, vol. 66.

Copyright © 1995 by The Society for Research in Child Development. Reprinted with permission.

"Effects of Community Violence on Inner-City Preschoolers and Their Families" by Jo Ann M. Farver, Lucia X. Natera, and Dominick L. Frosch, *Journal of Applied Developmental Psychology,* 1999, vol. 20. Copyright © 1999 by Elsevier Science. Reprinted with permission.

"Gender Effects in Children's Beliefs About School Performance: A Cross-Cultural Study" by Anna Stetsenko, Todd D. Little, Tamara Gordeeva, Matthias Grasshof, and Gabriele Oettingen, *Child Development,* 2000, vol. 71. Copyright © 2000 by The Society for Research in Child Development. Reprinted with permission.

"Phonetic Awareness: Knowledge of Orthography–Phonology Relationships in the Character Acquisition of Chinese Children" by Hua Shu, Richard C. Anderson, and Ningning Wu, *Journal of Educational Psychology,* 2000, vol. 92. Copyright © 2000 by American Psychological Association. Reprinted with permission.

"A Prospective Study of the Effects of Marital Status and Family Relations on Young Children's Adjustment Among African American and European American Families" by Daniel S. Shaw, Emily B. Winslow, and Clare Flanagan, *Child Development,* 1999, vol. 70. Copyright © 1999 by The Society for Research in Child Development. Reprinted with permission.

"Children of the National Longitudinal Survey of Youth: Choices in After-School Care and Child Development" by Deborah Lowe Vandell and Janaki Ramanan, *Developmental Psychology,* 1991, vol. 27. Copyright © 1991 by American Psychological Association. Reprinted with permission.

"Costa Rican Children's Perceptions of Their Social Networks" by Melissa E. DeRosier and Janis B. Kupersmidt, *Developmental Psychology,* 1991, vol. 27. Copyright © 1991 by American Psychological Association. Reprinted with permission.

"Effects of Body Fat on Weight Concerns, Dating, and Sexual Activity: A Longitudinal Analysis of Black and White Adolescent Girls" by Carolyn Tucker Halpern, J. Richard Udry, Benjamin Campbell, and Chirayath Suchindran, *Developmental Psychology,* 1999, vol. 35. Copyright © 1999 by American Psychological Association. Reprinted by permission.

"The Collectivistic Nature of Ethnic Identity Among Asian-American College Students" by Christine J. Yeh and Karen Huang, *Adolescence,* 1996, vol. 31. Reprinted by permission of Libra Publishers, Inc.

"Depression in Adolescence" by Anne C. Petersen, Bruce E. Compas, Jeanne Brooks-Gunn, Mark Stemmler, Sydney Ey, and Kathryn E. Grant, *American Psychologist,* 1993, vol. 48.

"Adolescent Same-Sex and Opposite-Sex Best Friend Interactions" by Cami K. McBride and Tiffany Field, *Adolescence,* 1997, vol. 32. Reprinted by permission of Libra Publishers, Inc.

"Searching for the Magic Johnson Effect: AIDS, Adolescents, and Celebrity Disclosure" by Bruce Brown Jr., Marc D. Baranowski, John W. Kulig, John N. Stephenson, and Barbara Perry, *Adolescence,* 1996, vol. 31. Reprinted with permission of Libra Publishers, Inc.

"Constant Hierarchic Patterns of Physical Functioning Across Seven Populations in Five Countries" by Luigi Ferrucci, Jack M. Guralnik, Francesca Cecchi, Niccoló Marchionni, Bernardo Salani, Judith Kasper, Romano Celli, Sante Giardini, Eino Heikkinen, Marja Jylhä, and Alberto Baroni, *The Gerontologist,* 1998, vol. 38. Reprinted by permission of Copyright Clearance Center, on behalf of the Gerontological Society of America.

"Awareness and Utilization of Long-Term Care Services by Elderly Korean and Non-Hispanic White Americans" by Ailee Moon, James E. Lubben, and Valentine Villa, *The Gerontologist,* 1998, vol. 38. Reprinted by permission of Copyright Clearance Center, on behalf of The Gerontological Society of America.

"Women and Objectified Body Consciousness: Mothers' and Daughters' Body Experience in Cultural, Developmental, and Familial Context" by Nita Mary McKinley, *Developmental Psychology,* 1999, vol. 35. Copyright © 1999 by American Psychological Association. Reprinted with permission.

"Age Differences in Personality Across the Adult Life Span: Parallels in Five Countries" by Robert R. McRae, Paul T. Costa Jr., Margarida Pedroso de Lima, António Simões, Fritz Ostendorf, Alois Angleitner, Iris Marŭsić, Denis Bratko, Gian Vittorio Caprara, Claudio Barbaranelli, Joon-Ho Chae, and Ralph L. Piedmont, *Developmental Psychology,* 1999, vol. 35.

"Ethnicity, Gender, and Depressive Symptoms in Older Workers" by Maria E. Fernandez, Elizabeth J. Mutran, Donald C. Reitzes, and S. Sudha, *The Gerontologist,* 1998, vol. 38. Reprinted by permission of Copyright Clearance Center, on behalf of the Gerontological Society of America.

"Personality and Demographic Factors in Older Adults' Fear of Death" by Victor G. Cicirelli, *The Gerontologist,* 1999, vol. 39. Reprinted by permission of Copyright Clearance Center, on behalf of the Gerontological Society of America.

"Changing Community Responses to Wife Abuse: A Research and Demonstration Project in Iztacalco, Mexico" by Gillian M. Fawcett, Lori L. Heise, Leticia Isita-Espejel, and Susan Pick, *American Psychologist,* 1999, vol. 54. Copyright © 1999 by American Psychological Association. Reprinted with permission.

"Raising Grandchildren: The Experiences of Black and White Grandmothers" by Rachel Pruchno, *The Geronotologist,* 1999, vol. 39. Reprinted by permission of Copyright Clearance Center, on behalf of The Gerontological Society of America.

"Bicultural Identification: Experience of Internationally Adopted Children and Their Parents" by Myrna L. Friedlander, Lucille C. Larney, Marianne Skau, Marcus Hotaling, Marsha L. Cutting, and Michelle Schwam, *Journal of Counseling Psychology,* 2000, vol. 47. Copyright © 2000 by American Psychological Association. Reprinted with permission.

Index

academic achievement, in middle childhood, 97–100, 107–11
adolescence, 131–79
  cognitive development in, 135–37
    body image, 135–37, 147–54
  defined, 3–4, 132
  emotional development in, 137–41
    depression, 139–41, 158–70
    identity development, 137–39, 154–58
  physical development in, 133–35
  social development in, 141–43
    peer group, 141–43, 170–73
    sexual activity and risk-taking behavior, 143–46, 173–77
  substages of, 4
Adolescent Same-Sex and Opposite-Sex Best Friend Interactions (McBride and Field), 170–73
adoption, bicultural identity and, 237–41
adulthood, 180–242
  cognitive development in, 184–87
    long-term care services, 184–85, 200–204
    objectified body consciousness, 185–87, 205–12
  defined, 4
  emotional development in, 187–91
    continuity of personality across life cycle, 187–88, 212–16
    depression, 188–90, 216–20
    fear of death, 190–91, 220–25
  physical development in, 182–84, 196–99
  social development in, 191–95
    bicultural identity, 194–95, 237–41
    family violence, 191–93, 226–31
    grandparenting, 193–94, 231–36
  substages of, 4
African American Fathers in Low Income, Urban Families: Development, Behavior, and Home Environment of Their Three-Year-Old Children (Black et al.), 80–84
African Americans
  in adolescence
    body image, 147–54
    sexual behavior, 173–77
  in adulthood
    depression, 216–20
    fear of death, 220–25
    grandparenting, 231–36
  in middle childhood, divorce of parents, 117–22
  in preschool years
    language development, 65–69
    role of father, 80–84
after-school care, in middle childhood, 103–4, 123–26
Age Differences in Personality Across the Adult Life Span: Parallels in Five Cultures (McCrae et al.), 212–16
AIDS/HIV, in adolescence, 145–46, 173–77
Ainsworth's Strange Situation, 22–23
ambivalent children, 22
Anderson, Richard C., 112–17
androcentrism, 6
Angleitner, Alois, 212–16
anorexia nervosa, 135–36
Arcus, Doreen, 37–41
Argentina
  infant-directed speech in, 25–31
  play in infancy, 45–50

Asian-Americans
identity development in adolescence, 154–58
identity in adulthood, 237–41
long-term care services, 200–204
play in preschool years, 84–88
assimilation, 138
associative play, 62
Aviezer, Ora, 41–44
avoidant children, 22
Awareness and Utilization of Community Long-Term Care Services by Elderly Korean and Non-Hispanic White Americans (Moon et al.), 200–204
Azuma, Hiroshi, 25–31

Baranowski, Marc D., 173–77
Barbaranelli, Claudio, 212–16
Baronj, Alberto, 196–99
Bicultural Identification: Experiences of Internationally Adopted Children and Their Parents (Friedlander et al.), 237–41
Black, Maureen M., *African American Fathers in Low Income, Urban Families: Development, Behavior, and Home Environment of Their Three-Year-Old Children*, 80–84
body image
in adolescence, 135–37, 147–54
in adulthood, 185–87, 205–12
Bornstein, Marc H.
Functional Analysis of the Contents of Maternal Speech to Infants of 5 and 13 Months in Four Cultures: Argentina, France, Japan, and the United States, 25–31
Play in Two Societies: Pervasiveness of Process, Specificity of Structure, 45–50
Bratko, Denis, 212–16
Brooks-Gunn, Jeanne, 158–70
Brown, Bruce R., Jr., *Searching for the Magic Johnson Effect: AIDS, Adolescents, and Celebrity Disclosure*, 173–77
bulimia, 136
Burchinal, Margaret, 65–69

Campbell, Benjamin, 147–54
Caprara, Gian Vittorio, 212–16
Cecchi, Francesca, 196–99
Celli, Romano, 196–99
Chae, Joon-Ho, 212–16
Changing Community Responses to Wife Abuse: A Research and Demonstration Project in Iztacalco, Mexico (Fawcett et al.), 226–31
checklists, 12
child care, in preschool years, 57–59, 70–73
Child Care for Children in Poverty: Opportunity or Inequity? (Phillips et al.), 70–73
Children of the National Longitudinal Survey of Youth: Choices in After-School Care and Child Development (Vandell and Ramanan), 123–26
China
language development in middle childhood, 112–17
temperament in infancy, 37–41
Cicirelli, Victor G., *Personality and Demographic Factors in Older Adults' Fear of Death*, 220–25
cliques, 142
cognitive development
in adolescence, 135–37
body image, 135–37, 147–54
in adulthood, 184–87
long-term care services, 184–85, 200–204
objectified body consciousness, 185–87, 205–12
defined, 4
in infancy, 17–19
infant-directed speech (motherese), 17–19, 25–31
interdependence with other dimensions, 4
in middle childhood, 97–101
academic achievement and adjustment, 97–100, 107–11
language development, 100–101, 112–17
in preschool years, 55–59
child care, 57–59, 70–73
language advances, 55–57, 65–69
Collectivistic Nature of Ethnic Identity Development Among Asian-American College Students, The (Yeh and Huang), 154–58
Compas, Bruce E., 158–70
Constant Hierarchic Patterns of Physical Functioning Across Seven Populations in Five Countries (Ferrucci et al.), 196–99
constructive play, 61–62
cooperative play, 62
Costa, Paul T., Jr., 212–16

Costa Rican Children's Perceptions of Their Social Networks (DeRosier and Kupersmidt), 126–29
Croatia, personality continuity across life cycle, 212–16
cultural assimilators, 9–11
Cultural Differences in Korean- and Anglo-American Preschoolers' Social Interaction and Play Behaviors (Farver et al.), 84–88
Cultural Variation in Infants' Sleeping Arrangements: Questions of Independence (Morelli et al.), 31–37
culture, concept of, 4–5
Cutting, Marsha L., 237–41
Czechoslovakia, cognitive development in middle childhood, 107–11

death, fear of, 190–91, 220–25
decentering, 97
depression
  in adolescence, 139–41, 158–70
  in adulthood, 188–90, 216–20
Depression in Adolescence (Petersen et al.), 158–70
DeRosier, Melissa E., *Costa Rican Children's Perceptions of Their Social Networks,* 126–29
disorganized-disoriented children, 22
divorce, in middle childhood, 101–3, 117–22
Donnell, Frank, 41–44
Dubowitz, Howard, 80–84
Durham, Meghan, 65–69

early childhood. *See* preschool years
eating disorders, 135–36
Effects of Body Fat on Weight Concerns, Dating, and Sexual Activity: A Longitudinal Analysis of Black and White Adolescent Girls (Halpern et al.), 147–54
Effects of Community Violence on Inner-City Preschoolers and Their Families (Farver et al.), 88–91
emotional development
  in adolescence, 137–41
    identity development, 137–39, 154–58
  in adulthood, 187–91
    continuity of personality across life cycle, 187–88, 212–16
    depression, 188–90, 216–20
    fear of death, 190–91, 220–25
  defined, 4
  in infancy, 19–21
    sleeping arrangements, 19–20, 31–37
    temperament, 20–21, 37–41
  interdependence with other dimensions, 4
  in middle childhood, 101–4
    divorce, 101–3, 117–22
    self-care after school, 103–4, 123–26
  in preschool years, 59–61
    role of father, 60–61, 80–84
    role of mother, 59–60, 74–79
Emotion Regulation in Early Childhood: A Cross-Cultural Comparison Between German and Japanese Toddlers (Friedlmeier and Trommsdorff), 74–79
ethnicity
  concept of, 5
  ethnic identity, 138
  race versus, 5
  socioeconomic class and, 7
Ethnicity, Gender, and Depressive Symptoms in Older Workers (Fernandez et al.), 216–20
ethnocentrism, 6
experimenter bias, 7–8
exploratory play, 23–24
Ey, Sydney, 158–70

Farver, Jo Ann M.
  Cultural Differences in Korean- and Anglo-American Preschoolers' Social Interaction and Play Behaviors, 84–88
  Effects of Community Violence on Inner-City Preschoolers and Their Families, 88–91
fathers, and preschool emotional development, 60–61, 80–84
Fawcett, Gillian M., *Changing Community Responses to Wife Abuse: A Research and Demonstration Project in Iztacalco, Mexico,* 226–31
Feng, Wang Yu, 37–41
Fernandez, Maria E., *Ethnicity, Gender, and Depressive Symptoms in Older Workers,* 216–20
Ferrucci, Luigi, *Constant Hierarchic Patterns of Physical Functioning Across Seven Populations in Five Countries,* 196–99

Field, Tiffany, *Adolescent Same-Sex and Opposite-Sex Best Friend Interactions,* 170–73
Finland, physical development in adulthood, 196–99
Flanagan, Clare, 117–22
France, infant-directed speech in, 25–31
Friedlander, Myrna L., *Bicultural Identification: Experiences of Internationally Adopted Children and Their Parents,* 237–41
Friedlmeier, Wolfgang, *Emotion Regulation in Early Childhood: A Cross-Cultural Comparison Between German and Japanese Toddlers,* 74–79
friendship. *See* peer group
Frosch, Dominick L., 88–91
Functional Analysis of the Contents of Maternal Speech to Infants of 5 and 13 Months in Four Cultures: Argentina, France, Japan, and the United States (Bornstein et al.), 25–31
functional play, 61

Galperín, Celia Z., 25–31, 45–50
gender
- concept of, 5
- in middle childhood, 107–11
- puberty and, 134–35
- sex versus, 5

gendercentrism, 6
Gender Effects in Children's Beliefs About School Performance: A Cross-Cultural Study (Stetsenko et al.), 107–11
Germany
- cognitive development in middle childhood, 107–11
- emotion regulation in preschool years, 74–79
- personality continuity across life cycle, 212–16
- physical development in adulthood, 196–99

Giardini, Sante, 196–99
Goldsmith, Denise, 31–37
Gordeeva, Tamara, 107–11
grandparenting, 193–94, 231–36
Grant, Kathryn E., 158–70
Grasshof, Matthias, 107–11
Greene, Sheila, 37–41
Guralnik, Jack M., 196–99

Halpern, Carolyn Tucker, *Effects of Body Fat on Weight Concerns, Dating, and Sexual Activity: A Longitudinal Analysis of Black and White Adolescent Girls,* 147–54
Haynes, O. Maurice, 45–50
Heikkinen, Eino, 196–99
Heise, Lori L., 226–31
Hendler, John, 37–41
heterosexism, 6
homosexuality, 140
Hotaling, Marcus, 237–41
Howes, Carollee, 70–73
Huang, Karen, *The Collectivistic Nature of Ethnic Identity Development Among Asian-American College Students,* 154–58

identity
- in adolescence, 137–39, 154–58
- in adulthood, 194–95, 237–41

infancy, 15–52
- cognitive development in, 17–19
  - infant-directed speech (motherese), 17–19, 25–31
- defined, 3, 16
- emotional development in, 19–21
  - sleeping arrangements, 19–20, 31–37
  - temperament, 20–21, 37–41
- physical development in, 16–17
- social development in, 21–24
  - mother-infant attachment, 21–23, 41–44
  - play, 23–24, 45–50

infant-directed speech (motherese), 17–19, 25–31
initiation rites, 132
integration, 138
interviews, 12
Ireland, temperament in infancy, 37–41
Isita-Espejel, Leticia, 226–31
Israel, mother-infant attachment, 41–44
Italy
- personality continuity across life cycle, 212–16
- physical development in adulthood, 196–99

Japan
- cognitive development in middle childhood, 107–11

emotion regulation in preschool years, 74–79
infant-directed speech in, 25–31
journal-writing, 14
Jylhä, Marja, 196–99

Kagan, Jerome, *Reactivity in Infants: A Cross-National Comparison*, 37–41
Kasper, Judith, 196–99
Kim, Yonnie Kwak, 84–88
Kisker, Ellen, 70–73
Korea, personality continuity across life cycle, 212–16
Korean-Americans
identity in adulthood, 237–41
long-term care services, 200–204
play in preschool years, 84–88
Kulig, John W., 173–77
Kupersmidt, Janis B., *Costa Rican Children's Perceptions of Their Social Networks*, 126–29

Lamour, Martine, 25–31
language development
infant-directed speech (motherese), 17–19, 25–31
in middle childhood, 100–101, 112–17
in preschool years, 55–57, 65–69
Larney, Lucille C., 237–41
latchkey children, 104
Latin Americans, identity in adulthood, 237–41
Lee, Yoolim, 84–88
lesbianism, 140
life-cycle developmental psychology
infancy in, 3, 15–52
multiculturalism in, 4–11
nature of, 3–4
Little, Todd D., 107–11
long-term care services, 184–85, 200–204
Lubben, James E., 200–204

machismo, 144–45
Marchionni, Niccoló, 196–99
marianismo, 144–45
Marušić, Iris, 212–16
Mayan community, infancy in, 31–37
Mayseless, Ofra, 41–44
McBride, Cami K., *Adolescent Same-Sex and Opposite-Sex Best Friend Interactions*, 170–73
McCrae, Robert R., *Age Differences in Personality Across the Adult Life Span: Parallels in Five Cultures*, 212–16
McKinley, Nita Mary, *Women and Objectified Body Consciousness: Mothers' and Daughters' Body Experience in Cultural, Developmental, and Familial Context*, 205–12
metalinguistic awareness, 100
Mexico, family violence in, 226–31
middle childhood, 94–130
cognitive development in, 97–101
academic achievement and adjustment, 97–100, 107–11
language development, 100–101, 112–17
defined, 3, 95
emotional development in, 101–4
divorce, 101–3, 117–22
self-care after school, 103–4, 123–26
physical development in, 95–97
social development in, 104–6
peer group, 104–6, 126–29
Moon, Ailee, *Awareness and Utilization of Community Long-Term Care Services by Elderly Korean and Non-Hispanic White Americans*, 200–204
Morelli, Gilda A., *Cultural Variation in Infants' Sleeping Arrangements: Questions of Independence*, 31–37
motherese. *See* infant-directed speech
mothers
after-school care in middle childhood, 103–4, 123–26
body image and, 185–87, 205–12
as grandmothers, 193–94, 231–36
and infant-directed speech, 17–19, 25–31
and mother-infant attachment, 21–24, 41–44
and preschool emotional development, 59–60, 74–79
multiculturalism
concept of culture and, 4–5
in life-cycle developmental psychology, 4–11
marginality versus inclusion in, 6–8
Mutran, Elizabeth J., 216–20

Natera, Lucia X., 88–91
naturalistic observation, 12
North American bias, 8

Oettingen, Gabriele, 107–11
Ogino, Misako, 25–31
onlooker play, 62
Oppenheim, David, 31–37
Ostendorf, Fritz, 212–16
overnutrition, in middle childhood, 96

Painter, Kathleen M., 45–50
parallel play, 62
Parents' Report of Vocabulary and Grammatical Development of African American Preschoolers: Child and Environmental Associations (Roberts et al.), 65–69
Pascual, Liliana, 45–50
Pêcheux, Marie-Germaine, 25–31
Pedroso de Lima, Margarida, 212–16
peer group
  in adolescence, 141–43, 170–73
  in middle childhood, 104–6, 126–29
Perry, Barbara, 173–77
personality
  continuity across life cycle, 187–88, 212–16
  fear of death, 190–91, 220–25
Personality and Demographic Factors in Older Adults' Fear of Death (Cicirelli), 220–25
Petersen, Anne C., *Depression in Adolescence,* 158–70
Phillips, Deborah A., *Child Care for Children in Poverty: Opportunity or Inequity?* 70–73
phonemes, 100
Phonetic Awareness: Knowledge of Orthography-Phonology Relationships in the Character Acquisition of Chinese Children (Shu et al.), 112–17
physical development
  in adolescence, 133–35
  in adulthood, 182–84, 196–99
  defined, 4
  in infancy, 16–17
  interdependence with other dimensions, 4
  in middle childhood, 95–97
  in preschool years, 54–55
Pick, Susan, 226–31
Piedmont, Ralph L., 212–16
play
  in infancy, 23–24, 45–50
  in preschool years, 61–63, 84–88
Play in Two Societies: Pervasiveness of Process, Specificity of Structure (Bornstein et al.), 45–50
Portugal, personality continuity across life cycle, 212–16
preschool years, 53–93
  cognitive development in, 55–59
    child care, 57–59, 70–73
    language advances, 55–57, 65–69
  defined, 3
  emotional development in, 59–61
    role of father, 60–61, 80–84
    role of mother, 59–60, 74–79
  physical development in, 54–55
  social development in, 61–64
    exposure to violence, 63–64, 88–91
    play, 61–63, 84–88
private speech, 55–56
Prospective Study of the Effects of Marital Status and Family Relations on Young Children's Adjustment Among African American and European American Families (Shaw et al.), 117–22
Pruchno, Rachel, *Raising Grandchildren: The Experiences of Black and White Grandmothers,* 231–36
puberty, 133–35. *See also* adolescence
pubescence, 133–35. *See also* adolescence

questionnaires, 12

race
  concept of, 5
  ethnicity versus, 5
  socioeconomic class and, 7
Rahn, Charles, 25–31
Raising Grandchildren: The Experiences of Black and White Grandmothers (Pruchno), 231–36
Ramanan, Janaki, *Children of the National Longitudinal Survey of Youth: Choices in After-School Care and Child Development,* 123–26

Reactivity in Infants: A Cross-National Comparison (Kagan et al.), 37–41
Reitzes, Donald C., 216–20
Republic of Serbia, physical development in adulthood, 196–99
risk-taking behavior, in adolescence, 143–46, 173–77
rites of passage, 132
Roberts, Joanne E., *Parents' Report of Vocabulary and Grammatical Development of African American Preschoolers: Child and Environmental Associations*, 65–69
Rogoff, Barbara, 31–37
Russia, cognitive development in middle childhood, 107–11

Sagi, Abraham, *Sleeping Out of Home in a Kibbutz Communal Arrangement: It Makes a Difference for Infant-Mother Attachment*, 41–44
Salani, Bernardo, 196–99
school-age period. *See* middle childhood
Schwam, Michelle, 237–41
Searching for the Magic Johnson Effect: AIDS, Adolescents, and Celebrity Disclosure (Brown et al.), 173–77
securely attached children, 22
sex
  concept of, 5
  gender versus, 5
sexism, guidelines to avoid, 14
sexual activity, in adolescence
  body image, 135–37, 147–54
  risk-taking behavior, 143–46, 173–77
sexual orientation, 140
Shaw, Daniel S., *Prospective Study of the Effects of Marital Status and Family Relations on Young Children's Adjustment Among African American and European American Families*, 117–22
Shu, Hua, *Phonetic Awareness: Knowledge of Orthography-Phonology Relationships in the Character Acquisition of Chinese Children*, 112–17
Simões, António, 212–16
Skau, Marianne, 237–41
sleeping arrangements in infancy, 19–20, 21–23, 31–37, 41–44
Sleeping Out of Home in a Kibbutz Communal Arrangement: It Makes a Difference for Infant-Mother Attachment (Sagi et al.), 41–44
Snidman, Nancy, 37–41
social development
  in adolescence, 141–43
    peer group, 141–43, 170–73
    sexual activity and risk-taking behavior, 143–46, 173–77
  in adulthood, 191–95
    bicultural identity, 194–95, 237–41
    family violence, 191–93, 226–31
    grandparenting, 193–94, 231–36
  defined, 4
  in infancy, 21–24
    mother-infant attachment, 21–23, 41–44
    play, 23–24, 45–50
  interdependence with other dimensions, 4
  in middle childhood, 104–6
    peer group, 104–6, 126–29
  in preschool years, 61–64
    exposure to violence, 63–64, 88–91
    play, 61–63, 84–88
social play, 23–24
socioeconomic class, 5–6
  ethnicity and, 7
  in preschool years
    child care, 70–73
    role of father, 80–84
    violence, 88–91
  race and, 7
South Korea, personality continuity across life cycle, 212–16
standardized testing, 12–13
Starr, Raymond H., Jr., 80–84
Stemmler, Mark, 158–70
Stephenson, John N., 173–77
Stetsenko, Anna, *Gender Effects in Children's Beliefs About School Performance: A Cross-Cultural Study*, 107–11
Suchindran, Chirayath, 147–54
Sudha, S., 216–20
Switzerland, cognitive development in middle childhood, 107–11
symbolic play, 23–24

Tal, Joseph, 25–31
Tamis-LeMonda, Catherine S., 25–31

temperament
  concept of, 20–21
  in infancy, 20–21, 37–41
Toda, Sueko, 25–31
Trommsdorff, Gisela, *Emotion Regulation in Early Childhood: A Cross-Cultural Comparison Between German and Japanese Toddlers,* 74–79

Udry, J. Richard, 147–54
Ukraine, physical development in adulthood, 196–99
United States
  adolescence in
    body image, 147–54
    depression, 158–70
    identity development, 154–58
    peer group, 170–73
    sexual behavior, 173–77
  adulthood in
    body image, 205–12
    depression, 216–20
    fear of death, 220–25
    grandparenting, 231–36
    identity, 237–41
    long-term care services, 200–204
  infancy in
    infant-directed speech, 25–31
    play, 45–50
    sleeping arrangements, 31–37
    temperament, 37–41
  middle childhood in
    after-school care, 123–26
    cognitive development, 107–11
    divorce, 117–22
  preschool years in
    language development, 65–69
    play, 84–88
    role of father, 80–84
    violence, 88–91

Vandell, Deborah Lowe, *Children of the National Longitudinal Survey of Youth: Choices in After-School Care and Child Development,* 123–26
van IJzendoorn, Marinus H., 41–44
Villa, Valentine, 200–204
violence
  in adulthood, 191–93, 226–31
  in preschool years, 63–64, 88–91
Voran, Miriam, 70–73

wait time, 98–99
Whitebook, Marcy, 70–73
Winslow, Emily B., 117–22
Women and Objectified Body Consciousness: Mothers' and Daughters' Body Experience in Cultural, Developmental, and Familial Context (McKinley), 205–12
Wu, Ningning, 112–17

Yeh, Christine J., *The Collectivistic Nature of Ethnic Identity Development Among Asian-American College Students,* 154–58